READINGS IN SOCIAL PSYCHOLOGY

PRENTICE-HALL, INC.

Englewood Cliffs, New Jersey

READINGS IN
SOCIAL PSYCHOLOGY

edited by

Jonathan L. Freedman
Columbia University

J. Merrill Carlsmith
Stanford University

David O. Sears
University of California
Los Angeles

Library of Congress Catalog Card Number 78-146739
Printed in the United States of America

Current printing (last digit):

12 11 10 9 8 7 6 5 4

Prentice-Hall International, Inc., London
Prentice-Hall of Australia, Pty. Ltd., Sydney
Prentice-Hall of Canada, Ltd., Toronto
Prentice-Hall of India Private Limited, New Delhi
Prentice-Hall of Japan, Tokyo

CONTENTS

GROUP DYNAMICS

CONFORMITY

ATTITUDE FORMATION AND CHANGE — THEORETICAL BACKGROUND

ATTITUDE CHANGE

DISSONANCE AND ATTITUDE-DISCREPANT BEHAVIOR

COMPLIANCE, OBEDIENCE, AND ALTRUISM

PREFACE

This collection contains forty-two of the most oustanding articles in social psychology. Some are classic; most are recent. But whether old or new, they deal with problems which are of current and continuing interest. In a field as varied and heterogeneous as social psychology, no single book of readings can represent all areas. Therefore we have had to make the difficult decision of including some fields and omitting others. Our choices have been guided by the principle that preference should be given to those areas which are being most actively investigated at present and which are likely to continue to receive the attention of large numbers of research workers. The problem areas represented here are those which appear most regularly in the journals, in symposia, and in research proposals. The book thus reflects the major interests of the large majority of active social psychologists.

Even more difficult decisions had to be made about which articles to present in a particular area. There are so many excellent articles that it is almost painful to be forced to choose just a few to represent a large area of important research. These decisions are somewhat arbitrary and necessarily reflect the biases of the editors, but the articles chosen represent a wide range of approaches, methodologies, and theoretical orientations. There is, however, a clear bias toward articles that present data rather than purely theoretical, conceptual, or methodological work. Although the latter kinds of articles are extremely valuable for the field, the primary purpose of this book is to present research findings and to give the reader a first-hand impression of how evidence is gathered in social psychology. The articles accordingly all present data—but we have attempted to be catholic in the kinds of data represented. Data are derived from laboratory experiments, field experiments, surveys, psychiatric interviews, and field observations; the populations on which the data are based include tropical fish, subprimates, children, college sophomores, and normal adults.

The book is designed primarily to accompany a textbook in an introductory course in social psychology. Students can read the text for general discussions and be assigned all or part of this book for exposure to more detailed descriptions of research and for a better understanding of how research is done. The readings were specifically selected to accompany our own text (*Social Psychology* by Freedman, Carlsmith, and Sears; Prentice-Hall, Inc.). The organization follows that text exactly, with three or more articles corresponding to a chapter. This book may, however, be used profitably as an adjunct to any text which treats current problems in social psychology. Or the readings could be used without an accompanying text or with a methodology text in a course that focused on research methods in social psychology.

We are grateful to all of the authors of the papers collected here for their permission to reprint them.

Stanford, California, 1971

JONATHAN L. FREEDMAN
J. MERRILL CARLSMITH
DAVID O. SEARS

READINGS IN SOCIAL PSYCHOLOGY

AFFILIATION

Anxiety, Fear, and Social Affiliation

IRVING SARNOFF AND PHILIP G. ZIMBARDO

In his recent monograph, Schachter (1959) reports that anticipated exposure to a painful external stimulus determines the degree to which persons wish to affiliate with each other: the greater the anticipated pain, the stronger the desire to await the onset of that pain in the company of others in the same predicament. In attempting to account theoretically for this finding, Schachter mentions such motivational forces as the subjects' needs for reassurance, distraction, escape, and information. However, among the various possible explanations, Schachter appears to favor one derived from Festinger's (1954) theory of social comparison processes. Adapting that theory to the phenomena under investigation, Schachter postulates that the arousal of any strong emotion evokes a need for comparison. Emotions are assumed to be quite unspecific states of affect. Hence, persons can only evaluate the quality, intensity, and appropriateness of their emotions properly by comparing their own reactions with those of others. Moreover, novel emotion producing stimuli should induce a greater tendency to affiliate than familiar stimuli. By definition, a novel stimulus is one that is more difficult to fit into a person's established frame of reference for emotive states. Accordingly, the individual is more obliged to seek out others in order to define the emotional effects of novel stimuli.

The explication of Schachter's (1959) results in terms of the theory of social comparison processes is appealingly parsimonious. However, it requires the assumption that *all* emotive states have the same effect on affiliative behavior. Thus, Schachter, like many contemporary psychologists, does not deal with the possible conceptual distinctions between fear and anxiety. Yet, it seems to us that, by adopting an alternative assumption about the psychological properties of emotions, to be presented briefly below, it is possible to formulate predictions concerning affiliative responses that could not have been derived from the theory of social comparison processes. Indeed, by employing Freud's (1949a, 1949b) conceptual distinctions between fear and anxiety, we are led to predict a tendency toward social isolation—rather than affiliation—as a consequence of certain conditions of emotional arousal.

The present experiment was, thus, undertaken with two objectives: to assess the empirical validity of conceptual differentiation between fear and anxiety, and to evaluate the extent to which the theory of social comparison processes may be applied to the relationship between all emotions and affiliative behavior. In order to implement these objectives, we have conducted an experimental investigation of the differential effects of fear and anxiety upon social affiliation.

Functional Relationship between Emotions and Motives

The guiding assumption of our experiment holds that all emotions are consciously experienced epiphenomena of motives.[1] When our motives are aroused, we experience subjective reactions to which we learn, over time, to attach commonly agreed upon labels that signify the various emotions.

Motive, on the other hand, is defined as a tension producing stimulus that provokes behavior designed to reduce the tension. Each of our motives (innate or learned) requires the performance of a *different* response for the maximal reduction of its tension.

Fear and Anxiety Viewed as Motives

The motive of fear (which Freud called objective anxiety) is aroused whenever persons are confronted by an external object or event that is inherently dan-

---

[1] The concept of motivation which we have chosen to employ has been elaborated elsewhere (Sarnoff, 1960a).

gerous and likely to produce pain. Only one type of overt[2] response can maximally reduce our fear: separation from the threatening aspects of the feared object, accomplished by flight from the object, at one extreme, and conquest, at the other. In the case of fear, then, one's energies are mobilized toward dealing with the external stimulus; to eliminate, through some mode of escape or attack, the threat that is clearly and objectively present in the stimulus.

If we examine the consequences of anxiety (which Freud termed neurotic anxiety), we see no such correspondence between the internal disturbance of the person and an objectively harmful environmental stimulus. Instead, anxiety is typically aroused by stimuli which, objectively considered, are *innocuous*.[3] For example, in the case of the classical phobias, harmless objects possess a special motivational significance for certain people. These objects activate some motive other than fear, and this other motive, in turn, arouses the consciously perceived motive of anxiety. Hence, the emotional reaction of the anxious person is inappropriate to the inherent characteristics of the external stimulus.

Regardless of their content, the motives whose arousal evokes anxiety share a common property: they are all *repressed*. These repressed motives continue unconsciously to press for the reduction of their tensions; and anxiety signals the threat of possible expression of these repressed motives. Consequently, the person develops a number of additional ego defenses that function to safeguard the initial effects of repression. If the ego defenses do their work effectively, the motives are kept under repression, the inner danger passes and the individual's anxiety is reduced.

Implications of the Motives of Anxiety and Fear for Affiliative Behavior

It follows from the foregoing discussion that, when their anxieties are aroused, people are more inclined to become preoccupied with the reassertion of inner self-control than with modes of dealing with the anxiety evoking external object. Because the anxious person tends to be aware of the element of *inappropriateness* in his feelings, he is loath to communicate his anxieties to others. To avoid being ridiculed or censured, he conceals anxiety aroused by stimuli which he guesses do not have a similar effect upon others, and which, he feels, ought not so to upset him. Thus, when anxiety is aroused, a person should tend to seek isolation from others. On the other hand, when fear is aroused and he is unable to flee from the threatening object, he welcomes the opportunity to affiliate. Since the usual responses to fear, flight and fight, are restricted in the experi-

[2] Space limitations do not permit a consideration of the two types of covert (ego defensive) responses, denial and identification with the aggressor, which persons may employ in their efforts to cope with external threat. A full discussion of these ego defenses is presented by Sarnoff (1960a).

[3] In fact, since anxiety arousing stimuli are often related to unconscious libidinal motives, they may be regarded by most people as intrinsically pleasurable, rather than in any way painful. For example, owing to the manner in which their heterosexual motives have been socialized, some men may tend severely to repress their sexual cravings for women. Hence, when such men are shown photographs of voluptuous nudes, stimuli which might be quite evocative of pleasurable fantasies among most of their fellows, they are likely to experience anxiety (Sarnoff & Corwin, 1959).

mental situation, the subject seeks other fear reducing responses. Therefore, the probability of affiliation increases because it mediates fear reduction through the potentiality for catharsis and distraction as well as the emotional comparison offered by interpersonal contact.

We are led, therefore, to the hypothesis that the motives of fear and anxiety should influence social affiliation behavior differently: the greater the fear aroused, the more the subjects should choose to be together with others while they await actual contact with the fear arousing object. Conversely, the greater the anxiety elicited, the more the subjects should choose to be alone while they await contact with the anxiety arousing object.

METHOD

The experiment was presented to the subjects as a physiological investigation of the cutaneous sensitivity of various parts of the body. A 2×2 design was used in which two levels of fear and of anxiety were experimentally aroused. The dependent variable of social affiliation was measured by having the subjects state whether they preferred to spend an anticipated waiting period alone or in the company of others.

Subjects

The subjects were 72 unpaid, male undergraduate volunteers from six introductory psychology classes in Yale University. An additional 36 subjects were used to pretest the manipulations and measuring devices, and an additional 13 subjects were excluded from the analyses because they did not qualify as acceptable subjects, i.e., were friends, misunderstood the instructions, did not believe the rationale.

Procedure

Background information was collected by an accomplice alleged to be from the counseling program of the Student Health Department. A questionnaire was designed to obtain background information on the subjects and also their preferred mode of defense mechanism. The latter data were in response to four Blacky cards. As in a recent experiment by Sarnoff (1960b), each card was accompanied by three alternatives that were to be rank ordered according to the subjects' reaction to the theme of the card (sibling rivalry, achievement, and two of sucking). The alternatives reflected predominantly an acceptance of the motive, projection of the motive upon others, or a reaction formation against the motive.

About one month later, the experimenter was introduced to the psychology classes as a physiological psychologist studying physiological responses to sensory stimuli. The subjects were subsequently recruited individually, and randomly assigned to the four experimental treatments. The specious purpose of the experiment and of the conditions of waiting were further established by marking the experimental room "Sensory Physiology Laboratory" and two nearby rooms "Waiting Room A" and "Waiting Room T." Because of absentees, the size of the groups tested varied from three to five, and was usually composed of four subjects. In order to avoid the development of superficial friendships during the experiment, and eliminate the possibility that the subjects might react to cues from each other or from the experimenter, the subjects were isolated in adjacent cubicles, no communication was allowed, and the tape-recorded instructions were presented through earphones.

The experimental conditions and instructions common to all subjects will be presented first. After rolling up their sleeves, removing their watches from their wrists, and gum or cigarettes from their mouths ("They interfere with the recording electrodes"), the subjects were told:

Our experiment falls in the general area of physiological psychology. As you may know, one branch of physiological psychology is concerned with the reactions of the sense organs to various kinds of stimulation. Our present experiment deals with the skin [or mouth] as an organ of sensation. We are interested in studying individual differences in response to particular stimuli applied to it.

There has been a good deal of controversy about the relative sensitivity of the fingertips [lips] as compared to the palms [tongue], and upper surface of the hand [palate]. Our experiment will help to provide data upon which we may be able ultimately to draw a detailed map of the cutaneous sensitivity of the human hand [mouth].

In order to measure your physiological reactions, we are now going to attach some instruments to your arm and finger [corner of your mouth]. These instruments are electrodes which are connected to a machine which records exactly the strength of your response to each stimulus.... Electrode jelly will be applied first to the area to insure that we get a good electrical contact. (The electrodes were then attached by a female laboratory assistant of middle age.)

In order to provide a reasonable basis for asking the subjects to wait in other rooms (and, thus, for making the choice of affiliation or isolation), the subjects were told that it was necessary to assess their basal rates of responding prior to the application of the actual stimuli. They were led to believe that their individual sensitivities were being recorded while they viewed a series of slides of a typical subject who had participated in the experiment. They anticipated that a waiting period would come after the slides, and then in the second—and purportedly major—part of the experiment their direct reactions to the actual stimuli would be measured. Accordingly, they were told:

Now that your basal rates have been recorded on our polygraph recorder, it will take us about 10 minutes while we tally the data and reset our measuring instruments so that they will be geared to your individual basal rates as you are run one at a time through the rest of the experiment. While we are doing these things, we are going to ask you to wait in other rooms which are available to us. We will come to get you when it is your turn to go through with the experiment. Incidentally, we have found that some of our subjects prefer to do their waiting alone, while others prefer to wait together with other subjects. Therefore, we are going to give you your choice of waiting alone or with others. In either case, you will be ushered to a comfortable room furnished with adequate reading material.

After indicating their preference of waiting alone or together with others, the subjects also indicated the intensity of this preference on an "open-ended" scale in which 0 represented a very weak preference and 100 a very strong preference. On this relatively unstructured scale there was as much as 175 points of difference between subjects (from "75-alone" to "100-together").

Presentation of the slides during the experiment served two purposes in addition to the one previously mentioned. The content of the slides (appropriate to each experimental treatment) served to reinforce the subjects' differential expectations of the nature and severity of the stimulus situation. Furthermore, the subject seen in the slides became a focal point for measuring the effectiveness of the experimental manipulations. It was assumed that a direct attempt (by means of a scaled question) to appraise the level of the subjects' fear or anxiety would be likely to: sensitize them to the true purpose of the experiment; yield unreliable results since the subjects might neither be consciously aware of, nor able to verbalize, their anxiety reaction; and evoke resistance since some subjects might not want to admit to being anxious or fearful calling their masculinity into question.

Therefore, it was necessary to use an indirect, disguised measure to evaluate whether the experimental inductions had actually aroused two levels of both fear and anxiety. Immediately after the slides had been shown (but before the affiliation choices had been made), the subjects were told:

As you may know, an individual shows his physiological reaction in a variety of behavioral forms. We are interested in seeing whether it is possible to estimate how ill-at-ease or upset individuals are at the prospect of receiving the stimulation in this experiment. Recalling the subject whom you just saw in the slides, how upset or ill-at-ease did he seem to you? Please assign a number anywhere from zero to 100 to indicate your feeling. (Zero = unconcerned, at ease; 100 = extremely concerned and ill-at-ease.)

Since the subject in the slides was a posed model instructed to remain poker faced throughout, it was assumed that there was no objective difference in his expression. Thus, any systematic difference in ratings between groups should reflect a projection of the subjects' own motives upon this screen.

However, because the content of the slides was not identical for every group but rather "tailored" to each specific treatment, it was possible that the model may have actually looked more fearful in the slides shown to the subjects in the High Fear than in the Low Fear condition. As a control check on this possibility, four additional introductory psychology classes ($N = 108$) served as judges. They were told that the slides were of a typical subject in a recently completed experiment, and their task was to estimate how ill-at-ease and concerned he appeared (on the same scale used by the experimental subjects). Two of the classes saw only the face of the model (the rest of the slide was blacked out) and were told only that he was a subject in a physiological experiment in which stimuli were applied and responses measured. The other two classes saw the entire stimulus field of the slides and were given the same complete description that the experimental subjects received. Since each class of judges rated the slides for all four experimental treatments, the order of presentation was counterbalanced.

After the projective measure of motive arousal and the measure of affiliation, the electrodes were removed and a measure taken of the subjects' reasons for choosing to affiliate or be isolated. This was done with the rationale that a social psychologist had become interested in the fact that some of our subjects preferred to be together while others preferred to be alone, and he had asked us to get some information for him about the reasons underlying this preference.

The questionnaire, designed by Gerard and Rabbie (1960), contained both open-ended and structured questions asking for reasons for the affiliation choice. Finally, the subjects noted whether or not they wished to continue in the experiment. Only one subject (in the High Fear condition) refused to remain for the "stimulation" part of the experiment.

The true purpose, hypothesis, design, and reasons for the various deceptions (and, at a later time, the results) were explained fully to each subject.

High Fear

A high level of fear was induced by leading the subjects to anticipate a series of painful electrical shocks. Although they expected to endure each of the shocks for 2 minutes, the subjects were assured that the shocks would not cause damage or injury.

The female assistant (dressed in a white lab coat, as was the experimenter) then attached electrodes to each subject's arm and fingertip and strapped his arm onto a cotton-padded board. The leads from the electrodes appeared to go to a polygraph recorder, which also was seen in the series of slides of the typical subjects. Another slide showed an enormous electrical stimulator, and the implication was that it was behind a curtain in the experimental room. It was called to the subjects' attention that:

The four dials shown in the upper right-hand corner of the stimulator enable us to regulate automatically the frequency, duration, delay, and intensity of the shock you will get.

The other slides portrayed the subject with earphones and electrodes attached (like the subjects themselves), "listening to the instructions," and then "about to receive his first painful shock," administered by the experimenter, who could be seen in the background manipulating the dials on the stimulator. A final situational factor that may have enhanced the effectiveness of the High Fear manipulation was that the experimental room housed electrical generators which made a continuous buzzing sound, a cue interpreted by the High Fear subjects as the electrical stimulator "warming up," but unnoticed or quickly adapted to by the other subjects. An unobtrusively posted sign reading "Danger/High Voltage," present only for the High Fear subjects, gave further credence to this notion.

Low Fear

In the Low Fear condition the word "shock" was never used, and all cues in the situation associated with shock, fear, or pain were removed; i.e., no white lab coats, arms not strapped to boards, etc. The expectations of these subjects were guided by instructions stating that our methodology was to apply a 10-second stimulus of very low intensity that would be just sufficient to elicit a measurable physiological response.

In the series of slides viewed by these subjects, the imposing electrical stimulator was replaced by a small innocuous looking apparatus (actually a voltmeter), and the experimenter was seen not in the active role as an agent of pain, but in the passive role of recording data from the polygraph recorder.

High Anxiety

Anxiety was manipulated by arousing a motive that was assumed to have been repressed by most of the subjects. In Freudian terminology, the motive might be called "oral libido," a desire to obtain pleasurable gratification by sucking on objects that are clearly related to infantile nursing experiences. The female breast is, of course, the prototype of such objects, but others include nipples, baby bottles, and pacifiers. Thus, to arouse this oral motive and, hence, the anxiety that should follow its arousal, subjects in the High Anxiety condition were led to believe that they would have to suck on a number of objects commonly associated with infantile oral behavior. They were told that their task would be to suck on these objects for 2 minutes while we recorded their physiological responses from the skin surfaces stimulated by the objects. In clear view in front of the subjects were the following items: numerous baby bottles, oversized nipples, pacifiers, breast shields (nipples women often wear over their breasts while nursing), and lollipops.

The same variety of stimulus objects was shown arrayed in front of the subject in the slides. He could be seen, tongue hanging out, lips puckered, about to suck his thumb (as one of the objects of stimulation) or one of the other objects. Subjects were told that the contact taped to the mouth recorded the direct reaction to the oral stimulation, while the arm contact recorded peripheral reactions.

Low Anxiety

The instructions to the Low Anxiety subjects did not mention "suck," nor any stimulation that they would receive from putting the objects in their mouths. Moreover, they were led to believe that they would keep each object in their mouths for only 10 seconds. The stimulus objects were not in immediate proximity to the subjects while their electrodes were being attached. The stimulus objects which they anticipated putting in their mouths were shown in the slides: whistles, balloons, "kazoos," and pipes. Since these objects do not require sucking (but rather, in general, blowing), the model's tongue was not seen as he prepared to use the stimuli in the slides.

RESULTS

Evidence of the Effectiveness of the Experimental Manipulations

In using the subjects' estimates of the degree to which the model seen in the slides was upset by the prospect of receiving the stimulation in the experiment, it was assumed that the subjects would tend to project their induced level of fear and anxiety. Table 1, which presents the mean projection scores for each experimental treatment, offers evidence that this assumption was valid and the manipulations effective. The High Arousal subjects perceived the model to be significantly[4] more upset, concerned, and ill-at-ease than did the Low Arousal subjects.

Table 1 MEAN PROJECTION SCORES FOR EACH EXPERIMENTAL TREATMENT

| MOTIVE | LEVEL OF AROUSAL | | p VALUE |
	LOW	HIGH	
Fear	24	42	$< .01$ ($t = 3.05$)
Anxiety	14	31a	$< .01$ ($t = 2.95$)
	ns	*ns*	

Note.—The larger the score, the greater the degree of projection.
  a Variance greater than in High Fear group, $p < .10$; SD for High Anxiety = 24, for High Fear = 16.

Our theoretical distinction between fear and anxiety, and the way these concepts were operationally defined in this experiment, lead to the prediction that, assuming similarity of past experience, persons facing the same clearly, objectively present threat should react in a relatively homogeneous fashion. This close correspondence between stimulus and response is not assumed to hold for anxiety. We have already noted that a stimulus that produces anxiety for some persons is not an anxiety producing cue for many others. Since the significance of the stimulus depends upon its symbolic and generally idiosyncratic associations, one would expect that a stimulus which elicited anxiety for persons with relevant predispositions (repressed motives) would have less effect on those who had more adequately resolved the conflict over the expression of the same motives. Thus, one way of determining whether our experimental manipulations produced two different motives, fear and anxiety (rather than only two levels of one motive), is to compare the variability in response between treatments.

The heterogeneity of response in the High Anxiety group is, as predicted, greater than in the High Fear and the Low Arousal conditions. The same difference in response variability between the High Anxiety group and all other groups is manifested as well in the dependent variable of social affiliation. The questionnaire data to be presented in a later section offer further support to the distinction between fear and anxiety.

Before presenting the major results, it is necessary to account for two possible sources of artifact in the just reported data on projection. They are: by chance sampling, the High Arousal groups could have contained more subjects who characteristically used projection as a mechanism of defense than the Low Arousal groups; and the subject seen in the High Fear and High Anxiety slides was objectively more upset and concerned than he was in the Low Fear and Low Anxiety slides. If either of these alternatives were true, then the projection measure would not be a reflection of differences due to the experimental arousal of levels of fear and anxiety.

[4] All *p* values reported throughout the paper are based on two-tailed tests of significance.

The pretest data of the subjects' mode of defense preference on the Blacky Projection test show no initial significant difference between any of the groups in their tendency to use projection.

Among the groups of neutral judges who evaluated all the slides shown in the study, from 68%–98% reported perceiving either no difference in the degree to which the model appeared upset, or a difference opposite to that reported in Table 1. This result holds for both fear and anxiety, and regardless of the order of presentation or amount of the stimulus field seen (model's face only or entire slide). Thus, it appears that the projection measure can be used as an index of the efficacy of the experimental conditions and manipulations.

Effects of Fear and Anxiety on Social Affiliation

The results bearing upon the hypothesis of the study are presented in Table 2, where for each condition the mean intensity of desire to affiliate, as well as the number of subjects choosing to affiliate and to be alone, are presented. It is evident that there is a strong positive relationship between fear and the index of affiliative tendency, but a strong negative relationship between anxiety and affiliation, so that as fear increases affiliation also increases, while an increase in anxiety results in a decrease in affiliation. Thus, our prediction of an interaction between kind of motive and level of arousal is clearly supported by the data. While some 95% of the High Fear subjects chose the "together" alternative (with more than 0 intensity), only 46% of the High Anxiety subjects chose to wait together. The marked mean difference between these groups in intensity of choice (51.0–8.0) is significant well beyond the .01 level ($t = 3.63$). The large mean difference in affiliative tendency between the High and Low Fear groups ($p < .07$, $t = 1.96$) represents a replication of Schachter's (1959, p. 18) results. While the mean difference between High and Low Anxiety was even larger than that between the Fear conditions, it only approached significance ($p = .16$, $t = 1.46$) due to the marked heterogeneity of variance of the High Anxiety group.

Table 2 RELATIONSHIP OF MOTIVE TO SOCIAL AFFILIATION

	MEAN AFFILIATION STRENGTH[a]	*NUMBER OF SUBJECTS CHOOSING*	
		TOGETHER	*ALONE OR "0-TOGETHER"*
Fear			
Low	34.0	12	3
High	51.0	19	1
Anxiety			
Low	27.0	11	4
High	8.0	10	12

Interaction: (Motive × Level) $p < .05$, $t = 2.30$, $df = 68$.

[a]*The larger the score, the greater the affiliation tendency; isolation intensity score subtracted from affiliation intensity score.*

Reasons Given for Affiliation Choice

The final measure taken was a questionnaire that explored the reasons the subjects gave for choosing to wait together with others or to wait alone. The 11 structured items on the questionnnaire each presented a possible motive for affiliation; and each was accompanied by a 70-point scale on which the subject indicated how important he thought the motive was in determining his choice. The highly significant interaction between experimental treatment and questions ($p < .001$, $F = 3.74$, $df = 30.570$) on a repeated-measurement analysis of variance justified a search for those questions (motives for affiliation) that differentiated the groups.

Since there were too few subjects choosing the alone condition, the analysis is limited to those wanting to affiliate. The motives for affiliation that were most important for the High Fear subjects and most distinguished them from the Low Fear subjects were (the lower the mean, the greater the importance; 10 = extremely important):

1. I am not sure whether I am reacting in the same way as the others to the prospect of getting shocked and would like to compare my reactions to theirs. [Emotional comparison] High Fear $\bar{x}$ = 38, Low Fear $\bar{x}$ = 54, $p < .001$.
2. I feel worried about getting shocked and would like to know to what extent the others are worried too. [Extent of comparison] High Fear $\bar{x}$ = 40, Low Fear $\bar{x}$ = 61, $p < .001$.
3. I want to be distracted in order to take my mind off the prospect of getting shocked. [Distraction] High Fear $\bar{x}$ = 44, Low Fear $\bar{x}$ = 59, $p < .01$.
4. I am worried about the prospect of getting shocked and felt that talking with someone about it would get it off my chest. [Catharsis] High Fear $\bar{x}$ = 50, Low Fear $\bar{x}$ = 59, $p < .05$.

The reasons for affiliation given spontaneously to a single open-ended question also reflect the importance of these same considerations. Among High Anxiety subjects choosing to be alone, the major reason given spontaneously and supported by the scaled questions is the desire "to be alone to think about personal affairs and school work."

Curiosity as to "what the others were like" was important, but equally so across all conditions. Of least importance among all subjects are the following motives for affiliation ("oral stimulation" substituted for "shock" for Anxiety groups):

"It would be clearer in my own mind as to how I feel about getting shocked if I could express my reactions to someone else." "I anticipated that the others would offer reassuring comments." "I want to be with others to reassure myself that I am not the only one who was singled out to be shocked." "I feel that perhaps together we could somehow figure out a way to avoid getting shocked."

There are several large differences between the High Fear and High Anxiety groups; with the former finding the following motives as significantly more important: emotional comparison, extent of comparison, distraction, catharsis, and the physical presence of others ($p < .05$ in each instance). Similarly, an internal analysis of the High Fear group reveals these same motives (especially catharsis and emotional comparison) to be more important for those subjects who chose to affiliate most strongly than for those below the group median in affiliation strength.

Ordinal Position and Its Relation to Affiliation

While the reasoning used in the planning of the present study did not include predictions of the effects of ordinal position upon affiliation, data relevant to this question was nevertheless obtained, to check on Schachter's (1959) finding that affiliation tendencies increased with emotional arousal only among first- and only-born children. This finding is duplicated in the present study. First-born children want to affiliate significantly more than later-borns under conditions of high fear, but not when the level of fear is low. While the mean affiliation intensity for the first-born High Fear subjects was 62, it was only 23 for the later-born High Fear subjects ($p = .05$, $t = 2.10$). This same general finding holds for the High Anxiety group, but again the within-group variability does not permit the large mean difference obtained (16 for first-borns and –3 for later-borns) to be statistically significant.

DISCUSSION

Since our basic hypothesis has been supported, our results lend credence to the previously drawn conceptual distinction between fear and anxiety. In view of the fact that our anxiety arousing stimulus was specifically designed to tap only one kind of repressed motive, it of course remains an empirical question whether or not the evocation of other types of presumably repressed motives also leads to social isolation.

In order to predict the consequences of the arousal of a motive, therefore, it is necessary to know which responses are required to reduce its tension. The probability of the social comparison response is, thus, a function of: the kind of motive aroused, the intensity of the motive, the degree of novelty of the emotional experience, the response hierarchy associated with the specific motive, and certain attributes of those with whom the person is to affiliate.

We do not question the assumption that the need for some kind of cognitive-emotional clarity and structure is a basic human motive. However, we feel that the need for self-evaluation is not the *most* salient motive aroused in the experimental situations that Schachter (1959) and we employed. We do not view the cognitive need to structure a vague emotional state as the primary motive in these experiments; we see social comparison not as an end in itself but merely as one of the several responses that are *instrumental* in reducing the tension associated with the situationally more salient motives of fear and anxiety.

Strict application of the theory of emotional comparison processes to the present experimental situation should lead one to predict greater affiliation tendencies for the High Anxiety subjects than the High Fear subjects, since the Anxiety situation was more unusual than that of Fear, and the emotion aroused was probably more novel and vague. The opposite prediction, supported by the results, demands an approach, such as the one followed here, that specifies the probability of the response alternatives evoked by the dominant motives aroused.

As the emotional experience becomes very novel and unusual, the need for comparison of one's reactions with others should increase, and, hence, intensify affiliation tendencies. The induction of esoteric states of consciousness by "anxiety producing drugs" (being studied presently by Schachter) may be the kind of situation in which emotional comparison theory offers the best explanations and predictions. Under such circumstances, it may be possible to create emotional states that are epiphenomena of motives whose neurophysiological bases had never previously been set into motion. A more natural counterpart of this novel emotional experience occurs the first time a person experiences the emotions associated with the death of a loved one.

The predictive importance of knowing the specific responses appropriate to the motive aroused is clearly illustrated by the following examples. If a person's guilt is aroused, his response to feelings of guilt should be to seek out others only if they could be expected to punish him and, thus, to expiate his guilt, but not to affiliate with individuals perceived as unable to fill this role. Similarly, if repressed homosexual anxieties are aroused, isolation should generally be preferred to affiliation, as with oral anxiety in the present study. However, affiliation tendencies should increase if the subject is allowed to wait with females, but not if he can wait only in the company of males.

While our questionnaire data offer support for the importance of emotional comparison, they also point up the role of other motives such as need for catharsis and distraction. The marked difference in the importance of the reasons given for affiliation between the High Fear and High Anxiety groups is perhaps the most substantial evidence that the experimental manipulations have indeed led to the arousal of two quite different motives.

A final point of interest concerns the data about ordinal position. The finding that first-born children show greater affiliation tendencies than later-born children when either fear or anxiety are aroused supports Schachter's (1959) results. Theoretical and experimental attempts to uncover the dynamics underlying this "static" variable should prove interesting and fruitful.

SUMMARY

This experiment tests the utility of the psychoanalytic distinction between fear and anxiety for making differential predictions about social affiliation. It also assesses the breadth of generalization of Schachter's (1959) empirical finding of a positive relation between emotional arousal and affiliation. Seventy-two subjects were randomly assigned to four experimental treatments in which low and high levels of fear and anxiety were manipulated. The success of these inductions was established by a projective device and questionnaire data. The dependent variable of social affiliation was measured by having the subjects choose to await the anticipated exposure to the stimulus situation either alone or together with others.

The results show that, while the desire to affiliate increases as fear increases (a replication of Schachter's, 1959, results), the opposite is true for anxiety; as anxiety increases the desire to affiliate decreases. Thus, as predicted, our findings lend empirical support to the theoretical distinction between fear and anxiety. At the same time, our results suggest that the theory of social comparison processes may not be adequate to account for the general relationship between emotions and affiliative tendencies.

REFERENCES

Festinger, L. A theory of social comparison processes. *Hum. Relat.,* 1954, *7,* 117–40.

Freud, S. *Inhibitions, symptoms, and anxiety.* (Originally published 1936) London: Hogarth, 1949. (a)

Freud, S. *New introductory lectures on psychoanalysis.* (Originally published 1933) London: Hogarth, 1949. (b)

Gerard, H. B., & Rabbie, J. M. Fear and social comparison. Unpublished manuscript, Bell Telephone Research Laboratories, 1960.

Sarnoff, I. Psychoanalytic theory and social attitudes. *Publ. opin. Quart.,* 1960, *24,* 251–79. (a)

Sarnoff, I. Reaction formation and cynicism. *J. Pers.,* 1960, *28,* 129–43. (b)

Sarnoff, I., & Corwin, S. M. Castration anxiety and the fear of death. *J. Pers.,* 1959, *27,* 374–85.

Schachter, S. *The psychology of affiliation.* Stanford: Stanford Univer. Press, 1959.

Emotional Uncertainty and Social Comparison

HAROLD B. GERARD

An experiment was run to test an assumption, basic to social comparison theory, that evaluational uncertainty regarding some aspect of the self, such as an emotional experience, produces a desire to compare one's self with others. Under threat of a strong shock, 2 levels of uncertainty were induced. Cross-cutting this induction were treatments in which information about others due to undergo the same experience was manipulated. Following Schachter, the desire for comparison information was measured by the strength of S's affiliation tendency. The findings suggest that: (a) uncertainty does produce a desire to compare one's self with others, (b) the individual's uncertainty relative to available comparison persons will determine his comparison tendency, and (c) a discrepancy in position (in this case, emotionality) reduces the desire to compare.

Reprinted from Journal of Abnormal and Social Psychology, 66, *1963, 568–73.* *Copyright 1963 by the American Psychological Association, and reproduced by permission.*

The discomfort associated with an uncertain evaluation of some aspect of the self (e.g., an opinion or an ability) is a function both of its indeterminateness and its importance for the person. This discomfort, being drive-like, will lead to behavior enabling the individual to achieve greater certainty in his evaluation. When information relevant to an uncertain evaluation is available the individual will therefore attempt to acquire it. When this information is in the form of the opinions or performances of others, a process is generated whereby the individual's uncertainty is reduced through comparison of himself with others. Some aspects of this process have been elaborated by Festinger (1954). Nowhere, however, has the fundamental relationship between uncertainty and social comparison been examined directly. This is the purpose of the present experiment.

Schachter's (1959) recent work attempts to bring emotional experience within the context of social comparison theory. He found that an individual, when emotionally aroused, will seek the company of others who are confronted by the same emotion provoking situation. Schachter infers, from indirect evidence, that a major motivation accounting for this affiliation is the individual's desire to evaluate his experience by checking his own emotional reactions to the situation against the reaction of others.

If Schachter's finding is indeed due to the individual's desire to compare himself with others, then providing him with information about the others would have a consummatory effect and thus reduce affiliation. Using Schachter's basic experimental situation, Gerard and Rabbie (1961) found such evidence in a study designed to test this derivation. Their results, however, were not entirely explicable in comparison theory terms, leaving the matter still open.

A social comparison interpretation of Schachter's data rests entirely upon the assumption that less uncertainty is aroused in the low than in the high fear treatment. The argument is as follows. The situation confronting the subject evokes an emotional response which is far greater in the high as compared with the low fear treatment. Since the threat of being shocked is novel, cognitive uncertainty exists regarding the bodily state produced by the anticipation; the greater the threat, the greater both the bodily response and the cognitive uncertainty. This assumption of a positive relationship between emotional level and uncertainty may not be tenable. It is just as likely that greater uncertainty is associated with weak, vague feelings and that a situation posing an obvious danger like a strong shock is very clearly cognized. Another motive or set of motives which was not ruled out by Schachter's procedures may account for the positive relation between level of fear and affiliation. The fact that uncertainty may not have an obvious relationship to emotional level is suggested by the parallel effects of information under both fear levels in the Gerard-Rabbie experiment.

Since, in comparison theory, it is not the level of fear arousal but uncertainty which is assumed to mediate the relationship between arousal and affiliation, it is important to bring *this* relationship into experimental focus by a more direct check.

Rabbie (1961) attempted such a direct examination, again using Schachter's basic experimental situation, and varying the likelihood that the individual would receive a strong shock. Under one treatment, the subject was informed that each of the four people present would receive a strong shock whereas under another treatment he was told that only one of the four would receive the shock. Although the treatments produced no difference in reported emotional arousal, there was greater affiliation under the "one-in-four" likelihood treatment. Rabbie's results support the uncertainty-comparison relationship, if we assume that varying the likelihood of getting shocked varies cognitive uncertainty regarding the *internal* emotional state. An obvious alternative interpretation of his data is that the greater affiliation in the one-in-four treatment may have been due to aroused curiosity as to who specifically would be the victim.

The present experiment approaches more directly an examination of the assumption that uncertainty produces information seeking behavior. This was done by attempting to do the obvious, namely, to vary uncertainty regarding the aroused bodily state.

Since affiliation in these experiments is assumed to be a measure of the motivation to compare one's self with others, providing the individual with information about the others should reduce affiliation, as in the Gerard-Rabbie experiment. This reduction in affiliation should be more marked the greater his uncertainty since the information would presumably have a greater consummatory effect the greater the drive. Evidence exists indicating that an individual will cease comparing himself with others to the extent that they differ in the aspect being compared (Festinger, Gerard, Hymovitch, Kelley, & Raven, 1952; Hoffman, Festinger, & Lawrence, 1954; Schachter, 1951). Therefore further evidence for social comparison would be a reduced desire to be with others to the extent that they differ in emotionality.

METHOD

Subjects

Each four-person group consisted either of all men or all women seated in adjacent cubicles. All subjects were students at Drew University. When only three subjects showed up for the experiment, as happened occasionally, it was made to appear, by appropriate deception, that all four cubicles were occupied.

Procedure

After the subject was seated in his cubicle, a pair of nonpolarizing electrodes, designed for electrodermal measurements by O'Connell and Tursky (1960), were attached to the subject's nonpreferred hand. One of these electrodes was attached to the palm and the other fixed in position just above the wrist on the dorsal side of the forearm. A dummy EKG electrode was attached to the dorsal side of the forearm just above the reference skin resistance electrode. The arm was then immobilized by strapping it into a specially made armrest. The skin resistance electrodes were connected across one of the inputs of a four-channel constant current (40 microamperes) galvanometer circuit.

All of the instructions for each experimental condition were prerecorded and heard by the subject over earphones which had a rubber cup over each earpiece.

Each subject was exposed to the same high fear threat which was induced by a procedure similar to that used in the Schachter, Gerard-Rabbie, and Rabbie experiments. The two experimenters wore white coats and each had a stetho-scope bulging from one pocket. A sphygmomanometer, some gauze, cotton, and medicaments were conspicuously on display as was a sign on some formidable looking electronic gear which read "Caution, High Voltage." After the electrodes were in place, the subject was informed that he was taking part in an investiga-tion of the effects of electrical shock and that these shocks would be painful. For the exact wording of these instructions, the reader is referred either to Schachter (1959, p. 13) or Gerard and Rabbie (1961, p. 587).

The certainty and information treatments were then administered after which the subject was informed that there would be a 10- or a 15-minute wait before we were ready to administer the shocks. He was given a choice of waiting together with the others in a room nearby or alone in a separate room and was told that on the basis of the choices made, we would arrange the most appropriate waiting situation. He depressed one of two buttons to indicate his choice and was then asked to indicate the strength of his desire for the waiting situation he had chosen. He did this by setting a pointer on a dial in the center of his console at a position between "1" and "11." His dial setting was read on a meter in the control room which transformed it to a score from 0 to 100. This was the basic information required to test the comparison hypothesis. When informed that they were not actually going to be shocked, the subjects were generally quite relieved. They were apprised of the deceptions and asked not to reveal the nature of the experiment to fellow students who had not as yet participated.

Manipulation of Uncertainty

The subject had a meter on his table which was a disguised VU (volume unit) meter. It was labeled "Emotionality Index" and its dial was painted to read from 0 to 100. Since a VU meter registers the amplitude of an audio signal, it was possible to control the magnitude and variability of the bogus emotionality index reading with a tone which was recorded on the instruction tape. While this tone was on, the subject's earphones were disconnected from the output of the tape recorder.

He was told:

We are interested not only in how you react to the shocks but also in your reactions while anticipating these shocks. With the aid of the electrodes attached to you now, we can determine your present emotional state. With a formula that has been carefully worked out, we take your skin conductance as measured by the little polystyrene cup electrodes attached to your hand and above your wrist and combine it with your muscle tremor, which is detected by the large electrode attached to your forearm, and arrive at an emotionality index. We have found the measure to be very accurate in reflecting the worked-up state of the body.

In this experiment we have decided to let you see your own emotionality index which will appear on the meter in front of you. The needle may waver somewhat indicating momentary changes in your emotionality. We are going to record your index on our equipment for a three minute period. After that, we will proceed with the shock administration. Zero is complete calm, whereas 100 indicates extreme emotionality. Now watch your meter.

In the "uncertain" treatment, the needle made rather erratic and wide excursions for the 3-minute period with an average reading of 75. In the "certain" treatment, the needle remained at or very close to 75 during the entire 3-minute period.

Information Treatments

In order to examine the effects of information upon tendencies to engage in social comparison two information treatments were superimposed on the two levels of uncertainty. A procedure similar to the Gerard-Rabbie one was used. In one treatment the subject received no information about the others. In the other treatment the instructions continued:

We thought that you would like to know how emotional the other subjects were during that three minute period. Rather than give you a running record of each of their emotionality indexes, we will indicate, on the meter, the average for the other subjects for the three minute interval. The average for each of you for the interval is computed automatically. It will take a few more seconds to combine these averages. Separate computations have to be made since each of you will see the average of the three others.

After a reasonable pause, the meter indicated the others' average in the Others-same treatment, as 75.

Two additional information conditions which, due to a subject shortage, were run only under the unsteady meter display, purported to show the others as either much higher (an average of 95) or much lower (an average of 50) in emotionality than the subject. These treatments were applied in order to further detect social comparison. Positive evidence would be lower affiliation in both of these treatments as compared with the Others-same treatment. Of course, any conclusions that we may draw are necessarily limited by the lack of counter-balancing.

Summary of the Design

Two degrees of emotional uncertainty in the face of a threat of electrical shock were induced. This was accomplished by displaying to the subject a steady and an unsteady meter reading which purported to indicate to the subject the level of his emotionality.

Each of these treatments was run under two levels of information about the others. Under one, he was given no information about the others whereas under the other he was shown data indicating that the others were similar to himself in emotionality level. Two additional treatments of discrepant information were run only under the uncertain condition.

RESULTS

Since affiliation varies with level of threat (Gerard & Rabbie, 1961; Schachter, 1959), it is important to establish at the outset that the manipulation of differential uncertainty did not induce a difference in emotionality. The change in base level conductance during the uncertainty induction was taken as a measure of the change in emotionality produced by the induction (Gerard & Rabbie, 1961). A comparison of the change in skin conductance from the beginning to the end of the induction shows no differential increase between the certain and uncertain treatments. We are therefore relatively safe in assuming a lack of difference in emotionality between the two treatments.

Induction of Uncertainty

During the 3-minute uncertainty induction, a continuous record was made of the subject's skin conductance. In order to determine if this induction produced a differential in emotional variability, we measured the variability of 13 arbitrary points taken at 10-second intervals from the beginning to the end of the uncertainty induction. The unsteady needle treatment does show somewhat greater variability ($p < .15$ by a t test comparing the average variance per subject in each uncertainty treatment).[1]

Affiliation

Table 1[2] presents the mean desire for affiliation for the six experimental conditions. For the four counterbalanced conditions we see an effect of uncertainty in the predicted direction ($p < .01$ by t) as well as an interaction with information. Information that the others are at the same emotional level reduces affiliation under the steady meter ($p < .01$ by t) but not under the unsteady meter display.[3] Both discrepant conditions show some reduction in affiliation. However, only the Others-higher condition is significantly different ($p < .01$ by t) from the Others-same condition.

[1] Two "maverick" scores were exceptionally large and added considerably to the standard error. Were it not for these two scores, the difference would have been significant at beyond the .05 level. Unfortunately no other check on emotional variability could be taken immediately after the uncertainty induction since the interposition of a questionnaire measure might have further complicated what is a somewhat awkward procedure to begin with. The "take" of the variable might have been adversely affected. We therefore only have the conductance variability data to rely on.

[2] The data for those six subjects who chose to be alone are not presented in this table. In all of the experiments thus far, a constant proportion of approximately 10% of the subjects choose to be alone.

[3] There is a good deal of interest currently in certain phenomena which appear to be linked with the order of birth in the family (Dittes, 1961; Gerard & Rabbie, 1961; Glass, Horwitz, Firestone, & Grinker, 1963; Sarnoff & Zimbardo, 1961; Schachter, 1959). Schachter, using all female subjects, found greater affiliation among first as compared to later borns. Gerard and Rabbie, on the other hand, found an interaction with sex. Their females behaved like those of Schachter whereas males showed the opposite trend. As Glass et al. have pointed out, it is probably misleading to consider birth order as a variable in psychological research independently of the sociocultural context of the particular family since there are such wide variations in child rearing practices. However, for the record, birth order data were collected. Once again we find the same interaction found in the Gerard-Rabbie experiment. That is, first born females want to affiliate more than later borns whereas for males, the relationship is reversed ($p < .05$ for the interaction). In response to the Gerard-Rabbie results, some have argued (informally) that the interaction may be due to the fact that the subjects were from a large urban college with a large Jewish population. The present results were for subjects from a small Methodist suburban college.

Table 1 AFFILIATION PRODUCED BY DEGREE OF CERTAINTY (STEADINESS OF METER DISPLAY) AND INFORMATION ABOUT THE OTHER'S EMOTIONALITY

UNSTEADY METER				STEADY METER	
No Info	Others-Same	Others-Higher	Others-Lower	No Info	Others-Same
79.6(12)[a]	79.6(12)	51.1(9)	71.2(12)	69.0(10)	54.2(12)

[a]*Ns are indicated in parentheses.*

DISCUSSION

We shall first discuss the data from the four counterbalanced conditions reserving some remarks at the end for the other two conditions. When fear is aroused we find greater affiliation the greater the uncertainty. This basic finding is direct support for the assumption underlying comparison theory. However, we had predicted that information indicating that the others were similar to the subject would have a greater effect on reducing affiliation under the uncertain rather than the certain treatment. The data indicate that the opposite obtained. How can we account for this reversal?

One possible interpretation is that the mere fact of knowing the level of the others' emotion is not sufficient to reduce comparison motivation in the uncertain treatment. The general level of uncertainty may be much too high for this information to have had any effect. The steady meter treatment on the other hand, does have at least some uncertainty associated with it. Perhaps this level is sufficiently low for the information to produce a change in comparison motivation. Admittedly, this is not a very compelling interpretation.

There is a more plausible, although somewhat more complicated, interpretation which makes three assumptions: the individual not only compares his emotional level with that of the others but makes variability comparisons as well, variability comparison occurs only when the individual's own variability is high, and variability comparison takes precedence over level comparison. Thus, under the unsteady display information about the others' level failed to reduce affiliation since this information has only second priority, as it were. The high degree of affiliation here presumably reflects the desire for variability information. Following our assumptions, the subject who saw the steady meter was more concerned with level than with variability since his variability was low. The information as to the others' level was information which he could utilize in reducing whatever uncertainty there was regarding his own level.

Variability comparison is assumed to have priority over the comparison of positions or levels since it is tantamount to the attribution, by the individual, of reliability or credibility "weightings" to his own and the others' positions. This says that relative rather than absolute uncertainty is the prime mover in social comparison. Under circumstances where there is easy access to information from others it is conceivable that the individual will attempt to check his self-evaluation against direct "physical" facts even when these facts are quite difficult to obtain. He could do this if he attributed low credibility to the information available from others.

There is still another explanation for the reversal which relates to some data from a recent experiment (Gerard, 1962) where it was found that a comparison person takes on positive value for the individual to the extent that he serves to reduce uncertainty. The relatively high affiliation level for the unsteady meter subject in the Others-same condition may reflect such an increased attraction. There may be two opposing tendencies at work, a reduction in comparison motivation due to having information which has reduced uncertainty and an increase in affiliation due to the attraction produced by uncertainty reduction. Further research is necessary to examine these tendencies separately. Such research would, however, require a measure of comparison motivation which is purer than simple affiliation since affiliation contains motivational components other than comparison motivation which are probably affected by the experimental manipulations of the kind that we impose upon the situation.

Since comparison theory does predict reduced affiliation where the others differ in level, the evidence from the treatments in which the others were higher or lower than the subject in emotionality does suggest that levels were being compared under the uncertain treatment. The fact that affiliation is higher in the Others-low condition suggests the possibility that, in addition to a desire to compare levels, the subject was seeking reassurance that the prospects were not as dire as he anticipated. Since the design was not counterbalanced, the findings here cannot be properly evaluated. If we are correct in assuming that variability comparison was salient in the uncertain treatment then a discrepancy would have relatively little effect on affiliation as compared with the steady meter display where the individual is primarily concerned with information as to the others' level. Therefore, if the design were to be filled out by running these variations under the steady display we would predict an even greater decrement in affiliation due to a discrepancy in emotionality.

REFERENCES

Dittes, J. E. Birth order and vulnerability to differences in acceptance. *Amer. Psychologist,* 1961, *16*, 358. (Abstract)

Festinger, L. A theory of social comparison processes. *Hum. Relat.,* 1954, *7*, 117–40.

Festinger, L., Gerard, H. B., Hymovitch, B., Kelley, H. H., & Raven, B. H. The influence process in the presence of extreme deviates. *Hum. Relat.,* 1952, *5*, 327–46.

Gerard, H. B. Attitudes toward an agent of uncertainty reduction. *J. Pers.,* 1962, *30*, 485–95.

Gerard, H. B., & Rabbie, J. M. Fear and social comparison. *J. abnorm. soc. Psychol.,* 1961, *62*, 586–92.

Glass, D. C., Horwitz, M., Firestone, I., & Grinker, J. Birth order and reactions to frustration. *J. abnorm. soc. Psychol.,* 1963, *66*, 192–94.

Hoffman, P. J., Festinger, L., & Lawrence, D. H. Tendencies toward group comparability in competitive bargaining. *Hum. Relat.,* 1954, *7*, 141–59.

O'Connell, D. N., & Tursky, B. Silver-silver chloride sponge electrodes for skin potential recording. *Amer. J. Psychol.,* 1960, *73*, 302–304.

Rabbie, J. M. Factors influencing the magnitude and direction of affiliative tendencies under stress. Unpublished doctoral dissertation, Yale University, 1961.

Sarnoff, I., & Zimbardo, P. G. Anxiety, fear, and social affiliation. *J. abnorm. soc. Psychol.*, 1961, *62*, 356–63.

Schachter, S. Deviation, rejection, and communication. *J. abnorm. soc. Psychol.*, 1951, *46*, 190–207.

Schachter, S. *The psychology of affiliation.* Minneapolis: Univer. Minnesota Press, 1959.

Cognitive, Social, and Physiological Determinants of Emotional State

STANLEY SCHACHTER AND JEROME E. SINGER

The problem of which cues, internal or external, permit a person to label and identify his own emotional state has been with us since the days that James (1890) first tendered his doctrine that "the bodily changes follow directly the perception of the exciting fact, and that our feeling of the same changes as they occur *is* the emotion" (p. 449). Since we are aware of a variety of feeling and emotion states, it should follow from James' proposition that the various emotions will be accompanied by a variety of differentiable bodily states. Following James' pronouncement, a formidable number of studies were undertaken in search of the physiological differentiators of the emotions. The results, in these early days, were almost uniformly negative. All of the emotional states experimentally manipulated were characterized by a general pattern of excitation of the sympathetic nervous system but there appeared to be no clear-cut physiological discriminators of the various emotions. This pattern of results was so consistent from experiment to experiment that Cannon (1929) offered, as one of the crucial criticisms of the James-Lange theory, the fact that "the same visceral changes occur in very different emotional states and in non-emotional states" (p. 351).

More recent work, however, has given some indication that there may be differentiators. Ax (1953) and Schachter (1957) studied fear and anger. On a large number of indices both of these states were characterized by a similarly high level of autonomic activation but on several indices they did differ in the degree of activation. Wolf and Wolff (1947) studied a subject with a gastric fistula and were able to distinguish two patterns in the physiological responses of the stomach wall. It should be noted, though, that for many months they studied their subject during and following a great variety of moods and emotions and were able to distinguish only two patterns.

Whether or not there are physiological distinctions among the various emotional states must be considered an open question. Recent work might be taken

Reprinted from Psychological Review, 69, *1962, 379–99. Copyright 1962 by the American Psychological Association and reproduced by permission.*

to indicate that such differences are at best rather subtle and that the variety of emotion, mood, and feeling states are by no means matched by an equal variety of visceral patterns.

This rather ambiguous situation has led Ruckmick (1936), Hunt, Cole, and Reis (1958), Schachter (1959) and others to suggest that cognitive factors may be major determinants of emotional states. Granted a general pattern of sympathetic excitation as characteristic of emotional states, granted that there may be some differences in pattern from state to state, it is suggested that one labels, interprets, and identifies this stirred-up state in terms of the characteristics of the precipitating situation and one's apperceptive mass. This suggests, then, that an emotional state may be considered a function of a state of physiological arousal[1] and of a cognition appropriate to this state of arousal. The cognition, in a sense, exerts a steering function. Cognitions arising from the immediate situation as interpreted by past experience provide the framework within which one understands and labels his feelings. It is the cognition which determines whether the state of physiological arousal will be labeled as "anger," "joy," "fear," or whatever.

In order to examine the implications of this formulation let us consider the fashion in which these two elements, a state of physiological arousal and cognitive factors, would interact in a variety of situations. In most emotion inducing situations, of course, the two factors are completely interrelated. Imagine a man walking alone down a dark alley; a figure with a gun suddenly appears. The perception-cognition "figure with a gun" in some fashion initiates a state of physiological arousal; this state of arousal is interpreted in terms of knowledge about dark alleys and guns and the state of arousal is labeled "fear." Similarly a student who unexpectedly learns that he has made Phi Beta Kappa may experience a state of arousal which he will label "joy."

Let us now consider circumstances in which these two elements, the physiological and the cognitive, are, to some extent, independent. First, is the state of physiological arousal alone sufficient to induce an emotion? Best evidence indicates that it is not. Marañon[2] (1924), in a fascinating study, (which was replicated by Cantril & Hunt, 1932, and Landis & Hunt, 1932) injected 210 of his patients with the sympathomimetic agent adrenalin and then simply asked them to introspect. Seventy-one percent of his subjects simply reported their physical symptoms with no emotional overtones; 29% of the subjects responded in an apparently emotional fashion. Of these the great majority described their feelings in a fashion that Marañon labeled "cold" or "as if" emotions, that is, they made statements such as "I feel *as if* I were afraid" or "*as if* I were awaiting a great happiness." This is a sort of emotional "déjà vu" experience; these subjects are neither happy nor afraid, they feel "as if" they were. Finally a very few cases apparently reported a genuine emotional experience. However, in order to produce this reaction in most of these few cases, Marañon (1924) points out:

[1] Though our experiments are concerned exclusively with the physiological changes produced by the injection of adrenalin, which appear to be primarily the result of sympathetic excitation, the term physiological arousal is used in preference to the more specific "excitation of the sympathetic nervous system" because there are indications, to be discussed later, that this formulation is applicable to a variety of bodily states.

[2] Translated copies of Marañon's (1924) paper may be obtained by writing to the senior author.

One must suggest a memory with strong affective force but not so strong as to produce an emotion in the normal state. For example, in several cases we spoke to our patients before the injection of their sick children or dead parents and they responded calmly to this topic. The same topic presented later, during the adrenal commotion, was sufficient to trigger emotion. This adrenal commotion places the subject in a situation of 'affective imminence' (pp. 307–308).

Apparently, then, to produce a genuinely emotional reaction to adrenalin, Marañon was forced to provide such subjects with an appropriate cognition.

Though Marañon (1924) is not explicit on his procedure, it is clear that his subjects knew that they were receiving an injection and in all likelihood knew that they were receiving adrenalin and probably had some order of familiarity with its effects. In short, though they underwent the pattern of sympathetic discharge common to strong emotional states, at the same time they had a completely appropriate cognition or explanation as to why they felt this way. This, we would suggest, is the reason so few of Marañon's subjects reported any emotional experience.

Consider now a person in a state of physiological arousal for which no immediately explanatory or appropriate cognitions are available. Such a state could result were one covertly to inject a subject with adrenalin or, unknown to him, feed the subject a sympathomimetic drug such as ephedrine. Under such conditions a subject would be aware of palpitations, tremor, face flushing, and most of the battery of symptoms associated with a discharge of the sympathetic nervous system. In contrast to Marañon's (1924) subjects he would, at the same time, be utterly unaware of why he felt this way. What would be the consequence of such a state?

Schachter (1959) has suggested that precisely such a state would lead to the arousal of "evaluative needs" (Festinger, 1954), that is, pressures would act on an individual in such a state to understand and label his bodily feelings. His bodily state grossly resembles the condition in which it has been at times of emotional excitement. How would he label his present feelings? It is suggested, of course, that he will label his feelings in terms of his knowledge of the immediate situation.[3] Should he at the time be with a beautiful woman he might decide that he was wildly in love or sexually excited. Should he be at a gay party, he might, by comparing himself to others, decide that he was extremely happy and euphoric. Should he be arguing with his wife, he might explode in fury and hatred. Or, should the situation be completely inappropriate he could decide that he was excited about something that had recently happened to him or, simply, that he was sick. In any case, it is our basic assumption that emotional states are a function of the interaction of such cognitive factors with a state of physiological arousal.

---

[3] This suggestion is not new for several psychologists have suggested that situational factors should be considered the chief differentiators of the emotions. Hunt, Cole, and Reis (1958) probably make this point most explicitly in their study distinguishing among fear, anger, and sorrow in terms of situational characteristics.

This line of thought, then, leads to the following propositions:

1. Given a state of physiological arousal for which an individual has no immediate explanation, he will "label" this state and describe his feelings in terms of the cognitions available to him. To the extent that cognitive factors are potent determiners of emotional states, it could be anticipated that precisely the same state of physiological arousal could be labeled "joy" or "fury" or "jealousy" or any of a great diversity of emotional labels depending on the cognitive aspects of the situation.

2. Given a state of physiological arousal for which an individual has a completely appropriate explanation (e.g., "I feel this way because I have just received an injection of adrenalin") no evaluative needs will arise and the individual is unlikely to label his feelings in terms of the alternative cognitions available.

Finally, consider a condition in which emotion inducing cognitions are present but there is no state of physiological arousal. For example, an individual might be completely aware that he is in great danger but for some reason (drug or surgical) remain in a state of physiological quiescence. Does he experience the emotion "fear"? Our formulation of emotion as a joint function of a state of physiological arousal and an appropriate cognition, would, of course, suggest that he does not, which leads to our final proposition.

3. Given the same cognitive circumstances, the individual will react emotionally or describe his feelings as emotions only to the extent that he experiences a state of physiological arousal.[4]

PROCEDURE

The experimental test of these propositions requires (*a*) the experimental manipulation of a state of physiological arousal, (*b*) the manipulation of the extent to which the subject has an appropriate or proper explanation of his bodily state, and (*c*) the creation of situations from which explanatory cognitions may be derived.

In order to satisfy the first two experimental requirements, the experiment was cast in the framework of a study of the effects of vitamin supplements on vision. As soon as a subject arrived, he was taken to a private room and told by the experimenter:

In this experiment we would like to make various tests of your vision. We are particularly interested in how certain vitamin compounds and vitamin supplements affect the visual skills. In particular, we want to find out how the vitamin compound called 'Suproxin' affects your vision.

What we would like to do, then, if we can get your permission, is to give you a small injection of Suproxin. The injection itself is mild and harmless; however, since some people do object to being injected we don't want to talk you into anything. Would you mind receiving a Suproxin injection?

[4] In his critique of the James-Lange theory of emotion, Cannon (1929) also makes the point that sympathectomized animals and patients do seem to manifest emotional behavior. This criticism is, of course, as applicable to the above proposition as it was to the James-Lange formulation. We shall discuss the issues involved in later papers.

If the subject agrees to the injection (and all but 1 of 185 subjects did) the experimenter continues with instructions we shall describe shortly, then leaves the room. In a few minutes a physician enters the room, briefly repeats the experimenter's instructions, takes the subject's pulse and then injects him with Suproxin.

Depending upon condition, the subject receives one of two forms of Suproxin—epinephrine or a placebo.

Epinephrine or adrenalin is a sympathomimetic drug whose effects, with minor exceptions, are almost a perfect mimicry of a discharge of the sympathetic nervous system. Shortly after injection systolic blood pressure increases markedly, heart rate increases somewhat, cutaneous blood flow decreases, while muscle and cerebral blood flow increase, blood sugar and lactic acid concentration increase, and respiration rate increases slightly. As far as the subject is concerned the major subjective symptoms are palpitation, tremor, and sometimes a feeling of flushing and accelerated breathing. With a subcutaneous injection (in the dosage administered to our subjects), such effects usually begin within 3–5 minutes of injection and last anywhere from 10 minutes to an hour. For most subjects these effects are dissipated within 15–20 minutes after injection.

Subjects receiving epinephrine received a subcutaneous injection of ½ cubic centimeter of a 1 : 1000 solution of Winthrop Laboratory's Suprarenin, a saline solution of epinephrine bitartrate.

Subjects in the placebo condition received a subcutaneous injection of ½ cubic centimeter of saline solution. This is, of course, completely neutral material with no side effects at all.

Manipulating an Appropriate Explanation

By "appropriate" we refer to the extent to which the subject has an authoritative, unequivocal explanation of his bodily condition. Thus, a subject who had been informed by the physician that as a direct consequence of the injection he would feel palpitations, tremor, etc. would be considered to have a completely appropriate explanation. A subject who had been informed only that the injection would have no side effects would have no appropriate explanation of his state. This dimension of appropriateness was manipulated in three experimental conditions which shall be called: Epinephrine Informed (Epi Inf), Epinephrine Ignorant (Epi Ign), and Epinephrine Misinformed (Epi Mis).

Immediately after the subject had agreed to the injection and before the physician entered the room, the experimenter's spiel in each of these conditions went as follows:

Epinephrine Informed. I should also tell you that some of our subjects have experienced side effects from the Suproxin. These side effects are transitory, that is, they will only last for about 15 or 20 minutes. What will probably happen is that your hand will start to shake, your heart will start to pound, and your face may get warm and flushed. Again these are side effects lasting about 15 or 20 minutes.

While the physician was giving the injection, she told the subject that the injection was mild and harmless and repeated this description of the symptoms that the subject could expect as a consequence of the shot. In this condition, then, subjects have a completely appropriate explanation of their bodily state. They know precisely what they will feel and why.

Epinephrine Ignorant. In this condition, when the subject agreed to the injection, the experimenter said nothing more relevant to side effects and simply left the room. While the physician was giving the injection, she told the subject that the injection was mild and harmless and would have no side effects. In this condition, then, the subject has no experimentally provided explanation for his bodily state.

Epinephrine Misinformed. I should also tell you that some of our subjects have experienced side effects from the Suproxin. These side effects are transitory, that is, they will only last for about 15 or 20 minutes. What will probably happen is that your feet will feel numb, you will have an itching sensation over parts of your body, and you may get a slight headache. Again these are side effects lasting 15 or 20 minutes.

And again, the physician repeated these symptoms while injecting the subject.

None of these symptoms, of course, are consequences of an injection of epinephrine and, in effect, these instructions provide the subject with a completely inappropriate explanation of his bodily feelings. This condition was introduced as a control condition of sorts. It seemed possible that the description of side effects in the Epi Inf condition might turn the subject introspective, self-examining, possibly slightly troubled. Differences on the dependent variable between the Epi Inf and Epi Ign conditions might, then, be due to such factors rather than to differences in appropriateness. The false symptoms in the Epi Mis condition should similarly turn the subject introspective, etc., but the instructions in this condition do not provide an appropriate explanation of the subject's state.

Subjects in all of the above conditions were injected with epinephrine. Finally, there was a placebo condition in which subjects, who were injected with saline solution, were given precisely the same treatment as subjects in the Epi Ign condition.

Producing an Emotion Inducing Cognition

Our initial hypothesis has suggested that given a state of physiological arousal for which the individual has no adequate explanation, cognitive factors can lead the individual to describe his feelings with any of a diversity of emotional labels. In order to test this hypothesis, it was decided to manipulate emotional states which can be considered quite different—euphoria and anger.

There are, of course, many ways to induce such states. In our own program of research, we have concentrated on social determinants of emotional states and have been able to demonstrate in other studies that people do evaluate their own feelings by comparing themselves with others around them (Schachter 1959; Wrightsman 1960). In this experiment we have attempted again to manipulate emotional state by social means. In one set of conditions, the subject is placed together with a stooge who has been trained to act euphorically. In a second set of conditions the subject is with a stooge trained to act in an angry fashion.

Euphoria

Immediately[5] after the subject had been injected, the physician left the room and the experimenter returned with a stooge whom he introduced as another subject, then said:

Both of you have had the Suproxin shot and you'll both be taking the same tests of vision. What I ask you to do now is just wait for 20 minutes. The reason for this is simply that we have to allow 20 minutes for the Suproxin to get from the injection site into the bloodstream. At the end of 20 minutes when we are certain that most of the Suproxin has been absorbed into the bloodstream, we'll begin the tests of vision.

The room in which this was said had been deliberately put into a state of mild disarray. As he was leaving, the experimenter apologetically added:

The only other thing I should do is to apologize for the condition of the room. I just didn't have time to clean it up. So, if you need any scratch paper or rubber bands or pencils, help yourself. I'll be back in 20 minutes to begin the vision tests.

As soon as the experimenter had left, the stooge introduced himself again, made a series of standard icebreaker comments, and then launched his routine. For observation purposes, the stooge's act was broken into a series of standard units, demarcated by a change in activity or a standard comment. In sequence, the units of the stooge's routine were the following:

    1. Stooge reaches for a piece of paper and starts doodling saying, "They said we could use this for scratch, didn't they?" He doodles a fish for some 30 seconds, then says:

    2. "This scrap paper isn't even much good for doodling" and crumples paper and attempts to throw it into wastebasket in far corner of the room. He misses but this leads him into a "basketball game." He crumples up other sheets of paper, shoots a few baskets, says "Two points" occasionally. He gets up and does a jump shot saying, "The old jump shot is really on today."

    3. If the subject has not joined in, the stooge throws a paper basketball to the subject saying, "Here, you try it."

    4. Stooge continues his game saying, "The trouble with paper basketballs is that you don't really have any control."

    5. Stooge continues basketball, then gives it up saying, "This is one of my good days. I feel like a kid again. I think I'll make a plane." He makes a paper airplane saying, "I guess I'll make one of the longer ones."

    6. Stooge flies plane. Gets up and retrieves plane. Flies again, etc.

    7. Stooge throws plane at subject.

    8. Stooge, flying plane, says, "Even when I was a kid, I was never much good at this."

[5] It was, of course, imperative that the sequence with the stooge begin before the subject felt his first symptoms for otherwise the subject would be virtually forced to interpret his feelings in terms of events preceding the stooge's entrance. Pretests had indicated that, for most subjects, epinephrine-caused symptoms begin within 3–5 minutes after injection. A deliberate attempt was made then to bring in the stooge within 1 minute after the subject's injection.

9. Stooge tears off part of plane saying, "Maybe this plane can't fly but at least it's good for something." He wads up paper and making a slingshot of a rubber band begins to shoot the paper.

10. Shooting, the stooge says, "They [paper ammunition] really go better if you make them long. They don't work right if you wad them up."

11. While shooting, stooge notices a sloppy pile of manila folders on a table. He builds a tower of these folders, then goes to the opposite end of the room to shoot at the tower.

12. He misses several times, then hits and cheers as the tower falls. He goes over to pick up the folders.

13. While picking up, he notices, behind a portable blackboard, a pair of hula hoops which have been covered with black tape with a few wires sticking out of the tape. He reaches for these, taking one for himself and putting the other aside but within reaching distance of the subject. The stooge tries the hula hoop, saying, "This isn't as easy as it looks."

14. Stooge twirls hoop wildly on arm, saying, "Hey, look at this—this is great."

15. Stooge replaces the hula hoop and sits down with his feet on the table. Shortly thereafter the experimenter returns to the room.

This routine was completely standard, though its pace, of course, varied depending upon the subject's reaction, the extent to which he entered into this bedlam and the extent to which he initiated activities of his own. The only variations from this standard routine were those forced by the subject. Should the subject originate some nonsense of his own and request the stooge to join in, he would do so. And, he would, of course, respond to any comments initiated by the subject.

Subjects in each of the three "appropriateness" conditions and in the placebo condition were submitted to this setup. The stooge, of course, never knew in which condition any particular subject fell.

Anger

Immediately after the injection, the experimenter brought a stooge into the subject's room, introduced the two and after explaining the necessity for a 20 minute delay for "the Suproxin to get from the injection site into the bloodstream" he continued, "We would like you to use these 20 minutes to answer these questionnaires." Then handing out the questionnaires, he concludes with, "I'll be back in 20 minutes to pick up the questionnaires and begin the tests of vision."

Before looking at the questionnaire, the stooge says to the subject,

I really wanted to come for an experiment today, but I think it's unfair for them to give you shots. At least, they should have told us about the shots when they called us; you hate to refuse, once you're here already.

The questionnaires, five pages long, start off innocently requesting face sheet information and then grow increasingly personal and insulting. The stooge, sitting directly opposite the subject, paces his own answers so that at all times subject and stooge are working on the same question. At regular points in the questionnaire, the stooge makes a series of standardized comments about the questions. His comments start off innocently enough, grow increasingly querulous, and finally he ends up in a rage. In sequence, he makes the following comments.

1. Before answering any items, he leafs quickly through the questionnaire saying, "Boy, this is a long one."

2. Question 7 on the questionnaire requests, "List the foods that you would eat in a typical day." The stooge comments, "Oh for Pete's sake, what did I have for breakfast this morning?"

3. Question 9 asks, "Do you ever hear bells?_____. How often? _____." The stooge remarks, "Look at Question 9. How ridiculous can you get? I hear bells every time I change classes."

4. Question 13 requests, "List the childhood diseases you have had and the age at which you had them" to which the stooge remarks, "I get annoyed at this childhood disease question. I can't remember what childhood diseases I had, and especially at what age. Can you?"

5. Question 17 asks "What is your father's average annual income?" and the stooge says, "This really irritates me. It's none of their business what my father makes. I'm leaving that blank."

6. Question 25 presents a long series of items such as "Does not bathe or wash regularly," "Seems to need psychiatric care," etc. and requests the respondent to write down for which member of his immediate family each item seems most applicable. The question specifically prohibits the answer "None" and each item must be answered. The stooge says, "I'll be damned if I'll fill out Number 25. 'Does not bathe or wash regularly'—that's a real insult." He then angrily crosses out the entire item.

7. Question 28 reads:
"How many times each week do you have sexual intercourse?" 0–1_____ 2–3_____ 4–6_____ 7 and over_____. The stooge bites out, "The hell with it! I don't have to tell them all this."

8. The stooge sits sullenly for a few moments; then he rips up his questionnaire, crumples the pieces and hurls them to the floor, saying, "I'm not wasting any more time. I'm getting my books and leaving," and he stamps out of the room.

9. The questionnaire continues for eight more questions ending with: "With how many men (other than your father) has your mother had extramarital relationships?"
4 and under_____: 5–9_____: 10 and over_____.

Subjects in the Epi Ign, Epi Inf and Placebo conditions were run through this "anger" inducing sequence. The stooge, again, did not know to which condition the subject had been assigned.

In summary, this is a seven condition experiment which, for two different emotional states, allows us (a) to evaluate the effects of "appropriateness" on emotional inducibility and (b) to begin to evaluate the effects of sympathetic activation on emotional inducibility. In schematic form the conditions are the following:

	EUPHORIA	*ANGER*
	Epi Inf	Epi Inf
	Epi Ign	Epi Ign
	Epi Mis	Placebo
	Placebo	

The Epi Mis condition was not run in the Anger sequence. This was originally conceived as a control condition and it was felt that its inclusion in the Euphoria conditions alone would suffice as a means of evaluating the possible artifactual effect of the Epi Inf instructions.

Measurement

Two types of measures of emotional state were obtained. Standardized observation through a one-way mirror was the technique used to assess the subject's behavior. To what extent did he act euphoric or angry? Such behavior can be considered in a way as a "semiprivate" index of mood for as far as the subject was concerned, his emotional behavior could be known only to the other person in the room—presumably another student. The second type of measure was self-report in which, on a variety of scales, the subject indicated his mood of the moment. Such measures can be considered "public" indices of mood for they would, of course, be available to the experimenter and his associates.

Observation

Euphoria.   For each of the first 14 units of the stooge's standardized routine an observer kept a running chronicle of what the subject did and said. For each unit the observer coded the subject's behavior in one or more of the following categories:

Category 1:   Joins in activity. If the subject entered into the stooge's activities, e.g., if he made or flew airplanes, threw paper basketballs, hula hooped, etc., his behavior was coded in this category.
Category 2:   Initiates new activity. A subject was so coded if he gave indications of creative euphoria, that is, if on his own, he initiated behavior outside of the stooge's routine. Instances of such behavior would be the subject who threw open the window and, laughing, hurled paper basketballs at passersby; or, the subject who jumped on a table and spun one hula hoop on his leg and the other on his neck.
Categories 3 and 4:   Ignores or watches stooge. Subjects who paid flatly no attention to the stooge or who, with or without comment, simply watched the stooge without joining in his activity were coded in these categories.

For any particular unit of behavior, the subject's behavior was coded in one or more of these categories. To test reliability of coding two observers independently coded two experimental sessions. The observers agreed completely on the coding of 88% of the units.

Anger.   For each of the units of stooge behavior, an observer recorded the subject's responses and coded them according to the following category scheme:

Category 1:   Agrees. In response to the stooge the subject makes a comment indicating that he agrees with the stooge's standardized comment or that he, too, is irked by a particular item on the questionnaire. For example, a subject who responded to the stooge's comment on the "father's income" question by saying, "I don't like that kind of personal question either" would be so coded (scored +2).

Category 2: Disagrees. In response to the stooge's comment, the subject makes a comment which indicates that he disagrees with the stooge's meaning or mood; e.g., in response to the stooge's comment on the "father's income" question, such a subject might say, "Take it easy, they probably have a good reason for wanting the information" (scored −2).

Category 3: Neutral. A noncommittal or irrelevant response to the stooge's remark (scored 0).

Category 4: Initiates agreement or disagreement. With no instigation by the stooge, a subject, so coded, would have volunteered a remark indicating that he felt the same way or, alternatively, quite differently than the stooge. Examples would be "Boy I hate this kind of thing" or "I'm enjoying this" (scored +2 or −2).

Category 5: Watches. The subject makes no verbal response to the stooge's comment but simply looks directly at him (scored 0).

Category 6: Ignores. The subject makes no verbal response to the stooge's comment nor does he look at him; the subject, paying no attention at all to the stooge, simply works at his own questionnaire (scored −1).

A subject was scored in one or more of these categories for each unit of stooge behavior. To test reliability, two observers independently coded three experimental sessions. In order to get a behavioral index of anger, observation protocol was scored according to the values presented in parentheses after each of the above definitions of categories. In a unit-by-unit comparison, the two observers agreed completely on the scoring of 71% of the units jointly observed. The scores of the two observers differed by a value of 1 or less for 88% of the units coded and in not a single case did the two observers differ in the direction of their scoring of a unit.

Self Report of Mood and Physical Condition

When the subject's session with the stooge was completed, the experimenter returned to the room, took pulses and said:

Before we proceed with the vision tests, there is one other kind of information which we must have. We have found, as you can probably imagine, that there are many things beside Suproxin that affect how well you see in our tests. How hungry you are, how tired you are, and even the mood you're in at the time—whether you feel happy or irritated at the time of testing will affect how well you see. To understand the data we collect on you, then, we must be able to figure out which effects are due to causes such as these and which are caused by Suproxin.

The only way we can get such information about your physical and emotional state is to have you tell us. I'll hand out these questionnaires and ask you to answer them as accurately as possible. Obviously, our data on the vision tests will only be as accurate as your description of your mental and physical state.

In keeping with this spiel, the questionnaire that the experimenter passed out contained a number of mock questions about hunger, fatigue, etc., as well as questions of more immediate relevance to the experiment. To measure mood or emotional state the following two were the crucial questions:

1. How irritated, angry or annoyed would you say you feel at present?

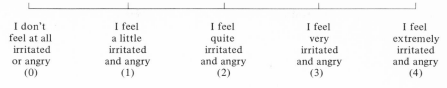

| I don't feel at all irritated or angry (0) | I feel a little irritated and angry (1) | I feel quite irritated and angry (2) | I feel very irritated and angry (3) | I feel extremely irritated and angry (4) |

2. How good or happy would you say you feel at present?

| I don't feel at all happy or good (0) | I feel a little happy and good (1) | I feel quite happy and good (2) | I feel very happy and good (3) | I feel extremely happy and good (4) |

To measure the physical effects of epinephrine and determine whether or not the injection had been successful in producing the necessary bodily state, the following questions were asked:

1. Have you experienced any palpitation (consciousness of your own heart beat)?

| Not at all (0) | A slight amount (1) | A moderate amount (2) | An intense amount (3) |

2. Did you feel any tremor (involuntary shaking of the hands, arms or legs)?

| Not at all (0) | A slight amount (1) | A moderate amount (2) | An intense amount (3) |

To measure possible effects of the instructions in the Epi Mis condition, the following questions were asked:

1. Did you feel any numbness in your feet?
2. Did you feel any itching sensation?
3. Did you experience any feeling of headache?

To all three of these questions was attached a four-point scale running from "Not at all" to "An intense amount."

In addition to these scales, the subjects were asked to answer two open-end questions on other physical or emotional sensations they may have experienced during the experimental session. A final measure of bodily state was pulse rate which was taken by the physician or the experimenter at two times—immediately before the injection and immediately after the session with the stooge.

When the subjects had completed these questionnaires, the experimenter announced that the experiment was over, explained the deception and its necessity in detail, answered any questions, and swore the subjects to secrecy. Finally, the subjects answered a brief questionnaire about their experiences, if any, with adrenalin and their previous knowledge or suspicion of the experimental setup. There was no indication that any of the subjects had known about the experiment beforehand but 11 subjects were so extremely suspicious of some crucial feature of the experiment that their data were automatically discarded.

Subjects

The subjects were all male, college students taking classes in introductory psychology at the University of Minnesota. Some 90% of the students in these classes volunteer for a subject pool for which they receive two extra points on their final exam for every hour that they serve as experimental subjects. For this study the records of all potential subjects were cleared with the Student Health Service in order to insure that no harmful effects would result from the injections.

Evaluation of the Experimental Design

The ideal test of our propositions would require circumstances which our experiment is far from realizing. First, the proposition that: "A state of physiological arousal for which an individual has no immediate explanation will lead him to label this state in terms of the cognitions available to him" obviously requires conditions under which the subject does not and cannot have a proper explanation of his bodily state. Though we toyed with such fantasies as ventilating the experimental room with vaporized adrenalin, reality forced us to rely on the disguised injection of Suproxin—a technique which was far from ideal for no matter what the experimenter told them, some subjects would inevitably attribute their feelings to the injection. To the extent that subjects did so, differences between the several appropriateness conditions should be attenuated.

Second, the proposition that: "Given the same cognitive circumstances the individual will react emotionally only to the extent that he experiences a state of physiological arousal" requires for its ideal test the manipulation of states of physiological arousal and of physiological quiescence. Though there is no question that epinephrine effectively produces a state of arousal, there is also no question that a placebo does not prevent physiological arousal. To the extent that the experimental situation effectively produces sympathetic stimulation in placebo subjects, the proposition is difficult to test, for such a factor would attenuate differences between epinephrine and placebo subjects.

Both of these factors, then, can be expected to interfere with the test of our several propositions. In presenting the results of this study, we shall first present condition by condition results and then evaluate the effect of these two factors on experimental differences.

RESULTS

Effects of the Injections on Bodily State

Let us examine first the success of the injections at producing the bodily state required to examine the propositions at test. Does the injection of epinephrine produce symptoms of sympathetic discharge as compared with the placebo injection? Relevant data are presented in Table 1 where it can be immediately seen that on all items subjects who were in epinephrine conditions show considerably more evidence of sympathetic activation than do subjects in placebo conditions. In all epinephrine conditions pulse rate increases significantly when compared with the decrease characteristic of the placebo conditions. On the scales it is clear that epinephrine subjects experience considerably more palpitation and tremor than do placebo subjects. In all possible comparisons on these symptoms, the mean scores of subjects in any of the epinephrine conditions are greater than the corresponding scores in the placebo conditions at better that the .001 level of significance. Examination of the absolute values of these scores makes it quite clear that subjects in epinephrine conditions were, indeed, in a state of physiological arousal, while most subjects in placebo conditions were in a relative state of physiological quiescence.

Table 1 THE EFFECTS OF THE INJECTIONS ON BODILY STATE

| CONDITION | N | PULSE | | SELF-RATING OF | | | | |
		PRE	POST	PALPITATION	TREMOR	NUMBNESS	ITCHING	HEADACHE
Euphoria								
Epi Inf	27	85.7	88.6	1.20	1.43	0	0.16	0.32
Epi Ign	26	84.6	85.6	1.83	1.76	0.15	0	0.55
Epi Mis	26	82.9	86.0	1.27	2.00	0.06	0.08	0.23
Placebo	26	80.4	77.1	0.29	0.21	0.09	0	0.27
Anger								
Epi Inf	23	85.9	92.4	1.26	1.41	0.17	0	0.11
Epi Ign	23	85.0	96.8	1.44	1.78	0	0.06	0.21
Placebo	23	84.5	79.6	0.59	0.24	0.14	0.06	0.06

The epinephrine injection, of course, did not work with equal effectiveness for all subjects; indeed for a few subjects it did not work at all. Such subjects reported almost no palpitation or tremor, showed no increase in pulse and described no other relevant physical symptoms. Since for such subjects the necessary experimental conditions were not established, they were automatically excluded from the data and all further tabular presentations will not include such subjects. Table 1, however, does include the data of these subjects. There were four such subjects in euphoria conditions and one of them in anger conditions.

In order to evaluate further data on Epi Mis subjects it is necessary to note the results of the "numbness," "itching," and "headache" scales also presented in Table 1. Clearly the subjects in the Epi Mis condition do not differ on these scales from subjects in any of the other experimental conditions.

Effects of the Manipulations on Emotional State

Euphoria: Self-report. The effects of the several manipulations on emotional state in the euphoria conditions are presented in Table 2. The scores recorded in this table are derived, for each subject, by subtracting the value of the point he checks on the irritation scale from the value of the point he checks on the happiness scale. Thus, if a subject were to check the point "I feel a little irritated and angry" on the irritation scale and the point "I feel very happy and good" on the happiness scale, his score would be +2. The higher the positive value, the happier and better the subject reports himself as feeling. Though we employ an index for expositional simplicity, it should be noted that the two components of the index each yield results completely consistent with those obtained by use of this index.

Let us examine first the effects of the appropriateness instructions. Comparison of the scores for the Epi Mis and Epi Inf conditions makes it immediately clear that the experimental differences are not due to artifacts resulting from the informed instructions. In both conditions the subject was warned to expect a variety of symptoms as a consequence of the injection. In the Epi Mis condition, where the symptoms were inappropriate to the subject's bodily state the self-report score is almost twice that in the Epi Inf condition where the symptoms were completely appropriate to the subject's bodily state. It is reasonable, then, to attribute differences between informed subjects and those in other conditions to differences in manipulated appropriateness rather than to artifacts such as introspectiveness or self-examination.

It is clear that, consistent with expectations, subjects were more susceptible to the stooge's mood and consequently more euphoric when they had no explanation of their own bodily states than when they did. The means of both the Epi Ign and Epi Mis conditions are considerably greater than the mean of the Epi Inf condition.

It is of interest to note that Epi Mis subjects are somewhat more euphoric than are Epi Ign subjects. This pattern repeats itself in other data shortly to be presented. We would attribute this difference to differences in the appropriateness dimension. Though, as in the Epi Ign condition, a subject is not provided with an explanation of his bodily state, it is, of course, possible that he will provide one for himself which is not derived from his interaction with the stooge. Most reasonably he could decide for himself that he feels this way

Table 2 SELF-REPORT OF EMOTIONAL STATE IN THE EUPHORIA CONDITIONS

CONDITION	N	SELF-REPORT SCALES	COMPARISON	p [a]
Epi Inf	25	0.98	Epi Inf vs. Epi Mis	< .01
Epi Ign	25	1.78	Epi Inf vs. Epi Ign	.02
Epi Mis	26	1.90	Placebo vs. Epi Mis,	*ns*
Placebo	26	1.61	Ign, or Inf	

[a]*All p values reported throughout paper are two-tailed.*

because of the injection. To the extent that he does so he should be less susceptible to the stooge. It seems probable that he would be less likely to hit on such an explanation in the Epi Mis condition than in the Epi Ign condition for in the Epi Mis condition both the experimenter and the doctor have told him that the effects of the injection would be quite different from what he actually feels. The effect of such instructions is probably to make it more difficult for the subject himself to hit on the alternative explanation described above. There is some evidence to support this analysis. In open-end questions in which subjects described their own mood and state, 28% of the subjects in the Epi Ign condition made some connection between the injection and their bodily state compared with the 16% of subjects in the Epi Mis condition who did so. It could be considered, then, that these three conditions fall along a dimension of appropriateness, with the Epi Inf condition at one extreme and the Epi Mis condition at the other.

Comparing the placebo to the epinephrine conditions, we note a pattern which will repeat itself throughout the data. Placebo subjects are less euphoric than either Epi Mis or Epi Ign subjects but somewhat more euphoric than Epi Inf subjects. These differences are not, however, statistically significant. We shall consider the epinephrine-placebo comparisons in detail in a later section of this paper following the presentation of additional relevant data. For the moment, it is clear that, by self-report manipulating appropriateness has had a very strong effect on euphoria.

Behavior. Let us next examine the extent to which the subject's behavior was affected by the experimental manipulations. To the extent that his mood has been affected, one should expect that the subject will join in the stooge's whirl of manic activity and initiate similar activities of his own. The relevant data are presented in Table 3. The column labeled "Activity index" presents summary figures on the extent to which the subject joined in the stooge's activity. This is

Table 3   BEHAVIORAL INDICATIONS OF EMOTIONAL STATE IN THE EUPHORIA CONDITIONS

CONDITION	N	ACTIVITY INDEX	MEAN NUMBER OF ACTS INITIATED
Epi Inf	25	12.72	.20
Epi Ign	25	18.28	.56
Epi Mis	25	22.56	.84
Placebo	26	16.00	.54

	p VALUE	
COMPARISON	ACTIVITY INDEX	INITIATES[a]
Epi Inf vs. Epi Mis	.05	.03
Epi Inf vs. Epi Ign	ns	.08
Plac vs. Epi Mis, Ign, or Inf	ns	ns

[a]Tested by X^2 comparison of the proportion of subjects in each condition initiating new acts.

a weighted index which reflects both the nature of the activities in which the subject engaged and the amount of time he was active. The index was devised by assigning the following weights to the subject's activities: 5—hula hooping; 4—shooting with slingshot; 3—paper airplanes; 2—paper basketballs; 1—doodling; 0—does nothing. Pretest scaling on 15 college students ordered these activities with respect to the degree of euphoria they represented. Arbitrary weights were assigned so that the wilder the activity, the heavier the weight. These weights are multiplied by an estimate of the amount of time the subject spent in each activity and the summed products make up the activity index for each subject. This index may be considered a measure of behavioral euphoria. It should be noted that the same between-condition relationships hold for the two components of this index as for the index itself.

The column labeled "Mean number of acts initiated" presents the data on the extent to which the subject deviates from the stooge's routine and initiates euphoric activities of his own.

On both behavioral indices, we find precisely the same pattern of relationships as those obtained with self-reports. Epi Mis subjects behave somewhat more euphorically than do Epi Ign subjects who in turn behave more euphorically than do Epi Inf subjects. On all measures, then, there is consistent evidence that a subject will take over the stooge's euphoric mood to the extent that he has no other explanation of his bodily state.

Again it should be noted that on these behavioral indices, Epi Ign and Epi Mis subjects are somewhat more euphoric than placebo subjects but not significantly so.

Anger: Self-report. Before presenting data for the anger conditions, one point must be made about the anger manipulation. In the situation devised, anger, if manifested, is most likely to be directed at the experimenter and his annoyingly personal questionnaire. As we subsequently discovered, this was rather unfortunate, for the subjects, who had volunteered for the experiment for extra points on their final exam, simply refused to endanger these points by publicly blowing up, admitting their irritation to the experimenter's face or spoiling the questionnaire. Though as the reader will see, the subjects were quite willing to manifest anger when they were alone with the stooge, they hesitated to do so on material (self-ratings of mood and questionnaire) that the experimenter might see and only after the purposes of the experiment had been revealed were many of these subjects willing to admit to the experimenter that they had been irked or irritated.

This experimentally unfortunate situation pretty much forces us to rely on the behavioral indices derived from observation of the subject's presumably private interaction with the stooge. We do, however, present data on the self-report scales in Table 4. These figures are derived in the same way as the figures presented in Table 2 for the euphoria conditions, that is, the value checked on the irritation scale is subtracted from the value checked on the happiness scale. Though, for the reasons stated above, the absolute magnitude of these figures (all positive) is relatively meaningless, we can, of course, compare condition means within the set of anger conditions. With the happiness-irritation index employed, we should, of course, anticipate precisely the reverse results from those obtained in the euphoria conditions; that is, the Epi Inf subjects in

Table 4 SELF-REPORT OF EMOTIONAL STATE IN THE ANGER CONDITIONS

CONDITION	N	SELF-REPORT SCALES	COMPARISON	p
Epi Inf	22	1.91	Epi Inf vs. Epi Ign	.08
Epi Ign	23	1.39	Placebo vs. Epi Ign or Inf	*ns*
Placebo	23	1.63		

the anger conditions should again be less susceptible to the stooge's mood and should, therefore, describe themselves as in a somewhat happier frame of mind than subjects in the Epi Ign condition. This is the case; the Epi Inf subjects average 1.91 on the self-report scales while the Epi Ign subjects average 1.39.

Evaluating the effects of the injections, we note again that, as anticipated, Epi Ign subjects are somewhat less happy than Placebo subjects but, once more, this is not a significant difference.

Behavior. The subject's responses to the stooge, during the period when both were filling out their questionnaires, were systematically coded to provide a behavioral index of anger. The coding scheme and the numerical values attached to each of the categories have been described in the methodology section. To arrive at an "Anger index" the numerical value assigned to a subject's responses to the stooge is summed together for the several units of stooge behavior. In the coding scheme used, a positive value to this index indicates that the subject agrees with the stooge's comment and is growing angry. A negative value indicates that the subject either disagrees with the stooge or ignores him.

The relevant data are presented in Table 5. For this analysis, the stooge's routine has been divided into two phases—the first two units of his behavior (the "long" questionnaire and "What did I have for breakfast?") are considered essentially neutral revealing nothing of the stooge's mood; all of the following units are considered "angry" units for they begin with an irritated remark about the "bells" question and end with the stooge's fury as he rips up his questionnaire and stomps out of the room. For the neutral units, agreement or disagreement with the stooge's remarks is, of course, meaningless as an index of mood and we should anticipate no difference between conditions. As can be seen in Table 5, this is the case.

For the angry units, we must, of course, anticipate that subjects in the Epi Ign condition will be angrier than subjects in the Epi Inf condition. This is indeed the case. The Anger index for the Epi Ign condition is positive and large, indicating that these subjects have become angry, while in the Epi Inf condition the Anger index is slightly negative in value indicating that these subjects have failed to catch the stooge's mood at all. It seems clear that providing the subject with an appropriate explanation of his bodily state greatly reduces his tendency to interpret his state in terms of the cognitions provided by the stooge's angry behavior.

Finally, on this behavioral index, it can be seen that subjects in the Epi Ign condition are significantly angrier than subjects in the Placebo condition. Behaviorally, at least, the injection of epinephrine appears to have led subjects to an angrier state than comparable subjects who received placebo shots.

Table 5 BEHAVIORAL INDICATIONS OF EMOTIONAL STATE IN THE ANGER
CONDITIONS

CONDITION	N	NEUTRAL UNITS	ANGER UNITS
Epi Inf	22	+0.07	−0.18
Epi Ign	23	+0.30	+2.28
Placebo	22[a]	−0.09	+0.79

COMPARISON FOR ANGER UNITS	p
Epi Inf vs. Epi Ign	< .01
Epi Ign vs. Placebo	< .05
Placebo vs. Epi Inf	ns

[a]*For one subject in this condition the sound system went dead and the observer could
not, of course, code his reactions.*

Conformation of Data to Theoretical Expectations

Now that the basic data of this study have been presented, let us examine closely
the extent to which they conform to theoretical expectations. If our hypotheses
are correct and if this experimental design provided a perfect test for these
hypotheses, it should be anticipated that in the euphoria conditions the degree
of experimentally produced euphoria should vary in the following fashion:

$$\text{Epi Mis} \geq \text{Epi Ign} > \text{Epi Inf} = \text{Placebo}$$

And in the anger conditions, anger should conform to the following pattern:

$$\text{Epi Ign} > \text{Epi Inf} = \text{Placebo}$$

In both sets of conditions, it is the case that emotional level in the Epi Mis
and Epi Ign conditions is considerably greater than that achieved in the corresponding Epi Inf conditions. The results for the Placebo condition, however,
are ambiguous for consistently the Placebo subjects fall between the Epi Ign and
the Epi Inf subjects. This is a particularly troubling pattern for it makes it
impossible to evaluate unequivocally the effects of the state of physiological
arousal and indeed raises serious questions about our entire theoretical structure.
Though the emotional level is consistently greater in the Epi Mis and Epi Ign
conditions than in the Placebo condition, this difference is significant at
acceptable probability levels only in the anger conditions.

In order to explore the problem further, let us examine the experimental
factors identified earlier, which might have acted to restrain the emotional level
in the Epi Ign and Epi Mis conditions. As was pointed out earlier, the ideal test
of our first two hypotheses requires an experimental setup in which the subject
has flatly no way of evaluating his state of physiological arousal other than by
means of the experimentally provided cognitions. Had it been possible to
physiologically produce a state of sympathetic activation by means other than
injection, one could have approached this experimental ideal more closely than
in the present setup. As it stands, however, there is always a reasonable
alternative cognition available to the aroused subject—he feels the way he does

because of the injection. To the extent that the subject seizes on such an explanation of his bodily state, we should expect that he will be uninfluenced by the stooge. Evidence presented in Table 6 for the anger condition and in Table 7 for the euphoria conditions indicates that this is, indeed, the case.

As mentioned earlier, some of the Epi Ign and Epi Mis subjects in their answers to the open-end questions clearly attributed their physical state to the injection, e.g., "the shot gave me the shivers." In Tables 6 and 7 such subjects are labeled "Self-informed." In Table 6 it can be seen that the self-informed subjects are considerably less angry than are the remaining subjects; indeed, they are not angry at all. With these self-informed subjects eliminated the difference between the Epi Ign and the Placebo conditions is significant at the .01 level of significance.

Table 6 THE EFFECTS OF ATTRIBUTING BODILY STATE TO THE INJECTION ON ANGER IN THE ANGER EPI IGN CONDITION

	N	*ANGER INDEX*
Self-informed subjects	3	−1.67
Others	20	+2.88
Self-informed versus Others		$p = .05$

Precisely the same pattern is evident in Table 7 for the euphoria conditions. In both the Epi Mis and the Epi Ign conditions, the self-informed subjects have considerably lower activity indices than do the remaining subjects. Eliminating self-informed subjects, comparison of both of these conditions with the Placebo

Table 7 THE EFFECTS OF ATTRIBUTING BODILY STATE TO THE INJECTION ON EUPHORIA IN THE EUPHORIA EPI IGN AND EPI MIS CONDITIONS

EPI IGN		
	N	*ACTIVITY INDEX*
Self-informed subjects	8	11.63
Others	17	21.14
Self-informed versus Others		$p = .05$

EPI MIS		
	N	*ACTIVITY INDEX*
Self-informed subjects	5	12.40
Others	20	25.10
Self-informed versus Others		$p = .10$

condition yields a difference significant at the .03 level of significance. It should be noted, too, that the self-informed subjects have much the same score on the activity index as do the experimental Epi Inf subjects (Table 3).

It would appear, then, that the experimental procedure of injecting the subjects, by providing an alternative cognition, has, to some extent, obscured the effects of epinephrine. When account is taken of this artifact, the evidence is good that the state of physiological arousal is a necessary component of an emotional experience for when self-informed subjects are removed, epinephrine subjects give consistent indications of greater emotionality than do placebo subjects.

Let us examine next the fact that consistently the emotional level, both reported and behavioral, in Placebo conditions is greater than that in the Epi Inf conditions. Theoretically, of course, it should be expected that the two conditions will be equally low, for by assuming that emotional state is a joint function of a state of physiological arousal and of the appropriateness of a cognition we are, in effect, assuming a multiplicative function, so that if either component is at zero, emotional level is at zero. As noted earlier this expectation should hold if we can be sure that there is no sympathetic activation in the Placebo conditions. This assumption, of course, is completely unrealistic for the injection of placebo does not prevent sympathetic activation. The experimental situations were fairly dramatic and certainly some of the placebo subjects gave indications of physiological arousal. If our general line of reasoning is correct, it should be anticipated that the emotional level of subjects who give indications of sympathetic activity will be greater than that of subjects who do not. The relevant evidence is presented in Tables 8 and 9.

As an index of sympathetic activation we shall use the most direct and unequivocal measure available—change in pulse rate. It can be seen in Table 1 that the predominant pattern in the Placebo condition is a decrease in pulse rate. We shall assume, therefore, that those subjects whose pulse increases or remains the same give indications of sympathetic activity while those subjects whose pulse decreases do not. In Table 8, for the euphoria condition, it is immediately clear that subjects who give indications of sympathetic activity are considerably more euphoric than are subjects who show no sympathetic activity. This relationship is, of course, confounded by the fact that euphoric subjects are considerably more active than noneuphoric subjects—a factor which independent of mood could elevate pulse rate. However, no such factor operates in the anger condition where angry subjects are neither more active nor talkative than calm

Table 8 SYMPATHETIC ACTIVATION AND EUPHORIA IN THE EUPHORIA PLACEBO CONDITION

SUBJECT WHOSE:	N	*ACTIVITY INDEX*
Pulse decreased	14	10.67
Pulse increased or remained same	12	23.17
Pulse decreasers versus pulse increasers or same		$p = .02$

Table 9 SYMPATHETIC ACTIVATION AND ANGER IN ANGER PLACEBO
CONDITION

SUBJECT WHOSE:	Na	ANGER INDEX
Pulse decreased	13	+0.15
Pulse increased or remained same	8	+1.69
Pulse decreasers versus pulse increasers or same		p = .01

aN *reduced by two cases owing to failure of sound system in one case and experimenter's failure to take pulse in another.*

subjects. It can be seen in Table 9 that Placebo subjects who show signs of sympathetic activation give indications of considerably more anger than do subjects who show no such signs. Conforming to expectations, sympathetic activation accompanies an increase in emotional level.

It should be noted, too, that the emotional levels of subjects showing no signs of sympathetic activity are quite comparable to the emotional level of subjects in the parallel Epi Inf conditions (see Tables 3 and 5). The similarity of these sets of scores and their uniformly low level of indicated emotionality would certainly make it appear that both factors are essential to an emotional state. When either the level of sympathetic arousal is low or a completely appropriate cognition is available, the level of emotionality is low.

DISCUSSION

Let us summarize the major findings of this experiment and examine the extent to which they support the propositions offered in the introduction of this paper. It has been suggested, first, that given a state of physiological arousal for which an individual has no explanation, he will label this state in terms of the cognitions available to him. This implies, of course, that by manipulating the cognitions of an individual in such a state we can manipulate his feelings in diverse directions. Experimental results support this proposition for following the injection of epinephrine, those subjects who had no explanation for the bodily state thus produced, gave behavioral and self-report indications that they had been readily manipulable into the disparate feeling states of euphoria and anger.

From this first proposition, it must follow that given a state of physiological arousal for which the individual has a completely satisfactory explanation, he will not label this state in terms of the alternative cognitions available. Experimental evidence strongly supports this expectation. In those conditions in which subjects were injected with epinephrine and told precisely what they would feel and why, they proved relatively immune to any effects of the manipulated cognitions. In the anger condition, such subjects did not report or show anger; in the euphoria condition, such subjects reported themselves as far less happy than subjects with an identical bodily state but no adequate knowledge of why they felt the way they did.

Finally, it has been suggested that given constant cognitive circumstances, an individual will react emotionally only to the extent that he experiences a state of physiological arousal. Without taking account of experimental artifacts, the evidence in support of this proposition is consistent but tentative. When the effects of "self-informing" tendencies in epinephrine subjects and of "self-arousing" tendencies in placebo subjects are partialed out, the evidence strongly supports the proposition.

The pattern of data, then, falls neatly in line with theoretical expectations. However, the fact that we were forced, to some extent, to rely on internal analyses in order to partial out the effects of experimental artifacts inevitably makes our conclusions somewhat tentative. In order to further test these propositions on the interaction of cognitive and physiological determinants of emotional state, a series of additional experiments, published elsewhere, was designed to rule out or overcome the operation of these artifacts. In the first of these, Schachter and Wheeler (1962) extended the range of manipulated sympathetic activation by employing three experimental groups—epinephrine, placebo, and a group injected with the sympatholytic agent, chlorpromazine. Laughter at a slapstick movie was the dependent variable and the evidence is good that amusement is a direct function of manipulated sympathetic activation.

In order to make the epinephrine-placebo comparison under conditions which would rule out the operation of any self-informing tendency, two experiments were conducted on rats. In one of these Singer (1961) demonstrated that under fear inducing conditions, manipulated by the simultaneous presentation of a loud bell, a buzzer, and a bright flashing light, rats injected with epinephrine were considerably more frightened than rats injected with a placebo. Epinephrine-injected rats defecated, urinated, and trembled more than did placebo-injected rats. In nonfear control conditions, there were no differences between epinephrine and placebo groups, neither group giving any indication of fear. In another study, Latané and Schachter (1962) demonstrated that rats injected with epinephrine were notably more capable of avoidance learning than were rats injected with a placebo. Using a modified Miller-Mowrer shuttlebox, these investigators found that during an experimental period involving 200 massed trials, 15 rats injected with epinephrine avoided shock an average of 101.2 trials while 15 placebo-injected rats averaged only 37.3 avoidances.

Taken together, this body of studies does give strong support to the propositions which generated these experimental tests. Given a state of sympathetic activation, for which no immediately appropriate explanation is available, human subjects can be readily manipulated into states of euphoria, anger, and amusement. Varying the intensity of sympathetic activation serves to vary the intensity of a variety of emotional states in both rats and human subjects.

Let us examine the implications of these findings and of this line of thought for problems in the general area of the physiology of the emotions. We have noted in the introduction that the numerous studies on physiological differentiators of emotional states have, viewed en masse, yielded quite inconclusive results. Most, though not all, of these studies have indicated no differences among the various emotional states. Since as human beings, rather than as scientists, we have no difficulty identifying, labeling, and distinguishing among our feelings, the results of these studies have long seemed rather puzzling and paradoxical. Perhaps because of this, there has been a persistent tendency to discount such results as due to ignorance or methodological inadequacy and to pay far more attention to the very few studies which demonstrate *some* sort of physiological differences among emotional states than to the very many studies which indicate no differences at all. It is conceivable, however, that these results should be taken at face value and that emotional states may, indeed, be generally characterized by a high level of sympathetic activation with few if any physiological distinguishers among the many emotional states. If this is correct, the findings of the present study may help to resolve the problem. Obviously this study does *not* rule out the possibility of physiological differences among the emotional states. It is the case, however, that given precisely the same state of epinephrine-induced sympathetic activation, we have, by means of cognitive manipulations, been able to produce in our subjects the very disparate states of euphoria and anger. It may indeed be the case that cognitive factors are major determiners of the emotional labels we apply to a common state of sympathetic arousal.

Let us ask next whether our results are specific to the state of sympathetic activation or if they are generalizable to other states of physiological arousal. It is clear that from our experiments proper, it is impossible to answer the question for our studies have been concerned largely with the effects of an epinephrine created state of sympathetic arousal. We would suggest, however, that our conclusions are generalizable to almost any pronounced internal state for which no appropriate explanation is available. This suggestion receives some support from the experiences of Nowlis and Nowlis (1956) in their program of research on the effects of drugs on mood. In their work the Nowlises typically administer a drug to groups of four subjects who are physically in one another's presence and free to interact. The Nowlises describe some of their results with these groups as follows:

At first we used the same drug for all 4 men. In those sessions seconal, when compared with placebo, increased the checking of such words as expansive, forceful, courageous, daring, elated, and impulsive. In our first statistical analysis we were confronted with the stubborn fact that when the same drug is given to all 4 men in a group, the N that has to be entered into the analysis is 1, not 4. This increases the cost of an already expensive experiment by a considerable factor, but it cannot be denied that the effects of these drugs may be and often are quite contagious. Our first attempted solution was to run tests on groups in which each man had a different drug during the same session, such as 1 on seconal, 1 on benzedrine, 1 on dramamine, and 1 on placebo. What does seconal do? Cooped up with, say, the egotistical benzedrine partner, the withdrawn, indifferent dramamine partner, and the slightly bored lactose man, the second subject reports that he is distractible, dizzy, drifting, glum, defiant, languid, sluggish, discouraged, dull, gloomy, lazy, and slow! This is not the report of mood that we got when all 4 men were on seconal. It thus appears that the moods of the partners do definitely influence the effect of seconal (p 350).

It is not completely clear from this description whether this "contagion" of mood is more marked in drug than in placebo groups, but should this be the case, these results would certainly support the suggestion that our findings are generalizable to internal states other than that produced by an injection of epinephrine.

Finally, let us consider the implications of our formulation and data for alternative conceptualizations of emotion. Perhaps the most popular current conception of emotion is in terms of "activation theory" in the sense employed by Lindsley (1951) and Woodworth and Schlosberg (1958). As we understand this theory, it suggests that emotional states should be considered as at one end of a continuum of activation which is defined in terms of degree of autonomic arousal and of electroencephalographic measures of activation. The results of the experiment described in this paper do, of course, suggest that such a formulation is not completely adequate. It is possible to have very high degrees of activation without a subject either appearing to be or describing himself as "emotional." Cognitive factors appear to be indispensable elements in any formulation of emotion.

SUMMARY

It is suggested that emotional states may be considered a function of a state of physiological arousal and of a cognition appropriate to this state of arousal. From this follow these propositions:

1. Given a state of physiological arousal for which an individual has no immediate explanation, he will label this state and describe his feelings in terms of the cognitions available to him. To the extent that cognitive factors are potent determiners of emotional states, it should be anticipated that precisely the same state of physiological arousal could be labeled "joy" or "fury" or "jealousy" or any of a great diversity of emotional labels depending on the cognitive aspects of the situation.
2. Given a state of physiological arousal for which an individual has a completely appropriate explanation, no evaluative needs will arise and the individual is unlikely to label his feelings in terms of the alternative cognitions available.
3. Given the same cognitive circumstances, the individual will react emotionally or describe his feelings as emotions only to the extent that he experiences a state of physiological arousal.

An experiment is described which, together with the results of other studies, supports these propositions.

REFERENCES

Ax, A. F. Physiological differentiation of emotional states. *Psychosom. Med.*, 1953, *15*, 433–42.

Cannon, W. B. *Bodily changes in pain, hunger, fear and rage.* (2nd ed.) New York: Appleton, 1929.

Cantril, H., & Hunt, W. A. Emotional effects produced by the injection of adrenalin. *Amer. J. Psychol.*, 1932, *44*, 300–307.

Festinger, L. A theory of social comparison processes. *Hum. Relat.*, 1954, *7*, 114–40.

Hunt, J. McV., Cole, M. W., & Reis, E. E. Situational cues distinguishing anger, fear, and sorrow. *Amer. J. Psychol.*, 1958, *71*, 136–51.

James, W. *The principles of psychology.* New York: Holt, 1890.

Landis, C., & Hunt, W. A.   Adrenalin and emotion. *Psychol. Rev.*, 1932, *39,* 467–85.

Latané, B., & Schachter, S.   Adrenalin and avoidance learning. *J. Comp. physiol. Psychol.*, 1962, *65,* 369–72.

Lindsley, D. B.   Emotion. In S. S. Stevens (Ed.), *Handbook of experimental psychology.* New York: Wiley, 1951. Pp. 473–516.

Marañon, G.   Contribution à l'étude de l'action émotive de l'adrénaline. *Rev. Francaise Endocrinol.*, 1924, *2,* 301–25.

Nowlis, V., & Nowlis, H. H.   The description and analysis of mood. *Ann. N.Y. Acad. Sci.*, 1956, *65,* 345–55.

Ruckmick, C. A.   The psychology of feeling and emotion. New York: McGraw-Hill, 1936.

Schachter, J.   Pain, fear, and anger in hyptertensives and normotensives: A psychophysiologic study. *Psychosom. Med.*, 1957, *19,* 17–29.

Schachter, S.   *The psychology of affiliation.* Stanford, Calif.: Stanford Univer. Press, 1959.

Schachter, S., & Wheeler, L.   Epinephrine, chlorpromazine, and amusement. *J. abnorm. soc. Psychol.*, 1962, *65,* 121–28.

Singer, J. E.   The effects of epinephrine, chlorpromazine and dibenzyline upon the fright responses of rats under stress and non-stress conditions. Unpublished doctoral dissertation, University of Minnesota, 1961.

Wolf, S., & Wolff, H. G.   *Human gastric functions.* New York: Oxford Univer. Press, 1947.

Woodworth, R. S., & Schlosberg, H.   *Experimental psychology.* New York: Holt, 1958.

Wrightsman, L. S.   Effects of waiting with others on changes in level of felt anxiety. *J. abnorm. soc. Psychol.*, 1960, *61,* 216–22.

PERSON PERCEPTION

2

The Warm-Cold Variable in First Impressions of Persons

HAROLD H. KELLEY

This experiment is one of several studies of first impressions (3), the purpose of the series being to investigate the stability of early judgments, their determinants, and the relation of such judgments to the behavior of the person making them. In interpreting the data from several nonexperimental studies on the stability of first impressions, it proved to be necessary to postulate inner-observer variables which contribute to the impression and which remain relatively constant through time. Also some evidence was obtained which directly demonstrated the existence of these variables and their nature. The present experiment was designed to determine the effects of one kind of inner-observer variable, specifically,

Reprinted from Journal of Personality, 18, *1950, 431–39. Copyright 1950 by Duke University Press. Reprinted by permission of the publisher.*

expectations about the stimulus person which the observer brings to the exposure situation.

That prior information or labels attached to a stimulus person make a difference in observers' first impressions is almost too obvious to require demonstration. The expectations resulting from such preinformation may restrict, modify, or accentuate the impressions he will have. The crucial question is: What changes in perception will accompany a given expectation? Studies of stereotyping, for example, that of Katz and Braly (2), indicate that from an ethnic label such as "German" or "Negro," a number of perceptions follow which are culturally determined. The present study finds its main significance in relation to a study by Asch (1) which demonstrates that certain crucial labels can transform the entire impression of the person, leading to attributions which are related to the label on a broad cultural basis or even, perhaps, on an autochthonous basis.

Asch read to his subjects a list of adjectives which purportedly described a particular person. He then asked them to characterize that person. He found that the inclusion in the list of what he called *central* qualities, such as "warm" as opposed to "cold," produced a widespread change in the entire impression. This effect was not adequately explained by the halo effect since it did not extend indiscriminately in a positive or negative direction to all characteristics. Rather, it differentially transformed the other qualities, for example, by changing their relative importance in the total impression. Peripheral qualities (such as "polite" versus "blunt") did not produce effects as strong as those produced by the central qualities.[1]

The present study tested the effects of such central qualities upon the early impressions of *real* persons, the same qualities, "warm" vs. "cold," being used. They were introduced as preinformation about the stimulus person before his actual appearance; so presumably they operated as expectations rather than as part of the stimulus pattern during the exposure period. In addition, information was obtained about the effects of the expectations upon the observers' behavior toward the stimulus person. An earlier study in this series has indicated that the more incompatible the observer initially perceived the stimulus person to be, the less the observer initiated interaction with him thereafter. The second purpose of the present experiment, then, was to provide a better controlled study of this relationship.

No previous studies reported in the literature have dealt with the importance of first impressions for behavior. The most relevant data are found in the sociometric literature, where there are scattered studies of the relation between choices among children having some prior acquaintance and their interaction behavior. For an example, see the study by Newstetter, Feldstein, and Newcomb (8).

---

[1] Since the present experiment was carried out, Mensch and Wishner (6) have repeated a number of Asch's experiments because of dissatisfaction with his sex and geographic distribution. Their data substantiate Asch's very closely. Also, Luchins (5) has criticized Asch's experiments for their artificial methodology, repeated some of them, and challenged some of the kinds of interpretations Asch made from his data. Luchins also briefly reports some tantalizing conclusions from a number of studies of first impressions of actual persons.

PROCEDURE

The experiment was performed in three sections of a psychology course (Economics 70) at the Massachusetts Institute of Technology.[2] The three sections provided 23, 16, and 16 subjects respectively. All 55 subjects were men, most of them in their third college year. In each class the stimulus person (also a male) was completely unknown to the subjects before the experimental period. One person served as stimulus person in two sections, and a second person took this role in the third section. In each case the stimulus person was introduced by the experimenter, who posed as a representative of the course instructors and who gave the following statement:

Your regular instructor is out of town today, and since we of Economics 70 are interested in the general problem of how various classes react to different instructors, we're going to have an instructor today you've never had before, Mr.——. Then, at the end of the period, I want you to fill out some forms about him. In order to give you some idea of what he's like, we've had a person who knows him write up a little biographical note about him. I'll pass this out to you now and you can read it before he arrives. *Please read these to yourselves and don't talk about this among yourselves until the class is over so that he won't get wind of what's going on.*

Two kinds of these notes were distributed, the two being identical except that in one the stimulus person was described among other things as being "rather cold" whereas in the other form the phrase "very warm" was substituted. The content of the "rather cold" version is as follows:

Mr.—— is a graduate student in the Department of Economics and Social Science here at M. I. T. He has had three semesters of teaching experience in psychology at another college. This is his first semester teaching Ec. 70. He is 26 years old, a veteran, and married. People who know him consider him to be a rather cold person, industrious, critical, practical, and determined.

The two types of preinformation were distributed randomly within each of the three classes and in such a manner that the students were not aware that two kinds of information were being given out. The stimulus person then appeared and led the class in a twenty-minute discussion. During this time the experimenter kept a record of how often each student participated in the discussion. Since the discussion was almost totally leader-centered, this participation record indicates the number of times each student initiated verbal interaction with the instructor. After the discussion period, the stimulus person left the room, and the experimenter gave the following instructions:

Now, I'd like to get your impression of Mr.——. This is not a test of you and can in no way affect your grade in this course. This material will not be identified as belonging to particular persons and will be kept strictly confidential. It will be of most value to us if you are completely honest in your evaluation of Mr.——. Also, please understand that what you put down will not be used against him or cause him to lose his job or anything like that. This is not

---

[2] Professor Mason Haire, now of the University of California, provided valuable advice and help in executing the experiment.

a test of him but merely a study of how different classes react to different instructors.

The subjects then wrote free descriptions of the stimulus person and finally rated him on a set of 15 rating scales.

RESULTS AND DISCUSSION

1. Influence of warm-cold variable on first impressions.   The differences in the ratings produced by the warm-cold variable were consistent from one section to another even where different stimulus persons were used. Consequently, the data from the three sections were combined by equating means (the S.D.'s were approximately equal) and the results for the total group are presented in Table I. Also in this table is presented that part of Asch's data which refers to the qualities included in our rating scales. From this table it is quite clear that those given the "warm" preinformation consistently rated the stimulus person more favorably than do those given the "cold" preinformation. Summarizing the statistically significant differences, the "warm" subjects rated the stimulus person as more considerate of others, more informal, more sociable, more popular, better natured, more humorous, and more humane. These findings are very similar to Asch's for the characteristics common to both studies. He found more frequent attribution to his hypothetical "warm" personalities of sociability, popularity, good naturedness, generosity, humorousness, and humaneness. So these data strongly support his finding that such a central quality as "warmth" can greatly influence the total impression of a personality. This effect is found to be operative in the perception of real persons.

This general favorableness in the perceptions of the "warm" observers as compared with the "cold" ones indicates that something like a halo effect may have been operating in these ratings. Although his data are not completely persuasive on this point, Asch was convinced that such a general effect was *not* operating in his study. Closer inspection of the present data makes it clear that the "warm-cold" effect cannot be explained altogether on the basis of simple halo effect. In Table I it is evident that the "warm-cold" variable produced differential effects from one rating scale to another. The size of this effect seems to depend upon the closeness of relation between the specific dimension of any given rating scale and the central quality of "warmth" or "coldness." Even though the rating of intelligence may be influenced by a halo effect, it is not influenced to the same degree to which considerateness is. It seems to make sense to view such strongly influenced items as considerateness, informality, good naturedness, and humaneness as dynamically more closely related to warmth and hence more perceived in terms of this relation than in terms of a general positive or negative feeling toward the stimulus person. If first impressions are normally made in terms of such general dimensions as "warmth" and "coldness," the power they give the observer in making predictions and specific evaluations about such disparate behavior characteristics as formality and considerateness is considerable (even though these predictions may be incorrect or misleading).

The free report impression data were analyzed for only one of the sections. In general, there were few sizable differences between the "warm" and "cold"

Table 1 COMPARISON OF "WARM" AND "COLD" OBSERVERS IN TERMS OF AVERAGE RATINGS GIVEN STIMULUS PERSONS

ITEM	LOW END OF RATING SCALE	HIGH END OF RATING SCALE	AVERAGE RATING		LEVEL OF SIGNIFICANCE OF WARM-COLD DIFFERENCE	ASCH'S DATA: PER CENT OF GROUP ASSIGNING QUALITY AT LOW END OF OUR RATING SCALE*	
			WARM $N = 27$	COLD $N = 28$		WARM	COLD
1	Knows his stuff	Doesn't know his stuff	3.5	4.6	1%		
2	Considerate of others	Self-centered	6.3	9.6	1%		
3†	Informal	Formal	6.3	9.6			
4†	Modest	Proud	9.4	10.6			
5	Sociable	Unsociable	5.6	10.4	1%	91%	38%
6	Self-assured	Uncertain of himself	8.4	9.1			
7	High intelligence	Low intelligence	4.8	5.1			
8	Popular	Unpopular	4.0	7.4	1%	84%	28%
9†	Good natured	Irritable	9.4	12.0	5%	94%	17%
10	Generous	Ungenerous	8.2	9.6		91%	08%
11	Humorous	Humorless	8.3	11.7	1%	77%	13%
12	Important	Insignificant	6.5	8.6		88%	99%
13†	Humane	Ruthless	8.6	11.0	5%	86%	31%
14†	Submissive	Dominant	13.2	14.5			
15	Will go far	Will not get ahead	4.2	5.8			

*Given for all qualities common to Asch's list and this set of rating scales.
†These scales were reversed when presented to the subjects.

observers. The "warm" observers attributed more nervousness, more sincerity, and more industriousness to the stimulus person. Although the frequencies of comparable qualities are very low because of the great variety of descriptions produced by the observers, there is considerable agreement with the rating scale data.

Two important phenomena are illustrated in these free description protocols, the first of them having been noted by Asch. *Firstly,* the characteristics of the stimulus person are interpreted in terms of the precognition of warmth or coldness. For example, a "warm" observer writes about a rather shy and retiring stimulus person as follows: "He makes friends slowly but they are lasting friendships when formed." In another instance, several "cold" observers describe him as being "...intolerant: would be angry if you disagree with his views ..."; while several "warm" observers put the same thing this way: "Unyielding in principle, not easily influenced or swayed from his original attitude." *Secondly,* the preinformation about the stimulus person's warmth or coldness is evaluated and interpreted in the light of the direct behavioral data about him. For example, "He has a slight inferiority complex which leads to his coldness," and "His conscientiousness and industriousness might be mistaken for coldness." Examples of these two phenomena occurred rather infrequently, and there was no way to evaluate the relative strengths of these countertendencies. Certainly some such evaluation is necessary to determine the conditions under which behavior which is contrary to a stereotyped label resists distortion and leads to rejection of the label.

A comparison of the data from the two different stimulus persons is pertinent to the last point in so far as it indicates the interaction between the properties of the stimulus person and the label. The fact that the warm-cold variable generally produced differences in the same direction for the two stimulus persons, even though they are very different in personality, behavior, and mannerisms, indicates the strength of this variable. However, there were some exceptions to this tendency as well as marked differences in the *degree* to which the experimental variable was able to produce differences. For example, stimulus person A typically appears to be anything but lacking in self-esteem and on rating scale 4 he was generally at the "proud" end of the scale. Although the "warm" observers tended to rate him as they did the other stimulus person (i.e., more "modest"), the difference between the "warm" and "cold" means for stimulus person A is very small and not significant as it is for stimulus person B. Similarly, stimulus person B was seen as "unpopular" and "humorless," which agrees with his typical classroom behavior. Again the "warm" observers rated him more favorably on these items, but their ratings were not significantly different from those of the "cold" observers, as was true for the other stimulus person. Thus we see that the strength or compellingness of various qualities of the stimulus person must be reckoned with. The stimulus is not passive to the forces arising from the label but actively resists distortion and may severely limit the degree of influence exerted by the preinformation.[3]

[3] We must raise an important question here: Would there be a tendency for "warm" observers to distort the perception in the favorable direction regardless of how much the stimulus deviated from the expectation? Future research should test the following hypothesis, which is suggested by Gestalt perception theory (4, pp. 95–98): If the stimulus differs but slightly from the expectation, the perception will tend to be *assimilated* to the expectation; however, if the difference between the stimulus and expectation is too great, the perception will occur by contrast to the expectation and will be distorted in the opposite direction.

2. Influence of warm-cold variable on interaction with the stimulus person.   In the analysis of the frequency with which the various students took part in the discussion led by the stimulus person, a larger proportion of those given the "warm" preinformation participated than of those given the "cold" preinformation. Fifty-six per cent of the "warm" subjects entered the discussion, whereas only 32 per cent of the "cold" subjects did so. Thus the expectation of warmth not only produced more favorable early perceptions of the stimulus person but led to greater initiation of interaction with him. This relation is a low one, significant at between the 5 per cent and 10 per cent level of confidence, but it is in line with the general principle that social perception serves to guide and steer the person's behavior in his social environment.

As would be expected from the foregoing findings, there was also a relation between the favorableness of the impression and whether or not the person participated in the discussion. Although any single item yielded only a small and insignificant relation to participation, when a number are combined the trend becomes clear cut. For example, when we combine the seven items which were influenced to a statistically significant degree by the warm-cold variable, the total score bears considerable relation to participation, the relationship being significant as well beyond the 1 per cent level. A larger proportion of those having favorable total impressions participated than of those having unfavorable impressions, the biserial correlation between these variables being .34. Although this relation may be interpreted in several ways, it seems most likely that the unfavorable perception led to a curtailment of interaction. Support for this comes from one of the other studies in this series (3). There it was found that those persons having unfavorable impressions of the instructor at the end of the first class meeting tended less often to initiate interactions with him in the succeeding four meetings than did those having favorable first impressions. There was also some tendency in the same study for those persons who interacted least with the instructor to change least in their judgments of him from the first to later impressions.

It will be noted that these relations lend some support to the autistic hostility hypothesis proposed by Newcomb (7). This hypothesis suggests that the possession of an initially hostile attitude toward a person leads to a restriction of communication and contact with him which in turn serves to preserve the hostile attitude by preventing the acquisition of data which could correct it. The present data indicate that a restriction of interaction is associated with unfavorable preinformation and an unfavorable perception. The data from the other study support this result and also indicate the correctness of the second part of the hypothesis, that restricted interaction reduces the likelihood of change in the attitude.

What makes these findings more significant is that they appear in the context of a discussion class where there are numerous *induced* and *own* forces to enter the discussion and to interact with the instructor. It seems likely that the effects predicted by Newcomb's hypothesis would be much more marked in a setting where such forces were not present.

SUMMARY

The warm-cold variable had been found by Asch to produce large differences in the impressions of personality formed from a list of adjectives. In this study the same variable was introduced in the form of expectations about a real person and was found to produce similar differences in first impressions of him in a classroom setting. In addition, the differences in first impressions produced by the different expectations were shown to influence the observers' behavior toward the stimulus person. Those observers given the favorable expectation (who, consequently, had a favorable impression of the stimulus person) tended to interact more with him than did those given the unfavorable expectation.

REFERENCES

1. Asch, S. E. Forming impressions of personality. *J. abnorm. soc. Psychol.*, 1946, *41*, 258–90.

2. Katz, D., and Braly, K. W. Verbal stereotypes and racial prejudice. In Newcomb, T. M. and Hartley, E. L. (eds.), *Readings in social psychology.* New York: Holt, 1947. Pp. 204–10.

3. Kelley, H. H. First impressions in interpersonal relations. Ph.D. thesis, Massachusetts Institute of Technology, Cambridge, Mass. Sept., 1948.

4. Krech, D., and Crutchfield, R. S. *Theory and problems of social psychology.* New York: McGraw-Hill, 1948.

5. Luchins, A. S. Forming impressions of personality: a critique. *J. abnorm. soc. Psychol.*, 1948, *43*, 318–25.

6. Mensh, I. N., and Wishner, J. Asch on "Forming impressions of personality": further evidence. *J. Personal.*, 1947, *16*, 188–91.

7. Newcomb, T. M. Autistic hostility and social reality. *Hum. Relations.*, 1947, *1*, 69–86.

8. Newstetter, W. I., Feldstein, M. J., and Newcomb, T. M. *Group adjustment: a study in experimental sociology.* Cleveland: Western Reserve University, 1938.

Application of a Linear-Serial Model to a Personality-Impression Task Using Serial Presentation

NORMAN H. ANDERSON

In social situations, one's opinions and judgments are usually based on various different pieces of information. The processes that govern the integration of this information are of considerable interest. This experiment studies this integration problem in an experimental task based on serial presentation of trait information about personalities.

A substantial amount of related work has already been done in connection with testing a linear model for information integration (cf., Anderson, 1962, 1968b). In this formulation, the judgment is assumed to be, in effect, a weighted sum of the subjective values of relevant stimuli. With appropriate experimental design, analysis of variance may then be used to give a rigorous, quantitative test of the model. For the case of stimuli presented simultaneously, several experiments have given considerable support to this formulation. For serial presentation, however, previous experiments using social stimuli (e.g., Anderson, 1959, 1965b) have not employed a corresponding test of goodness of fit.

Serial presentation is more realistic because one's daily judgments are usually based on information accumulated over time. But it is also more complicated because the effect of a given stimulus may depend on its temporal position. Indeed, order of presentation is known to be important in a variety of tasks (e.g., Hovland, 1957; Lana, 1964; McGuire, 1966; Rosnow, Holz, & Levin, 1966).

Fortunately, the linear integration model can still be directly applied to serial presentation by allowing the weight, or importance, of each stimulus to depend on serial position. With appropriate experimental procedure, analysis of variance may still be used to get an exact test of the goodness of fit of the data to the model (Anderson, 1964a). Such a test of the model is also important in the estimation and interpretation of the serial position curve, including primacy and recency effects.

A special feature of the present design is that each stimulus sequence contains only positive or only negative information. This is important, and considerable pains were taken to implement it by preselection of the stimuli on an individual basis. Stimulus sequences constructed in this way do not have the potential inconsistencies of the usual order effect sequences, which include both positive and negative information. As a consequence, the data bear on the interpretation of the primacy effect usually obtained with the present task in terms of a

Reprinted from Journal of Personality and Social Psychology, 10, *1968, 354–62.* *Copyright 1968 by the American Psychological Association and reproduced by permission.*

discounting (Anderson & Jacobson, 1965) of the later adjectives from being inconsistent with the earlier adjectives. In addition, the use of unipolar sequences allows a critical test between the averaging and adding forms of the general model, parallel to that given previously for simultaneous presentation (Anderson, 1965a).

METHOD

Subjects were shown sequences of three or six personality-trait adjectives one at a time. They were told that the adjectives described a person whom they were to rate on a likableness scale. The main independent variables were the value and the serial pattern of the adjectives in the various sequences, and these were chosen to test specified hypotheses. In addition, three different response modes were employed. In the continuous, final, and intermittent conditions, respectively, subjects rated after each successive adjective, after the last adjective only, or after the third and sixth adjectives only.

Stimulus construction.   To get high precision in the critical tests, it was necessary to construct sequences with adjectives of specified value for each individual subject. Accordingly, a preliminary session was given in which each subject selected groups of six adjectives that were about equal for him.

The basic adjectives were four sublists of 32 adjectives chosen from a master list on which normative data were available (Anderson, 1968b). These four sublists, the same as used in previous work, are denoted by H, M^+, M^-, and L, standing for high, moderately high, moderately low, and low, respectively. All adjectives were typed on 3×5-inch cards, and each sublist was split into two packets of 16 cards. From each packet, the subject was given 12 cards and selected a group of 6 that seemed about equally likable or dislikable as personality traits. After all eight groups had been thus chosen, the subjects checked each one and were allowed to improve it by exchanging with the four remaining cards of each packet.

In this way, each subject selected two groups of six equated adjectives from each of the four scale ranges, H, M^+, M^-, and L. From these selections, 32 sequences of adjectives were constructed for each subject. The 16 sequences of favorable adjectives are shown in Table 1. There were 16 complementary sequences constructed of L and M^- adjectives in the same manner.

Twelve of the 16 sets of Table 1 were constructed from one group of six H adjectives and one group of six M^+ adjectives. The subscripts 1–6, which were paired with particular adjectives by random choice, indicate the stimulus balancing that was employed. For example, Sets 3a and 3b are equivalent, while Set 10a is merely Set 3a in reversed order. The subscripts 11–16 in Sets 2ab and 4ab denote a different group of adjectives.

Sets 2ab and 4ab of Table 1 were used to give additional data on a central question of this experiment. That is, an additive formulation would predict a higher response to Sets 4ab then to Sets 2ab. The second groups of six H and M^+ adjectives were used for these last four sets, and the subscripts 11–16 were assigned to particular adjectives by random choice.

Table 1 Experimental Sequences of Favorable Adjectives

SET NO.	ADJECTIVE SEQUENCE
1a	$H_3 H_1 H_2$
1b	$H_4 H_6 H_5$
2a	$H_{11} H_{12} H_{13}$
2b	$H_{14} H_{15} H_{16}$
3a	$H_1 H_2 H_3 M_1^+ M_2^+ M_3^+$
3b	$H_4 H_5 H_6 M_4^+ M_5^+ M_6^+$
4a	$H_{13} H_{12} H_{11} M_{11}^+ M_{12}^+ M_{13}^+$
4b	$H_{16} H_{15} H_{14} M_{14}^+ M_{15}^+ M_{16}^+$
9a	$M_3^+ M_1^+ M_2^+$
9b	$M_4^+ M_6^+ M_5^+$
10a	$M_3^+ M_2^+ M_1^+ H_3 H_2 H_1$
10b	$M_6^+ M_5^+ M_4^+ H_6 H_5 H_4$
13a	$H_2 H_3 H_1 H_6 H_4 H_5$
13b	$H_5 H_4 H_6 H_1 H_3 H_2$
14a	$M_2^+ M_3^+ M_1^+ M_6^+ M_4^+ M_5^+$
14b	$M_5^+ M_4^+ M_6^+ M_1^+ M_3^+ M_2^+$

Note.—Set numbers correspond to Table 2; a and b denote the two instances of each set type. Subscripts 1-6 denote six particular adjectives at each polarity; Subscripts 11-16 (Sets 2ab and 4ab) denote a second group of six particular adjectives. Sequences of negative adjectives were constructed similarly.

Procedure. The adjectives of each set were typed on 8½ × 11-inch sheets and positioned in a flat exposure apparatus on a table. The experimenter exposed the adjectives by stepping a 7 × 15-inch mask down the sheet of paper. In the mask were two slits, 3 × ¾ inches in size. One slit exposed the adjectives; the other exposed a 2-inch line when a response was required, and otherwise a blank space. The two slits were offset so that no adjective was visible when the response was made.

The 2-inch line exposed by the second slit represented a like-dislike scale. Subjects gave their judgments by making a slash mark on the line. This graphic scale was used in preference to a numerical scale in order to avoid memory effects in the continuous condition in which subjects revised their ratings after each added adjective. The graphic scale has the added potentialities of being sensitive to small changes in response and of avoiding number preferences.

The subject read each adjective aloud as it was shown. Each adjective was exposed for approximately 1 second. The mask was then advanced one step to expose a blank space under each slit for approximately 1 second, and then advanced again to expose the next adjective or a response line. Between the last adjective and the final response there was a 4-second interval during which the subject was to "think about your overall impression of the person."

Three response modes were used. In the final condition, subjects rated the person only once, after all the adjectives had been presented. In the continuous condition, the person was rated after each successive adjective. In the intermittent condition, ratings were given after the third and sixth adjectives of the sequence.

For the continuous condition, the total times required for sequences of three and six words were approximately 16 and 27 seconds, respectively.

The 32 experimental sets were presented in shuffled order for each subject. Four common filler sets were also included, after the third, eighth, fifteenth, and twenty-fourth experimental sets. Each filler contained both positive and negative adjectives, less extreme than the H or L adjectives, and without obvious inconsistency. Their main purpose was to break up the patterning in the experimental sets which were all homogeneous in polarity.

Instructions.   The subject was told to imagine that the adjectives on each sheet described a single person, and that each adjective was accurate and equally important; that he should decide how much he himself would like the person, that there was no right or wrong answer; that he should simply give his own opinion; and that he should try to spread his responses over the whole response line.

The serial presentation procedure was explained by analogy to real life in which one ordinarily gets to know a person step by step.

Further, subjects in the continuous and intermittent conditions were told that each response should be made on the basis of all the accumulated information, and that changes in opinion were only natural as more information was obtained.

Four practice sets were given, common to all subjects. Two of these were mixed M^+ and M^- adjectives, and two were end anchors consisting of very high and very low adjectives. Questions were then answered, and the main points of the instructions repeated before proceeding to the experimental sets.

Subjects.   Subjects were 88 undergraduates who were paid $2.50 for the two ½-hour sessions. There were 40 subjects in the final condition, and 24 each in the other two conditions. Half the subjects were of either sex, and within each sex they were randomly assigned to conditions.

RESULTS

Terminal Response

The terminal responses, given after all the adjectives had been presented, are the most important. Table 2 gives the response means, averaged over subjects and over the two instances of each set type. These data answer several specific questions that will be considered in turn.

Order of presentation.   The experimental design assesses the effect of presenting the same adjectives in different orders. For positive stimuli, the comparison is between Sets 3 and 10, that is, between $3H3M^+$ and $3M^+3H$. The response to the first set is somewhat lower, a recency effect. However, the difference of .33 fell short of significance.

The corresponding comparison for negative stimuli is based on Sets 7 and 11. The response of 3.10 to $3L3M^-$ is larger than the response of 2.44 to $3M^-3L$, again a recency effect. The difference of .66 is significantly greater than 0 ($F = 10.37$, $df = 1/82$).

The theoretical interpretation of these order effects is quite uncertain. Within the present formulation, they are considered to reflect differential weighting of the initial and later stimuli. This problem will be discussed in more detail below when the complete response curves for the continuous condition are examined.

Table 2 MEAN LIKABLENESS RESPONSE AT END OF ADJECTIVE SEQUENCE AS A
FUNCTION OF SEQUENCE OF ADJECTIVES AND RESPONSE CONDITION

SET NO.	SET WORDS	RESPONSE CONDITION			
		FINAL	CONTINUOUS	INTERMITTENT	M
1	HHH	16.44	16.98	16.00	16.47
2	HHH	16.46	16.46	16.06	16.35
3	HHHM⁺M⁺M⁺	14.46	14.23	14.23	14.33
4	HHHM⁺M⁺M⁺	15.20	15.25	15.19	15.21
5	LLL	1.49	1.48	1.58	1.51
6	LLL	1.02	1.58	1.69	1.36
7	LLLM⁻M⁻M⁻	3.12	2.92	3.23	3.10
8	LLLM⁻M⁻M⁻	2.62	3.71	3.10	3.05
9	M⁺M⁺M⁺	11.96	11.04	10.08	11.20
10	M⁺M⁺M⁺HHH	14.92	14.88	14.02	14.66
11	M⁻M⁻M⁻LLL	2.51	2.23	2.52	2.44
12	M⁻M⁻M⁻	5.28	6.06	6.65	5.86
13	HHHHHH	17.41	17.79	17.48	17.53
14	M⁺M⁺M⁺M⁺M⁺M⁺	12.29	11.23	11.67	11.83
15	M⁻M⁻M⁻M⁻M⁻M⁻	4.42	5.79	5.75	5.16
16	LLLLLL	.91	1.00	1.35	1.06

Note.—Adjectives listed in the order presented. H, M⁺, M⁻, and L denote adjectives of high, mildly favorable, mildly unfavorable, and low value. Because of the balancing in the experimental design, Sets 2, 4, 6, and 8 figure in comparisons only in the upper half of the table, not in the lower half.

Serial integration model. The design provides two tests of quantitative predictions of the general model, one for positive and one for negative stimuli. These two predictions are:

$$R(6H) + R(6M^+) = R(3H3M^+) + R(3M^+3H),$$

and

$$R(6L) + R(6M^-) = R(3L3M^-) + R(3M^-3L),$$

where R denotes the response to the stimulus sequence in parentheses. The model derivation allows weight or importance to vary with serial position, but assumes that all stimuli at a given serial position have the same effective weight.

To test the first prediction, the combined response to Sets 13 and 14 is to be compared to the combined response to Sets 3 and 10 in Table 2. The corresponding means are 14.68 and 14.50, respectively, and the difference of .18 points does not approach significance. It may be noted, incidentally, that the four sets form a 2×2 design in which the cited difference score is just the interaction.

The second prediction, for negative stimuli, compares Sets 15 and 16 to Sets 7 and 11. The means are 3.11 and 2.77, respectively, and the difference of .34 points is just significant ($F = 4.30$, $df = 1/82$).

This pair of results parallels that for simultaneous presentation (Anderson, 1965a). There also the prediction was verified for positive stimuli but not for negative stimuli. In the earlier report, it was noted that the discrepancy could be interpreted as evidence for a special case of the general formulation in which the stimulus values are averaged. This interpretation rested on the assumption that the L adjectives had greater natural weight than the M⁻adjectives. The response to a set with equally many Ls and M's would then be shifted from the stimulus midpoint toward the stimulus with greater weight. The direction of the discrepancy is the same in the present data which supports the earlier interpretation, and suggests that the test of fit reflects no more than an inaccuracy in the simplifying assumption of equal weighting.

There is one further aspect of the discrepancy with the negative stimuli that needs comment. In the statistical analysis, response condition was also significant. Inspection of Table 2 shows that the continuous and intermittent, but not the final, response conditions are discrepant from the model prediction. This naturally casts doubt on the interpretation of the discrepancy in terms of differential weighting since that would, presumably, imply that the final condition should show the same discrepancy as the other two conditions. More detailed inspection of the data suggests that the between-conditions difference is located in the lower response to 6M⁻ in the final condition. This between-conditions difference is consistent since it appears also for 3M⁻, but it does not shed any obvious light on the above interpretation.

Averaging versus adding. Further evidence on the averaging interpretation is also embodied in the design. The empirical test is straightforward. Sets 1 and 2 contain three H adjectives; Sets 3 and 4 contain added favorable information, namely, three M⁺ adjectives. This added favorable information must raise the response according to any summative formulation. In contradiction, the response to the 3H3M⁺ sets is 1.64 points lower than the response to the 3H sets.

A similar critical test, for negative information, is given by Sets 5 to 8. An additive model would predict a more negative response from 3L3M⁻ than from 3L, but the observed difference is again in the other direction. In both cases, of course, the result is consistent with an averaging formulation.

Both results are quite reliable. For the comparison between 3H and 3H3M⁺, the analysis yielded $F = 36.86$, $df = 1/82$. For the difference between 3L and 3L3M⁻, $F = 75.06$, $df = 1/82$.

These results are not peculiarities of the order of presentation. In Set 10 (3M⁺3H) the order of presentation is reversed compared to Sets 3 and 4. Because of the stimulus balancing, Set 10 is properly compared only with Set 1. However, the difference of 1.81 points favors the averaging formulation and is statistically significant ($F = 31.09$, $df = 1/82$. The similar comparison for negative stimuli is based on Sets 5 and 11. Here the difference between the response of 2.44 to 3M⁻3L and 1.51 to 3L again favors an averaging formulation ($F = 23.19$, $df = 1/82$).

Set-size effect. The data show the usual effect of set size. For each stimulus value the response to sets of six adjectives is more extreme than the response to sets of three adjectives. This effect has some immediate relevance since it validates the choice of M⁺ and M⁻stimuli.

The present set-size effect is consistent with previous experiments that have also employed serial presentation (Anderson, 1959; Fishbein & Hunter, 1964; Stewart, 1965). It has theoretical interest since it rules out the most simple averaging model. That is, if the response were the average of the scale values of the stimuli actually presented, a set of three Hs and a set of six Hs would yield the same response. This situation can be handled theoretically by assuming that the subject averages an initial or neutral impression in with the values of the overt stimuli (Anderson, 1959, 1967b). In this form, the averaging model then predicts the response to be a growth curve function of set size, and this has been verified in all the above cited work. The effect can be seen more directly when continuous responding is used as illustrated in Figure 1 below.

Response mode and sex.   Each of the above analyses included Response Condition and Sex as between-subjects variables. All tests were made by analysis of variance, and all results significant at the .05 level are reported. Somewhat surprisingly, there was relatively little effect of Response Condition on the size of the terminal response. It was significant only in the one test already mentioned. The data show some scattered between-conditions differences with some tendency for the final condition to give lower responses to negative stimuli. However, two further tests, based on the five homogeneous sets of each polarity, failed to yield significant differences.

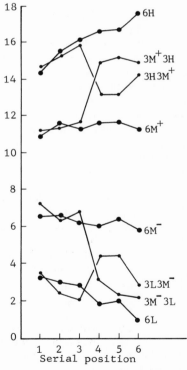

Fig. 1.   Mean impression as function of serial position in continuous responding condition.

Sex was significant in most of the separate analyses, with the female response being more extreme. In the two tests just cited, the female mean was 1.43 higher for positive stimuli and .72 lower for negative stimuli, both differences being significant. As is usually the case, comparison of different populations presents methodological difficulties, and these data naturally give no warrant for concluding that the underlying impression is different in males and females. The given result may simply reflect different semantic habits in using the response scale.

Intermediate Responses

Subjects in the continuous condition responded after each adjective so that a complete response curve may be obtained for each sequence. These response curves for sets of six adjectives are shown in Figure 1. The curves reflect the development of the person-impression as additional information is received.

The curves for the sets of three adjectives are not included since they duplicated information in Figure 1. The data for the intermittent condition at Serial Position 3 are also omitted. They were, on the whole, about the same as the corresponding data for the continuous condition; the between-conditions differences were somewhat less than the differences at Serial Position 6 in Table 2 and showed no systematic pattern.

The most interesting comparison in Figure 1 concerns order of presentation. Sets 4 and 8 of Table 2 were excluded to allow comparison of order of presentation unconfounded with stimulus differences. Thus, $3M^+3H$ and $3H3M^+$ represent equivalent information presented in opposite orders, and similarly for $3M^-3L$ and $3L3M^-$. Each pair of curves shows two effects: recency and finality.

The recency effect is represented graphically by the crossing of the paired curves at Serial Position 4. Thus, $3M^+3H$ yields a higher response than $3H3M^+$ at each of the last three serial positions. Similarly, $3M^-3L$ yields a lower response than $3L3M^-$ over the last three serial positions, also a recency effect.

To test this recency effect, the two orders of presentation and the three last serial positions were combined as a 2×3 design. The overall recency was significant both for the positive and the negative stimuli ($F = 7.32$ and 7.58, respectively, $df = 1/22$.)

The finality effect is seen in the reversal of trend at the last point for Sets $3H3M^+$ and $3L3M^-$. The marked upward jump at the last point would seem to reflect a latent effect of the initial H adjectives. Similarly, the downward jump at the last point of Set $3L3M^-$ suggests a latent effect of the initial L adjectives.

This finality effect was unexpected, and a completely suitable test of its reliability is not available. On a post hoc basis, however, it seemed reasonable to test the null hypothesis that the difference in response at Positions 5 and 6 was 0. The mean upjump for the $3H3M^+$ curve in Figure 1 was 1.10; the other $3H3M^+$ data showed an even larger upjump of 1.82 points. The test was made on the combined data and yielded $F = 18.65$, $df = 1/22$. For the negative stimuli, the mean downjump from Position 5 to 6 is 1.50 in the plotted curve. The other $3L3M^-$ data showed a downjump of 1.02. The test on the combined data yielded $F = 14.22$, $df = 1/22$.

These tests were suggested by inspection of the data and must therefore be interpreted cautiously. However, the effect occurs consistently in the data and the F ratios are large enough to give some warrant for considering the finality effect to be real.

The order effect curves of Figure 1 require a brief discussion in relation to two previous reports. They differ in two respects from curves obtained by Stewart (1965) with a fairly similar task. The second limb of Stewart's curves shows a gradual change toward recency, whereas here the recency appears abruptly at Serial Position 4. Also, Stewart found differences between his final and continuous conditions, with primacy in the former, and no primacy or recency in the latter. The present final condition exhibits recency and this difference, as well as the abrupt recency in the continuous condition, may reflect the present use of adjectives of the same polarity in each set as discussed below. The general agreement between the present continuous and final data provides a safeguard on the main theoretical results of this report.

Finally, it may be noted that the finality effect, if real, may be interpretable in terms of a two-component hypothesis of opinion structure (Anderson, 1959). In this view, the immediate shift to recency at Serial Position 4 would reflect the action of the superficial component, whereas the basal component would produce the finality effect during the terminal pause in the stimulus presentation. Here, of course, as above, it must be realized that the shape of the continuous curves may depend heavily on the time intervals used in the sequence.

The remaining curves of Figure 1 are for sets in which all six adjectives have equivalent value. These curves have theoretical interest since they represent the set-size effect for serial presentation. Although the sequences are too short to be conclusive, the curves for Sets $6M^+$ and $6M^-$ seem to have reached an asymptote as would be predicted by an averaging model. The shape of the curves for Sets 6H and 6L is not entirely clear since the last point on each shows a larger change than might be expected in view of the first five points. Since this may only reflect a tendency to use the endpoints of the response scale (Anderson, 1967b), detailed analysis of these curves does not seem justified here. Further work in this direction will probably require closer attention to scale end effects and more extensive use of end anchors.

Several people (e.g., M. Brewer, G. S. Leventhal, R. S. Wyer, Jr.)[1] have suggested that this set-size effect results simply from an increase in confidence as information accumulates. No doubt confidence does increase with each successive adjective in Set 6H, for instance, but this may merely reflect the processes involved in the information integration without playing any causative role in the impression response. The present data suggest that confidence alone is not a sufficient explanation. In Sets $6M^+$ and $6M^-$ confidence should increase steadily over successive stimuli. On the confidence interpretation, then, there is no reason to expect the impression curves to level off at intermediate values as they do in Figure 1. The mixed sets, such as Sets $3H3M^+$ and $3M^+3H$, also pose difficulties for a confidence interpretation. It might not be unreasonable to argue, for instance, that the M^+ adjectives in Set $3H3M^+$ decrease confidence since, even though they add positive information, they increase the variance of that information. That argument, however, would not be able to account for the

[1] Personal communications.

increase in the curve for Set $3M^+3H$ as the H adjectives are added. Nevertheless, the confidence question is quite interesting. However, further speculation is unwarranted here since the problem is open to direct experimental attack.

DISCUSSION

Two main theoretical questions will be considered here. The first concerns the general model for serial information integration; the second concerns the interpretation of the serial order effects.

On the first question, the results are fairly straightforward. The quantitative predictions were satisfied under all three response conditions for positive stimuli, but there was a discrepancy in two conditions for negative stimuli. The pattern of these results is similar to that obtained previously with simultaneous presentation (Anderson, 1965a). As noted above, it is possible to account for this discrepancy if the general formulation is specialized to an averaging model, with greater weighting of the more polarized stimuli.

Added support for an averaging interpretation is found in two qualitative tests. For both positive and negative stimuli, adding mildly polarized to highly polarized information decreased the polarity of the response. This contradicts an additive model, but is consistent with an averaging interpretation, just as in the cited report on simultaneous presentation.

On the whole, therefore, the present and previous reports allow some optimism over this approach to information integration. Although the empirical tests have been mainly limited to the personality-impression task, similar results may be expected with other stimuli (Anderson, 1965a, 1967b).

In this connection, one methodological comment deserves special note. In the present data, the critical test between averaging and adding was considerably more reliable than in the previous report. Although comparison of serial with simultaneous presentation is risky, it seems likely that the increase in reliability flows in large part from the stimulus preselection employed here. This allows a very close matching of stimulus values for each individual with a consequent reduction in error variability (cf., Anderson, 1965b; Table 2). Constructing sets of stimuli for each separate subject is costly, of course, but may well be worth the gain in precision as well as in validity.

The data also bear on a second theoretical problem; the cause of the primacy effect that is usually obtained in this task under a standard set of conditions. This primacy was first obtained by Asch (1946), who interpreted it in terms of assimilation of the meaning of the later adjectives toward the meaning of the earlier adjectives. Recent work has uniformly favored an alternative hypothesis that the primacy results from a decrease in the weight rather than a shift in the meaning of the later adjectives (Anderson, 1965b; Anderson & Barrios, 1961; Anderson & Hubert, 1963; Anderson & Norman, 1964; Stewart, 1965). These experiments also supported the idea that the serial decrease in weight stemmed from a decrement in attention over successive serial positions, and this seemed especially clear in the straight-line primacy curves obtained from a generalized order effect paradigm (Anderson, 1965b).

However, a second possible cause of a serial decrease in weight was suggested by the finding that subjects discount, that is, give lower weight to, affectively inconsistent stimuli (Anderson & Jacobson, 1965). That experiment used simultaneous presentation, but it was noted that primacy with serial presentation could result from discounting. It is easy to see that any such discounting would be directional, producing lower weights for the later stimuli. In LLLHHH, for instance, the first H is to be integrated by itself into the weightier impression based on the three Ls. Discounting would then tend to work against the first H. Somewhat the same situation would then also apply to the second and third Hs.

The present design allows a test between these two explanations of a serial decrease in weight. Previous work has used sequences with both positive and negative stimuli, whereas the present sequences contain stimuli of only one polarity.

Simple attention decrement would produce primacy for either kind of sequence. On the discounting hypothesis, in contrast, primacy would not obtain with the present sequences since they do not embody affective or semantic inconsistency. That primacy was not obtained here argues, therefore, that the primacy in previous experiments was caused by a discounting process.

At the same time, the present recency effect is consistent with recency effects that have been obtained under comparable conditions with averaging of psychophysical stimuli (Anderson, 1967a; Parducci, Thaler, & Anderson, 1968) and numbers (Anderson, 1964b). The cause of this recency is not known, but it probably stems jointly from forgetting of the earlier stimuli (e.g., Miller & Campbell, 1959), and from a natural tendency to overweight the immediately present stimulus in a sequence as assumed in the linear operator model of previous work (Anderson, 1964a; Anderson & Hovland, 1957).

On the above view, recency would be generally expected, and a necessary though not sufficient condition for primacy would be inconsistency among the stimulus items. Whether this view has any generality is difficult to say since the primacy-recency area is especially marked by conflicting results (e.g., Hovland, 1957; Lana, 1964; McGuire, 1966; Rosnow et al., 1966). However, since most work in the area has in fact used stimuli of mixed polarity, conflicting results might be expected on the present view. With such stimuli, tendencies toward primacy and toward recency would be operating together, and the net resultant could depend heavily on experimental details. For the personality-adjective task, at least, this seems to be true empirically. Ordinarily strong primacy is obtained, but this is eliminated or changed to recency by relatively simple experimental manipulations (Anderson & Hubert, 1963; Stewart, 1965). The above view, it should be noted, allows for but does not explain this shift from primacy to recency. Some additional mechanism, such as attention, would still be needed for this purpose.

The checkered history of the primacy-recency problem indicates the need for courage if not caution in any theoretical analysis. The present view at least has the merit of being easily tested. For instance, it requires primacy to vary directly with amount of discounting, and discounting can be manipulated fairly easily.

REFERENCES

Anderson, N. H.   Test of a model for opinion change. *Journal of Abnormal and Social Psychology*, 1959, *59*, 371–81.

Anderson, N. H.   Application of an additive model to impression formation. *Science*, 1962, *138*, 817–18.

Anderson, N. H.   Note on weighted sum and linear operator models. *Psychonomic Science*, 1964, *1*, 189–90. (a)

Anderson, N. H.   Test of a model for number-averaging behavior. *Psychonomic Science*, 1964, *1*, 191–92. (b)

Anderson, N. H.   Averaging versus adding as a stimulus-combination rule in impression formation. *Journal of Experimental Psychology*, 1965, *70*, 394–400. (a)

Anderson, N. H.   Primacy effects in personality impression formation using a generalized order effect paradigm. *Journal of Personality and Social Psychology*, 1965, *2*, 1–9. (b)

Anderson, N. H.   Component ratings in impression formation. *Psychonomic Science*, 1966, *6*, 279–80.

Anderson, N. H.   Application of a weighted average model to a psychophysical averaging task. *Psychonomic Science*, 1967, *8*, 227–28. (a)

Anderson, N. H.   Averaging model analysis of set size effect in impression formation. *Journal of Experimental Psychology*, 1967, *75*, 158–65. (b)

Anderson, N. H.   A simple model for information integration. In R. P. Abelson, E. Aronson, W. J. McGuire, T. M. Newcomb, M. J. Rosenberg, & P. H. Tannenbaum (Eds.), *Theories of cognitive consistency: A sourcebook*. Chicago: Rand McNally, 1968. (a)

Anderson, N. H.   Likableness ratings of 555 personality-trait words. *Journal of Personality and Social Psychology*, 1968, *9*, 272–79. (b)

Anderson, N. H., & Barrios, A. A.   Primacy effects in personality impression formation. *Journal of Abnormal and Social Psychology*, 1961, *63*, 346–50.

Anderson, N. H., & Hovland, C. I.   The representation of order effects in communication research. In C. I. Hovland (Ed.), *The order of presentation in persuasion*, New Haven: Yale University Press, 1957.

Anderson, N. H., & Hubert, S.   Effects of concomitant verbal recall on order effects in personality impression formation. *Journal of Verbal Learning and Verbal Behavior*, 1963, *2*, 379–91.

Anderson, N. H., & Jacobson, A.   Effects of stimulus inconsistency and discounting instructions in personality impression formation. *Journal of Personality and Social Psychology*, 1965, *2*, 531–39.

Anderson, N. H., & Norman, A.   Order effects in impression formation in four classes of stimuli. *Journal of Abnormal and Social Psychology*, 1964, *69*, 467–71.

Asch, S. E.   Forming impressions of personality. *Journal of Abnormal and Social Psychology*, 1946, *41*, 258–90.

Fishbein, M., & Hunter, R.   Summation versus balance in attitude organization and change. *Journal of Abnormal and Social Psychology,* 1964, *69,* 505–10.

Hovland, C. I.   Summary and implications. In C. I. Hovland (Ed.), *The order of presentation in persuasion.* New Haven: Yale University Press, 1957.

Lana, R. E.   Three interpretations of order effects in persuasive communications. *Psychological Bulletin,* 1964, *61,* 314–20.

McGuire, W. J.   Attitudes and opinions. In P. Farnsworth (Ed.), *Annual review of psychology.* Vol. 17. Palo Alto: Annual Review Press, 1966.

Miller, N., & Campbell, D. T.   Recency and primacy in persuasion as a function of the timing of speeches and measurement. *Journal of Abnormal and Social Psychology,* 1959, *59,* 1–9.

Parducci, A., Thaler, H., & Anderson, N. H.   Stimulus averaging and the context for judgment. *Perception and Psychophysics,* 1968, *3,* 145–50.

Rosnow, R. L., Holz, R. F., & Levin, J.   Differential effects of complementary and competing variables in primacy-recency. *Journal of Social Psychology,* 1966, *69,* 135–47.

Stewart, R. H.   Effect of continuous responding on the order effect in personality impression formation. *Journal of Personality and Social Psychology,* 1965, *1,* 161–65.

The Perceiver and the Perceived: Their Relative Influence on the Categories of Interpersonal Cognition

SANFORD M. DORNBUSCH, ALBERT H. HASTORF,
STEPHEN A. RICHARDSON, ROBERT E. MUZZY,
AND REBECCA S. VREELAND

This paper reports an empirical approach to the nature of the individual's structuring of his interactions with other people. More specifically, it will describe a method of determining the salient cognitive categories employed by a person in his descriptions of others. Substantively, we shall report an analysis of the categories of interpersonal cognition employed by children, emphasizing the relative strength of category determination by the perceiver and by the person perceived.

If each person employs a rather consistent set of categories for the interpretation of his social world, the same general categories should be present in descriptions of other people who vary considerably in their characteristics. On the other hand, category selection might be so heavily determined by the stimulus object that there would be little reappearance of categories as one person describes a number of others.

Reprinted from Journal of Personality and Social Psychology, 1, *1965, 434–40. Copyright 1965 by the American Psychological Association and reproduced by permission.*

Researchers interested in social perception or person cognition (the terms often are used with a common meaning) have long been concerned with the relative impact of the perceiver and the perceived, but the emphasis of their empirical research has been on variations in the psychological state of the perceiver. Most commonly, investigators have used experimental manipulations (for example, frustrating one group) or taken advantage of individual differences on some trait (for example, authoritarianism) and then observed differences in the perception of a social object. This orientation is consonant with prevailing conceptions of accuracy, distortion, projection, and empathic ability. As we have noted elsewhere (Hastorf, Richardson, & Dornbusch, 1958), the desire for quantification and control has led researchers to specify the categories upon which the subject is required to report his perceptions. In these types of studies, the relevance of the categories has been defined by the investigator, not by the subject.

Our approach demands an exploration of the cognitive structure of the perceiver, following interaction in a natural setting with a series of individuals. To operationalize the problem, what categories does he use in describing other persons when the investigator does not specify the relevant dimensions? The veridicality of his reports is not evaluated. Instead, prior questions are explored. What categories do people employ in a free response situation? Do these change as different individuals are described?

We shall study reappearing categories as our index of salience. The term "salience" refers to that which a perceiver tends to notice in others or that which tends to be noticeable about a perceived person. When a describer uses a category in several descriptions, we assume that the specific category is salient to him. If several perceivers use the same category in describing a particular person, we assume that this is a salient characteristic of the perceived person in his interaction with others. Salience in one case refers to cognitive or perceptual organization and in the other to prominence in the perceived stimulus object, yet, using reappearance as the measure, one can explore the more general issue of the relative strength of the perceiver and the perceived in determining category usage.

The analysis of verbal reports in unstructured interviews will necessarily center on that sample of categories used by the respondent. Quite clearly, questions may arise in regard to subjects withholding certain descriptive statements or to the operation of certain hypothetical unconscious processes. We shall concern ourselves only with the manifest content of the descriptions, the words used by the subjects. In Heider's sense, we are seeking information about the naive psychology of the layman.

The focus is on children in this beginning step of a cumulative series of researches. They are likely to be less sophisticated, less able to conceal material, and perhaps less motivated to control the impression they make upon the interviewer. It is assumed that all people tell us something about themselves as they describe others. It is also assumed that children will be somewhat less guarded. Studying children has some further advantages. They talk less than adults and use simpler concepts. This simplifies our task of developing reliable content analysis procedures.

The remainder of this report will describe the methods by which we obtained and analyzed a set of descriptions of others in free response interviews.

METHOD

Sample

The children whose descriptions of others are reported here came from the lower-class areas of metropolitan New York. They were white, Negro, and Puerto Rican boys and girls between the ages of 9 and 11. Three summer camps operated by a charitable organization provided the setting. The children were referred to a camp by social agencies and spent 2 or 3 weeks in residence engaging in organized recreational activities.

The three camps differed primarily in the characteristics of the children in attendance. Therefore, we have used their diversity to provide us with opportunities to replicate the findings. Data analysis never combines either camps or sexes. Camp A accommodated both handicapped and able-bodied children. It had four different encampments, but we must combine encampments to develop a large enough sample. It contained separate groups of boys and girls. The tent, which had five or six children, is the basic unit for interaction and the planning of activities. The assignment of children to tents was specifically designed by us to provide heterogeneity of race and handicap in each tent, while seeking homogeneity of age and sex. Children were not previously acquainted with their tent mates. Camps B and C had no handicapped children, and each had only one sex. Camp B had only boys, and C had only girls. The general organization and activities of the three camps were similar. Nonhandicapped children showed no statistically significant differences in age, occupation of father, ethnicity, or other bases for assignment to the three camps.

Method of Interviewing

The interviews were conducted during four encampments at Camp A, two at Camp B, and three at Camp C. The interviewers were trained by the authors prior to reaching the camp. Each interviewer was present during various camp activities before he began interviewing. He was careful not to act as a counselor. The child knew his interviewer as a member of the camp community who was interested in children, but not as a representative of the camp authorities. Before each interview, the child was encouraged to play with the tape recorder and listen to his voice played back. The child was further assured that the other children and the counselors would not be told what he had said. The interviewer explained to the child that he was interested in learning about children in the camp.

The interviews were completely nondirective, so that the descriptions given would not be influenced by the responses of the interviewer. The entire interview was tape recorded, transcribed, and later coded. Each child in the study was interviewed twice—first, a few days after arrival at camp, and second, shortly before departure. There was usually a 1-week interval between interviews. Information solicited in each interview included a description of two other children in the child's tent. The second interview followed exactly the same procedure, except that two different children were described. Thus, each child described four children. The children to be described were assigned in order by random numbers.

The interviewer began by stating that he was interested in learning about the camp and the children in the camp. Following this, he said, "Tell me about Johnny Doe." The interviewer was not permitted to illustrate the type of statement desired. If the child asked for more specific instructions, the answer was, "Just tell me anything you can think of." When the respondent stopped talking, the probes were variants of, "Anything else?" and "Can you tell me any more?" The next description was requested only when a probe did not elicit further verbal material.

College students of the same sex as the respondent were used as interviewers. Neither sex nor personal variability of interviewers had a major effect on the findings of this study, for camp and sex differences in Table 2 are negligible.

Content-Analysis Procedure

Our goal in content analysis was to stay as close to the child's verbal report as possible. It would be impossible to analyze the verbatim record of the children's responses without a more abstract method of categorizing the words they used. Yet, the very act of categorizing for content analysis may distort the perceptual categories of the children. In this dilemma, we developed an empirically based set of content-analysis categories from an exploratory study at Camp A. The coding scheme consists of two parts: 69 content categories (68 plus a residual category), and 19 somewhat more abstract second-order categories, which emphasize the descriptive style of the describer. This paper is concerned only with the 69 content categories, as listed in Table 1.[1]

The unit of coding is an idea, and a sentence may contain several such units. For example, "He played baseball with his father," would be coded as both "physical recreation" (He played baseball) and "relations with father." A single idea unit can be coded in only 1 of the 69 mutually exclusive categories. Ideas not codable in the first 68 categories were coded in the sixty-ninth, or residual category. We analyzed only descriptions with six or more idea units so that we could assume at least minimal ability to communicate.

It should be noted that many categories are really continuous. For example, "He can run very fast," and "He is the slowest runner in our tent," would both be coded "physical ability." We were interested in the describer's making use of a category, rather than where he located another on a specific continuum.

The proportion of residual statements provides some test of the relevance of our coding scheme. If the coding scheme departed drastically from the categories employed by the children, the proportion of residuals would be high. The average residual was 11.8% of the total number of idea units and was mainly a product of lengthy anecdotes straying from the topic.

The reliability of the coding is high. Specific interviews for reliability analysis were selected at random. Studies of reliability by the two coders were performed throughout the coding process. There was no tendency for reliability to change as the coding continued. Reliability using the strictest criterion was 86.4%. This

---

[1] The coding manual has been deposited with the American Documentation Institute. Order Document No. 8014 from ADI Auxiliary Publications Project, Photoduplication Service, Library of Congress, Washington, D. C. 20540. Remit in advance $1.75 for microfilm or $2.50 for photocopies and make checks payable to: Chief, Photoduplication Service, Library of Congress.

Table 1 FIRST ORDER CATEGORIES

Demographic variables
1. Spatial location
2. Age
3. Race
4. Ethnicity
5. Religion

Organic Variables
6. Handicap
7. Health
8. Physical description
9. Physical attractiveness

Recreational variables
10. Physical recreation
11. Nonphysical recreation

Aggression
12. Physical aggression
13. Verbal aggression
14. General aggression

Quality of interaction
15. Described to describer
16. Describer to described
17. Others to described
18. Described to others
19. Described and describer to others
20. Others to describer and described
21. Reciprocal relationships

Frequency of interaction
22. Described and describer
23. Others and described
24. Described, describer, and others

Interpersonal relations
25. Relations with describer
26. Relations with father
27. Relations with mother
28. Relations with siblings
29. Relations with other family members
30. Relations with nonfamily adults
31. Relations with nonfamily children

Group status
32. Membership in a specific collective
33. Inclusion or exclusion by others in a group
34. Executive-holding an office in a specific collective
35. Socioeconomic status

Modes of interaction
36. Generosity
37. Giving aid
38. Needing aid
39. Cooperation
40. Competition
41. Trust
42. Humor
43. Dominance-submission
44. Interpersonal skill

Moods of interaction
45. Happiness
46. Excitability
47. Confidence

Total personality
48. Adult terms
49. Children's terms
50. Undifferentiated positive comments
51. Undifferentiated negative comments

Abilities
52. Verbal communication
53. Physical ability
54. Mental ability
55. School ability

Norms
56. Grooming and manners
57. Honest-dishonest
58. Swearing, cursing, drinking, smoking
59. Conformity to expectations of peers
60. Conformity to expectations of family adults
61. Conformity to expectations of nonfamily adults

Miscellaneous
62. Possessions of the child
63. Possessions of the family
64. Magic and autism
65. Occupation of child
66. Occupation of adult
67. Family
68. Sexual
69. Residual

means that for any idea which one interviewer coded in a specific category, more than 17 out of 20 times the other interviewer coded in the identical category. If idea units on which both coders agreed on residual classification were included in the reliability analysis, the coding reliability is above 90%.

A second problem of analysis is the measurement of overlap or reappearance of categories. A number of indices could be used. We selected two indices that appeared to have meaningful relationship to our concept of salience. Let us examine the psychological bases of these indices before turning to the specific measures.

First a category may be considered salient if it is employed in a number of descriptions. This is a binary concept, present or absent, related to reappearance or nonreapparence. This definition views salience in terms of a sampling process which the describer uses to select samples from some finite number of categories available to him. Of two descriptions we compared, salient categories would then be those which appear in both descriptions.

A second conception views salient categories as more likely to be frequently employed. Instead of noting merely the reappearance of a category used in another description, this conception takes account of the number of times it has been used. Viewed in the same sampling terms, this notion of salience incorporates not only the reappearance criterion, but also the number of elements in each sample assigned to the reappearing category. This second conception of salience appears to be superior. One possible disadvantage, however, is the extent to which it can be affected by individual differences in linguistic style.

These two conceptions of salience would dictate differing measures. Both these measures could be employed for the determination of those categories which are salient for a particular perceiver (he tends to notice these things) or salient about a particular social object (these things about him are noticeable) or even salient in a specific interaction situation. The focus of attention in this report, however, is not on the level of specific salient categories, but rather on the more abstract question of the relative influence of the perceiver and the perceived. For example, if we compare two descriptions given by the same perceiver of two different persons, do we find more reappearing categories than when we compare two descriptions given by different perceivers of the same person? This provides a comparison of the relative influence of the perceiver and the perceived on the amount of category overlap or reappearance.

The two measures used can now be specified. The "presence" measure is the mean proportion of the categories used in one description that were used at least once in the other description. The denominator for the computation of the proportion of reappearing categories varies with the number of categories in the description selected as the base. Therefore, the mean proportion is used, with each description in turn as the base. For example, if eight categories are used in one description and six categories in another, the presence of three reappearing categories would produce the mean of 3/8 and 3/6, or .44.

The second, a "frequency" measure, is the mean proportion of idea units in reappearing categories. This measure considers both the reappearance of categories and the distribution of idea units among the categories. With 15 units and 10 units in the two descriptions, for example, 6 idea units in the reappearing categories would give the mean of 6/10 and 6/15, or .50.

RESULTS

Before presenting data on the relative strength of the perceiver and the perceived in determining reappearance, it may be appropriate to give the reader a general idea of the most frequently used categories. For this purpose, the high incidence categories for the nonhandicapped white boys and girls in Camp A will be noted. It is interesting that of the top 12 categories for the boys, 11 of these were also among the top 12 categories for the girls. They were: relations to describer, relations to peers, relations to nonfamily adults, conformity to peers, conformity to nonfamily adults, physical recreation, physical ability, humor, giving aid, verbal communication, and undifferentiated positive comments. The boys also stressed physical aggression, while happiness appeared to be more salient for the girls.

Two caveats are in order here. First, the near identity in the set of the top 12 categories in usage for both boys and girls does not indicate equivalence in category usage. There are, in fact, major sex differences which will be discussed in a separate report. Second, no single category is used so frequently in these groups that overlap between descriptions is a product of its incidence, for the most used category is only 12% of the idea units.

To return to the central problem, the relative influence of the perceiver and the perceived, the descriptions can be organized to attack this issue. Let us now define "1 on 2," "2 on 1," and "2 on 2." One on 2 refers to overlap for a single describer when comparing 2 of his descriptions of others. Two on 1 refers to the amount of overlap found when 2 perceivers have described the same person. Two on 2 refers to the overlap when 2 different perceivers have each described different persons. Let us use A, B, C, and D as symbols for persons to illustrate these concepts. If A and B both describe C, we get 2 on 1. If A describes both B and C, the result is 1 on 2. When A describes B, and C describes D, the result is 2 on 2. These three measures of overlap make it possible to ask such questions as: "Is there greater overlap when a single perceiver describes two different people than when two different perceivers describe the same individual?" or, more simply, "Is there greater overlap with a common perceiver, or is there greater overlap with a common person as object?" The 2 on 2 analysis provides some evidence as to the amount of overlap that can be ascribed to what might be called "common culture."

It is tempting to look at these data within the framework of how much overlap can be attributed to the perceiver, how much to the perceived, and how much to "culture." It is, however, crucial to note at this point that there clearly is not a common object of description in this study. Each person participates in relatively unique interaction with another, so that no two persons can be said to have the same experiential basis for describing John Jones. In 1 on 2, the common participant in the interaction is the perceiver. In 2 on 1, he is the person perceived. In 2 on 2, there is no common participant. The results of our overlap analysis are presented in Table 2.

There is remarkable order in these overlap data. There are no exceptions to the finding that 1 on 2 is higher than 2 on 1, and that 2 on 1 is higher than 2 on 2. Not only is this regularity found for both presence and frequency measures, but the three distributions do not overlap in range. The lowest 1 on 2 proportion, for example, is higher than the highest 2 on 1. Quite clearly, the greatest overlap is obtained with a common perceiver.

The interpretation of these data, attributing the greatest overlap to the existence of a common perceiver, is complicated by the possibility that the respondent is affected by his own immediate prior responses. To say of a girl

Table 2 CATEGORY OVERLAP BY CAMP AND SEX

| | PERCENTAGE OF OVERLAP | | | | | |
| CAMP GROUP | PRESENCE | | | FREQUENCY | | |
	1 on 2	2 on 1	2 on 2	1 on 2	2 on 1	2 on 2
A—Males	48	41	34	59	47	39
	(251)	(444)	(80)	(251)	(444)	(80)
B—Males	48	38	34	58	45	41
	(223)	(452)	(40)	(223)	(452)	(40)
A—Females	47	38	32	54	44	35
	(284)	(536)	(74)	(284)	(536)	(74)
C—Females	48	36	32	57	45	39
	(100)	(162)	(40)	(100)	(162)	(40)
A + B—Males	48	39	34	59	46	40
	(474)	(896)	(120)	(474)	(896)	(120)
A + C—Females	47	38	32	55	44	36
	(384)	(698)	(114)	(384)	(698)	(114)
Total	48	39	33	57	45	38
	(858)	(1594)	(234)	(858)	(1594)	(234)

Note.—Figures in parentheses represent the number of pairs averaged in a group.

that "She is a good student" may make it markedly more probable that a description of another girl a few minutes later will mention school ability. Are we studying salience or merely the recall of a prior response in a somewhat similar situation? Recall is a possible complication only for 1 on 2, since 2 on 1 and 2 on 2 employ different describers. A test of this possible deficiency is provided by the separation of a week between the first and second interviews. A random sample of 40 boys and 40 girls was selected from Camp A. For each, both presence and frequency overlap were computed for two descriptions by a single perceiver within the same interview and for two descriptions given in interviews 1 week apart. Table 3 reports these data.

The differences in overlap for descriptions separated by only a few minutes as compared to descriptions given a week apart are so slight that the high 1 on 2 overlap is clearly not a function of a temporary set.

Table 3 WITHIN-INTERVIEW AND BETWEEN-INTERVIEW OVERLAP

| | WITHIN-INTERVIEW OVERLAP | | BETWEEN-INTERVIEW OVERLAP | |
	PRESENCE INDEX	FREQUENCY INDEX	PRESENCE INDEX	FREQUENCY INDEX
Camp A				
Males	47%	59%	45%	56%
(N = 40)				
Females	48%	51%	45%	53%
(N = 40)				
Total	47%	55%	45%	55%
(N = 80)				

DISCUSSION

The ordering of the overlap data is highly consistent: reference to Table 2 indicates the presence and the frequency measures maintain a constant relationship to each other, with the frequency measure consistently higher. For the frequency measure, the total 1 on 2 overlap is 57%, while the 2 on 1 is 45%, and the 2 on 2 is 38%. Obviously, the absolute values of these measures could shift rather easily with a different coding scheme. Yet, these figures are remarkably high, given the fact that there are 68 categories used in the analysis (the residual category is excluded).

In one sense, the 2 on 2 measure represents the model for overlap due to chance, given the distribution of category usage in the population. One might ask what overlap would be present if all categories were equally likely to occur. For both the presence and the frequency measures, the chance overlap is the ratio of the mean number of categories in a description to the 68 categories in the analysis. Applied to this data, the chance presence and frequency measures would be .12. As in the research of Yarrow and Campbell (1963), the chance model for the reappearance of categories can be rejected, for the lowest overlap is .32. In this paper, we attempt to go beyond the rejection of chance to the development of techniques for measuring the relative contribution of the perceiver and the perceived.

Special stress should be placed on the relative differences indicated by our measures. Let us compare 2 on 1 with 2 on 2; in both situations, we have different perceivers, but in 2 on 1 we have a common individual being described. Yet, the increase in overlap over the 2 on 2 situation is only 6 and 7%, whereas if attention is shifted to the 1 on 2 analysis (where two different individuals are being described by a single perceiver), the increase over the 2 on 2 is 15 and 19%. Certainly, the magnitude of the 2 on 2 finding is a function of the homogeneity of the camp situation, as well as of the common general culture the children share. However, the small difference introduced by specifying a common social object reinforces our finding of the greater impact of the perceiver.

In the process of comparing the relative contribution to overlap of the perceiver and the perceived, we want to emphasize an important next step for investigation. It will be important to explore the relative contribution of the perceiver and the perceived to overlap of specific categories. Are there certain categories that appear to be mainly perceiver determined, whereas others may be mainly a function of the perceived? This is an interaction situation, but it still may be possible to separate certain categories as being mainly determined by the object of description, whereas others are more a function of the perceiver. Evidence of this sort should contribute to the exploration of interpersonal perception, especially in terms of the categories selected to be the basis of ratings in experimental situations. For example, one might ask the effect of various sets upon the descriptions given. Providing an "objective stimulus set" ought to increase the number of categories that are a function of the perceived, while altering the cognitive orientation of the perceiver should have the most impact on perceiver-determined categories.

Some further questions that need investigation are the effect of the interpersonal relationship on category usage. For example, how does the description of another vary with one's own interpersonal attraction to that person? Does category usage shift when a liked and a disliked other are described, or does one merely shift position on category continua? Questions can also be raised as to the relation between category usage and interpersonal behavior. Do people who behave aggressively talk a lot about aggression in their descriptions of others?

A number of questions can also be raised as to group differences in category usage in the description of others. How do descriptions of others differ between rural and urban groups, sociocultural groups, etc.? Sex differences in category usage should be of considerable interest. Beach and Wertheimer (1962) have demonstrated the existence of category usage differences as a function of sex.

A final comment: our findings indicate that the most powerful influence on interpersonal description is the manner in which the perceiver structures his interpersonal world. However, we wish to draw attention to the complement of each of the proportions in Table 2. If there is overlap for 1 on 2, there is also shift, as another person is described. It is irresponsible to treat this shift as merely "noise." In this same-status, same-age, same-sex world, the descriptions do change as each describer discusses a new person with whom he interacts. The world of our subjects is not just a Rorschach card. A major task of social psychology, we believe, is the development of concepts to order the interaction phenomena that lead to these changes, for we have here focused only on stability.

REFERENCES

Beach, L., & Wertheimer, M. A free response approach to the study of personal cognition. *Journal of Abnormal and Social Psychology,* 1962, *62,* 367–74.

Hastorf, A. H., Richardson, S. A., & Dornbusch, S. M. The problem of relevance in the study of person perception. In R. Tagiuri & L. Petrullo (Eds.), *Person perception and interpersonal behavior.* Stanford: Stanford Univer. Press, 1958. Pp. 54–62.

Yarrow, Marian R., & Campbell, J. D. Person perception in children. *Merrill-Palmer Quarterly,* 1963, *9,* 57–72.

3

LIKING

Gain and Loss of Esteem as Determinants of Interpersonal Attractiveness

ELLIOT ARONSON AND DARWYN LINDER

One of the major determinants of whether or not one person (P) will like another (O) is the nature of the other's behavior in relation to the person. Several investigators have predicted and found that if P finds O's behavior "rewarding," he will tend to like O (Newcomb, 1956, 1961; Thibaut and Kelley, 1959; Homans, 1961; Byrne, 1961; Byrne and Wong, 1962). One obvious source of reward for P is O's attitude regarding him. Thus, if O expresses invariably positive feelings and opinions about P, this constitutes a reward and will tend to increase P's liking for O.

Reprinted from The Journal of Experimental Social Psychology, 1, *1965, 156–71. Copyright 1965 by Academic Press Inc. and reproduced by permission.*

Although this has been demonstrated to be true (Newcomb, 1956, 1961), it may be that a more complex relationship exists between being liked and liking others. It is conceivable that the sequence of O's behavior toward P might have more impact on P's liking for O than the total number of rewarding acts emitted by O toward P. Stated briefly, it is our contention that the feeling of gain or loss is extremely important—specifically, that a gain in esteem is a more potent reward than invariant esteem, and similarly, the loss of esteem is a more potent "punishment" than invariant negative esteem. Thus, if O's behavior toward P was initially negative but gradually became more positive, P would like O more than he would had O's behavior been uniformly positive. This would follow even if, in the second case, the sum total of rewarding acts emitted by O was less than in the first case.

This "gain-loss" effect may have two entirely different causes. One is largely affective, the other cognitive. First, when O expresses negative feelings toward P, P probably experiences some negative affect, e.g., anxiety, hurt, self-doubt, anger, etc. If O's behavior gradually becomes more positive, his behavior is not only rewarding for P in and of itself, but it also serves to reduce the existing negative drive state previously aroused by O. The total reward value of O's positive behavior is, therefore, greater. Thus, paradoxically, P will subsequently like O better *because* of O's early negative, punitive behavior.

This reasoning is similar to that of Gerard and Greenbaum (1962). Their experiment involved an Asch-type situation in which they varied the behavior of the stooge whose judgments followed those of the subject. In one condition the investigators varied the trial on which the stooge switched from disagreeing with the judgment of the subject (and agreeing with that of the majority) to agreeing with the judgment of the subject. The results showed a curvilinear relationship between the point at which the stooge switched and his attractiveness for the subjects—the subjects liked him best if he switched either very early or very late in the sequence of judgments. The investigators predicted and explained the high degree of liking for the "late-switcher" as being due to the fact that he was reducing a greater degree of uncertainty. Our reasoning is also consistent with that of Walters and Ray (1960) who, in elaborating on an experiment by Gewirtz and Baer (1958), demonstrated that prior anxiety arousal increases the effectiveness of social reinforcement on children's performance. In their experiment social approval had a greater effect on performance in the anxiety conditions because it was reducing a greater drive.

We are carrying this one step further. What we are suggesting is that the existence of a prior negative drive state will increase the attractiveness of an individual who has both created and reduced this drive state. The kind of relationship we have in mind was perhaps best expressed by Spinoza (1955) in proposition 44 of *The Ethics:* "Hatred which is completely vanquished by love passes into love: and love is thereupon greater than if hatred had not preceded it. For he who begins to love a thing, which he has wont to hate or regard with pain, from the very fact of loving feels pleasure. To this pleasure involved in love is added the pleasure arising from aid given to the endeavour to remove the pain involved in hatred, accompanied by the idea of the former object of hatred as cause."

The same kind of reasoning (in reverse) underlies the "loss" part of our notion. Here, *P* will like *O* better if *O*'s behavior toward *P* is invariably negative than if *O*'s initial behavior had been positive and gradually became more negative. Although in the former case *O*'s behavior may consist of a greater number of negative acts, the latter case constitutes a distinct loss of esteem and, therefore, would have a greater effect upon reducing *P*'s liking for *O*. When negative behavior follows positive behavior, it is not only punishing in its own right but also eradicates the positive affect associated with the rewarding nature of *O*'s earlier behavior. Therefore, *P* dislikes the positive-negative *O* more than the entirely negative *O* precisely because of the fact that, in the first case, *O* had previously rewarded him.

The predicted gain-loss effect may also have a more cognitive cause. By changing his opinion about *P*, *O* forces *P* to take his evaluation more seriously. If *O* expresses uniformly positive or uniformly negative feelings about *P*, *P* can dismiss this behavior as being a function of *O*'s style of response, i.e., that *O* likes everybody or dislikes everybody, and that is *his* problem. But if *O* begins by evaluating *P* negatively and then becomes more positive, *P* must consider the possibility that *O*'s evaluations are a function of *O*'s perception of him and not merely a style of responding. Because of this he is more apt to be impressed by *O* than if *O*'s evaluation had been invariably positive. It is probably not very meaningful to be liked by a person with no discernment or discrimination. *O*'s early negative evaluation proves that he has discernment and that he's paying attention to *P*—that he's neither blind nor bland. This renders his subsequent positive evaluation all the more meaningful and valuable.

By the same token, if *O*'s evaluation of *P* is entirely negative, *P* may be able to write *O* off as a misanthrope or a fool. But if *O*'s initial evaluation is positive and then becomes negative, *P* is forced to conclude that *O* can discriminate among people. This adds meaning (and sting) to *O*'s negative evaluation of *P* and, consequently, will decrease *P*'s liking for *O*.

The present experiment was designed to test the major prediction of our gain-loss notion, that is, the primary intent of this experiment was to determine whether or not *changes* in the feelings of *O* toward *P* have a greater effect on *P*'s liking for *O* than the total number of rewarding acts emitted by *O*. A secondary purpose was to shed some light on the possible reasons for this relationship. The specific hypotheses are (1) *P* will like *O* better if *O*'s initial attitude toward *P* is negative but gradually becomes more positive, than if his attitude is uniformly positive; (2) *P* will like *O* better if his attitude is uniformly negative than if his initial attitude toward *P* is positive and becomes increasingly negative.

METHOD

Subjects and Design

In order to provide a test of the hypotheses, it was necessary to design an experiment in which a subject interacts with a confederate over a series of discrete meetings. During these meetings the confederate should express either a uniformly positive attitude toward the subject, a uniformly negative attitude toward the subject, a negative attitude which gradually becomes positive, or a positive attitude which gradually becomes negative. It was essential that the interactions between subject and confederate be constant throughout experimental conditions except for the expression of attitude. At the close of the experiment, the subject's liking for the confederate could be assessed.

The subjects were 80 female students[1] at the University of Minnesota. Virtually all of them were sophomores; they were volunteers from introductory classes in psychology, sociology, and child development. All subjects were randomly assigned to one of the four experimental conditions.

Procedure

The experimenter greeted the subject and led her to an observation room which was connected to the main experimental room by a one-way window and an audio-amplification system. The experimenter told the subject that two students were scheduled for this hour, one would be the subject and the other would help the experimenter perform the experiment. He said that since she arrived first, she would be the helper. He asked her to wait while he left the room to see if the other girl had arrived yet. A few minutes later, through the one-way window, the subject was able to see the experimenter enter the experimental room with another female student (the paid confederate). The experimenter told the confederate to be seated for a moment and that he would return shortly to explain the experiment to her. The experimenter then returned to the observation room and began the instructions to the subject. The experimenter told the subject that she was going to assist him in performing a verbal conditioning experiment on the other student. The experimenter explained verbal conditioning briefly and told the subject that his particular interest was in the possible generalization of conditioned verbal responses from the person giving the reward to a person who did not reward the operant response. The experimenter explained that he would condition the other girl to say plural nouns to him by rewarding her with an "mmm hmmm" every time she said a plural noun. The experimenter told the subject that his procedure should increase the rate of plural nouns employed by the other girl. The subject was then told that her tasks were: (1) to listen in and record the number of plural nouns used by the other girl, and (2) to engage her in a series of conversations (not rewarding plural nouns) so that the experimenter could listen and determine whether generalization occurred. The experimenter told the subject that they would alternate in talking to the girl (first the subject, then the experimenter, then the subject) until each had spent seven sessions with her.

The experimenter made it clear to the subject that the other girl must not know the purpose of the experiment lest the results be contaminated. He explained that, in order to accomplish this, some deception must be used. The experimenter said that he was going to tell the girl that the purpose of the experiment was to determine how people form impressions of other people. He said that the other girl would be told that she was to carry on a series of seven

---

[1] Actually, 84 subjects were run in these four conditions. Four of the subjects were unusable because they were able to guess the real purpose of the experiment.

short conversations with the subject, and that between each of these conversations both she and the subject would be interviewed, the other girl by the experimenter and the subject by an assistant in another room, to find out what impressions they had formed. The experimenter told the subject that this "cover story" would enable the experimenter and the subject to perform their experiment on verbal behavior since it provided the other girl with a credible explanation for the procedure they would follow. In actuality, this entire explanation was, in itself, a cover story which enabled the experimenter and his confederate to perform their experiment on the formation of impressions.

The independent variable was manipulated during the seven meetings that the experimenter had with the confederate. During their meetings the subject was in the observation room, listening to the conversation and dutifully counting the number of plural nouns used by the confederate. Since the subject had been led to believe that the confederate thought that the experiment involved impressions of people, it was quite natural for the experimenter to ask the confederate to express her feelings about the subject. Thus, without intending to, the subject heard herself evaluated by a fellow student on seven successive occasions.

There were four experimental conditions: (1) Negative-Positive, (2) Positive-Negative, (3) Negative-Negative, and (4) Positive-Positive. In the Negative-Positive condition the confederate expressed a negative impression of the subject during the first three interviews with the experimenter. Specifically, she described her as being a dull conversationalist, a rather ordinary person, not very intelligent, as probably not having many friends, etc. During the fourth session she began to change her opinion about her. The confederate's attitude became more favorable with each successive meeting until, in the seventh interview, it was entirely positive. In the Positive-Positive condition the confederate's stated opinions were invariably positive. During the seventh interview her statements were precisely the same as those in the seventh meeting of the Negative-Positive condition. In the Negative-Negative condition the confederate expressed invariably negative feelings about the subject throughout the seven interviews. The Positive-Negative condition was the mirror image of the Negative-Positive condition. The confederate began by stating that the subject seemed interesting, intelligent, and likeable, but by the seventh session she described the subject as being dull, ordinary, etc.

In the Positive-Positive condition the confederate made 28 favorable statements about the subject and zero unfavorable statements. In the Negative-Negative condition the confederate made 24 unfavorable statements about the subject and zero favorable ones. In both the Negative-Positive and Positive-Negative conditions the confederate made 14 favorable and 8 unfavorable statements about the subject.

At the opening of the first interview, the experimenter informed the confederate that she should be perfectly frank and honest and that the subject would never be told anything about her evaluation. This was done so that the subject, upon hearing favorable statements, could not readily believe that the confederate might be trying to flatter her.

Interactions between Subjects and Confederate

Prior to each interview with the experimenter, the confederate and the subject engaged in a 3-minute conversation. This provided a credible basis upon which the confederate might form and change her impression of the subject. During these sessions it was essential that the confederate's conversations with the subject be as uniform as possible throughout the four experimental conditions. This was accomplished by informing the subject, prior to the first session, of the kind of topics she should lead the confederate into. These included movies, teachers, courses, life goals, personal background information, etc. Once the subject brought up one of these topics, the confederate spewed forth a prepared set of facts, opinions, and anecdotes which were identical for all experimental subjects. Of course, since a social interaction was involved, it was impossible for the confederate's conversations to be entirely uniform for all of the subjects. Occasionally the confederate was forced to respond to a direct question which was idiosyncratic to a particular subject. However, any variations in the statements made by the confederate were minor and nonsystematic.

The subject and confederate met in the same room but they were separated at all times by a cardboard screen which prevented visual communication. This was done for two reasons. First, it made it easier for the confederate to play the role of the naive subject. We feared that the confederate, after saying negative things about the subject, might be reluctant to look her squarely in the eye and engage in casual conversation. In addition, the use of the screen allowed for a more precise control of the conversation of the confederate by enabling her to read her lines from a prepared script which was tacked to the screen. The use of the screen was easily explained to the subject (in terms of the verbal reinforcement cover story) as a necessary device for eliminating inadvertant nonverbal reinforcement, like nods and smiles.

The confederate carried on her end of the conversation in a rather bland, neutral tone of voice, expressing neither great enthusiasm nor monumental boredom. The same girl (an attractive 20-year-old senior) was used as the confederate throughout the experiment. In order to further convince the subject of the validity of the cover story, the confederate used increasingly more plural nouns throughout the course of the experiment.

The Dependent Variable

At the close of the experiment the experimenter told the subject that there was some additional information he needed from her, but that it was also necessary for him to see the other girl to explain the true nature of the experiment to her. He said that, since he was pressed for time, the subject would be interviewed by his research supervisor while he, the experimenter, explained the experiment to the other girl. The experimenter then led the subject into the interviewer's office, introduced them, and left.

A separate interviewer[2] was used in order to avoid bias, the interviewer being ignorant of the subject's experimental condition. The purpose of the interview was to measure the subject's liking for the confederate; but this could not be done in any simple manner because the bare outlines of this experiment were extremely transparent: the confederate evaluated the subject, then the subject evaluated the confederate. Unless the interviewer could provide the subject with a credible rationale (consistent with the cover story) for asking her to evaluate the other girl, even the most naive of our subjects might have guessed the real purpose of the experiment. Therefore, the interviewer took a great deal of time and trouble to convince the subject that these data were essential for an understanding of the other girl's verbal behavior. The essence of his story was that the attitudes and feelings that the "helpers" in the experiment had for the "subjects" in the experiment often found expression in such subtle ways as tone of voice, enthusiasm, etc. "For example, if you thought a lot of the other girl you might unwittingly talk with warmth and enthusiasm. If you didn't like her you might unwittingly sound aloof and distant." The interviewer went on to explain that, much to his chagrin, he noticed that these subtle differences in inflection had a marked effect upon the gross verbal output of the other girls, that is, they talked more when they were conversing with people who seemed to like them than when they were conversing with people who seemed not to like them. The interviewer said that this source of variance was impossible to control but must be accounted for in the statistical analysis of the data. He explained that if he could get a precise indication of the "helpers'" feelings toward the "subjects," he could then "plug this into a mathematical formula as a correction term and thereby get a more or less unbiased estimate of what her gross verbal output would have been if your attitude toward her had been neutral."

The interviewer told the subject that, in order to accomplish this, he was going to ask her a number of questions aimed at getting at her feelings about the other girl. He emphasized that he wanted her *feeling*, her "gut response"; i.e., that it was essential that she give her frank impression of the other girl regardless of whether or not she had solid, rational reasons for it.

After the subject indicated that she understood, the interviewer asked her whether she liked the other girl or not. After she answered, the interviewer showed her a card on which was printed a 21-point scale, from −10 to +10. The interviewer asked her to indicate the magnitude of her feeling as precisely as possible. He verbally labeled the scale: "+10 would mean you like her extremely, −10 that you dislike her extremely. Zero means that you are completely indifferent. If you liked her a little, you'd answer +1, +2, or +3; if you liked her moderately well, you'd answer +4, +5, or +6; if you liked her quite a bit, you'd answer with a higher number. What point on the scale do you feel reflects your feeling toward the girl most accurately?"

[2] It should be reported that in an earlier attempt to test this hypothesis, a questionnaire was administered instead of an interview. This was a more economical procedure, but it proved to be less effective. Although the results in the four experimental conditions were in the predicted order, the variance was extremely large. Postexperimental discussions with the subjects led us to suspect that one reason for the large variance might be due to the fact that the subjects were treating the questionnaires in a rather casual manner, believing that this aspect of the experiment was of little importance. It was primarily for this reason that we decided to use a high-status interviewer, whose earnest presence forced the subjects to treat the interview seriously and to respond in an honest and thoughtful manner.

This was the dependent measure. In addition, the interviewer asked the subjects to rate the confederate on 14 evaluative scales including intelligence, friendliness, warmth, frankness, etc. Most of these were asked in order to ascertain whether or not general liking would manifest itself in terms of higher ratings on specific attributes; a few were asked as possible checks on the manipulations.

Finally, the interviewer asked the subject if it bothered, embarrassed, annoyed, or upset her to hear the other girl evaluate her to the experimenter. After recording her answer, the interviewer probed to find out whether or not the subject suspected the real purpose of the experiment. He then explained, in full, the true nature of the experiment and the necessity for the deception. The subjects, especially those who had been negatively evaluated, were relieved to learn that it was not "for real." Although several of the girls admitted to having been quite shaken during the experiment, they felt that it was a worthwhile experience, inasmuch as they learned the extent to which a negative evaluation (even by a stranger) can affect them. They left the interview room in good spirits.

In most cases the interviewer remained ignorant of which of the four experimental conditions the subject was in until the conclusion of the interview. On a few occasions, however, a subject said something casually, in the midst of the interview, from which the interviewer could infer her experimental condition. It should be emphasized, however, that the dependent variable was the first question asked; in no case was the interviewer aware of a subject's experimental condition before she responded to that question.

RESULTS AND DISCUSSION

Our hypotheses were that the confederate would be liked better in the Negative-Positive condition than in the Positive-Positive condition and that she would be liked better in the Negative-Negative condition than in the Positive-Negative condition. To test these hypotheses we compared the subjects' ratings of their liking for the confederate across experimental conditions. The significance of the differences were determined by t-test.[3] Table 1 shows the means, *SDs, t*-values, and significance levels. An examination of the table reveals that the means are ordered in the predicted direction. Moreover, it is clear that the confederate was liked significantly more in the Negative-Positive condition than in the Positive-Positive condition ($p < .02$, two-tailed). The difference between the Negative-Negative condition and the Positive-Negative condition showed a strong trend in the predicted direction, although it did not reach an acceptable level of significance ($p < .15$, two-tailed). There is a great deal of variability in these two conditions. This large variability may be partly a function of the well-known reluctance of college students to express negative feelings about their fellow

[3] A t-test was used because it is the most direct statistical technique and it also allowed us to perform an internal analysis to be described later. However, it is not the most powerful method of analyzing the data. An analysis of variance was also performed, and the results were slightly more significant than those of the t-test. The difference between Negative-Positive and Positive-Positive conditions reached the .02 level of significance; the difference between the Negative-Negative and the Positive-Negative conditions reached the .07 level of significance. The over-all treatment effect was highly significant ($p < .0005$).

Table 1 MEANS AND STANDARD DEVIATIONS FOR LIKING OF THE
CONFEDERATE

EXPERIMENTAL CONDITION	MEAN	SD	t-VALUES	
1. Negative-Positive	+7.67	1.51	1 vs. 2	2.71**
2. Positive-Positive	+6.42	1.42	2 vs. 3	7.12***
3. Negative-Negative	+2.52	3.16	3 vs. 4	1.42*
4. Positive-Negative	+0.87	3.32		

*$p < .15$.
**$p < .02$.
***$p < .001$ (all p levels are two-tailed).

students, even when the behavior of the latter is objectively negative (e.g., Aronson and Mills, 1959). Typically, in social psychological experiments, regardless of how obnoxiously a stooge behaves toward a subject, many subjects find it difficult to verbalize negative evaluations of the stooge. In these two conditions the behavior of the stimulus person would seem to have brought forth a negative evaluation; although most of the subjects were able to do this, several came out with highly positive evaluations. Thus, the range for the Negative-Negative and Positive-Negative conditions was 15 scale units (from +7 to –7). In the other two conditions negative evaluations were *not* in order; thus, this difficulty was not encountered. The range for these two conditions was only seven scale units (from +9 to +3). Therefore, although the mean difference between the Positive-Negative and Negative-Negative conditions was actually larger than the mean difference between the Positive-Positive and Negative-Positive conditions, it fell short of statistical significance.

Table 1 also indicates that there is a very large difference between those conditions in which the confederate ended by expressing a positive feeling for the subject and those in which she ended with a negative feeling for the subject. For example, a comparison of the Positive-Positive condition with the Negative-Negative condition yields a *t* of 7.12, significant at far less than the .001 level. As predicted, the widest mean difference occurs between the Negative-Positive condition (M = +7.67) and the Positive-Negative condition (M = +0.87). This is interesting in view of the fact that the confederate made the same number of positive and negative statements in these two conditions; only the sequence was different.

It will be recalled that the subjects were asked to rate the confederate on 14 evaluative scales in order to ascertain whether or not greater liking would manifest itself in terms of higher ratings on specific attributes. No evidence for this was found; e.g., although the subjects liked the confederate better in the Negative-Positive condition than in the Positive-Positive condition, they did not find her significantly more intelligent or less conceited. In fact, the only ratings that reached an acceptable level of significance showed a reverse effect: In the Positive-Positive condition the confederate was rated more friendly ($p < .01$), nicer ($p < .01$), and warmer ($p < .01$) than in the Negative-Positive condition. Our failure to predict this effect may be attributable to a naive belief in generalization which served to blind us to more obvious factors. Thus, although we did not predict this result, it is not startling if one considers the simple fact that in the Positive-Positive condition the confederate's evaluations of the subject, because they were entirely positive, *did* reflect greater friendliness, niceness, and warmth. That is, when forced to consider such things as friendliness, niceness, and warmth, the subjects in the Negative-Positive condition could not give the confederate a very high rating. The confederate, here, is not the kind of person who exudes niceness; by definition she is capable of saying negative things. Nevertheless, when asked for their "gut-response" regarding how much they liked the confederate, the subjects in the Negative-Positive condition tended to give her a high rating. To speculate, we might suggest the following: When one is asked to rate a person on a particular attribute, one tends to sum the person's relevant behavior in a rather cognitive, rational manner. On the other hand, when one is asked how much one likes a person, one tends to state a current feeling rather than to add and subtract various components of the person's past behavior.

Degree of Liking as a Function of "Upset"

The major results are consistent with the hypotheses derived from the gain-loss notion. Although, in this experiment, it was not our intention to test the underlying assumptions of this notion, there are some data which may be of relevance. Recall that one of the suggested causes of the gain-loss effect is that, in the negative conditions, the subjects experienced negative feelings such as anxiety, anger, self-doubt, etc. That is, it was predicted that the subjects in the Negative-Positive condition would like the confederate better than would the subjects in the Positive-Positive condition because in the Negative-Positive condition the confederate's behavior was reducing a negative drive state. If this assumption is correct, the effect should not occur if, for some reason, the confederate's negative behavior did not produce a negative drive state in the subjects. For example, in the Negative-Positive condition, if the subjects did not take the negative evaluation personally there would be no negative drive state to be reduced. Similarly, in the Positive-Negative condition, loss would not be experienced if the confederate's negative behavior, for some reason, were not taken personally by the subject. As mentioned earlier, near the end of the experiment the interviewer asked the subject if it bothered, embarrassed, or upset her to listen to herself being evaluated by the other girl. As one might expect, in the Positive-Positive condition none of the subjects were at all bothered, upset, or embarrassed by the situation. In the Negative-Positive condition, however, 11 subjects admitted to having been somewhat upset when the other girl was evaluating them negatively; similarly, nine girls in the Negative-Negative condition and nine in the Positive-Negative condition admitted that they were upset by the negative evaluation. In these latter conditions the subjects who claimed that they were not upset by the negative evaluation tended to explain this by saying that the situation was so restricted that they lacked the freedom and relaxation to "be themselves" and "make a good impression" on the other girl. Typically, they felt that it was reasonable for the other girl to think of them as dull and stupid—the situation *forced* them to appear dull. Thus, many of the girls refused to take a negative evaluation personally; instead, they felt that the confederate would have liked them better if the situation had been freer, allowing them to express their usual, loveable personalities.

For what it is worth, let us compare those who were upset by a negative evaluation with those who were not in terms of how much they liked the confederate. Within the Negative-Positive condition those subjects who were upset by the negative evaluation liked the confederate *more* than those who were not upset ($t = 3.36$, $p < .01$, two-tailed). Similarly, within the Positive-Negative condition those who were upset by the negative evaluation liked the confederate *less* than those who were not upset ($t = 4.44$, $p < .01$). In the Negative-Negative condition, as might be expected, there was a tendency for those who were not upset to like the confederate better than those who were upset ($t = 1.26$, N.S.). We can also compare degree of liking across experimental conditions, eliminating those subjects who were not upset by a negative evaluation. The difference between the Negative-Positive and Positive-Positive conditions is highly significant ($t = 4.57$, $p < .005$, two-tailed). When the "upset" subjects only are compared, the difference between the Negative-Negative and Positive-Negative conditions approaches significance ($t = 1.91$, $p < .08$, two-tailed).

These data are consistent with the affective assumption of the gain-loss notion inasmuch as they suggest that a feeling of upset is a necessary precondition for the great liking in the Negative-Positive condition and the great dislike in the Positive-Negative condition. However, since these data are based on an internal analysis, they are not unequivocal; those subjects who were upset (strictly speaking, those who admitted to being upset) by a negative evaluation may be different kinds of animals from those who did not admit to being upset. The differences in their liking for the stimulus person may be a reflection of some unknown individual differences rather than of the manipulated differences in the independent variable. For example, considering the explanations given by those subjects who were not upset, it is conceivable that these individuals may be extreme on "ego-defensiveness"; or, conversely, those subjects who *were* upset may be extremely "hypersensitive." From our data it is impossible to judge whether or not such individual differences could be correlated with the dependent variable. In sum, although the results from the internal analysis are suggestive, they are equivocal because they do not represent a systematic experimental manipulation.

A Neutral-Positive Condition

If, for the moment, one ignores the internal analysis, the possibility exists that *any* increase in the confederate's positive evaluation of the subject would have produced an increase in the subject's liking for the confederate, even if pain had not been involved. For example, suppose the confederate's initial evaluation of the subject had been neutral rather than negative, and then had become increasingly positive; would the subject like the confederate as much in this condition as in the Negative-Positive condition? If so, then, clearly, pain and suffering are not necessary factors. To test this possibility, 15 additional subjects were run in a Neutral-Positive condition.[4] This condition is identical to the Negative-Positive condition except that during the first three meetings, instead

---

[4] We wish to thank Ellen Berscheid, who first suggested this condition.

of expressing negative evaluations of the subject, the confederate was non-committal, saying such things as "She seems to be pretty intelligent, but perhaps just a little on the dull side...." "I'm not sure; she kind of strikes me both ways...." "I just can't make up my mind about her. My feelings are rather neutral." The subjects were randomly assigned to this condition, although assignment did not commence until after two or three subjects had been run in each of the other four conditions. In this condition the mean liking score was 6.66. This is almost identical with the mean in the Positive-Positive condition. The difference between the Neutral-Positive and Negative-Positive conditions approaches statistical significance ($t = 1.96, p < .07$, two-tailed).

These data, coupled with the data from the internal analysis, suggest that some upset on the subject's part increased her liking for the stimulus person. However, other factors may contribute to the effect. One such contributing factor has already been discussed as the cognitive assumption underlying the gain-loss notion. Specifically, when O changes his evaluation of P, it is indicative of the fact that he (O) has some discernment and that his evaluation is a considered judgment. Consequently, his evaluation of P should have greater impact on P than an invariably positive or invariably negative evaluation. This would lead to greater liking in the Negative-Positive condition and less liking in the Positive-Negative condition. We made no great attempt to investigate the validity of this assumption in the present experiment. We did ask the subjects to rate the degree of discernment of the stimulus person. Here, we found a faint glimmer of support. There was some tendency for the subjects in the Negative-Positive condition to rate the stimulus person higher ($M = 6.75$) than did the subjects in the Positive-Positive condition ($M = 5.35$), but this difference was not statistically significant ($t = 1.40, p < .15$). There was no difference in the ratings made by the subjects in the other two conditions.

Alternative Explanations

Flattery.   Recent work by Jones (1964) on flattery and ingratiation suggests the possibility that a person who makes exclusively positive statements might be suspected of using flattery in order to manipulate the subject, and therefore might be liked less than someone whose evaluations include negative statements. However, this is not a compelling explanation of the results of the present experiment because the subject was led to believe that the confederate was unaware that she (the subject) was eavesdropping during the evaluation. One cannot easily attribute these ulterior motives to a person who says nice things about us in our absence.

Contrast.   Another possible alternative explanation involves the phenomenon of contrast (Helson, 1964). After several negative and neutral statements, a positive evaluation may seem more positive than the same statement preceded by other positive statements. Similarly, a negative evaluation following several positive and neutral statements may appear to be more negative than one that formed part of a series of uniformly negative statements. Thus, a contrast effect, if operative, could have contributed to our results. At the same time, it should be noted that in the Neutral-Positive condition, where some degree of contrast should also occur, there is little evidence of the existence of this phenomenon. Specifically, the mean liking score in the Neutral-Positive condition was almost identical to that in the Positive-Positive condition and quite different from that in the Negative-Positive condition ($p < .07$). These data suggest that, although a contrast effect could conceivably have contributed to the results, it is doubtful that such an effect was strong enough, in this experimental situation, to have generated the results in and of itself.

Competence. In the Negative-Positive condition the subject has succeeded in showing the confederate that he (the subject) is not a dull clod but is, in fact, a bright and interesting person. This is no mean accomplishment and therefore might lead the subject to experience a feeling of competence or efficacy (White, 1959). Thus, in this condition, part of the reason for O's great attractiveness may be due to the fact that he has provided the subject with a success experience. Indeed, during the interview many subjects in this condition spontaneously mentioned that, after hearing O describe them as dull and stupid, they tried hard to make interesting and intelligent statements in subsequent encounters with O. It is reasonable to suspect that they were gratified to find that these efforts paid off by inducing a change in O's evaluations. This raises an interesting theoretical question; it may be that the feeling of competence is not only a contributing factor to the "gain" effect but may actually be a necessary condition. This possibility could be tested in future experimentation by manipulating the extent to which the subject feels that O's change in evaluation is contingent upon the subject's actual behavior.

Possible Implications

One of the implications of the gain-loss notion is that "you always hurt the one you love," i.e., once we have grown certain of the good will (rewarding behavior) of a person (e.g., a mother, a spouse, a close friend), that person may become less potent as a source of reward than a stranger. If we are correct in our assumption that a gain in esteem is a more potent reward than the absolute level of the esteem itself, then it follows that a close friend (by definition) is operating near ceiling level and therefore cannot provide us with a gain. To put it another way, since we have learned to expect love, favors, praise, etc. from a friend, such behavior cannot possibly represent a gain in his esteem for us. On the other hand, the constant friend and rewarder has great potential as a punisher. The closer the friend, the greater the past history of invariant esteem and reward, the more devastating is its withdrawal. Such withdrawal, by definition, constitutes a loss of esteem.

An example may help clarify this point. After 10 years of marriage, if a doting husband compliments his wife on her appearance, it may mean very little to her. She already knows that her husband thinks she's attractive. A sincere compliment from a relative stranger may be much more effective, however, since it constitutes a gain in esteem. On the other hand, if the doting husband (who used to think that his wife was attractive) were to tell his wife that he had decided that she was actually quite ugly, this would cause a great deal of pain since it represents a distinct loss of esteem.

This reasoning is consistent with previous experimental findings. Harvey (1962) found a tendency for subjects to react more positively to a stranger than a friend when they were listed as sources of a relatively positive evaluation of the subject. Moreover, subjects tended to react more negatively to a friend than a stranger when they were listed as sources of negative evaluations of the subject. Similarly, experiments with children indicate that strangers are more effective as agents of social reinforcement than parents, and that strangers are also more effective than more familiar people (Shallenberger and Zigler, 1961; Stevenson and Knights, 1962; Stevenson, Keen, and Knights, 1963). It is reasonable to assume that children are accustomed to receiving approval from parents and familiar people. Therefore, additional approval from them does not represent much of a gain. However, approval from a stranger *is* a gain and, according to the gain-loss notion, should result in a greater improvement in performance. These latter results add credence to our speculations regarding one of the underlying causes of the gain-loss effect. Specifically, children probably experience greater social anxiety in the presence of a stranger than a familiar person. Therefore, social approval from a stranger may be reducing a greater drive than social approval from a friend. As previously noted, this reasoning is identical to that of Walters and his colleagues regarding the effect of prior anxiety on subsequent performance (Walters and Ray, 1960; Walters and Foote, 1962).

SUMMARY

In a laboratory experiment, coeds interacted in two-person groups over a series of brief meetings. After each meeting the subjects were allowed to eavesdrop on a conversation between the experimenter and her partner in which the latter (actually a confederate) evaluated the subject. There were four major experimental conditions: (1) the evaluations were all highly positive; (2) the evaluations were all quite negative; (3) the first few evaluations were negative but gradually became positive; (4) the first few evaluations were positive but gradually became negative.

The major results showed that the subjects liked the confederate best when her evaluations moved from negative to positive and least when her evaluations moved from positive to negative. The results were predicted and discussed in terms of a "gain-loss" notion of interpersonal attractiveness.

REFERENCES

Aronson, E., and Mills, J. The effect of severity of initiation on liking for a group. *J. abnorm. soc. Psychol.,* 1959, *59,* 177–81.

Byrne, D. Interpersonal attraction and attitude similarity. *J. abnorm. soc. Psychol.,* 1961, *62,* 713–15.

Byrne, D., and Wong, T. J. Racial prejudice, interpersonal attraction, and assumed dissimilarity of attitudes. *J. abnorm. soc. Psychol.,* 1962, *65,* 246–53.

Gerard, H. B., and Greenbaum, C. W. Attitudes toward an agent of uncertainty reduction. *J. Pers.,* 1962, *30,* 485–95.

Gewirtz, J. L., and Baer, D. M. The effect of brief social deprivation on behaviors for a social reinforcer. *J. abnorm. soc. Psychol.*, 1958, *56*, 49–56.

Harvey, O. J. Personality factors in resolution of conceptual incongruities. *Sociometry,* 1962, *25*, 336–52.

Helson, H. Current trends and issues in adaptation-level theory. *Amer. Psychologist,* 1964, *19*, 26–38.

Homans, G. *Social behavior: Its elementary forms.* New York: Harcourt, Brace, and World, 1961.

Jones, E. E. *Ingratiation: A social psychological analysis.* New York: Appleton, Century, Crofts, 1964.

Newcomb, T. M. *The acquaintance process.* New York: Holt, Rinehart, and Winston, 1961.

Newcomb, T. M. The prediction of interpersonal attraction. *Amer. Psychologist,* 1956, *11*, 575–86.

Shallenberger, Patricia, and Zigler, E. Rigidity, negative reaction tendencies and cosatiation effects in normal and feebleminded children. *J. abnorm. soc. Psychol.,* 1961, *63*, 20–26.

Spinoza, B. *The ethics.* New York: Dover Press, 1955. Prop. *44*, p. 159.

Stevenson, H. W., Keen, Rachel, and Knights, R. M. Parents and strangers as reinforcing agents for children's performance. *J. abnorm. soc. Psychol.,* 1963, *67*, 183–85.

Stevenson, H. W., and Knights, R. M. Social reinforcement with normal and retarded children as a function of pretraining, sex of *E,* and sex of *S. Amer. J. ment. Defic.,* 1962, *66*, 866–71.

Thibaut, J., and Kelley, H. H. *The social psychology of groups.* New York: Wiley, 1959.

Walters, R. H., and Foote, Ann. A study of reinforcer effectiveness with children. *Merrill-Palmer quart. Behav. Develpm.,* 1962, *8*, 149–57.

Walters, R. H., and Ray, E. Anxiety, social isolation, and reinforcer effectiveness. *J. Pers.,* 1960, *28*, 258–67.

White, R. W. Motivation reconsidered: the concept of competence. *Psychol. Rev.,* 1959, *66*, 297–334.

Attitudinal Effects of Mere Exposure

ROBERT B. ZAJONC

On February 27, 1967, the Associated Press carried the following story from Corvallis, Oregon:

A mysterious student has been attending a class at Oregon State University for the past two months enveloped in a big black bag. Only his bare feet show. Each Monday, Wednesday, and Friday at 11:00 A.M. the Black Bag sits on a small table near the back of the classroom. The class is Speech 113—basic persuasion.... Charles Goetzinger, professor of the class, knows the identity of the person inside. None of the 20 students in the class do. Goetzinger said *the students' attitude changed from hostility toward the Black Bag to curiosity and finally to friendship* [italics added].

This monograph examines the general hypothesis implied by the above phenomenon: mere repeated exposure of the individual to a stimulus is a sufficient condition for the enhancement of his attitude toward it. By "mere exposure" is meant a condition which just makes the given stimulus accessible to the individual's perception.

Even though the hypothesis seems to be in conflict with such celebrated laws as *familiarity breeds contempt* and *absence makes the heart grow fonder,* it is not particularly original or recent (Fechner, 1876, pp. 240–243; James, 1890, p. 672; Maslow, 1937; Meyer, 1903; Pepper, 1919). The foremost proponent of this hypothesis, the advertising industry, has always attributed to exposure formidable advertising potential. But—apparently, in respect for the law of enhancement by association—it seldom dared to utilize *mere* exposure. The product, its name, or its hallmark is always presented to the public in contiguity with other and always attractive stimuli, commonly females, exposed more bodily than the product itself. At the same time, however, the advertising industry also likes to warn against *over*exposure, relying, it would appear, on the above law of familiarity (Erdelyi, 1940; Wiebe, 1940).

It isn't altogether clear just what evidence supports these advertising principles. And direct evidence that attitudes are enhanced by *mere* exposure or *mere* contact with the stimulus object is scant. Moreover, it is the product of antiquated methods, and almost all of it concerns music appreciation (Downey & Knapp, 1927; Krugman, 1943; Meyer, 1903; Moore & Gilliland, 1924; Mull, 1957; Verveer, Barry, & Bousfield, 1933; Washburn, Child, & Abel, 1927). The problem of attitudinal effects of social contact and interaction has also been of some interest in the study of interracial attitudes (Cook & Selltiz, 1952). But these studies have invariably examined the effects not of *mere* perceptual exposure of people to each other, but of processes considerably more complex: prolonged social interaction, group interdependence, cooperation, etc. (Deutsch

Reprinted from Journal of Personality and Social Psychology, *9, 1968, Monograph, 1–29. Copyright 1968 by the American Psychological Association and reproduced by permission.*

& Collins, 1951; Kramer, 1950; MacKenzie, 1948; Wilner, Walkley, & Cook, 1952). Although the independent variables in these studies have generally been featured under the labels "contact" and "exposure," the effects they report cannot, because of confounding with a multitude of other events (and with reinforcement in particular), be regarded as produced alone by contact or exposure. Thus, it has been known for some time that social interaction enhances the attitudes of interactors toward each other (Bovard, 1951; Festinger, 1951; Homans, 1961; Newcomb, 1963). But it is not known just what contribution to the relationship between social interaction and attitudes is made by *mere* exposure on the one hand, and by the variety of psychologically significant processes that necessarily accompany mere exposure during the course of social interaction, on the other.

The main empirical support for the exposure hypothesis comes, therefore, not from work on interaction, interracial attitudes, or attitudes in general, but from an entirely different and seemingly unrelated area of research. It comes from some recent work on word frequencies. This recent research shows that there exists an intimate relationship between word frequency and meaning. And this relationship, in my opinion (for which I shall later present support), may be a special case of the more general relationship between mere exposure and attitude enhancement.

The strength and pervasiveness of the relationship between word frequency and meaning—the *evaluative* aspect of meaning, in particular—is truly remarkable. For, if there is any correspondence between the frequency with which words are used and the actual preponderance of the things and events for which these words stand, then we may congratulate ourselves on living in a most happy world. According to the Thorndike-Lorge count (1944), the word "happiness" occurs 761 times, "unhappiness" occurs only 49 times. "Beauty" is to be found at least 41 times as often as "ugliness," and "wealth" outdoes "poverty" by a factor of 1.6. We "laugh" 2.4 times as often as we "cry"; we "love" almost 7 times more often than we "hate"; we are "in" at least 5 times more often than we are "out"; "up" twice as often as we are "down"; much more often "successful" than "unsuccessful"; and we "find" things 4.5 times more often than we "lose" them—all because most of us are "lucky" (220) rather than "unlucky" (17).

We have all the reasons in the world to be "happy" (1449) and "gay" (418) rather than "sad" (202) and "gloomy" (72), for things are 5 times more often "good" than "bad," almost 3 times more often "possible" than "impossible," and about five times more "profitable" than "unprofitable." That is, perhaps, why "boom" and "prosperity" outdo "recession" by a factor of just about 30, "abundance" outdoes "scarcity" by at least 3:1, and "affluence" is 6 times more prevalent than "deprivation." Catering to our corporeal sensibilities, things are 3 times more often "fragrant" than they are "foul," 12 times more often "fresh" than "stale," and almost 7 times more often "sweet" than "sour," and everything that can be filled is three times as often "full" as it is "empty." If we have anything, we have "more" of it 6 times more often than we have "less" of it,[1] and 3 times more often "most" of it than "least" of it. And those things that we

---

[1] N.B. The more-less ratio in this text is 7:1 up to now.

have so frequently more of are 5 times more often "better" than they are "worse," 6 times more often "best" than "worst," and 4 times more often "superior" than "inferior." Still, they "improve" at least 25 times as often as they "deteriorate."

These examples suffice to convince one that the world represented by a one-to-one correspondence with word frequencies is as unreal as it is spectacular. Bitterly aware of it, Sartre (1964) confessed in his autobiography, "... as a result of discovering the world through language, for a long time, I took language for the world [p. 182]."

But, while they are unfaithful in representing reality, word frequencies are extraordinarily accurate in representing real values: words that stand for good, desirable, and preferred aspects of reality are more frequently used.

It isn't entirely clear who discovered this remarkable relationship between word frequency and the evaluative dimension of word meaning. Postman (1953) seems to be one of the early workers to note its generality, while Howes and Solomon (1950) observed in their critique of McGinnies' (1949) perceptual defense experiment that the so-called "taboo" words he used as stimuli are particularly infrequent. However, the first systematic research effort that demonstrates the word-frequency–word-value relationship is due to Johnson, Thomson, and Frincke (1960). These authors were the first, I believe, to collect empirical data showing that words with "positive" meaning have higher frequency counts than words with "negative" meanings. They have also gathered experimental evidence showing that the repeated use of a nonsense word tends to enhance its rating on the good-bad scale of the semantic differential. Johnson, Thomson, and Frincke (1960) have not tried to explain either of these two aspects of the frequency-value relationship, being primarily concerned with its implications for the study of word-recognition thresholds.

This paper examines the frequency-value relationship, proposing that it is considerably more pervasive and general than implied by the Johnson-Thomson-Frincke results, and that it is, moreover, a special case of a broader and more basic phenomenon: the enhancement of attitudes by mere repeated exposure. I shall first review evidence on the correlation between word frequency and word value, and between stimulus frequency and attitude. Experimental evidence on these two relationships, and on the likely causal direction, will then be examined.

Word Frequency–Word Value: Correlational Evidence

Johnson, Thomson, and Frincke (1960) obtained correlations of .63, .40, and .38 between the L-count (Thorndike & Lorge, 1944) and the good-bad scale values for three samples of randomly chosen words. In a further attempt, they constructed 30 pairs, each consisting of one frequent and one infrequent word. These pairs were given to a group of subjects with the instructions to "encircle the most pleasantly toned word of each pair." In 87% of the pairs the majority of subjects endorsed the more frequent word. Finally, 64 nonsense syllables of low, medium, and high association were rated by a group of subjects on the good-bad scale of the semantic differential. Johnson, Thomson, and Frincke reported a clear relationship between association value and "goodness" ratings.

The rationale of this study invoked the assumed relationship between association of the given nonsense syllable and the probability of occurrence of the corresponding letter combination in meaningful words (Underwood, 1959).

In an attempt to examine the generality of this phenomenon, we studied the evaluations of 154 antonym pairs. First, a large pool of antonym pairs was amassed. From this pool all symmetric[2] pairs were chosen in the following manner. For each antonym pair 10 judges, 1 at a time, were asked to give the antonym of one member of the pair. Ten other judges—independently of the first 10—were asked to give the antonym of the other member of the pair. Only those pairs were retained about which the 20 judges showed unanimous agreement with the dictionary sources. A list of 154 antonym pairs was thus obtained. These were given to 100 subjects, all college students, for judgments as to which member had "the more favorable meaning, represented the more desirable object, event, state of affairs, characteristic, etc." A different random order of the antonym pairs was given to each subject, and the lateral positions of the members of each pair were reversed at random for half of the group.

Table 1 shows the list of these 154 antonym pairs, together with the "desirability" and the frequency data (the Thorndike-Lorge L-count). The preferred member of each pair is always listed first. The "desirability" figures are simply the percentages of subjects choosing the left member of the pair as the preferred alternative.

It is of some interest, however incidental, that there is considerable agreement about desirability of the meanings. On half of the items the agreement exceeded 95%. Agreement is high even for words which are not genuinely evaluative. For instance, 97 of the 100 students preferred "on" to "off," 98 preferred "add" to "subtract," 96 "above" to "below," and 92 "upward" to "downward."

For the overwhelming majority of the items the preferred word is also the more frequent one. Only 28 of the 154 antonym pairs (18%) show a negative relationship between frequency and desirability. Moreover, these "reversals" occur primarily for antonym pairs on which there is relatively little agreement. For pairs with agreement greater than 95% (i.e., the upper half of the list) there are only six reversals out of the 77 possible. It is significant, moreover, that in three of these six antonym pairs the less desirable member (which in these cases is the more frequent one) has more meanings and linguistic uses than the more desirable one. "Invalid" means both "not valid" and "cripple," but "valid" is just "valid." "Yes" is an adverb, but "no" is an adverb *and* an adjective. And "front" is a noun, a verb, and an adjective, while "back" is all that and an adverb to boot.

Toward the end of the list where the desirability preferences are divided fairly evenly between the two members of the antonym pairs, the frequencies of the

[2] One finds in the course of this endeavor that the antonymic relation is seldom symmetric. According to the standard sources, if Y is listed as the antonym of X, then chances are that not X but Z is listed as the antonym of Y. For instance, in the 1960 edition of Webster's New Collegiate Dictionary, "extend" is given as the antonym of "contract." Looking up "extend" we find, however, that its antonym is "reduce." The antonym of "reduce," on the other hand is "increase." The antonym of "increase" is "decrease," the antonym of "decrease" is "amplify," the antonym of "amplify" is "condense," and the antonym of "condense" is "expand." We can ultimately close the circle, because "contract," according to this source, is the antonym of "expand."

Table 1 SEMANTIC PREFERENCE AND FREQUENCY OF 154 ANTONYM PAIRS

% AGREEMENT	PREFERRED ALTERNATIVE (a)	NONPREFERRED ALTERNATIVE (b)	FREQUENCY OF (a)	FREQUENCY OF (b)
100	able	unable	930	239
100	attentive	inattentive	49	4
100	better	worse	2354	450
100	encourage	discourage	205	147
100	friendly	unfriendly	357	19
100	honest	dishonest	393	41
100	possible	impossible	1289	459
99	advance	retreat	452	105
99	best	worst	1850	292
99	clean	dirty	781	221
99	comfortable	uncomfortable	348	112
99	favorable	unfavorable	93	25
99	good	bad	5122	1001
99	grateful	ungrateful	194	13
99	peace	war	472	1118
99	present	absent	1075	65
99	pure	impure	197	4
99	responsible	irresponsible	267	30
99	reward	punishment	154	80
99	right	wrong	3874	890
99	smile	frown	2143	216
99	tolerant	intolerant	42	13
99	victory	defeat	118	166
98	add	subtract	2018	6
98	advantage	disadvantage	404	41
98	agreeable	disagreeable	58	43
98	capable	incapable	176	30
98	desirable	undesirable	160	42
98	find	lose	2698	593
98	fortunate	unfortunate	136	108
98	forward	backward	736	139
98	friend	enemy	2553	883
98	high	low	1674	1224
98	honorable	dishonorable	58	8
98	kind	unkind	1521	34
98	legal	illegal	180	34
98	life	death	4804	815
98	love	hate	5129	756
98	mature	immature	91	17
98	moral	immoral	272	19
98	pleasant	unpleasant	457	114
98	polite	impolite	115	3
98	reliable	unreliable	78	9
98	success	failure	573	262
98	valid	invalid	22	56
98	voluntary	involuntary	28	26
97	adequate	inadequate	95	59
97	competent	incompetent	69	23
97	found	lost	2892	1074
97	important	unimportant	1130	40
97	likely	unlikely	364	25
97	on	off	30224	3644
97	patience	impatience	139	39
97	patient	impatient	392	79
97	patiently	impatiently	85	82
97	popular	unpopular	418	12
97	positive	negative	92	28
97	profitable	unprofitable	57	12
97	promote	demote	90	2
97	remember	forget	1682	882

Table 1 Continued

% AGREEMENT	PREFERRED ALTERNATIVE (a)	NONPREFERRED ALTERNATIVE (b)	FREQUENCY OF (a)	FREQUENCY OF (b)	% AGREEMENT	PREFERRED ALTERNATIVE (a)	NONPREFERRED ALTERNATIVE (b)	FREQUENCY OF (a)	FREQUENCY OF (b)
97	satisfactory	unsatisfactory	154	32	94	together	apart	1835	276
97	willingly	unwillingly	66	13	93	agreement	disagreement	143	21
96	above	below	941	529	93	certain	uncertain	800	107
96	active	passive	186	29	93	first	last	5154	3517
96	early	late	1022	2859	93	major	minor	366	83
96	front	back	1094	6587	93	normal	abnormal	335	43
96	full	empty	1129	395	93	regular	irregular	340	44
96	live	die	4307	1079	93	unselfish	selfish	32	137
96	presence	absence	277	163	93	upwards	downwards	9	40
96	probable	improbable	64	14	93	wide	narrow	593	391
96	rational	irrational	33	9	92	more	less	8015	1357
96	reasonable	unreasonable	155	56	92	now	then	7665	10208
96	resolutely	irresolutely	30	4	92	up	down	11718	5534
96	strong	weak	770	276	92	upward	downward	111	27
96	succeed	fail	264	620	92	visible	invisible	110	74
96	superior	inferior	166	40	92	yes	no	2202	11742
96	timely	untimely	27	6	91	always	never	3285	5715
95	accept	reject	667	51	91	familiar	unfamiliar	345	39
95	direct	indirect	416	23	91	maximum	minimum	43	86
95	include	exclude	533	38	91	optimism	pessimism	28	11
95	increase	decrease	781	86	90	agree	disagree	729	38
95	most	least	3443	1259	90	necessary	unnecessary	715	107
95	practical	impractical	340	12	90	over	under	7520	2961
95	regularly	irregularly	122	5	90	sweet	sour	679	102
95	rich	poor	656	857	90	whole	part	1663	1585
95	wealth	poverty	243	146	89	light	dark	2387	1005
94	approve	disapprove	171	45	88	deep	shallow	881	104
94	conscious	unconscious	299	116	88	smooth	rough	346	294
94	leader	follower	373	45	86	white	black	2663	1083
94	obedient	disobedient	70	4	85	in	out	75253	13649

Table 1 Continued

% AGREE-MENT	PREFERRED ALTERNATIVE (a)	NONPREFERRED ALTERNATIVE (b)	FRE-QUENCY OF (a)	FRE-QUENCY OF (b)	% AGREE-MENT	PREFERRED ALTERNATIVE (a)	NONPREFERRED ALTERNATIVE (b)	FRE-QUENCY OF (a)	FRE-QUENCY OF (b)
85	independent	dependent	134	18	67	internal	external	36	26
84	fast	slow	514	434	65	coming	going	1486	4623
83	comedy	tragedy	126	189	64	informal	formal	64	166
83	fasten	unfasten	142	16	63	answer	question	2132	1302
79	day	night	4549	3385	63	men	women	3614	2552
78	dry	wet	592	319	61	different	same	1194	1747
78	long	short	5362	887	59	inward	outward	43	54
78	unshaken	shaken	6	83	59	man	woman	7355	2431
77	usually	unusually	718	91	58	husband	wife	1788	1668
74	upstairs	downstairs	314	226	58	usual	unusual	516	273
72	inner	outer	143	97	57	offense	defense	86	223
72	interior	exterior	185	48	55	hot	cold	1006	1092
70	near	far	1338	1835	55	import	export	86	88
70	unlimited	limited	43	67	55	inwardly	outwardly	32	33
68	inside	outside	656	921	54	inconspicuous	conspicuous	33	59
68	wrap	unwrap	293	17	52	play	work	2606	2720
67	infinite	finite	71	2	51	mortal	immortal	54	26

two antonyms often are nearly the same. "Play" is preferred to "work" only by a majority of two (a curious commentary on the contemporary college population!), and the respective frequency counts of these antonyms are 2606 and 2720. The "hot-cold" preference is 55 to 45 and their frequency counts 1006 and 1092. The "husband-wife" perference is 58 to 42 and their respective frequencies, 1788 and 1668.

Three antonym items about which agreement was complete or nearly complete show a curious pattern of results. They are "good-bad" (5122:1001), "better-worse" (2354:450), and "best-worst" (1850:292). Since "better" is presumably better than "good," "worse" worse than "bad," and since "best" is presumably better than "better," and "worst" worse than "worse," we would expect the greatest separation between the frequencies of "best" and "worst," smallest between the frequencies of "good" and "bad," and medium between the frequencies of "better" and "worse." Since absolute differences are deceiving, we best take the ratios of the frequencies, which are 6.34, 5.23, and 5.12 for "best-worst," "better-worse," and "good-bad," respectively. It is indeed the case that the frequency ratios increase from "good-bad" to "best-worst." However, if frequency reflects "desirability," we would also expect the frequency of "best" to exceed the frequency of "better," and that of "better" to exceed the frequency of "good." In fact, however, "good" is more frequent than "better," and "better" more frequent than "best"! But *is* "better" better than "good"? In an extensive study of meanings Mosier (1941) found that "good" was consistently rated as better than "better."

Startling as this may appear to grammarians, it is psychologically sound, since GOOD is a positive assertion, whereas BETTER implies comparison with some standard which might, in many cases, be itself unfavorable. Compare the often heard comment, "He is getting better, but he is still far from good" [p. 134].

For purposes of comparison the frequencies of French, German, and Spanish equivalents of some of the antonyms examined are given in Table 2 below. Systematic data on indigenous desirability ratings are unfortunately not available, but it would be surprising if the French, German, and Spanish judgments differed from those obtained in the United States. An informal inquiry among foreign visitors marshalled a good deal of support for this conjecture. Comparing the data in Tables 1 and 2, the agreement is rather striking. In 15 out of the 44 cases the frequency relation in the antonym pairs is the same in the three foreign languages as in English: the more favorable item is more frequent, a result exceeding chance expectation by a large margin. The results in Table 2, furthermore, give a ready expression to our favorite ethnic prejudices. The relatively low frequency of the two Romance equivalents of "early" and the high frequency of these equivalents of "late," in comparison to their Germanic counterparts, make generalizations about national character tempting, as does the relatively low frequency of the German equivalent of "reward." The foreign equivalents of answer-question, hot-cold, import-export, peace-war, etc., however, show patterns of differences that may reflect more than superficial linguistic idiosyncrasies.

Table 2 FREQUENCY RANKS OF ENGLISH, FRENCH, GERMAN, AND SPANISH
ANTONYM PAIRS

ENGLISH	*FRENCH*	*GERMAN*	*SPANISH*
able (3)	capable (3)	fähig (4)	capaz (3)
unable (9)	incapable (4)	unfähig (11)	incapaz (7)
accept (3)	accepter (2)	annehmen (2)	acceptar (3)
reject (9)	rejeter (5)	ablehnen (5)	rechazar (5)
active (6)	actif (6)	tätig (5)	activo (6)
passive (14)	passif (?)	untätig (?)	pasivo (10)
answer (2)	réponse (4)	Antwort (3)	respuesta (4)
question (3)	question (2)	Frage (2)	pregunta (4)
better (2)	meilleur (2)	besser (2)	mejor (2)
worse (4)	pire (5)	schlechter (?)	peor (2)
certain (2)	certain (2)	sicher (2)	cierto (2)
uncertain (9)	incertain (10)	unsicher (9)	incierto (9)
clean (3)	propre (2)	sauber (9)	limpio (3)
dirty (7)	sale (7)	schmutzig (12)	sucio (6)
comedy (9)	comédie (6)	Komödie (9)	comedia (4)
tragedy (9)	tragédie (9)	Tragödie (11)	tragedia (8)
comfortable (5)	à l'aise (4)	bequem (5)	cómodo (7)
uncomfortable (11)	inconfortable (9)	unbequem (10)	incómodo (10)
day (2)	jour (2)	Tag (2)	día (2)
night (2)	nuit (2)	Nacht (2)	noche (2)
direct (3)	direct (6)	direkt (3)	directo (4)
indirect (12)	indirect (12)	indirekt (8)	indirecto (8)
dry (3)	sec (3)	trocken (5)	seco (3)
wet (4)	mouillé (5)	nass (9)	mojado (6)
early (2)	tôt (3)	früh (2)	temprano (4)
late (2)	tard (2)	spät (2)	tarde (2)
fast (2)	vite (2)	schnell (2)	pronto (2)
slow (3)	lent (4)	langsam (3)	lento (4)
find (2)	trouver (2)	finden (2)	encontrar (2)
lose (3)	perdre (2)	verlieren (2)	perder (2)
friend (2)	ami (2)	Freund (2)	amigo (2)
enemy (3)	ennemi (2)	Feind (2)	enemigo (2)
full (2)	plein (2)	voll (2)	lleno (2)
empty (4)	vide (4)	leer (4)	vacio (4)
good (2)	bon (2)	gut (2)	buen (2)
bad (2)	mauvais (2)	schlecht (3)	mal (2)
high (2)	haut (2)	hoch (2)	alto (2)
low (2)	bas (2)	niedrig (4)	bajo (2)
hot (2)	chaud (3)	heiss (5)	caliente (5)
cold (2)	froid (3)	kalt (3)	frío (2)
husband (3)	mari (3)	Mann (2)	esposo (2)
wife (3)	femme (2)	Frau (2)	esposa (2)

Table 2 Continued

ENGLISH	FRENCH	GERMAN	SPANISH
import (7)	importation (11)	Einfuhr (11)	importación (?)
export (11)	exportation (10)	Ausfuhr (12)	exportación (13)
increase (3)	augmentation (10)	Vermehrung (6)	aumento (5)
decrease (8)	reduction (11)	Verminderung (11)	diminución (?)
independent (6)	indépendent (7)	selbstständig (4)	independiente (5)
dependent (14)	dépendent (?)	abhängig (6)	dependiente (9)
life (2)	vie (2)	Leben (2)	vida (2)
death (2)	mort (2)	Tod (2)	muerte (2)
light (2)	clair (3)	hell (4)	claro (2)
dark (2)	sombre (3)	dunkel (3)	obscuro (2)
live (2)	vivre (2)	leben (2)	vivir (2)
die (2)	mourir (2)	sterben (2)	morir (2)
long (2)	long (2)	lang (2)	largo (2)
short (2)	court (3)	kurz (2)	corto (3)
love (2)	aimer (2)	lieben (2)	amar (2)
hate (4)	haïr (6)	hassen (6)	odiar (7)
more (2)	plus (2)	mehr (2)	más (2)
less (2)	moins (2)	weniger (2)	menos (2)
near (2)	près (3)	nah (2)	cerca (2)
far (2)	loin (2)	fern (2)	lejos (2)
peace (3)	paix (3)	Friede (3)	paz (2)
war (2)	guerre (3)	Krieg (2)	guerra (2)
positive (9)	positif (6)	positiv (8)	positivo (7)
negative (11)	negatif (11)	negativ (?)	negativo (7)
possible (3)	possible (2)	möglich (2)	posible (2)
impossible (5)	impossible (3)	unmöglich (3)	imposible (2)
presence (4)	présence (2)	Anwesenheit (9)	presencia (3)
absence (7)	absence (5)	Abwesenheit (9)	ausencia (4)
reward (6)	récompense (6)	Anerkennung (5)	premio (4)
punishment (6)	punition (12)	Strafe (4)	castigo (4)
right (2)	juste (2)	richtig (2)	justo (3)
wrong (3)	faux (3)	falsch (3)	mal (2)
strong (2)	fort (2)	stark (2)	fuerte (2)
weak (3)	faible (3)	schwach (3)	debil (4)
sweet (2)	doux (2)	süss (4)	dulce (2)
sour (9)	amer (4)	sauer (9)	amargo (4)
together (2)	ensemble (2)	zusammen (2)	junto (2)
apart (4)	séparé (2)	getrennt (3)	separado (3)
victory (5)	victoire (4)	Sieg (4)	victoria (5)
defeat (7)	défaite (8)	Niederlage (8)	derrota (9)
wealth (4)	richesse (5)	Vermögen (4)	riqueza (3)
poverty (7)	pauvreté (12)	Armut (10)	pobreza (5)

Table 2   Continued

ENGLISH	FRENCH	GERMAN	SPANISH
white (2)	blanc (2)	weiss (2)	blanco (2)
black (2)	noir (2)	schwartz (3)	negro (2)
wide (2)	large (2)	breit (4)	ancho (3)
narrow (3)	étroit (3)	schmal (6)	angosto (8)

Note.—The figures in brackets indicate frequency ranks: (1) means that the word is among the 500 most frequent words, (2) that it is among the 1000 most frequent words, (3) that it is among the 1500 most frequent words, etc. The source of these counts is Eaton (1940).

Several questions can immediately be raised about the above results. First, are these figures up to date? The Thorndike-Lorge count is based on samples of material published during the late twenties and the early thirties. The German equivalents come from a source dating to the late 19th century (Käding, 1898). The French count was published in 1929 (Van der Beke, 1929), and the Spanish in 1927 (Buchanan, 1927). Secondly, do these results reflect general verbal habits? Word counts are based on printed material alone. Do people show the same linguistic predilections in ordinary speech as they do in writing? Admittedly, both questions indicate caution in generalizing from the above results. But this caution needn't be excessive. Howes (1954) has recently asked Harvard and Antioch undergraduates to estimate the probabilities of various words. The correlations between the students' estimates of several word samples and the L-count of the Thorndike-Lorge source varied around .80. There is also evidence from word association studies showing that word counts do reflect general verbal habits of the population. A word which has a high frequency of occurrence in print is also a highly probable associate. The association norms to 200 words were recently collected by Palermo and Jenkins (1964) from a sample of 4,500 school children and college students in Minneapolis. The list of the 200 stimulus words represents a systematic sample of verbs, nouns, pronouns, adverbs, adjectives, participles, etc., all having fairly high frequency on the Thorndike-Lorge counts. Since in the word association task each subject makes one response to each stimulus word, Palermo and Jenkins collected from their subjects 900,000 word responses. Among them "good" occurred 4890 times, "bad" only 1956. The response "right" was given 477 times, the response "wrong" only 100 times. "Full" was found 431 times among the associations, "empty" only 62 times. "Strong" was given 557, "weak" 96 times. "Together" occurred 575 times, "apart" 29 times. "Light" was a response 8655 times (N.B., some subjects must have given it more than once), "dark" 4274 times. But as in the case of the Thorndike-Lorge count, "front" occurred 22 times, while "back" occurred 265 times; "rich" was given 36 times, while "poor" was a response 95 times. "Near" was given 981 times, "far" 1218. "Coming" was given 166 times, "going" 714 times. And, as in L-count, "play" and "work" showed 791 and 957 occurrences, respectively.

However, the best evidence about the relationship between the individual's verbal habits and the evaluative aspect of meaning is found in a recent study by Siegel,[3] although it wasn't the purpose of her study to explore this relationship. Siegel's experiment dealt with the effects of verbal reinforcement on the emission of words differing in affective connotation and in frequency. Eighteen six-letter words of known frequencies and previously judged on the good-bad and the pleasant-unpleasant scales were selected from a larger sample. Six of these words were of high frequency (100 and more in 1 million), six of medium (20 to 30), and six of low frequency (1 to 5). Within each frequency class two words were previously judged to be good, two neutral, and two bad. Three groups of subjects, other than those involved in the affective judgments, participated in the experiment, each having to deal with six words of the same frequency. The procedure consisted of presenting the subject with the list of six words, all high, medium, or low in frequency, depending on the condition in which he was, and giving him at the same time a stack of cards on which appeared illegible six-letter "words." Ostensibly, each card contained one of the six words in the subjects' list. Actually, the "words" consisted of random sequences of six letters, printed over several thicknesses of paper and one carbon. Their legibility was further reduced by placing each card in an onionskin paper envelope. The subjects' task was to "read" or to guess what word appeared on each card. Of interest for the present purposes are the first 50 trials which served to establish operant rate, and during which, of course, no reinforcement of any sort was given. Table 3 shows data on the guessing behavior of Siegel's subjects as a function of word frequency and affective connotation. Reported in each cell is the average number of times a word of a given frequency and affective value was used as a guess during the 50 operant trials. Since there are six words to choose from, 8.33 represents a chance response rate. It is clear, however, that both frequency and affective connotation displace response rate away from the chance level. High frequency seems to result in overcalling, and low frequency in undercalling. But it is striking to discover that affective connotation had an even stronger effect on response emission, the marginals for that variable showing a somewhat greater range of differences.

Table 3 FREE RESPONSE EMISSION AS A FUNCTION OF WORD-FREQUENCY AND WORD VALUE[a]

WORD VALUE	WORD FREQUENCY			$\bar{X}$
	LOW	MEDIUM	HIGH	
Good	7.43	9.43	9.68	8.85
Medium	6.28	8.57	8.71	7.85
Bad	6.28	5.86	7.71	6.61
$\bar{X}$	6.66	7.95	8.70	

[a]From Siegel, 1960.

[3] Siegel, Felicia S. Effects of word frequency and affective connotation on verbal responding during extinction. (Mimeo)

Some words in the language have primarily an evaluative function. These words should show the frequency-value relationship with particular clarity. Several instances of this relationship are examined.

Let us first consider the scales of the Semantic Differential (Osgood, Suci, & Tannenbaum, 1957). We have chosen only those scales which have high and relatively pure loadings on one of the three main factors, *evaluation, potency,* and *activity.* Table 4 shows the polar opposites of these scales, together with their frequencies according to the Thorndike-Lorge L-count. The left-hand polar opposites in the three columns are the favorable, potent, and active ends of the scales. It is significant that among the 19 evaluative scales the favorable polar opposite has always higher frequency than the unfavorable opposite. For the scales which do not load high on the evaluative factor the high frequencies are divided fairly evenly among the potent and nonpotent opposites. In 9 of the 15 potency scales the highly potent end of the scale is more frequent. In 3 of the 8 activity scales the active polar opposite is more frequent.

There are two other instances of a high correlation between frequency and value for adjectives. The first comes from the work by Gough (1953). Gough has given the items of his Adjective Checklist to 30 judges who rated each adjective for favorability. The most favorable and the least favorable quartiles of Gough's checklist are reported in his publication. The average word frequency of the upper quartile is 140, and of the lower quartile 48. The second illustration comes from data collected by Anderson (1964). A list of 555 adjectives was recently used by Anderson in his work on impression formation. The list was constructed out of a large sample of items. The 555 selected items were given by Anderson to a group of 100 subjects with the instructions to rate on a 7-point scale "how much you yourself would like the person described by that word." We have simply computed the correlation between these likeability ratings and the logarithm of the Thorndike-Lorge L-count.[4] Figure 1 shows this relationship graphically, where means of log frequencies are plotted for six categories of adjectives in increasing order of favorability. Considering that the reliabilities of the Thorndike-Lorge count and of Anderson's favorability ratings are less than perfect, the coefficient of correlation of .83 is particularly impressive.

Miller, Newman, and Friedman (1958) have shown that word frequency is a negative function of word length. The problem immediately arises, therefore, as to which of these two variables is critical for word value and word meaning. In order to examine this possible confounding between frequency and word length, the above correlation was recomputed holding the number of letters constant. No appreciable change in the previously obtained coefficient was observed.

The relationship between word frequency and word length is generally explained in terms of the principle of least effort. Words that require considerable effort in writing and in speech are less likely candidates for use. In an attempt to control for effort Frincke and Johnson (1960) have asked subjects to choose the "most pleasantly toned word" from each of 108 homophone pairs. The greatest majority of these pairs consisted of words of the same length, and

---

[4] Items for which there was no frequency information in the Thorndike-Lorge count were not included in computing this coefficient. These items were primarily of the hyphenated form, such as open-minded, good-humored, well-spoken, fault-finding, ultra-critical, wishy-washy, etc.

Table 4 POLAR OPPOSITES OF THE SEMANTIC DIFFERENTIAL AND THEIR
FREQUENCIES

	EVALUATIVE FACTOR		
beautiful	ugly	987	178
clean	dirty	781	221
fair	unfair	561	59
fragrant	foul	66	39
good	bad	5122	1001
grateful	ungrateful	194	13
happy	sad	1449	202
harmonious	dissonant	26	9
honest	dishonest	393	41
kind	cruel	1521	165
nice	awful	630	370
pleasant	unpleasant	457	114
positive	negative	92	28
reputable	disreputable	23	21
sacred	profane	102	13
successful	unsuccessful	352	14
sweet	sour	679	102
true	false	1711	209
wise	foolish	420	223

	POTENCY FACTOR		
bass	treble	28	17
brave	cowardly	216	26
deep	shallow	881	104
hard	soft	1909	549
heavy	light	680	1005
large	small	1697	1818
masculine	feminine	54	40
mature	youthful	91	99
rough	smooth	294	346
rugged	delicate	37	248
severe	lenient	119	9
strong	weak	770	276
tenacious	yielding	22	7
thick	thin	443	646
wide	narrow	593	391

	ACTIVITY FACTOR		
active	passive	514	434
bright	dark	645	1005
excitable	calm	7	267
fast	slow	514	434
heretical	orthodox	2	21
hot	cold	1006	1092
rash	cautious	37	48
sharp	dull	324	289

all pairs, of course, consisted of words that required the same effort in uttering
them. Out of 3,132 possible choices, the more frequent member of the pair was
chosen 1,836 times.

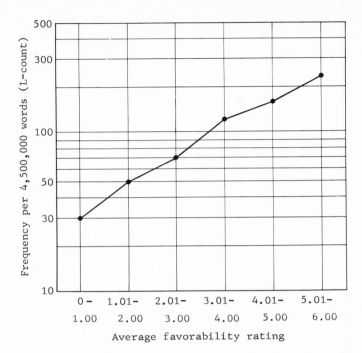

Fig. 1.   Average frequencies of 555 adjectives rated for favorability. (Based on data from Anderson, 1964.)

Dixon and Dixon (1964) have given a list of 200 verbs (in past-tense form) to 60 female and 60 male judges who rated them on an 11-point good-bad scale. The instructions were to rate what "kind of impression the subject thought a psychologist would get of him when he used each verb in a sentence." These impression ratings have correlations with log frequencies (the Thorndike-Lorge L-count) equal to .48 for females and to .50 for males. But it must be pointed out that these coefficients represent correlations severely attenuated by unreliability of the frequency variable. The Thorndike-Lorge count lists verbs in the present-tense form. If an adjectival form of the verb exists, then it is also listed. In our own research, in computing correlation coefficients, only the present-tense frequencies were used.

Miron (1961) had American and Japanese subjects rate a sample of three-element phonetic combinations on various scales of the Semantic Differential. The subjects also rated these stimulus materials for their familiarity. It is interesting that the correlations between familiarity and the composite of evaluative scales were .59 and .50 for the American and the Japanese samples, respectively. But the correlations of familiarity with the composites of the potency and activity factors were low and negative.

As a final example of the relationship between word frequency and the evaluative aspect of meaning, two poems by William Blake are called to the reader's attention:

Infant Joy

"I have no name:
I am but two days old,"
What shall I call thee?
"I happy am,
Joy is my name."
Sweet joy befall thee!

Pretty joy!
Sweet joy but two days old,
Sweet joy I call thee:
Thou dost smile,
I sing the while,
Sweet joy befall thee!

Infant Sorrow

My mother groaned! My father wept;
Into the dangerous world I leapt;
Helpless, naked, piping loud,
Like a fiend hid in a cloud,

Struggling in my father's hands,
Striving against my swadling bands,
Bound and weary I thought best
To sulk upon my mother's breast.

In these two poems, expressing opposite qualities of affect, the frequencies of the critical words (i.e., words which convey the major content, and hence not articles, pronouns, or auxiliary verbs) were averaged. The average frequency of *Infant Joy* is 2,037. The average for *Infant Sorrow* is 1,116. Two formally similar verses, one by Browning and the other by Shelley, show the same pattern:

Song. R. Browning	*Dirge.* P. B. Shelley
The year's at the spring,	Rough wind, that moanest loud
And day's at the morn;	Grief too sad for song;
Morning's at seven;	Wild wind, when sullen cloud
The hillside's dew-pearled;	Knells all the night long;
The lark's on the wing;	Sad storm, whose tears are in vain,
The snail's on the thorn;	Bare woods, whose branches strain,
God's in his Heaven—	Deep caves and dreary main—
All's right with the world.	Wail, for the world's wrong.

The average word frequency of Browning's poem is 1,380. The poem by Shelley—which comes to a rather different and sadder conclusion—has an average frequency of 728.

Stimulus Frequency Attitude: Correlational Evidence

We may now turn to the more general question of the effect of exposure on attitude, still limiting ourselves to correlational studies. Here, less evidence exists, and the evidence which is available is often indirect. But the results are quite similar to those just reviewed. For instance, Alluisi and Adams (1962) found a correlation of .843 between the preference subjects expressed for the appearance of letters and their frequency in the language. Strassburger and Wertheimer (1959) had subjects rate for "pleasantness" nonsense syllables varying in association value. Higher association values consistently received higher "pleasantness" ratings. Wilson and Becknell (1961) and Braun (1962) successfully replicated these results. Braun also found that eight-letter pseudowords, varying in their order of approximation to English (Miller, 1951), show the same pattern. These two studies differ from the similar ones by Johnson, Thomson, and Frincke, discussed earlier, in that subjects in the former ones were asked to judge how pleasant were the stimuli themselves, or how much subjects liked them (Wilson & Becknell, 1961), while in the latter whether they *meant* something close to "good" or close to "bad."

In 1947 the National Opinion Research Center conducted an extensive survey on the "prestige" of various occupations and professions. Nearly 100 occupational categories were rated for "general standing." Twenty-four of these occupations are labeled by single words, such as "physician," "scientist," "janitor," etc. The remainder is described less economically: "owner-operator of a printing shop," or "tenant farmer—one who owns livestock and machinery and manages the farm." Thus, one is able to determine the frequency of usage for only a part of this list—the 24 single-word occupations. The correlation between rated occupational prestige of these 24 items and the log of frequency of usage is .55.

Similar to the ratings of occupational prestige are the social distance ratings of ethnic and racial groups, first developed by Bogardus (1925) over 30 years ago. Recent replications show that these social distance ratings enjoy remarkable stability (Bogardus, 1959). The correlation between the so-called "racial-distance quotients," which are numerical equivalents of these ratings, and the log frequency of usage of these ethnic labels is .33.

In order to explore relationships of this sort further, I have selected 10 countries whose names are found in the Thorndike-Lorge L-count, and whose frequencies can be arranged in increasing order in approximately constant log units. These countries were then given to high-school students with the instructions to rank-order them in terms of liking. Table 5 shows the average rank each country received and its frequency of usage according to the L-count. There seems to be little question about the frequency-attitude relationship. The same relationship is found with American cities. Selected were 10 cities that (*a*) are listed in the Thorndike-Lorge L-count, and (*b*) can be arranged in increasing order of frequency in approximately constant log units. University students were asked how much they would like to live in each of these 10 cities. Their task, specifically, was to rank-order these cities according to their preferences "as a place to live." The average ranks, together with frequency counts of these 10 cities, are shown in Table 5.

Table 5 PREFERENCE RANKS AND FREQUENCY COUNTS FOR 10 COUNTRIES
AND 10 CITIES

COUNTRIES			CITIES		
COUNTRY	FREQUENCY	AVERAGE PREFERENCE RANK	CITY	FREQUENCY	AVERAGE PREFERENCE RANK
England	497	2.67	Boston	255	2.75
Canada	130	3.33	Chicago	621	3.08
Holland	59	3.42	Milwaukee	124	3.83
Greece	31	4.00	San Diego	9	4.25
Germany	224	4.92	Dayton	14	5.75
Argentina	15	6.08	Baltimore	68	6.08
Venezuela	9	6.58	Omaha	28	7.08
Bulgaria	3	7.75	Tampa	5	7.08
Honduras	1	7.92	El Paso	1	7.50
Syria	4	8.34	Saginaw	2	7.58

Other subjects, also high-school students in the Midwest, were asked to rate on a 7-point scale how much they liked various trees, fruits, vegetables, and flowers. In each case 10 items were selected which were listed in the Thorndike-Lorge count and which could be ordered according to a constant log frequency unit. Table 6 shows both the average ratings (0 = dislike; 6 = like) and the frequency counts for the four types of items. The rank correlations between the frequency and average attitude are .89, .85, .84, .81, .85, and .89, for countries, cities, trees, fruits, vegetables, and flowers, respectively.

Of course, word counts do not faithfully represent the frequencies with which one encounters the above items. And it is difficult to discover precisely how often the average Midwestern high school student encounters a yew, a cowslip, or a radish. But a fair index of frequency of exposure can be found in farm production data. For seven of the vegetables in Table 6 farm production figures for 1963 are available, and they are shown below in thousands of tons:

corn (4.17)	2,340.9
potatoes (4.13)	13,777.1
lettuce (4.00)	1,937.6
carrots (3.57)	843.8
asparagus (2.33)	187.8
cauliflower (1.96)	123.4
broccoli (1.96)	123.9

Included also (in brackets) are average preference ratings of these seven vegetables. The rank correlation between the production figures and the average preference ratings is .96.

Of course, this impressive correlation coefficient, like those we observed above, may not reflect the effect of frequency on attitude but the effect of attitude on frequency. Thus, it can be argued that many roses are grown because people like roses. But it can also be argued that people like roses because there are many roses growing. There is less ambiguity, however, with regard to the correlation between frequency of letters and the preference for their appearance

Table 6 PREFERENCE RATINGS OF TREES, FRUITS, VEGETABLES,
AND FLOWERS, AND THEIR CORRESPONDING FREQUENCIES

TREES	f	APR	FRUITS	f	APR
pine	172	4.79	apple	220	5.13
walnut	75	4.42	cherry	167	5.00
oak	125	4.00	strawberry	121	4.83
rosewood	8	3.96	pear	62	4.38
birch	34	3.83	grapefruit	33	4.00
fir	14	3.75	cantaloupe	1.5	3.75
sassafras	2	3.00	avocado	16	2.71
aloes	1	2.92	pomegranate	8	2.63
yew	3	2.83	gooseberry	5	2.63
acacia	4	2.75	mango	2	2.38

VEGETABLES	f	APR	FLOWERS	f	APR
corn	227	4.17	rose	801	5.55
potato	384	4.13	lily	164	4.79
lettuce	142	4.00	violet	109	4.58
carrot	96	3.57	geranium	27	3.83
radish	43	3.13	daisy	62	3.79
asparagus	5	2.33	hyacinth	16	3.08
cauliflower	27	1.96	yucca	1	2.88
broccoli	18	1.96	woodbine	4	2.87
leek	3	1.96	anemone	8	2.54
parsnip	8	1.92	cowslip	2	2.54

Note.—f = frequency of usage; APR = average preference rating.

(Alluisi & Adams, 1962). There aren't so many e's in English just because we like the way e's look. Still, until there is experimental evidence, the question of which is the cause and which the effect remains a matter of conjecture. We shall now turn, therefore, to such experimental evidence.

Exposure—Meaning: Experimental Evidence

Experiment I. The first experimental study on the relationship between exposure and word meaning was carried out by Johnson, Thomson, and Frincke (1960). These authors first asked subjects to rate a number of nonsense words on the good-bad scale of the semantic differential. The subjects were then instructed that "this is an experiment concerning the effectiveness of repetition in learning to pronounce strange words correctly." Some of these words were shown once, others twice, 5 times, or 10 times. Subjects were required to look at these words and to pronounce them on each presentation. Following this training procedure the words were again rated on the good-bad scale. A significant exposure effect was obtained, with the words shown frequently increasing on the evaluative scale. Strangely, however, words which were seen only once in training were judged afterwards not quite as "good" as before training. Thus, as a result of 2, 5, and 10 exposures words improved in meaning, and as a result of but 1 exposure they deteriorated. This finding, however, may be an artifact of the before-after procedure used by Johnson, Thomson, and Frincke. Moreover, frequencies and stimuli were fully confounded in their study.

Our experiment used the same stimuli which, incidentally, came from the familiar experiment by Solomon and Postman (1952) on the effects of word frequency on recognition threshold, but our design differed from the one used by Johnson, Thomson, and Frincke in several respects. In the Johnson-Thomson-Frincke experiment the same words always appeared in the same frequencies to all subjects. Thus, the word "jandara," for instance, was given 10 times to each subject, and the word "mecburi" was given once to each subject. It is possible that the effects these authors obtained are not due to the frequency manipulation alone, but that they depend on the stimulus material with which the frequency variable was fully confounded. In our study words and training frequencies were, therefore, counterbalanced in a Latin-square design. Because words and the number of exposures were counterbalanced, an after-only design could be employed, requiring no premeasures. The effects of repeated exposure could be observed for each word by comparing the favorability rating it received after having been exposed during training once, twice, five times, etc. Eliminating premeasures also eliminated for each stimulus one full exposure that necessarily preceded and therefore accompanied the frequency manipulation.

The present experiment differs from that of Johnson, Thomson, and Frincke (1960) in several other respects which are less critical for the interpretation of results. The procedure of this experiment, therefore, is described in some detail. Except for some specific changes, the same general methodology is followed throughout this series of studies.

Twelve seven-letter "Turkish" words, shown in Figure 3, were counterbalanced against six frequencies (0, 1, 2, 5, 10, and 25) in six replications of the experiment. Seventy-two subjects were run, one at a time, 12 subjects in each replication. The initial instructions informed the subject that the experiment dealt with "pronouncing foreign words." He was told that he would be shown some foreign words, hear the experimenter pronounce them, and that he would be required to pronounce them himself. The words were typed on 3×5-inch cards. On each trial a card was shown to the subject for approximately 2 seconds. Simultaneously the experimenter pronounced the word, requiring the subject to follow him. Since each frequency class contained two word-stimuli, there were 86 trials altogether. The position of a given stimulus in the sequence of these 86 trials was determined at random. Following the above frequency training subjects were told that the words they had just learned to pronounce were in fact Turkish adjectives, and that their next task would be to guess what they meant. The experimenter told the subject that he realized how nearly impossible this task was, and he therefore did not require him to guess the word meanings exactly. Instead, it would suffice if the subject indicated on a 7-point (0 to 6) good-bad scale whether each word meant something good or something bad and to what extent, because these Turkish adjectives all meant something good or bad. These ratings were made of the 10 stimuli which the subject received during the frequency training, and of 2 additional ones previously never seen by him.

The results of the experiment are shown in Figure 2 and in Figure 3. In Figure 2 are shown the ratings of "goodness" averaged for each of the six

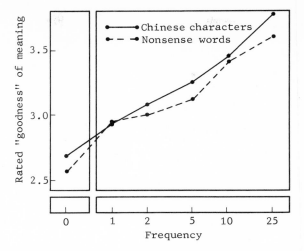

Fig. 2.   Average rated affective connotation of nonsense words and Chinese-like characters as a function of frequency of exposure.

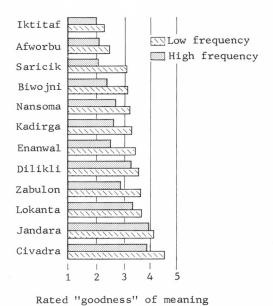

Fig. 3.   Average rated affective connotation of nonsense words exposed with low and high frequencies.

frequencies, and plotted on a log scale. Each point on that curve is based on 144 observations, and it is clear that a strong exposure effect was obtained ($F = 5.64$; $df = 5/355$; $p < .001$). Figure 3 shows the exposure effect for each of the 12 words separately. The ratings of "goodness" were averaged for each word when it was given during training with the lower frequencies of 0, 1, and 2 (hatched bars), and when it was given with the higher frequencies of 5, 10, and 25 (solid bars). This was possible because each word was used in each frequency equally often but for different subjects. It is evident from Figure 3 that some words are rated as having more positive meaning than others, and this effect is indeed significant ($F = 8.35$; $df = 11/781$; $p < .001$). Apparently, some of these words "sound better" than others. But independently of word content, subjects consistently rated the given word to mean something "better" if they had seen it (and had said it) more often. This is true for all the 12 words used in the experiment, a result that has a chance likelihood equal to .00024.

Experiment II. Since the hypothesis proposed above holds that it is *mere* exposure that is a sufficient condition of attitude change, the procedure used in Experiment I is not optimal for testing its validity. Subjects in Experiment I were required to pronounce the nonsense words during training, and it is possible that a decrease in difficulty in pronouncing the words associated with successive presentations was responsible for the results. In other words, subjects rated the frequent stimuli more favorably because they found them easier to pronounce than stimuli which they saw and pronounced only once or twice. And, there were stimuli which they never pronounced and, in fact, did not really know how to pronounce. Wilson and Becknell (1961) suggested that the evaluative ratings of nonsense syllables of high association value are higher than of low association value because they are easier to pronounce. In order to follow up their suggestion a group of 22 University of Michigan subjects were given the above "Turkish adjectives" with the instructions to rate them according to "how easy or difficult it is to pronounce" them. Using a 7-point scale, a significant item-effect was revealed by an analysis of variance ($F = 14.28$; $df = 11/263$; $p < .001$), showing that there are indeed differences among the nonsense words in the ease with which they can be pronounced upon their first presentation. The Wilson-Becknell conjecture is supported by a correlation of .46 between the average ease of pronouncing the words and the evaluative scores obtained in Experiment I. These latter scores were obtained by averaging for each word the rating it obtained in all frequencies.

These results, however, in themselves do not preclude a relationship between exposure and evaluative rating. With ease of pronouncing held constant the exposure effect may still be obtained. This expectation is strengthened by the results of a study described above (Frincke & Johnson, 1960) in which homophone pairs differing in word-frequency were rated for "pleasantness." Since homophones do not differ in pronunciation, the obtained frequency effects show that ease of pronouncing may be a sufficient factor in affecting evaluative ratings but not a necessary one. In order to eliminate the pronunciation factor and to reduce the subjects' active participation while exposure is being manipulated, the following experiment was carried out.

To meet the requirements of the definition of "mere exposure," Chinese characters were substituted for the nonsense words. These stimuli were taken from Hull's (1920) concept formation study, and I am told that not only are most of them meaningless, but that they are also far from the absolutely minimal standards of Chinese caligraphy. Nevertheless, they were quite adequate for our experimental purposes. The subjects were again told that the experiment dealt with the learning of a foreign language, but now they were not required to pronounce the characters. Nor were they able to pronounce them subvocally. They were simply instructed to pay close attention to the characters whenever they were exposed to them. In all other respects the experiment was identical to the one employing nonsense words. Now, too, following training subjects were told that the characters stood for adjectives, and that their task was to guess their meaning on the good-bad scale. Characters and exposures were again counterbalanced. Figures 2 and 4 show the results, and it is obvious that the exposure-favorability relationship previously found with nonsense words obtains ($F = 4.72$; $df = 5/335$; $p < .001$) even if the individual's exposure to the stimulus consists of his passively looking at it for a period of about 2 seconds. Figure 4 shows that the exposure effect is found for all stimuli but one.

The above results add strength to the hypothesis that mere exposure is a sufficient condition for attitude enhancement. But again the last experiment did not succeed in completely eliminating a learning factor from the exposure manipulation, for it is possible that this manipulation is now confounded with the ease of recognition. This danger of confounding, however, is probably minimal because at no time were the subjects ever required to recognize or discriminate the idiograms.

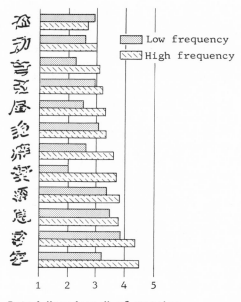

Rated "goodness" of meaning

Fig. 4. Average rated affective connotation of Chinese-like characters exposed with low and high frequencies.

The results of Experiments I and II are in an apparent conflict with results reported by Amster and Glasman (1966). These researchers report a negative result using a procedure similar to that employed by Johnson, Thomson, and Frincke (1960). The experiment was similar in all respects except that meaningful English words were substituted for the nonsense stimuli. No exposure effect was observed by Amster and Glasman for these meaningful words. But this finding is not at all surprising. Nor is it especially significant for the understanding of exposure effects. Adding one more occasion (or even 10 more occasions) to see and say a perfectly well-known English word to all the times this word had been seen and uttered by the individual in the past—a figure often in the thousands—really shouldn't have much effect on the meaning he attributes to it. The expectation of a change in the evaluative aspect of meaning as a function of a few additional exposures becomes even less reasonable when we consider that the change in affective connotation is a linear function of the logarithm of frequency, as we noted in Figures 1 and 2. If n is the frequency of the subject's preexperimental exposure to the word, then the comparisons made by Amster and Glasman involved the following four frequencies: $n + 1$, $n + 2$, $n + 5$, and $n + 10$. Since n is large, perhaps as large as 1000, the differences in exposures amounted to fractions of 1%.

Word-Frequency–Word-Value Relationship as a Special Case of the Exposure-Attitude Relationship

In the first section of this paper some evidence was presented suggesting that words with positive affective connotations are used more frequently (both in print and in speech) than words with negative affective connotations. In the second section evidence was given to suggest that the affective connotation of a word improves with their repeated use. Because the second item of evidence rests on experimental proof, in which the frequency of usage was systematically and independently manipulated, one cannot question the causal direction implied in these data. But finding that the frequency of usage affects meaning needn't necessarily preclude the posibility that meaning determines the frequency of usage. It is necessary, therefore, to examine more closely the results on the correlational evidence between word-frequency and word value.

Why are positive words used more frequently? Besides the rather wistful and unlikely explanation that there are more positive than negative referents (i.e., we live in a paradise), one real possibility suggests itself. The evidence reviewed so far deals only with usage *per word*. The totality of "good" and "bad" usage, however, depends on the numbers of different "good" and "bad" words in the language. It is entirely possible, therefore, that the superiority of "good" words in frequency *per word* exists side by side with the superiority of "bad" words in their greater variety. This possibility receives some support from the fact that in English (and in a host of other languages) prefixes and suffixes that serve to negate or reverse meaning, such as anti, de, im, in, ir, less, un, etc., are most commonly attached to words having a positive connotation. Once attached to a word they almost universally form a word with a negative affective connotation. Positive words with these prefixes or suffixes are exceptional: unselfish, independent, are some examples.

It would appear, therefore, that there are indeed more negative than positive words. And if there are more different negative words, the usage *per word* would naturally be attenuated for these words, because the total usage would be distributed among a larger universe of items.

Norman[5] has asked a group of students to separate a large sample of adjectives into "good" ones and "bad" ones. On the average 2.31 more items were placed in the "bad" pile than in the "good" pile. The frequency figures in Table 1 above show a pattern consistent with Norman's independent finding. The average frequency of the preferred antonyms is 2.3 times larger than the average frequency of the nonpreferred antonyms! Therefore, for the material considered here, the ratio of total positve and negative usage is equal to unity.

If repeated usage enhances the affective meaning of words, a relatively large supply of negative words would in fact be needed. It would be equally reasonable to expect that there exist devices in language protecting words from a deterioration of meaning. It is entirely possible that the prefixes and suffixes discussed above serve this function. Because the negative qualities of these prefixes and suffixes are independent of their referents, because they are essentially abstract, and because they derive their negativity from the semantic function they perform, words formed by means of these prefixes and suffixes are perhaps better able than root words to resist an enhancement of affective connotation as a result of repeated usage. I was unable to find evidence corroborating this point of view, although there is a good deal of philological literature on both positive changes in meaning (see for instance vanDongen, 1933) and negative changes in meaning (see, for instance, Schreuder, 1929). Most of the sources, however, consider changes in meaning of root words only.

If there are many remaining doubts that frequency of words is a function of the value of their referents, then the following frequencies of a few well-chosen but significant words should once and for all dispel them:

Psychologist	36
Chemist	32
Economist	32
Sociologist	14
Astronomer	12
Geologist	9
Physicist	8
Geographer	7
Botanist	6
Biologist	5

Exposure-Attitude Relationship: Experimental Evidence

Experiment III.   In all the experiments above the question asked of the subjects in rating the stimuli following exposure dealt with the evaluative aspect of their meaning. The subjects were never required to say just how much they "liked" the nonsense words or "Chinese" characters. In all probability, the results would

[5] Warren T. Norman, personal communication, 1965.

have been the same if they were asked directly to state their attitude toward these words and characters, and the Wilson-Becknell (1961) results support this conjecture. But because their stimuli were essentially verbal, subjects' answers could in these studies be strongly influenced by semantic factors. This would have been less likely, of course, in the case of Chinese characters than in the case of nonsense words.

As was pointed out above, there is some direct evidence on the attitudinal effects of mere exposure, dealing almost exclusively with music appreciation. Meyer (1903), for example, played to his students oriental music 12 to 15 times in succession. In most cases the students' introspective protocols indicated a better liking for the pieces on the last than on the first presentation. One of the students who took part in Meyers' experiment (H. T. Moore), and who showed enhancement effects of repeated exposure ("I liked the last time better than the first, because I became more used to the successive chords"), followed up this work in a study of his own 20 years later. Moore and Gilliland (1924) played to their students jazz and classical records once a week for 25 weeks. Liking for classical records increased, but no change was found for jazz music. Similar results are reported by other writers (Krugman, 1943; Verveer, Barry, & Bousfield, 1933; Washburn, Child, & Abel, 1927). Downey and Knapp (1927) played to 33 students a variety of musical selections (e.g., Tschaikowsky's *Marche Slave,* Massenet's *Meditation* from "Thais," *Columbia, The Gem of the Ocean,* etc.) once a week for five weeks. All pieces of music except one (*Columbia, The Gem of the Ocean*) became better liked at the close of the sessions. Alpert (1953) presented subjects with sounds having unfamiliar rhythms. His subjects found these sounds at first unpleasant. After repeated presentations, however, the liking for them increased. Additional exposures of subjects to the tones resulted in increasing indifference on the part of the listeners. More recently, Mull (1957) found that upon repeated exposure to their music subjects enjoyed Schoenberg and Hindemith more.

In the area of visual arts, Pepper (1919) found that repeated exposure resulted in more positive esthetic judgments of unusual color combinations. Krugman and Hartley (1960), however, using famous paintings, could only find ambiguous results. Maslow (1937) projected for 4 days in succession 15 paintings of great masters. Six days following the last presentation the 15 paintings were presented once again, and interspersed among them were 15 others (matched for the artist) which the subjects had never seen. The results indicated a greater liking for the familiar paintings. Maslow (1937) also made tests of preference, frequently with similar results, for other familiar and unfamiliar objects, such as rubber bands, paper clips, blotters, pens, pencils, etc. A similar experiment to the one with paintings, but using instead Russian girls' names, showed the same results. The same subjects were used in all these studies and the sessions took place in the same room, the subjects always sitting in the same chairs. Toward the end of the testing program Maslow asked if anyone would like to change seats. No one did, preferring, apparently, to remain in the familiar one.

Although the results of the above studies are fairly consistent, the conditions under which they were carried out make their conclusions somewhat less than compelling. In the majority of instances, the circumstances of the repeated exposure were quite ambiguous. The experiments were usually conducted in classes, the instructor serving as the experimenter. Subjects often responded aloud, thus being able to influence each other's judgments and opinions. Prior to the sessions the experimenter often expressed his own preferences. The stimuli, repeatedly shown, were not always exposed under the same conditions, and the material, exposures, and sequences were seldom counterbalanced. But in all of these experiments a pattern of results emerges showing that the frequency manipulation has more pronounced attitude effects for stimuli that are novel, unfamiliar, or unusual than for familiar stimuli. This pattern is, of course, consistent with the observation that attitude enhancement is a function of the logarithm of frequency.

Becknell, Wilson, and Baird (1963) have recently reported more convincing support for the exposure-attitude hypothesis. Slides of nonsense syllables were presented with different frequencies (1, 4, 7, and 10). Following this exposure training (which also included interspersed presentations of slides with landscapes and with ads) female subjects were given pairs of boxes containing nylon stockings, and they were asked to choose the "brand" they preferred. These "brands" corresponded to the nonsense syllables previously shown, and they were printed on the boxes. Each subject received two different pairs of boxes for comparison. The paired-comparison data showed a tendency of subjects to prefer the box marked by the more frequent syllable. Again, however, the semantic component is not excluded from the effects obtained in these two studies.

There is one more item of evidence, somewhat indirect, on the problem of the effects of exposure. In a study by Munsinger (1964) subjects were given the opportunity to present to themselves CVC trigrams whose association value, evaluation scale value, and prepotency score (Mandler, 1955) were previously assessed. By pressing a response key the subject would expose in a small window a trigram which he would then have to spell. The rate at which he key-pressed constituted the dependent measure. In one of Munsinger's experimental groups subjects could expose to themselves, by means of that key response, trigrams that were matched for association and prepotency. All these trigrams, however, previously scored low on the evaluative scales of the semantic differential. After subjects reached an asymptotic key-pressing rate, the experimental conditions changed such that now the subjects' response would expose trigrams that were high in evaluation, although they were still matched for association and pre-potency. A significant increase in key-pressing rates is reported by Munsinger following the change in the affective value of the trigrams. Again, however, the semantic component is not entirely excluded from the effects obtained in these two studies.

Because they are less a matter of semantic factors, we have chosen to manipulate interpersonal attitudes by means of exposure. Using the same experimental design as with the Chinese characters, faces of men (photographs of graduating Michigan State University seniors taken from the MSU Yearbook) were employed as attitude objects. The experiment was introduced to subjects—all students at the University of Michigan—as dealing with the problem of "visual memory." Following the exposure manipulation, which consisted of presenting each photograph a different number of times for a period of 2 seconds, subjects were asked to rate on a 7-point scale how much they might like the man on each photograph. The results of this study are shown in Figures 5 and 6. While the exposure effect is not as clear as previously (only 9 of the 12 stimuli show it), it is still rather impressive ($F = 9.96$; $df = 5/355$; $p < .001$).

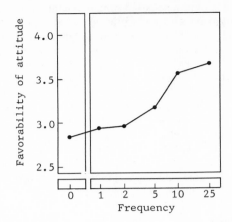

Fig. 5. Average attitude toward photographs as a function of frequency of exposure.

The Exposure-attitude Hypothesis and Related Theoretical Issues

The above results raise a series of empirical and theoretical questions. Are all attitudes enhanced by mere repeated exposure? Is there a number of repetitions beyond which attitude begins to become negative? Does this number vary systematically across attitude objects? Are these effects stable? These and similar questions can only be answered by further empirical work. On a theoretical level these questions address themselves primarily to those psychological processes that mediate exposure effects.

Let us first consider a possible biological significance of an exposure-enhancement mechanism. A stimulus presented for the first time evokes in the organism an instinctive fear reaction. Lorenz (1956) noted that a young raven,

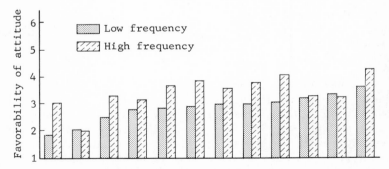

Fig. 6. Average attitude toward photographs exposed with low and high frequencies.

confronted with a new object, which may be a camera, an old bottle, a stuffed polecat, or anything else, first reacts with escape responses. He will fly up to an elevated perch, and, from this point of vantage, stare at the object literally for hours. After this he will begin to approach the object very gradually ...

Bühler, Hetzer, and Mabel (1928) observed that human infants reacted to a strange sound by crying out with fear. Upon the second exposure of the sound stimulus, movement and vocalization that indicated displeasure were observed. On the third exposure, the infants listened to the sound showing some signs of attention, but did not seem to show any displeasure. On the fourth exposure, they looked in the direction of the sound with detectable interest. These facts, of course, are borne out by common observation. Hunt (1965) reported that young infants he observed preferred a familiar mobile to a new one. And the "Black Bag" story cited in the introduction represents another example of phenomena in this category. At the outset the "Black Bag," in fact, attracted a good deal of hostility. Cairns (1966) has recently presented a very convincing argument that the affiliative behavior and social attachments among animals are solely determined by the animals' exposure to one another. Examining evidence on affiliative preferences of animals observed under conditions of inter- and intraspecific cohabitation and of animals deprived of social contact, Cairns concluded that such affiliative preferences vary directly with the length of the association and with the importance of the cues which are generated in the course of the association. Cairns, moreover, did not limit his conclusion to inter-animal social attachments but proposed that "animals tend to remain in the presence of [any] objects to which they have been continually exposed [p. 409]."

The survival value of an avoidance reflex to a novel stimulus is obvious. But there is no direct evidence that all organisms are equipped with an avoidance reaction occurring upon the encounter of a novel stimulus. However, if we assume that they are, then the exposure-attitude hypothesis becomes more reasonable. The first encounter with the novel stimulus produces fear reaction. If no negative consequences are associated with this first encounter, the avoidance reaction upon the second encounter will naturally be weaker. If such encounters continue, and if no other events—negative in their consequences for the organism—accompany these encounters, then the organism's attitude toward the stimulus must improve. To be sure, the hypothesis does not deny or preclude the effects of reinforcement. The exposure of a stimulus coupled with reward will strengthen the animal's approach behavior; and the exposure of stimulus coupled with a noxious event will strengthen his avoidance reactions. But in the absence of reward or punishment, mere exposure will result in the enhancement of the organism's attitude toward the given stimulus object.

If novel stimuli evoke fear, conflict, or uncertainty, one should be able to detect these states, and to observe their dissipation upon repeated exposure. To the extent that GSR measures arousal that is associated with the above states, we would expect greater GSRs upon the presentation of novel stimuli than upon the presentation of familiar ones, and we would also expect a drop in GSR reactivity to be the consequence of repeated stimulus exposure.

Experiment IV. Changes in affective arousal that occur as a result of repeated exposure of a novel stimulus were examined in an independent experiment. Fifteen subjects were presented with nonsense words (the same as in Experiment I) in a series of 86 trials. Two words appeared 25 times, two 10 times, two 5 times, two twice, and two once. The position of a word in the series of trials was determined by a random device. Words were counterbalanced against frequencies in three experimental replications. Due to a mechanical failure of the apparatus, data for one subject could not be used, and were not included in the analysis.

On a given trial, the stimulus word was projected onto a screen for a period of 2 seconds, and the subject's GSR was recorded. The interstimulus interval was 20 seconds. GSR was measured only during the first 10 seconds following stimulus onset, and all GSRs occurring during the last 12 seconds of the interstimulus interval were treated as artifacts. The Kaplan-Hobart technique of GSR measurement (Kaplan & Hobart, 1964), which requires current of only 10 microamperes, was employed. Zinc-zinc sulphate electrodes (Kaplan & Fisher, 1964; Lykken, 1959) were applied to the forefinger and the middle finger of the subject's nonpreferred hand.

The results of the experiment are shown in Figure 7 and Figure 8. In Figure 7 changes in conductance are plotted for each successive presentation of the stimulus-word. For purposes of clarity data for only one stimulus are graphed in each frequency class. The results for the other set of stimuli are the same. It can be seen that, in general, successive presentations result in a lower autonomic reactivity. After about seven or eight exposures a stable asymptote is reached. Hence, only stimuli shown 25 and 10 times attain an asymptote. Words shown five times, twice, or once generate greater changes in conductance even on their last exposure. This effect is seen better in Figure 8 in which GSRs on the last exposure of the stimuli were plotted. As prior frequency of exposure increases there is a lesser change in conductance upon stimulus presentation. This effect is significant at the .05 level ($F = 4.01$; $df = 4/117$).

These results cannot be due to an overall adaptation that may be occurring as the series of the 86 trials progresses. It is clear that the stimulus shown just once

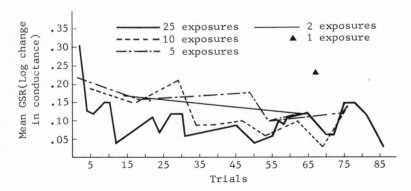

Fig. 7. GSR obtained upon repeated exposures of nonsense words.

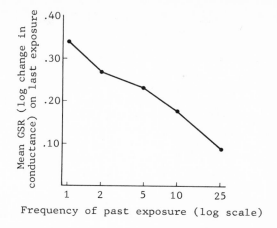

Fig. 8. GSR obtained on the last exposure of nonsense words exposed with various frequencies.

generated a substantial GSR although it occurred as late as on the 67th trial. As a matter of fact, its GSR does not differ from the GSR obtained for the *first* presentation of the other stimuli. The last presentation of the stimulus word that had just one prior exposure also resulted in a substantial GSR although it occurred on the 64th trial. And on the whole, although there is variability over trials, at any one point during the series GSR's are higher for stimuli with infrequent prior exposures than for stimuli previously seen by the subject many times. It seems, therefore, that with increased exposure there is a genuine reduction in stimulus-evoked arousal. These findings are in agreement with those reported by Berlyne, Craw, Salapatek, and Lewis (1963). In their study subjects were shown visual patterns differing in complexity and in incongruity. The patterns were presented for 3 seconds on three successive occasions. A significant drop in GSR was obtained between the first and the second presentation. But no significant GSR effects were associated with complexity or incongruity.

DISCUSSION

While the bulk of the results presented and reviewed in this monograph supports the hypothesis that repeated exposure is a sufficient condition of attitude enhancement, there are findings and theoretical formulations which appear to be in conflict with the hypothesis. The most pronounced source of ostensibly contradictory results is in the area of exploration and curiosity. There is impressive evidence today that in a free situation the subject (human or animal) will turn toward a novel stimulus in preference to a familiar one (e.g., Berlyne, 1960). If such orienting and exploratory "approach" behavior is a symptom of a favorable attitude toward the stimulus object, the wealth of data on exploration and orienting behavior (Berlyne, 1950, 1955; Berlyne & Slater, 1957; Dember &

Milbrook, 1956; Montgomery, 1953; Thiessen & McGaugh, 1958; Thomson & Solomon, 1954) stands in clear contradiction to those reported in this monograph.

But there is at present no direct evidence to support the above assumption. And, on the contrary, it is more likely that orienting toward a novel stimulus in preference to a familiar one may indicate that it is less liked rather than it is better liked. Ordinarily, when confronted with a novel stimulus the animal's orienting response enables it to discover if the novel stimulus constitutes a source of danger. It need not explore familiar stimuli in this respect. Novelty is thus commonly associated with uncertainty and with conflict—states that are more likely to produce negative than positive affect. Most recent work by Harrison (1967) indicates quite clearly that exploration and favorable attitudes are in fact negatively related. Using nonsense words, Chinese characters, and photographs of men's faces, Harrison obtained measures of liking from one group of subjects and measures of exploration from another group. The correlations between exploration and liking were −.69, −.69, and −.60 for nonsense words, characters, and photographs, respectively. If the function of orienting behavior is eventually to change the novel stimulus into a familiar one, it is also its consequence to render the stimulus object eventually more attractive (or perhaps merely less repulsive).

In his research Harrison also obtained data on the behavioral consequences of exposure, and in particular, on response conflict that novelty seems to arouse. It is a truism, of course, to assert that novel stimulus is one to which *no* specific response, beside orienting, has as yet been attached. But the novel stimulus cannot fail being similar to an entire host of other stimuli that the individual had encountered in the past, and to which he had attached specific responses. And it is entirely likely that some of these generalized response tendencies that the novel stimulus simultaneously excites are mutually incompatible; that is, they cannot all be emitted at the same time. This antecedent condition is what makes response conflict (of some, however small, magnitude) a necessary concomitant of novelty.

Using latency of free associations as a measure of response conflict, Harrison was able to demonstrate that response conflict is markedly reduced upon repeated exposure of a novel stimulus. Chinese ideographs were shown to a group of subjects once, twice, 5 times, 10 times, and 25 times, in a manner similar to that used in other experiments described above. Following this exposure manipulation, Harrison presented each stimulus once again requiring the subject to respond "with the first thing that came to mind." Included now were also Chinese ideographs that the subject had never seen. The latency of these free associations was obtained on each such trial, and the results revealed a systematic and significant drop in latencies as a function of the frequency of prior exposure.

Another set of data which may also be of some consequence for the exposure-attitude hypothesis is to be found in the area of semantic satiation. In a typical semantic-satiation experiment the subject is asked to repeat words, two or three per second, for a period of 15 seconds. The general findings in this area indicate that following this sort of rapid repetition the word seems to "lose" its meaning (for a review of the literature see Amster, 1964). Loss of meaning is measured by a departure from polarity on semantic differential scales, such as good-bad, strong-weak, etc. (Lambert & Jakobovits, 1960). When repeated in rapid succession and rated on some semantic differential scale, immediately thereafter the words tend to be placed neither toward one (e.g., good) nor the other (e.g., bad) end of the scale, but are rated toward the neutral point of the scale. While several studies have demonstrated a reduction of polarization following rapid repetition of a word (Das, 1964; Kanungo & Lambert, 1963a, 1963b; Messer, Jakobovitz, Kanungo, & Lambert, 1964), there is an equal amount of conflicting evidence (Amster & Glasman, 1965; Floyd, 1962; Reynierse & Barch, 1963; Schulz, Weaver, & Radtke, 1965). Yelen and Schulz (1963) attribute satiation findings to a regression artifact. A reduction of polarity of *positive* words as a result of repetition would indeed be embarrassing for the exposure-attitude hypothesis. A reduction of polarity of *negative* words (i.e., words with a semantic score below the neutral point) would, of course, be entirely in agreement with the present results, for they would simply be showing an enhancement effect along the evaluative dimension. It should be noted that all our stimuli initially received negative ratings, that is, below the neutral point, 3, on the 0–6 good-bad scale. Given no exposure at all, the evaluative ratings for the Turkish nonsense words, Chinese-like characters, and photographs were 2.56, 2.67, and 2.79, respectively. In terms of polarity these averages are −.44, −.33, and −.21. Contrary to the semantic satiation hypothesis, absolute polarities increased after 25 exposures, for they were +.61, +.78, and +.61, respectively. Admittedly, the controversy within semantic satiation literature may have to be resolved before clear implications for the exposure effect can be drawn. Parenthetically it should be noted, however, that the form of exposure used in the semantic satiation paradigm (i.e., 30 to 45 repetitions in 15 seconds) is not what has been above defined as the sufficient condition of attitude enhancement. Moreover, in semantic satiation studies the stimulus is commonly a verbal response made by the subject himself. Whether such a response-produced stimulus should constitute what is meant by mere exposure is a matter of some doubt.

The above hypothesis and data seem to be consistent with the theory of reinforcement recently proposed by Premack (1959). This new and engaging approach to reinforcement effects, for which a good deal of impressive evidence has already been accumulated (Premack, 1961, 1962, 1963, 1965; Premack & Bahwell, 1959; Premack & Collier, 1962), holds that if the emission of one response, A, is made contingent upon the emission of another response, B, and if A occurs with greater frequency than B, B will gain in the rate of emission. A can, therefore, be considered as having positive reinforcement value which seems to depend alone upon its frequency of occurrence. Contingencies between responses can be introduced by controlling manipulanda or the availability of goal objects. Thus, for instance, in studying these effects in Cebus monkeys, Premack (1963) used four manipulanda: a plunger, a hinged door, a vertically operated lever, and a horizontally operated lever. It was possible to make any manipulandum inoperable at any time, and to make it operable only in the case of a prior manipulation of another manipulandum. Thus, each manipulandum could serve for the reinforc*ing* or for the reinforc*ed* response. After establishing for each monkey the probabilities of operating each item under free access to all, contingencies were arranged between pairs of items, such that, for instance, the vertical lever could not be operated unless the animal pulled the plunger, or the hinged door remained locked unless the subject pressed the horizontal lever, etc. The introduction of these contingencies resulted in the predicted effects. In general, responses that were less probable increased in the rate of emission when more probable responses were made contingent upon them. When two responses were equal in probability of emission little or no change in response rates was observed.

Viewed in the present context, the individual's response probabilities can be taken as an indication of his "attitudinal liking" or "attraction" to the goal objects of these responses, or to the instrumental stimuli associated with them. To the extent that the reward value of a given response, A, which is contingent upon another response, B, is a direct function of A's probability of emission, then increasing its probability of emission will increase its reward value. Premack (1961) was able to demonstrate such an effect in rats for licking and bar pressing. Changing the language somewhat, it may be said that the individual's "attitudinal liking" for the goal object of the response A increases with the individual's exposure to the goal object of A. In Premack's work continuous reinforcement schedules are used and, hence, the individual's frequency of exposure to the goal object of A is equal to the frequency of emission of A.

There are important differences between the phenomena observed by Premack and those reported in the present paper. In most of his experiments the frequency of occurrence of responses results from an independent, perhaps genetically given or previously acquired, response preference of the subject. In the experimental work on attitudinal effects of exposure, the frequency of occurrence of the stimulus-object is deliberately manipulated. Moreover, the subject usually does not have a prior preference for the stimulus exposed. On the contrary, he may often manifest avoidance tendencies. But the parallel is compelling.

While there is a great deal in common between Premack's work on reinforcement and the research on attitudinal effects of exposure, a clear understanding of the implications of one for the other requires a systematic determination of what "reinforcement value" and "attitudes" have in common that makes them both equally vulnerable to simple frequency effects.

CONCLUSION

The balance of the experimental results reviewed and reported in this paper is in favor of the hypothesis that mere repeated exposure of an individual to a stimulus object enhances his attitude toward it. But, as yet, the account books cannot be closed. Further research must examine the boundary conditions of the exposure-attitude relationship, for it is possible that the neat linear log-frequency–attitude relationship, repeatedly observed here, may well break down under some conditions. This future research must, in particular, concentrate on the effects of large frequencies of exposure, on duration of exposure, on interexposure intervals, and on many other similar parameters of mere exposure. This research must also assess the applicability of the exposure-attitude relationship to a greater variety of stimulus objects. The question of generalization of specific exposure effects is of equal theoretical importance. Does repeated exposure to a given stimulus result in the enhancement of attitudes toward similar or related stimuli?

Because the above effects seem to be a function of the *logarithm* of frequency of exposure, they are more apparent and more pronounced for differences among small frequencies than for differences among large frequencies. For the same reason, attitudinal enhancement produced by means of exposure will be more readily effected for novel objects than for familiar ones. It is likely that exposure effects for very familiar objects are absent completely or are so small that they cannot be detected at all by methods now available. As we have seen above, Amster and Glasman (1966) failed to obtain the exposure effect for common English words. It will be important for future research, therefore, to determine the range of familiarity for which the exposure effect is obtained.

Mere exposure is a necessary precondition of a vast variety of experimental manipulations. For example, in attempts to change attitudes by means of persuasive communications the attitude object is mentioned repeatedly, regardless of whether the attempt is directed toward making the attitude more favorable or toward making it less favorable. Making attitudes more favorable should, therefore, be easier than making them less favorable. It is interesting that studies on the effectiveness of persuasion in attitude change seldom try to effect a negative change, and almost never compare the relative success of a pro-persuasion with the success of a con-persuasion. In an attitude-change study Tannenbaum and Gengel (1966) have recently obtained only positive shifts, although both a positive as well as a negative manipulation were employed.

The partial reinforcement manipulation, too, is subject to possible confounding with the number of stimulus presentations. Erlebacher and Archer (1961), for instance, reported the curious result that at the completion of training greater numbers of correct responses were associated with smaller percentages of reinforcement. However, in the various conditions of reinforcement subjects worked until they performed in succession a predetermined number of correct responses, the same for all percentages of reinforcement. Therefore, percentage of reinforcement was in this study completely confounded with the number of stimulus exposures (and also with the number of reinforcements). Although many authors have tried to cope with this confounding in one way or another (e.g., Festinger, 1961; Kanfer, 1954; O'Connell, 1965), the methodological difficulties have not been completely overcome. None of the four variables that are associated with the partial reinforcement effect—percentage of reinforced trials, number of trials, number of positive reinforcements, number of nonreinforcements—can be studied independently of the others.

REFERENCES

Alluisi, E. A., & Adams, O. S. Predicting letter preferences: Aesthetics and filtering in man. *Perceptual and Motor Skills,* 1962, *14,* 123–31.

Alpert, R. Perceptual determinants of affect. Unpublished master's thesis, Wesleyan University, 1953.

Amster, H. Semantic satiation and generation: Learning? Adaptation? *Psychological Bulletin,* 1964, *62,* 273–86.

Amster, H., & Glasman, L. D. Verbal repetition and connotative change. *Journal of Experimental Psychology,* 1966, *71,* 389–95.

Anderson, N. H. *Likeableness ratings of 555 personality-trait adjectives.* Los Angeles: University of California, 1964. (Mimeo)

Becknell, J. C., Jr., Wilson, W. R., & Baird, J. C. The effect of frequency of presentation on the choice of nonsense syllables. *Journal of Psychology,* 1963, *56,* 165–70.

Berlyne, D. E. Novelty and curiosity as determinants of exploratory behavior. *British Journal of Psychology,* 1950, *41,* 68–80.

Berlyne, D. E. The arousal and satiation of perceptual curiosity in the rat. *Journal of Comparative and Physiological Psychology,* 1955, *48,* 232–46.

Berlyne, D. E. *Conflict, curiosity, and exploratory behavior.* New York: McGraw-Hill, 1960.

Berlyne, D. E., Craw, M. A., Salapatek, P. H., & Lewis, J. L. Novelty, complexity, incongruity, extrinsic motivation, and the GSR. *Journal of Experimental Psychology,* 1963, *66,* 560–67.

Berlyne, D. E., & Slater, J. Perceptual curiosity, exploratory behavior, and maze learning. *Journal of Comparative and Physiological Psychology,* 1957, *50,* 228–32.

Bogardus, E. S. Measuring social distance. *Journal of Applied Sociology,* 1925, *9,* 299–308.

Bogardus, E. S. *Social distance.* Yellow Springs, Ohio: Antioch Press, 1959.

Bovard, E. W., Jr. Group structure and perception. *Journal of Abnormal and Social Psychology,* 1951, *46,* 398–405.

Braun, J. R. Three tests of the McClelland discrepancy hypothesis. *Psychological Reports,* 1962, *10,* 271–74.

Buchanan, M. A. *Graded Spanish word book.* Toronto: Toronto University Press, 1927.

Bühler, C., Hetzer, H., & Mabel, F. Die Affektwirksamkeit von Fremdheitseindrücken im ersten Lebensjahr. *Zeitschrift für Psychologie,* 1928, *107,* 30–49.

Cairns, R. B. Attachment behavior of mammals. *Psychological Review,* 1966, *73,* 409–26.

Cook, S. W., & Selltiz, C. *Contact and intergroup attitudes: Some theoretical considerations.* New York: Research Center for Human Relations, 1952.

Das, J. P. Hypnosis, verbal satiation, vigilance, and personality factors: A correlational study. *Journal of Abnormal and Social Psychology,* 1964, *68,* 72–78.

Dember, W. N., & Millbrook, B. A. Free choice by the rat of the greater of two brightness changes. *Psychological Reports,* 1956, *2,* 465–67.

Deutsch, M., & Collins, M. E. *Interracial housing: A psychological evaluation of a social experiment.* Minneapolis: University of Minnesota Press, 1951.

Dixon, T. R., & Dixon, J. F. The impression value of verbs. *Journal of Verbal Learning and Verbal Behavior,* 1964, *3,* 161–65.

Downey, J. E., & Knapp, G. E. The effect on a musical programme of familiarity and of sequence of selections. In M. Schoen (Ed.), *The effects of music.* New York: Harcourt, Brace, 1927.

Eaton, H. S. *An English, French, German, Spanish word frequency dictionary.* New York: Dover, 1940.

Erdélyi, M. The relation between "Radio Plugs" and sheet sales of popular music. *Journal of Applied Psychology,* 1940, *24,* 696–702.

Erlebacher, A., & Archer, E. J. Perseveration as a function of degree of learning and percentage of reinforcement in card sorting. *Journal of Experimental Psychology,* 1961, *62,* 510–17.

Fechner, G. T. *Vorschule der Aesthetik.* Leipzig: Breitkopf & Härtel, 1876.

Festinger, L. Group attraction and membership. *Journal of Social Issues,* 1951, *7,* 152–63.

Festinger, L. The psychological effects of insufficient reward. *American Psychologist,* 1961, *16,* 1–11.

Floyd, R. L. Semantic satiation: Replication and test of further implications. *Psychological Reports,* 1962, *11,* 274.

Frincke, G., & Johnson, R. C. Word value and word frequency in homophone pairs. *Psychological Reports,* 1960, *7,* 470.

Gough, H. G. *Reference handbook for the Gough Adjective Check List.* Berkeley: University of California Institute of Personality Assessment and Research, April 1955. (Mimeo)

Harrison, A. A. Response competition and attitude change as a function of repeated stimulus exposure. Unpublished doctoral dissertation, University of Michigan, 1967.

Homans, G. C. *Social behavior: Its elementary forms.* New York: Harcourt, Brace, 1961.

Howes, D. On the interpretation of word frequency as a variable affecting speed of recognition. *Journal of Experimental Psychology,* 1954, *48,* 106–12.

Howes, D. H., & Solomon, R. L. A note on McGinnies' "Emotionality and perceptual defense." *Psychological Review,* 1950, *57,* 229–34.

Hull, C. L. Quantitative aspects of the evolution of concepts. *Psychological Monographs,* 1920, *28*(1, Whole No. 123).

Hunt, J. McV. Traditional personality theory in the light of recent evidence. *American Scientist,* 1965, *53,* 80–96.

James, W. *The principles of psychology.* Vol. 2. New York: Holt, 1890.

Johnson, R. C., Thomson, C. W., & Frincke, G. Word values, word frequency, and visual duration thresholds. *Psychological Review,* 1960, *67,* 332–42.

Käding, F. W. *Häufigkeitswörterbuch der deutschen Sprache.* Berlin: Mittler, 1948.

Kanfer, F. H. The effect of partial reinforcement in acquisition and extinction of a class of verbal responses. *Journal of Experimental Psychology,* 1954, *48,* 424–32.

Kanungo, R. N., & Lambert, W. E. Paired-associate learning as a function of stimulus and response satiation. *British Journal of Psychology*, 1963, *54*, 135–44 (a).

Kanungo, R. N., & Lambert, W. E. Semantic satiation and meaningfulness. *American Journal of Psychology*, 1963, *76*, 421–28 (b).

Kaplan, S., & Fisher, G. R. A modified design for the Lykken zinc electrodes. *Psychophysiology*, 1964, *1*, 88–89.

Kaplan, S., & Hobart, J. L. A versatile device for the measurement of skin resistance in rats and humans. *American Journal of Psychology*, 1964, *77*, 309–10.

Kramer, M. Residential contact as a determinant of attitudes toward Negroes. Unpublished doctoral dissertation, University of Chicago, 1950.

Krugman, H. E. Affective response to music as a function of familiarity. *Journal of Abnormal and Social Psychology*, 1943, *38*, 388–92.

Krugman, H. E., & Hartley, E. C. The learning of tastes. *Public Opinion Quarterly*, 1960, *24*, 621–31.

Lambert, W. E., & Jakobovits, L. A. Verbal satiation and changes in the intensity of meaning. *Journal of Experimental Psychology*, 1960, *60*, 376–83.

Lorenz, K. *L'instinct dans le comportement de l'animal et de l'homme.* Paris: Masson, 1956.

Lykken, D. T. Properties of electrodes used in electrodermal measurements. *Journal of Comparative and Physiological Psychology*, 1959, *52*, 629–34.

MacKenzie, B. K. The importance of contact in determining attitudes toward Negroes. *Journal of Abnormal and Social Psychology*, 1948, *43*, 4.

Mandler, G. Associative frequency and associative prepotency as measures of response to nonsense syllables. *American Journal of Psychology*, 1955, *68*, 662–65.

Maslow, A. H. The influence of familiarization on preference. *Journal of Experimental Psychology*, 1937, *21*, 162–80.

McGinnies, E. Emotionality and perceptual defense. *Psychological Review*, 1949, *56*, 244–51.

Messer, S., Jakobovits, L. A., Kanungo, R. N., & Lambert, W. A. Semantic satiation of words and numbers. *British Journal of Psychology*, 1964, *55*, 156–63.

Meyer, M. Experimental studies in the psychology of music. *American Journal of Psychology*, 1903, *14*, 456–76.

Miller, G. A., Newman, E. B., & Friedman, E. A. Length-frequency statistics for written English. *Information and Control*, 1958, *1*, 370–98.

Miron, M. S. A cross-linguistic investigation of phonetic symbolism. *Journal of Abnormal and Social Psychology*, 1961, *62*, 623–30.

Montgomery, K. C. Exploratory behavior as a function of "similarity" of stimulus situations. *Journal of Comparative and Physiological Psychology*, 1953, *46*, 129–33.

Moore, H. T., & Gilliland, A. R. The immediate and long time effects of classical and popular phonograph selections. *Journal of Applied Psychology*, 1924, *8*, 309–23.

Mosier, C. I. A psychometric study of meaning. *Journal of Social Psychology*, 1941, *13*, 123–40.

Mull, H. K. The effect of repetition upon enjoyment of modern music. *Journal of Psychology*, 1957, *43,* 155–62.

Munsinger, H. L. Meaningful symbols as reinforcing stimuli. *Journal of Abnormal and Social Psychology*, 1964, *68,* 665–68.

National Opinion Research Center. Jobs and occupations: A popular evaluation. In R. Bendix & S. B. Lipsit (Eds.), *Class, status, and power: A research in social stratification.* Glencoe, Ill.: Free Press, 1953.

Newcomb, T. M. Stabilities underlying changes in interpersonal attraction. *Journal of Abnormal and Social Psychology,* 1963, *66,* 376–86.

O'Connell, D. C. Concept learning and verbal control under partial reinforcement and subsequent reversal and non-reversal shifts. *Journal of Experimental Psychology,* 1965, *69,* 144–51.

Osgood, C. E., Suci, G. J., & Tannenbaum, P. H. *The measurement of meaning.* Urbana: University of Illinois Press, 1957.

Palermo, D. S., & Jenkins, J. J. *Word association norms–grade school through college.* Minneapolis: University of Minnesota Press, 1964.

Pepper, S. C. Changes of appreciation for color combinations. *Psychological Review,* 1919, *26,* 389–96.

Postman, L. The experimental analysis of motivational factors in perception. In J. S. Brown (Ed.), *Current theory and research in motivation.* Lincoln: University of Nebraska Press, 1953.

Premack, D. Toward empirical behavior laws: I. Positive reinforcement. *Psychological Review,* 1959, *66,* 219–33.

Premack, D. Predicting instrumental performance from the independent rate of the contingent response. *Journal of Experimental Psychology,* 1961, *61,* 163–71.

Premack, D. Reversibility of the reinforcement relation. *Science,* 1962, *136,* 255–57.

Premack, D. Rate differential reinforcement in monkey manipulation. *Journal of the Experimental Analysis of Behavior,* 1963, *6,* 81–89.

Premack, D. Reinforcement theory. *Nebraska Symposium on motivation,* 1965, *13,* 123–80.

Premack, D., & Bahwell, R. Operant-level lever pressing by a monkey as a function of interest interval. *Journal of the Experimental Analysis of Behavior,* 1959, *2,* 127–31.

Premack, D., & Collier, G. Joint effects of stimulus deprivation and intersession interval: Analysis of nonreinforcement variables affecting response probability. *Psychological Monographs,* 1962, *76*(5, Whole No. 524).

Reynierse, J. H., & Barch, A. M. Semantic satiation and generalization. *Psychological Reports,* 1963, *13,* 790.

Sartre, J. P. *Words.* New York: Braziller, 1964.

Schreuder, H. *Pejorative sense development.* Groningen: Noordhoff, 1929.

Schulz, R. W., Weaver, G. E., & Radtke, R. C. Verbal satiation?? *Psychonomic Science,* 1965, *2,* 43–44.

Solomon, R. L., & Postman, L. Usage as a determinant of visual duration thresholds of words. *Journal of Experimental Psychology,* 1952, *43,* 195–201.

Strassburger, F., & Wertheimer, M. The discrepancy hypothesis of affect and association value of nonsense syllables. *Psychological Reports,* 1959, *5,* 528.

Tannenbaum, P. H., & Gengel, R. W. Generalization of attitude change through congruity principle relationships. *Journal of Personality and Social Psychology,* 1966, *3,* 299–304.

Thiessen, D. D., & McGaugh, J. L. Conflict and curiosity in the rat. Paper presented at the meeting of the Western Psychological Association, Monterey, California, 1958.

Thomson, W. R., & Solomon, L. M. Spontaneous pattern discrimination in the rat. *Journal of Comparative and Physiological Psychology,* 1954, *47,* 104–7.

Thorndike, E. L., & Lorge, I. *The teacher's word-book of 30,000 words.* New York: Teachers College, Columbia University, 1944.

Underwood, B. J. Verbal learning and the educative process. *Harvard Educational Review,* 1959, *29,* 107–17.

van der Beke, G. E. *French word book.* New York: Macmillan, 1929.

van Dongen, G. A. *Amelioratives in English.* Rotterdam: De Vries, 1933.

Verveer, E. M., Barry, H., Jr., & Bousfield, W. A. Change in affectivity with repetition. *American Journal of Psychology,* 1933, *45,* 130–34.

Washburn, M. F., Child, M. S., & Abel, T. M. The effects of immediate repetition on the pleasantness or unpleasantness of music. In M. Schoen (Ed.), *The effects of music.* New York: Harcourt, Brace, 1927.

Wiebe, G. The effects of radio plugging on students' opinions of popular songs. *Journal of Applied Psychology,* 1940, *24,* 721–27.

Wilner, D. M., Walkley, R. P., & Cook, S. W. Residential proximity and intergroup relations in public housing projects. *Journal of Social Issues, 8,* 1, 1952.

Wilson, L. R., & Becknell, J. C. The relation between the association value, pronounciability, and affectivity of nonsense syllables. *Journal of Psychology,* 1961, *52,* 47–49.

Yelen, D. R., & Schulz, R. W. Verbal satiation? *Journal of Verbal Learning and Verbal Behavior,* 1963, *1,* 372–77.

Race and Belief: An Open and Shut Case

DAVID D. STEIN, JANE ALLYN HARDYCK, AND M. BREWSTER SMITH

One of the many ideas presented in *The Open and Closed Mind* (Rokeach, 1960) is that prejudice may be in large part the result of perceived dissimilarity of belief systems. That is, Rokeach, Smith, and Evans (1960) contend that the prejudiced person does not reject a person of another race, religion, or nationality because of his ethnic membership per se, but rather because he perceives that the other differs from him in important beliefs and values. He reports two studies in which subjects were asked to rate pairs of stimulus individuals on a 9-point scale, defined at the ends by the statements, "I *can't* see myself being friends with such a person" and "I can *very easily* see myself being friends with

Reprinted from Journal of Personality and Social Psychology, 1, *1965, 281–89. Copyright 1965 by the American Psychological Association and reproduced by permission.*

such a person." In one experiment, the stimulus individuals were white or Negro; in the other they were Jewish or gentile. Racial and religious attitudes and general beliefs of the stimulus individuals were also varied. In this situation, it was found that the friendship preferences expressed were determined primarily on the basis of congruence in beliefs rather than on racial or religious grounds.

Triandis (1961) took issue with this position, stating that:

People do not exclude other people from their neighborhood, for instance, because the other people have different belief systems, but they do exclude them because they are Negroes [p. 186].

He has reported results contrary to Rokeach's contention regarding the primacy of belief congruence over race as a determinant of prejudice. Since he objected to Rokeach's use of the single criterion of friendship as the measure of prejudice, he employed a social distance scale of 15 items. For his manipulation of belief congruence, he used "same philosophy" or "different philosophy" as determined by the subjects' most and least preferred of Morris' (1956) "13 ways to live." Stimulus individuals in the study were varied in race, religion, and occupational status as well as in philosophy. He obtained a "race effect" that accounted for about four times as much variance, in terms of the percentage of the total sum of squares, as any of the other three effects singly, although all four main effects were highly significant.

Rokeach (1961) replied with the objection that the long and involved passages of Morris' "ways to live" could not be equated with belief systems as he defined them; the "ways to live" were too vague and were not salient to the subjects. He concluded that the results of Triandis' study were therefore irrelevant to the point at issue. In a more recent study, Byrne and Wong (1962) essentially supported Rokeach's position, employing personal feelings of friendliness and willingness to work together in an experiment as dependent variables.

The present study was designed with the intent of reconciling these disparate findings. It seemed reasonable to assume that there might be some truth in each position, and that the large differences between the results obtained by Rokeach et al. and by Byrne and Wong, on the one hand, and by Triandis, on the other, followed primarily from the methods used.

In the design of the present study, our first concern was that of making our "stimulus individuals" appear real to our subjects. In Rokeach's studies, pairs of individuals, described in very sketchy fashion, were presented in such a way that it was rather obvious to the subject that a choice was to be made between race and belief. In Triandis' study, there was less of a suggestion of choice, but the descriptions were equally sketchy and the measure of belief was, indeed, very vague. Our intent has been, following an improved procedure devised by Byrne (1961), to present to our subjects, as nearly as is possible on paper, realistic stimulus individuals. In this study, as in Byrne and Wong (1962), stimulus individuals were varied in race and in the similarity of their beliefs to those previously expressed by the subjects. This procedure makes it possible to elicit absolute rather than comparative judgments so as to minimize self-consciously ideological responses. As our dependent variables, we employed both a measure of friendly feelings and a social distance scale, on which responses to each individual item could be separately analyzed.

METHOD

The sample consisted of 23 male and 21 female white teen-agers in two ninth grade classes of a California high school. The subjects, all of whom were 14 years of age, came mainly from working class homes in a nonmetropolitan industrial community. They participated in the study during their advisory periods.[1]

At the beginning of the period, the experimenter introduced himself as "a research worker from the University of California" and handed out a mimeographed booklet to each student, by name. The instructions were printed on the front page of the booklet and read as follows:

As you remember, a few months ago we asked you to answer some questions concerning your interests and attitudes about yourself, your friends, and certain groups of teenagers. You may also recall that there were some questions asking you to give first impressions about people when you knew only a few things about them, such as the person's religion or type of job. We are very much interested in how people form these impressions.

In fact, we would like to know how you would feel about some teenagers who took the same questionnaires as you did, but in other parts of the country. Therefore, we have taken some of their answers and presented them on the following pages.

We want you to look at the descriptions of *four* teenage boys [girls] and then answer some questions about how you feel toward them. The four teenagers will be called: TEENAGER I, II, III, and IV. If you have any questions, please raise your hand and the research worker will help you. Be sure to read everything carefully.[2]

As the instructions indicate, 2 months prior to this study the students had filled out the pretest version of a questionnaire being developed for a large-scale study of teen-age attitudes towards minority groups.[3] A value scale on the pretest questionnaire had asked the students, "Do you think teenagers in general *ought* to ..." about each of 25 items. Five response alternatives were provided, ranging from "Strongly feel they should" to "Strongly feel they shouldn't." The students' own responses to these items on the pretest provided the basis for the manipulation of belief congruence in the present study (Figure 1).

[1] We would like to thank Wayne Henderson, his teaching staff, and the students at Pacifica High School, Pittsburg, California, for their cooperation in this research, and Herbert Weissman who served as experimenter in one classroom.

[2] Male subjects answered questions about boys; female subjects answered questions about girls. Wording throughout the questionnaire was adapted to the sex of the subject.

[3] This study of teen-age attitudes is a part of a 5-year program of research on various aspects of anti-Semitism being conducted at the Survey Research Center of the University of California under the general direction of Charles Y. Glock. The research is supported by a grant to the Survey Research Center from the Anti-Defamation League of B'nai B'rith. We gratefully acknowledge our indebtedness to the Anti-Defamation League, but this organization is not to be held responsible for our interpretations.

For each of the subjects, two "stimulus teen-agers" were constructed who were like him in values, and two were constructed who were unlike him, following a procedure similar to that used by Byrne (1961). One "like" stimulus teen-ager was made up whose responses were identical with those given by the subject. In order to avoid raising the suspicions of the subjects, the other "like" teen-ager was made to differ slightly from the first by moving the responses to six items, chosen at random, one step on the 5-point scale.[4] Each "unlike" teen-ager was created by choosing at random three of the items the subject had answered "Strongly feel they should" and changing them to "feel they shouldn't." Three more modest alterations were made as well, depending on the subject's original pretest response pattern.[5]

Besides the information on how the stimulus teen-agers had "answered" the value items, the subjects were given the sex, grade and program in school, last year's grades, and race of the teen-ager (Figure 2). For half the subjects, this additional information preceded that on values throughout the booklet, and for the other half, the value scale information was presented first. The sex and grade in school were always the same as that of the subject, the program in school was college preparatory, and grades were "about a B average." Only race was varied. Thus, by combining like and unlike responses on the value scale with "Negro" and "white," four stimulus teen-agers were created. These will be referred to as white-like, white-unlike, Negro-like, and Negro-unlike. These four were presented in eight different orders, the only restriction in ordering being that like and unlike teen-agers were alternated.

As the subject opened his booklet, he was confronted with the description of one of the four stimulus teen-agers, called Teenager I. The subject read this first description, at his own speed, and then turned to the next pair of pages and answered three questions. One of these served as a check on the manipulation of belief congruence, and the other two were measures of friendliness and social distance towards the stimulus teen-ager. The questions will be discussed in more detail under Results. The subject then went on to read the description of Teenagers II, III, and IV and in turn to answer the questions about them. When he had finished, usually in 20–25 minutes, he turned over his booklet and waited for the rest of the class to complete their booklets.

---

[4] A check of responses to the question, "How much like you is this teen-ager?" showed that responses to an "exact-like" stimulus teen-ager differed somewhat from those to a "modified-like" teen-ager ($t = 1.76$, $p < .05$, one-tailed test). Since half of the white-like stimulus teen-agers were "exact like" and half of each were "modified like," this difference cannot have affected our results.

[5] A pilot study revealed that more drastic changes than the ones finally used made the stimulus teen-agers appear unreal. Details of procedure for constructing the stimulus teen-agers may be had by writing to the first author listed.

Fig. 1. Example of information concerning values provided to describe a "stimulus teen-ager." (Underlined responses reflect the subject's own responses from the pretest questionnaire.)

On this page and the one facing it are the answers given by TEENAGER I. After you have looked over the answers and have a good picture of what you think this person is like, turn the page and answer the questions about how you feel toward this person.

Every teenager has his own ideas about how his fellow students ought to be. We would like you to tell us, for each of the items on the list below, whether or not you think teenagers in general ought to be like that, and how strongly you feel about it.

"Do you think teenagers in general *ought* to...."	STRONGLY FEEL THEY SHOULD	FEEL THEY SHOULD	DON'T CARE	FEEL THEY SHOULDN'T	STRONGLY FEEL THEY SHOULDN'T
1. Try to please their parents by the things they do.	**	*	0	—	—
2. Have school spirit; know what's going on in school and take part in activities.	**	*	0	—	—
3. Be able to express their feelings freely and "let themselves go."	**	*	0	—	—
4. Try to get average grades, not go "all out" for "A's."	**	*	0	—	—
5. Be intelligent, be able to think clearly about things.	**	*	0	—	—
6. Be well groomed, keep themselves neat and attractive.	**	*	0	—	—
7. Have good taste in clothes.	**	*	0	—	—
8. Be concerned about other people, *not* be self-centered.	**	*	0	—	—
9. Be modest, *not* try to draw attention to themselves.	**	*	0	—	—
10. Be good at athletics.	**	*	0	—	—
11. Be sincerely religious.	**	*	0	—	—
12. Have respect for other students' wishes and beliefs; *not* be bossy.	**	*	0	—	—

Fig. 1. Continued

"Do you think teenagers in general *ought* to...."	STRONGLY FEEL THEY SHOULD	FEEL THEY SHOULD	DON'T CARE	FEEL THEY SHOULDN'T	STRONGLY FEEL THEY SHOULDN'T
13. Let everybody have his fair say in running things in the school.	**	*	0	—	—
14. Be honest and trustworthy.	**	*─	0	—	—
15. Be generally friendly and sociable, mix with different kinds of students.	**	*─	0	—	—
16. Treat other students as equals, *not* be conceited or snobbish.	**─	*	0	—	—
17. Be quiet and well behaved in school, *not* get into fights.	**	*─	0	—	—
18. Follow all the rules and laws that have been made by those in authority.	**	*─	0	—	—
19. Stay in groups where they are welcome, *not* be "social climbers."	**	*	0─	—	—
20. Live up to strict moral standards.	**	*─	0	—	—
21. Be good at expressing their opinions.	**	*─	0	—	—
22. Be good at dancing.	**	*─	0─	—	—
23. Be able to stick to hard problems, try to do well in school work.	**	*─	0	—	—
24. Go along with what most other students do and stand for, *not* be too different.	**	*	0─	—	—
25. Stand on their own feet, work for things, not seek special favors.	**	*─	0	—	—

137

Fig. 2. Example of information, other than values, provided to describe a white-like or white-unlike stimulus teen-ager.

TEENAGER I

---

1. Sec ____M____ Grade ____9____

2. What program are you taking in school? (If undecided, mark the program you think you will take.)

    0_____ Vocational
    1_____ Commercial
    2__X__ College preparatory
    3_____ General
    4_____ Other_____ (write in)

3. Last year, what kind of grades did you get?

0_____ about an A average	4_____ about a C average
1_____ between an A & B average	5_____ between a C & D average
2__X__ about a B average	6_____ about a D average
3_____ between a B & C average	7_____ below a D average

4. What is your race?

    0__X__ white   1_____Negro   2_____Oriental
    3_____ other (What?_____)

RESULTS AND DISCUSSION

Check on the Manipulation of Belief Congruence

One question answered by the subjects about each of the four stimulus teen-agers was the following:

How much like you would you say Teenager X is?

    0 _____ as much like me as any teenager I can think of
    1 _____ very much like me
    2 _____ a little like me
    3 _____ a little unlike me
    4 _____ very much unlike me
    5 _____ as much unlike me as any teenager I can think of

The subjects' responses to this question served as a check on the manipulation of similarity between the subject and the stimulus teen-agers. Mean responses to this question, for each of the four stimulus teen-agers, may be found in Table 1. It is clear that the white-like (1.63) and Negro-like (1.91) teen-agers are seen as more like the subjects than are the white-unlike (2.76) and Negro-unlike (3.27) teen-agers. The mean of responses to both like teen-agers combined (3.56) differs from the mean of responses to both unlike teen-agers (6.05) at well beyond the .001 level ($t = 6.99$). All individual like-unlike comparisons also yield

Table 1   MEAN RESPONSE TO STIMULUS TEEN-AGERS

QUESTION	N	STIMULUS TEEN-AGER			
		WHITE-LIKE	WHITE-UNLIKE	NEGRO-LIKE	NEGRO-UNLIKE
1. "How friendly"[a]	42	.59	1.69	.83	1.86
2. Social distance scale total score[b]	44	9.84	5.90	7.81	5.54
2A. Individual items on social distance scale[c]					
Invite home to dinner	44	.82	.36	.39	.20
Go to party to which this person was invited	44	1.00	.80	.93	.70
Go to same school	44	1.00	.91	1.00	.91
Have as member of social group	44	.91	.32	.82	.48
Have as speaking acquaintance	44	.91	.59	.91	.59
Live in same apartment house with this person and his (her) family	44	.89	.45	.43	.27
Eat lunch at school with	44	.93	.57	.84	.57
Sit next to in class	44	.98	.70	.93	.73
Close personal friend	44	.80	.27	.59	.32
Work on comittee with	44	.93	.68	.91	.73
Date my sister (brother)	44	.68	.25	.09	.05
3. "How much like you?"[a]	43	1.63	2.76	1.91	3.27

[a]*For these questions, a low score signifies greater friendliness and perceived similarity, respectively.*
[b]*Scoring: 1 for "yes," 0 for "no"; 11 points possible.*
[c]*Scores run from 0 to 1. A mean of 1.0 signifies endorsement of the item by everyone.*

t values significant at beyond the .001 level (*p* values reported henceforth are all two-tailed). From these data we may conclude that the manipulation of similarity or dissimilarity between the subjects and the stimulus teen-agers has been successful.

"Friendliness" Question

The first question the subject answered about each stimulus teen-ager was the following:

If you met this teenager for the first time, what would your immediate reaction be?

I think I would feel:

    0 _____ quite friendly
    1 _____ a little friendly
    2 _____ nothing either way
    3 _____ a little unfriendly
    4 _____ quite unfriendly

This question was intended to be a nearly pure measure of "affect"; that is, a measure of the subject's overall reaction to each stimulus teen-ager. The mean responses with respect to each of the teen-agers are given in Row 1 of Table 1.

Subjects would feel most friendly towards the white-like teen-ager (.59), followed by the Negro-like (.83), white-unlike (1.69), and Negro-unlike (1.86) teen-agers. An analysis of variance[6] using McNemar's (1955, p. 330) Case XIV mixed model reveals that belief congruence accounts for a much larger part of the variance of responses than does race, although the effects for both race and belief are significant. (F for the belief effect = 37.72, $p < .001$; F for the race effect = 5.21, $p < .05$.) This result, of course, is consistent with Rokeach's theory.

This question was also asked, in a somewhat different format, on the "pretest" questionnaire mentioned earlier. At that time subjects were asked to respond to a list of many different individuals, of which one was "A Negro teen-ager." Of the subjects in the present experiment, 35 answered this item on the pretest. An interesting finding emerges when we compare responses to "A Negro teen-ager," with no other information, with responses to Negro-like and Negro-unlike in the present study.

A rather obvious expectation is that the mean of responses to "A Negro teen-ager" should fall between the means for Negro-like and Negro-unlike. This is the case. Means for those subjects present on both occasions ($N = 35$) are given in Table 2. (They are .91, 1.34, and 1.80 for Negro-like, Negro teen-ager, and Negro-unlike, respectively.) Subjects feel significantly more friendly towards the Negro-like teen-ager than towards the Negro teen-ager ($t = 2.08$, $p < .05$) and significantly more friendly towards the Negro teenager than towards the Negro-unlike teen-ager ($t = 2.88$, $p < .01$).

One should also expect that subjects' responses to the Negro teen-ager should correlate moderately both with responses to Negro-like and Negro-unlike. This

Table 2 ANALYSIS OF RESPONSES ON THE "FRIENDLINESS" SCALE TOWARDS VARIOUS STIMULUS TEEN-AGERS (N = 35)

STIMULUS TEEN-AGER	M[a]	σ^2	COMPARISON	CORRELATION	t BETWEEN MEANS	t BETWEEN VARIANCES
Negro-like	.91	.48	Negro-like versus Negro teen-ager	.15	2.08*	2.31*
Negro teen-ager[b]	1.34	.99	Negro teen-ager versus Negro-unlike	.62***	2.88**	< 1
Negro-unlike	1.80	1.13	Negro-like versus Negro-unlike	.29	4.68***	3.01**

[a]*A low score indicates greater friendliness towards the stimulus teen-ager.*
[b]*From pretest questionnaire.*
*$p < .05$.
**$p < .01$.
***$p < .001$.

[6] All analyses of variance reported follow this model.

should be the case unless, for some reason, subjects have an expectation that Negro teen-agers in general are either like them or unlike them. Again referring to Table 2, we note that the correlation between Negro-like and Negro teen-ager is .15 and the correlation between Negro-like and Negro-unlike is .29. Neither of these correlations is large enough to be considered significantly different from zero. (The *CR* for the correlation of .29 reaches the .09 level of significance.) The correlation between Negro teen-ager and Negro-unlike, however, is .62, significant at beyond the .001 level, and also significantly different from the other two correlations, at the .01 and .05 levels, respectively.

These differences would seem to demonstrate an important point: namely, when our white subjects are given no information at all about a Negro teen-ager, they apparently assume that he is different from them in values and react towards him accordingly. It should be noted here, referring again to Table 2, that the variance of responses to the Negro-like teen-ager is significantly smaller than the variance of the other two distributions. Some caution must be exercised in the interpretation of the differences between the correlations for this reason. Our data from the question "How much like you would you say Teenager X is?" add further information, however. On that question, the subjects perceived the Negro stimulus teen-agers to be significantly less like them than were the white teen-agers, even when given the same information about both. The mean of responses to Negro-like and Negro-unlike teen-agers combined was 5.33, while the mean for like and unlike white teen-agers was 4.44 (t for this difference is 3.29, $p < .01$). That is, with belief similarity held constant, the subjects perceived that the white stimulus teen-agers were more like them, given *identical* information about the whites and Negroes. These results parallel findings reported by Byrne and Wong (1962, p. 247, Table 1), in which white subjects attributed greater similarity of attitudes to unknown whites than to unknown Negroes. Our data further indicate the expectation held by the subjects that a Negro teen-ager, simply by virtue of his being a Negro, will be different from them. It seems likely that their propensity to react negatively towards the Negro is based on this expectation, or, equally compatible with the obtained relationship, for persons sharing the anti-Negro prejudices endemic in American society, the sheer fact that a person is Negro marks him as significantly "different," however similar he may be in other respects.

Social Distance Scale

Our major measure of reactions to the four stimulus teen-agers was the following "teen-age social distance scale":

Everyone has his own preferences about the people he wants to associate with. There are probably some people with whom you would be willing to be very good friends, and others whom you would just as soon not ever be with. We would like you to tell us how close a relationship you think you would be willing to have with TEENAGER X. Check the blank under "yes" for each statement you agree with, and the blank under "no" for each statement you disagree with for TEENAGER X. Guess if you aren't really sure.

I think I would be willing:

Yes No

        to invite this person home to dinner
        to go to a party to which this person was invited
        to go to the same school with this person
        to have this person as a member of my social group or club
        to have this person as one of my speaking acquaintances
        to live in the same apartment house with this person and his family
        to eat lunch with this person in school
        to sit next to this person in class
        to have this person as a close personal friend
        to work on a committee at school with this person
        to have this person date my sister [brother]

This social distance scale, which was devised for the pretest questionnaire, was patterned after that of Triandis. Items were changed, omitted, and added to make the scale suitable for teen-age subjects; for example, no negative items were used, on the assumption that they would not discriminate between the subjects. Total scores on the scale were obtained by simply summing responses to the 11 items, each scored "1" for "yes" and "0" for "no."

Responses to the social distance scale were analyzed in two ways. First, an analysis of variance of the total scores was computed; results are presented in Table 3. As in the analysis of the "friendliness" question, belief accounts for by far the largest amount of the variance, although effects for both race and belief are highly significant. (F for race $= 7.20$, $p < .02$; F for belief $= 48.51$, $p < .001$.) Then, t tests for both race and belief effects were calculated for each of the 11 items. That is, each subject's responses to the two Negro stimulus teen-agers were combined, and his responses to the two white stimulus teen-agers were combined. The t between the means of these scores evaluates the race effect. The belief effect was tested similarly, by combining responses to the two like teen-agers and comparing the mean of these scores with the mean of the summed responses to the two unlike teen-agers.

The t-test analysis, presented in Table 4, adds more specific information concerning the areas in which race and belief effects are strongest. It is clear that

Table 3 ANALYSIS OF VARIANCE OF TOTAL SOCIAL DISTANCE SCALE SCORES

SOURCE	SS	df	F
Individuals (A)	528.11	43	—
Race (B)	62.64	1	7.20*
Belief (C)	423.46	1	48.51**
A × B	374.11	43	< 1
A × C	375.29	43	< 1
B × C	30.28	1	< 1
A × B × C	9,225.11	43	—
		175	

*$p < .02$.
**$p < .001$.

Table 4   SOCIAL DISTANCE SCALE ITEM COMPARISONS WITH RESPECT TO
BELIEF AND RACE ($N = 44$)

ITEMS IN SOCIAL DISTANCE SCALE	t FOR BELIEF[a]	t FOR RACE[b]
1. Invite home to dinner	4.57**	5.00**
2. Go to party to which this person was invited	4.30**	2.00
3. Go to same school	2.57*	< 1
4. Have as member of social group	7.75**	< 1
5. Have as speaking acquaintance	4.92**	< 1
6. Live in same apartment house	5.36**	4.92**
7. Eat lunch at school with	4.92**	< 1
8. Sit next to in class	4.00**	< 1
9. Close personal friend	6.15**	1.23
10. Work on committee with	3.75**	< 1
11. Date my sister (brother)	4.80**	6.67**

[a] *Based on the difference in mean response to like and unlike stimulus teen-agers, regardless of race: (white-like + Negro-like) − (white-unlike + Negro-unlike).*
[b] *Based on the difference in mean response to white and Negro stimulus teen-agers, regardless of whether like or unlike: (white-like + white-unlike) − (Negro-like + Negro-unlike).*
$*p < .02.$
$**p < .001.$

belief has a very strong effect on all 11 items. All but one of the differences between responses to like and unlike teen-agers are significant at beyond the .001 level; the difference on the item concerning "Go to the same school" is significant at the .02 level. The race effect, however, appears to be specific to three items: "Invite him home to dinner," "Live in the same apartment house," and "Have him date my sister [brother]." These 3 items on which the race effect is significant at beyond the .001 level seem to be "sensitive areas," ones in which there is widespread resistance, in American society, to Negro-white contacts. Rokeach (Rokeach et al., 1960) has stated that his theory applies "insofar as psychological processes are involved ... [p. 135]." As an example of institutionalized racial prejudice outside the framework of his theory he later states "the southern white bigot would not want his daughter to marry the 'good' Negro any more than the 'bad' one [p. 165]." In Rokeach's sense, the present "sensitive" items would seem to fall in the latter category. Clearly, an empirical definition of institutional prejudice in terms of an obtained "race effect" would be circular and meaningless. For purposes of future research, we would suggest two criteria for situations that may be expected to produce a "race effect": intimacy of contact and presence of others—in this case parents—who are the enforcers of social norms. At present, all we can state from our empirical finding is that a belief effect is strong on all the items, whereas a race effect occurs on items that appear to involve publicly visible relationships that are "sensitive" or controversial by prevailing cultural standards.

One further set of data is available, from the pretest, which provides an important comparison with the results of the social distance scale in the present study. On the pretest, subjects were asked to respond, on the same "teen-ager social distance scale," to stimulus teen-agers who resembled quite closely the stimulus individuals used by Triandis. "Same or different philosophy" and "same or different religion" which he used as variables were omitted. Our stimulus teen-agers were all stated to be Christians, and varied only in race, white versus Negro, and in status. For the status variable, program in school and grades were varied. The teen-agers were thus described as either "in the college preparatory program getting Bs" or "in the vocational program getting failing grades." Again, there were four stimulus teen-agers: white, low status; white, high status; Negro, low status; and Negro, high status.

The results of the analysis of variance of total scores on the social distance scale, in response to these four stimulus teen-agers, are given in Table 5. In this case, there is a very large race effect ($F = 45.50$, $p < .001$), about twice as large as a smaller, but still highly significant status effect ($F = 28.52$, $p < .001$), in terms of percentage of variance explained. These results, obtained on 37 of the 44 subjects used in the later study, resemble quite closely those obtained by Triandis. When belief is not a variable, as in these data, or when the belief effect is weakened by the ambiguity of the information provided, as in Triandis' data, both race and status account for appreciable portions of the variance, with race being by far the more important variable.

The explanation for all of these data, it would seem, is to be found in a very simple fact. Individuals make judgments about others on the basis of all of the relevant information they possess. If little information is provided, and a judgment is demanded, it is made on the basis of inferences from past experiences or information obtained from others. That first impressions are seldom accurate is due to the fact that very little information is available, and the person must be judged on the basis of some known group membership. The correlations presented earlier, between responses to Negro-like, Negro teen-ager, and Negro-unlike, seem to indicate that the inference made by most subjects about a Negro teen-ager, in the absence of other information, is that he is *unlike* them.

If the foregoing interpretation is correct, the very large race effects obtained by Triandis and also demonstrated in the pretest data are easily accounted for. The subjects are forced to guess at the belief systems of the stimulus individuals, and their guess is that the Negro is unlike them. Our subjects in this situation respond with a very large "race effect." When essentially the same subjects were provided, in the later study, with actual information about the belief systems of the stimulus individuals, they no longer had to guess, and they responded

Table 5 ANALYSIS OF VARIANCE OF TOTAL SOCIAL DISTANCE SCALE SCORES, PRETEST DATA

SOURCE	SS	df	F
Individuals (A)	408.77	36	—
Race (B)	283.95	1	45.50*
Status (C)	134.33	1	28.52*
A × B	224.80	36	< 1
A × C	169.42	36	< 1
B × C	10.28	1	< 1
A × B × C	8,695.45	36	—

*p < .001.

primarily, though not exclusively, in terms of the information about belief congruence with which they had been provided.

CONCLUSIONS

The data presented strongly support Rokeach's theory that the variable of belief congruence accounts for a major portion of the variance in prejudice, if it does not tell the "whole truth" about it. The teen-age subjects in this study, when given extensive information concerning the belief systems of stimulus teen-agers, react primarily in terms of similarity of beliefs and only very secondarily in terms of race. This was the case in an analysis of total scores on a social distance scale, and in an analysis of "friendliness" responses. Strong "race effects" were obtained on "sensitive" items on the social distance scale, perhaps reflecting institutionalized areas of prejudice, and on total social distance scores when information concerning belief systems was not provided.[7]

Not only do our results support Rokeach's contention regarding the primacy of belief congruence, but they also account for the discrepancy between the findings reported by Rokeach et al. (1960) and by Byrne and Wong (1962), on the one hand, and those reported by Triandis (1961), on the other. When subjects are forced to evaluate stimulus individuals in terms of their beliefs, then belief congruence is more important than race. But when the belief component is not provided, spelled out in considerable detail, subjects will react in racial terms on the basis of assumptions concerning the belief systems of others, and of emotional or institutionalized factors. The practical implications of these results are obvious. If people of different races encounter one another under conditions favoring the perception of belief congruence (as, for example, in equal-status contacts), then racial prejudice should be substantially reduced.

REFERENCES

Byrne, D. Interpersonal attraction and attitude similarity. *Journal of Abnormal and Social Psychology,* 1961, *62,* 713–15.

Byrne, D., & Wong, T. J. Racial prejudice, interpersonal attraction, and assumed dissimilarity of attitudes. *Journal of Abnormal and Social Psychology,* 1962, *65,* 246–53.

McNemar, Q. *Psychological statistics.* New York: Wiley, 1955.

Morris, C. *Varieties of human value.* Chicago: Univer. Chicago Press, 1956.

Rokeach, M.(Ed.) *The open and closed mind.* New York: Basic Books, 1960.

Rokeach, M. Belief versus race as determinants of social distance: Comment on Triandis' paper. *Journal of Abnormal and Social Psychology,* 1961, *62,* 187–88.

Rokeach, M., Smith, Patricia W., & Evans, R. I. Two kinds of prejudice or one? In M. Rokeach (Ed.), *The open and closed mind.* New York: Basic Books, 1960, 132–68.

Triandis, H. C. A note on Rokeach's theory of prejudice. *Journal of Abnormal and Social Psychology,* 1961, *62,* 184–86.

[7]Current research by one of the authors (DDS) replicates these findings for white ninth grade subjects in an Eastern school system in which there were substantial numbers of Negro students.

The Spatial Ecology of Group Formation

LEON FESTINGER, STANLEY SCHACHTER, KURT BACK

Human ecology has dealt mainly with the study of the distribution of persons, institutions, or any social phenomena in space. Among the concerns of the human ecologist have been studies of the spatial distribution and patterning of such things as delinquency, truancy, crime, vice, suicide, mental disorders, divorce, desertion, poverty, mortality, etc. Almost without exception these studies have followed a common pattern—a relatively large area, such as a metropolitan region, is subdivided into a number of zones or enumeration districts in each of which the rate of occurrence of a particular social phenomenon is computed. Little attention has been devoted to the possible effects of the spatial arrangement of smaller areas such as neighborhoods, nor has attention been focused on the relations between ecological factors and the formation of friendship and face-to-face groups.

Stouffer[1] in a study of mobility says, "Whether one is seeking to explain 'why' persons go to a particular place to get jobs, 'why' they go to trade at a particular store, 'why' they go to a particular neighborhood to commit a crime, or 'why' they marry the particular spouse they choose, the factor of spatial distance is of obvious significance."

Direct research on the ecological determinants of friendship and group formation has, however, been minimal. A few studies[2,3] have examined the relationship between distance and marriage selection. Such studies show that there is an inverse relationship between the distance separating potential marriage partners and the number of marriages. Thus, in New Haven, 76 per cent of the marriages in 1940 were between persons living within twenty blocks of each other and 35 per cent between persons living within five blocks of each other.[3]

While such findings may not seem surprising, it is less obvious that differences in distance as small as twenty or thirty feet would play a major part in determining friendships. Within the Westgate and Westgate West housing projects, however, even these small differences in distance are effective in determining patterns of friendship. This chapter outlines the relationships

[1] Stouffer, S.A., "Intervening Opportunities: A Theory Relating Mobility and Distance." *American Sociological Review*, Vol. 5, pp. 845–67, 1940.

[2] Abrams, R.H., "Residential Propinquity as a Factor in Marriage Selection." *American Sociological Review*, Vol. 8, pp. 288–94, 1943.

[3] Kennedy, R., "Premarital Residential Propinquity." *American Journal of Sociology*, Vol. 48, pp. 580–84, 1943.

between the physical environment and the sociometric structure of these two communities.

THE ECOLOGICAL BASES OF FRIENDSHIP

In communities such as Westgate or Westgate West, where people moving into the area have few or no previous contacts in the community, friendships are likely to develop on the basis of the brief and passive contacts made going to and from home or walking about the neighborhood. These brief meetings, if they are frequent enough, may develop into nodding acquaintanceships, then into speaking relationships, and eventually, if psychological factors are right, into friendships. Such casual or involuntary meetings we will call passive contacts.

Passive contacts are determined by the required paths followed in entering or leaving one's home for any purpose. For example, in going from one's door to the stairway one must pass certain apartments; in walking to the butcher shop one must go by certain houses. These specific required paths are determined by the physical structure of the area.

In relating physical structure to the formation of friendships, it is necessary to distinguish between two ecological factors, (1) physical distance, and (2) positional relationships and features of design which we may call functional distance.

1. Physical distance is measured distance and is one of the major determinants of whether or not passive contacts will occur. Obviously there is a high negative relationship between the physical distance separating the homes of two people and the probability that these people will make passive contact. The smaller the physical distance the greater the number of required paths neighbors are likely to share and the greater the probability of passive contacts. For example, in hanging clothes out to dry, or putting out the garbage, or simply sitting on the porch one is much more likely to meet next-door neighbors than people living four or five houses away.

2. Factors such as the design of a building or the positional relationships among a group of houses are also important determinants of which people will become friends. It is these functional factors of design and position which determine the specific pattern of required paths in an area and consequently determine which people will meet. For example, if there is a stairway at each end of a floor, there is a good chance that people living at opposite ends of the floor will never or rarely meet. Functional distance is measured by the number of passive contacts that position and design encourage.

Both physical distance and functional distance, therefore, will affect the pattern and number of passive contacts. Obviously, they cannot be considered as independent variables, for we can expect a high relationship between the two. In particular cases, however, the distinction becomes clear. For example, two back-to-back houses which are thirty feet apart and have neither back doors nor back yards would be considered functionally farther apart than two back-to-back houses, also thirty feet apart, which do have back doors and yards. Thus we can have varying functional distances while physical distance remains constant.

THE EFFECT OF PHYSICAL DISTANCE ON THE
FORMATION OF FRIENDSHIPS

Figure 3 is a schematized representation of the front of a Westgate West building. The porch area provides the only means of entering or leaving the building and is, therefore, the only place within the building in which passive contacts can occur. Each of the doorways is the entrance to a different apartment and the numbers on the doorways will be used to designate each apartment position. Each floor consists of five directly adjoining apartments and the two floors are connected by stairways at each end of the porch. With two exceptions the doorways of all adjoining apartments are separated by almost 19 feet. Apartments 3 and 4 and apartments 8 and 9 are separated by 32 feet. The maximum separation on any one floor is the 88 feet between the end apartments.

In order to simplify the presentation of data we have adopted a unit of approximate physical distance to describe the difference between any two apartments in a building. Each unit is the equivalent of the physical distance separating any two neighboring doorways. Thus, in Figure 3, apartments 1 and 2 are one unit of approximate physical distance apart; apartments 1 and 3 are two units apart; apartments 1 and 5 and apartments 6 and 10 are four units apart, and so on. In specifying the distance between apartments on different floors, the letter S is employed as a symbol for the stairways between the first and second floors. Thus, apartments 9 and 1 are separated by two units of physical distance and a stairway and this distance is designated as 2S; apartments 2 and 7 are separated by 1 unit and a stairway and are 1S units apart, and so on. Despite the fact that the stairway on the right-hand side of the building ends midway between apartments 9 and 10, the units are calculated as if this stairway ended right in front of the door of apartment number 9. This procedure has been adopted for simplicity's sake and makes little difference in our results. Where there are two possible routes connecting any apartment on one floor to any apartment on the other floor, the units are always computed for the shorter route.

In order to study the effect of these physical design features on the formation of friendships we may relate such things as physical distance to sociometric choices. These sociometric data were gathered on all residents of Westgate and 166 of the 170 Westgate West residents by asking, "What three people in Westgate or Westgate West do you see most of socially?"

Table 1 presents the data for Westgate West on choices given to people living in the same building and on the same floor as the person who chooses them. The

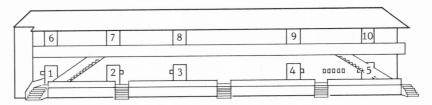

Fig. 3. Schematic Diagram of a Westgate West Building

data for all seventeen Westgate West buildings are grouped since all of these buildings are exactly the same.

In column (1) of Table 1 are listed all the approximate physical distances which can separate any two persons living on the same floor. Column (2) presents the total number of choices given to persons living at each distance away from the people who are choosing. These figures, however, are inadequate in this form because there are great differences in the total number of potential choices between people separated by the various distances. There are, for example, many more 1 unit choices than 4 unit choices possible. These figures in column (2) must, consequently, be corrected on the basis of the total number of such possible choices.

Table 1 THE RELATIONSHIP BETWEEN SOCIOMETRIC CHOICE AND PHYSICAL
DISTANCE ON ONE FLOOR OF A WESTGATE WEST BUILDING

(1)	*(2)*	*(3)*	*(4)*
UNITS OF APPROXIMATE PHYSICAL DISTANCE	*TOTAL NUMBER OF CHOICES GIVEN*	*TOTAL NUMBER OF POSSIBLE CHOICES*	$\dfrac{\textit{CHOICES GIVEN (2)}}{\textit{POSSIBLE CHOICES (3)}}$
1	112	8 × 34	.412
2	46	6 × 34	.225
3	22	4 × 34	.162
4	7	2 × 34	.103

Column (3) presents the correction factors for each distance of separation between apartments. The figures in this column represent the total number of choices that could exist in the entire Westgate West project at each separation distance. Thus, at three units distance, there are four possible choices within any one floor; apartments 4 to 1, 5 to 2, 1 to 4, and 2 to 5 on the first floor or, symmetrically, apartments 9 to 6, 10 to 7, 6 to 9, and 7 to 10 on the second floor. Since there are seventeen buildings, each with two floors, the number of possible choices at each distance is multiplied by thirty-four. Column (4) presents the corrected sociometric choices at each distance. These figures are arrived at by dividing the figures in column (2) by those in column (3). They state specifically the percentage of possible choices at each distance that were actually made. Thus, 41.2 per cent of the 272 possible one unit choices were actually made; 22.5 per cent of the 204 possible two unit choices were made.

The data in Table 1 show unequivocally that within the floor of a Westgate West building there is a high relationship between friendships and physical distance. The greatest percentage of possible choices are made to next-door neighbors. These percentages decrease constantly with distance to a minimum of 10.3 per cent of all choices that could be exchanged between people four units apart, that is, between those who live at opposite ends of the same floor. It must be remembered that these distances are actually small. Neighboring apartments are about 22 feet apart and apartments at opposite ends of the same floor are only 88 feet apart. Yet these small differences in distance seem to be major determinants of whether or not friendships will form.

These choices given to people living on the same floor represent a very sizeable proportion of the total number of choices given. Forty-four per cent of the 426 choices made were given to people living on the same floor as the chooser.

We find a similar relationship of sociometric choice to physical distance in choices given to people living in the same building but on a different floor. Table 2 presents data for between-floor choices. The meaning of each of the columns is the same as in Table 1. The letter S in column (1) is the symbol for stairway.

Table 2 THE RELATIONSHIP OF SOCIOMETRIC CHOICES BETWEEN FLOORS OF A WESTGATE WEST BUILDING TO PHYSICAL DISTANCE

(1)	(2)	(3)	(4)
UNITS OF APPROXIMATE PHYSICAL DISTANCE	TOTAL NUMBER OF CHOICES GIVEN	TOTAL NUMBER OF POSSIBLE CHOICES	CHOICES GIVEN (2) / POSSIBLE CHOICES (3)
S	14	2 × 34	.206
1S	39	6 × 34	.191
2S	20	8 × 34	.074
3S	14	7 × 34	.059
4S	4	2 × 34	.059

The data in Table 2 show a high relationship between choices exchanged among people living on different floors of the same barracks and the distance between these people. Again, those people having the smallest physical separation give each other the highest proportion of the total number of possible choices. Thus, 20.6 per cent of the 68 possible choices are made at S units, the shortest possible distance between apartments on different floors. These percentages decrease constantly with increasing distance to a low point of 5.9 per cent of possible choices between apartments with a separation of 3S or 4S units of approximate physical distance.

Whereas 44 per cent of the total number of sociometric choices in Westgate West were made to others on their own floor, only 21 per cent of the total choices were made between floors.

The data in columns (4) of Tables 1 and 2 are presented graphically in Figure 4. This figure plots the percentage of the total possible choices made at each approximate physical distance for choices within the same floor and choices between floors. Both curves are monotonically decreasing curves.

Though both curves decrease there are differences between them. The curve for same-floor choices drops sharply from point to point. The first two points of the curve for between-floor choices are at about the same level. The curve then drops and the next three points again are all at about the same low level. Both curves are, in part, affected by functional factors but positional relationships have played so strong a part in shaping the between-floor curve that it may well be considered more a curve of functional than of physical distance.

Data on the effects of physical distance on friendship formation are more difficult to obtain for Westgate. Within any one court there are houses next to

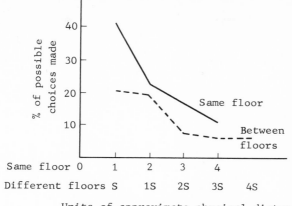

Fig. 4. Relationship Between Physical Distance and Sociometric Choices in Westgate West

one another and houses facing one another. Some of the back-to-back houses have back doors while others do not, and so on. Even if one wishes to ignore the possible effects of different functional relationships throughout this community, it would be almost impossible to compute the relationship of physical distance per se to friendship formation because of the extreme difficulty of determining the necessary correction factors for the number of possible choices at various distances.

However, for part of each side of a large Westgate U-shaped court it is possible partially to isolate the effect of physical distance. Figure 5 is a schematic representation of any pair of the six identically designed courts which face one another across the street dividing the project in two (see Figure 2). Each of the letters in Figure 5 represents a different house. The houses lettered *b, c, d, e, f,* and those lettered *l, k, j, i, h* are approximately arranged in rows and are somewhat similar in this respect to the five apartments on each floor of a Westgate West building. The end houses *a* and *m* are not included in this grouping because they face onto the street whereas all of the other houses in the row face into the courtyard.

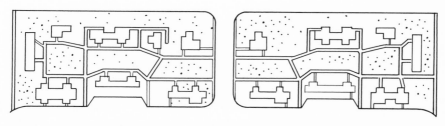

Fig. 5. Schematic Diagram of the Arrangement of the Westgate Court

Analysis of the sociometric choices exchanged among the people living in each row of houses follows the same pattern as the analysis of choices among apartments on the same floor of a Westgate West building. Distance between houses is again handled in terms of units of approximate physical distance. Thus, *b* is separated from *c* by one unit, from *d* by two units, and so on. The average measured distance between houses is about 45 feet. Choices are again categorized according to the units of distance separating the house of the person chosen from that of the person choosing. The data for all twelve rows are pooled and are presented in Table 3. Again, there is the same marked relationship between sociometric choice and physical distance. The greatest proportion of possible choices is made to next-door neighbors. This proportion decreases with increasing distance to the low point of no choices at all to people living four units away.

Table 3 THE RELATIONSHIP OF SOCIOMETRIC CHOICES AMONG THE HOUSES IN A ROW IN WESTGATE COURTS TO PHYSICAL DISTANCE

(1) *UNITS OF APPROXIMATE PHYSICAL DISTANCE*	*(2)* *TOTAL NUMBER OF CHOICES GIVEN*	*(3)* *TOTAL NUMBER OF POSSIBLE CHOICES*	*(4)* *CHOICES GIVEN (2)* *POSSIBLE CHOICES (3)*
1	26	8 × 12	.271
2	6	6 × 12	.083
3	2	4 × 12	.042
4	0	2 × 12	.000

These data are presented graphically in Figure 6. The curve is similar to the one obtained for choices within one floor of a Westgate West building.

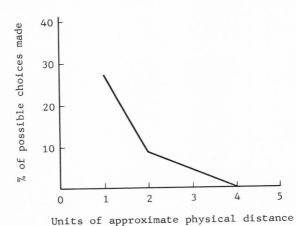

Fig. 6. Relationship Between Physical Distance and Sociometric Choices Along Each Side of the Westgate Courts

In summary, data for two differently designed housing projects show a strong relationship between sociometric choice and physical distance. In both projects the greatest number of choices were made to people living closest to the person choosing and the choices decreased continuously as distance from the home of the chooser increased. The actual measured distances involved were quite small, in no case being larger than 180 feet. Yet the effect of even these small distances is so marked that in a Westgate row no choices at all were made between houses with the maximum separation of four units or 180 feet.

THE EFFECT OF PHYSICAL DISTANCE ON CHOICES OUTSIDE OF OWN COURT OR BUILDING

The data presented so far have explored the relationships between sociometric choices and physical distances within a court or building. This same relationship holds for choices outside of the court or building. The greater the physical separation between any two points in these communities, the fewer the friendships. Table 4 presents the data for choices given by Westgaters to people living anywhere in the two projects. Column (1) lists the places of residence of the people chosen. "Own court" refers to a choice made within the court of the chooser; "adjacent court" refers to choices given to people living in immediately neighboring courts. "Other courts" refers to any choice within Westgate which does not fall into the first two categories. "Westgate West" includes all choices given by Westgaters to people in Westgate West. In the order given, these categories approximate a continuum of physical distance. In general, though not in all cases, "own court" choices are physically closer than "adjacent court" choices and so on.

Table 4 SOCIOMETRIC CHOICES GIVEN BY WESTGATERS TO PEOPLE LIVING ANYWHERE IN THE TWO PROJECTS

(1) LOCATION OF PERSON CHOSEN	(2) TOTAL NUMBER OF CHOICES	(3) TOTAL NUMBER OF POSSIBILITIES	(4) $\dfrac{\text{CHOICES GIVEN (2)}}{\text{POSSIBLE CHOICES (3)}}$
Own court	143	1076	.133
Adjacent court	51	2016	.025
Other courts	47	6794	.007
Westgate West	17	17,000	.001

Table 4 makes it obvious that the relationship between physical distance and sociometric choice holds for out-of-court choices as well as in-court choices. Column (4) again shows that the percentage of possible choices made decreases with increasing distance.

The data for Westgate West presents a similar picture. Table 5 shows that for Westgate West, too, there is an inverse relationship between the percentage of possible choices actually made and physical distance.

Table 5 SOCIOMETRIC CHOICES GIVEN BY WESTGATE WEST PEOPLE TO
PEOPLE LIVING ANYWHERE IN THE TWO PROJECTS

(1) LOCATION OF PERSON CHOSEN	(2) TOTAL NUMBER OF CHOICES MADE	(3) TOTAL NUMBER OF POSSIBILITIES	(4) CHOICES GIVEN (2) / POSSIBLE CHOICES (3)
Own buildings	278	1530	.182
Own quadrangle	49	4000	.012
Other buildings	66	23,200	.003
Westgate	33	17,000	.002

THE EFFECT OF FUNCTIONAL DISTANCE ON THE FORMATION OF FRIENDSHIPS

In describing the six large Westgate courts we mentioned that, with the exception of the end houses at the tips of the U, all of the houses constituting a court face into the courtyard area. All but two of these end houses face out onto the street which runs through the project. In Figure 2, such houses would be numbers 8 and 20 in Tolman court, 21 and 33 in Carson court, and so on. The only exceptions are number 34 in Williams and 59 in Howe. These two end houses face into the courtyard.

Because of these differences in position we can expect marked functional differences between these end houses and the rest of the houses in the court. It is possible to come and go from the end houses facing the street without ever passing the homes of court neighbors. One can work in the garden or sit out on the porch and only rarely meet court neighbors. None of these things are true for the houses facing into the court. Therefore, we can expect that the people living in the end houses facing the street will have far fewer passive contacts with their court neighbors than will people living in houses facing into the court. If the hypothesis be true that in this community the formation of friendships depends upon the extent of passive contacts, the people living in these end houses will receive fewer sociometric choices from their court neighbors than will the people living in houses facing into the court.

Table 6 shows the number of choices given to people living in each house position for the six large courts. The letters in Row 1 symbolize each house position and correspond to the letters in Figure 5. The letters *a* and *m* stand for the end houses in each court. Row 2 is the total number of choices received by people living in each house position from people living in their own court. The mean number of choices received by people in each position is presented in Row 3. The unbracketed figures in column *a* are the total and mean choices received by all six of the end houses in this position. It should be kept in mind, however, that only four of these six houses face out on the street, the other two facing into the court. The figures in brackets are the total and mean choices received by the four houses facing the street.

Table 6 THE NUMBER OF SOCIOMETRIC CHOICES RECEIVED FROM THEIR COURT NEIGHBORS BY PEOPLE LIVING IN EACH HOUSE POSITION IN THE SIX LARGE WESTGATE COURTS

	a	b	c	d	e	f	g	h	i	j	k	l	m
1. House position	a	b	c	d	e	f	g	h	i	j	k	l	m
2. Total number of choices received	(1)* 4	9	7	10	11	6	13	11	9	8	10	9	5
3. Mean number of choices received	(.25)* .67	1.50	1.17	1.67	1.83	1.00	2.17	1.83	1.50	1.33	1.67	1.50	.83

Mean number of choices received by all inner houses facing into the court (b–l) = 1.56
Mean number of choices received by all end houses facing the street (a and m) = 0.60
*Total and mean not including the end houses facing into their courts

Examination of the figures in this table makes it clear that the people living in these end houses receive fewer choices than the people living in any other house position. The mean number of choices received by people living in end houses facing the street is 0.60 and by people living in inner court houses is 1.56. This difference is consistent throughout. In each of the six courts the inner court residents receive a larger mean number of choices than the residents in end houses facing the street.[4]

Let us now examine the effects of functional distance in Westgate West. Figure 3 shows that each building has a long porch on each floor with the entrances to each apartment opening out onto the porch. Short stairways lead up to each of the lower-floor apartments. Outside stairways at each end of the lower-floor porch connect the two floors, and form the only paths by which upper-floor people can reach their floor.

The left-hand stairway connecting the two floors passes directly in front of the doorway of apartment 1 and close to the door of apartment 7. The connecting stairway on the right passes close by, though not directly in front of, the doorway to apartment 5, and directly between the doorways of the two right-hand apartments, 9 and 10, on the upper floor.

Each of the lower-floor apartments has a small mailbox directly adjoining its doorway. Near the lower-floor apartment 5 is a cluster of five mailboxes which serve all of the upper-floor apartments.

These are the details of construction which of themselves will determine the required paths followed in moving in or out of the building. From the nature of these details of design and the required paths they impose on the residents of these buildings, it is possible to make a number of derivations about the relative frequency of passive contacts and, consequently, the sociometric choices exchanged among particular people or groups of people living in each of the buildings. These derivations demand only one assumption—that the people living in these barracks will most frequently use the shortest path between their apartment and their destination.

---

[4] Significant at the 3 per cent level of confidence.

1. *The people living in the end apartments 1 and 5 on the lower floor should receive from and give to the upper-floor residents more sociometric choices than the people living in any other apartment on the lower floor.*

We can expect this because apartments 1 and 5 are at the foot of the stairways connecting the two floors and are, therefore, the only lower-floor apartments which upper-floor residents must pass in entering or leaving the building. In using the left-hand stairway, upper-floor people must pass directly in front of the doorway of apartment 1. In using the right-hand stairway, upper-floor people pass close to, though not directly in front of, the doorway of apartment 5. In going to their mailboxes upper-floor people do pass the doorway of apartment 5.

Table 7 presents the number of sociometric choices lower-floor people give to and receive from people living on the upper floor. The figures in Row 1 are the apartment numbers as diagrammed in Figure 3. Row 2 presents the number of choices the people in each apartment position on the lower floor give to people on the upper floor of their building, and row 3 presents the number of choices lower-floor people receive from their upstairs neighbors. The figures in Rows 2 and 3 are the combined totals for all seventeen buildings.

We see, then, that the end apartments on the lower floor give far more choices to upper-floor people than do any of the other apartments. The end apartments average 12 choices each to upstairs neighbors, compared to only 6.33 for the three middle apartments. Choices given by apartments 1 and 5 are significantly higher than choices given by 2, 3, and 4 at the 5 per cent level of confidence.[5]

Table 7 THE NUMBER OF SOCIOMETRIC CHOICES THE LOWER-FLOOR PEOPLE GIVE TO AND RECEIVE FROM PEOPLE LIVING ON THE UPPER FLOORS OF THE WESTGATE WEST BUILDINGS

	1	2	3	4	5
1. Apartment position	1	2	3	4	5
2. Choices given to upper floor	13	5	8	6	11
3. Choices received from upper floor	14	3	12	4	15

Similarly, the end apartments receive more choices from the upper floor than do any of their lower-floor neighbors. They receive an average of 14.5 choices each and the three middle apartments receive only an average of 6.33 choices apiece. Apartments 1 and 5 differ from apartments 2 and 4 at the 5 per cent level of significance. They do not, however, differ significantly from middle apartment 3.

Clearly the derivation is upheld. The end apartments on the lower floor both give and receive more upper-floor choices than do any of the other lower-floor apartments. A theoretical difficulty, however, exists in the unusually high number of choices which middle apartment 3 receives from the upper floor. Apartment 3 receives twelve choices, while its immediate neighbors,

---

[5] Significance of differences, unless otherwise noted, were calculated by means of an analysis of variance. The significance consequently depends upon the consistency of the results among all the separate buildings.

apartments 2 and 4, receive only three and four choices respectively. Even if, for some reason we know nothing about, upper-floor people should have to pass by apartment 3, they would also have to pass apartments 2 and 4 and passive contacts with upper-floor people should be about the same for all three apartments. We have not been able to find an unequivocal explanation for the large number of choices of apartment 3 by their upstairs neighbors. One possible explanation is that the people in apartment 3, as will be shown later, receive the greatest number of lower-floor choices, and perhaps could meet more upper-floor people through their many lower-floor friends. However, this possible factor seems hardly sufficient to account for the observed data and the high number of upper-floor choices received by apartment 3 remains the one puzzling inconsistency in the body of data.

Table 7 helps to explain the peculiar shape noted in the lower curve in Figure 4 which plots the choices exchanged between floors. This curve has about the same high level for distance units S and 1S, then a sudden drop to a low level at which distances 2S, 3S, and 4S all have about the same value. Distance units S and 1S are made up largely of choices exchanged between end apartments 1 and 5 and the upper floor, while distances 2S, 3S, and 4S are made up predominantly of choices exchanged between the upper floor and the middle apartments 2, 3, and 4. This explanation of the shape of this curve also suggests that for choices between floors, functional distance is far more important than physical distance.

In line with this explanation, we would expect that the end apartments on the first floor would give and receive a high number of upper-floor choices whereas the middle apartments, 2, 3, and 4, would give and receive a uniformly low number of upper-floor choices. Table 7 shows that this is true for choices given to the upper floor and, with the exception of apartment 3, also true for choices received from the upper floor.

2. *Apartments 1 and 6 should exchange more choices than apartments 2 and 7. Similarly, apartments 5 and 10 should exchange more choices than apartments 4 and 9.*

Apartments 1 and 6 and apartments 2 and 7 are both exactly 53 feet apart. However in using the left-hand stairway, the people in apartment 6 must pass by apartment 1, whereas the people living in 7 will not pass by apartment 2. Therefore we can expect that there will be many more passive contacts between 1 and 6 than between 2 and 7, and there should consequently be more choices between 1 and 6 than between 2 and 7. The data substantiate this derivation. Apartments 1 and 6 exchange eleven choices and apartments 2 and 7 only four choices.

The same considerations should apply for choices between 5 and 10 as compared with 4 and 9. These apartments are within seven feet of being equidistant. Apartments 5 and 10 exchange nine choices while 4 and 9 give each other four choices. The Chi Square test for both sets of differences combined is significant at almost the 1 per cent level.

These data give clear evidence that it is possible to have equal physical distances but very different functional distances.

3. *Apartment 7 will choose 6 more than it will choose 8; apartment 9 will choose 10 more than it will choose 8. This will not be true for first-floor apartments in similar positions.*

Apartments 6 and 7 will use predominantly the left-hand stairway. Apartments 9 and 10 will use predominantly the right-hand stairway. Apartment 8, however, which is approximately equidistant from both stairways should sometimes use one end and sometimes the other. Therefore, there should be a greater number of passive contacts between 6 and 7 and between 9 and 10 than between 7 and 8 or 9 and 8. Again the sociometric data bear out the derivation. The choices from apartment 7 to 6 and from apartment 9 to 10 add up to a total of nineteen. They give to apartment 8, however, a total of only ten choices. The Chi Square for this difference is significant at almost the 2 per cent level.

We should not expect this result on the first floor since each of the apartments has its own short stairway leading to the outside of the building. Apartment 2 gives to apartment 1, and 4 gives to 5, a total of twenty choices. Apartments 2 and 4 give seventeen choices to apartment 3. This difference is not significant.

4. *The upper-floor choices apartment 1 gives and receives should be concentrated in apartments 6 and 7 and should taper off for apartments 8, 9, and 10. The upper-floor choices apartment 5 gives and receives should still be heaviest for apartments 9 and 10 but should decrease more gradually for apartments 8, 7 and 6.*

Only apartments 6 and 7 use the left-hand stairway consistently; 8, located between the two stairways, uses it occasionally, and 9 and 10 only rarely if at all. Therefore, apartment 1 will make most contacts with 6 and 7, a few with 8, and almost none at all with 9 and 10. The data in Table 8 support this derivation. Apartment 1 gives ten of its thirteen choices to 6 and 7, two choices to 8, one to 9, and none at all to 10. Of the fourteen choices 1 receives, ten come from apartments 6 and 7, two from 8, and one each from 9 and 10.

Table 8 UPPER-FLOOR CHOICES APARTMENTS 1 AND 5 GIVE AND RECEIVE

Apartment position	6	7	8	9	10
Choices 1 gives	6	4	2	1	0
Choices 1 receives	5	5	2	1	1
Choices 5 gives	1	1	3	2	4
Choices 5 receives	2	1	4	3	5

Numbers 9 and 10 are the only upstairs apartments that use the right-hand connecting stairway consistently in order to leave the building. Though this stairway does not pass directly in front of number 5, the people using it also use the short stairway out from the lower porch which is used by apartment 5 and are likely, therefore, to make contacts with 5. Apartment 8 will use the right-hand stairway occasionally in leaving the building, and 6 and 7 only rarely. In addition, however, upper-floor people who wish to go to their mailboxes will pass apartment 5. Therefore, apartment 5 will make contacts with all upper-floor persons, but the most frequent contacts will be made with 9 and 10. Again the data support the derivation. Table 8 shows that 9 and 10 receive six of the eleven choices apartment 5 makes, 8 receives three choices, and 7 and 6 one choice apiece. Similarly, apartments 9 and 10 give eight of the fifteen upstairs choices 5 receives, and the remaining seven are received from apartments 6, 7, and 8. As predicted, apartment 1 has a heavier concentration of choices in 6 and 7 than does apartment 5 in 9 and 10. Twenty of the twenty-seven choices apartment 1 gives and receives are concentrated in apartments 6 and 7, whereas only fourteen of the twenty-six choices made by and to apartment 5 are centered in apartments 9 and 10. For this difference Chi Square is significant at about the 12 per cent level.

The data so far presented all support the hypotheses from which the numerous derivations about the effects of physical and functional factors were made. These hypotheses stated simply that in these two communities friendships will depend upon the occurrence of passive contacts and that the pattern and frequency of passive contacts among particular people will depend upon the ecological factors of physical and functional distance. The only finding inconsistent with these hypotheses is the large number of choices which the lower-floor middle apartment receives from upper-floor residents. There are, however, implicit in these hypotheses a series of rather interesting derivations which it has been impossible to check because of the great difficulty of isolating the effects of physical and functional distance.

Let us assume that we have a row of five identically designed houses with equal physical distance between any two adjoining houses. For reference we may label these houses a, b, c, d, and e in order along the row.

It is apparent that of all five house positions, the middle house, c, has the minimum total separation from all other houses in the row. The farther a house is from the middle position, the greater is its total physical separation from all other houses in the row.

Let us assume that within any given time interval the probability of a passive contact occurring between residents of houses which are one unit apart is greater than the probability of a contact occurring between residents of houses 2 units apart and so on. The probability of a passive contact occurring between residents living 4 units apart would be lowest.

The resident of house c will generally have made contact with all others living in the row sooner than any other resident. If enough time is allowed to elapse one might be relatively certain that all residents would have had at least one passive contact with all others in the row, but the resident in house c will have had the greatest number of such contacts, the residents of houses b and d the next largest number, and the residents of houses a and e would have had the least number. Therefore, we can expect that if a sociometric test were administered c would receive the greatest number of choices, b and d somewhat fewer choices, and a and e fewest choices of all. Thus, if we plotted a curve of number of choices against house position, we would expect a symmetrical curve monotonically decreasing with distance from the central position. Further, we would expect that as more and more contacts are made among all people living in this row with the passage of time, the curve would tend to flatten out.

To check these derivations specifically against the data available for Westgate and Westgate West is impossible, because in all cases both physical and functional distance have influenced the assignment of sociometric choices. A specific case may illustrate the difficulties involved. The lower floors of the Westgate West buildings resemble the theoretical arrangement of houses suggested above. There are five apartments arranged in a row with roughly equal physical separations between all apartments. Functionally, however, the two end apartments are very different from the middle apartments, for they are at the foot of the stairways connecting the two floors and therefore make many passive contacts with upstairs people. This increased number of between-floor contacts affects the relation the people in the end apartments have with others on their own floor. Table 9 presents the data on the number of choices given to each apartment position by people living on the lower floor. Indeed, there is a peak at the middle apartment. The number of choices received by apartment 3 is greater at the 5 per cent level of significance than the number received by the other lower-floor apartments. Contrary to expectations, apartment 1 receives more choices than 2, and 5 receives more choices than 4.

Table 9 NUMBER OF SOCIOMETRIC CHOICES GIVEN TO EACH LOWER-FLOOR APARTMENT POSITION BY PEOPLE LIVING ON THE LOWER FLOOR

Apartment position	1	2	3	4	5
Number of sociometric choices	22	19	28	11	17

In analyzing the data specifically for choices exchanged between particular apartment positions, we learn that apartment 4 gives 5 a total of nine choices whereas 5 gives 4 only four choices. Similarly, 2 gives eleven choices to apartment 1 and receives nine choices from 1. Thus, the major part of the differences between 5 and 4, and 1 and 2, is made up of unreciprocated choices from 4 and 2 to 5 and 1. The fact that many of these choices go unreciprocated is explained by the functional relationships between the end apartments 1 and 5, and the upper floor. Since these end apartments make so many passive contacts with the upper-floor residents, many of their choices will inevitably go to upper-floor people (see Table 7). Since the sociometric question limited the number of choices to three, it necessarily follows that many of the lower-floor choices to the end apartments must go unreciprocated.

THE ECOLOGICAL BASIS FOR FORMATION OF GROUPS

The data presented have been stated largely in terms of specific friendships between people living in particular house positions. We have shown that, in these two communities, friendships will be determined in large part by physical and functional distance. In terms of these ecological considerations we can further expect that a large proportion of all sociometric choices will be exchanged among people living within the same court or building. We know that in a Westgate court the houses are close to one another and with a few exceptions face into the same area. In general, the people living in each court are both physically and functionally closer to one another than to anyone else living in Westgate. This is obviously also true for the people living in each Westgate West building. The data corroborate the expectation. Of the 426 choices made by

Westgate West people, 278 or 65.3 per cent were given to people living in the same building as the choosers. Similarly for Westgate, 143 or 55.5 per cent of the 258 choices made were given to people living in the same court as the choosers. Further, 85.5 per cent of all people in Westgate West chose at least one person living in the same building and 80 per cent of Westgaters chose at least one person in their court. If the end houses facing the street, which positionally at least are not members of the court, are excluded from this count, the figure for Westgate rises to 87.4 per cent. Thus, a large share of all friendships in both of these communities was among people living in the same court or building.

If one accepts the definition of a group as a number of interacting and sociometrically connected people, it follows that these ecological factors determine not only specific friendships but the composition of groups within these communities as well. Each court and building is populated by people who have most of their friends in the same living unit. Thus the people in each court or building will work together, play together, and, in general, see more of each other than of any other individuals living in the projects.

SUMMARY

The hypothesis has been advanced that friendships and group membership will be determined in these communities by passive contacts between neighbors. The pattern and number of such contacts among particular people will depend upon physical and functional distance. Data have been presented which reveal a striking relationship between these ecological factors and sociometric choice.

Obviously, there are other methods of making friends. The men of the project undoubtedly meet one another in class and school activities. People probably meet at parties, and so on. However, the relationships between ecological and sociometric structures is so very marked that there can be little doubt that in these communities passive contacts are a major determinant of friendship and group formation. Further, we know from the data presented in Chapter 2 that these friendships are very active relationships and compose the major portion of the social lives of these people.

It should be remembered that Westgate and Westgate West represent homogeneous communities. Whether these ecological factors would be as effective in more heterogeneous communities is, of course, a question for further empirical study. It seems likely that in such communities ecological factors will play some part, though a less important one, in determining sociometric structure.

AGGRESSION

4

Transmission of Aggression Through Imitation of Aggressive Models

ALBERT BANDURA, DOROTHEA ROSS, AND SHEILA A. ROSS

A previous study, designed to account for the phenomenon of identification in terms of incidental learning, demonstrated that children readily imitated behavior exhibited by an adult model in the presence of the model (Bandura & Huston, 1961). A series of experiments by Blake (1958) and others (Grosser, Polansky, & Lippitt, 1951; Rosenblith, 1959; Schachter & Hall, 1952) have likewise shown that mere observation of responses of a model has a facilitating effect on subjects' reactions in the immediate social influence setting.

While these studies provide convincing evidence for the influence and control exerted on others by the behavior of a model, a more crucial test

Reprinted from Journal of Abnormal and Social Psychology, 63, *1961, 575–82. Copyright 1961 by the American Psychological Association and reproduced by permission.*

of imitative learning involves the generalization of imitative response patterns to new settings in which the model is absent.

In the experiment reported in this paper children were exposed to aggressive and nonaggressive adult models and were then tested for amount of imitative learning in a new situation in the absence of the model. According to the prediction, subjects exposed to aggressive models would reproduce aggressive acts resembling those of their models and would differ in this respect both from subjects who observed nonaggressive models and from those who had no prior exposure to any models. This hypothesis assumed that subjects had learned imitative habits as a result of prior reinforcement, and these tendencies would generalize to some extent to adult experimenters (Miller & Dollard, 1941).

It was further predicted that observation of subdued nonaggressive models would have a generalized inhibiting effect on the subjects' subsequent behavior, and this effect would be reflected in a difference between the nonaggressive and the control groups, with subjects in the latter group displaying significantly more aggression.

Hypotheses were also advanced concerning the influence of the sex of model and sex of subjects on imitation. Fauls and Smith (1956) have shown that preschool children perceive their parents as having distinct preferences regarding sex appropriate modes of behavior for their children. Their findings, as well as informal observation, suggest that parents reward imitation of sex appropriate behavior and discourage or punish sex inappropriate imitative responses, e.g., a male child is unlikely to receive much reward for performing female appropriate activities, such as cooking, or for adopting other aspects of the maternal role, but these same behaviors are typically welcomed if performed by females. As a result of differing reinforcement histories, tendencies to imitate male and female models thus acquire differential habit strength. One would expect, on this basis, subjects to imitate the behavior of a same-sex model to a greater degree than a model of the opposite sex.

Since aggression, however, is a highly masculine-typed behavior, boys should be more predisposed than girls toward imitating aggression, the difference being most marked for subjects exposed to the male aggressive model.

METHOD

Subjects

The subjects were 36 boys and 36 girls enrolled in the Stanford University Nursery School. They ranged in age from 37 to 69 months, with a mean age of 52 months.

Two adults, a male and a female, served in the role of model, and one female experimenter conducted the study for all 72 children.

Experimental Design

Subjects were divided into eight experimental groups of six subjects each and a control group consisting of 24 subjects. Half the experimental subjects were exposed to aggressive models and half were exposed to models that were subdued and nonaggressive in their behavior. These groups were further subdivided into male and female subjects. Half the subjects in the aggressive and nonaggressive conditions observed same-sex models, while the remaining subjects in each group viewed models of the opposite sex. The control group had no prior exposure to the adult models and was tested only in the generalization situation.

It seemed reasonable to expect that the subjects' level of aggressiveness would be positively related to the readiness with which they imitated aggressive modes of behavior. Therefore, in order to increase the precision of treatment comparisons, subjects in the experimental and control groups were matched individually on the basis of ratings of their aggressive behavior in social interactions in the nursery school.

The subjects were rated on four five-point rating scales by the experimenter and a nursery school teacher, both of whom were well acquainted with the children. These scales measured the extent to which subjects displayed physical aggression, verbal aggression, aggression toward inanimate objects, and aggressive inhibition. The latter scale, which dealt with the subjects' tendency to inhibit aggressive reactions in the face of high instigation, provided a measure of aggression anxiety.

Fifty-one subjects were rated independently by both judges so as to permit an assessment of interrater agreement. The reliability of the composite aggression score, estimated by means of the Pearson product-moment correlation, was .89.

The composite score was obtained by summing the ratings on the four aggression scales; on the basis of these scores, subjects were arranged in triplets and assigned at random to one of two treatment conditions or to the control group.

Experimental Conditions

In the first step in the procedure subjects were brought individually by the experimenter to the experimental room and the model who was in the hallway outside the room, was invited by the experimenter to come and join in the game. The experimenter then escorted the subject to one corner of the room, which was structured as the subject's play area. After seating the child at a small table, the experimenter demonstrated how the subject could design pictures with potato prints and picture stickers provided. The potato prints included a variety of geometrical forms; the stickers were attractive multicolor pictures of animals, flowers, and western figures to be pasted on a pastoral scene. These activities were selected since they had been established, by previous studies in the nursery school, as having high interest value for the children.

After having settled the subject in his corner, the experimenter escorted the model to the opposite corner of the room which contained a small table and chair, a tinker toy set, a mallet, and a 5-foot inflated Bobo doll. The experimenter explained that these were the materials provided for the model to play with and, after the model was seated, the experimenter left the experimental room.

With subjects in the *nonaggressive condition,* the model assembled the tinker toys in a quiet subdued manner totally ignoring the Bobo doll.

In contrast, with subjects in the *aggressive condition,* the model began by assembling the tinker toys but after approximately a minute had elapsed, the model turned to the Bobo doll and spent the remainder of the period aggressing toward it.

Imitative learning can be clearly demonstrated if a model performs sufficiently novel patterns of responses which are unlikely to occur independently of the observation of the behavior of a model and if a subject reproduces these behaviors in substantially identical form. For this reason, in addition to punching the Bobo doll, a response that is likely to be performed by children independently of a demonstration, the model exhibited distinctive aggressive acts which were to be scored as imitative responses. The model laid Bobo on its side, sat on it and punched it repeatedly in the nose. The model then raised the Bobo doll, picked up the mallet and struck the doll on the head. Following the mallet aggression, the model tossed the doll up in the air aggressively and kicked it about the room. This sequence of physically aggressive acts was repeated approximately three times, interspersed with verbally aggressive responses such as, "Sock him in the nose ...," "Hit him down ...," "Throw him in the air ...," "Kick him ...," "Pow ...," and two nonaggressive comments, "He keeps coming back for more" and "He sure is a tough fella."

Thus in the exposure situation, subjects were provided with a diverting task which occupied their attention while at the same time insured observation of the model's behavior in the absence of any instructions to observe or to learn the responses in question. Since subjects could not perform the model's aggressive behavior, any learning that occurred was purely on an observational or covert basis.

At the end of 10 minutes, the experimenter entered the room, informed the subject that he would now go to another game room, and bid the model goodbye.

Aggression Arousal

Subjects were tested for the amount of imitative learning in a different experimental room that was set off from the main nursery school building. The two experimental situations were thus clearly differentiated; in fact, many subjects were under the impression that they were no longer on the nursery school grounds.

Prior to the test for imitation, however, all subjects, experimental and control, were subjected to mild aggression arousal to insure that they were under some degree of instigation to aggression. The arousal experience was included for two main reasons. In the first place, observation of aggressive behavior exhibited by others tends to reduce the probability of aggression on the part of the observer (Rosenbaum & deCharms, 1960). Consequently, subjects in the aggressive condition, in relation both to the nonaggressive and control groups, would be under weaker instigation following exposure to the models. Second, if subjects in the nonaggressive condition expressed little aggression in the face of appropriate instigation, the presence of an inhibitory process would seem to be indicated.

Following the exposure experience, therefore, the experimenter brought the subject to an anteroom that contained these relatively attractive toys: a fire engine, a locomotive, a jet fighter plane, a cable car, a colorful spinning top, and a doll set complete with wardrobe, doll carriage, and baby crib. The experimenter explained that the toys were for the subject to play with but, as soon as the subject became sufficiently involved with the play material (usually in about 2 minutes), the experimenter remarked that these were her very best toys, that she did not let just anyone play with them, and that she had decided to reserve these toys for the other children. However, the subject could play with any of the toys that were in the next room. The experimenter and the subject then entered the adjoining experimental room.

It was necessary for the experimenter to remain in the room during the experimental session; otherwise a number of the children would either refuse to remain alone or would leave before the termination of the session. However, in order to minimize any influence her presence might have on the subject's behavior, the experimenter remained as inconspicuous as possible by busying herself with paper work at a desk in the far corner of the room and avoiding any interaction with the child.

Test for Delayed Imitation

The experimental room contained a variety of toys including some that could be used in imitative or nonimitative aggression, and others that tended to elicit predominantly nonaggressive forms of behavior. The aggressive toys included a 3-foot Bobo doll, a mallet and peg board, two dart guns, and a tether ball with a face painted on it which hung from the ceiling. The nonaggressive toys, on the other hand, included a tea set, crayons and coloring paper, a ball, two dolls, three bears, cars and trucks, and plastic farm animals.

In order to eliminate any variation in behavior due to mere placement of the toys in the room, the play material was arranged in a fixed order for each of the sessions.

The subject spent 20 minutes in this experimental room during which time his behavior was rated in terms of predetermined response categories by judges who observed the session through a one-way mirror in an adjoining observation room. The 20-minute session was divided into 5-second intervals by means of an electric interval timer, thus yielding a total number of 240 response units for each subject.

The male model scored the experimental sessions for all 72 children. Except for the cases in which he served as model, he did not have knowledge of the subjects' group assignments. In order to provide an estimate of interscorer agreement, the performances of half the subjects were also scored independently by a second observer. Thus one or the other of the two observers usually had no knowledge of the conditions to which the subjects were assigned. Since, however, all but two of the subjects in the aggressive condition performed the models' novel aggressive responses while subjects in the other conditions only rarely exhibited such reactions, subjects who were exposed to the aggressive models could be readily identified through their distinctive behavior.

The responses scored involved highly specific concrete classes of behavior and yielded high interscorer reliabilities, the product-moment coefficients being in the .90s.

Response Measures

Three measures of imitation were obtained:

Imitation of physical aggression: This category included acts of striking the Bobo doll with the mallet, sitting on the doll and punching it in the nose, kicking the doll, and tossing it in the air.

Imitative verbal aggression: Subject repeats the phrases, "Sock him," "Hit him down," "Kick him," "Throw him in the air," or "Pow."

Imitative nonaggressive verbal responses: Subject repeats, "He keeps coming back for more," or "He sure is a tough fella."

During the pretest, a number of the subjects imitated the essential components of the model's behavior but did not perform the complete act, or they directed the imitative aggressive response to some object other than the Bobo doll. Two responses of this type were therefore scored and were interpreted as partially imitative behavior.

Mallet aggression: Subject strikes objects other than the Bobo doll aggressively with the mallet.

Sits on Bobo doll: Subject lays the Bobo doll on its side and sits on it, but does not aggress toward it.

The following additional nonimitative aggressive responses were scored:

Punches Bobo doll: Subject strikes, slaps, or pushes the doll aggressively.

Nonimitative physical and verbal aggression: This category included physically aggressive acts directed toward objects other than the Bobo doll and any hostile remarks except for those in the verbal imitation category; e.g., "Shoot the Bobo," "Cut him," "Stupid ball," "Knock over people," "Horses fighting, biting."

Aggressive gun play: Subject shoots darts or aims the guns and fires imaginary shots at objects in the room.

Ratings were also made of the number of behavior units in which subjects played nonaggressively or sat quietly and did not play with any of the material at all.

RESULTS

Complete Imitation of Models' Behavior

Subjects in the aggression condition reproduced a good deal of physical and verbal aggressive behavior resembling that of the models, and their mean scores differed markedly from those of subjects in the nonaggressive and control groups who exhibited virtually no imitative aggression (see Table 1).

Table 1 MEAN AGGRESSION SCORES FOR EXPERIMENTAL AND CONTROL
SUBJECTS

| | EXPERIMENTAL GROUPS | | | | |
| | AGGRESSIVE | | NONAGGRESSIVE | | CONTROL GROUPS |
RESPONSE CATEGORY	F MODEL	M MODEL	F MODEL	M MODEL	
Imitative physical aggression					
Female subjects	5.5	7.2	2.5	0.0	1.2
Male subjects	12.4	25.8	0.2	1.5	2.0
Imitative verbal aggression					
Female subjects	13.7	2.0	0.3	0.0	0.7
Male subjects	4.3	12.7	1.1	0.0	1.7
Mallet aggression					
Female subjects	17.2	18.7	0.5	0.5	13.1
Male subjects	15.5	28.8	18.7	6.7	13.5
Punches Bobo doll					
Female subjects	6.3	16.5	5.8	4.3	11.7
Male subjects	18.9	11.9	15.6	14.8	15.7
Nonimitative aggression					
Female subjects	21.3	8.4	7.2	1.4	6.1
Male subjects	16.2	36.7	26.1	22.3	24.6
Aggressive gun play					
Female subjects	1.8	4.5	2.6	2.5	3.7
Male subjects	7.3	15.9	8.9	16.7	14.3

Since there were only a few scores for subjects in the nonaggressive and control conditions (approximately 70% of the subjects had zero scores), and the assumption of homogeneity of variance could not be made, the Friedman two-way analysis of variance by ranks was employed to test the significance of the obtained differences.

The prediction that exposure of subjects to aggressive models increases the probability of aggressive behavior is clearly confirmed (see Table 2). The main effect of treatment conditions is highly significant both for physical and verbal imitative aggression. Comparison of pairs of scores by the sign test shows that the obtained over-all differences were due almost entirely to the aggression displayed by subjects who had been exposed to the aggressive models. Their scores were significantly higher than those of either the nonaggressive or control groups, which did not differ from each other (Table 2).

Imitation was not confined to the model's aggressive responses. Approximately one-third of the subjects in the aggressive condition also repeated the model's nonaggressive verbal responses while none of the subjects in either the nonaggressive or control groups made such remarks. This difference, tested by means of the Cochran Q test, was significant well beyond the .001 level (Table 2).

Partial Imitation of Models' Behavior

Differences in the predicted direction were also obtained on the two measures of partial imitation.

Table 2 SIGNIFICANCE OF THE DIFFERENCES BETWEEN EXPERIMENTAL AND CONTROL GROUPS IN THE EXPRESSION OF AGGRESSION

				COMPARISON OF PAIRS OF TREATMENT CONDITIONS		
RESPONSE CATEGORY	$\chi^2 r$	Q	p	AGGRESSIVE VS. NONAGGRESSIVE p	AGGRESSIVE VS. CONTROL p	NONAGGRESSIVE VS. CONTROL p
Imitative responses						
Physical aggression	27.17		< .001	< .001	< .001	.09
Verbal aggression	9.17		< .02	.004	.048	.09
Nonaggressive verbal responses		17.50	< .001	.004	.004	ns
Partial imitation						
Mallet aggression	11.06		< .01	.026	ns	.005
Sits on Bobo doll		13.44	< .01	.018	.059	ns
Nonimitative aggression						
Punches Bobo doll	2.87		ns			
Physical and verbal	8.96		< .02	.026	ns	ns
Aggressive gun play	2.75		ns			

Analysis of variance of scores based on the subjects' use of the mallet aggressively toward objects other than the Bobo doll reveals that treatment conditions are a statistically significant source of variation (Table 2). In addition, individual sign tests show that both the aggressive and the control groups, relative to subjects in the nonaggressive condition, produced significantly more mallet aggression, the difference being particularly marked with regard to female subjects. Girls who observed nonaggressive models performed a mean number of 0.5 mallet aggression responses as compared to mean values of 18.0 and 13.1 for girls in the aggressive and control groups, respectively.

Although subjects who observed aggressive models performed more mallet aggression ($M = 20.0$) than their controls ($M = 13.3$), the difference was not statistically significant.

With respect to the partially imitative response of sitting on the Bobo doll, the over-all group differences were significant beyond the .01 level (Table 2). Comparison of pairs of scores by the sign test procedure reveals that subjects in the aggressive group reproduced this aspect of the models' behavior to a greater extent than did the nonaggressive ($p = .018$) or the control ($p = .059$) subjects. The latter two groups, on the other hand, did not differ from each other.

Nonimitative Aggression

Analyses of variance of the remaining aggression measures (Table 2) show that treatment conditions did not influence the extent to which subjects engaged in aggressive gun play or punched the Bobo doll. The effect of conditions is highly significant ($\chi^2_r = 8.96$, $p < .02$), however, in the case of the subjects' expression of nonimitative physical and verbal aggression. Further comparison of treatment pairs reveals that the main source of the overall difference was the aggressive and nonaggressive groups which differed significantly from each other (Table 2), with subjects exposed to the aggressive models displaying the greater amount of aggression.

Influence of Sex of Model and Sex of Subjects on Imitation

The hypothesis that boys are more prone than girls to imitate aggression exhibited by a model was only partially confirmed. t tests computed for subjects in the aggressive condition reveal that boys reproduced more imitative physical aggression than girls ($t = 2.50$, $p < .01$). The groups do not differ, however, in their imitation of verbal aggression.

The use of nonparametric tests, necessitated by the extremely skewed distributions of scores for subjects in the nonaggressive and control conditions, preclude an over-all test of the influence of sex of model per se, and of the various interactions between the main effects. Inspection of the means presented in Table 1 for subjects in the aggression condition, however, clearly suggests the possibility of a Sex × Model interaction. This interaction effect is much more consistent and pronounced for the male model than for the female model. Male subjects, for example, exhibited more physical ($t = 2.07$, $p < .05$) and verbal imitative aggression ($t = 2.51$, $p < .05$), more nonimitative aggression ($t = 3.15$, $p < .025$), and engaged in significantly more aggressive gun play ($t = 2.12$, $p < .05$) following exposure to the aggressive male model than the female subjects. In contrast, girls exposed to the female model performed considerably more imitative verbal aggression and more nonimitative aggression than did the boys (Table 1). The variances, however, were equally large and with only a small N in each cell the mean differences did not reach statistical significance.

Data for the nonaggressive and control subjects provide additional suggestive evidence that the behavior of the male model exerted a greater influence than the female model on the subjects' behavior in the generalization situation.

It will be recalled that, except for the greater amount of mallet aggression exhibited by the control subjects, no significant differences were obtained between the nonaggressive and control groups. The data indicate, however, that the absence of significant differences between these two groups was due primarily to the fact that subjects exposed to the nonaggressive female model did not differ from the controls on any of the measures of aggression. With respect to the male model, on the other hand, the differences between the groups are striking. Comparison of the sets of scores by means of the sign test reveals that, in relation to the control group, subjects exposed to the non-aggressive male model performed significantly less imitative physical aggression ($p = .06$), less imitative verbal aggression ($p = .002$), less mallet aggression ($p = .003$), less nonimitative physical and verbal aggression ($p = .03$), and they were less inclined to punch the Bobo doll ($p = .07$).

While the comparison of subgroups, when some of the over-all tests do not reach statistical significance, is likely to capitalize on chance differences, nevertheless the consistency of the findings adds support to the interpretation in terms of influence by the model.

Nonaggressive Behavior

With the exception of expected sex differences, Lindquist (1956) Type III analyses of variance of the nonaggressive response scores yielded few significant differences.

Female subjects spent more time than boys playing with dolls ($p < .001$), with the tea set ($p < .001$), and coloring ($p < .05$). The boys, on the other hand, devoted significantly more time than the girls to exploratory play with the guns ($p < .01$). No sex differences were found in respect to the subjects' use of the other stimulus objects, i.e., farm animals, cars, or tether ball.

Treatment conditions did produce significant differences on two measures of nonaggressive behavior that are worth mentioning. Subjects in the nonaggressive condition engaged in significantly more nonaggressive play with dolls than either subjects in the aggressive group ($t = 2.67$, $p < .02$), or in the control group ($t = 2.57, p < .02$).

Even more noteworthy is the finding that subjects who observed non-aggressive models spent more than twice as much time as subjects in aggressive condition ($t = 3.07$, $p < .01$) in simply sitting quietly without handling any of the play material.

DISCUSSION

Much current research on social learning is focused on the shaping of new behavior through rewarding and punishing consequences. Unless responses are emitted, however, they cannot be influenced. The results of this study provide strong evidence that observation of cues produced by the behavior of others is one effective means of eliciting certain forms of responses for which the original probability is very low or zero. Indeed, social imitation may hasten or short-cut the acquisition of new behaviors without the necessity of reinforcing successive approximations as suggested by Skinner (1953).

Thus subjects given an opportunity to observe aggressive models later reproduced a good deal of physical and verbal aggression (as well as nonaggressive responses) substantially identical with that of the model. In contrast, subjects who were exposed to nonaggressive models and those who had no previous exposure to any models only rarely performed such responses.

To the extent that observation of adult models displaying aggression communicates permissiveness for aggressive behavior, such exposure may serve to weaken inhibitory responses and thereby to increase the probability of aggressive reactions to subsequent frustrations. The fact, however, that subjects expressed their aggression in ways that clearly resembled the novel patterns exhibited by the models provides striking evidence for the occurrence of learning by imitation.

In the procedure employed by Miller and Dollard (1941) for establishing imitative behavior, adult or peer models performed discrimination responses following which they were consistently rewarded, and the subjects were similarly reinforced whenever they matched the leaders' choice responses. While these experiments have been widely accepted as demonstrations of learning by means of imitation, in fact, they simply involve a special case of discrimination learning in which the behavior of others serves as discriminative stimuli for responses that are already part of the subject's repertoire. Auditory or visual environmental cues could easily have been substituted for the social stimuli to facilitate the discrimination learning. In contrast, the process of imitation studied in the present experiment differed in several important respects from the one investigated by Miller and Dollard in that subjects learned to combine fractional responses into relatively complex novel patterns solely by observing the performance of social models without any opportunity to perform the models' behavior in the exposure setting, and without any reinforcers delivered either to the models or to the observers.

An adequate theory of the mechanisms underlying imitative learning is lacking. The explanations that have been offered (Logan, Olmsted, Rosner, Schwartz, & Stevens, 1955; Maccoby, 1959) assume that the imitator performs the model's responses covertly. If it can be assumed additionally that rewards and punishments are self-administered in conjunction with the covert responses, the process of imitative learning could be accounted for in terms of the same principles that govern instrumental trial-and-error learning. In the early stages of the developmental process, however, the range of component responses in the organism's repertoire is probably increased through a process of classical conditioning (Bandura & Huston, 1961; Mowrer, 1950).

The data provide some evidence that the male model influenced the subjects' behavior outside the exposure setting to a greater extent than was true for the female model. In the analyses of the Sex × Model interactions, for example, only the comparisons involving the male model yielded significant differences. Similarly, subjects exposed to the nonaggressive male model performed less aggressive behavior than the controls, whereas comparisons involving the female model were consistently nonsignificant.

In a study of learning by imitation, Rosenblith (1959) has likewise found male experimenters more effective than females in influencing children's behavior. Rosenblith advanced the tentative explanation that the school setting may involve some social deprivation in respect to adult males which, in turn, enhances the male's reward value.

The trends in the data yielded by the present study suggest an alternative explanation. In the case of a highly masculine-typed behavior such as physical aggression, there is a tendency for both male and female subjects to imitate the male model to a greater degree than the female model. On the other hand, in the case of verbal aggression, which is less clearly sex linked, the greatest amount of imitation occurs in relation to the same-sex model. These trends together with the finding that boys in relation to girls are in general more imitative of physical aggression but do not differ in imitation of verbal aggression, suggest that subjects may be differentially affected by the sex of the model but that predictions must take into account the degree to which the behavior in question is sex-typed.

The preceding discussion has assumed that maleness-femaleness rather than some other personal characteristics of the particular models involved, is the significant variable—an assumption that cannot be tested directly with the data at hand. It was clearly evident, however, particularly from boys' spontaneous remarks about the display of aggression by the female model, that some subjects at least were responding in terms of a sex discrimination and their prior learning about what is sex appropriate behavior (e.g., "Who is that lady. That's not the way for a lady to behave. Ladies are supposed to act like ladies...." "You should have seen what that girl did in there. She was just acting like a man. I never saw a girl act like that before. She was punching and fighting but no swearing."). Aggression by the male model, on the other hand, was more likely to be seen as appropriate and approved by both the boys ("Al's a good socker, he beat up Bobo. I want to sock like Al.") and the girls ("That man is a strong fighter, he punched and punched and he could hit Bobo right down to the floor and if Bobo got up he said, 'Punch your nose.' He's a good fighter like Daddy.").

The finding that subjects exposed to the quiet models were more inhibited and unresponsive than subjects in the aggressive condition, together with the obtained difference on the aggression measures, suggests that exposure to inhibited models not only decreases the probability of occurrence of aggressive behavior but also generally restricts the range of behavior emitted by the subjects.

"Identification with aggressor" (Freud, 1946) or "defensive identification" (Mowrer, 1950), whereby a person presumably transforms himself from object to agent of aggression by adopting the attributes of an aggressive threatening model so as to allay anxiety, is widely accepted as an explanation of the imitative learning of aggression.

The development of aggressive modes of response by children of aggressively punitive adults, however, may simply reflect object displacement without involving any such mechanism of defensive identification. In studies of child training antecedents of aggressively antisocial adolescents (Bandura & Walters, 1959) and of young hyperaggressive boys (Bandura, 1960), the parents were found to be nonpermissive and punitive of aggression directed toward themselves. On the other hand, they actively encouraged and reinforced their sons' aggression toward persons outside the home. This pattern of differential reinforcement of aggressive behavior served to inhibit the boys' aggression toward the original instigators and fostered the displacement of aggression toward objects and situations eliciting much weaker inhibitory responses.

Moreover, the findings from an earlier study (Bandura & Huston, 1961), in which children imitated to an equal degree aggression exhibited by a nurturant and a nonnurturant model, together with the results of the present experiment in which subjects readily imitated aggressive models who were more or less neutral figures suggest that mere observation of aggression, regardless of the quality of the model-subject relationship, is a sufficient condition for producing imitative aggression in children. A comparative study of the subjects' imitation of aggressive models who are feared, who are liked and esteemed, or who are essentially neutral figures would throw some light on whether or not a more parsimonious theory than the one involved in "identification with the aggressor" can explain the modeling process.

SUMMARY

Twenty-four preschool children were assigned to each of three conditions. One experimental group observed aggressive adult models; a second observed inhibited nonaggressive models; while subjects in a control group had no prior exposure to the models. Half the subjects in the experimental conditions observed same-sex models and half viewed models of the opposite sex. Subjects were then tested for the amount of imitative as well as nonimitative aggression performed in a new situation in the absence of the models.

Comparison of the subjects' behavior in the generalization situation revealed that subjects exposed to aggressive models reproduced a good deal of aggression resembling that of the models, and that their mean scores differed markedly from those of subjects in the nonaggressive and control groups. Subjects in the aggressive condition also exhibited significantly more partially imitative and nonimitative aggressive behavior and were generally less inhibited in their behavior than subjects in the nonaggressive condition.

Imitation was found to be differentially influenced by the sex of the model with boys showing more aggression than girls following exposure to the male model, the difference being particularly marked on highly masculine-typed behavior.

Subjects who observed the nonaggressive models, especially the subdued male model, were generally less aggressive than their controls.

The implications of the findings based on this experiment and related studies for the psychoanalytic theory of identification with the aggressor were discussed.

REFERENCES

Bandura, A. Relationship of family patterns to child behavior disorders. Progress Report, 1960, Stanford University, Project No. M-1734, United States Public Health Service.

Bandura, A., & Huston, Aletha C. Identification as a process of incidental learning. *J. abnorm. soc. Psychol.,* 1961, *63,* 311–18.

Bandura, A., & Walters, R. H. *Adolescent aggression.* New York: Ronald, 1959.

Blake, R. R. The other person in the situation. In R. Tagiuri & L. Petrullo (Eds.), *Person perception and interpersonal behavior.* Stanford, Calif: Stanford Univer. Press, 1958. Pp. 229–42.

Fauls, Lydia B., & Smith, W. D. Sex-role learning of five-year olds. *J. genet. Psychol.,* 1956, *89,* 105–17.

Freud, Anna. *The ego and the mechanisms of defense.* New York: International Univer. Press, 1946.

Grosser, D., Polansky, N., & Lippitt, R. A laboratory study of behavior contagion. *Hum. Relat.,* 1951, *4,* 115–42.

Lindquist, E. F. *Design and analysis of experiments.* Boston: Houghton Mifflin, 1956.

Logan, F., Olmsted, O. L., Rosner, B. S., Schwartz, R. D., & Stevens, C. M. *Behavior theory and social science.* New Haven: Yale Univer. Press, 1955.

Maccoby, Eleanor E. Role-taking in childhood and its consequences for social learning. *Child Develpm.,* 1959, *30,* 239–52.

Miller, N. E., & Dollard, J. *Social learning and imitation.* New Haven: Yale Univer. Press, 1941.

Mowrer, O. H. (Ed.) Identification: A link between learning theory and psychotherapy. In, *Learning theory and personality dynamics.* New York: Ronald, 1950, Pp. 69–94.

Rosenbaum, M. E., & deCharms, R. Direct and vicarious reduction of hostility. *J. abnorm. soc. Psychol.,* 1960, *60,* 105–11.

Rosenblith, Judy F. Learning by imitation in kindergarten chldren. *Child Develpm.,* 1959, *30,* 69–80.

Schachter, S., & Hall, R. Group-derived restraints and audience persuasion. *Hum. Relat.,* 1952, *5,* 397–406.

Skinner, B. F. *Science and human behavior.* New York: Macmillan, 1953.

The Stimulating Versus Cathartic Effects of a Vicarious Aggressive Activity

SEYMOUR FESHBACH

The present study is concerned with the complex effects of participation in a presumably vicarious aggressive activity upon subsequent aggressive behavior. A number of studies have demonstrated that the expression of aggression—whether directly or in symbolic form—results in a lowering of subsequent aggression (Berkowitz, 1960; Feshbach, 1955; Pepitone & Reichling, 1955; Rosenbaum & de Charms, 1960; Thibaut & Coules, 1952). However, there is also experimental evidence to the effect that aggressive activity has a stimulating effect upon the manifestation of other aggressive acts (Feshbach, 1956; Kenny, 1953); that is, aggression may breed aggression.

Since both possibilities—reduction and stimulation—have been experimentally observed, the pertinent issue then is under what conditions a vicarious aggressive act increases and under what conditions it decreases the probability of subsequent aggressive behavior. One such condition suggested by differences in procedure between the studies that obtained evidence of a cathartic effect and those demonstrating a stimulating effect is the emotional state of the subject at the time the aggressive act is performed; that is, if the subject is angry at the time he engages in the aggressive activity, he can then use the act to satisfy and thereby reduce his hostility.

The general hypothesis is suggested that in order for an activity to have drive reducing properties, components of the drive must be present or evoked during performance of the activity; that is, there must be some functional connection between the vicarious act and the original drive instigating conditions. While it is undoubtedly true that the vicissitudes of life will arouse hostilities that cannot be directly discharged, it does not follow that any indirect aggressive act will have the property of reducing hostility that has been evoked under markedly different circumstances. According to the present view, a child's anger toward its mother will not be reduced by an aggressive act toward a doll figure unless its anger toward the mother is aroused when the aggressive act is performed. The evocation of anger may not be a sufficient condition—the doll figure may have to be similar to the mother—but it is probably a necessary condition for drive reduction to take place.

If the subject is not hostile at the time of participating in an aggressive act, his subsequent aggressive behavior will not merely remain unaffected but is very likely to be increased. An increase in aggression following a vicarious aggressive act could result from a number of different processes: a reduction in inhibition or aggression anxiety, reinforcement of aggressive responses, and finally conditioned stimulation of aggressive drive and/or aggressive responses.

On the basis of the foregoing considerations, the following hypotheses are proposed: Participation in a vicarious aggressive act results in a reduction in subsequent aggressive behavior if aggressive drive has been aroused at the time of such participation; if aggressive drive has not been aroused at the time of participation in a vicarious aggressive act, such participation results in an increase in subsequent aggressive behavior.

METHOD

The experimental procedure consisted of arousing a subject's aggressive drive before participation in a vicarious aggressive act or before participation in a neutral act and then obtaining measures of aggression subsequent to these interpolated activities. The variation in level of aggression was accomplished by means of an insult versus noninsult condition and the variation in the interpolated activity consisted of exposure to a fight film versus a neutral film.

Subjects

The subjects were male college student volunteers who were assigned at random to one of the four treatment groups generated by the two experimental variables. One hundred and one subjects were used in the study, with approximately equal numbers in each experimental condition. The subjects were seen in small groups by the experimenter so that nine experimental sessions in all were held, three for the Noninsult Fight Film condition and two sessions for each of the other experimental conditions.

Procedure

Insult versus Noninsult condition.   Subjects assigned to the insult groups were subjected to a number of unwarranted and extremely critical remarks. These comments essentially disparaged the intellectual motivation and the emotional maturity of the students. Previous studies (Feshbach, 1955; Gellerman, 1956) have provided abundant evidence that this technique successfully arouses hostility toward an experimenter. Subjects assigned to the Noninsult condition were given standard test instructions.

Aggressive Film versus Neutral Film condition.   Subjects in the Insult and Noninsult groups then witnessed either a Fight Film or a Neutral Film. The Fight Film consisted of a film clip of a rather exciting prize fight sequence taken from the motion picture *Body and Soul* while the neutral film depicted the consequence of the spread of rumors in a factory. The duration of each of the films was approximately 10 minutes.

As a rationale for the presentation of the film, the subjects were told before the film was presented that they would be asked to judge the personality of the main character in the film. Following the completion of the film, each subject indicated his impression of the personality of the hero of the film on a questionnaire provided for that purpose.

Dependent Measures of Aggression. All subjects were given a modified word association test which, in a previous study (Gellerman, 1956) had been shown to be sensitive to differences in the arousal of aggression. The test involves the presentation of five aggressive words interspersed among six neutral stimuli as follows: wash, choke, travel, massacre, walk, murder, relax, stab, sleep, torture, listen. The subjects were asked to give in written form a series of associations to each word. The stimuli are presented orally and also visually, the experimenter holding up a 5" × 8" card on which the stimulus word is printed. The subject's Aggression score is based on the number of aggressive word associations among the first 10 responses to each of the aggressive stimulus words. The maximum score that can therefore be obtained on this measure is 50.

Subsequent to the administration of the word association test, the first experimenter left the room having presumably completed the study. A second experimenter then entered and informed the subjects that the psychology department wished to assess students' opinions of the value of participating in psychological experiments. A questionnaire was then administered dealing with the subjects' attitudes toward the experimenter and with their evaluation of the experiment. The questionnaire which consists of six items, each of which has six alternatives, is described in more detail in a previous study (Feshbach, 1955). It is scored so that the least aggressive choice for a particular item is given a score of 1 and the most aggressive choice, a score of 6.

RESULTS

By hypothesis, it was predicted that the Insult group exposed to the Fight Film would manifest *less* subsequent aggression on each of the two measures of aggression than the Insult group exposed to the Neutral Film while the Non-insult group exposed to the Fight Film would display *more* subsequent aggression than the Noninsult group exposed to the Neutral Film. The word association data bearing upon these predictions are presented in Table 1. The mean differences are in accordance with expectation, the Insult-Fight (IF) Film group responding with fewer aggressive associations than the Insult-Neutral (IN) Film group and the Noninsult-Fight (NIF) Film group responding with more aggressive associations than the Noninsult-Neutral (NIN) Film group. The results of an analysis of variance of the data indicate that the interaction between the Insult and the Film variable is statistically significant. The difference between the IF Film and the IN Film groups falls short of the 5% confidence level, the value of *t* being 1.9. The difference between the NIF Film and NIN Film groups yields a *t* value of approximately 1 which is clearly not significant.

The contrast between the IF Film and IN Film groups is more sharply delineated by a simple median split. The chi square for the fourfold table presented in Table 2 is 6.02 which yields a *p* value of <.02. The word association data, then, indicate that under conditions of anger-arousal, witnessing a fight film results in a lowering of aggression. However, the hypothesized stimulating effect of an aggressive film under nonaroused conditions is not borne out by the data.

Table 1

A. MEAN AGGRESSIVE WORD ASSOCIATION RESPONSES OBTAINED UNDER EACH EXPERIMENTAL CONDITION

DRIVE (D)	FILM (F)	
	FIGHT (N)	NEUTRAL (N)
Insult	24.5 (25)[a]	28.9 (21)
Noninsult	27.7 (29)	25.3 (25)

B. SUMMARY OF ANALYSIS OF VARIANCE OF AGGRESSIVE WORD ASSOCIATION RESPONSES

SOURCE	SS	df	MS	F
D	8.93	1	8.93	
F	38.43	1	38.43	
DF	291.59	1	291.59	4.58*
Within	6,111.80	96	63.66	
Total	6,450.75	99		

[a]*The word associations of one subject were not scored due to illegibility.*
*$p < .05$.

Table 2   DISTRIBUTION OF AGGRESSIVE WORD ASSOCIATION RESPONSES FALLING ABOVE AND BELOW THE MEDIAN AS A FUNCTION OF INSULT FIGHT FILM AND INSULT NEUTRAL FILM TREATMENTS

TREATMENT	< 27	> 27
Insult Fight Film	17	8
Insult Neutral Film	10	19

Note.$-\chi^2 = 6.02; p < .05$.

The questionnaire data are presented in Table 3. Because of the lack of homogeneity of variance between the IN and NIF Film groups, separate comparisons were made between pertinent groups and, in these comparisons, the variances of the respective distributions are not reliably different. As was the case with the word association data, the IF Film group displays significantly less aggression on the questionnaire than does the IN group. The difference between the Noninsult groups is not in the predicted direction but is small and unreliable.

The difference in subsequent aggressive attitudes between the insulted group exposed to fight film and the insulted group exposed to the neutral film is further illustrated by a simple median split. The chi square for the fourfold table presented in Table 4 is 15.1, which is significant at less than the .001 level.

Table 3 A COMPARISON OF MEAN SCORES ON THE AGGRESSION QUESTION-
NAIRE

INSULT-FIGHT (IF) (N = 26)	INSULT-NEUTRAL (IN) (N = 29)	NONINSULT-FIGHT (NIF) (N = 20[a])	NONINSULT-NEUTRAL (NIN) (N = 25)
M 14.6	19.5	13.7	15.0
σ 3.72	3.90	2.52	2.95

Note.—$IF-IN = 4.7; p < .01.$
[a]*One subject failed to complete questionnaire.*

Table 4 DISTRIBUTION OF AGGRESSION QUESTIONNAIRE SCORES FALLING
ABOVE AND BELOW THE MEDIAN AS A FUNCTION OF INSULT FIGHT
FILM AND INSULT NEUTRAL FILM TREATMENTS

TREATMENT	< 17.5	> 17.5
Insult Fight Film	20	6
Insult Neutral Film	7	22

Note.— $\chi^2 = 15.1; p < .001.$

DISCUSSION

The experimental results are consistent with the hypothesis that the drive
reducing effect of a vicarious aggressive act is dependent upon the aggressive
state of the subject at the time of the vicarious aggressive activity. Witnessing the
prize fight film resulted in a significant relative decrement in aggression in
comparison to witnessing the neutral film only for those subjects in whom
aggression had been previously aroused by the insulting comments of the
experimenter. The predicted increase in aggression for the noninsulted subjects
following exposure to the fight film did not occur, however. Each of these two
outcomes warrants further comment.

With regard to the difference between the two Insult groups in subsequent
aggression, a possible alternative to a catharsis or drive reduction hypothesis is
one that assumes that guilt or revulsion stimulated by the fight film is the
primary mechanism responsible for the lowered aggression. Berkowitz (1958,
1960) has strongly argued for such an explanation of a reduction in aggressive
behavior following an aggressive act: However, it must be noted that the
evidence for a guilt or inhibition process is most indirect and inferential.

With regard to the present study, the guilt alternative is certainly possible,
although, for various reasons to be suggested below, not a likely one. If guilt
arousal were a ubiquitous process, occurring whenever people are given the
opportunity to indulge in aggressive fantasies, then the fight film should
similarly have inhibited the aggressive response output of the Noninsult group.
The possibility still remains that guilt arousal can account for the aggression

reducing effects of fantasy under conditions where aggression has recently been stimulated, as in the Insult condition. As a check on whether the lowered aggression of the IF Film group was due to some inhibitory factor, the word associations were scored for defensiveness. A previous study of the effects of inhibition upon aggressive word associations has shown that when inhibition is experimentally aroused, the number of aggressive responses decreases while the number of defensive responses increases (Gellerman, 1956). While, in the present study, a difference was observed in the number of aggressive associations, the difference between the two Insult groups in the number of defensive associations was negligible and insignificant. The absence of an increment in defensive responses, while not decisive since the experiment cited employed an inhibition procedure more closely resembling fear rather than guilt, is more consistent with a drive reduction rather than guilt explanation of the decrease in aggression following the exposure of the insulted subjects to the Fight Film.

The problem remains of accounting for the failure to obtain the expected increase in aggression in the Noninsult group. One possible reason is the limitation of the questionnaire instrument as a measure of aggression. Although one's preference for or attitude toward another person is frequently used as an index of aggression, as was the case in the present experiment, dislike and aggression are not equivalent dimensions. At the extreme, aversion and aggression are likely to be strongly correlated; but within moderate ranges of feeling, the association between dislike and aggression may well be negligible. For this reason, the word association measure is probably a better instrument than the attitude questionnaire for detecting changes in aggression in the noninsulted groups. However, although the relative increment in aggressive associations following exposure of the Noninsult group to the Fight Film was in the predicted direction, it was not statistically significant. Whether this failure to obtain evidence of a stimulating effect of a vicarious aggressive activity under relaxed emotional conditions is due to inadequacies in the theoretical analysis or to limitations in the methods utilized cannot be ascertained from the present data.

On the other hand, the data consistently reflect the dependence of the drive reduction effect upon the arousal of aggression at the time the subject is engaging in the vicarious aggressive activity. Presumably vicarious aggressive acts do not wllly-nilly serve as outlets for aggressive motivation. This latter process warrants further attention. Aggression is not an ever-present tension system pervading all of an individual's activities. Like other acquired motives, its appearance is very much dependent upon situational factors; and, the more specific the category of objects toward which the aggression is directed, the narrower is both the range of stimuli that can elicit the motivation and the range of situations that can serve as substitute outlets for the aggression.

What would appear to be a relatively simple matter—the effects of a vicarious aggressive activity upon subsequent aggressive behavior—is in actuality a quite complex process. The present study has examined the influence of the drive state of the organism upon this process. Beyond the requirement of replication in a variety of situations, further research is needed to establish the extent to which other variables determine the effects of so-called vicarious aggressive activities and to establish the precise mechanism by which the performance, direct or vicarious, of an aggressive act influences subsequent aggressive behavior.

SUMMARY

Studies of the effects of a presumably vicarious aggressive activity upon subsequent aggressive activity suggest that under certain conditions the activity will tend to increase, and under other conditions decrease, the probability of subsequent aggressive behavior. The purpose of this experiment was to study the effects of one such condition—namely, the emotional state of the subject at the time the vicarious aggressive activity is performed. Specifically, it was proposed that a vicarious aggressive activity results in a *reduction* in subsequent aggressive behavior if the subject is emotionally aroused at the time he is engaging in this activity, but if anger has not been aroused, the activity results in an *increase* in subsequent aggressive behavior. The two independent variables manipulated in the study consisted of an Insult versus Noninsult condition and an Aggressive Film versus Neutral Film condition. One hundred and one college students were assigned at random to the four treatment groups generated by the two experimental variables. The subjects met the experimenter in small groups so that nine experimental sessions in all were held. Subjects assigned to the Noninsult condition were given standard test instructions while subjects in the Insult groups were subjected to a number of unwarranted and extremely critical remarks. The subjects then witnessed either an Aggressive Film or a Neutral Film. The former consisted of a film clip depicting a prize fight sequence while the latter depicted the consequences of the spread of rumors in a factory. They were then administered a word association test and under the guise of a departmental assessment of the value of students' serving as experimental subjects, a second experimenter administered a questionnaire dealing with the subjects' attitudes toward the first experimenter and with their evaluation of the experiment. The degree of aggression manifested on the attitude questionnaire and the number of aggressive responses on the word association test constituted the dependent measures.

A significant interaction in the predicted direction was obtained for the Word Association measure—the Insult-Aggressive Film group responding with fewer aggressive associations than the IN Film group, and the Noninsult-Aggressive Film group responding with more aggressive associations than the NIN Film group. A similar significant difference between the two Insult groups was found on the attitude questionnaire, but the difference between the two Noninsult groups on this measure was unreliable and was not in the predicted direction.

The results were interpreted as being consistent with a drive reduction theory, although an inhibitory process (guilt arousal) cannot be excluded by the evidence at hand. The dependence of the *aggression* reducing effect of exposure to a film depicting violent activity upon the prior or simultaneous arousal of aggressive drive was stressed.

REFERENCES

Berkowitz, L. The expression and reduction of hostility. *Psychol. Bull.*, 1958, *55*, 257–83.

Berkowitz, L. Some factors effecting the reduction of overt hostility. *J. abnorm. soc. Psychol.*, 1960, *60*, 14–22.

Feshbach, S.   The drive-reducing function of fantasy behavior. *J. abnorm. soc. Psychol.,* 1955, *50,* 3–11.

Feshbach, S.   The catharsis hypothesis and some consequences of interaction with aggressive and neutral play objects. *J. Pers.,* 1956, *24,* 449–62.

Gellerman, S.   The effects of experimentally induced aggression and inhibition on word association response sequences. Unpublished doctoral dissertation, University of Pennsylvania, 1956.

Kenny, D. T.   An experimental test of the catharsis theory of aggression. Unpublished doctoral dissertation, University of Michigan, 1953.

Pepitone, A., & Reichling, G.   Group cohesiveness and the expression of hostility. *Hum. Relat.,* 1955, *3,* 327–37.

Rosenbaum, M. E., & de Charms, R.   Direct and vicarious reduction of hostility. *J. abnorm. soc. Psychol.,* 1960, *60,* 105–11.

Thibaut, J. W., & Coules, J.   The role of communication in the reduction of interpersonal hostility. *J. abnorm. soc. Psychol.,* 1952, *47,* 770–77.

The Stimulus Qualities of the Scapegoat

LEONARD BERKOWITZ AND JAMES A. GREEN

Generally speaking, most explanations of social prejudice are somewhat one-sided. They concentrate on factors either in the prejudiced individual *or* in the victimized group, but typically do not effectively relate the attacker to the attacked. The present paper will attempt to show that the object serving as the target for the intolerant person's aggression usually has certain stimulus qualities for this person, and that objects not possessing these characteristics are less likely to be attacked. In dealing with ethnic prejudice, in other words, it is necessary to consider both the aggressor and the available targets. To focus on either alone is to give only part of the picture.

Such one-sidedness is particularly apparent in the scapegoat theory of prejudice. The details often vary from one writer to another, but all versions of this common social science doctrine seem agreed on at least the following features: Frustration generates aggressive tendencies, which cannot be directed against the actual thwarting agent because this agent is not visible, or is capable of retaliating with severely punitive actions. A needed outlet is then found for the pent-up aggressive "energy" through attacks upon some innocent minority group. The displaced aggression is rationalized by blaming the minority for the

Reprinted from Journal of Abnormal and Social Psychology, 64, *1962, 293–301. Copyright 1962 by the American Psychological Association and reproduced by permission.*

frustrations the aggressor has experienced, and/or attributing undesirable characteristics to this group.

Several authorities (e.g., Allport, 1954; Zawadski, 1948) have noted that the above type of theorizing leaves many important questions unanswered. It does not tell us, for example, why a particular minority is attacked when any number of groups are available. Why are Jews more likely to be the victim of the displaced aggression than, say, people of Scottish descent? Considerations other than that an individual is frustrated and unable to attack the source of his frustration obviously must be introduced in order to handle this problem. As Zawadski (1948) pointed out, analyses of the scapegoating process tend to be "pure drive" theories, explaining the origin of the aggressive tendencies, but not the target selection. Other variables must be employed to deal with the choice of object for aggression.

Many writers (e.g., Williams, 1947), basing their reasoning on the psycho-analytic "energy" model of behavior, have assumed, almost as a matter of course, that the thwarted individual who is afraid to attack the actual anger instigator will aggress against the person least likely to harm him by retaliatory aggression. An aggressive outlet must be found and presumably is found in attacks upon objects who cannot inflict injury in return. The most likely target for displaced aggression, then, supposedly is the safest available target. This formulation has also been seriously questioned (e.g., Allport, 1954). White and Lippitt (1960) have been among the most recent critics of this "safety" hypothesis in their latest report of their now classic leadership study. They observed a number of instances of scapegoating in the frustrated autocratically led groups, but claimed that the victims were never the weakest or most passive boys in the club. The boys singled out for aggression in one autocratic group "were both boys who could hold their own against any of the others taken singly," while in another club the scapegoat was the largest and heaviest boy. White and Lippitt suggested that these particular boys were attacked in an attempt to recover status or self-esteem. Frustrations, they maintained, elicit hostility only when they lower self-esteem. By aggressing against these boys who were fairly strong and dangerous but without being excessively formidable, the attackers presumably could regard themselves as strong and potent in their own right, and thus their self-esteem supposedly would be restored (p. 166).

It is doubtful, however, whether status recovery can satisfactorily account for every case of target selection in displaced aggression. Why would attacks upon Jews provide a greater restoration of self-esteem than attacks upon minorities of Nordic origin? The solution to this problem of object choice must involve the stimulus properties of the various available objects. Along these lines, Williams (1947), among others, proposed that scapegoats frequently are visibly different or strange. It is the strangeness of the available objects that determines their likelihood of evoking displaced hostility. Strangeness or difference itself supposedly is disturbing. Allport (1954) has been inclined to accept such a thesis, contending that whatever instinctive basis there may be for group prejudice can perhaps be found in the "hesitant response ... human beings have to strangeness" (p. 130). Babies of about 6 months of age cry or become emotionally upset when a stranger draws near them, and such a reaction tendency may persist into adulthood. The present writers, believe, nevertheless, that strangeness is upsetting only under certain limiting conditions. Animal research (cf. White, 1959) and the rush of tourists to foreign countries indicate that strange and novel stimuli may be enticing in some circumstances.

Fear of a stranger largely arises when the individual expects the unknown person to be potentially dangerous. If a person is afraid of strangers or people who are greatly different from himself he probably views most people as being dangerous; the stranger is an "inkblot" eliciting the responses the person customarily makes to people. Ethnocentric personalities, of course, are relatively likely to be antagonistic to those who are different (Adorno, Frenkel-Brunswik, Levinson, & Sanford, 1950), and evidence suggests these people often are fairly insecure. They supposedly are uncertain of themselves, the world about them, and their place in the world. Thus, according to a study by Allport and Kramer (1946), highly prejudiced adults are much more likely than their more tolerant peers to agree that, "The world is a hazardous place in which men are basically evil and dangerous." Having this outlook, it is not surprising that they are unfriendly toward outgroups. Since the world is a threatening place for them, an unknown person from this world also is potentially dangerous.

The above analysis explains the ethnocentric individual's relatively strong tendency to generalize his frustration induced aggressive tendencies toward strangers (Berkowitz, 1959). The stranger, and more generally, the alien group, is somewhat threatening and, because it is threatening, is disliked. Dislike, we contend, mediates the generalization of aggression. *Aggression will generalize from the anger-instigator to another person in direct proportion to the degree of dislike for this latter individual.* If this hypothesis is correct, we would have a means of integrating the scapegoat theory of prejudice with those other accounts of intergroup conflict focusing upon the characteristics of the socially victimized ethnic groups. Where the scapegoat theory is a "pure drive" theory, to employ Zawadski's (1948) terminology, these latter notions—such as the so-called "well-earned reputation" doctrine—can be described as "pure stimulus" theories (Zawadski, 1948). Though they differ in important ways, these "stimulus" theories have at least one aspect in common; they all provide reasons why given minority groups are disliked. Putting it simply, the present argument holds that the aggressive tendencies engendered by frustrations are generalized to those groups whose perceived characteristics result in their being disliked. The individual may absorb his family's or his culture's negative attitudes towards a particular group, or he may have had unpleasant experiences with members of this group. The genesis of the negative attitude is unimportant as far as we can see. As long as a group is disliked, whatever the reason, it is a likely target for displaced aggression.

This is not to say that particular characteristics of the minority group have no part in determining its likelihood of becoming a scapegoat. While investigators of the authoritarian personality usually maintain only that a group is attacked merely because it is an "outgroup" (cf. Adorno et al., 1950, p. 233), they sometimes, in company with other psychoanalytically oriented writers, also emphasize the importance of the group's perceived qualities. The prejudiced individual, for example, supposedly projects his own disapproved sexual wishes onto Negroes because the stereotype of this group easily accommodates such a projection, and then hates Negroes because of their perceived sexuality.

Similarly, Jews are said to symbolize other properties the authoritarian personality unconsciously sees and detests in himself.

The problem we are addressing ourselves to is the theoretical significance of the characteristics attributed to (or actually possessed by) the outgroups. Jews share few, if any, specific features with Negroes. In the United States at least, sexual qualities typically are not assigned to the former (Allport, 1954), but both groups are likely targets for the same prejudiced individual's hostility. Just what do Jews, Negroes, and other outgroups have in common that results in their all being victimized? Most investigators of authoritarianism have been too concerned with the detailed depths of the prejudiced personality to look for the abstract principle that effectively integrates the various instances of scapegoating.

The specific characteristics perceived in a group do four things from our point of view. Most important, they determine whether the minority is disliked and, if so, how strongly. This is the quality shared by the victims of displaced hostility. They are disliked for different reasons (the *Authoritarian Personality* and other writings give us some of these reasons), but all are detested. As a result of being the object of negative attitudes, then, hostility engendered by some frustration will generalize fairly readily to these outgroups. Two, the extent of hostility generalization, we believe, is a function of the total degree of association between the immediate frustrator and the objects available for scapegoating. The perceived properties of these latter objects, as well as the dislike for them, contribute to the psychological ties the thwarted person can draw between his frustrator and the available targets. The generalized aggressive tendencies of course will not lead to overt attacks if the intolerant person fears he will be punished for displaying aggression and/or believes such hostility is morally improper. The outgroup characteristics also may affect these factors. They can determine, three, whether the prejudiced individual believes it is safe to attack a given outgroup and, four, whether he is ethically justified in doing this.

The present reasoning obviously is based on the stimulus generalization of displacement (cf. Miller, 1948). Although our specific predictions do not necessarily require postulating stimulus generalization, we assume the negative attitudes associated with both the immediate frustrator and the disliked group give rise to a generalization continuum linking these two objects. In other words, because the thwarted individual makes the same implicit responses to the two objects the disliked group is associated with the frustrator. There may be an association between the two solely because they have elicited the same negative emotions in the individual. Another possibility is that the frustrated person implicitly applies the same label to both disliked objects, placing them in the same negatively evaluated category. Dollard and Miller (1950), in advancing the somewhat similar concept, "acquired equivalence of cues," contended that a previously neutral stimulus will produce the response elicited by a particular category of stimuli after the subject has learned to apply the category name to this stimulus. But however it comes about, there presumably is an acquired (i.e., response induced) equivalence between the frustrator and the minority group which mediates the generalization of aggressive responses from the former to the latter.

Two earlier papers by Berkowitz and Holmes (1959, 1960) provide evidence supporting the "dislike hypothesis." In the first, findings were reported suggesting that hostility is indeed generalized from the immediate frustrator to another stimulus person (P) the subject had previously learned to dislike. Subjects were first induced either to like or dislike their experimental partners (the Ps). After this, half of the subjects in each of these conditions were frustrated by the experimenter, with the others receiving a more pleasant treatment from him. Then, in the last phase of the study, pairs of subjects (each subject regarding the other as P) were brought together again for a cooperative task. It was shown that the subjects who had expressed relatively intense hostility to the experimenter after having been frustrated by him and who then were assembled with a disliked P on the final task generally expressed the strongest unfriendliness to this P on a questionnaire evaluation of him at the end of the session. The presumably intense hostility engendered by the experimenter apparently had generalized to the disliked P to a greater extent than to the more highly liked partner.

The second experiment (Berkowitz & Holmes, 1960) obtained similar findings with stronger and more direct acts of aggression. Pairs of subjects were put through the same procedures employed in the first study, but this time during the last phase of the experiment each subject was given a socially sanctioned opportunity to administer electric shocks to his partner. The subject was to evaluate P's performance on an assigned task by giving P electric shocks: one if the product was very good, more than this if the performance was thought to be poor. In actuality, each subject was shown the same product. There was the greatest increase in the number of shocks administered to the partner (in comparison to the number given during a baseline period at the start of the study) when the subject had been frustrated by the experimenter and then had an opportunity to shock the disliked P. Again it seems as if the aggressive tendencies evoked by the unpleasant experimenter had transferred to the unpleasant P.

However, there is at least one important difficulty confronting this interpretation. The subjects sending the greatest number of shocks to P had been frustrated twice: once during the manipulation creating the dislike to P, and again by the experimenter. Although internal evidence contrary to this possibility was reported, it is conceivable that the relatively great amount of aggression exhibited by these subjects was due solely to the intense anger aroused within them by the two thwartings. They could have been so angry they would have attacked anyone strongly, whether this target was disliked or not.

The present experiment seeks to test this alternative explanation. Essentially the same procedures utilized in the earlier experiments are again employed. However, the subject is now given two people to evaluate during the final phase of the experiment. One of these, as in the first two studies, had previously been either friendly or unfriendly to him. The second person is presumably fairly neutral since the subject had not interacted with him before. If the intense anger created by the two thwartings was the crucial determinant of the previous results, there should be no difference in the final evaluation of these two stimulus people, and both should be regarded more unfavorably after the subject is frustrated twice than after the subject is thwarted once or not at all. On the other hand, only the disliked P should receive the harshest evaluation, and not the "neutral" stimulus person, after the subject is thwarted by the experimenter if the existing attitude towards the available target affects this object's likelihood of receiving generalized aggression.

METHOD

Subjects

The subjects were male students from introductory psychology classes at the University of Wisconsin who volunteered without knowing the nature of the experiment. Four subjects were discarded after the pretesting was terminated— one because he had not completed the final questionnaire and three who indicated they were suspicious of the treatment accorded them. No more than two of these "discards" came from any one condition. There were 18 subjects in each of the four experimental conditions in the final sample.

Procedure

Two subjects who did not know each other were scheduled for any one experimental period. After both had arrived at the laboratory they were joined by a third male posing as the third experimental subject but who was, in actuality, the experimenter's confederate. The experimenter explained the ostensible purpose of the study, saying the experiment was to investigate the effects of stress upon creativity. They were told each subject would first make a judgment of the personalities of his two partners (supposedly because creative people were good at making "snap judgments"), and then two of the three would work on a problem solving task under mild stress, while the third person would be alone in a natural condition as a "control." The stress, they were told, would come from knowing they might receive several electric shocks if their performance was not too good. Each of the two people in the Stress condition was to work independently of the other on the assigned task. When they had finished they were to exchange their problem solutions so that each would serve as the judge of the other's performance. Each subject would transmit his evaluation of his partner's product by giving him electric shocks. There would be one shock if the product was very good and more than this if it was thought to be inadequate. Following this, the experimenter said, each subject would work alone and he would be judged (without shocks) by the experimenter. Finally, in the last part of the session, the three men would work together on a group task.

At this time the subjects were told the shocks would be relatively mild and they were given an opportunity to withdraw from the experiment if they objected to receiving shocks. None did. Letters were then assigned to the three men, the two "real subjects" being called A and C, and the confederate B. A and C were told that they would work under the Stress condition, and all three men were led to separate rooms where the naive subjects indicated their first impressions of their partners on an adjective checklist. The code letters were used in all of the ratings made throughout the experiment.

When the first personality evaluations were completed, both men were given the task of designing a "novel, imaginative, and creative" floor plan for a house. Each subject was informed that he would have 5 minutes to work on this problem and that his partner was to have the same task. After 5 minutes had passed by, the experimenter collected the subject's work, strapped shock electrodes onto his wrist, and then showed him what was supposedly the partner's (P's) performance but actually was previously constructed to be standard for all conditions. Each subject was told he was to go first in evaluating the other's performance by means of the electric shocks. He was to press a button on a nearby table one or more times depending upon his judgment of the other's work. The experimenter then left the room ostensibly to deliver the subject's product to his partner. When his instruments (to which the shock buttons were connected) informed him that both subjects had given shocks, the experimenter administered the shocks the subjects believed came from their partners.

Experimental Manipulations

The first manipulation, as in the preceding investigations, was designed to create differences in initial liking for P. Subjects in the Initial Liking for P condition received one shock, indicating that P had given them the most favorable evaluation. The other half of the subjects, those in the Initial Dislike for P condition, were given six electric shocks. Thus, on top of whatever physical hurt they felt, these subjects knew P had derogated their performance.

Subjects worked alone on the next problem (suggesting an original idea for attracting new customers to a gasoline station) without exchanging papers, but this time the experimenter, rather than P, was the perceived anger instigator. Half of the subjects in each of the above two conditions (those receiving the Frustrated by the Experimenter "treatment") were criticized and insulted by the experimenter during this problem by standardized messages transmitted to them via earphones. The remaining subjects (in the Nonfrustrated by the Experimenter condition) heard a friendlier evaluation of their work. Following this interaction with the experimenter, subjects were asked to fill out a short questionnaire, supposedly an evaluation of psychological experiments to go to the Chairman of the Department. This form, of course, was primarily intended to test the success of the manipulation (Frustration by the Experimenter) in arousing unfriendliness toward the experimenter.

In the third and final part of the study the two subjects and the confederate were brought together for 5 minutes to assemble a footbridge from materials stacked in the room. The three men returned to their individual rooms at the end of the work period. Once there, the subjects completed an alternate form of adjective checklist indicating their assessments of their two peers supposedly based on all the information they had obtained throughout the experiment.[1]

---

[1] The subjects also filled out a brief four-item scale assessing their attitudes toward each of their two peers. The results with this measure, not reported here because of indications that the adjective checklist had affected these later scale responses in the most strongly aroused condition (cf. Berkowitz & Holmes, 1960), are generally consistent with the adjective checklist findings. Thus the Initial Dislike for P-Frustrated by the Experimenter group was the only group experiencing some thwarting which gave P significantly more unfavorable ratings than as assigned to him in the Initial Liking for P-Not Frustrated by the Experimenter condition. The harsh treatment given the subjects by P, furthermore, did not significantly affect the attractiveness of the confederate on this measure, although (as was also found with the adjective checklist scores) there was some hostility generalized to the confederate when the experimenter had been a frustrator.

When this was done, the experimenter explained the actual purpose of the experiment and informed them of the deceptions he had practiced. Many of the subjects expressed a good deal of interest in the study and all promised not to talk about it to their friends.

Dependent Variables

The measure of each subject's attitudes toward P (with whom he had interacted throughout the study), and toward the confederate (the presumably neutral person), was based on the adjective checklist, a version of a technique used with apparent success in other research in the present program (e.g., Berkowitz, 1960). As mentioned above, two alternate forms were employed, one at the beginning, the other at the end of the session. Each form consisted of 33 adjectives. The subjects in responding to these forms were to mark a True-False IBM sheet (using separate IBM sheets but the same form for P and the confederate), stating which of the adjectives characterized the given stimulus person and which did not. Unknown to the subjects, a large group of judges had previously scaled the adjectives as to their overall social desirability. Thus it was possible to assess the level of unfriendliness in the subject's judgments of each of the other two men by adding the number of undesirable traits attributed to the person to the number of favorable characteristics he was said not to possess. As a working assumption, high unfriendliness is taken to signify relatively intense aggressive tendencies.

Two questions embedded in a group of four were employed in assessing the success of the Frustration by the Experimenter. One asked, "How much did you enjoy the experiment?" and the other, "How favorable was your reaction to the experimenter?" In answering each question the subjects were to place a mark at an appropriate position on a linear rating scale anchored at each end by a suitable phrase (e.g., "not at all"). The scores were distances from the favorable end of the continuum in 1 centimeter units. Subjects criticized and insulted by the experimenter should enjoy the experiment less and have a more unfavorable opinion of the experimenter than subjects receiving a friendlier treatment from him.

RESULTS

Success of the Experimental Manipulation

There were no measures taken in the present study of the subjects' feelings toward P immediately after they had obtained his first "evaluation" of their work. Results from the preceding investigations in this series (Berkowitz & Holmes, 1959, 1960), which employed virtually the same procedure, suggest, nevertheless, that the shock "evaluations" probably affected the level of the subjects' unfriendliness toward P. The subjects in these earlier experiments responded to a questionnaire within a few minutes of receiving the first shocks from P. Those getting the most shocks were more likely than the subjects getting one shock to indicate the P was "unfair," and to say that they had relatively little desire to know this person better. However, since these first investigations employed a greater number of shocks in the Initial Dislike for P condition, the earlier subjects receiving this treatment may have been more strongly angered than the comparable subjects in the present study.

The questionnaire ratings of the experimenter obtained in this experiment clearly indicate that his criticisms and insults in the Frustrated by the Experimenter condition had succeeded in provoking the subjects. Analyses of variance on each of the two relevant measures revealed significant main effects ($p < .01$ in both cases) for the frustration manipulation and no significant interactions. Thus the "aroused" subjects expressed reliably less enjoyment of the experiment and a significantly more unfavorable evaluation of the experimenter than the subjects receiving friendlier treatment from him.

Level of Unfriendliness toward P and the Confederate

The results obtained with the alternate forms of the adjective checklist administered at the beginning and end of the experimental session are summarized in Table 1.

It can be seen that the two stimulus people were not equally attractive to the subjects at the start of the study; the subjects in each condition had a significantly more favorable "first impression" of P than of the confederate. However, these initial attitudes apparently were only tentative and not too strongly held. Most subjects exhibited a considerable decline in unfriendliness to both of their partners by the end of the experiment.[2]

This decreased unfriendliness, nevertheless, did not occur to the same extent in all conditions. As we would expect from the earlier investigations, the only stimulus people not getting reliably more favorable evaluations at the end of the session were those men whom the subjects presumably had previously learned to dislike and who were being judged by subjects frustrated by the experimenter. Both of these independent variables had to combine in order to retard the growth of friendship. The subjects receiving only one of the harsh treatments, whether from P or the experimenter, showed a considerable decline in unfriendliness toward P. The table also indicates this impeded friendship development was not due simply to an accumulation of frustration effects. Subjects insulted by both P and the experimenter still became less unfriendly toward the confederate. Clearly, then, *the resentment aroused by the experimenter primarily affected the judgment of the disliked P.* It did not interfere with the growth of friendship for the confederate. The previously learned attitude toward the available stimulus person affected the degree to which he was the victim of anger created by someone else. Stimulus objects the subjects had not grown to dislike (i.e., the liked P and the confederate) did not receive anywhere as much generalized aggression.

There was *some* hostility generalization to the confederate, however. As the table notes, this person was regarded significantly more favorably by those

[2] The decreased unfriendliness may have been merely an effect of differences in adjective checklist forms. We think this is unlikely since the two forms were quite comparable in terms of the overall favorability of the traits listed.

Table 1 MEAN UNFRIENDLINESS TO THE PARTNER AND TO THE EXPERIMENTERS' CONFEDERATE

STIMULUS PERSON:	INITIAL DISLIKE FOR P				INITIAL LIKING FOR P			
	FRUSTRATED BY THE EXPERIMENTER		NOT FRUSTRATED BY THE EXPERIMENTER		FRUSTRATED BY THE EXPERIMENTER		NOT FRUSTRATED BY THE EXPERIMENTER	
TIME	P	CONFEDERATE	P	CONFEDERATE	P	CONFEDERATE	P	CONFEDERATE
First impression	9.0cd	11.1e	9.5d	11.0e	8.9bcd	12.2f	8.4bc	10.9e
End of study	8.4bc	8.2b	6.4a	8.5bc	6.2a	8.7bc	5.8a	6.5a
Change scores	−0.6	−2.9	−3.1	−2.5	−2.7	−3.5	−2.6	−4.4

Note.—*The absolute scores obtained at the start and conclusion of the study were subjected to one "repeated measures" analysis of variance. In the above table the higher the mean the more unfriendly the attitude toward the given stimulus person. Cells having the same subscript are not significantly different from each other by Duncan (1955) multiple range test.*

subjects who were not thwarted at all than by the subjects suffering at least one frustration. Nevertheless, these provocations did not retard the development of some friendliness toward the confederate. He may have been associated with the frustrators, but clearly was not one of them.

DISCUSSION

The above results, by and large, support the expectations underlying the present experiment. They indicate that the antagonism created by one unpleasant person has a stronger adverse effect on the individual's feelings toward another unpleasant person than on his attitudes toward someone he does not dislike.[3] This enhanced resentment, furthermore, can lead to relatively intense acts of hostility, as was shown in the preceding experiment in this series (Berkowitz & Holmes, 1960). In that study people given an opportunity to injure a disliked person (by administering electric shocks) in a socially sanctioned manner after having been insulted and criticized by the experimenter, generally performed more of these injurious acts than did the subjects also responding to a disliked person who had not been frustrated by the experimenter or the thwarted subjects given an opportunity to attack someone they presumably liked. Generalizing from these findings to the area of intergroup relations, we can hypothesize that the ethnic groups most likely to become the victim of displaced aggression are those groups the frustrated people had come to regard as being unpleasant for one reason or another (that is, assuming these thwarted individuals interact with these groups or otherwise become aware of them).

These data do not require postulating a stimulus induced generalization of aggressive tendencies from the immediate frustrator to the disliked individual. Many writers (e.g., Freud) have conceived of the aggressive drive as energy continually seeking an outlet. The attacked person supposedly merely provides this opportunity for release. From this point of view, then, we might say the aggressive tendencies aroused, strengthened, or released by the frustrating experimenter were inhibited when the subjects evaluated the neutral confederate or the presumably liked P. The degree of aggression inhibition could have been in direct ratio to the attractiveness of these stimulus objects. Such a formulation, of course, is compatible with "balance" (Newcomb, 1959) or "dissonance-avoiding" (Festinger, 1957) propositions. Dissonance (plus aggression-anxiety) would be aroused within a person if he knew he had deliberately injured someone he liked. He would have to suppress any inclinations he might have to hurt the attractive person if he is to avoid this dissonance (and aggression-anxiety).

We agree that this type of phenomenon probably occurs. However, we also believe, perhaps only as an article of faith, that the people the frustrated individual encounters after he is thwarted can serve as stimuli evoking aggressive responses from him. According to our present reasoning the perception of a disliked object is sufficient to elicit such hostility. However, it may be that only

---

[3] It is important to note that these results have been obtained with both male and female college students.

people who have inflicted injury on the individual, as was the case in this study, will evoke such generalized aggression, and not every disliked person.

The increased unfriendliness toward the confederate following the frustration of the experimenter can perhaps also be explained as the result of a stimulus generalization process. The provoked subjects could have associated the confederate with the instigator for several reasons. Both were involved in the experiment; both were somewhat unpleasant (although, as noted earlier, the unfavorable attitude toward the confederate might have been held with little conviction); and emotion arousal seems to reduce the use of peripheral cues, resulting in relatively gross discriminations among the available stimulus objects—in essence, flattening and extending the generalization gradient (Easterbrook, 1959). Nevertheless, the generalization of hostility to the confederate in the present study was unexpected and further research is necessary to determine which, if any, of these factors gave rise to the generalization.

The present argument, then, offers a relatively simple solution to the problem of target selection in scapegoating. At least some of the displacement of hostility upon certain minority groups can be accounted for by the thwarted individual's prior dislike for these groups. Feeling this way about them, he presumably associates these people with his most recent frustrators. An industrial worker may became more aggressive to the Jews in his community after receiving a pay cut because he associates the disliked Jews with the disliked factory owners and managers.

Other variables, however, can also intervene to affect the total strength of the association between ethnic group and immediate frustrator. This linkage may be weakened somewhat by knowledge forcing a discrimination between the particular minority and the frustrating source. It may also be strengthened by additional characteristics shared by the minority and the frustrator. Going back to the illustration of the disgruntled factory worker, suppose he has negative feelings towards both Turks and Jews and encounters a member of each of these groups. His knowledge that Turks generally are not involved in business management may weaken the total associative bond between this ethnic group and the factory owners. Jews, on the other hand, often are businessmen and, more than this, may also be regarded as rich and unscrupulous—just like the owners of the plant. There are several attributes held in common by Jews and the immediate frustrators as far as this individual is concerned, resulting in a heightened association between these people. Conditioned S-R bonds may summate (Hull, 1943, pp. 209–210). Furthermore, as we mentioned earlier, the perceived properties of the disliked minority can lower the individual's internal restraints against aggression. The stereotyped conception of Jews—e.g., that they are grasping and unscrupulous—acts to justify the aggressive inclinations the individual might feel toward this particular group. Believing the stereotype, he need not feel guilty about attacking this group. Knowing the group is in the minority and fairly widely disliked also means it is fairly safe to aggress against Jews. He need not fear retaliatory aggression either from the Jews in the street or from his peers. The consequence of all this is that the Jew is a more probable target for the thwarted worker's hostile tendencies than is the Turk.

SUMMARY

Most explanations of social prejudice do not relate the prejudiced individual to the victimized group. They generally are either "pure drive theories," dealing only with the source of the aggressive tendencies, or "pure stimulus theories," explaining only the characteristics of the attacked minority. The present paper attempts to construct a theoretical bridge between the aggressor and the aggressed-against. The central thesis is that aggression generalizes from the anger instigator to another person in direct proportion to the degree of dislike for this person. Hostile tendencies engendered by frustrations are generalized to those groups whose perceived characteristics result in their being disliked.

In the present study 72 college men were distributed evenly among four experimental conditions created by a 2×2 factorial design. Each subject (working in pairs) was first induced to either like or dislike his partner (the P). After this, half of the subjects in each of these conditions were individually frustrated by the experimenter, with the others receiving a more pleasant treatment from him. Then, in the last phase of the study, the two pair members and a neutral peer (actually the experimenter's confederate) were brought together to work on a cooperative task. Each subject's evaluations of his partner (P) and the confederate constituted the dependent variables. The results indicated that the disliked P was the primary victim of the resentment aroused by the frustrating experimenter.

REFERENCES

Adorno, T. W., Frenkel-Brunswik, Else, Levinson, D. J., & Sanford, R. N. *The authoritarian personality*. New York: Harper, 1950.

Allport, G. W.   *The nature of prejudice*. Cambridge, Mass.: Addison-Wesley, 1954.

Allport, G. W., & Kramer, B. M.   Some roots of prejudice. *J. Psychol.,* 1946, *22,* 9–39.

Berkowitz, L.   Anti-Semitism and the displacement of aggression. *J. abnorm. soc. Psychol.,* 1959, *59,* 182–87.

Berkowitz, L., & Holmes, D. S.   The generalization of hostility to disliked objects. *J. Pers.,* 1959, *27,* 565–77.

Berkowitz, L., & Holmes, D. S.   A further investigation of hostility generalization to disliked objects. *J. Pers.,* 1960, *28,* 427–42.

Dollard, J., & Miller, N. E.   *Personality and psychotherapy*. New York: McGraw-Hill, 1950.

Duncan, D.   Multiple range and multiple *F* tests. *Biometrics,* 1955, *11,* 1–45.

Easterbrook, J. A.   The effect of emotion on cue utilization and the organization of behavior. *Psychol. Rev.,* 1959, *66,* 183–201.

Festinger, L.   *A theory of cognitive dissonance*. Evanston, Ill.: Row, Peterson, 1957.

Hull, C. L.   *Principles of behavior*. New York: Appleton-Century, 1943.

Miller, N. E.   Theory and experiment relating psychoanalytic displacement to stimulus-response generalization. *J. abnorm. soc. Psychol.,* 1948, *43,* 155–78.

Newcomb, T. M.   Individual systems of orientation. In S. Koch (Ed.), *Psychology: A study of a science.* Vol. III. New York: McGraw-Hill, 1959. Pp. 384–422.

White, R. K., & Lippitt, R.   *Autocracy and democracy: An experimental inquiry.* New York: Harper, 1960.

White, R. W.   Motivation reconsidered: The concept of competence. *Psychol. Rev.,* 1959, *66,* 297–333.

Williams, R. M., Jr.   The reduction of intergroup tensions. *Soc. Sci. Res. Coun. Bull.,* 1947, No. 57.

Zawadski, B.   Limitations of the scapegoat theory of prejudice. *J. abnorm. soc. Psychol.,* 1948, *43,* 127–41.

Prologue in the Sea

KONRAD LORENZ

My childhood dream of flying is realized: I am floating weightlessly in an invisible medium, gliding without effort over sunlit fields. I do not move in the way that Man, in philistine assurance of his own superiority, usually moves, with belly forward and head upward, but in the age-old manner of vertebrates with back upward and head forward. If I want to look ahead, the discomfort of bending my neck reminds me painfully that I am really an inhabitant of another world. But I seldom want to do this, for my eyes are directed downward at the things beneath me, as becomes an earthly scientist.

Peacefully, indolently, fanning with my fins, I glide over fairy-tale scenery. The setting is the coast of one of the many little islands of coral chalk, the so-called Keys, that stretch in a long chain from the south end of the Florida peninsula. The landscape is less heroic than that of a real coral reef with its wildly cleft living mountains and valleys, but just as vivid. All over the ground, which consists of ancient coral rubble, can be seen strange hemispheres of brain coral, wavy bushes of Gorgonia, and, rarely, richly branched stems of staghorn coral, while between them are variegated patches of brown, red, and gold seaweed, not to be found in the real coral reefs further out in the ocean. At intervals are loggerhead sponges, man-broad and table-high, almost appearing man-made in their ugly but symmetrical forms. No bare surfaces of lifeless stone are visible, for any space between all these organisms is filled with a thick growth of moss animals, hydroid polyps and sponges whose violet and orange-red species cover large areas; among this teeming assortment I do not even know, in some cases, whether they belong to the plant or the animal kingdom.

Reprinted from Konrad Lorenz, On Aggression, Harcourt, Brace, and World, 1966, 3–48. Copyright 1966 by Konrad Lorenz and reproduced by permission.

My effortless progress brings me gradually into shallower water where corals become fewer, but plants more numerous. Huge forests of decorative algae, shaped exactly like African acacia trees, spread themselves beneath me and create the illusion that I am floating not just man-high above Atlantic coral ground, but a hundred times higher above an Ethiopian steppe. Wide fields of turtle grass and smaller ones of eelgrass glide away beneath me, and now that there is little more than three feet of water beneath me, a glance ahead reveals a long, dark, irregular wall stretching as far as I can see to each side and completely filling the space between the illuminated seabed and the mirror of the surface: it is the border between sea and land, the coast of Lignum Vitae Key.

The number of fish increases rapidly; dozens shoot from under me, reminding me of photographs of Africa where herds of wild animals flee in all directions from the shadow of an airplane. In some places, above the fields of thick turtle grass, comical fat puffers remind me of partridges taking off from a cornfield, zooming up only to glide down to land again in the next field or so. Other fish, many of which have incredible but always harmonious colors, do the opposite, diving straight into the grass as I approach. A fat porcupine with lovely devil's horns over ultramarine blue eyes lies quite quietly and grins at me. I have not hurt him, but he—or one of his kind—has hurt me! A few days ago I thoughtlessly touched one of this species, the Spiny Boxfish, and the needle-sharp parrot-beak, formed by two opposing teeth, pinched me and removed a considerable piece of skin from my right forefinger. I dive down to the specimen just sighted and, using the labor-saving technique of a duck in shallow water, leaving my backside above the surface, I seize him carefully and lift him up. After several fruitless attempts to bite, he starts to take the situation seriously and blows himself up; my hand clearly feels the "cylinder strokes" of the little pump formed by the pharyngeal muscles of the fish as he sucks in water. When the elasticity of his outer skin has reached its limit and he is lying like a distended prickly ball in my hand, I let him go and am amused at the urgency with which he squirts out the pumped-in water and disappears into the seaweed.

Then I turn to the wall separating sea from land. At first glance one could imagine it to be made of volcanic tuff, so fantastically pitted is its surface and so many are the cavities which stare like the eyeholes of skulls, dark and unfathomable. In fact, the rock consists of coral skeletons, relics of the pre-ice age. One can actually see in the ancient formations the structure of coral species still extant today and, pressed between them, the shells of mussels and snails whose living counterparts still frequent these waters. We are here on *two* coral reefs: an old one which has been dead for thousands of years and a new one growing on the old, as corals, like cultures, have the habit of growing on the skeletons of their forebears.

I swim up to and along the jagged waterfront, until I find a handy, not too spiky projection which I grasp with my right hand as an anchorage. In heavenly weightlessness, cool but not cold, a stranger in a wonderland far removed from earthly cares, rocked on gentle waves, I forget myself and am all eye, a blissful breathing captive balloon!

All around me are fish, and here in the shallow water they are mostly small fish. They approach me curiously from a distance or from the hiding places to which my coming had driven them; they dart back as I clear my snorkel by blowing out the water that has condensed in it; when I breathe quietly again they come nearer, swaying up and down in time with me in the gently undulating sea. It was by watching fish that, still with a clouded vision, I first noticed certain laws of animal behavior, without at the time understanding them in the least, but ever since I have endeavored to reach this understanding.

The multiplicity of the forms surrounding me—many so near that my far-sighted eyes cannot discern them sharply—seems at first overwhelming. But after a while their individual appearances become more familiar and my gestalt perception, that most wonderful of human faculties, begins to achieve a clearer, general view of the swarms of creatures. Then I find that there are not so many species as I thought at first. Two categories of fish are at once apparent: those which come swimming in shoals, either from the open sea or along the wall, and those which, after recovering from their panic at my presence, come slowly and cautiously out of a cave or other hiding place—always singly. Of the latter I already know that even after days or weeks the same individuals are always to be found in the same dwelling. Throughout my stay at Key Largo I visited regularly, every few days, a beautiful ocellated butterfly fish in its dwelling under a capsized landing stage and I always found it at home. Among the fish wandering hither and thither in shoals are myriads of little silversides, various small herrings which live near the coast, and their untiring hunters, the needle-fish, swift as arrows. Then there are gray-green snappers loitering in thousands under landing stages, breakwaters, and cliffs, and delightful blue-and-yellow-striped grunts, so called because they make a grunting noise when removed from the water. Particularly numerous and particularly lovely are the blue-striped, the white, and the yellow-striped grunts, misnomers because all three are blue-and-yellow-striped, each with a different pattern. According to my observations, all three kinds swim frequently in mixed shoals. These fish have a buccal mucous membrane of a remarkable burning-red color, only visible when, with widely opened mouth, a fish threatens a member of its own species, which naturally responds in the same manner. However, neither in the aquarium nor in the sea have I ever seen this impressive sparring lead to a serious fight.

One of the charms of these and other colorful grunts, and also of many snappers, is the fearless curiosity with which they accompany the snorkel diver. Probably they follow harmless large fish and the now almost extinct manatee, the legendary sea cow, in the same way, in the hope of catching little fish or other tiny creatures that have been scared out of cover by the large animal. The first time I swam out from my home harbor, the landing pier of Key Haven Motel in Tavernier on Key Largo, I was deeply impressed by the enormous crowd of grunts and snappers which surrounded me so densely that it obscured my view, and which seemed to be just as strong in numbers wherever I swam. Gradually I realized that I was always escorted by exactly the same fish and that at a modest estimate there were at least a few thousand. If I swam parallel with the shore to the next pier about half a mile away, the shoal followed me for about half this distance and then suddenly turned around and raced home as fast as it could swim. When the fish under the other landing stage noticed my coming, a startling thing happened: from the darkness of the stage emerged a monster several yards high and wide, and many times this length, throwing a deep black shadow on the sunlit sea bottom as it shot toward me, and only as it drew very near did it become resolved into a crowd of friendly grunts and snappers. The first time this happened to me, I was terrified, but later on these fish became a source of reassurance rather than fear, because while they remained with me I knew that there was no large barracuda anywhere near.

Entirely different are those daring little predators, needlefish and halfbeaks, which hunt in small bands of five or six just under the surface. Their whiplike forms are almost invisible from my submarine viewpoint, for their silver flanks reflect the light in exactly the same way as the under surface of the air, more familiar to us in its Janus face as the upper surface of the water. Seen from above, they are even more difficult to discern, since they shimmer blue-green just like the water surface. In widely spread flank formation they comb the highest layers of water hunting the little silversides which frequent the water in millions, thick as snowflakes in a blizzard and gleaming like silver tinsel. These dwarfs, the silversides, are not afraid of me, for fishes of their size would be no prey for fishes of mine. I can swim through the midst of their shoals and they give way so little that sometimes I hold my breath involuntarily to avoid breathing them in, as if I were passing through an equally dense cloud of mosquitoes. The fact that I am breathing through my snorkel in another medium does not in the least inhibit this reflex. If even the smallest needlefish approaches, the little silversides dart at lightning speed in all directions, upward, downward, and even leaping above the surface, producing in a few seconds a large clear space of water, which only gradually fills up again when the predator has passed.

Although the shapes of the fat-headed grunts and snappers are so different from those of the fine, streamlined needlefish, they have one thing in common: they do not deviate too much from the usual conception of the term "fish." Among the resident cave-dwellers the situation is different: the blue anglefish, decorated in youth with yellow vertical stripes, can still be called a "normal fish," but this thing pushing its way out of a crevice between two coral blocks, weaving with hesitating backward and forward movements, this velvet-black disk with bright yellow semicircular transverse bands and a luminous ultramarine-blue border to its lower edge, is this really a fish? Or those two round little things, the size and shape of a bumblebee, hurrying by and displaying on the *rear* end a round eye bordered with blue? Or the little jewel shining from that hollow, whose body is divided by a diagonal line from the lower anterior to the upper posterior end into a deep violet-blue and a lemon-yellow half? Or this unique little piece of dark-blue starry sky, strewn with tiny pale blue lights, which in paradoxical inversion of space is emerging from a coral block *below* me? On closer examination, all these fairy-tale figures are of course perfectly ordinary fishes, not too distantly related to my old friends and collaborators, the cichlids. The starry sky, the Marine Jewel Fish, and the little fish with the blue head and back and the yellow belly and tail, called Beau Gregory by the Floridians, are in fact close relations. The orange-red bumblebee is a baby of the "Rock Beauty," and the black and yellow disk is a young black Angelfish. But what colors, and what incredible designs: one could almost imagine they were planned to create a distant effect, like a flag or a poster.

The great, rippling mirror above me; starry skies—if only tiny ones—below;

swaying weightlessly in a translucent medium, surrounded by angels, lost in contemplation and awed admiration of the creation and its beauty, I thank the creator that I am still able to observe essential details: of the dull-colored fishes or the pastel-colored grunts I nearly always see several of the same species at once, swimming in close shoal formation; but of the brightly colored species within my field of vision, there is *one* blue and *one* black angelfish. Of the two baby rock beauties that have just raced by, one is in furious pursuit of the other.

I continue to observe, although, in spite of the warmth of the water, my captive-balloon position is making me feel cold. Now in the far distance—that is, only ten or twelve yards even in clear water—I see a beau gregory approaching, in search of food. The other beau, which is close to me, sees the intruder later than I do from my lookout post, and he only notices him when he is within about four yards. Then he shoots toward him furiously, whereupon the stranger, although he is a little bigger than his adversary, switches around and flees with vigorous strokes in wild zigzags, trying to avoid the ramming movements of his pursuer; these, if they met their mark, could inflict severe wounds, and indeed one of them does for I see a glinting scale flutter to the bottom like a wilted leaf. As soon as the stranger has disappeared into the dusky blue-green distance, the victor returns to his hollow, threading his way calmly through a dense shoal of young grunts who are in search of food in front of the entrance, and the absolute equanimity with which he passes through the shoal gives the impression that he is dodging stones or other inanimate obstacles. Even the little blue angelfish, not unlike himself in shape and color, rouses not the least sign of aggression.

Shortly afterward I observe a similar altercation between two black angelfish, scarcely a finger in length; but this time it is even more dramatic. The anger of the aggressor and the panicky flight of the intruder are even more apparent— though perhaps this is because my slow human eye is better able to follow the movements of the angelfish than those of the far swifter beau gregorys, whose performance is too quick for me.

I now realize that I am rather cold, and as I climb the coral wall into the warm air and golden sun of Florida, I formulate my observations in a few short sentences: the brilliant "poster-colored" fish are all local residents, and it is only these that I have seen defending a territory. Their furious attack is directed toward members of their own species only, except, of course, in the case of predatory fish in which, however, the motive of the pursuit is hunger and not real aggressiveness. Never have I seen fish of two different species attacking each other, even if both are highly aggressive by nature.

Coral Fish in the Laboratory

In the previous chapter I made use of poetic license: I did not mention that I already knew from observations in the aquarium how furiously the brightly colored coral fish fight their own species, and that I had already formed an opinion on the biological meaning of these fights. I went to Florida to test this hypothesis, and if the facts disproved it I was ready to throw it overboard—or rather to spit it out through my snorkel, for one can hardly throw something overboard when one is swimming under water. It is a good morning exercise for a research scientist to discard a pet hypothesis every day before breakfast. It keeps him young.

Some years ago I began to study brightly colored reef fish in the aquarium, impelled not only by my aesthetic pleasure in their beauty but also by my flair for interesting biological problems. The first question that occurred to me was: Why are these fish so colorful? When a biologist asks "What is the aim or purpose of something?" he is not trying to plumb the depth of meaning of the universe or of this problem in particular, but he is attempting much more humbly to find out something quite simple and, in principle, open to solution. Since we have learned, through Charles Darwin, about evolution and even something about its causes, the question "What for?" has, for the biologist, a sharply circumscribed meaning. We know that it is the *function* of an organ that alters its form, in the sense of functional improvement; and when, owing to a small, in itself fortuitous hereditary change, an organ becomes a little better and more efficient, the bearer of this character, and his descendants, will set a standard with which other, less talented members of his species cannot compete; thus in the course of time those less fit to survive will disappear from the earth's surface. This ever present phenomenon is called natural selection and is one of the two great constructors of evolution. It is mutation, plus the recombination of hereditary factors in sexual reproduction, which provides the material for natural selection. Though the process of mutation had not yet been discovered in his time, and even the word had not been coined in its present connotation, Darwin, with remarkable foresight, postulated mutation as a necessity although he never used the word.

All the innumerable, complex, and expedient structures of plant and animal bodies owe their existence to the patient work performed in the course of millions of years by mutation and selection. We are even more convinced of this than Darwin was, and, as we shall soon see, with more justification. To some people it may seem disappointing that the many forms of life, whose harmonious laws evoke our awe and whose beauty delights our aesthetic senses, have originated in such a prosaic and causally determined way. But to the scientists it is a constant source of wonder that nature has created its highest works without ever violating its own laws.

Our question "What for?" can receive a meaningful answer only in cases where both constructors of evolution have been at work in the manner just described. Our question simply asks what function the organ or character under discussion performs in the interests of the survival of the species. If we ask,

"What does a cat have sharp, curved claws for?" and answer simply by saying, "To catch mice with," this does not imply a profession of any mythical teleology, but the plain statement that catching mice is the function whose survival value, by the process of natural selection, has bred cats with this particular form of claw. Unless selection is at work, the question "What for?" cannot receive an answer with any real meaning. If we find, in a central European village, a population of mongrel dogs some of whom have straight tails and others curly ones, there is no point whatever in asking what they have such tails for. This random variety of forms—mostly more or less ugly—is the product of mutation working by itself, in other words, pure chance. But whenever we come upon highly regular, differentiated, and complicated structures, such as a bird's wing or the intricate mechanism of an instinctive behavior pattern, we must ask what demands of natural selection caused them to evolve, in other words, what they are for. We ask this question with assurance, in the confident hope of an intelligible answer, for we have found that we usually get one provided the questioner perseveres enough. This is not disproved by the few exceptional cases where scientific research has not yet been able to solve some of the most important of all biological problems, such as the question of what the wonderful forms and colors of mollusk shells are for, as the inadequate eye of these animals cannot see them, even when they are not—as they often are— hidden by the skin-fold of the mantle and in the darkness of the deep sea-bed.

The loud colors of coral fish call loudly for explanation. What species-preserving function could have caused their evolution? I bought the most colorful fishes I could find and, for comparison, a few less colorful and even some really drab species. Then I made an unexpected discovery: in the case of most of the really flamboyant "poster"-colored coral fish, it is quite impossible to keep more than one individual of a species in a small aquarium. If I put several members of the same species into the tank, there were vicious fights and within a short time only the strongest fish was left alive. Later, in Florida, it impressed me deeply to watch in the sea the same scene that I had always observed in my aquarium after the fatal battles: several fish, but only one of each species, each brightly colored but each flying a different flag, living peaceably together. At a small breakwater near my hotel, *one* beau gregory, *one* small black angelfish and *one* butterfly fish lived in peaceful association. Peaceful coexistence between two individuals of a "poster"-colored species occurs, in the aquarium or in the sea, only among those fishes that live in a permanent conjugal state. Such couples were observed, in the sea, among Blue Angelfish and Beau Gregory, and in the aquarium among white-and-yellow Butterfly Fish. The partners are inseparable and it is interesting to note that they are more aggressive toward members of their own species than single fish are. I shall explain the reason for this later.

In the sea, the principle "Like avoids like" is upheld without bloodshed, owing to the fact that the conquered fish flees from the territory of his conqueror who does not pursue him far; whereas in the aquarium, where there is no escape, the winner often kills the loser, or at least claims the whole container as his territory and so intimidates the weaker fish with continual attacks that they grow much more slowly than he does; and so his dominance increases till it leads to the fatal conclusion.

In order to observe how territory "owners" normally behave, one needs a container big enough for at least two territories of a size normally commanded by the species under examination. We therefore built an aquarium six feet long, holding more than two tons of water and big enough for several such territories of various species of smaller, coastal fish. In the "poster"-colored species, the young are nearly always not only more colorful and fiercer but also more firmly attached to their territories than the adults are. Since the young are small, we could observe their behavior in a comparatively limited space.

Into this aquarium my coworker Doris Zumpe and I put small fish, one to two inches in length, of the following: seven species of butterfly fish, two species of angelfish, eight species of demoiselles (the group to which the starry skies and the beau gregory belong), two species of triggerfish, three species of wrasse, one species of doctorfish, and several species of nonposter-colored, nonaggressive fish, such as trunkfish, puffers, and others. Thus there were about twenty-five species of "poster"-colored fish, with an average of four per species, more of some, only one of others, a total of roughly a hundred individuals. They settled in very well, with almost no losses; they started to flourish—and according to program, they began to fight.

Now came the chance of counting something. When the "exact" scientist can count or measure something, he experiences a pleasure which, to the outsider, is hard to understand. Admittedly we would know only a little less about intraspecific aggression if we had not counted but our results would be much less convincing if we could only say, "Brightly colored coral fishes hardly ever bite any other species than their own"; however, we, or to be more exact, Doris, counted the bites, with the following result: since there were about one hundred fish in the aquarium and each species was represented by an average of four, the chances of a fish biting one of its own species were three to ninety-six; but the proportion of bites inflicted on members of the same species to the bites given to other species was roughly eighty-five to fifteen. And even this small number of fifteen was misleading, because these bites came almost entirely from the demoiselles which in the aquarium stay in their caves all the time, invisible from without, and attack every intruder regardless of the species. In nature, they, too, ignore fishes of other species. Later on we omitted this group and obtained much more impressive figures.

A further proportion of the bites inflicted on fishes of different species came from those individuals which had no members of their own species in the container and therefore had to discharge their anger on other objects. Their choice of objects confirmed the correctness of my supposition as convincingly as did the more exact figures. For example, there was a single member of an uncertain species of butterfly fish whose form and markings were so exactly intermediate between the white-and-gold and the white-and-black butterfly fish that we called him the white-gold-black, and he evidently shared our opinion of his classification for he divided his attacks almost equally between the representatives of those two species and was never seen to bite a member of the third species. The behavior of our single blue trigger (Odonus niger) was even more interesting. The zoologist who gave this fish its Latin name can only have seen it as a corpse in formalin, for the live fish is not black but luminous blue, suffused with a delicate violet and pink, particularly evident at the edges of the fins. I bought only one specimen of this fish because I realized, from the fights in the dealer's tank, that my own tank would be too small for two of these two-and-a-half-inch fishes. In the absence of a fellow member of his species, my blue triggerfish behaved peaceably for a time, administering only a few bites, significantly distributing them between two quite different species. Firstly he pursued the so-called blue devils, near relations of the blue gregory, which had the same beautiful blue color as himself; and secondly he attacked the two members of another triggerfish species, the so-called Picasso fish. As its name indicates, the markings of this fish are extraordinarily colorful and bizarre, but it resembles the blue trigger in its outward form if not in its color. After a few months, the stronger of the two Picassos had dispatched the weaker into the realm of formalin, and a strong rivalry sprang up between the survivor and the blue trigger. Doubtless the increased aggression of the latter toward the Picasso was influenced by the fact that his old enemies, the blue devils, had meanwhile changed from the bright blue of their youth to their drab, dove-gray adult dress which had a less fight-eliciting effect. Finally, the blue trigger killed the Picasso. I could quote many more such cases where, in similar experiments, only one fish survived. In cases where, as a result of pairing, two fishes behaved as one, one pair remained, as in the brown, and the white-and-gold butterfly fish. Numerous cases are also known where other animals, besides fish, in the absence of a member of their own species discharged their aggression on other objects, choosing for the purpose close relations or species with coloring similar to their own.

These aquarium observations, confirmed by my sea studies, prove the rule that fish are far more aggressive toward their own species than toward any other. Now there are, as I have already described, a number of species which are not nearly so aggressive as the coral fish of my experiments. When one examines the aggressive and the more or less nonaggressive species, it is evident that there is a connection between coloring, aggressiveness, and sedentary territorial habits. Among the fish that I examined in the free state, extreme aggressiveness, associated with territorial behavior and concentrated on members of the same species, is found almost exclusively in those forms whose bright poster-like color patterns proclaim their species from afar. In fact, it was this extraordinary kind of coloring that aroused my curiosity and drew my attention to the existence of a problem. Fresh-water fish can also be beautifully colorful, and in this respect many of them can hold their own with marine fish, but apart from their beauty they contrast oddly with the coral fish.

The charm of the coloring of most fresh-water fish lies in its changeability: Cichlids, Labyrinth Fish, the red, green, and blue male Stickleback, the rainbow-colored Bitterling of our home waters, and many other forms well known to us through the home aquarium, illuminate their jewels only when they are glowing with love or anger. In many of these fish the degree of their emotion can be measured by their coloring, which also shows whether aggressiveness, sexual excitement or the flight urge is uppermost. Just as a rainbow disappears when a cloud covers the sun, so the beauty of the fish fades when the emotion that produced it wanes or is superseded by another conflicting emotion, such as fear, which quickly covers the fish with drab protective coloring. In other words, the colors of all these fish are a means of expression, only appearing when they are needed. Correspondingly, the young and often the females of these species have plain camouflage coloring.

The situation is different among the aggressive coral fish. By day, their glorious dress is as constant as if it had been painted on them in fast colors. It is only before going to sleep that most of them show their capacity for changing color by putting on a nightdress whose design is amazingly different from their day attire; but as long as they are awake and active, they keep their flamboyant colors at all costs, whether they are hotly pursuing a fellow member of their species or are themselves escaping in wild zigzags from a pursuer. They would no more think of lowering their flag than would an English battleship in a novel by Forester. And even in transport containers, where they are certainly not at ease, and during illness their gorgeous colors remain unchanged; even after death it is a long time before they disappear entirely.

In all typical poster-colored coral fish, not only are male and female both brightly colored but even the tiny babies show brilliant colors which, strangely enough, are often quite different from those of the adults, and sometimes even more striking. Most amazing of all: in several forms, only the babies are multicolored, for example the starry skies mentioned on page 9, and the blue devils (page 17), both of which change with sexual maturity into drab dove-gray fish with pale yellow tail fins.

The coloring of coral fish is distributed in large, sharply contrasting areas of the body. This is quite different from the color patterns not only of most fresh-water fish but of nearly all less aggressive and less territorial fish, whose charm lies in the delicacy of their designs, the harmony of their soft coloring, and the careful "attention to detail." When you see a grunt from a distance, you see an insignificant, greenish-silver fish, and only when he is right in front of you—a thing that may easily happen with these inquisitive creatures—do you notice the gold and sky-blue hieroglyphs clothing his body like an attractively designed brocade. Without any doubt these patterns are signals for the recognition of the species by its own members, but their design is such that it can be seen only at very close quarters by members of the species in the immediate vicinity. Conversely, the poster colors of the territorially aggressive coral fish are so arranged that they can be seen and recognized from the greatest possible distance, and we know only too well that recognition of their own species provokes furious aggression in these fish.

Many people, even those with an understanding of nature, think that we biologists show a strange desire for superfluous knowledge when we want to know what functions every single colored patch on an animal fulfills in the preservation of the species, and what causes could have led to its evolution. Indeed this curiosity is often attributed to materialism and a distorted sense of values. But every question that has a reasonable answer is justifiable, and the value and beauty of a natural object is in no way affected by our finding out why it is made in this, and no other way. The scientist's attitude cannot be better expressed than as William Beebe once formulated it in his quaint manner: "The isness of things is well worth studying; but it is their whyness that makes life worth living." The rainbow is no less beautiful because we have learned to understand the laws of light refraction to which it owes its existence, and the beauty and symmetry of design, color, and movement in our fishes must excite our admiration even more when we know that their purpose is preservation of the species that they adorn. We know, with tolerable certainty, the species-preserving function of the glorious war paint of coral fish: it elicits furious reactions of territorial defense in every fish of the same species—and only of the same species—when the reacting individual is in its own territory; and it proclaims fear-inspiring readiness to fight to the intruder encroaching on foreign ground. Both functions are practically identical with those of another natural phenomenon whose beauty has inspired our poets—bird song.

If we test this theory by comparing the fighting behavior of poster-colored and non-poster-colored fishes of the same genera and in the same environment, it proves itself particularly impressively when a poster-colored and plain-colored fish belong to the same genus; for example, the Sergeant Major, with its plain transverse bands, is a peaceful schooling fish, while its generic relation, the sharp-toothed Abudefduf, a gorgeous velvet-black fish with bright blue stripes on head and thorax and a yellow transverse band on its body, is about the fiercest of all the fierce territory owners that I met with during my coral fish studies. Our large aquarium proved too small for two tiny youngsters, scarcely an inch long, of this species; one claimed for itself the whole container and the other eked out its existence in the left upper front corner behind the bubbles of the air generator which hid it from the view of its disagreeable brother. Another good example is provided by comparing fish of the butterfly fish genera. The only peaceful one I know is the four-eyed butterfly, and this is the only one whose characteristic design is broken up into such small details that it can be recognized only at very close quarters.

The most remarkable thing of all is that coral fish which are poster-colored in youth and plain-colored at sexual maturity show the same correlation between coloring and aggression: as babies they are furious defenders of their territory but as adults they are far more peaceable; in some, one has the impression that they are obliged to divest themselves of their fight-eliciting colors in order to make friendly contact between the sexes possible. This certainly applies to the demoiselle group; several times I saw a brilliantly black and white species spawning in the aquarium, for this purpose changing their striking color for a monotonous dull gray, only to hoist the flag again as soon as spawning was over.

What Aggression Is Good For

What is the value of all this fighting? In nature, fighting is such an ever-present process, its behavior mechanisms and weapons are so highly developed and have so obviously arisen under the selection pressure of a species-preserving function, that it is our duty to ask this Darwinian question.

The layman, misguided by sensationalism in press and film, imagines the relationship between the various "wild beasts of the jungle" to be a bloodthirsty struggle, all against all. In a widely shown film, a Bengal tiger was seen fighting with a python, and immediately afterward the python with a crocodile. With a clear conscience I can assert that such things never occur under natural conditions. What advantage would one of these animals gain from exterminating the other? Neither of them interferes with the other's vital interests.

Darwin's expression, "the struggle for existence," is sometimes erroneously interpreted as the struggle between different species. In reality, the struggle Darwin was thinking of and which drives evolution forward is the competition between near relations. What causes a species to disappear or become transformed into a different species is the profitable "invention" that falls by chance to one or a few of its members in the everlasting gamble of hereditary change. The descendants of these lucky ones gradually outstrip all others until the particular species consists only of individuals who possess the new "invention."

There are, however, fightlike contests between members of different species: at night an owl kills and eats even well-armed birds of prey, in spite of their vigorous defense, and when these birds meet the owl by day they attack it ferociously. Almost every animal capable of self-defense, from the smallest rodent upward, fights furiously when it is cornered and has no means of escape. Besides these three particular types of inter-specific fighting, there are other, less typical cases; for instance, two cave-nesting birds of different species may fight for a nesting cavity. Something must be said here about these three types of inter-specific fighting in order to explain their peculiarity and to distinguish them from the *intra*-specific aggression which is really the subject of this book.

The survival value of inter-specific fights is much more evident than that of intra-specific contests. The way in which a predatory animal and its prey influence each other's evolution is a classical example of how the selection pressure of a certain function causes corresponding adaptations. The swiftness of the hunted ungulate forces its feline pursuers to evolve enormous leaping power and sharply armed toes. Paleontological discoveries have shown impressive examples of such evolutionary competition between weapons of attack and those of defense. The teeth of grazing animals have achieved better and better grinding power, while, in their parallel evolution, nutritional plants have devised means of protecting themselves against being eaten, as by the storage of silicates and the development of hard, wooden thorns. This kind of "fight" between the eater and the eaten never goes so far that the predator causes extinction of the prey: a state of equilibrium is always established between them, endurable by both species. The last lions would have died of hunger long before they had killed the last pair of antelopes or zebras; or, in terms of human commercialism, the whaling industry would go bankrupt before the last whales became extinct. What directly threatens the existence of an animal species is never the "eating enemy" but the competitor. In prehistoric times man took the Dingo, a primitive domestic dog, to Australia. It ran wild there, but it did not exterminate a single species of its quarry; instead, it destroyed the large marsupial beasts of prey which ate the same animals as it did itself. The large marsupial predators, the Tasmanian Devil and the Marsupial Wolf, were far superior to the Dingo in strength, but the hunting methods of these "old-fashioned," relatively stupid and slow creatures were inferior to those of the "modern" mammal. The Dingo reduced the marsupial population to such a degree that their methods no longer "paid," and today they exist only in Tasmania, where the Dingo has never penetrated.

In yet another respect the fight between predator and prey is not a fight in the real sense of the word: the stroke of the paw with which a lion kills his prey may resemble the movements that he makes when he strikes his rival, just as a shotgun and a rifle resemble each other outwardly; but the inner motives of the hunter are basically different from those of the fighter. The buffalo which the lion fells provokes his aggression as little as the appetizing turkey which I have just seen hanging in the larder provokes mine. The differences in these inner drives can clearly be seen in the expression movements of the animal: a dog about to catch a hunted rabbit has the same kind of excitedly happy expression as he has when he greets his master or awaits some longed-for treat. From many excellent photographs it can be seen that the lion, in the dramatic moment before he springs, is in no way angry. Growling, laying the ears back, and other well-known expression movements of fighting behavior are seen in predatory animals only when they are very afraid of a wildly resisting prey, and even then the expressions are only suggested.

The opposite process, the "counteroffensive" of the prey against the predatory, is more nearly related to genuine aggression. Social animals in particular take every possible chance to attack the "eating enemy" that threatens their safety. This process is called "mobbing." Crows or other birds "mob" a cat or any other nocturnal predator, if they catch sight of it by day.

The survival value of this attack on the eating enemy is self-evident. Even if the attacker is small and defenseless, he may do his enemy considerable harm. All animals which hunt singly have a chance of success only if they take their prey by surprise. If a fox is followed through the wood by a loudly screaming jay, or a sparrow hawk is pursued by a flock of warning wagtails, his hunting is spoiled for the time being. Many birds will mob an owl, if they find one in the daytime, and drive it so far away that it will hunt somewhere else the next night. In some social animals such as jackdaws and many kinds of geese, the function of mobbing is particularly interesting. In jackdaws, its most important survival value is to teach the young, inexperienced birds what a dangerous eating enemy looks like, which they do not know instinctively. Among birds, this is a unique case of traditionally acquired knowledge.

Geese and ducks "know" by very selective, innate releasing mechanisms that anything furry, red-brown, long-shaped, and slinking is extremely dangerous, but nonetheless mobbing, with its intense excitement and the gathering together of geese from far and wide, has an essentially educational character as well as a survival value; anyone who did not know it already learns: foxes may be found *here!* At a time when only part of the shore of our lake was protected by a foxproof fence, the geese kept ten or fifteen yards clear of all unfenced cover likely to conceal a fox, but in the fenced-in area they penetrated fearlessly into the thickets of young fir trees. Besides this didactic function, mobbing of predators by jackdaws and geese still has the basic, original one of making the enemy's life a burden. Jackdaws actively attack their enemy, and geese apparently intimidate it with their cries, their thronging, and their fearless advance. The great Canada geese will even follow a fox over land in a close phalanx, and I have never known a fox in this situation try to catch one of his tormentors. With ears laid back and a disgusted expression on his face, he glances back over his shoulder at the trumpeting flock and trots slowly—so as not to lose face—away from them.

Among the larger, more defense-minded herbivores which, en masse, are a match for even the biggest predators, mobbing is particularly effective; according to reliable reports, zebras will molest even a leopard if they catch him on a veldt where cover is sparse. The reaction of social attack against the wolf is still so ingrained in domestic cattle and pigs that one can sometimes land oneself in danger by going through a field of cows with a nervous dog which, instead of barking at them or at least fleeing independently, seeks refuge between the legs of its owner. Once, when I was out with my bitch Stasi, I was obliged to jump into a lake and swim for safety when a heard of young cattle half encircled us and advanced threateningly; and when he was in southern Hungary during the First World War my brother spent a pleasant afternoon up a tree with his Scotch terrier under his arm, because a herd of half-wild Hungarian swine, disturbed while grazing in the wood, encircled them, and with bared tusks and unmistakable intentions began to close in on them.

Much more could be said about these effective attacks on the real or supposed enemy. In some birds and fishes, to serve this special purpose brightly colored "aposematic" or warning colors have evolved, which predators notice and associate with unpleasant experiences with the particular species. Poisonous, evil-tasting, or otherwise specially protected animals have, in many cases, "chosen" for these warning signals the combination of red, white, and black; and it is remarkable that the Common Sheldrake and the Sumatra Barb, two creatures which have nothing in common either with each other or the above-named groups, should have done the same thing. It has long been known that Common Sheldrake mob predatory animals and that they so disgust the fox with the sight of their brightly colored plumage that they can nest safely in inhabited foxholes. I bought some Sumatra Barbs because I had asked myself why these fishes looked so poisonous; in a large communal aquarium, they immediately answered by question by mobbing big Cichlids so persistently that I had to save the giant predators from the only apparently harmless dwarfs.

There is a third form of fighting behavior, and its survival value is as easily demonstrated as that of the predator's attack on its prey or the mobbing by the prey of the eating enemy. With H. Hediger, we call this third behavior pattern the *critical reaction*. The expression "fighting like a cornered rat" has become symbolic of the desperate struggle in which the fighter stakes his all, because he cannot escape and can expect no mercy. This most violent form of fighting behavior is motivated by fear, by the most intense flight impulses whose natural outlet is prevented by the fact that the danger is too near; so the animal, not daring to turn its back on it, fights with the proverbial courage of desperation. Such a contingency may also occur when, as with the cornered rat, flight is prevented by lack of space, or by strong social ties, like those which forbid an animal to desert its brood or family. The attack which a hen or goose makes on everything that goes too near her chicks or goslings can also be classified as a critical reaction. Many animals will attack desperately when surprised by an enemy at less than a certain critical distance, whereas they would have fled if they had noticed his coming from farther away. As Hediger has described, lion tamers maneuver their great beasts of prey into their positions in the arena by playing a dangerous game with the margin between flight distance and critical distance; and thousands of big game hunting stories testify to the dangerousness of large beasts of prey in dense cover. The reason is that in such circumstances the flight distance is particularly small, because the animal feels safe, imagining that it will not be noticed by a man even if he should penetrate the cover and get quite close; but if in so doing the man oversteps the animal's critical distance, a so-called hunting accident happens quickly and disastrously.

All the cases described above, in which animals of different species fight against each other, have one thing in common: every one of the fighters gains an obvious advantage by its behavior or, at least, in the interests of preserving the species it "ought to" gain one. But intra-specific aggression, aggression in the proper and narrower sense of the word, also fulfills a species-preserving function. Here, too, the Darwinian question "What for?" may and must be asked. Many people will not see the obvious justification for this question, and those accustomed to the classical psychoanalytical way of thinking will probably regard it as a frivolous attempt to vindicate the life-destroying principle or, purely and simply, evil. The average normal civilized human being witnesses aggression only when two of his fellow citizens or two of his domestic animals fight, and therefore sees only its evil effects. In addition there is the alarming progression of aggressive actions ranging from cocks fighting in the barnyard to dogs biting each other, boys thrashing each other, young men throwing beer mugs at each other's heads, and so on to bar-room brawls about politics, and finally to wars and atom bombs.

With humanity in its present cultural and technological situation, we have good reason to consider intra-specific aggression the greatest of all dangers. We shall not improve our chances of counteracting it if we accept it as something metaphysical and inevitable, but on the other hand, we shall perhaps succeed in finding remedies if we investigate the chain of its natural causation. Wherever man has achieved the power of voluntarily guiding a natural phenomenon in a certain direction, he has owed it to his understanding of the chain of causes which formed it. Physiology, the science concerned with the normal life processes and how they fulfill their species-preserving function, forms the essential foundation for pathology, the science investigating their disturbances. Let us forget for a moment that the aggression drive has become derailed under conditions of civilization, and let us inquire impartially into its natural causes. For the reasons already given, as good Darwinians we must inquire into the species-preserving function which, under natural—or rather precultural—conditions, is fulfilled by fights within the species, and which by the process of selection has caused the advanced development of intra-specific fighting behavior in so many higher animals. It is not only fishes that fight their own species: the majority of vertebrates do so too, man included.

Darwin had already raised the question of the survival value of fighting, and he has given us an enlightening answer: It is always favorable to the future of a species if the stronger of two rivals takes possession either of the territory or of the desired female. As so often, this truth of yesterday is not the untruth of today but only a special case; ecologists have recently demonstrated a much more essential function of aggression. Ecology—derived from the Greek *oikos*, the house—is the branch of biology that deals with the manifold reciprocal relations of the organism to its natural surroundings—its "household"—which of course includes all other animals and plants native to the environment. Unless the special interests of a social organization demand close aggregation of its members, it is obviously most expedient to spread the individuals of an animal species as evenly as possible over the available habitat. To use a human analogy: if, in a certain area, a larger number of doctors, builders, and mechanics want to exist, the representatives of these professions will do well to settle as far away from each other as possible.

The danger of too dense a population of an animal species settling in one part of the available biotope and exhausting all its sources of nutrition and so starving can be obviated by a mutual repulsion acting on the animals of the same species, effecting their regular spacing out, in much the same manner as electrical charges are regularly distributed all over the surface of a spherical conductor. This, in plain terms, is the most important survival value of intra-specific aggression.

Now we can understand why the sedentary coral fish in particular are so crazily colored. There are few biotopes on earth that provide so much and such varied nutrition as a coral reef. Here fish species can, in an evolutionary sense, take up very different professions: one can support itself as an "unskilled laborer," doing what any average fish can do, hunting creatures that are neither poisonous nor armor-plated nor prickly, in other words hunting all the defenseless organisms approaching the reef from the open sea, some as "plankton," others as active swimmers "intending" to settle on the reef, as millions of free-swimming larvae of all coral-dwelling organisms do. On the other hand, another fish species may specialize in eating forms of life that live on the reef itself and are therefore equipped with some sort of protective mechanism which the hunting fish must render harmless. Corals themselves provide many different kinds of nourishment for a whole series of fish species. Pointed-jawed butterfly fish get their food parasitically from corals and other stinging animals. They search continuously in the coral stems for small prey caught in the stinging tentacles of coral polyps. As soon as they see these, they produce, by fanning with their pectoral fins, a current so directly aimed at the prey that at the required point a "parting" is made between the polyps, pressing their tentacles flat on all sides and thus enabling the fish to seize the prey almost without getting its nose stung. It always gets it just a little stung and can be seen "sneezing" and shaking its nose, but, like pepper, the sting seems to act as an agreeable stimulant. My beautiful yellow and brown butterfly fishes prefer a prey, such as a piece of fish, stuck in the tentacles of a stinging sea anemone, to the same prey swimming free in the water. Other related species have developed a stronger immunity to stings and they devour the prey together with the coral animal that has caught it. Yet other species disregard the stinging capsules of coelenterates altogether, and eat coral animals, hydroid polyps, and even big, strong, stinging sea anemones, as placidly as a cow eats grass. As well as this immunity to poison, parrot fish have evolved a strong chisellike dentition and they eat whole branches of coral including their calcareous skeleton. If you dive near a grazing herd of these beautiful, rainbow-colored fish, you can hear a cracking and crunching as though a little gravel mill were at work—and this actually corresponds with the facts, for when such a fish excretes, it rains a little shower of white sand, and the observer realizes with astonishment that most of the snow-clean coral sand covering the glades of the coral forest has obviously passed through parrot fish.

Other fish, plectognaths, to which the comical puffers, trunk, and porcupine fish belong, have specialized in cracking hard-shelled mollusks, crabs, and sea urchins; and others again, such as angelfish, specialize in snatching the lovely feather crowns that certain feather worms thrust out of their hard, calcareous tubes. Their capacity for quick retraction acts as a protection against slower predators, but some angelfish have a way of sidling up and, with a lightning sideways jerk of the mouth, seizing the worm's head at a speed surpassing its capacity for withdrawal. Even in the aquarium, where they seize prey which has no such quick reactions, these fish cannot do otherwise than snap like this.

The reef offers many other "openings" for specialized fish. There are some which remove parasites from others and which are therefore left unharmed by the fiercest predators, even when they penetrate right into the mouth cavities of their hosts to perform their hygienic work. There are others which live as parasites on large fish, punching pieces from their epidermis, and among these are the oddest fish of all: they resemble the cleaner fish so closely in color, form, and movement that, under false pretenses, they can safely approach their victims.

It is essential to consider the fact that all these opportunities for special careers, known as ecological niches, are often provided by the same cubic yard of ocean water. Because of the enormous nutritional possibilities, every fish, whatever its specialty, requires only a few square yards of sea bottom for its support, so in this small area there can be as many fish as there are ecological niches, and anyone who has watched with amazement the thronging traffic on a coral reef knows that these are legion. However, every one of this crowd is determined that no other fish of his species should settle in his territory. Specialists of other "professions" harm his livelihood as little as, to use our analogy again, the practice of a doctor harms the trade of a mechanic living in the same village.

In less densely populated biotopes where the same unit of space can support three or four species only, a resident fish or bird can "afford" to drive away all living beings, even members of species that are no real threat to his existence; but if a sedentary coral fish tried to do the same thing, it would be utterly exhausted and, moreover, would never manage to keep its territory free from the swarms of noncompetitors of different "professions." It is in the occupational interests of all sedentary species that each should determine the spatial distribution that will benefit its own individuals, entirely without consideration for other species. The colorful "poster" patterns, described in Chapter One, and the fighting reactions elicited by them, have the effect that the fish of each species keep a measured distance only from nutritional competitors of the same species. This is the very simple answer to the much discussed question of the function of the colors of coral fish.

As I have already mentioned, the species-typical song of birds has a very similar survival value to that of the visual signals of fishes. From the song of a certain bird, other birds not yet in possession of a territory recognize that in this particular place a male is proclaiming territorial rights. It is remarkable that in many species the song indicates how strong and possibly how old the singer is, in other words, how much the listener has to fear him. Among several species of birds that mark their territory acoustically, there is great individual difference of sound expression, and some observers are of the opinion that, in such species, the personal visiting card is of special significance. While Heinroth interpreted the crowing of the cock with the words, "Here is a cock!" Baeumer, the most knowledgeable of all domestic-fowl experts, heard in it the far more special announcement, "Here is the cock Balthazar!"

Among mammals, which mostly "think through their noses," it is not surprising that marking of the territory by scent plays a big role. Many methods have been tried; various scent glands have been evolved, and the most remarkable ceremonies developed around the depositing of urine and feces; of these the leg-lifting of the domestic dog is the most familiar. The objection has been raised by some students of mammals that such scent marks cannot have anything to do with territorial ownership because they are found not only in socially living mammals which do not defend single territories, but also in animals that wander far and wide; but this opinion is only partly correct. First, it has been proved that dogs and other pack-living animals recognize each other by the scent of the marks, and it would at once be apparent to the members of a pack if a nonmember presumed to lift its leg in their hunting grounds. Secondly, Leyhausen and Wolf have demonstrated the very interesting possibility that the distribution of animals of a certain species over the available biotope can be effected not only by a space plan but also by a time plan. They found that, in domestic cats living free in open country, several individuals could make use of the same hunting ground without ever coming into conflict, by using it according to a definite time-table, in the same way as our Seewiesen housewives use our communal washhouse. An additional safeguard against undesirable encounters is the scent marks which these animals—the cats, not the housewives—deposit at regular intervals wherever they go. These act like railway signals whose aim is to prevent collision between two trains. A cat finding another cat's signal on its hunting path assesses its age, and if it is very fresh it hesitates, or chooses another path; if it is a few hours old it proceeds calmly on its way.

Even in the case of animals whose territory is governed by space only, the hunting ground must not be imagined as a property determined by geographical confines; it is determined by the fact that in every individual the readiness to fight is greatest in the most familiar place, that is, in the middle of its territory. In other words, the threshold value of fight-eliciting stimuli is at its lowest where the animal feels safest, that is, where its readiness to fight is least diminished by its readiness to escape. As the distance from this "headquarters" increases, the readiness to fight decreases proportionately as the surroundings become stranger and more intimidating to the animal. If one plotted the graph of this decrease the curve would not be equally steep for all directions in space. In fish, the center of whose territory is nearly always on the bottom, the decline in readiness to fight is most marked in the vertical direction because the fish is threatened by special dangers from above.

The territory which an animal apparently possesses is thus only a matter of variations in readiness to fight, depending on the place and on various local factors inhibiting the fighting urge. In nearing the center of the territory the aggressive urge increases in geometrical ratio to the decrease in distance from this center. This increase in aggression is so great that it compensates for all differences ever to be found in adult, sexually mature animals of a species. If we know the territorial centers of two conflicting animals, such as two garden redstarts or two aquarium sticklebacks, all other things being equal, we can predict, from the place of encounter, which one will win: the one that is nearer home.

When the loser flees, the inertia of reaction of both animals leads to that phenomenon which always occurs when a time lag enters into a self-regulating process—to an oscillation. The courage of the fugitive returns as he nears his own headquarters, while that of the pursuer sinks in proportion to the distance covered in enemy territory. Finally the fugitive turns and attacks the former pursuer vigorously and unexpectedly and, as was predictable, he in his turn is beaten and driven away. The whole performance is repeated several times till both fighters come to a standstill at a certain point of balance where they threaten each other without fighting.

The position, the territorial "border," is in no way marked on the ground but is determined exclusively by a balance of power and may, if this alters in the least, for instance if one fish is replete and lazy, come to lie in a new position somewhat nearer the headquarters of the lazy one. An old record of our observations on the territorial behavior of two pairs of cichlids demonstrates this oscillation of the territorial borders. Four fish of this species were put into a large tank and at once the strongest male, A, occupied the left, back, lower corner and chased the other three mercilessly around the whole tank; in other words, he claimed the whole tank as his territory. After a few days, male B took possession of a tiny space immediately below the surface in the diagonally opposite right, front, upper corner. There he bravely resisted the attacks of the first male. This occupation of an area near the surface is in a way an act of desperation for one of these fish, because it is risking great danger from aerial predators in order to hold its own against an enemy of its own species, which, as already explained, will attack less resolutely in such a locality. In other words, the owner of such a dangerous area has, as an ally, the fear which the surface inspires in its bad neighbor. During succeeding days, the space defended by B grew visibly, expanding downward until he finally took his station in the right, front, lower corner, so gaining a much more satisfactory headquarters. Now at last he had the same chances as A, whom he quickly pressed so far back that their territories divided the tank into two almost equal parts. It was interesting to see how both fishes patrolled the border continuously, maintaining a threatening attitude. Then one morning they were doing this on the extreme right of the tank, again around the original headquarters of B, who could now scarcely call a few square inches his own. I knew at once what had happened: A had paired, and since it is characteristic of all large cichlids that both partners take part in territorial defense, B was subjected to double pressure and his territory had decreased accordingly. Next day the fish were again in the middle of the tank, threatening each other across the "border," but now there were four, because B had also taken a mate, and thus the balance of power with the A family was restored. A week later I found the border far toward the left lower area, and encroaching on A's former territory. The reason for this was that the A couple had spawned and since one of the partners was busy looking after the eggs, only one at a time was able to attend to frontier defense. As soon as the B couple had also spawned, the previous equal division of space was re-established. Julian Huxley once used a good metaphor to describe this behavior: he compared the territories to air-balloons in a close container, pressing against each other and expanding or contracting with the slightest change of pressure in each individual one. This territorial aggression, really a very simple mechanism of behavior-physiology, gives an ideal solution to the problem of the distribution of animals of any one species over the available area in such a way that it is favorable to the species as a whole. Even the weaker specimens can exist and reproduce, if only in a very small space. This has special significance in creatures which reach sexual maturity long before they are fully grown. What a peaceful issue of the "evil principle"!

In many animals the same result is achieved without aggressive behavior. Theoretically it suffices that animals of the same species "cannot bear the smell of each other" and avoid each other accordingly. To a certain extent this applies to the smell signals deposited by cats, though behind these lies a hidden threat of active aggression. There are some vertebrates which entirely lack intra-specific aggression but which nevertheless avoid their own species meticulously. Some frogs, in particular tree frogs, live solitary lives except at mating time, and they are obviously distributed very evenly over the available habitat. As American scientists have recently discovered, this distribution is effected quite simply by the fact that every frog avoids the quacking sound of his own species. This explanation, however, does not account for the distribution of the females, for these, in most frogs, are dumb.

We can safely assume that the most important function of intra-specific aggression is the even distribution of the animals of a particular species over an inhabitable area, but it is certainly not its only one. Charles Darwin had already observed that sexual selection, the selection of the best and strongest animals for reproduction, was furthered by the fighting of rival animals, particularly males. The strength of the father directly affects the welfare of the children in those species in which he plays an active part in their care and defense. The correlation between male parental care and rival fighting is clear, particularly in those animals which are not territorial in the sense which the Cichlids demonstrate but which wander more or less nomadically, as, for example, large ungulates, ground apes, and many others. In such animals, intra-specific aggression plays no essential part in the "spacing out" of the species. Bisons, antelopes, horses, etc., form large herds, and territorial borders and territorial jealousy are unknown to them since there is enough food for all. Nevertheless the males of these species fight each other violently and dramatically, and there is no doubt that the selection resulting from this aggressive behavior leads to the evolution of particularly strong and courageous defenders of family and herd; conversely, there is just as little doubt that the survival value of herd defense has resulted in selective breeding for hard rival fights. This interaction has produced impressive fighters such as bull bison or the males of the large baboon species; at every threat to the community, these valiantly surround and protect the weaker members of the herd.

In connection with rival fights attention must be drawn to a fact which, though it seems paradoxical to the nonbiologist, is, as we shall show later on in this book, of the very greatest importance: purely intra-specific selective breeding can lead to the development of forms and behavior patterns which are not only nonadaptive but can even have adverse effects on species preservation. This is why, in the last paragraph, I emphasized the fact that family defense, a form of strife with the extra-specific environment, has evolved the rival fight, and this in its turn has developed the powerful males. If sexual rivalry, or any other form of intra-specific competition, exerts selection pressure uninfluenced by any environmental exigencies, it may develop in a direction which is quite unadaptive to environment, and irrelevant, if not positively detrimental, to survival. This process may give rise to bizarre physical forms of no use to the species. The antlers of stags, for example, were developed in the service of rival fights, and a stag without them has little hope of producing progeny. Otherwise antlers are useless, for male stags defend themselves against beasts of prey with their fore-hoofs only and never with their antlers. Only the reindeer has based an invention on this necessity and "learned" to shovel snow with a widened point of its antlers.

Sexual selection by the female often has the same results as the rival fights. Wherever we find exaggerated development of colorful feathers, bizarre forms, etc., in the male, we may suspect that the males no longer fight but that the last word in the choice of a mate is spoken by the female, and that the male has no means of contesting this decision. Birds of Paradise, the Ruff, the Mandarin Duck, and the Argus Pheasant show examples of such behavior. The Argus hen pheasant reacts to the large secondary wing feathers of the cock; they are decorated with beautiful eye spots and the cock spreads them before her during courtship. They are so huge that the cock can scarcely fly, and the bigger they are the more they stimulate the hen. The number of progeny produced by a cock in a certain period of time is in direct proportion to the length of these feathers, and, even if their extreme development is unfavorable in other ways—his unwieldiness may cause him to be eaten by a predator while a rival with less absurdly exaggerated wings may escape—he will nevertheless leave more descendants than will a plainer cock. So the predisposition to huge wing feathers is preserved, quite against the interests of the species. One could well imagine an Argus hen that reacted to a small red spot on the wings of the male, which would disappear when he folded his wings and interfere neither with his flying capacity nor with his protective color, but the evolution of the Argus pheasant has run itself into a blind alley. The males continue to compete in producing the largest possible wing feathers, and these birds will never reach a sensible solution and "decide" to stop this nonsense at once.

Here for the first time we are up against a strange and almost uncanny phenomenon. We know that the techniques of trial and error used by the great master builders sometimes lead inevitably to plans that fall short of perfect efficiency. In the plant and animal worlds there are, besides the efficient, quantities of characteristics which only just avoid leading the particular species to destruction. But in the case of the Argus pheasant we have something quite different: it is not only like the strict efficiency expert "closing an eye" and letting second-rate construction pass in the interests of experiment, but it is selection itself that has here run into a blind alley which may easily result in destruction. This always happens when competition between members of a species causes selective breeding without any relation to the extra-specific environment.

My teacher, Oskar Heinroth, used to say jokingly, "Next to the wings of the Argus pheasant, the hectic life of Western civilized man is the most stupid product of intra-specific selection!" The rushed existence into which indus-trialized, commercialized man has precipitated himself is actually a good example of an inexpedient development caused entirely by competition between members of the same species. Human beings of today are attacked by so-called manager diseases, high blood pressure, renal atrophy, gastric ulcers, and torturing neuroses; they succumb to barbarism because they have no more time for cultural interests. And all this is unnecessary, for they could easily agree to take things more easily; theoretically they could, but in practice it is just as impos-sible for them as it is for the Argus pheasant to grow shorter wing feathers.

There are still worse consequences of intra-specific selection, and for obvious reasons man is particularly exposed to them: unlike any creature before him, he has mastered all hostile powers in his environment, he has exterminated the bear and the wolf and now, as the Latin proverb says, "*Homo homini lupus.*" Striking support for this view comes from the work of modern American sociologists, and in his book *The Hidden Persuaders* Vance Packard gives an impressive picture of the grotesque state of affairs to which commercial competition can lead. Reading this book, one is tempted to believe that intra-specific competition is the "root of all evil" in a more direct sense than aggression can ever be.

In this chapter on the survival value of aggression, I have laid special stress on the potentially destructive effects of intra-specific selection: because of them, aggressive behavior can, more than other qualities and functions, become exaggerated to the point of the grotesque and inexpedient. In later chapters we shall see what effects it has had in several animals, for example, in the Egyptian Goose and the Brown Rat. Above all, it is more than probable that the destructive intensity of the aggression drive, still a hereditary evil of mankind, is the consequence of a process of intra-specific selection which worked on our forefathers for roughly forty thousand years, that is, throughout the Early Stone Age. When man had reached the stage of having weapons, clothing, and social organization, so overcoming the dangers of starving, freezing, and being eaten by wild animals, and these dangers ceased to be the essential factors influencing selection, an evil intra-specific selection must have set in. The factor influencing selection was now the wars waged between hostile neighboring tribes. These must have evolved in an extreme form of all those so-called "warrior virtues" which unfortunately many people still regard as desirable ideals. We shall come back to this in the last chapter of this book.

I return to the theme of the survival value of the rival fight, with the statement that this only leads to useful selection where it breeds fighters fitted for combat with extra-specific enemies as well as for intra-specific duels. The most important function of rival fighting is the selection of an aggressive family defender, and this presupposes a further function of intra-specific aggression: brood defense. This is so obvious that it requires no further comment. If it should be doubted, its truth can be demonstrated by the fact that in many animals, where only one sex cares for the brood, only that sex is really aggressive toward fellow members of the species. Among sticklebacks it is the male, in several dwarf cichlids the female. In many gallinaceous birds, only the females tend the brood, and these are often far more aggressive than the males. The same thing is said to be true of human beings.

It would be wrong to believe that the three functions of aggressive behavior dealt with in the last three chapters—namely, balanced distribution of animals of the same species over the available environment, selection of the strongest by rival fights, and defense of the young—are its only important functions in the preservation of the species. We shall see later what an indispensable part in the great complex of drives is played by aggression; it is one of those driving powers which students of behavior call "motivation"; it lies behind behavior patterns that outwardly have nothing to do with aggression, and even appear to be its very opposite. It is hard to say whether it is a paradox or a commonplace that, in the most intimate bonds between living creatures, there is a certain measure of aggression. Much more remains to be said before discussing this central problem in our natural history of aggression. The important part played by aggression in the inter-action of drives within the organism is not easy to understand and still less easy to expound.

We can, however, here describe the part played by aggression in the structure of society among highly developed animals. Though many individuals interact in a social system, its inner workings are often easier to understand than the interaction of drives within the individual. A principle of organization without which a more advanced social life cannot develop in higher vertebrates is the so-called ranking order. Under this rule every individual in the society knows which one is stronger and which weaker than itself, so that everyone can retreat from the stronger and expect submission from the weaker, if they should get in each other's way. Schjelderup-Ebbe was the first to examine the ranking order in the domestic fowl and to speak of the "pecking order," an expression used to this day by writers. It seems a little odd though, to me, to speak of a pecking order even for large animals which certainly do not peck, but bite or ram. However, its wide distribution speaks for its great survival value, and therefore we must ask wherein this lies.

The most obvious answer is that it limits fighting between the members of a society, but here in contrast one may ask: Would it not have been better if aggression among the members of a society were utterly inhibited? To this, a whole series of answers can be given. First, as we shall discuss very thoroughly in a later chapter (Ten, "The Bond"), the case may arise that a society, for example, a wolf pack or monkey herd, urgently needs aggression against other societies of the same species, therefore aggression should be inhibited only *inside* the horde. Secondly, a society may derive a beneficial firmness of structure from the state of tension arising inside the community from the aggression drive and its result, ranking order. In jackdaws, and in many other very social birds, ranking order leads directly to protection of weaker ones. All social animals are "status seekers," hence there is always particularly high tension between individuals who hold immediately adjoining positions in the ranking order; conversely, this tension diminishes the further apart the two animals are in rank. Since high-ranking jackdaws, particularly males, interfere in every quarrel between two inferiors, this graduation of social tension has the desirable effect that the higher-ranking birds always intervene in favor of the losing party.

In jackdaws, another form of "authority" is already linked with the ranking position which the individual has acquired by its aggressive drive. The expression movements of a high-ranking jackdaw, particularly of an old male, are given much more attention by the colony members than those of a lower-ranking, young bird. For example, if a young bird shows fright at some meaningless stimulus, the others, especially the older ones, pay almost no attention to his expressions of fear. But if the same sort of alarm proceeds from one of the old males, all the jackdaws within sight and earshot immediately take flight. Since, in jackdaws, recognition of predatory enemies is not innate but is learned by every individual from the behavior of experienced old birds, it is probably of considerable importance that great store is set by the "opinion" of old, high-ranking, and experienced birds.

With the higher evolution of an animal species, the significance of the role played by individual experience and learning generally increases, while innate behavior, though not losing importance, becomes reduced to simpler though not less numerous elements. With this general trend in evolution, the significance attached to the experienced old animal becomes greater all the time, and it may even be said that the social coexistence of intelligent mammals has achieved a new survival value by the use it makes of the handing down of individually acquired information. Conversely, it may be said that social coexistence exerts selection pressure in the direction of better learning capacity, because in social animals this faculty benefits not only the individual but also the community. Thus longevity far beyond the age of reproductive capacity has considerable species-preserving value. We know from Fraser Darling and Margaret Altmann that in many species of deer the herd is led by an aged female, no longer hampered in her social duties by the obligations of motherhood.

All other conditions being equal, the age of an animal is, very consistently, in direct proportion to the position it holds in the ranking order of its society. It is thus advantageous if the "constructors" of behavior rely upon this consistency and if the members of the community—who cannot read the age of the experienced leader animal in its birth certificate—rate its reliability by its rank. Some time ago, collaborators of Robert M. Yerkes made the extraordinarily interesting observation that chimpanzees, animals well known to be capable of learning by imitation, copy only higher-ranking members of their species. From a group of these apes, a low-ranking individual was taken and taught to remove bananas from a specially constructed feeding apparatus by very complicated manipulations. When this ape, together with his feeding apparatus, was brought back to the group, the higher-ranking animals tried to take away the bananas which he had acquired for himself, but none of them thought of watching their inferior at work and learning something from him. Then the highest-ranking chimpanzee was removed and taught to use the apparatus in the same way, and when he was put back in the group the other members watched him with great interest and soon learned to imitate him.

S. L. Washburn and Irven de Vore observed that among free-living baboons the band was led not by a single animal but by a "senate" of several old males who maintained their superiority over the younger and physically stronger members by firmly sticking together and proving, as a united force, stronger than any single young male. In a more exactly observed case, one of the three "senators" was seen to be an almost toothless old creature while the other two were well past their prime. On one occasion when the band was in a treeless area and in danger of encountering a lion, the animals stopped and the young, strong males formed a defensive circle around the weaker animals. But the oldest male went forward alone, performed the dangerous task of finding out exactly where the lion was lying, without being seen by him, and then returned to the horde and led them, by a wide detour around the lion, to the safety of their sleeping trees. All followed him blindly, no one doubting his authority.

Let us look back on all that we have learned in this chapter from the objective observation of animals, and consider in what ways intra-specific aggression assists the preservation of an animal species. The environment is divided between the members of the species in such a way that, within the potentialities offered, everyone can exist. The best father, the best mother are chosen for the benefit of the progeny. The children are protected. The community is so organized that a few wise males, the "senate," acquire the authority essential for making and carrying out decisions for the good of the community. Though occasionally, in territorial or rival fights, by some mishap a horn may penetrate an eye or a tooth an artery, we have never found that the aim of aggression was the extermination of fellow members of the species concerned. This of course does not negate the fact that under unnatural circumstances, for example confinement, unforseen by the "constructors" of evolution, aggressive behavior may have a destructive effect.

Let us now examine ourselves and try, without self-conceit but also without regarding ourselves as miserable sinners, to find out what we would like to do, in a state of highest violent aggressive feeling, to the person who elicited that emotion. I do not think I am claiming to be better than I am when I say that the final, drive-assuaging act, Wallace Craig's consummatory act, is not the killing of my enemy. The satisfying experience consists, in such cases, in administering a good beating, but certainly not in shooting or disemboweling; and the desired objective is not that my opponent should lie dead but that he should be soundly thrashed and humbly accept my physical and, if I am to be considered as good as a baboon, my mental superiority. And since, on principle, I only wish to thrash such fellows as deserve these humiliations, I cannot entirely condemn my instincts in this connection. However, it must be admitted that a slight deviation from nature, a coincidence that put a knife into one's hand at the critical moment, might turn an intended thrashing into manslaughter.

Summing up what has been said in this chapter, we find that aggression, far from being the diabolical, destructive principle that classical psychoanalysis makes it out to be, is really an essential part of the life-preserving organization of instincts. Though by accident it may function in the wrong way and cause destruction, the same is true of practically any functional part of any system. Moreover, we have not yet considered an all-important fact which we shall hear about in Chapter Ten. Mutation and selection, the great "constructors" which make genealogical trees grow upward, have chosen, of all unlikely things, the rough and spiny shoot of intra-specific aggression to bear the blossoms of personal friendship and love.

5

GROUP STRUCTURE
AND LEADERSHIP

Experiments on the Alteration
of Group Structure

ALEX BAVELAS, ALBERT H. HASTORF, ALAN E. GROSS,
AND W. RICHARD KITE

A fundamental problem in social psychology is the relationship between an individual's behavior and how that behavior is perceived and evaluated by others. For example, there has been persistent interest in the process which generates a status hierarchy in small face-to-face groups such that some members are perceived as "leaders" and others not. Most of the research on this question has attempted to chart the course of a naturally emerging structure, sociometrically define the leader, and then attempt to define those aspects of his behavior that led to his being perceived as the leader. However, the behavior of the leader is normally so complex that it has been exceedingly difficult to isolate the behaviors that significantly influence the perceptions of the other group members. Bales (1950) has explored this approach most thoroughly, with one of the most persistent findings being that the people seen as leaders talk a great deal.

This report will describe a series of studies in which an attempt is made to alter experimentally the verbal behavior of an individual in a group discussion by the use of an operant conditioning procedure. Our primary concern was to develop a workable procedure for increasing one group member's verbal output, to define some of the variables which appear crucial to this procedure, and to explore the other group members' perceptions of this change in behavior on such dimensions as quality of ideas and leadership.[1]

Previous research with operant conditioning techniques in group situations has most commonly made use of confederates. Pepinsky, Hemphill, and Shevitz (1958) demonstrated that "accepting" or "rejecting" reactions on the part of confederates influenced the number of leadership attempts made by a naive subject. By making a straightforward application of a standard verbal conditioning procedure to a group situation, Bachrach, Candland, and Gibson (1961) have shown that the verbal output of a naive group member can be increased by the headnods, "umm humms," and agreements of two confederates. It should be noted that in both of these studies, the "group" aspects of the experimental situations were severely attenuated by the use of confederates. In such an experimental set-up it is impossible to obtain data on other group members' perceptions of the "target" subject whose behavior was being altered.

Oakes, Droge, and August (1960) demonstrated that verbal behavior can be either increased or decreased by the use of lights as reinforcers or punishers. Aiken (1964) has described a similar procedure in which lights as reinforcers or punishers were used for subjects in a group situation where each subject is provided with private feedback on his performance. This procedure has the significant advantage of bringing about a change in the verbal behavior of a subject in the presence of other subjects who are unaware of the exact nature of the reinforcements given the "target" person.

The studies reported below are directed toward answering the following questions. When lights are used as signals or reinforcers in a group situation, how much change in verbal behavior can be obtained? Must the reinforcing lights be directly contingent on talking or will a random pattern of lights also increase verbal output in a group discussion atmosphere? If an increase in the verbal output of a group member is obtained, will that person maintain his new verbal level in a following session where no lights are expected? Finally, how do the other group members evaluate the contributions of the "target" person? Do they increase his status on such dimensions as quality of ideas and leadership?

---

[1] Some of these issues are discussed in a preliminary report of this research (Hastorf, 1964).

EXPERIMENT I

Method

Subjects.   Seventy-two male students from industrial psychology and industrial engineering classes at Stanford University were recruited "to participate in group discussions of case problems." The Ss were divided into eighteen four-man groups, half of which were assigned to the Experimental condition and half to the Control condition. Group members were not well acquainted with each other prior to the experimental session.

Apparatus.   Each of four positions at a discussion table was equipped with a reflector box which contained two small lights, one green and one red. These boxes were flared toward each participant so that only he could see the lights facing his position. The lights were controlled from an observation room which was separated from the discussion room by one-way glass. Clocks and counters were used to record talking time and frequency for each S. Whenever an S talked, or whenever a red or green light was turned on, an Esterline-Angus pen recorder was activated, thereby providing a sequential event record.

Procedure.   The Ss were told that the discussions would be observed and recorded from behind the one-way glass. The E explained that he was interested in the study of group discussion techniques from an educational viewpoint. It was further explained that several different human relations problems would be discussed so that the dynamics of the group discussion process could be analyzed. Following these brief and purposely vague introductory remarks, the four Ss read the first case problem and were instructed to begin a 10-minute discussion period during which they "should discuss the pertinent facts which will affect a decision."

This initial discussion was intended to provide an operant level or baseline measurement of verbal activity. An observer operated the clocks and counters, which provided, respectively, a record of cumulative talking time and a record of the total number of times each S talked. This recording procedure was also followed in the two subsequent discussions.

At the end of each discussion period, E re-entered the discussion room and administered a short sociometric questionnaire. The Ss were required to rank all group members, including themselves, on four key items: amount of participation, quality of ideas, effectiveness in guiding the discussion, and general leadership ability.

After reading the second case problem, the groups were given further oral instructions. The E stated that in contrast to the usual nonfeedback procedure, group discussions might be more effective "if the participants are given an occasional sign that they are doing the kinds of things that will help the group arrive at intelligent solutions while at the same time yielding the maximum educational benefit to the group." The Ss were then told that some discussion groups work on their own and some groups "are provided with feedback information as to how they are doing as the discussion proceeds." At this point the experimental groups were told that they would be receiving feedback. The *E* directed attention to the small red and green lights which had previously been dismissed as extraneous equipment that "we won't be using now," and told the group that these lights would serve as the source of the feedback information. Control groups were told that they would receive no feedback.

Both Experimental and Control groups received vague descriptions of the criteria that were to be used in evaluating their discussion:

Many psychologists have studied group discussion of problems such as this one. Most of these investigators have found that maximum benefit is gained from such discussions when the group proceeds in an orderly way through various stages of development. For instance, one psychologist has cautioned against proceeding into the problem-solving stage of discussion too rapidly before there has been enough orientation. Other research has given us clues as to the value of cooperation, suggestion, conciliation, and other forms of group behavior during certain stages of the discussion process.

The case you have just read has been thoroughly analyzed in terms of how it can be discussed most effectively. Although, of course, there is no single correct solution to the problem, we have developed a definite set of principles, such as those I have just mentioned, which enable us to know whether or not you are following the best course; that is, using the best techniques in contributing to the discussion for the benefit of the group. Note that although this will be a group discussion, it will be your individual contributions to the discussion that will be judged.

At this point the Control groups were reminded that they would not receive any feedback as to how they were being evaluated. However, the Experimental groups were told that they would receive feedback which would be contingent upon the vaguely defined quality of their contributions:

Thus, whenever you make a contribution to the discussion which is helpful or functional in facilitating the group process, your green light will go on like this (green lights turned on). Are all your green lights on? Fine. Whenever you behave in a way which will eventually hamper or hinder the group process, your red light will go on like this (red lights turned on). Are all your red lights on? Good. It is conceivable that even remaining silent when you might have been clarifying a point that had been made earlier is a dysfunctional or hindering type of behavior. This would rate a red light indicating you should have said something at that point. On the other hand, silence might be good when talking would serve to confuse a good point that had already been made.

Since it is often impossible for us to determine the effect that a single statement or thought will have on the group discussion, a feedback light might be referring to the cumulative effect of two or three successive contributions to the discussion. Of course much of the time neither of your lights will be on, indicating that your behavior has been neither helping nor hindering the group, or that we simply can't validly analyze what has been going on in the group at that time.

Note that the discussion table is constructed so that each participant can see only the lights directly in front of him. During the discussion the fact that your lights are either on or off should not be mentioned. This would, of course, tend to disrupt the natural discussion atmosphere.

Group members in both conditions were told the discussion would last for 20 minutes and that they should "try to bring in the various possible facts that can be considered relevant to the problem in the case."

At the end of the first discussion period, the Ss were rank-ordered on the basis of objective behavior measured by the clocks and counters and on the basis of the perceptions of the group members measured by the responses to the four sociometric items. There was usually a close correspondence between amount of talking and average ranking on the four sociometric items. In the few cases in which these measures were inconsistent or contradicted each other, the ranking adopted was made on the basis of total talking times.

The third or fourth ranked man in this hierarchy was designated as the target person (TP). One of the less talkative men was selected so that here would be "room" to effect a relatively large change in verbal behavior. An exceedingly quiet man was not selected as the TP because it was felt that if he had been extremely quiet it would be difficult to alter his behavior. The man who was ranked first was designated M-1; the other two men were labeled M-2 and M-3, respectively.

The experimental manipulation consisted of flashing TP's green light whenever he made declarative statements or stated an opinion, and flashing the others' red lights if they (M-1, M-2, M-3) engaged in these same behaviors. Occasionally, TP received a red light for remaining silent, and other group members received green lights for interacting with TP, especially for agreeing with him.

No definite criteria or set of rules were followed for administering lights or for controlling the number of lights distributed. The light operator's task was to increase the TP's verbal output during the second discussion and to decrease or inhibit talking by the other group members. The operator was to select for reinforcement those statements by the TP which would intuitively appear to result in increased sociometric status.

After the second discussion, the Ss again completed the sociometry questionnaire and then read the third case problem. The Experimental groups were told that the lights would "not be operating—just as in the first case discussion; so don't pay any attention to the equipment." At the end of this final 10-minute discussion, the last sociometric questionnaire was administered, followed by a postsession questionnaire. Each S was asked to rank the three case problems from most to least liked and to indicate whether he felt that he had talked more, less, or about the same as usual during each of three discussions. Experimental Ss responded to items which asked how much attention was paid to the lights and whether the lights were perceived as helping or hindering the discussion.

After this questionnaire was completed, the purpose and design of the experiment was fully explained to the Ss, and questions were answered.

Results

The experimental procedure is clearly effective in altering both the distribution of verbal outputs and the sociometric structure of the group. In all nine Experimental groups, TP's talking time and frequency of talking increased during the second discussion when lights were being used. Furthermore, this change was strongly reflected in the sociometric votes of the other group members: all nine Experimental *TPs* received higher average rankings after the second discussion than after the first discussion (Table 1). Frequency of talking data, which are correlated with total talking time ($r = .91$) are omitted from Table 1. Since the rankings for guidance, best ideas, participation, and leadership turned out to be highly correlated, the sociometric data is reported as the mean ranking of these four items. The *TPs'* self-rankings are excluded from these averages.

In eight of nine cases *TPs'* ratings drop somewhat following the discussion of the third case, but in only one group do the ratings the *TP* receives drop back below the baseline level of the first period.

Increased sociometric ratings and length of talking time in the second period for Experimental *TPs* are significantly greater than the slight increase shown for Control group *TPs*. The drop-off from the second to third discussions is significant for the objective talking measures and the sociometric data. Despite the drop-off, *TPs'* level of output and sociometric ratings remain significantly higher than they were after the first discussion.

Table 1ᵃ SOCIOMETRIC RANK AND VERBAL OUTPUT OF TARGET PERSON

EXPERIMENT	MEAN RANKINGS RECEIVED BY TP FROM OTHER GROUP MEMBERS (1 TO 4) DISCUSSION PERIOD			TIME TALKED BY TP EXPRESSED AS A PERCENTAGE OF TOTAL GROUP TALKING TIME DISCUSSION PERIOD		
	1	2	3	1	2	3
Control (N = 9 groups)	3.05	2.81	2.80	17.3	20.2	19.5
Exp. I (N = 9 groups)	2.23 1 vs. 2 & 3, $p < .01$ 2 vs. 3, $p < .05$	1.70	2.30	15.7 1 vs. 2 & 3, $p < .01$ 2 vs. 3, $p < .01$	37.0	26.9
Exp. II (N = 7 groups)	3.18 1 vs. 2 & 3, $p < .02$	2.13	2.36	17.4 1 vs. 2, $p < .05$ 1 vs. 3, $p = .02$	31.1	29.0
Exp. III (N = 7 groups)	3.12	2.80	2.75	19.8	20.4	20.9
Exp. IV (N = 7 groups)	3.24	2.95	3.11	20.9	22.2	18.6
Exp. V (N = 7 groups)	3.08	2.66	2.82	19.3	24.3	22.2

ᵃ *Only p values of less than 0.10 are indicated. All p values are two-tailed. Differences for experimental groups between first and second discussions were compared with corresponding differences for control groups by the Mann-Whitney Test. Significance levels for differences between the second and third discussions and first and third discussions were computed by the sign test.*

The *TPs'* perception of their own behavior as reflected in their self-ratings followed a similar pattern. Their self-ratings also rose after the second period and then dropped off somewhat when the lights were not used in the third period. The *TPs'* self-ratings are presented in Table 2. Although mean self-ratings for each discussion period are slightly higher than ratings received from others, the magnitude of change between discussions is very similar to changes in ratings made by others.

Table 2 MEAN SELF-RANKINGS OF TARGET PERSON

	DISCUSSION PERIOD		
EXPERIMENT	1	2	3
Control	2.67	2.31	2.39
I	2.91	1.36	2.05
	1 vs. 2, $p < .02$		
	2 vs. 3, $p < .05$		
II	2.79	1.64	1.64
	1 vs. 3, $p < .05$		
III	2.93	2.64	2.79
IV	3.04	2.14	2.50
V	2.68	2.07	2.39

Data from the postsession questionnaire are presented in Table 3. These data indicate: (1) a strong liking for the second case problem among Experimental *TPs*, while no such consistent preference exists for any one case among the other group members; (2) *TPs* were aware that they talked a great deal during the second discussion: 6 of 9 felt that they talked "more than usual" during this period while all but one of the other group members felt that they had talked "less than usual" or "about the same"; (3) 8 of 9 *TPs* responded that the feedback lights had "helped" them during the second discussion while the others were split between feelings of being "helped" and being "hindered."

EXPERIMENTS II AND III

In Experiment I red and green lights were distributed to the *S*s on the basis of the *E*s' intuitive judgments as to what behaviors should be encouraged or discouraged. It was thought that such a procedure would be most effective in bringing about the desired changes in the behavior of the *S*s. When the effectiveness of this procedure was demonstrated, the question arose as to how crucial were the *E*s' choices of which behaviors to reinforce in producing the observed effect. Did the *TP's* increase in sociometric status result from an increase in certain categories of verbal output, or was it simply the result of his talking more in general? Experiments II and III represent an attempt to answer this question by eliminating the *E*s' judgments from the administering of the lights. Fifty-six undergraduate *S*s were assigned to 14 four-man groups. Seven groups were run in each experiment.

Table 3 POSTSESSION QUESTIONNAIRE DATA

EXPERIMENT		N	CASE PREFERENCE (1 = MOST LIKED, 3 = LEAST LIKED)			ESTIMATE OF TALKING (1 = MORE, 0 = SAME, -1 = LESS)			INFLUENCE OF LIGHTS (FREQUENCIES)		
			CASE 1	CASE 2	CASE 3	PERIOD 1	PERIOD 2	PERIOD 3	HELP	NO DIFF.	HINDER
Control	TP	9	2.56	1.56	1.89	-0.22	+0.33	-0.11	-a	-a	-a
	Others	27	2.30	1.81	1.89	-0.04	+0.07	-0.04	-a	-a	-a
I	TP	9	2.56	1.00	2.44	-0.33	+0.67	+0.22	8	0	1
	Others	27	2.15	2.07	1.78	+0.04	-0.37	+0.07	8	9	10
II	TP	7	2.43	1.86	1.71	-0.43	+0.43	+0.57	4	3	0
	Others	21	1.86	2.67	1.48	+0.19	-0.48	+0.05	7	4	10
III	TP	7	2.29	2.14	1.57	-0.29	-0.29	+0.29	1	4	2
	Others	21	2.14	2.05	1.81	-0.04	+0.07	-0.04	3	12	6
IV	TP	7	2.17	1.50	2.33	-0.50	+0.33	.00	4b	2	0
	Others	21	2.17	2.17	1.67	-0.22	-0.05	-0.05	-a	-a	-a
V	TP	7	2.14	2.14	1.71	+0.14	-0.29	-0.14	-a	-a	-a
	Others	21	1.85	2.29	1.86	.00	-0.29	-0.10	4	7	10

a Did not receive feedback.
b One group did not complete postsession questionnaires.

Experiment II

Procedure. Experiment II was an exact replication of Experiment I in terms of the general procedure followed. The only modification was in the manner in which the red and green lights were administered to the Ss during their second case discussion. All "feedback" lights were administered automatically by a preprogrammed event-controlling unit which was activated by the same switches used to record the Ss verbal output. In this way it was possible to make the lights contingent upon the Ss' talking without regard to its content.

The program unit was connected to a 25-position stepping switch which moved to the next position with the recording of each discrete utterance by any of the Ss. Each S had a fixed sequence of 25 events programmed for him: he could receive a green light, a red light, or no lights each time he talked. TP received a "leadership encouraging" schedule of 15 green lights with the remaining 10 positions blank. A separate timing device was connected to the TP's circuit which delivered a red light to him for every 45 seconds of continuous silence. The other three Ss received identical "followership encouraging" schedules consisting of 7 red lights, 2 green lights, and 16 blanks. These two schedules were intended to approximate the schedules administered in Experiment I in terms of both absolute number of lights and ratios of red to green.

Instructions regarding the onset of the "feedback lights" prior to the second discussion were the same as in Experiment I. Subjects also filled out the same sociometric questionnaire after each of the three discussions and the same post-experimental questionnaire as were administered in Experiment I.

Results. Although it was the intention of the Es to provide Ss with schedules of red and green lights which at least approximated those received by their counterparts in Experiment I, this objective was not achieved. The actual mean numbers of lights received by the Ss in both experiments are shown in Table 4. It is obvious that all Ss in Experiment II received considerably fewer lights of both kinds than did the comparable Ss in Experiment I.

This deficit appears to have been mainly due to the fact that the programmed schedules were simply too sparse, particularly in terms of green lights. There is also, however, a methodological problem inherent in the design of this study. In order for the TP to receive green lights, it was necessary for him to talk. If the programmed schedule of green lights was insufficient to produce a sizeable increase in his talking over time, then this placed an obvious limitation on the number of green lights he would receive over the course of the entire discussion.

The major results of Experiment II are presented in Table 1. When compared with TPs in the Control groups, it can be seen that even making the green lights contingent upon sheer talking produces an increase in both the sociometric rankings received from others and verbal output. These increases are not, however, as great as those obtained in Experiment I.

From the first to the second discussion the TP shows a significant increase in sociometric rankings received from others and a significant increase in talking time. These gains in sociometry and talking time are maintained by the TP to a significant extent throughout the third discussion.

Unfortunately, the fact that fewer lights were given to the Ss in Experi-

Table 4 NUMBER OF LIGHTS RECEIVED

EXPERIMENT		TP	M-1	M-2	M-3
I	Green	38.1	15.2	15.1	13.8
	Red	7.6	7.8	9.6	9.3
II	Green	15.4	1.7	1.7	0.4
	Red	5.3	9.7	6.0	3.3
III	Green	38	15	16	14
	Red	7	8	10	9
IV	Green	14.0	—	—	—
	Red	5.0	—	—	—
V	Green	—	7.9	7.9	5.1
	Red	—	6.4	7.7	5.6

ment II than to the Ss in Experiment I makes it impossible to give an unequivocal answer to the question of how much the Es' judgments contributed to the over-all effect. It does appear safe to conclude, however, that such judgments as were being made in Experiment I were at least not indispensible in producing significant changes in both verbal behavior and sociometric rankings.

Experiment III

Procedure. As a second method of eliminating the Es' judgments from the administration of lights, seven groups of Ss received red and green lights on a time-contingency basis. A leadership schedule was derived by averaging the number of red and green lights received by TPs in Experiment I within each successive 5-minute interval and then distributing this number randomly over an equal period of time. In a like manner a different schedule was derived for M-1, M-2, and M-3 on the basis of the average number of lights received by their counterparts in Experiment I.

These schedules were administered manually by a single E who viewed a large clock with a sweep-second hand in conjunction with the four schedules written out on large sheets of cardboard. This procedure allowed Ss to receive the same number and ratio of lights received in Experiment I, but without regard to whether or not they were talking at the time. In all other respects, the procedure was the same as that followed in Experiment I.

Results. Table 4 shows the numbers of lights received by all Ss in Experiment III. It can be seen that these numbers correspond to the averages of Experiment I.

The changes in sociometric status and verbal output that resulted from this procedure were no greater, and in some cases were smaller, than those obtained in the control groups (see Table 1).

EXPERIMENTS IV AND V

The experiments described thus far have all involved an attempt to alter the verbal behavior of all four group members. This procedure consisted of essentially two operations: (1) an attempt to increase the *TP*'s output by rewarding his talking and punishing him for being silent, and (2) an attempt to decrease the other members' output by punishing their talking and rewarding their silence. Although these two operations can be conceptualized separately, they did not function independently in the experiments reported above. The behavior change of the *TP* in Experiments I and II may have been due to one or the other of these two techniques, or to an interaction of the two.

In order to determine the independent effects of these two operations, two additional experiments were conducted. Experiment IV provided only the *TP* with feedback, while Experiment V provided only the three nontarget *S*s with feedback.

Experiment I V

Procedure.   To provide only the *TP* with feedback during the second discussion, it was necessary to instruct the other three members of the group in such a way that they would not anticipate any feedback while at the same time instructing the *TP* in the usual manner. To achieve this, two sets of written instructions were prepared and were passed out to the group just prior to the second discussion. The instructions that the *TP* read were a written version of the standard instructions given to all *S*s in the experimental condition of Experiment I. The other three *S*s were given a written version of the control instructions of Experiment I. Both sets of instructions were carefully prepared so as to appear identical in terms of location of paragraph indentations, margins, and other typographical aspects. No *S*s in any of the groups reported awareness of this difference in the instructions.

A single *E* administered the red and green lights to the *TP* in the same manner that they were given to the *TP*s in Experiment I. No explicit attempt was made to replicate the mean numbers of each kind of light given in Experiment I.

Results.   The sociometric and verbal output measures for Experiment IV show virtually no changes over the three discussions and do not differ from the results obtained in the control condition (Table 1). The mean number of lights received by the *TP* are reported in Table 4. In comparison with the figures for Experiment I, the number of green lights received by the *TP*s is much smaller. This was due mainly to the fact that the *TP*s did not markedly increase their verbal output in the second discussion.

Experiment V

Procedure. This experiment was essentially the complement of Experiment IV. Instead of encouraging the *TP* to talk more, the procedure of Experiment V consisted of discouraging the other three members of the group and withholding all feedback from the *TP*. Written instructions were again used to instruct the *S*s differentially with regard to the administration of feedback in the second discussion. The *TP* received the control version while the other three were given the experimental version.

The *E* who administered the feedback lights to the three nontarget *S*s followed the same general rules that were observed in Experiment I in attempting to decrease their verbal output in the second discussion.

Results. The *TP*s in Experiment V increased slightly in sociometric ranking and verbal output from the first to the second discussion (Table 1). None of these increases were significant, however. As shown in Table 4, the nontarget *S*s received slightly fewer red lights and about half as many green lights as did the nontarget *S*s in Experiment I.

DISCUSSION

The results of Experiment I clearly demonstrate that the procedure used is an effective method of changing the verbal output of selected group members in a desired direction. Furthermore, changes in the sociometric structure of the group are highly correlated with verbal output changes ($r = .84$). It had been anticipated that a crucial element necessary for the success of this manipulation was the manner in which the experimenters determined the appropriate times to reinforce group members. Therefore, the results of Experiment II were somewhat surprising in that the programmed machine produced not only an increase in the *TP*'s verbal output, but also a significant rise in his sociometric status.

One possible explanation for the similarity in the results of Experiments I and II is that the same general class of behaviors was being reinforced by both the experimenters and the programmed machine. Although there are no data to confirm this notion, it was the opinion of the experimenters that all discussions were relatively homogeneous in content and highly task-oriented, with very few irrelevant or disruptive statements being made by any of the participants. This being the case, it seems reasonable to assume that the majority of the *TP*s' statements that were reinforced in both Experiments I and II were task relevant in nature, and, therefore, that an increase in such verbal output would result in higher sociometric rankings for the *TP*s.

Some indirect support for this contention is provided by Oakes (1962), who used a reinforcement technique similar to the one described in this report in an attempt to determine which of the twelve Bales' categories of response are most susceptible to reinforcement. His findings show that only one of these categories, "giving opinion, evaluation, analysis, expresses feeling, wish," could be increased significantly during a group discussion. It should be noted that more than 50% of the total responses were coded in this one category. These findings appear to coincide with our contention that discussion content was both relevant to the case discussion and homogeneous across groups. Therefore, it is not surprising that the experimenter function of selecting statements to "reinforce" in Experiment I is not critical in the alteration of group structure. At the same time, the results of Experiment III indicate that lights must be contingent upon verbal behavior to be effective. Receiving encouraging lights at predetermined intervals did not prove sufficient to significantly alter the initial group structure.

The technique which was used successfully to modify group structure can be considered as two separate operations. One operation consisted of positively reinforcing or encouraging the target person to step up his verbal output. A complementary operation was employed simultaneously to depress the verbal output of the other group members except when they complied or agreed with the *TP*. It could be argued that one or the other of these two operations alone might account for most of the behavioral and sociometric changes. Experiments IV and V were designed to test the independent effects of each of these two component techniques. The results suggest that both operations are necessary to produce modification of the group behavior. The ineffectiveness of either operation used separately indicates that without some encouragement a quiet group member will not spontaneously increase his output when other members are artificially depressed; and conversely it is not enough to encourage a quiet individual to participate more unless "room" is provided for his increased verbal output. It is also possible that when both techniques are employed, agreeing and complying behaviors of other group members may increase and provide additional social reinforcement for the *TP*.

The previously mentioned high correlation between sociometric rankings and total talking time deserves further consideration. Given a situation in which four strangers are brought together, allowed to interact for a brief period, and then asked to evaluate one another on characteristics such as "best ideas," "guidance," and "leadership," one might expect that sheer amount of talking would be a salient factor in determining these evaluations. It would be misleading, however, to conclude that such a high correlation between talking and sociometry always obtains in group situations, or that talking, regardless of its quality or appropriateness, always leads to the perception of good ideas and leadership ability. Such a hypothesis would have to be tested under a wider variety of situations than the present experimental design affords. For instance, other group members may rate a talkative man highly on "best ideas" if he is perceived as talking a great deal because he had earned encouragement from expert evaluators. On the other hand, others may not positively evaluate a talkative man's ideas if they are aware that experimenters are manipulating rather than evaluating his behavior. These considerations have been explored by Hastorf *et al.* (1964).

The results of Experiments I and II show that the increase in the *TP*'s verbal output from the first to the second discussion is partly carried over to the third period when the lights are not used. The question of how long the effect lasts and whether or not it will generalize to other similar situations is unanswered. A series of experiments to test the perseveration and generalization of these effects is in progress.

If *TP* gains in sociometry and talks more, some one person or combination of other participants must lose sociometric votes and talk less. Because of this "degrees of freedom" restriction, it is of some interest to explore the dynamics of the change situation. For instance, one might ask which group member(s) loses when *TP* gains. It would be reasonable to predict that each man loses sociometric votes and talking time in proportion to what he has to lose, i.e., *M-1,* the man who was originally ranked the highest, would lose the most, and *M-2* and *M-3* should lose proportionally less. An analysis of ratings received by *M-1, M-2,* and *M-3* (Table 5) shows that in Experiment I, *M-1*'s losses alone account for *TP*'s gains. In Experiment II, although *M-1* suffers the greatest loss, *M-2* also talks somewhat less and receives lower ratings on the questionnaires.

Table 5 SOCIOMETRIC RANK AND VERBAL OUTPUT CHANGES FROM DISCUSSION PERIOD 1 TO DISCUSSION PERIOD 2

Experiment	TP	M-1	M-2	M-3
Sociometric rank[a] Control	+0.24	−0.12	−0.35	+0.25
Verbal output (%)	+2.9	−2.3	−3.9	+3.3
I Sociometric rank	+1.53	−0.72	−0.61	−0.31
Verbal output (%)	+21.3	−15.7	−5.0	−0.7
II Sociometric rank	+1.05	−0.36	−0.56	−0.05
Verbal output (%)	+13.7	−10.3	−7.1	+3.6
III Sociometric rank	+0.32	+0.06	−0.32	+0.10
Verbal output (%)	+0.6	−2.3	−0.2	+2.1
IV Sociometric rank	+0.29	−0.45	+0.11	−0.08
Verbal output (%)	+1.3	−3.5	+1.7	+0.6
V Sociometric rank	+0.42	−0.14	−0.38	+0.08
Verbal output (%)	+5.0	−4.8	−1.3	+1.2

[a] *Total positive and negative sociometric changes are not necessarily equal because self-rankings have been excluded from the averages which are presented in Table 1.*

It might also be asked if the increase in the *TP*s' sociometric rank from the first to the second discussion was largely due to the other members assigning lower ranks to themselves. This would result in an artificial elevation of the *TP*s' rank. The data were analyzed with all self-rankings eliminated and each subject's ratings of the other group members reranked from 1 to 3. This analysis revealed substantially the same pattern of results as those presented in Table 1.

Two opposing hypotheses may be entertained regarding the *TP*s' affective response to the experimental manipulation. It could be predicted that participants who are rewarded for talking will gain more satisfaction from the discussion and will generalize some of this affect to the case problem, or alternatively that the *TP* will feel uncomfortable in the unfamiliar role of a high participator. The postsession questionnaire results clearly support the former prediction in that *TP*s enjoyed participating in the second discussion and indicated strong preference for the second case problem. During the first discussion, before any lights were administered, high participators showed no more preference for the case than did low participators.

In summary, the experiments described above provide a workable technique for the alteration of verbal output and sociometric structure in a group situation and define some of the necessary conditions to obtain such changes.

Two problems emerge that are of significance to the understanding of social interaction. The first relates to the perseveration and the generalization of behavior change. What are the conditions under which behavior change would perseverate and generalize to other conditions? We have obtained evidence of some perseveration to a session which immediately followed the acquisition session. An important variable in this respect is the way in which the *TP* himself views the situation. We would hypothesize that the more an individual perceives changes in his behavior as being self-caused and not the result of external forces (in Heider's (1958) sense of the word), the more likely he will maintain some of this behavior change.

The second general problem concerns the perception and evaluation of one person's behavior change by others. In the experiments described above when a *TP's* verbal output was markedly changed, the other group members attributed high quality to the output. It is our hypothesis that observers who are able to see the rewarding or punishing lights would be more likely to attribute the change in behavior to the influence of the lights and would thus be less willing to attribute such qualities as leadership to the *TP*.

REFERENCES

Aiken, E. G.   Interpersonal behavior changes perceived as accompanying the operant conditioning of verbal output in small groups. *Technical Report Number II.* Western Behavioral Sciences Institute, 1963.

Bachrach, A. J., Candland, D. K., and Gibson, J. T.   Group reinforcement of individual response experiments in verbal behavior. In Irwin A. Berg and Bernard M. Bass (Eds.), *Conformity and deviation.* New York: Harper, 1961. Pp. 258–85.

Bales, R. F.   *Interaction process analysis: A method for the study of small groups.* Cambridge, Mass.: Addison-Wesley Co., Inc., 1950.

Hastorf, A. H.   The "reinforcement" of individual actions in a group situation. In L. Krasner and L. P. Ullmann (Eds.), *Research in behavior modification.* New York: Holt, 1964.

Hastorf, A. H., Kite, W. R., Gross, A. E., and Wolfe, Lyn J.   The perception and evaluation of behavior change. Unpublished manuscript. Stanford University, 1964.

Heider, F.   *The psychology of interpersonal relations.* New York: Wiley, 1958.

Oakes, W. F.   Reinforcement of Bales' categories in group discussion. *Psychol. Rep., 1962, 11,* 427–35.

Oakes, W. F., Droge, A. E., and August, B.   Reinforcement effects on participation in group discussion. *Psychol. Rep.,* 1960, *7,* 503–14.

Pepinsky, P. N., Hemphill, J. K., and Shevitz, R. N.   Attempts to lead, group productivity, and morale under conditions of acceptance and rejection. *J. Abnorm. soc. Psychol.,* 1958, *57,* 47–54.

Some Effects of Certain Communication Patterns on Group Performance

BY HAROLD J. LEAVITT

INTRODUCTION

Cooperative action by a group of individuals having a common objective requires, as a necessary condition, a certain minimum of communication. This does not mean that all the individuals must be able to communicate with one another. It is enough, in some cases, if they are each touched by some part of a network of communication which also touches each of the others at some point. The ways in which the members of a group may be linked together by such a network of communication are numerous; very possibly only a few of the many ways have any usefulness in terms of effective performance. Which of all feasible patterns are "good" patterns from this point of view? Will different patterns give different results in the performance of group tasks?

In a free group, the kind of network that evolves may be determined by a multitude of variables. The job to be done by the group may be a determinant, or the particular abilities or social ranks of the group members, or other cultural factors may be involved.

Even in a group in which some parent organization defines the network of communication, as in most military or industrial situations, the networks themselves may differ along a variety of dimensions. There may be differences in number of connections, in the symmetry of the pattern of connections, in "channel capacity" (how much and what kind of information), and in many other ways.

It was the purpose of this investigation to explore experimentally the relationship between the behavior of small groups and the patterns of communication in which the groups operate. It was our further purpose to consider the psychological conditions that are imposed on group members by various communication patterns, and the effects of these conditions on the organization and the behavior of its members. We tried to do this for small groups of a constant size, using two-way written communication and a task that required the simple collection of information.

Some Characteristics of Communication Structures

The stimulus for this research lies primarily in the work of Bavelas (1), who considered the problem of defining some of the dimensions of group structures. In his study, the structures analyzed consist of cells connected to one another. If we make persons analogous to "cells" and communication channels analogous to

Reprinted from Journal of Abnormal Social Psychology, 46, *1951, 38–50. Copyright 1951 by the American Psychological Association and reproduced by permission.*

"connections," we find that some of the dimensions that Bavelas defines are directly applicable to the description of communication patterns. Thus, one way in which communication patterns vary can be described by the sum of the neighbors that each individual member has, neighbors being defined as individuals to whom a member has communicative access. So, too, the concept of *centrality,* as defined by Bavelas, is of value in describing differences within and between structures. The most central position in a pattern is the position closest to all other positions. Distance is measured by number of communicative links which must be utilized to get, by the shortest route, from one position to another.

Bavelas also introduced a *sum of neighbors* measure—sum of neighbors being a summation, for the entire pattern, of the number of positions one link away from each position. Similarly, *sum of distances* is the summation, for all positions, of the shortest distances (in links) from every position to every other one.

Unfortunately, these dimensions we have mentioned do not in themselves uniquely define a pattern of communication. What defines a pattern is the *way* the cells are connected, regardless of how they are represented on paper. In essence, our criterion is this: if two patterns cannot be "bent" into the same shape without breaking a link, they are different patterns. A more precise definition of unique patterns would require the use of complex topological concepts.

Some Operational Characteristics of Communication Patterns

Consider the pattern depicted as A in Figure 1. If at each dot or cell (lettered *a*, *b,* etc.) we place a person; if each link (line between dots) represents a two-way channel for written communications; and if we assign to the five participants a

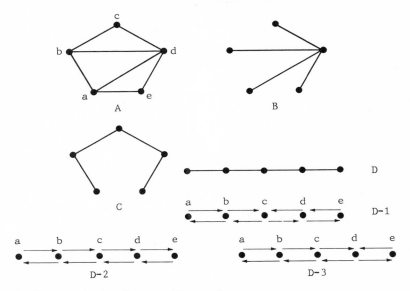

Fig. 1. Communication Patterns (See text)

task requiring that *every* member get an answer to a problem which can be solved only by pooling segments of information originally held separately by each member, then it is possible a priori to consider the ways in which the problem can be solved.

Pattern Flexibility. First we note that the subjects (*S*s) need not always use all the channels potentially available to them in order to reach an adequate solution of the problem. Although pattern A (Fig. 1) contains potentially seven links or channels of communication, it can be solved as follows with three of the seven channels ignored.

Step 1: *a* and *e* each send their separate items of information to *b* and *d* respectively.
Step 2: *b* and *d* each send their separate items of information along with those from *a* and *b* respectively.
Step 3: *c* organizes all the items of information, arrives at an answer, and sends the answer to *b* and then to *d*.
Step 4: *b* and *d* then send the answer to *a* and *e* respectively.

The use of these particular four channels yields pattern C (Fig. 1). The original seven-link pattern (A) can be used as a four-link pattern in various ways. For instance, each of the four *S*s diagrammatically labelled *c, b, a,* and *e* might send his item of information to *d* who would organize the items, arrive at the answer, and send it back to each respectively. Use of these particular four channels would yield the pattern B in Figure 1. The problem could also be solved by the *S*s using five, six, or all of the seven potential channels.

Operational Flexibility. Secondly, with the specification that a given number of links be used, any pattern can be operated in a variety of ways. Thus the pattern D (Fig. 1), which has no pattern flexibility, can be used as shown in D-1, with information funnelled in to C and the answer sent out from C. It is also possible to use it, as in D-2, with E as the key position; or as in D-3. These are operational differences that can be characterized in terms of the roles taken by the various positions. Thus in D-1, C is the decision-making position. In D-2, it is E or A. Some patterns can be operated with two or three decision-makers.

The Definition of Maximum Theoretical Efficiency

Before going further it may be helpful to state the task used in this research. To each *S*, labeled by color (see Fig. 2), was given a card on which there appeared a set of five (out of six possible) symbols. Each *S*'s card was different from all the others in that the symbol lacking, the sixth one, was a different symbol in each case.

Thus, in any set of five cards there was only one symbol in common. The problem was for every member to find the common symbol. To accomplish this each member was allowed to communicate, by means of written messages, with those other members of the group to whom he had an open channel (a link in our diagrams). Every separate written communication from one *S* (A) to another (B) was considered one message.

Six symbols used:	● ▲ ◆ ■ + ✳				
Trial no.	Symbol missing from:					Common symbol
	White	Red	Brown	Yellow	Blue	
1	▲	◆	✳	●	■	+
2	◆	●	■	▲	+	✳
3	+	✳	■	▲	◆	●
4	■	◆	▲	✳	+	●
5	●	✳	+	▲	■	◆
6	▲	●	■	✳	◆	+
7	■	+	●	◆	▲	✳
8	◆	✳	■	+	●	▲
9	✳	◆	■	▲	●	+
10	+	●	■	✳	◆	▲
11	●	+	▲	◆	✳	■
12	✳	●	■	▲	+	◆
13	▲	●	◆	■	+	✳
14	■	◆	+	✳	▲	●
15	+	●	■	◆	✳	▲

Fig. 2. Symbol Distribution by Trial

An *S* who had discovered the answer was allowed to pass the answer along.

Minimum Number of Communications.   For any pattern of *n* Ss, the minimum number of communications, *C*, is given by $C = 2(n-1)$.

Theoretically, then, with *number of messages as the sole criterion*, any pattern of *n* Ss is as efficient as any other *n*-sized pattern.

The Minimum Time Required for Solution.   If we assume "standard" *S*'s, all of whom work, think, and write at the same speed, it is possible to calculate the limit set by the communication pattern on the speed with which the problem can be solved. Toward this end, we can arbitrarily define a *time unit* as the time required to complete any message, from its inception by any *S* to its reception by any other.

For any *n* not a power of 2 and *with unrestricted linkage* when $2^x < n < 2^{x+1}$ and *x* is a power of 2, $x+1$ equals the minimum possible time units for solution of the problem. Thus, for a five-man group we have $2^x < 5 < 2^{x+1}$ becoming $2^2 < 5 < 2^3$, and $x+1 = 3$ time units. *No* five-man pattern can be done in less than three time units, although several require more than three time units. When n is an even power of 2, the formula $2^x = n$ holds, and x = minimum time.[1]

It will be noted that, although some patterns require fewer time units than others, they may also require more message (m) units. This phenomenon, effectively the generalization that it requires increased messages to save time units, holds for all the patterns we have examined. It is, however, true that certain patterns requiring different times can be solved in the same number of message units.

Some Possible Effects of Various Patterns on the Performance of Individuals

There are two general kinds of reasons which dictate against our theoretically perfect performance from real people. The first of these is the obvious one that people are not standardized. There are also the forces set up by the patterns themselves to be considered. The problem becomes one of analyzing the forces operating on an individual in any particular position in a communication pattern and then predicting how the effects of these forces will be translated into behavior.

It is our belief that the primary source of differential forces will be *centrality*. Centrality will be the chief (though perhaps not the sole) determinant of behavioral differences because centrality reflects the extent to which one position is strategically located relative to other positions in the pattern.

Our selection of centrality derives from the belief that availability of information necessary for the solution of the problem will be of prime importance in affecting one's behavior. Centrality is a measure of one's closeness to all other group members and, hence, is a measure of the availability of the information necessary for solving the problem.

Availability of information should affect behavior, in turn, by determining one's role in the group. An individual who can rapidly collect information should see himself and be seen by others in a different way from an individual to whom vital information is not accessible. Such roles should be different in the extent to which they permit independence of action, in the responsibility they entail, and in the monotony they impose. Finally, differences in independence, in responsibility, and in monotony should affect the speed, the accuracy, the aggressiveness, and the flexibility of behavior.

---

[1] This is an empirical generalization derived chiefly from an analysis of a four-man square pattern. In such a pattern, A and B, and C and D may swap information in one time unit. Then A and C, and B and D may swap in two time units to yield a complete solution. For an eight-man ladder pattern the same simultaneous swapping process yields a minimum time. For the intervening n's, at least "part" of a time unit is required, in addition to the minimum time for the four-man pattern. A detailed account of this analysis may be found in a paper, as yet unpublished, by J. P. Macy, Jr.

METHOD

The Problem to be Solved

We have already described the task to be given our *S*s—a task of discovering the single common symbol from among several symbols. When *all five* men indicated that they knew the common symbol, a trial was ended. Another set of cards, with another common symbol, was then given to the *S*s, and another trial was begun.

Each group of *S*s was given 15 consecutive trials. The composition of the standard sets of cards, used for all groups, is indicated in Figure 2, which indicates the symbol *not* on each person's card for each trial. By referring this missing symbol to the set of six symbols at the top, the reader may reconstruct the symbols actually on each man's card. The common symbol (the right answer) is also shown in Figure 2.

The Apparatus

The *S*s were seated around a circular table (Fig. 3) so that each was separated from the next by a vertical partition from the center to six inches beyond the table's edge. The partitions had slots permitting subjects to push written message cards to the men on either side of them.

To allow for communication to the other men in the group, a five-layered pentagonal box was built and placed at the center of the table. The box was placed so that the partitions just touched each of the five points of the pentagon. Each of the five resulting wedge-shaped work-spaces was then painted a different color. The *S*s were supplied with blank message cards whose colors matched that of their work spaces. Any message sent from a booth had to be on

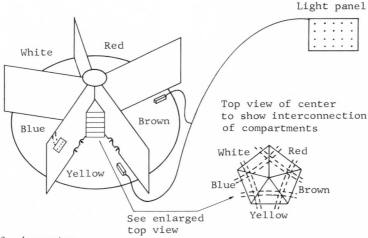

Fig. 3. Apparatus

a card of the booth's color. On the left wall of each partition, 16 large symbol cards, representing 16 trials, were hung in loose-leaf fashion. The cards were placed in order with numbered backs to S. At the starting signal, S could pull down the first card and go to work.

In addition, each work space was provided with a board on which were mounted six switches. Above each switch appeared one of the six symbols. When S got an answer to the problem, he was to throw the proper switch, which would turn on an appropriate light on a master board of 30 lights in the observer's room. When five lights (whether or not they were under the correct symbol), representing five different Ss, were lit, the observer called a halt to the trial. The observer could tell by a glance at the light panel whether (a) five different Ss had thrown their switches, (b) whether all five had decided on the same answer, and (c) whether the answer decided on was right or wrong. The same detailed instructions were given to all Ss.

A preliminary series of four problems, in which each S was given all the information required for solution, was used. This was done to note the extent of differences among Ss in the time required to solve such problems.

The Procedure

One hundred male undergraduates of M.I.T.,[2] drawn from various classes at the Institute, served as Ss for these experiments. These 100 were split up into 20 groups of five men each. These 20 groups were then further subdivided so that five groups could be tested on each of four experimental patterns.

Each group was given 15 consecutive trials on *one* pattern, a process which required one session of about fifty minutes. These Ss were *not used again.* The order in which we used our patterns was also randomized. Just in case the color or geographical position of one's work-space might affect one's behavior, we shifted positions for each new group. After a group had completed its 15 trials, and before members were permitted to talk with one another, each member was asked to fill out a questionnaire.

The Patterns Selected

The four five-man patterns selected for this research are shown in Figure 4.

These four patterns represented extremes in centrality (as in the circle vs. the wheel), as well as considerable differences in other characteristics (Table 1).

RESULTS

The data which have been accumulated are broken down in the pages that follow into (a) a comparison of total patterns and (b) a comparison of positions within patterns.

---

[2] Data on female graduate students are being gathered at M.I.T. by Smith and Bavelas, and the indications are that their behavior differs in some ways from the behavior of our male Ss.

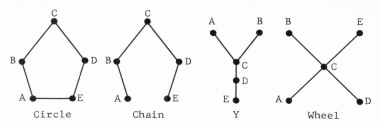

Fig. 4.   The Experimental Patterns

Table 1   CHARACTERISTICS OF THE EXPERIMENTAL PATTERNS

PATTERN	NO. OF LINKS	MOST CENTRAL POSITION	SUM OF NEIGHBORS	SUM OF DISTANCES	MIN. TIME UNITS	MIN. MESSAGES
Chain	4	C(6.7)	8	40	5(8m)	8(5t)
Y	4	C(7.2)	8	36	4(8m)	8(4t)
Wheel	4	C(8.0)	8	32	5(8m)	8(5t)
Circle	5	All(5.0)	10	30	3(14m)	8(5t)

A. Differences among Patterns

It was possible to reconstruct a picture of the operational methods actually used by means of: (a) direct observations, (b) post-experimental analysis of messages, and (c) post-experimental talks with Ss.

The *wheel* operated in the same way in all five cases. The peripheral men funnelled information to the center where an answer decision was made and the answer sent out. This organization had usually evolved by the fourth or fifth trial and remained in use throughout.

The *Y* operated so as to give the most central position, C (see Fig. 4 and Table 1), complete decision-making authority. The next-most-central position, D (see Fig. 4) served only as a transmitter of information and of answers. In at least one case, C transmitted answers first to A and B and only then to D. Organization for the Y evolved a little more slowly than for the wheel, but, once achieved, it was just as stable.

In the *chain* information was usually funnelled in from both ends to C, whence the answer was sent out in both directions. There were several cases, however, in which B or D reached an answer decision and passed it to C. The organization was slower in emerging than the Y's or the wheel's, but consistent once reached.

The *circle* showed no consistent operational organization. Most commonly messages were just sent in both directions until any S received an answer or worked one out. In every case, all available links were used at some time during the course of each trial.

Direct Measures of Differences among Patterns

Time. The curves in Figure 5 are for *correct* trials only, that is, for trials in which all five switches represented the correct common symbols. In most cases, the medians shown are for distributions of five groups, but in no case do they represent less than three groups.

The variability of the distributions represented by these medians is considerable. In the fifteenth trial, the distribution for the circle has a range of 50–96 seconds; for the chain, 28–220 seconds; for the Y, 24–52 seconds; and for the wheel, 21–46 seconds. Moreover, much of the time that went to make up each trial was a constant consisting of writing and passing time. Any differences attributable to pattern would be a small fraction of this large constant and would be easily obscured by accidents of misplacing or dropping of messages.

Despite all these factors, one measure of speed did give statistically significant differences. A measure of the *fastest single trial* of each group indicates that the wheel was considerably faster (at its fastest) than the circle (Table 2).

Table 2 FASTEST SINGLE CORRECT TRIAL

	CIRCLE	*CHAIN*	*Y*	*WHEEL*	*DIFF.*	*p**
Mean	50.4	53.2	35.4	32.0	Ci–W	<.01
Median	55.0	57.0	32.0	36.0	Ch–W	<.10
Range	44–59	19–87	22–53	20–41	Ci–Y	<.05
					Ch–Y	<.20

* Significance of differences between means were measured throughout by t-tests. The p-values are based on distributions of t which include both tails of the distribution (see Freeman [2]). Where differences are between proportions, p is derived from the usual measure of significance of differences between proportions. Ci–W means the circle-wheel difference, and so on.

Messages. The medians in Figure 6 represent a count of the number of messages sent by each group during a given (correct) trial. It seems clear that the circle pattern used more messages to solve the problem than the others.

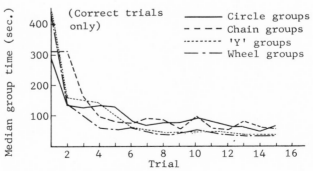

Fig. 5. Median Group-Times per Trial

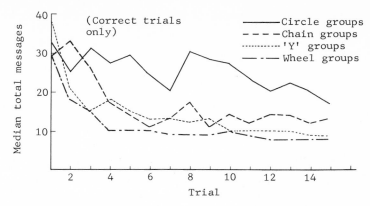

Fig. 6. Median Messages per Trial

Errors. An error was defined as the throwing of any incorrect switch by an *S* during a trial. Errors that were *not* corrected before the end of a trial are labelled "final errors"; the others are referred to as "corrected errors."

It should be pointed out that the error figures for the *wheel* in Table 3 are distorted by the peculiar behavior of one of the five wheel groups. The center man in this group took the messages which he received to be *answers* rather than simple information, and, in addition to throwing his own switch, passed the information on *as an answer*. This difficulty was cleared up after a few trials, and the figures for the last eight trials are probably more representative than the figures for the full 15 trials.

In addition to the differences in errors, there are differences in the proportion of total errors that were corrected. Although more errors were made in the circle pattern than any other, a greater proportion of them (61 per cent) were corrected than in any other pattern. Too, the frequency of unanimous five-man final errors is lower, both absolutely and percentage-wise, for the circle than for the chain.

Table 3 ERRORS

PATTERN	TOTAL ERRORS (15 TRIALS) MEAN	RANGE	TOTAL ERRORS (LAST 8 TRIALS) MEAN	RANGE	FINAL ERRORS MEAN	RANGE	MEAN NO. OF TRIALS WITH AT LEAST ONE FINAL ERROR
Circle	16.6	9–33	7.6	1–18	6.4	2–14	3.4
Chain	9.8	3–19	2.8	0–11	6.2	1–19	1.8
Y	2.6	1–8	0	0	1.6	0–5	.8
Wheel	9.8	0–34	0.6	0–2	2.2	0–7	1.2

p Values $Ci-Y < .02$
$\quad\quad Ci-Y < .02$

Questionnaire Results

1. *"Did your group have a leader? If so, who?"*

Only 13 of 25 people who worked in the circle named a leader, and those named were scattered among all the positions in the circle. For all patterns, the total frequency of people named increased in the order *circle, chain, Y, wheel*. Similarly, the unanimity of opinion increased in the same order so that, for the wheel pattern, all 23 members who recognized any leader agreed that position C was that leader.

2. *"Describe briefly the organization of your group."*

The word "organization" in this question was ambiguous. Some of the Ss understood the word to mean pattern of communication, while others equated it with their own duties or with status difference.

These differences in interpretation were not random, however. Sixteen people in the wheel groups fully reproduced the wheel structure in answer to this question, while only one circle member reproduced the circle pattern.

3. *"How did you like your job in the group?"*

In this question Ss were asked to place a check on a rating scale marked "disliked it" at one end and "liked it" at the other. For purposes of analysis, the scale was translated into numerical scores from 0 at the dislike end to 100. Each rating was estimated only to the closest decile.

Again, we find the order circle, chain, Y, wheel, with circle members enjoying their jobs significantly more than the wheel members.

4. *"See if you can recall how you felt about the job as you went along. Draw the curve below."*

The Ss were asked to sketch a curve into a space provided for it. We measured the height of these curves on a six-point scale at trials 1, 5, 10, and 15. These heights were averaged for each group, and the averages of the group averages were plotted.

Although the differences between groups are not statistically significant, trends of increasing satisfaction in the circle and decreasing satisfaction in the wheel seem to corroborate the findings in the question on satisfaction with one's job. Except for a modest Y-chain reversal, the order is, as usual, from circle to wheel.

5. *"Was there anything, at any time, that kept your group from performing at its best? If so, what?"*

The answers to this question were categorized as far as possible into several classes.

None of the circle members feels that "nothing" was wrong with his group; a fact that is suggestive of an attitude different from that held by members of the other patterns. So, too, is the finding that insufficient knowledge of the pattern does not appear as an obstacle to the circle member but is mentioned at least five times in each of the other patterns.

6. *"Do you think your group could improve its efficiency? If so, how?"*

Circle members place great emphasis on *organizing* their groups, on working out a "system" (mentioned 17 times). Members of the other patterns, if they felt that any improvement at all was possible, emphasized a great variety of possibilities.

7. *"Rate your group on the scale below."*

For purposes of analysis, these ratings (along a straight line) were transposed into numbers from 0, for "poor," to 100.

The same progression of differences that we have already encountered, the progression *circle, chain, Y, wheel,* holds for this question. Once again the circle group thinks less well of itself (Mean = 56) than do the other patterns (M_{ch} = 60; M_y = 70; M_w = 71).

Message Analysis

The messages sent by all Ss were collected at the end of each experimental run and their contents coded and categorized. Some of these categories overlapped with others, and hence some messages were counted in more than one category.

The now familiar progression, *circle, chain, Y, wheel,* continues into this area. Circle members send many more informational messages than members of the other patterns (M_{ci} = 283; M_w = 101). Circle members also send more answers (M_{ci} = 91; M_w = 65).

The same tendency remains in proportion to total errors as well as absolutely. The circle has a mean of 4.8 recognition-of-error messages for a mean of 16.6 errors; the chain has a mean of 1 recognition-of-error messages for a mean of 9.8 errors.

We were concerned, before beginning these experiments, lest Ss find short cuts for solving the problem, thus making certain comparisons among patterns difficult. One such short cut we have called "elimination." Instead of taking time to write their five symbols, many Ss, after discovering that only six symbols existed in all, wrote just the missing symbol, thus saving considerable time. This method was used by at least one member in two of the circle groups, in all the chain groups, in three of the Y groups, and in four of the wheel groups. In *both* the circle cases, the method was used by *all five members* during final trials. In the chain, though present in every group, elimination was used only once by all five members, twice by three members, and twice by just one member. In the Y, the method was adopted once by four members (the fifth man was *not* the center) and twice by two members. There was at least one case (in the wheel) in which a member who suggested the use of elimination was ordered by another member not to use it.

The questions raised here are two. Is the idea of elimination more likely to occur in some patterns than in others? Is an innovation like elimination likely to be more readily accepted in some patterns than in others? To neither of these questions do we have an adequate answer.

B. A Positional Analysis of the Data

Observation of the experimental patterns indicates that every position in the circle is indistinguishable from every other one. No one has more neighbors, is more central, or is closer to anyone else than anyone else. In the wheel, the four peripheral positions are alike, and so on. Despite our inability to differentiate these positions from one another, we have set up the data in the following sections as if all positions in each pattern were actually different from one another.

Direct Observations

Messages.   The most central positions, it will be seen from Table 4, send the greatest number of messages; the least central ones send the fewest.

Errors.   The analysis of total errors made in each position showed nothing of significance.

Questionnaire Results by Position

1.   *"How much did you enjoy your job?"*
The most central positions in other patterns enjoy their jobs more than any circle position. Peripheral positions, on the other hand, enjoy the job less than any circle position (Table 5).

2.   *"See if you can recall how you felt about the job as you went along. Draw the curve below."*
The data for this question are gathered after all most-peripheral and all most-central positions are combined. Peripheral positions were: positions A and E, in the chain; position E in the Y; and positions A, B, D, and E in the wheel. Central positions were all C positions with the exception of C in the circle. The data thus combined highlight the trend toward higher satisfaction with increasing centrality. The central positions progress from a mean of 2.1 at trial 1 to a mean of 3.9 at trial 15. Peripheral positions decline from 3.9 to 2.3.

Message Analysis by Position

One of the things that immediately stands out from an examination of the messages is an apparent peculiarity in the *informational message* category. Although the most central man in the chain sends more informational messages (52) than the other positions in that pattern, the same is not true of the most central men in the Y and the wheel. In the Y, it is position D, the next-most-central position, that sends most; while in the wheel all positions are about equal. This peculiarity becomes quite understandable if we take into account (a) the kind of organization used in each pattern and (b) the fact that these figures represent the entire 15 trials, some of which occurred before the group got itself stably organized. In the wheel, the Y, and the chain, the center man really needed to send *no* informational messages, only answers; but in the *early* trials, before his role was clarified, he apparently sent enough to bring his total up to or higher than the level of the rest.

It can also be noted that the number of *organizational messages* (messages which seek to establish some plan of action for future trials) is negatively correlated with positional centrality. The most peripheral men send the greatest numbers of organizational messages, the most central men least.

DISCUSSION

Patternwise, the picture formed by the results is of differences almost always in the order *circle, chain, Y, wheel.*
We may grossly characterize the kinds of differences that occur in this way: the circle, one extreme, is active, leaderless, unorganized, erratic, and yet is

Table 4 NUMBER OF MESSAGES SENT BY EACH POSITION

		A	B	C	D	E	DIFF.	p
Circle	Mean	78.4	90.0	83.6	86.2	81.0	A–B	<.30
	Range	64–101	63–102	60–98	60–122	72–90		
Chain	Mean	24.8	70.8	82.4	71.8	27.6	C–E	<.01
	Range	20–34	43–112	45–113	42–101	22–43		
Y	Mean	28.0	23.8	79.8	63.8	25.6	A–C	<.01
	Range	20–44	21–28	65–104	43–78	21–37	D–C	<.20
							D–E	<.01
Wheel	Mean	29.4	26.2	102.8	26.6	30.2	C–E	<.01
	Range	19–48	17–40	78–138	17–39	22–43		

Table 5 ENJOYMENT OF THE JOB

		A	B	C	D	E	DIFF.	p
Circle	Mean	58.0	64.0	70.0	65.0	71.0	A–E	<.70
	Range	0–100	0–100	20–100	40–100	25–100		
Chain	Mean	45.0	82.5	78.0	70.0	24.0	C–E	<.02
	Range	25–55	50–100	50–100	40–100	0–70	C–AE	<.01
Y	Mean	46.0	49.0	95.0	71.0	31.0	C–A	<.02
	Range	0–100	25–100	75–100	30–100	0–75	C–AB	<.01
							D–E	<.10
Wheel	Mean	37.5	20.0	97.0	25.0	42.5	B–C	<.01
	Range	0–50	0–40	85–100	0–75	0–100	C–E	<.02
							ABED–C	<.01

enjoyed by its members. The wheel, at the other extreme, is less active, has a distinct leader, is well and stably organized, is less erratic, and yet is unsatisfying to most of its members.

There are two questions raised by these behavioral differences. First, what was wrong with our a priori time-unit analysis? The results measured in clock time do not at all match the time-unit figures. And second, to what extent are behavioral differences matched by centrality differences?

The Time Unit

It was hypothesized earlier that the time taken to solve a problem should be limited at the lower end by the structure of the pattern of communication. If pattern does set such a limitation on speed, the limitation is not in the direction we would have predicted. Our analysis (Table 1), based on a theoretical time unit, led us falsely to expect greatest speed from the circle pattern.

There are three outstanding reasons for the failure of the time-unit analysis to predict clock time. First, the time unit, itself, was too gross a measure. We defined the time unit as the time required for the transmission of one message from its inception to its reception. In actuality, different kinds of messages required very different clock times for transmission. *S*s could send two messages simultaneously. They could also lay out and write several messages before sending any.

A second reason for the failure of the time-unit analysis was the assumption that *S*s would gravitate to the theoretically "best"-operating organization. Only the wheel groups used the theoretically "best" method (the minimum time method) consistently.

Finally, it should be pointed out that differences in speed between patterns were subject to major fluctuations for reasons of differences in writing speed, dexterity in passing messages, and other extraneous factors.

The Relation of the Centrality Measure to Behavior

Our second and more important question is: Are the behavioral differences among patterns and among positions related consistently to the centrality index? An examination of Table 1 indicates that the centrality index shows the same progression, *circle, chain, Y, wheel,* as do most of the behavioral differences. On a positional basis, centrality also differentiates members of a pattern in the same order that their behavior does.

Because such a relationship does exist between behavior and centrality, a more detailed consideration of the centrality concept is in order.

The central region of a structure is defined by Bavelas as "the class of all cells with the smallest p to be found in the structure." The quantity, p, in turn, is defined as the largest distance between one cell and any other cell in the structure. Distance is measured in link units. Thus the distance from A to B in the chain is one link; from A to C the distance is two links. The most central position in a pattern is the position that is closest to all other positions. Quantitatively, an index of the centrality of position A in any pattern can be found by (a) summing the shortest distances from *each* position to every other one and (b) dividing this summation by the total of the shortest distances from position A to every other position.

Centrality, then, is a function of the size of a pattern as well as of its structure. Thus, in a five-man circle, the centrality of each man is 5.0. In a six-man circle, the centrality of each man jumps to 6.0. The two most peripheral men in a five-man chain each have a centrality of 4.0. But in a seven-man chain, the two most peripheral men have centralities of 5.3.

In Figure 7 are given the centralities of each position in each of our four test patterns. The sum of centralities is also given. Both total centrality and distribution of centralities fall in the order *circle, chain, Y, wheel.*

These centrality figures correlate with the behavior we have observed. But it seems unreasonable to assume that the correlation would hold for larger *n*'s. Certainly we would not expect *more* message activity or *more* satisfaction from peripheral positions in a chain of a larger *n* than from a five-man chain.

To obviate this difficulty, a measure we have called "relative peripherality" may be established. The relative peripherality of any position in a pattern is the difference between the centrality of that position and the centrality of the most central position in that pattern. Thus, for the two end men in a five-man chain, the peripherality index is 2.7 (the difference between their centralities of 4.0 and the centrality of the most central position, 6.7). For a total pattern, the peripherality index may be taken by summating all the peripherality indices in the pattern (Fig. 7).

Examination of the data will show that observed differences in behavior correlate positively with these peripherality measures. *By total pattern*, messages, satisfaction, and errors (except for the wheel) vary consistently with total peripherality index. Similarly, by position, messages and satisfaction vary with peripherality. Errors, however, show no clear relationship with peripherality of position, a finding which is discussed in detail later in this section.

Recognition of a leader also seems to be a function of peripherality, but in a somewhat different way. A review of our leadership findings will show that

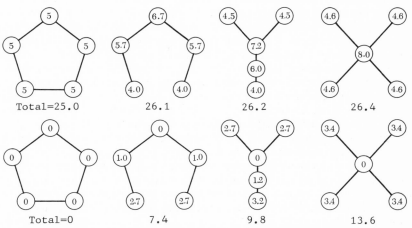

Fig. 7. Centrality Indices (above) and Peripherality Indices (below)

leadership becomes more clear-cut as the differences in peripherality *within a pattern become greater*. Recognition of a leader seems to be determined by the extent of the difference in centrality between the most central and next-most-central man.

There arises next the question: What is the mechanism by which the peripherality of a pattern or a position affects the behavior of persons occupying that pattern or position?

A reconstruction of the experimental situation leads us to this analysis of the peripherality-behavior relationship:

First, let us assume standard Ss, motivated to try to solve our experimental problem as quickly as possible. Let them be "intelligent" Ss who do not send the same information more than once to any neighbor. Let them also be Ss who, given several neighbors, will send, with equal probability, their first message to any one of those neighbors.

Given such standard Ss, certain specific positions will probably get an answer to the problem before other positions. In the chain, position C will be most likely to get the answer first, but, in the circle, all positions have an equal opportunity.

To illustrate, consider the chain pattern (see Fig. 4): During time unit 1, A may send only to B. B may send either to C or to A. C may send either to B or to D. D may send either to C or to E. E may send only to D. No matter where B, C, and D send their messages, B and D will have, at the end of one time unit, A's and E's information. During the second time unit, if B and/or D had sent to C the first time, they will now send to A and E. If they sent to A and E the first time, they will send to C, and C will have the answer. Even if B and D do not send to C until the third time unit, C will either get the answer before or simultaneously with B and D. In *no* case can any other position beat C to the answer. In the wheel, C cannot even be tied in getting an answer. He will *always* get it first.

Our second concern is with Ss' perceptions of these answer-getting potentials. We suggest that these random differences in answer-getting potentials rapidly structure members' perceptions of their own roles in the group. These differences affect one's independence from, or dependence on, the other members of the group. In the wheel, for example, a peripheral S perceives, at first, only that he gets the answer and information from C and can send only to C. C perceives that he gets information from everyone and must send the answer to everyone. The recognition of roles is easy. The peripheral men are dependent on C. C is autonomous and controls the organization.

In the circle, an S's perception must be very different. He gets information from both sides; sometimes he gets the answer, sometimes he sends it. He has two channels of communication. He is exclusively dependent on no one. His role is not clearly different from anyone else's.

Thirdly, having closed the gap between structural pattern and Ss' perceptions of their roles in the group, the problem reduces to one purely psychological. The question becomes: How do differences in one's perception of one's own dependence or independence bring about specific behavior differences of the sort we have observed?

Differences in satisfaction level are relatively easy to relate to independence. In our culture, in which needs for autonomy, recognition, and achievement are strong, it is to be expected that positions which limit independence of action (peripheral positions) would be unsatisfying.

A fairly direct relationship between centrality (and, hence, independence) and the speed with which a group gets organized is also perceptible. In the wheel, unless Ss act "unintelligently," an organization, with C as center, is forced on the wheel groups by the structural pattern. In the circle, no such differences in role and, hence, in organization are forced on the group.

Message-activity can also be related to centrality by means of the independence-of-action concept. A peripheral person in any pattern can send messages to only one other position. Only one informational message is called for. Extra messages would be repetitious. Central positions, however, are free to send more than one non-repetitious informational message until an organization evolves. Once the most central man perceives that he is most central, he need send *no* informational messages. But so long as the most central man does not perceive his own position, it is intelligent to send informational messages to whomever he feels may require some information. It is in keeping with this analysis that the circle should yield maximum messages and the wheel minimum messages.

If the behavior of one of the wheel groups can be discounted, then an explanation, in terms of peripherality, is also possible for both differences in tendencies to correct errors and total error differences.

If peripherality determines one's independence of action, it seems very likely that positions most limited in independence should begin to perceive themselves as subordinates whose sole function is to send information and await an answer. That they should then uncritically accept whatever answer they receive is perfectly in keeping with their subordinate, relatively unresponsible positions—hence, very little correction of errors in the patterns in which there are great differences in peripherality.

Total errors, it will be recalled, were correlated with total peripherality indices but showed no clear relationship with the relative peripherality of particular positions. A consideration of our definition of error may shed some light on this apparent anomaly.

The "errors" that we recorded were signals from the S that indicated a wrong answer. But these wrong answers derived from a variety of sources. First, Ss might wrongly interpret the correct information they received. They might also make errors in throwing switches; and they might also *correctly* interpret *wrong* information. In all three cases, "errors" were recorded.

We submit that this broad definition of error should yield a total pattern relationship with peripherality, but no positional relationship. Our reasoning can be illustrated by an example. Suppose that the central man in the wheel wrongly interprets information sent to him and, hence, throws an incorrect switch. This is a "real" error. He then funnels out the wrong answer to the other members. At least three of these intelligently conclude that the answer sent them is correct and also throw the wrong switches. We then have three "false" errors consequent to our single "real" one. When several independent answer decisions are made (as in the circle), we should expect several real errors, multiplication of these by a factor of about 3, and a larger total of errors. This process should lead to a correlation between total pattern behavior and peripherality but not to a correlation between positional behavior and peripherality. The process simply multiplies real errors more or less constantly for a whole pattern but obscures positional differences because the "real" and the "false" errors are indistinguishable in our data.

We submit, further, that pattern differences in real errors, if such there be, may be attributable to "over-information"; too much information to too many members which, under pressure, leads to errors. Central positions or positions which are no less central than others in the pattern should be the ones to yield the greatest number of real errors, while peripheral positions, which require no such rapid collation of information, should be the false error sources. Such an hypothesis would be in keeping with our total pattern findings and might also clarify our positional findings. Only an experiment designed to differentiate real from false errors can answer this question.

It is in keeping with this peripherality-independence analysis, also, that we should find the recognition of a single leader occurring most frequently in the wheel and Y groups. It is also to be expected that we should find circle members emphasizing need for organization and planning and seldom giving a complete picture of their pattern. Perhaps, too, it is reasonable to expect that the whole group should be considered good in the highly organized wheel (and not so good in the unorganized circle) even though one's own job is considered poor.

In summary, then, it is our feeling that centrality determines behavior by limiting independence of action, thus producing differences in activity, accuracy, satisfaction, leadership, recognition of pattern, and other behavioral characteristics.

SUMMARY AND CONCLUSIONS

Within the limits set by the experimental conditions—group size, type of problem, source of Ss—these conclusions seem warranted:

1. The communication patterns within which our groups worked affected their behavior. The major behavioral differences attributable to communication patterns were differences in accuracy, total activity, satisfaction of group members, emergence of a leader, and organization of the group. There may also be differences among patterns in speed of problem solving, self-correcting tendencies, and durability of the group as a group.

2. The positions which individuals occupied in a communication pattern affected their behavior while occupying those positions. One's position in the group affected the chances of becoming a leader of the group, one's satisfaction with one's job and with the group, the quantity of one's activity, and the extent to which one contributed to the group's functional organization.

3. The characteristic of communication patterns that was most clearly correlated with behavioral differences was *centrality*. Total pattern differences in behavior seemed to be correlated with a measure of centrality we have labelled the *peripherality index*. Positional differences in behavior seemed to be correlated with the positional peripherality indices of the various positions within patterns.

4. It is tentatively suggested that centrality affects behavior via the limits that centrality imposes upon independent action. Independence of action, relative to other members of the group is, in turn, held to be the primary determinant of the definition of who shall take the leadership role, total activity, satsifaction with one's lot, and other specific behaviors.

More precisely, it is felt that where centrality and, hence, independence are evenly distributed, there will be no leader, many errors, high activity, slow organization, and high satisfaction. Whatever frustration occurs will occur as a result of the inadequacy of the group, not the inadequacy of the environment.

Where one position is low in centrality relative to other members of the group, that position will be a follower position, dependent on the leader, accepting his dictates, falling into a role that allows little opportunity for prestige, activity, or self-expression.

REFERENCES

1. Bavelas, A. A mathematical model for group structures. *Appl. Anthrop.*, 1948, 7, 16–30.

2. Freeman, H. *Industrial statistics.* New York: Wiley, 1942.

6

GROUP DYNAMICS

Social Facilitation

ROBERT B. ZAJONC

Most textbook definitions of social psychology involve considerations about the influence of man upon man, or, more generally, of individual upon individual. And most of them, explicitly or implicitly, commit the main efforts of social psychology to the problem of how and why the *behavior* of one individual affects the behavior of another. The influences of individuals on each others' behavior which are of interest to social psychologists today take on very complex forms. Often they involve vast networks of inter-individual effects, such as one finds in studying the process of group decision-making, competition, or conformity to a group norm. But the fundamental forms of interindividual influence are

Reprinted from Science, 149, *July 16, 1965, 269–74. Copyright 1965 by the American Association for the Advancement of Science.*

represented by the oldest experimental paradigm of social psychology: social facilitation. This paradigm, dating back to Triplett's original experiments on pacing and competition, carried out in 1897 (1), examines the consequences upon behavior which derive from the sheer presence of other individuals.

Until the late 1930's, interest in social facilitation was quite active, but with the outbreak of World War II it suddenly died. And it is truly regrettable that it died, because the basic questions about social facilitation—its dynamics and its causes—which are in effect the basic questions of social psychology, were never solved. It is with these questions that this article is concerned. I first examine past results in this nearly completely abandoned area of research and then suggest a general hypothesis which might explain them.

Research in the area of social facilitation may be classified in terms of two experimental paradigms: audience effects and co-action effects. The first experimental paradigm involves the observation of behavior when it occurs in the presence of passive spectators. The second examines behavior when it occurs in the presence of other individuals also engaged in the same activity. We shall consider past literature in these two areas separately.

AUDIENCE EFFECTS

Simple motor responses are particularly sensitive to social facilitation effects. In 1925 Travis (2) obtained such effects in a study in which he used the pursuit-rotor task. In this task the subject is required to follow a small revolving target by means of a stylus which he holds in his hand. If the stylus is even momentarily off target during a revolution, the revolution counts as an error. First each subject was trained for several consecutive days until his performance reached a stable level. One day after the conclusion of the training the subject was called to the laboratory, given five trials alone, and then ten trials in the presence of from four to eight upper-classmen and graduate students. They had been asked by the experimenter to watch the subject quietly and attentively. Travis found a clear improvement in performance when his subjects were confronted with an audience. Their accuracy on the ten trials before an audience was greater than on any ten previous trials, including those on which they had scored highest.

A considerably greater improvement in performance was recently obtained in a somewhat different setting and on a different task (3). Each subject (all were National Guard trainees) was placed in a separate booth. He was seated in front of a panel outfitted with 20 red lamps in a circle. The lamps on this panel light in a clockwise sequence at 12 revolutions per minute. At random intervals one or another light fails to go on in its proper sequence. On the average there are 24 such failures per hour. The subject's task is to signal whenever a light fails to go on. After 20 minutes of intensive training, followed by a short rest, the National Guard trainees monitored the light panels for 135 minutes. Subjects in one group performed their task alone. Subjects in another group were told that from time to time a lieutenant colonel or a master sergeant would visit them in the booth to observe their performance. These visits actually took place about four times during the experimental session. There was no doubt about the results.

The accuracy of the supervised subjects was on the average 34 percent higher than the accuracy of the trainees working in isolation, and toward the end of the experimental session the accuracy of the supervised subjects was more than twice as high as that of the subjects working in isolation. Those expecting to be visited by a superior missed, during the last experimental period, 20 percent of the light failures, while those expecting no such visits missed 64 percent of the failures.

Dashiell, who, in the early 1930's, carried out an extensive program of research on social facilitation, also found considerable improvement in performance due to audience effects on such tasks as simple multiplication or word association (*4*). But, as is the case in many other areas, negative audience effects were also found. In 1933 Pessin asked college students to learn lists of nonsense syllables under two conditions, alone and in the presence of several spectators (*5*). When confronted with an audience, his subjects required an average of 11.27 trials to learn a seven-item list. When working alone they needed only 9.85 trials. The average number of errors made in the "audience" condition was considerably higher than the number in the "alone" condition. In 1931 Husband found that the presence of spectators interferes with the learning of a finger maze (*6*), and in 1933 Pessin and Husband (*7*) confirmed Husband's results. The number of trials which the isolated subjects required for learning the finger maze was 17.1. Subjects confronted with spectators, however, required 19.1 trials. The average number of errors for the isolated subjects was 33.7; the number for those working in the presence of an audience was 40.5.

The results thus far reviewed seem to contradict one another. On a pursuit-rotor task Travis found that the presence of an audience improves performance. The learning of nonsense syllables and maze learning, however, seem to be inhibited by the presence of an audience, as shown by Pessin's experiment. The picture is further complicated by the fact that when Pessin's subjects were asked, several days later, to recall the nonsense syllables they had learned, a reversal was found. The subjects who tried to recall the lists in the presence of spectators did considerably better than those who tried to recall them alone. Why are the learning of nonsense syllables and maze learning inhibited by the presence of spectators? And why, on the other hand, does performance on a pursuit-rotor, word-association, multiplication, or a vigilance task improve in the presence of others?

There is just one, rather subtle, consistency in the above results. It would appear that the emission of well-learned responses is facilitated by the presence of spectators, while the acquisition of new responses is impaired. To put the statement in conventional psychological language, performance is facilitated and learning is impaired by the presence of spectators.

This tentative generalization can be reformulated so that different features of the problem are placed into focus. During the early stages of learning, especially of the type involved in social facilitation studies, the subject's responses are mostly the wrong ones. A person learning a finger maze, or a person learning a list of nonsense syllables, emits more wrong responses than right ones in the early stages of training. Most learning experiments continue until he ceases to make mistakes—until his performance is perfect. It may be said, therefore, that during training it is primarily the wrong responses which are dominant and strong; they are the ones which have the highest probability of occurrence. But after the individual has mastered the task, correct responses necessarily gain ascendancy in his task-relevant behavioral repertoire. Now they are the ones which are more probable—in other words, dominant. Our tentative generalization may now be simplified: audience enhances the emission of dominant responses. If the dominant responses are the correct ones, as is the case upon achieving mastery, the presence of an audience will be of benefit to the individual. But if they are mostly wrong, as is the case in the early stages of learning, then these wrong responses will be enhanced in the presence of an audience, and the emission of correct responses will be postponed or prevented.

There is a class of psychological processes which are known to enhance the emission of dominant responses. They are subsumed under the concepts of drive, arousal, and activation (8). If we could show that the presence of an audience has arousal consequences for the subject, we would be a step further along in trying to arrange the results of social-facilitation experiments into a neater package. But let us first consider another set of experimental findings.

CO-ACTION EFFECTS

The experimental paradigm of co-action is somewhat more complex than the paradigm involved in the study of audience effects. Here we observe individuals all simultaneously engaged in the same activity and in full view of each other. One of the clearest effects of such simultaneous action, or co-action, is found in eating behavior. It is well known that animals simply eat more in the presence of others. For instance, Bayer had chickens eat from a pile of wheat to their full satisfaction (9). He waited some time to be absolutely sure that his subject would eat no more, and then brought in a companion chicken who had not eaten for 24 hours. Upon the introduction of the hungry co-actor, the apparently sated chicken ate two-thirds again as much grain as it had already eaten. Recent work by Tolman and Wilson fully substantiates these results (10). In an extensive study of social-facilitation effects among albino rates, Harlow found dramatic increases in eating (11). In one of his experiments, for instance, the rats, shortly after weaning, were matched in pairs for weight. They were then fed alone and in pairs on alternate days. Figure 1 shows his results. It is clear that considerably more food was consumed by the animals when they were in pairs than when they were fed alone. James (12), too, found very clear evidence of increased eating among puppies fed in groups.

Perhaps the most dramatic effect of co-action is reported by Chen (13). Chen observed groups of ants working alone, in groups of two, and in groups of three. Each ant was observed under various conditions. In the first experimental session each ant was placed in a bottle half filled with sandy soil. The ant was observed for 6 hours. The time at which nest-building began was noted, and the earth excavated by the insect was carefully weighed. Two days afterward the same ants were placed in freshly filled bottles in pairs, and the same observations were made. A few days later the ants were placed in the bottles in groups of three, again for 6 hours. Finally, a few days after the test in groups of three, nest-building of the ants in isolation was observed. Figure 2 shows some of Chen's data.

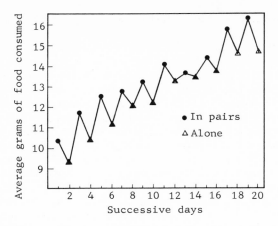

Fig. 1.   Data on feeding of isolated and paired rats. [Harlow (11)]

There is absolutely no question that the amount of work an ant accomplishes increases markedly in the presence of another ant. In all pairs except one, the presence of a companion increased output by a factor of at least 2. The effect of co-action on the latency of the nest-building behavior was equally dramatic. The solitary ants of session 1 and the final session began working on the nest in 192 minutes, on the average. The latency period for ants in groups of two was only 28 minutes. The effects observed by Chen were limited to the immediate situation and seemed to have no lasting consequences for the ants. There were no differences in the results of session 1, during which the ants worked in isolation, and of the last experimental session, where they again worked in solitude.

If one assumes that under the conditions of Chen's experiment nest-building *is* the dominant response, then there is no reason why his findings could not be embraced by the generalization just proposed. Nest-building is a response which

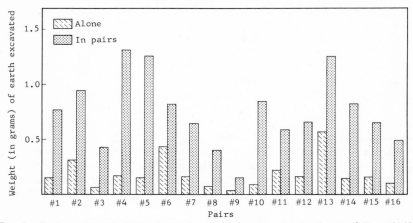

Fig. 2.   Data on nest-building behavior of isolated and paired ants. [Chen (13)]

Chen's ants have fully mastered. Certainly, it is something that a mature ant need not learn. And this is simply an instance where the generalization that the presence of others enhances the emission of dominant and well-developed responses holds.

If the process involved in audience effects is also involved in co-action effects, then learning should be inhibited in the presence of other learners. Let us examine some literature in this field. Klopfer (14) observed greenfinches—in isolation and in heterosexual pairs—which were learning to discriminate between sources of palatable and of unpalatable food. And, as one would by now expect, his birds learned this discrimination task considerably more efficiently when working alone. I hasten to add that the subjects' sexual interests cannot be held responsible for the inhibition of learning in the paired birds. Allee and Masure, using Australian parakeets, obtained the same result for homosexual pairs as well (15). The speed of learning was considerably greater for the isolated birds than for the paired birds, regardless of whether the birds were of the same sex or of the opposite sex.

Similar results are found with cockroaches. Gates and Allee (16) compared data for cockroaches learning a maze in isolation, in groups of two, and in groups of three. They used an E-shaped maze. Its three runways, made of galvanized sheet metal, were suspended in a pan of water. At the end of the center runway was a dark bottle into which the photophobic cockroaches could escape from the noxious light. The results, in terms of time required to reach the bottle, are shown in Fig. 3. It is clear from the data that the solitary cockroaches required considerably less time to learn the maze than the grouped animals. Gates and Allee believe that the group situation produced inhibition. They add, however (16, p. 357): "The nature of these inhibiting forces is speculative, but

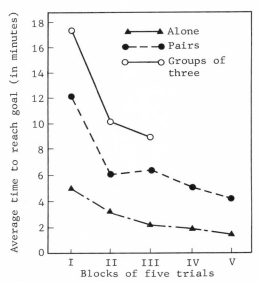

Fig. 3. Data on maze learning in isolated and grouped cockroaches. [Gates and Allee (16)]

the fact of some sort of group interference is obvious. The presence of other roaches did not operate to change greatly the movements to different parts of the maze, but did result in increased time per trial. The roaches tended to go to the corner or end of the runway and remain there a longer time when another roach was present than when alone; the other roach was a distracting stimulus."

The experiments on social facilitation performed by Floyd Allport in 1920 and continued by Dashiell in 1930 (4, 17), both of whom used human subjects, are the ones best known. Allport's subjects worked either in separate cubicles or sitting around a common table. When working in isolation they did the various tasks at the same time and were monitored by common time signals. Allport did everything possible to reduce the tendency to compete. The subjects were told that the results of their tests would not be compared and would not be shown to other staff members, and that they themselves should refrain from making any such comparisons.

Among the tasks used were the following: chain word association, vowel cancellation, reversible perspective, multiplication, problem solving, and judgments of odors and weights. The results of Allport's experiments are well known: in all but the problem-solving and judgments test, performance was better in groups than in the "alone" condition. How do these results fit our generalization? Word association, multiplication, the cancellation of vowels, and the reversal of the perceived orientation of an ambiguous figure all involve responses which are well established. They are responses which are either very well learned or under a very strong influence of the stimulus, as in the word-association task or the reversible-perspective test. The problem-solving test consists of disproving arguments of ancient philosophers. In contrast to the other tests, it does not involve well-learned responses. On the contrary, the probability of wrong (that is, logically incorrect) responses on tasks of this sort is rather high; in other words, wrong responses are dominant. Of interest, however, is the finding that while intellectual work suffered in the group situation, sheer output of words was increased. When working together, Allport's subjects tended consistently to write more. Therefore, the generalization proposed in the previous section can again be applied: if the presence of others raises the probability of dominant responses, and if strong (and many) incorrect response tendencies prevail, then the presence of others can only be detrimental to performance. The results of the judgment tests have little bearing on the present argument, since Allport gives no accuracy figures for evaluating performance. The data reported only show that the presence of others was associated with the avoidance of extreme judgments.

In 1928 Travis (18), whose work on the pursuit rotor I have already noted, repeated Allport's chain-word-association experiment. In contrast to Allport's results, Travis found that the presence of others decreased performance. The number of associations given by his subjects was greater when they worked in isolation. It is very significant, however, that Travis used stutterers as his subjects. In a way, stuttering is a manifestation of a struggle between conflicting response tendencies, all of which are strong and all of which compete for expression. The stutterer, momentarily hung up in the middle of a sentence, waits for the correct response to reach full ascendancy. He stammers because other competing tendencies are dominant at that moment. It is reasonable to assume that, to the extent that the verbal habits of a stutterer are characterized by conflicting response tendencies, the presence of others, by enhancing each of these response tendencies, simply heightens his conflict. Performance is thus impaired.

AVOIDANCE LEARNING

In two experiments on the learning of avoidance responses the performances of solitary and grouped subjects were compared. In one, rats were used: in the other, humans.

Let us first consider the results of the rat experiment, by Rasmussen (*19*). A number of albino rats, all litter mates, were deprived of water for 48 hours. The apparatus consisted of a box containing a dish of drinking water. The floor of the box was made of a metal grille wired to one pole of an electric circuit. A wire inserted in the water in the dish was connected to the other pole of the circuit. Thirsty rats were placed in the box alone and in groups of three. They were allowed to drink for 5 seconds with the circuit open. Following this period the shock circuit remained closed, and each time the rat touched the water he received a painful shock. Observations were made on the number of times the rats approached the water dish. The results of this experiment showed that the solitary rats learned to avoid the dish considerably sooner than the grouped animals did. The rats that were in groups of three attempted to drink twice as often as the solitary rats did, and suffered considerably more shock than the solitary subjects.

Let us examine Rasmussen's results somewhat more closely. For purposes of analysis let us assume that there are just two critical responses involved: drinking, and avoidance of contact with the water. They are clearly incompatible. But drinking, we may further assume, is the dominant response, and, like eating or any other dominant response, it is enhanced by the presence of others. The animal is therefore prevented, by the facilitation of drinking which derives from the presence of others, from acquiring the appropriate avoidance response.

The second of the two studies is quite recent and was carried out by Ader and Tatum (*20*). They devised the following situation with which they confronted their subjects, all medical students. Each subject is told on arrival that he will be taken to another room and seated in a chair, and that electrodes will be attached to his leg. He is instructed not to get up from the chair and not to touch the electrodes. He is also told not to smoke or vocalize, and is told that the experimenter will be in the next room. That is all he is told. The subjects are observed either alone or in pairs. In the former case the subject is brought to the room and seated at a table equipped with a red button which is connected to an electric circuit. Electrodes, by means of which electric shock can be administered, are attached to the calf of one leg. After the electrodes are attached, the experimenter leaves the room. From now on the subject will receive ½ second of electric shock every 10 seconds unless he presses the red button. Each press of the button delays the shock by 10 seconds. Thus, if he is to avoid shock, he must press the button at least once every 10 seconds. It should be noted that no information was given him about the function of the button, or about the purpose of the experiment. No essential differences are introduced when subjects are brought to the room in pairs. Both are seated at the table and both become part of the shock circuit. The response of either subject delays the shock for both.

The avoidance response is considered to have been acquired when the subject (or pair of subjects) receives less than six shocks in a period of 5 minutes. Ader and Tatum report that the isolated students required, on the average, 11 minutes, 35 seconds to reach this criterion of learning. Of the 12 pairs which participated in the experiment, only two reached this criterion. One of them required 46 minutes, 40 seconds; the other, 68 minutes, 40 seconds! Ader and Tatum offer no explanation for their curious results. But there is no reason why we should not treat them in terms of the generalization proposed above. We are dealing here with a learning task, and the fact that the subjects are learning to avoid shock by pressing a red button does not introduce particular problems. They are confronted with an ambiguous task, and told nothing about the button. Pressing the button is simply not the dominant response in this situation. However, escaping is. Ader and Tatum report that eight of the 36 subjects walked out in the middle of the experiment.

One aspect of Ader and Tatum's results is especially worth noting. Once having learned the appropriate avoidance response, the individual subjects responded at considerably lower rates than the paired subjects. When we consider only those subjects who achieved the learning criterion and only those responses which occurred *after* criterion had been reached, we find that the response rates of the individual subjects were in all but one case lower than the response rates of the grouped subjects. This result further confirms the generalization that, while learning is impaired by the presence of others, the performance of learned responses is enhanced.

There are experiments which show that learning is enhanced by the presence of other learners (21), but in all these experiments, as far as I can tell, it was possible for the subject to *observe* the critical responses of other subjects, and to determine when he was correct and when incorrect. In none, therefore, has the co-action paradigm been employed in its pure form. That paradigm involves the presence of others, and nothing else. It requires that these others not be able to provide the subject with cues or information as to appropriate behavior. If other learners can supply the critical individual with such cues, we are dealing not with the problem of co-action but with the problem of imitation or vicarious learning.

THE PRESENCE OF OTHERS AS A SOURCE OF AROUSAL

The results I have discussed thus far lead to one generalization and to one hypothesis. The generalization which organizes these results is that the presence of others, as spectators or as co-actors, enhances the emission of dominant responses. We also know from extensive research literature that arousal, activation, or drive all have as a consequence the enhancement of dominant responses (22). We now need to examine the hypothesis that the presence of others increases the individual's general arousal or drive level.

The evidence which bears on the relationship between the presence of others and arousal is, unfortunately, only indirect. But there is some very suggestive evidence in one area of research. One of the more reliable indicators of arousal and drive is the activity of the endocrine systems in general, and of the adrenal cortex in particular. Adrenocortical functions are extremely sensitive to changes in emotional arousal, and it has been known for some time that organisms subjected to prolonged stress are likely to manifest substantial adrenocortical hypertrophy (23). Recent work (24) has shown that the main biochemical component of the adrenocortical output is hydrocortisone (17-hydro-xycorticosterone). Psychiatric patients characterized by anxiety states, for instance, show elevated plasma levels of hydrocortisone (25). Mason, Brady, and Sidman (26) have recently trained monkeys to press a lever for food and have given these animals unavoidable electric shocks, all preceded by warning signals. This procedure led to elevated hydrocortisone levels; the levels returned to normal within 1 hour after the end of the experimental session. This "anxiety" reaction can apparently be attenuated if the animal is given repeated doses of reserpine 1 day before the experimental session (27). Sidman's conditioned avoidance schedule also results in raising the hydrocortisone levels by a factor of 2 to 4 (26). In this schedule the animal receives an electric shock every .20 seconds without warning, unless he presses a lever. Each press delays the shock for 20 seconds.

While there is a fair amount of evidence that adrenocortical activity is a reliable symptom of arousal, similar endocrine manifestations were found to be associated with increased population density (28). Crowded mice, for instance, show increased amphetamine toxicity—that is, susceptibility to the excitatory effects of amphetamine—against which they can be protected by the administration of phenobarbital, chlorpromazine, or reserpine (29). Mason and Brady (30) have recently reported that monkeys caged together had considerably higher plasma levels of hydrocortisone than monkeys housed in individual cages. Thiessen (31) found increases in adrenal weights in mice housed in groups of 10 and 20 as compared with mice housed alone. The mere presence of other animals in the same room, but in separate cages, was also found to produce elevated levels of hydrocortisone. Table 1, taken from a report by Mason and Brady (30), shows plasma levels of hydrocortisone for three animals which lived at one time in cages that afforded them the possibility of visual and tactile contact and, at another time, in separate rooms.

Mason and Brady also report urinary levels of hydrocortisone, by days of the week, for five monkeys from their laboratory and for one human hospital patient. These very suggestive figures are reproduced in Table 2 (30). In the monkeys, the low weekend traffic and activity in the laboratory seem to be associated with a clear decrease in hydrocortisone. As for the hospital patient, Mason and Brady report (30, p. 8), "he was confined to a thoracic surgery ward that bustled with activity during the weekdays when surgery and admissions occurred. On the weekends the patient retired to the nearby Red Cross building, with its quieter and more pleasant environment."

Admittedly, the evidence that the mere presence of others raises the arousal level is indirect and scanty. And, as a matter of fact, some work seems to suggest that there are conditions, such as stress, under which the presence of others may

Table 1 BASAL PLASMA CONCENTRATIONS OF 17-HYDROXYCORTICOSTERONE IN MONKEYS HOUSED ALONE (CAGES IN SEPARATE ROOMS), THEN IN A ROOM WITH OTHER MONKEYS (CAGES IN SAME ROOM). [LEIDERMAN AND SHAPIRO (*35, p.* 7)].

SUBJECT	TIME	*CONC. OF 17-HYDROXYCORTICOSTERONE IN CAGED MONKEYS (μg PER 100 ml OF PLASMA)*	
		IN SEPARATE ROOMS	*IN SAME ROOM*
M-1	9 a.m.	23	34
M-1	3 p.m.	16	27
M-2	9 a.m.	28	34
M-2	3 p.m.	19	23
M-3	9 a.m.	32	38
M-3	3 p.m.	23	31
Mean	9 a.m.	28	35
Mean	3 p.m.	19	27

Table 2 VARIATIONS IN URINARY CONCENTRATION OF HYDROCORTISONE OVER A 9-DAY PERIOD FOR FIVE LABORATORY MONKEYS AND ONE HUMAN HOSPITAL PATIENT. [LEIDERMAN AND SHAPIRO (*35, p.* 8)].

SUBJECTS	*AMOUNTS EXCRETED (mg/24 hr)*								
	MON.	*TUES.*	*WED.*	*THURS.*	*FRI.*	*SAT.*	*SUN.*	*MON.*	*TUES.*
Monkeys	1.88	1.71	1.60	1.52	1.70	1.16	1.17	1.88	
Patient		5.9	6.5	4.5	5.7	3.3	3.9	6.0	5.2

lower the animal's arousal level. Bovard (*32*), for instance, hypothesized that the presence of another member of the same species may protect the individual under stress by inhibiting the activity of the posterior hypothalamic centers which trigger the pituitary adrenal cortical and sympathetico-adrenal medullary responses to stress. Evidence for Bovard's hypothesis, however, is as indirect as evidence for the one which predicts arousal as a consequence of the presence of others, and even more scanty.

SUMMARY AND CONCLUSION

If one were to draw one practical suggestion from the review of the social-facilitation effects which are summarized in this article he would advise the student to study all alone, preferably in an isolated cubicle, and to arrange to take his examinations in the company of many other students, on stage, and in the presence of a large audience. The results of his examination would be beyond his wildest expectations, provided, of course, he had learned his material quite thoroughly.

I have tried in this article to pull together the early, almost forgotten work on social facilitation, and to explain the seemingly conflicting results. This explanation is, of course, tentative, and it has never been put to a direct experimental test. It is, moreover, not far removed from the one originally proposed by Allport. He theorized (*33*, p. 261) that "the sights and sounds of others doing the same thing" augment ongoing responses. Allport, however, proposed this effect only for *overt* motor responses, assuming (*33*, p. 274) that "*intellectual* or *implicit responses* of thought are hampered rather than facilitated" by the presence of others. This latter conclusion was probably suggested to him by the negative results he observed in his research on the effects of co-action on problem solving.

Needless to say, the presence of others may have effects considerably more complex than that of increasing the individual's arousal level. The presence of others may provide cues as to appropriate or inappropriate responses, as in the case of imitation or vicarious learning. Or it may supply the individual with cues as to the measure of danger in an ambiguous or stressful situation. Davitz and Mason (*34*), for instance, have shown that the presence of an unafraid rat reduces the fear of another rat in stress. Bovard (*32*) believes that the calming of the rat in stress which is in the presence of an unafraid companion is mediated by inhibition of activity of the posterior hypothalamus. But in their experimental situations (that is, the open field test) the possibility that cues for appropriate escape or avoidance responses are provided by the co-actor is not ruled out. We might therefore be dealing not with the effects of the mere presence of others but with the considerably more complex case of imitation. The animal may not be calming *because* of his companion's presence. He may be calming *after* having copied his companion's attempted escape responses. The paradigm which I have examined in this article pertains only to the effects of the mere presence of others, and to the consequences for the arousal level. The exact parameters involved in social facilitation still must be specified.

REFERENCES AND NOTES

1. N. Triplett, *Amer. J. Psychol. 9,* 507 (1897).

2. L. E. Travis, *J. Abnormal Soc. Psychol. 20,* 142 (1925).

3. B. O. Bergum and D. J. Lehr, *J. Appl. Psychol. 47,* 75 (1963).

4. J. F. Dashiell, *J. Abnormal Soc. Psychol. 25,* 190 (1930).

5. J. Pessin, *Amer. J. Psychol. 45,* 263 (1933).

6. R. W. Husband, *J. Genet. Psychol. 39,* 258 (1931). In this task the blindfolded subject traces a maze with his finger.

7. J. Pessin and R. W. Husband, *J. Abnormal Soc. Psychol. 28,* 148 (1933).

8. See, for instance, E. Duffy, *Activation and Behavior* (Wiley, New York, 1962); K. W. Spence, *Behavior Theory and Conditioning* (Yale Univ. Press, New Haven, 1956); R. B. Zajonc and B. Nieuwenhuyse, *J. Exp. Psychol. 67,* 276 (1964).

9. E. Bayer, *Z. Psychol. 112,* 1 (1929).

10. C. W. Tolman and G. T. Wilson, *Animal Behavior 13,* 134 (1965).

11. H. F. Harlow, *J. Genet. Psychol. 43*, 211 (1932).

12. W. T. James, *J. Comp. Physiol. Psychol. 46*, 427 (1953); *J. Genet. Psychol. 96*, 123 (1960); W. T. James and D. J. Cannon, *ibid. 87*, 225 (1956).

13. S. C. Chen, *Physiol. Zool. 10*, 420 (1937).

14. P. H. Klopfer, *Science 128*, 903 (1958).

15. W. C. Allee and R. H. Masure, *Physiol. Zool. 22*, 131 (1936).

16. M. J. Gates and W. C. Allee, *J. Comp. Psychol. 15*, 331 (1933).

17. F. H. Allport, *J. Exp. Psychol. 3*, 159 (1920).

18. L. E. Travis, *J. Abnormal Soc. Psychol. 23*, 45 (1928).

19. E. Rasmussen, *Acta Psychol. 4*, 275 (1939).

20. R. Ader and R. Tatum, *J. Exp. Anal. Behavior 6*, 357 (1963).

21. H. Gurnee, *J. Abnormal Soc Psychol. 34*, 529 (1939); J. C. Welty, *Physiol. Zool. 7*, 85 (1934).

22. See K. W. Spence, *Behavior Theory and Conditioning* (Yale Univ. Press, New Haven, 1956).

23. H. Selye, *J. Clin. Endocrin. 6*, 117 (1946).

24. D. H. Nelson and L. T. Samuels, *ibid. 12*, 519 (1952).

25. E. L. Bliss, A. A. Sandberg, D. H. Nelson, *J. Clin. Invest. 32*, 9 (1953); F. Board, H. Persky, D. A. Hamburg, *Psychosom. Med. 18*, 324 (1956).

26. J. W. Mason, J. V. Brady, M. Sidman, *Endocrinology 60*, 741 (1957).

27. J. W. Mason and J. V. Brady, *Science 124*, 983 (1956).

28. D. D. Thiessen, *Texas Rep. Biol. Med. 22*, 266 (1964).

29. L. Lasagna and W. P. McCann, *Science 125*, 1241 (1957).

30. J. W. Mason and J. V. Brady, in *Psychobiological Approaches to Social Behavior*, P. H. Leiderman and D. Shapiro, Eds. (Stanford Univ. Press, Stanford, Calif., 1964).

31. D. D. Thiessen, *J. Comp. Physiol. Psychol. 57*, 412 (1964).

32. E. W. Bovard, *Psychol. Rev. 66*, 267 (1959).

33. F. H. Allport, *Social Psychology* (Houghton-Mifflin, Boston, 1924).

34. J. R. Davitz and D. J. Mason, *J. Comp. Physiol. Psychol. 48*, 149 (1955).

35. P. H. Leiderman and D. Shapiro, Eds., *Psychobiological Approaches to Social Behavior* (Stanford Univ. Press, Stanford, Calif., 1964).

36. The preparation of this article was supported in part by grants Nonr-1224(34) from the Office of Naval Research and GS-629 from the National Science Foundation.

Effects of Increased Incentives upon the Use of Threat in Bargaining

PHILIP S. GALLO, JR.

The relationship of threat to interpersonal bargaining has been studied recently by Deutsch and Krauss (1960, 1962) and Borah (1963). The problem was investigated within the context of an ingenious two-person, nonzero-sum simulation game developed by Deutsch. A detailed description of the methodology and equipment used by Deutsch and Krauss would be beyond the scope of this paper, but the salient features of the situation should be noted.

The players were asked to imagine that they were the owners of trucking companies. With the aid of an electronic control panel and a road map, each player maneuvered an imaginary truck along a pathway to a destination. The amount of profit per trial was inversely related to the length of time needed to reach the destination. The task was complicated by the fact that the trucks started simultaneously, and if sent directly along the main route would meet head on in a one-lane section of that route. The players thus had to learn, without benefit of communication, to alternate going first on the main route. Failure to alternate would result in expensive stalemates on the one-lane section or the use of a costly alternate route to the goal.

Threat could be introduced by providing one or both players with a barrier which could be placed across the one-lane path. The players could use the barriers to prevent their opponent's truck from reaching its destination. Deutsch and Krauss predicted that the introduction of threat into such a conflict of interest situation would increase the competitive orientation of the players. Threat, if available, would tend to be used, and the use of threat would provoke counterthreat and/or resistance to yielding under duress. The result would be increased difficulty in reaching a tacit agreement concerning the use of the one-lane path and poorer payoffs. The results of their first experiment supported this prediction. When neither subject was given a barrier, the mean joint payoff per dyad, summed over the 20 trials of the experiment, was +$2.03. When both subjects were given barriers (bilateral threat) the mean joint payoff was –$8.75. The results of the second experiment indicated that neither free nor forced communication between the players substantially increased the payoffs in the bilateral-threat condition.

Borah disagreed with the theoretical position of Deutsch and Krauss. He argued that the level of competitiveness was probably equal in the no-threat and bilateral-threat conditions and was actually quite low in each. The poor outcomes in the bilateral threat condition could be explained by the increased use of the costly alternate path when the barriers were used. Borah replicated Deutsch and Krauss' experiment, using a game board with movable pawns rather

Reprinted from Journal of Personality and Social Psychology, 4, *1966, 14–20.*
Copyright 1966 by the American Psychological Association and reproduced by
permission.

than the original electronic equipment. His results indicated that despite the changed methodology, the mean joint payoffs were very similar to those obtained by Deutsch and Krauss, and there was no difference between the no-threat and bilateral-threat dyads in the amount of time lost in standoffs on the short path, a dependent measure that he felt would be sensitive to differences in competitiveness.

If it is true, as Borah assumes, that motivation to compete is at a fairly low level, it is probably also true that motivation to cooperate is at an even lower level. In all three experiments, payoffs to the subjects were in imaginary money. If the subjects cooperatively alternate, they will amass equal amounts of imaginary money. Despite the fact that they have been instructed to play exactly as though the money were real, it would appear that the utility of amassing imaginary money would be quite low for the players.

If this analysis is correct, it is probable that subjects invent a new game to play, one in which success is measured not by the absolute amount of imaginary money acquired, but by the discrepancy between their gains or losses and those of their opponent. However, such a game cannot really be played in the no-threat condition. The only behavioral alternatives are alternation or interminable stalemate on the one-lane path. It is probably to the subjects' advantage to alternate and get the game over with as quickly as possible. However, when the barriers are present, numerous opportunities exist to trick, deceive, outwit, and "beat" one's opponent. The two conditions may differ only in terms of the opportunities available for expressing whatever competitiveness may be present.

The present study was designed to test the hypothesis that the seemingly irreconcilable conflict present in the bilateral-threat condition is the result of the fact that the subjects have been presented with virtually no motivation to cooperate. Half of the subjects in the present study were given the opportunity to win sizable amounts of real money. The payoffs in the original studies were increased such that perfect cooperative alternation would result in a payoff to each subject of $16. It was predicted that the subjects playing for real money would attain significantly higher payoffs than the subjects playing for imaginary money, and in fact would do as well as the no-threat subjects in the previous experiments.

In addition to the main independent variable of real versus imaginary money, three other independent variables were investigated in a factorial design. These were:

1. Barriers for the last 10 trials only versus barriers for all 20 trials. It was predicted that subjects who did not receive the barriers until the last 10 trials would have experienced good outcomes and would be less tempted to try the barriers. Thus they should attain higher overall outcomes.

2. Relative value versus absolute value instructions. Half of the subjects were told to measure their success in terms of how much more money they won than their opponent (relative value). The other half were told to make as much money as they could for themselves (absolute value). It was predicted that the relative value instructions would induce a more competitive set than would the absolute value instructions.

3. Possession of winnings versus potential winnings. Half of the subjects were given the maximum possible winnings at the start of the experiment and penalties for incoordination, if any, were subtracted from the total after each

trial. The other half of the subjects were given their profit after each trial. It was predicted that the subjects who actually possessed the money at the start of the experiment would play more cautiously and attain higher payoffs.

METHOD

The Game

An alternate method of playing the game was developed which eliminated the need for expensive electronic equipment and at the same time provided information about the ways in which the conflict developed and was resolved. A logical analysis of the structure of the game indicated that the players in the no-threat condition are actually faced with only three basic decisions. At any given time the player must decide either to: go down or stay on the short, one-lane route; wait at the start or back up to the start on the one-lane path so that the other player's truck can go first; or, take the alternate path to the goal. In the bilateral-threat situation the player is faced with the same three decisions plus the independent decision of whether or not to use the barrier. If this analysis is correct, the game can be represented by a 3×3 game matrix. Actual play would involve allowing the players to make discrete, simultaneous choices of strategy.

The game matrix and road map, with appropriate Southern California labels, are shown in Figures 1 and 2. Every attempt was made to keep the behavioral alternatives identical to those available in the original game. If the players' choices resulted in blockage on the one-lane path, they were allowed to choose a second time and the payoffs were reduced. In all, the players were allowed to choose six times per trial. If they had not reached their destinations at the end of six choices, the trial was terminated and the players took a considerable loss.

San Fernando Valley Trucking Co.

		Freeway	Wait	Canyon
Los Angeles Trucking Co.	Freeway	Trucks blocking one another Choose again	Both reached destination	Both reached destination
	Wait	Both reached destination	Trucks both waited, then moved out at same time. Are blocking one another. Choose again	Both reached destination
	Canyon	Both reached destination	Both reached destination	Both reached destination

Fig. 1. The game matrix.

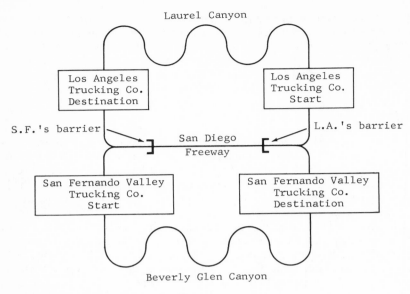

Fig. 2. The road map used in the game.

The fact that two games are logically equivalent does not insure that they will be actually equivalent in terms of motives and behaviors produced. Game-playing behavior can be influenced by such nonlogical factors as mode of presentation, timing, ability to evaluate partial responses, etc. Therefore, a pilot study was undertaken to determine whether this procedure would replicate the results obtained by Deutsch and Krauss. Twenty female undergraduates served as subjects for the pilot study. Two subjects at a time were brought into the experimental room and seated at a table in front of a large blackboard. The blackboard had a picture of the game matrix and the road map drawn on it. Each subject was assigned a trucking company, and the general nature of the situation was explained to her. When the subjects understood the nature of the game, specific instructions were given to them. Subjects indicated their choice of strategy by checking the appropriate strategy on a small, hand-held blackboard. The choices were made simultaneously, without knowledge of the other player's choice. In the bilateral-threat condition, barrier use or nonuse was also indicated by checking the appropriate space on the blackboard. When a barrier was in place, it effectively prevented the other person's truck from leaving the one-lane path and continuing to the destination. The player whose truck was blocked by the barrier had to either wait until it was removed, or take the alternate path.

Payoffs were determined by a careful inspection of the payoffs used in the original studies. For example, if on the first choice one player took the main route while the other waited, the first player made $.26 profit, the second made $.10. If either player took the alternate route on the first choice, that player lost $.16. If the players blocked one another on the first choice but reached their destination on the second choice, the payoffs for the main route and wait strategies were reduced by $.05. The payoff for the alternate route was reduced by $.22. The larger reduction for the alternate route took into account the fact that the subject, in the original game, would have had to back up the one-lane path and then go all the way around the alternate route. Each succeeding blockage reduced the payoffs by $.10. If the players were still blocked at the end of six choices, the payoff to each was $.10 less than the alternate route would have paid on the sixth choice.

In keeping with the original studies, the players in the bilateral-threat condition were not allowed to use their barriers until they were on the main route. In the context of the present game, this meant that they must first have blocked one another. As in the original experiment, they were allowed to remove their barriers at any time. Before play began, the subjects were given several practice trials, and the outcomes and payoffs associated with various strategy choices were explained to them.

The results of the pilot study indicated that the five no-threat dyads attained a mean joint payoff of $1.88. This compares favorably with the $2.03 obtained by Deutsch and Krauss. The five bilateral-threat dyads lost an average of $9.60 as compared to a loss of $8.75 in the original experiment. The median joint payoffs per trial indicated a pattern of play that was again in close correspondence to that obtained by Deutsch and Krauss. It was decided that the revised game was a suitable vehicle to use in the test of the hypotheses.

Procedure

The methodology employed in the main experiment was virtually identical to that used in the pilot study. The payoffs were multiplied by a factor of 4.5. This procedure raised the maximum payoff per trial to $1.15 and the total payoff for perfect alternation over the 20 trials of the experiment to $16 per subject.

The instructions were modified somewhat to make them appropriate to the various levels of the independent variables. The real-money subjects were told that money would actually be given to them if they made a profit. They were shown a letter from the vice-chairman of the department in which he made himself personally responsible for the truth of what the experimenter told them. In the imaginary-money condition the subjects understood that no money would change hands. However, the instructions stressed the necessity of playing exactly as though the money were real.

The subjects in the absolute-value condition were told that they were taking part in a decision-making experiment. They were instructed to make as much money for themselves as possible and not to concern themselves about the profits or losses of the other player. The subjects in the relative-value condition were told that they were taking a test of "social intelligence." It was mentioned that the more "socially intelligent" an individual is, the more likely it would be that he would win more money than his opponent.

Half of the subjects were given the barriers at the start of the experiment. They were told that the decision to use or not use them was strictly up to them. They were told under what conditions they could use them, and the results of their use, in terms of the effect upon the other person's truck, were explained to them. The other half of the subjects played 10 trials without the barriers. At that time the game was stopped, the barriers introduced, and the instructions as to their use given.

The players in the potential winnings condition were given the payoffs that have previously been mentioned. The players in the possession of winnings condition were given $16 in real or imaginary money at the start of the experiment. The payoffs per trial were changed such that perfect alternation would enable the subjects to keep the entire sum that they had been given. Lack of coordination would cause the subjects to lose some of their holdings. The payoffs in both conditions were figured such that similar play would result in identical payoffs by the end of the 20 trials.

Subjects

The subjects were 64 undergraduate females at UCLA who were fulfilling a psychology lab experimental requirement. The number and sex of the subjects were chosen to correspond to the original Deutsch and Krauss experiment. Each main effect was represented by 16 dyads at each level. The girls in the imaginary-money condition were run during the first 2 weeks of April. The real-money condition was run during the last 2 weeks. Subjects were sworn to secrecy at the end of the experiment, and those subjects who won money signed a receipt which obligated them to forfeit their winnings if they talked about the experiment. Interviews with the subjects at the end of the experimental session indicated that no subjects had any prior knowledge of the experimental situation.

RESULTS

The total joint payoffs per dyad were analyzed in a mixed design analysis of variance. The 20 trials were broken into two blocks of 10 trials each, thus providing the within-subjects variable. The mean joint payoffs for each of the main effects, summed over the other three, are presented in Table 1.

Table 1 MEAN TOTAL JOINT PAYOFF FOR EACH MAIN EFFECT, SUMMED OVER
THE OTHER THREE, BY FIRST AND SECOND HALVES

CONDITION	FIRST HALF	SECOND HALF	OVERALL
Imaginary money	−15.17	−23.63	−38.80
Real money	+ 4.30	+ 5.62	+ 9.92
Barriers, last 10 trials	+ 3.64	− 6.40	− 2.77
Barriers, all 20 trials	−14.51	−11.60	−26.11
Relative-value instructions	− 6.50	−15.56	−22.06
Absolute-value instructions	− 4.37	− 2.44	− 6.81
Possession of winnings	− 3.52	− 6.75	−10.27
Potential winnings	− 7.36	−11.25	−18.61

The presence or absence of real money had a highly significant effect upon the payoffs obtained by the subjects ($F = 19.74$, $df = 1/17$, $p < .005$). In addition to the effect upon the size of the payoffs, it was found that 12 of the 16 dyads who played for real money showed a profit at the end of the experiment, whereas only 2 of the imaginary-money dyads ended up winning money. A chi-square test performed on this distribution indicates that the relationship is significant beyond the .01 level. Thus the use of real money to motivate the players had an effect not only on the amount of money won, but also on the number of dyads who managed to win money.

The data also indicate a significant difference in payoffs between the dyads who had the barriers for the entire experiment and those who had them only for the last 10 trials ($F = 4.53$, $df = 1/17$, $p < .05$). This finding, however, must be interpreted in light of the fact that the interaction of barriers with trial blocks is also significant ($F = 4.61$, $df = 1/21$, $p < .05$). Inspection of this interaction indicates that most of the difference between these groups can be attributed to the outcomes in the first 10 trials, as shown in Table 1. Overall, the subjects who received the barriers at the end of the tenth trial received poorer payoffs in the second half of the experiment. The subjects who received the barriers at the start of the experiment tended to do somewhat better in the second half.

Neither the method of administering the payoffs nor the type of instructions given had a significant effect upon the payoffs. However, the instructions variable did enter into two interactions that attained borderline significance ($.10 > p > .05$). Because of the small sample used ($N = 32$), it is possible that these interactions would have reached significance with a larger N. These interactions seem to suggest that the two types of instructions had little effect upon outcomes in the first 10 trials. However, the players who had been given the relative-value instructions received considerably poorer payoffs in the second half of the experiment, whereas players given the absolute-value instructions improved slightly. Moreover, this effect seemed to be almost entirely confined to the subjects in the imaginary-money condition.

Data were also gathered concerning the style of play evidenced by subjects in the real-money and imaginary-money conditions. These data are summarized in Table 2. It can be seen that the real-money dyads used their barriers significantly less frequently than the imaginary-money dyads. The real-money dyads were also more likely to lower their barriers and let their opponent through on the main route, while the imaginary-money dyads more often forced their opponent to back up and take the costly alternate route. In keeping with these results, it was found that the real-money dyads engaged in five times as much cooperative alternation behavior as did the imaginary-money dyads.

DISCUSSION

In order to compare the results of the present experiment with the results obtained by Deutsch and Krauss, it is necessary to divide the payoffs by 4.5, the factor by which they were originally multiplied. Performing this operation results in a mean joint payoff for the imaginary-money dyads of −$8.62 and a

Table 2 FREQUENCY OF BARRIER USE, BARRIER LOWERING, AND COOPERATIVE ALTERNATION

BEHAVIOR	REAL-MONEY GROUPS		IMAGINARY-MONEY GROUPS		p VALUES[a] REAL-MONEY GROUPS VERSUS IMAGINARY-MONEY GROUPS
	BARRIERS LAST 10 TRIALS	BARRIERS ALL 20 TRIALS	BARRIERS LAST 10 TRIALS	BARRIERS ALL 20 TRIALS	
Mean number of trials on which one or both members of dyad used barriers	3.25	4.00	4.75	11.88	
Barrier use, expressed as percentage of trials on which use was possible	32.5	20.0	47.5	49.4	>.01
Mean number of trials on which one or both members of dyad lowered barriers, after having first raised them	2.88	2.62	2.00	2.25	
Barrier lowering, expressed as percentage of trials on which they were raised	88.6	65.5	42.1	18.9	<.025
Mean number of trials on which first choice was part of alternation sequence of two or more	10.25	10.38	2.00	2.13	
Percentage of trials on which first choice was part of alternation sequence of two or more	51.3	52.9	10.0	10.7	<.01

[a]The p values were obtained by applying one-way analysis of variance to the percentage scores.

mean joint payoff for the real-money dyads of +$2.20. It will be recalled that Deutsch and Krauss' bilateral-threat dyads averaged −$8.75 and their no-threat dyads averaged +$2.03. It would appear that our imaginary-money bilateral-threat dyads were as competitive as theirs were, whereas our real-money bilateral-threat dyads were as cooperative as their imaginary-money no-threat dyads.

It is clear that the presence of large monetary incentives had a dramatic effect upon the payoffs achieved by the subjects. There are a number of possible explanations for this effect. One of the more reasonable would seem to be that the large incentives produced a number of cooperative gestures on the part of subjects and that these gestures were then reciprocated. Support for this position can be adduced from the data gathered on style of play.

Subjects in the imaginary-money condition tended to demonstrate a pattern of play that was also evidenced in the earlier Deutsch and Krauss studies. After an initial period of fumbling and incoordination, the subjects fell into a pattern whereby each put up her barrier and then took the longer, alternate route. This style of play can be considered a withdrawal from interaction. The real-money dyads, for the most part, remained in interaction and persisted in cooperative gestures. Incoordination or barrier use was generally followed not by reciprocal barrier use but by a unilateral attempt on the part of one or both subjects to reestablish alternation by selecting the "wait" response. Trend analysis applied to the frequency of barrier use indicated that the real-money dyads who had the barriers for all 20 trials used them significantly less frequently as the game progressed. Barrier use remained at a fairly high, constant level for the imaginary-money dyads who had the barriers for the entire experiment. No trend was evidenced for the dyads who had the barriers for only the last 10 trials.

The foregoing interpretation must be tempered by the fact that there would seem to be considerable individual differences in the extent to which subjects actually understood the game and the implications of their behaviors. Four of the dyads in the real-money condition and one dyad in the imaginary-money condition played the entire game without ever using their barriers. It could be argued that these subjects realized the solution to the game before play ever began, and for them it was just a matter of achieving the proper coordination. The remaining 12 dyads in the real-money condition and the remaining 15 dyads in the imaginary-money condition used the barriers to some extent. However, 8 of these 12 real-money dyads who used the barriers won money.

It is possible that the presence of real money enabled some subjects, who perceived the solution before play began, to implement that solution. For other subjects it may have provided the incentive to produce cooperative gestures and remain in interaction until the solution could be discovered and worked out. And for still others, those who did not understand the implications of their strategy choices, it may have had no effect whatsoever.

Another alternative explanation that cannot be disregarded is that the meaning of the situation is changed for the subjects when real money is at stake. The subjects may perceive that the object of the game is to beat the situation rather than each other. They may form a tacit coalition against the experimenter to try and extract as much money from the situation as possible. They may perceive that their opponent is more interested in making money than in "beating" them, hence may be less likely to attribute exploitative intentions to their opponent. In addition, the meaning of various behaviors may be altered when real money is at stake. When a subject uses a barrier in a punitive way and causes her opponent to lose $4 in imaginary money, she can easily justify her behavior on the grounds that it is just a game. The same behavior performed when real money is involved has more serious consequences. The subject then faces the very real disapproval of her opponent and the presumed disapproval of the experimenter, who is observing the behavior. Thus, there may be social constraints operating against competition in this situation when the rewards are real.

The data do not provide an adequate basis for determining the relative importance of these factors. It would appear that the dynamics underlying the various behaviors that were observed are extremely complex. Further research is needed to determine the exact manner by which large incentives increase the prospects of cooperation and also to identify those situations within which large incentives will have that effect. Attention must be paid to the motives that are being expressed by the players and attributed to their opponents before, during, and after the game. In addition, research is needed to determine the importance of social constraints and the effect of the symmetrical power relationships that are present in the trucking game. The results of the present study would imply that caution should be applied in generalizing the results that have been obtained in experimental studies of conflict that have utilized small or imaginary rewards. On the other hand, caution must also be applied in generalizing the results of the present study to other conflict situations that may differ in important ways from the trucking game.

REFERENCES

Borah, L. A., Jr. The effects of threat in bargaining: Critical and experimental analysis. *Journal of Abnormal and Social Psychology,* 1963, *66,* 37–44.

Deutsch, M., & Krauss, R. M. The effect of threat upon interpersonal bargaining. *Journal of Abnormal and Social Psychology,* 1960, *61,* 181–89.

Deutsch, M., & Krauss, R. M. Studies of interpersonal bargaining. *Journal of Conflict Resolution,* 1962, *6,* 52–76.

The Effect of Group Participation on Brainstorming Effectiveness for Two Industrial Samples

MARVIN D. DUNNETTE, JOHN CAMPBELL, AND KAY JAASTAD

Proponents of brainstorming, as an idea eliciting or problem solving technique, emphasize the value of group participation as a facilitating factor in producing ideas. For example, Osborn (1957) concludes on the basis of experiments conducted at the University of Buffalo, that "the average person can think up twice as many ideas when working with a group that when working alone" (pp. 228–229). He adds that a combination of group and individual effort is probably best, but he fails to specify the exact nature of the optimal combination. A widely cited study by Taylor, Berry, and Block (1957) suggested that group participation actually inhibits the potential ideational output of individuals. Taylor et al. presented three different problems to 96 Yale juniors and seniors who had previously worked together in small group discussion sections. Forty-eight of the subjects were divided into 12 real groups of 4 men each; the other 48 brainstormed the problems alone. The number of different ideas produced by the real groups was compared with the number produced by so-called "nominal" groups formed after the experiment by randomly dividing the 48 individual subjects into 12 groups of 4 each. Scores of nominal groups represented, therefore, the expected level of achievement if actual group participation neither inhibits nor facilitates creativeness during brainstorming. For each of the three problems presented, the nominal groups produced an average of nearly twice as many different ideas as the real group. Taylor et al. concluded, therefore, that group participation actually has an inhibiting influence on creative thinking during brainstorming—a conclusion radically different from the one by Osborn cited earlier.

Our purpose has been to repeat the Taylor et al. study among two different occupational groups: research scientists and advertising men. Further, we have modified the design of the Taylor study in order to allow subjects to participate in *both* individual and group brainstroming sessions. We believe our results lend support to the conclusions reached by Taylor and his associates and that they also help to define the conditions for the optimal combination of group and individual effort mentioned by Osborn.

METHOD

The subjects of the experiment were 48 research personnel from one of the larger laboratories of Minnesota Mining and Manufacturing Co. (3M) and 48

Reprinted from Journal of Applied Psychology, 47, *1963, 30–37. Copyright 1963 by the American Psychological Association and reproduced by permission.*

persons employed with 3M's central staff Advertising Department. Our choice of research and advertising personnel was based on our hypothesis that advertising personnel would more likely profit from any facilitating influence of group interaction and that research persons would more likely be inhibited by group participation; thus, we hypothesized opposite effects of group interaction in the two groups. Each of the two sets of subjects was divided into 12 groups of 4 men each. The assignment was not random. Instead, persons were placed together who had worked together and who were well acquainted with one another. In no case, however, were persons of differing job levels placed in the same group; among the researchers no one with supervisory responsibilities participated in the study. Among the advertisers, different supervisory levels were represented but never in the same group, thereby reducing any possible inhibiting effects due to differing status levels within a group. In addition, no persons with advanced degrees participated in the study; the researchers included only persons with BA or equivalent degrees. The range of education represented in the advertising group was from high school through college.

Each subject in Taylor's study participated in only one of the two experimental conditions. Such an experimental design does not allow a test of possible effects of prior group experience on individual brainstorming behavior or vice versa, and it also, of course, depends on randomization to effect an equating of any individual differences in brainstorming ability between subjects in the two experimental conditions. Because of these factors, our experiment allowed each subject to take part in *both* group and individual brainstorming sessions. The experimental design shown in Table 1 was used separately for the researchers and the advertisers. It will be noted that individual and group performance, the two problem sets, and order of participation are counterbalanced.

Table 1 DESIGN OF THE EXPERIMENT

		ORDER	
GROUP	INDIVIDUALS	FIRST	SECOND
A	1, 2, 3, 4		
B	5, 6, 7, 8	I, 2	G, 2
C	9, 10, 11, 12		
D	13, 14, 15, 16		
E	17, 18, 19, 20	G, 1	I, 2
F	21, 22, 23, 24		
G	25, 26, 27, 28		
H	29, 30, 31, 32	I, 2	G, 1
I	33, 34, 35, 36		
J	37, 38, 39, 40		
K	41, 42, 43, 44	G, 2	I, 1
L	45, 46, 47, 48		

Note. − 1 = Problem Set 1, Thumbs and Education;
2 = Problem Set 2, People and Tourists;
G = Group; I = Individual.

The problems used in our study were the same as those used by Taylor et al. with the addition of a fourth, the People problem. The four problems are stated below:

Thumbs problem. We do not think this is likely to happen, but imagine for a moment what would happen if everyone after 1960 had an extra thumb on each hand. This extra thumb will be built just as the present one is, but located on the other side of the hand. It faces inward, so that it can press against the fingers, just as the regular thumb does now. Here is the question: What practical benefits or difficulties will arise when people start having this extra thumb?

Education problem. Because of the rapidly increasing birthrate beginning in the 1940s, it is now clear that by 1970 public school enrollment will be very much greater than it is today. In fact, it has been estimated that if the student-teacher ratio were to be maintained at what it is today, 50% of all individuals graduating from college would have to be induced to enter teaching. What different steps might be taken to insure that schools will continue to provide instruction at least equal in effectiveness to that now provided?

People problem. Suppose that discoveries in physiology and nutrition have so affected the diet of American children over a period of 20 years that the average height of Americans at age 20 has increased to 80 inches and the average weight has about doubled. Comparative studies of the growth of children during the last 5 years indicate that the phenomenal change in stature is stabilized so that further increase is not expected. What would be the consequences? What adjustments would this situation require?

Tourists problem. Each year a great many American tourists go to visit Europe. But now suppose that our country wished to get many more European tourists to come to visit America during their vacations. What steps can you suggest that would get more European tourists to come to this country?

The problems were pretested along with several others among University of Minnesota engineering and business administration students in order to select those problems which elicited a large volume and diversity of responses and to equate approximately the idea eliciting qualities of the two problem sets. The pretest problems were presented in counterbalanced order to each subject, and he was allowed 10 minutes for each problem to write his responses. The mean number of responses given by the pretest subjects was not significantly different for Thumbs and People (10.70 and 10.08) or for Education and Tourists (9.62 and 9.80); Thumbs and Education were, therefore, used for Problem Set 1 and People and Tourists for Problem Set 2.

About a week prior to the experiment, the senior author met with the subjects "over coffee" and discussed creative thinking with particular emphasis on brainstorming. The nature and purpose of the forthcoming experiment were explained and questions concerning scheduling and procedural details were answered. The importance of applying the "principles"[1] of brainstorming was heavily emphasized, and participants were urged to refrain from discussing their experimental sessions (particularly the problems used) with any of their coworkers who may not yet have participated in the experiment.

The same graduate student (Kay Jaastad) served as experimenter for *all* subjects. She began each experimental session by reading aloud the instructions which emphasized the importance of research study and which restated the techniques and principles of brainstorming. She then presented each problem by first reading it aloud and then distributing dittoed copies to each of the subjects. She allowed time for questions, if any, and then instructed the subjects to "begin brainstorming." Responses were recorded on a DeJur-Grundig *Stenorette* with conference microphone. Subjects were allowed to spend 15 minutes on each of the problems; in every session, nearly all ideas and solutions had been expressed at the end of 10–12 minutes. The time limit did not in any instance result in cutting off a flow of ideas. On the other hand, it did serve as a stimulus to the rapid and free wheeling expression of ideas and solutions. Each subject participated in both experimental conditions on the same afternoon.[2] The individual brainstorming condition was carried out by placing subjects in four widely separated offices where each would be free to brainstorm without interruption.[3]

RESULTS

After completing the experimental sessions, the responses of the 96 subjects in both individual and group situations were transcribed. Each idea or solution was placed on one side of a 3 X 5 card, and appropriate identifying information (e.g., problem set, condition, order) was entered on the opposite side. Using the cards, it was an easy (albeit voluminous and time consuming) task to sort responses, delete duplications, rate the quality of ideas, etc. The first step in the analysis of results was simply to compare the number of different ideas or solutions produced by group participation with the number of different ideas or solutions produced by the same group members during the individual brainstorming condition. It should be emphasized that the "score" (number of ideas) under the individual condition includes only *different* ideas. Thus, if two or more members of a group, during their individual sessions, suggested the same idea or solution to a problem, it was counted as only a single contribution to the total score of the nominal group. Comparisons were

[1] The following principles have been suggested by Osborn and were emphasized by Taylor in his study: the more ideas the better, the wilder the ideas the better, improve or combine ideas already suggested, and do not be critical.

[2] For example, members of Groups A, B, and C participated first as individuals using Problem Set 1 followed immediately by group brainstorming using Problem Set 2. Those in Groups D, E, and F participated first in the group situation using Problem Set 1 followed immediately by individual brainstorming using Problem Set 2—and so on.

[3] Unfortunately the individual sessions were not *entirely* free from interruption. In at least one instance, a man answered a phone in the middle of his session. At other times, men were interrupted briefly by passers-by who looked in to ask, "What the heck are you doing?" or to make similar comments. Of course, all such slip-ups worked to the disadvantage of individuals' achievements in comparison with groups.

made between individual and group brainstorming for the total of both problems in each set, for the Thumbs-People problems of each set, and for the Education-Tourists problems of each set. Results are shown in Tables 2, 3, and 4. For all comparisons, the condition effect is highly significant, the individual condition yielding a markedly greater number of ideas than group participation. Of the 24 groups, only one failed to produce more ideas under the individual condition than under the group condition, and the difference in this one instance was only 163–162 in favor of group participation. Only 5 of the 48 research subjects failed to produce more ideas when working individually than when participating in a group. Clearly, individual brainstorming achieves more ideas than group brainstorming. Our hypothesis that group interaction would facilitate the output of advertising personnel and inhibit the output of research personnel failed to be sustained. Apparently, the inhibiting influence of group participation cuts across the kinds of personal and occupational differences investigated in this study.

Table 2 MEAN TOTAL NUMBER OF DIFFERENT IDEAS AND/OR SOLUTIONS TO PROBLEMS BY SUBJECTS UNDER CONDITIONS OF INDIVIDUAL AND GROUP BRAINSTORMING

	RESEARCH PERSONNEL		ADVERTISING PERSONNEL	
PROBLEM	INDIVIDUAL	GROUP	INDIVIDUAL	GROUP
Thumbs and People	78.3	60.9	82.9	59.8
Education and Tourists	62.2	49.3	58.5	37.3
Total	140.5	110.2	141.4	97.1

It will be noted from Tables 3 and 4 that certain other effects also showed significance. The significant Order effect shown by researchers was most pronounced on the Thumbs and People problems. A larger number of ideas or solutions was produced when subjects experienced the individual brainstorming *after* having experienced the group session than when they "went in cold" to the individual session. Although the Order effect was not significant for the advertisers, the Order X Condition interaction was. A plot of Individual versus Group scores for each of the two orders shows that the relative superiority of individual brainstorming was greatest when it was preceded by the group session. For example, the mean number of ideas for Individual and Group sessions was 143 and 109, respectively, under Order A (Individual session followed by Group session); the corresponding means under Order B (Individual session preceded by Group session) were 140 and 95. These results help to specify the conditions for combining group and individual effort. Apparently, a brainstorming session (either group or individual) can serve the important function of a "warm up" for subsequent brainstorming. In this study, the net superiority of individual brainstorming over group brainstorming seems to have been enhanced by such a warm-up session.

Two other statistically significant effects are shown in Tables 3 and 4. The Set effect is significant for the advertising group. Problem Set 1 (Thumbs and Education) gave a higher yield than Problem Set 2 (People and Tourists). The

Table 3 ANALYSIS OF VARIANCE: TOTAL NUMBER OF DIFFERENT IDEAS AND/OR SOLUTIONS TO PROBLEMS BY RESEARCH PERSONNEL UNDER CONDITIONS OF INDIVIDUAL AND GROUP BRAINSTORMING

SOURCE	df	TOTAL (BOTH PROBLEMS OF EACH SET)		THUMBS AND PEOPLE PROBLEMS		EDUCATION AND TOURISTS PROBLEMS	
		MS	F	MS	F	MS	F
Between individuals							
Order	1	1001	6.37*	585	9.39*	56	1.57
S × C	1	1291	8.21*	277	4.44	372	10.54*
S × O × C	1	30	0.19	3	0.05	14	0.40
Error (b)	8	157.1		62.3		35.3	
Within individuals							
Conditions	1	1380	23.71**	455	15.12**	250	31.64**
C × O	1	40	0.69	10	0.33	10	1.26
Set	1	96	1.65	32	1.05	19	2.40
S × O	1	135	2.33	53	1.74	19	2.40
Error (w)	8	58.3		30.1		7.9	

Note. — S = Set, C = Condition, O = Order, (b) = between, (w) = within.
* p < .05.
** p < .01.

Table 4 ANALYSIS OF VARIANCE: TOTAL NUMBER OF DIFFERENT IDEAS AND/OR SOLUTIONS TO PROBLEMS BY ADVERTISING PERSONNEL UNDER CONDITIONS OF INDIVIDUAL AND GROUP BRAINSTORMING

SOURCE	df	TOTAL (BOTH PROBLEMS OF EACH SET) MS	F	THUMBS AND PEOPLE PROBLEMS MS	F	EDUCATION AND TOURISTS PROBLEMS MS	F
Between individuals							
Order	1	274	0.96	153	1.63	18	0.31
S × C	1	293	1.03	78	0.83	69	1.17
S × O × C	1	73	0.29	2	0.02	82	1.39
Error (b)	8	285.1		93.6		58.8	
Within individuals							
Condition	1	2949	93.61**	800	27.78**	677	34.02**
C × O	1	170	5.40*	101	3.51	9	0.45
Set	1	316	10.03*	196	6.81*	14	0.70
S × O	1	125	3.97	24	0.83	39	1.96
Error (w)	8	31.5		28.8		19.9	

Note. — See note in Table 3.
* $p < .05$.
** $p < .01$.

285

major source of the difference was between the Thumbs and People problems, probably reflecting the fact that they were somewhat less perfectly matched on the basis of the pretests than were the Education and Tourists problems. For the researchers, the interaction effect Set × Condition is significant. A plot of Individual versus Group scores for each of the two problem sets shows that the superiority of individual brainstorming was greatest (151–91) for Problem Set 1 and that it actually was negligible for Problem Set 2 (130–129). We are at a loss to explain this outcome, particularly in view of the consistent results obtained for *both* problem sets in the advertising group.

Although the total number of ideas and solutions was greater for individual than for group participation, it could be argued that this may have been accompanied by a corresponding decrease in the quality of ideas produced. Two of the scales used by Taylor et al. for rating the quality of ideas were employed in this study. The first two authors used Taylor's Effectiveness scale[4] to rate solutions to the Education and Tourists problems and his Probability scale[5] to rate responses to the Thumbs and People problems. Although not *all* responses were rated by both investigators, the interrater reliabilities were estimated on the basis of sampling randomly the ideas from each group of subjects for each of the four problems. The resulting coefficients ranged between .54 and .77 with a median value of .66. These reliabilities are *not* impressively high; even so, the ratings of the second author (which were done for *all* problems in *all* groups) were used to provide a rough index of the quality of each solution proposed. The ratings were summed for all the different ideas produced under each of the conditions. Comparisons of means and statistical tests of significance are shown in Tables 5, 6, and 7. It is apparent that quality was *not* sacrificed for quantity under the condition of individual brainstorming. It is noteworthy that the Set and Condition × Order effects are not significant among the advertisers for the quality score comparisons. For the advertisers, the Thumbs problem elicited a significantly larger number of responses than the People problem, but the total quality of output did not differ for the two problems.

Table 5 MEAN TOTAL QUALITY SCORES OBTAINED BY SUBJECTS UNDER CONDITIONS OF INDIVIDUAL AND GROUP BRAINSTORMING

	RESEARCH PERSONNEL		ADVERTISING PERSONNEL	
PROBLEM	INDIVIDUAL	GROUP	INDIVIDUAL	GROUP
Thumbs and People	171	131	192	131
Education and Tourists	128	94	116	65
Total	299	225	308	196

[4] Effectiveness scale: 0 = no conceivable contribution to solution of problem. Suggestion impossible of attainment; 1 = very little, if any, contribution to solution of problem; 2 = probably some contribution to solution of problem; 3 = definite minor contribution to solution of problem; and 4 = clearly a major contribution to solution of problem.

[5] Probability scale: 0 = very highly improbable or clearly impossible; 1 = conceivable, but improbable; 2 = possible; 3 = probable; and 4 = highly probable.

Table 6 ANALYSIS OF VARIANCE: TOTAL QUALITY SCORES FOR IDEAS AND/OR SOLUTIONS TO PROBLEMS BY RESEARCH PERSONNEL UNDER CONDITIONS OF INDIVIDUAL AND GROUP BRAINSTORMING

SOURCE	df	TOTAL (BOTH PROBLEMS OF EACH SET)		THUMBS AND PEOPLE PROBLEMS		EDUCATION AND TOURISTS PROBLEMS	
		MS	F	MS	F	MS	F
Between individuals							
Order	1	6225	8.18*	3385	9.45*	429	3.92
S × C	1	4916	6.46*	1734	4.84	811	7.41*
S × O × C	1	45	.06	0	.00	50	.46
Error (b)	8	761		358		109.5	
Within individuals							
Condition	1	8049	20.17**	2361	11.86**	1691	20.37**
C × O	1	340	.85	103	.52	69	.83
Set	1	995	2.49	425	2.14	119	1.43
S × O	1	172	.43	12	.06	94	1.13
Error (w)	8	399		199		83	

Note. – See note in Table 3.
* $p < .05$.
** $p < .01$.

Table 7 ANALYSIS OF VARIANCE: TOTAL QUALITY SCORES FOR IDEAS AND/OR SOLUTIONS TO PROBLEMS BY ADVERTISING PERSONNEL UNDER CONDITIONS OF INDIVIDUAL AND GROUP BRAINSTORMING

SOURCE	df	TOTAL (BOTH PROBLEMS OF EACH SET)		THUMBS AND PEOPLE PROBLEMS		EDUCATION AND TOURISTS PROBLEMS	
		MS	F	MS	F	MS	F
Between individuals							
Order	1	2063	1.67	1162	2.56	133	.63
S × C	1	2959	2.40	1162	2.56	404	1.92
S × O × C	1	1528	1.24	92	.20	883	4.20
Error (b)	8	1235		453		210	
Within individuals							
Condition	1	18676	54.44*	5460	16.25**	3966	60.00**
C × O	1	595	1.73	504	1.50	4	.06
Set	1	115	.34	140	.42	1	.02
S × O	1	10	.03	8	.02	0	.00
Error (w)	8	343		336		66	

Note. – *See note in Table 3.*
* $p < .05$.
** $p < .01$.

Table 8 MEAN QUALITY RATINGS FOR IDEAS AND/OR SOLUTIONS PRODUCED BY SUBJECTS UNDER CONDITIONS OF INDIVIDUAL AND GROUP BRAINSTORMING

PROBLEM	RESEARCH PERSONNEL			ADVERTISING PERSONNEL		
	INDIVIDUAL	GROUP	SIGNIFICANCE LEVEL [a]	INDIVIDUAL	GROUP	SIGNIFICANCE LEVEL [a]
Total (both problems of each set)	2.12	2.04	ns	2.18	2.02	$p < .05$
Thumbs and People	2.18	2.15	ns	2.32	2.19	ns
Education and Tourists	2.06	1.91	ns	1.96	1.74	$p < .01$

[a] The significance tests were made using the same analysis of variance design shown in Tables 3, 4, 6, and 7. Copies of additional analysis of variance tables may be obtained upon request from the senior author.

A remaining question has to do with the mean quality of ideas and solutions produced under the two experimental conditions. Table 8 summarizes the mean quality ratings and the significance levels of the mean differences between individual and group conditions. The values in Table 8 were obtained by dividing the mean total quality score (Table 5) by the mean total number of different ideas (Table 2). It is evident that individuals produce responses of quality equal to or greater than that of the ideas produced in groups. The evidence is clear-cut: brainstorming is most effective when undertaken by individuals working *alone* in an atmosphere free from the apparently inhibiting influences of group interaction.

DISCUSSION

Our results confirm those of Taylor et al. and tend to refute Osborn's argument that individuals are stimulated by group brainstorming to produce more ideas than when brainstorming alone. Of special interest is our finding that group interaction has an inhibiting influence for advertising people (that area in which brainstorming was developed and where it first came into widespread use) as well as for technical research personnel and for college students at Yale University (Taylor's study). Individuals not only produce *more* ideas when working alone, but they do this without sacrificing quality; indeed our results show that advertising personnel, working as individuals, produced ideas on the Tourists and Education problems of significantly higher mean quality than when they worked in groups. The net superiority of individual performance over group participation for these two sets of industrially employed subjects is highlighted by the fact that 23 of the 24 groups produced a larger number of different ideas under the individual condition. To the extent that we may generalize these findings to future situations, we can state that four persons, attacking a problem individually, and then pooling their efforts will, on the average, produce about 30% more ideas than if they attempted to solve the problem in a group session or meeting.

Our findings also suggest that group participation may be useful in "warming up" for individual brainstorming sessions. Research personnel produced more ideas when individual brainstorming followed group participation than when it preceded it. Advertising men also exhibited relatively greater superiority in the individual sessions when they had been preceded by a group session.

Neither the Taylor study nor our study has identified the exact nature of the inhibiting influence which apparently acts to reduce the productivity of group brainstorming. Taylor et al. suggested, and we concur, on the basis of our observations during these experiments, that a group tends to "fall in a rut" and to pursue the same train of thought. The effect of this is to limit the diversity of approaches to a problem, thereby leading to the production of fewer different ideas. It was also apparent that the output of many individuals who were highly productive when working alone was considerably less in the group situation. In spite of the stimulus of group brainstorming and our specific directive to avoid all criticism, it was apparent that these persons were inhibited simply by the presence of other group members. The central idea underlying brainstorming of placing a moratorium on all criticism is a good one. It appears, however, that group participation still contains certain inhibitory influences which are not easily dissipated. The "best bet" for creative thinking in attacking problems seems, therefore, to be the pooled individual efforts of many people with perhaps an initial group session to serve simply as a warm up to their efforts.

REFERENCES

Osborn, A. F. *Applied imagination.* (Rev. ed.) New York: Scribner, 1957.

Taylor, D. W., Berry, P. C., & Block, C. H. Does group participation when using brainstorming facilitate or inhibit creative thinking? Technical Report No. 1, 1957, Yale University, Department of Psychology, Office of Naval Research.

Group Decision Making Under Risk of Aversive Consequences

DARYL J. BEM, MICHAEL A. WALLACH, AND NATHAN KOGAN

In two previous studies of individual and group decision making, Wallach, Kogan, and Bem (1962, 1964) found that group decisions reached through discussion and consensus tended to be more risky than decisions made by the group members as individuals. In our first investigation, the decisions involved a number of hypothetical life situations in which a protagonist was faced with the choice between a more risky and a less risky course of action. The second experiment inquired whether these risk-taking tendencies in groups would be found in a decision situation in which the group members were actually exposed to the consequences of their decisions. Using risks and payoffs based on monetary gain and loss for problem-solving performance, we observed that groups were considerably more likely than individuals to select the more difficult, higher payoff (for correct solution) problems, even though problem solving itself was carried out by a single group member. In both of the above experiments, the "risky shift" phenomenon was interpreted as the outcome of a process of responsibility diffusion.

The present experiment seeks to extend the generality of our previous findings to a type of group decision making in which negative consequences are emphasized. In order to accomplish this end, we selected physical pain and

Reprinted from Journal of Personality and Social Psychology, 1, *1965. Copyright 1965 by the American Psychological Association and reproduced by permission.*

discomfort, coupled with monetary loss, as the potential negative outcomes of risk taking. A second purpose of the present investigation was to examine in more detail whether processes other than a diffusion of responsibility might account for, or contribute to, a risk-taking shift in group decision making. We consider two possible alternative processes in turn below.

First, there is the possibility that risk taking, by connoting boldness, may be more socially desirable than conservatism. Such an association might be quite strong in the present experiment where physical pain and discomfort are being risked, since conservatism under such circumstances could imply cowardice. Further, the association may be especially likely to appear in a group setting where one's "image" is on public display. Accordingly, an experimental condition involving anticipated disclosure of one's decisions to others has been incorporated in the study design.

Second, an expectation that the consequences of one's decisions will not be experienced alone, but in the company of group members who are undergoing the same experience, may enhance the level of risk selected. This possibility might well be derived from Schachter's (1959) observations concerning subjects' strong preference for awaiting impending painful stimulation in the company of others in the same predicament. In the present case, subjects may be inclined toward greater risk taking if they know that others will be present to serve as a potential source of comfort during the course of any negative consequences ensuing from their risk-taking behavior. Accordingly, we have included an experimental condition in which subjects were informed that like-minded peers would be present during any experimental session involving possible aversive stimulation.

The two conditions outlined above might or might not be sufficient, when considered separately, to elicit the "risky shift" effect. Suppose, however, that the processes at work in the preceding two conditions were allowed to operate simultaneously. Would such a state of affairs yield a shift in the direction of greater risk taking? To explore this third possibility, we added an experimental condition in which subjects would make their decisions on the basis of an anticipated discussion to consensus. The possible social desirability of high risk taking would be expected to emerge even more dramatically under these circumstances, for beyond having one's decisions disclosed to others, one anticipates defending the selected risk level in the discussion to follow. In addition, the presence of others while consequences of the decisions are being experienced is also anticipated in this condition. Thus, only the discussion to consensus itself is omitted in the present case.

If we can show that the conditions stated above are unable or insufficient to account for the observed shift of group decisions in the risky direction, then we will possess a strong basis for proposing that the group discussion to consensus is an active causal factor. Such a finding would, of course, reinforce the "diffusion of responsibility" interpretation discussed earlier. On the other hand, if the conditions described produce a risky shift as large as that obtained under group discussion to consensus, then we shall know that diffusion of responsibility cannot be the sole explanatory principle.

METHOD

Subjects and General Procedure

One hundred and twenty-six male subjects, students at the summer session of the University of Colorado, were recruited to serve in an experiment disguised as a study of various "physiological effects on problem solving." The mean age of the subjects was 22.6 years, and they were randomly assigned to five treatment conditions. The written description of the experiment used for recruiting subjects was designed to minimize self-selection; in particular, neither the risk-taking nature nor the possible aversive features of the experiment were mentioned. Potential subjects were told that there would be two sessions, a preliminary session of .5 hour during which they would fill out nonpersonal information forms, and a 1-hour experimental session to be arranged at their convenience sometime later. Payment of $2.00 was offered for the preliminary session in addition to payment (of unspecified amount) for the experiment itself. The "preliminary session," in actual fact, constituted the complete experiment. Subjects were paid $2.50 after all participants had completed the experiment at which time the deception was fully explained.

The experimental procedures were administered to groups of three previously unacquainted subjects at a time by a male experimenter. The subjects were seated along one side of a long table in a small experimental room which contained assorted pieces of mechanical and electrical apparatus. Movable wooden partitions separated the subjects' work spaces at the table. As soon as the subjects were seated, they were given a paper-and-pencil questionnaire with the request that they read the initial instructions and the first item and then wait for further instructions. The 6-item questionnaire was entitled, "Preliminary Session for Psychophysiological Experiment," and its instructions read as follows:

With the recent interest in manned space exploration, scientists have become increasingly concerned with the effects of various physiological stimulations on the ability to perform various tasks. For example, it is well known that background noise interferes with the ability to solve simple arithmetic problems. In our research we are interested in having people undergo various physiological stimulations for a period of fifteen minutes before engaging in a forty-five minute session of solving simple verbal and mathematical problems. An experimental session, then, lasts a total period of one hour.

Each of the following sheets describes one of the six experiments we are conducting. Through a random drawing procedure, you may be selected to participate in one of these; no person will serve in more than one. If you are so selected, the information you provide on these sheets will then be consulted for selecting the exact procedure to be employed. Within the next few weeks, you will be informed by mail whether or not you have been selected to participate in one of these experiments. Whether you are selected or not, you will be paid $2.00 for the present preliminary session at that time.

We are employing this rather unusual preliminary session and selection procedure in order to partially overcome a difficulty which has impeded the research. This is the occurrence of unwanted disruptive side effects which sometimes result from the physiological stimulations under investigation. When such side effects do occur, it is impossible for the individual to provide meaningful results on the problem-solving and his participation in the experiment must then necessarily be terminated. Although we do know that all of the side effects subside within an hour and never leave any permanent effect, it is still not possible to prevent such side effects nor to predict in advance who is likely to suffer them. For these reasons, then, we are offering more money to those willing to undergo stimulation which is more likely to produce a side effect, with the understanding that those suffering the side effect cannot be used in the problem-solving and, hence, will be excused from the experiment and paid a flat fee of $1.00 for their time and inconvenience. That is, the greater compensation is paid only to those who complete the experiment after undergoing stimulation which was more likely to have produced the side effect, but did not do so.

The forms of stimulation, side effects, and schedule of payments are described on the following sheets. For each experiment you are asked to indicate your preference on the stimulation to be employed; you are also given the option in each experiment of not undergoing the stimulation at all, but participating only in the problem-solving portion of the experiment.

The first "experiment" was entitled, "Olfactory Stimulation," and follows in its entirety:

In the olfactory experiment, we are interested in assessing the effects on subsequent problem-solving of a 15-minute exposure to an odor. Some of the odors we are testing are known to produce side effects of nausea and intense sinus pain in a portion of the population. The side effects subside within an hour and leave no permanent effect. The table below indicates the approximate percentage of the population likely to suffer these side effects. You will note that the payment is larger if you are willing to choose an odor for which the likelihood of the side effects is greater. That is, greater compensation is offered to those who complete the experiment after experiencing a stimulation which had a greater likelihood of producing the side effects. If you happen to suffer the side effects, you will be excused from the experiment and paid a flat fee of $1.00 for your time and inconvenience.

Please select one of the odors by circling its identification code letter. If you

ODOR	PERCENTAGE OF POPU-LATION EXPERIENCING SIDE EFFECTS	PAY IN ADDITION TO 75¢ FOR THE HOUR OF THE EXPERI-MENTAL SESSION
None	——	$ 0.00
a	10%	$ 2.80
b	20%	$ 3.15
c	30%	$ 3.60
d	40%	$ 4.20
e	50%	$ 5.00
f	60%	$ 6.25
g	70%	$ 8.35
h	80%	$12.50
i	90%	$25.00

are selected for an olfactory experiment, this will be the odor which you will experience. If you prefer not to expose yourself to any odor but only to participate in the problem-solving part of the experiment, circle "none."

The six experiments described in the questionnaire were identical in format to the one just presented, differing only in the stimulation employed and the possible side effects which might occur. The five other experiments were: (b) "Chromatic stimulation," in which bright color patterns would be presented for 15 minutes by means of special goggles containing prisms. Possible side effects were severe headache and intense burning sensation in the eyes. (c) "Movement stimulation," in which a motor-driven apparatus used for flight simulation would provide bodily and vibratory movement. Possible side effects were dizziness and loss of muscular control in the limbs. (d) "Taste stimulation," in which various tastes would be presented by means of flavored sticks held in the mouth. The possible side effect was an intense burning sensation in the mouth. (e) "Auditory stimulation," in which complex sound patterns would be presented through high-fidelity earphones. Possible side effects were intense, throbbing headache and ringing in the ears. (f) "Odorless gases," in which nontoxic odorless gases would be presented for the 15 minutes preceding the problem solving. The possible side effect was stomach cramps.

After subjects had read the instructions and examined the first experiment, further verbal clarification of the procedures was given. The following points were covered:

1. Subjects for the various experiments will be selected by a random procedure; in other words, responses on the questionnaire will not enter into the selection. Each individual will serve either in one or none of the experiments.

2. Responses on the questionnaire will be held confidential and the experimental sessions themselves will be private; you will undergo the stimulation and problem-solving alone.

3. We are equally interested in all of the stimulations; therefore, you should be guided only by your own preferences in making your decisions.

4. The side effects are all-or-none affairs; it is easy to tell when one is suffering from them, they appear almost immediately, and they cannot be hidden.

5. The scales of stimulations do not represent intensity scales; that is, the side effect from odor "a," for example, would be just as severe as the side effect from odor "i." The only feature which varies as one goes down the scale is the probability that the given side effect will occur. Similarly, the stimulations themselves are not unpleasant—including the movement stimulation—nor do they differ very much from one another within a particular experiment. It is only the side effects which would be unpleasant.

6. The salary scale has been arranged to suit the percentages. Thus, for example, if you select the 90% level, you have a 10% chance of being paid—of not suffering the side effect; if you select the 80% level, you then have a 20% chance of being paid. Since the chances have doubled, the salary has been halved. All of the salaries have been arranged in this way so that we can calculate our budget ahead of time.

These points were all emphasized so that they could not arise as new information in a group discussion and lead, thereby, to an artifactual shift in risk taking under the group-discussion condition. As the last point made clear to the subjects, the probability of being paid multiplied by the size of the payoff is a constant. Therefore, since the side effects have negative utilities, the expected values of the various alternatives *decrease* as one becomes more risky. Hence, a "rational" decision-making strategy of maximizing expected values would lead to conservatism in the present situation.

This first administration of the questionnaire provided the individual base lines against which all subsequent shifts in risk taking were evaluated. After all subjects had completed the initial questionnaire, they either were told to return the following week or were given a second questionnaire (as noted below in the appropriate treatment conditions).

Test-Retest Control (N = 18 Subjects)

Subjects in this control condition were asked to return the following week in order to receive their salary and, possibly, to provide additional information. At that time they were told that selection of subjects had not yet been made and that a number of people had expressed a desire to change their responses either up or down after thinking about their participation. Since it is very important that nobody be asked to undergo stimulation which they do not really want, the experimenter explained further, they were being encouraged to make any changes they desired before experimental subjects were actually selected. Thus, change was encouraged rather than discouraged. Separating partitions remained in place as in the first administration. This condition provides data on the test-retest reliability of the questionnaire as well as a practice or familiarity control for any shifts in risk levels observed in the other conditions.

Discussion to Consensus (N = 18 Groups)

Group decisions.   This condition was designed to answer the basic question: will discussion to consensus lead to increased risk taking in the present decision-making context? Subjects were told:

This questionnaire I have just handed you is identical to the one you have just completed. It is to be used for a second phase of our research. In this second phase, we are interested in examining an even more important problem than individual problem-solving, that of the effects of various stimulations on the ability of a crew or group of men who must perform joint tasks, tasks which require them to coordinate their efforts. It is for this reason that three of you were asked to be here at the same time. If you are selected for an individual experiment, then the information you gave on your first questionnaire will still be consulted; but we are also selecting groups of three, at random, to participate in a group problem-solving session after undergoing the same stimulation. In these sessions, if one person suffers a side effect, he will be paid his dollar and dismissed and a stand-in will replace him; if two suffer the side effects, then two replacements will be used. In any case, if you do not suffer the side effect, you will be solving problems with two other individuals who have experienced the same physiological stimulation. If you are selected for a group experiment, you will not also serve in an individual experiment.

Since this group may be selected for one of the six experiments, we would like you to go through the questionnaire and decide among yourselves which stimulation you would like to experience in each case. That is, you should discuss each experiment and come to a unanimous decision regarding the stimulation to be employed; be sure the decision is unanimous and that a majority is not just bulldozing the third member into something.

At this point, the partitions which had separated the subjects' working space on the table were removed. As in our previous experiments, the subjects were encouraged to take ample time for their deliberations.

Private decisions.   In order to assess the possible effects on individual risk-taking levels of the discussion to consensus, the above subjects went over the questionnaire again following the group decisions and indicated their private opinions. They did this, the subjects were told, since

it is important to us that nobody in this research be required to undergo an experience he has not chosen for himself, if possible. ... If it is at all possible, then, we will put you in a group of two others who have selected the same level of stimulation rather than placing you in this group.

Partitions were again placed between the subjects.

Anticipated Public Disclosure (N = 18 Subjects)

As one check on the possibility that the social desirability of increased risk taking might enhance the risk levels selected, this condition was identical to the test-retest control except that the subjects were further told at the retest session that each person's decisions would be made public and discussed after they filled out the questionnaire, since

a number of people have expressed an interest in knowing what the other people have been deciding.

In addition, the wooden partitions which had previously separated the work spaces were not present this time. Again, change was encouraged rather than discouraged. Note that subjects still anticipated that the experimental session itself would be private.

Anticipated Presence of Others (N = 18 Subjects)

This condition examined the effect on risk-taking levels of expecting to undergo the consequences of one's decisions in the company of others who have selected the same levels of risk. Subjects received the second questionnaire immediately after the first one. The first paragraph of instructions was identical to the first paragraph for the condition of discussion to consensus—group decisions. The subjects then were requested to go through the questionnaire and

mark the stimulation in each experiment you would prefer to undergo for this group problem-solving. If you are selected for an experiment on group problem-solving, then you will participate in the experiment with two other individuals who have selected the same stimulation.

Anticipated Discussion to Consensus (N = 18 Subjects)

This condition contained all the features of the discussion-to-consensus condition except for the discussion itself. Subjects were given the second questionnaire immediately following the first one. Again, the first paragraph of instructions was identical to the first paragraph for the condition of discussion to consensus—group decisions. The instructions then continued:

If this group is selected for an experiment, then it will be necessary for the three of you to reach an agreement as to which stimulation you will all undergo. For this reason, we would like each of you to go through the questionnaire, marking the stimulation in each experiment which you would prefer to undergo in the group experience. When and if you are selected for an experiment, then your decisions on that experiment will be made available to the three of you so you can discuss them and make a unanimous selection on just which stimulation is to be employed. In other words, you should now mark the stimulation in each experiment which you would want to suggest to the group for the stimulation to be used.

RESULTS

In the presentation of results, risk scores on the questionnaire represent the percentage level (probability of side effect) selected by a subject or group for the average of six "experiments." Thus, scores can range from 0% (for the "none" alternative) to 90%, with higher scores reflecting greater risk taking. A shift score for an individual is computed by subtracting his score on the first administration of the questionnaire from his score on the second administration (N = number of subjects). When group decisions are under consideration, a shift score represents the group questionnaire score minus the mean of the questionnaire scores obtained by the same three individuals in the first administration (N = number of groups). When private decisions after group consensus are under study, a shift score represents the mean of the postconsensus private decisions by a group's members minus the mean of their scores on the first administration (N = number of groups). All subjects thus serve as their own controls. Positive shift scores represent shifts in the risky direction. One-sample t tests of the difference scores (Walker & Lev, 1953, pp. 151–153) are used to evaluate the null hypothesis that the mean shift for a condition is zero.

The mean initial risk score for the 126 subjects was 65.5%, with a standard deviation of 16.8%. Table 1 displays the mean shift score obtained in each of the conditions, and its statistical test.

With regard to the test-retest control (Table 1, Row 1), permitting subjects to reconsider their decisions after a period of 1 week and under circumstances that encourage change, does not lead to any systematic shift in either direction. The r between the first and second administrations of the questionnaire is .79, thus indicating that the test-retest reliability of the instrument is quite satisfactory.

Concerning discussion to consensus, group decisions are significantly more

Table 1 PERCENTAGE OF DEGREE OF SHIFT IN RISK TAKING FOR EACH OF THE EXPERIMENTAL CONDITIONS

CONDITION	MEAN DEGREE OF SHIFT IN PERCENTAGE	SD	t
1. Test-retest control (N = 18 subjects)	+1.11	12.78	0.36
2a. Discussion to consensus – group decisions (N = 18 groups)	+5.43	7.82	2.86***
2b. Discussion to consensus – private decisions (N = 18 groups)[a]	+3.97	6.02	2.71***
3. Anticipated public disclosure (N = 18 subjects)	+1.85	11.86	0.64
4. Anticipated presence of others (N = 18 subjects)	−1.30	2.52	2.12*
5. Anticipated discussion to consensus (N = 18 subjects)	−4.91	8.14	2.48**

[a] Test based on subjects pooled within groups in order to preserve independence. Hence df = 17.

* p < .05, two-tailed test.
** p < .025, two-tailed test.
*** p < .02, two-tailed test.

299

risky than the mean of the decisions made by the group members as individuals (Table 1, Row 2a). The groups selected levels of risk which averaged over one-half a scale step more risky than individual decisions. Sixteen of the 18 groups in this condition display a shift in the risky direction, which argues for the consistency of the effect. Row 2b of Table 1 indicates, in turn, that the private decisions of these same subjects, obtained after completion of the group discussions, also shifted significantly in the risky direction. Thus, subjects did not revert to their original prediscussion decisions, but rather showed a high degree of personal acceptance of the greater risk taking ensuing from discussion to consensus.

Regarding anticipated public disclosure, there is no evidence for either a risky or conservative shift due to knowing that one's decisions are to be disclosed to others rather than being held confidential (Table 1, Row 3). The results are quite comparable to those for the test-retest control condition.

The data for anticipated presence of others (Table 1, Row 4) indicate that individuals actually tend to be more conservative when they anticipate undergoing the consequences of the decisions in the company of others who have selected the same levels of risk. Although the magnitude of the shift is small, it is statistically significant, given the consistency of the effect. Note the very small standard deviation relative to that of the other conditions.

Finally, concerning anticipated discussion to consensus, decisions made under this expectation are considerably more *conservative* than decisions made by those same individuals under conditions of confidentiality (Table 1, Row 5). The shift in the conservative direction under anticipated discussion to consensus is about as large as the shift in the risky direction which appears when the discussion is actually held.

DISCUSSION

The present investigation has demonstrated in a context of aversive consequences that unanimous group decisions concerning matters of risk show a shift toward greater risk taking when compared with individual decisions, and postdiscussion individual decisions that follow group consensus reflect the risky shift of the group rather than the original prediscussion decisions. Hence, the general conclusions drawn from our two previous experiments (Wallach et al., 1962, 1964) can now be extended to include decision-making contexts emphasizing negative consequences.[1]

The proposal that a diffusion of responsibility is the process underlying such group-induced risky shifts received further support in the present experiment. Each of the alternative explanations that has been suggested in order to account for the group-induced risky shift phenomenon has been found inapplicable.

Consider first the proposal that higher risk taking has greater social desirability than conservatism. If this were the causal factor at work in the group

---

[1] The content of the discussions revealed that the present experiment was indeed successful in shifting the focus of the decision making to the negative or aversive consequences of risk taking. In fact, the monetary payoffs were rarely mentioned in achieving consensus; rather, discussion centered around the relative aversiveness of the various side effects for the group members.

discussion, one would also expect higher risk taking to appear when a person knows that his decisions, rather than remaining private, will be made available to others for inspection. Yet, in the anticipated-public-disclosure condition, such enhanced risk taking failed to appear. Furthermore, a dramatic conservative shift appeared in the anticipated-discussion-to-consensus condition where each subject not only knew that his decisions would be disclosed to others, but also knew that he would be expected to defend his decisions before the other members of the group.

Second, the proposal that increased risk taking might be caused simply by knowing that one would be experiencing the consequences of one's decisions in the company of others who had made similar decisions, also was clearly disconfirmed. Such a proposal followed from the consideration that a person might accept greater risk of aversive consequences if he knew that others would be present as a source of potential sympathy and comfort during the period when those aversive consequences might be experienced. We find, however, a significant conservative shift in the anticipated-presence-of-others condition. Perhaps, male subjects faced with the uncertainty of how they will "take" the side effects of physiological stimulation are concerned about the possibility of conveying an impression of weakness in the presence of peers. Such a process would enhance conservatism.

In a previous experiment (Wallach et al., 1964), a conservative shift was displayed by individual decision makers when responsibility for others was introduced in the absence of group interaction. The conservative shift which appeared in the present experiment's condition of anticipated discussion to consensus seems to be an example of the same phenomenon, even though here the individual's decisions are not yet binding on the other members of the group. In the present condition, the individual is proposing a decision which he presumably intends to urge upon the group, a decision whose consequences, therefore, will be experienced by all. It seems likely that a feeling of responsibility for others would be generated under such circumstances. When no discussion to consensus has yet occurred but is only expected, the effect of these forces is to make the individual favor conservative decisions. When the discussion to consensus actually takes place, on the other hand, increased risk taking is the result. These findings offer direct support for explaining the group induced risky shift phenomenon in terms of a diffusion of responsibility.[2]

In our previous paper (Wallach et al., 1964), we touched upon some of the implications of our work for committee decision making concerning national and military policy. While recognizing that these latter concerns introduced risks and deterrents likely to be qualitatively different from those capable of study in

[2] Wallach, Kogan, and Bem (1962) reported low but significant positive correlations between initial risk-taking levels and perceived influence exerted in the group discussion. While this finding could well represent an outcome of a responsibility diffusion process, the possibility remains that high risk takers may dominate the group discussion and hence exert a disproportionate influence in the risky direction on the other members of the group. Although quantitative data on this point were not obtained in the discussion-to-consensus condition of the present study, the experimenter observed that group members appeared eager to defer to and sympathize with any member who found a given side effect particularly aversive. There appeared to be little indication of particular group members urging an across-the-board strategy of high risk taking.

a laboratory context, we nevertheless felt that our research might be of some relevance to the decision making characterizing affairs of state. Indeed, the present experiment may be viewed as a closer approximation to the real-life cases cited above, for the reason that the risk of aversive consequences is here an important ingredient of the decision-making process. It is precisely such risks that underlie the deterrence policies of the major powers. Of course, the decisions reached in this experiment affect only the group members participating in the study; the decisions have no impact on the larger populations from which the subjects are drawn. Despite this important qualification, it would be most surprising if the shifts toward risk taking observed here and in our previous experiments did not have some counterpart in the actions of governmental decision-making bodies. Such matters would clearly be worthy of careful study.

REFERENCES

Schachter, S. *The psychology of affiliation.* Stanford: Stanford Univer. Press, 1959.

Walker, Helen M., & Lev, J. *Statistical inference.* New York: Holt, 1953.

Wallach, M. A., Kogan, N., & Bem, D. J. Group influence on individual risk taking. *Journal of Abnormal and Social Psychology,* 1962, *65,* 75–86.

Wallach, M. A., Kogan, N., & Bem, D. J. Diffusion of responsibility and level of risk taking in groups. *Journal of Abnormal and Social Psychology,* 1964, *68,* 263–74.

CONFORMITY

A Study of Normative and Informational Social Influences upon Individual Judgment

MORTON DEUTSCH AND HAROLD B. GERARD

By now many experimental studies (e.g., 1, 3, 6) have demonstrated that individual psychological processes are subject to social influences. Most investigators, however, have not distinguished among different kinds of social influences; rather, they have carelessly used the term "group" influence to characterize the impact of many different kinds of social factors. In fact, a review of the major experiments in this area—e.g., those by Sherif (6), Asch (1), Bovard (3)—would indicate that the subjects (Ss) in these experiments as they made their judgments were *not* functioning as *members* of a group in any simple or obvious manner. The S, in the usual experiment in this area, made perceptual judgments in the physical

Reprinted from Journal of Abnormal and Social Psychology, 51, *1955, 629–36. Copyright 1955 by the American Psychological Association and reproduced by permission.*

presence of others after hearing their judgments. Typically, the *S* was *not* given experimental instructions which made him feel that he was a member of a group faced with a common task requiring cooperative effort for its most effective solution. If "group" influences were at work in the foregoing experiments, they were subtly and indirectly created rather than purposefully created by the experimenter.

HYPOTHESES

The purpose of this paper is to consider two types of social influence, "normative" and "informational," which we believe were operative in the experiments mentioned above, and to report the results of an experiment bearing upon hypotheses that are particularly relevant to the former influence. We shall define a *normative social influence* as an influence to conform with the positive expectations[1] of another.[2] An *informational social influence* may be defined as an influence to accept information obtained from another as *evidence* about reality. Commonly these two types of influence are found together. However, it is possible to conform behaviorally with the expectations of others and say things which one disbelieves but which agree with the beliefs of others. Also, it is possible that one will accept an opponent's beliefs as evidence about reality even though one has no motivation to agree with him, per se.

Our hypotheses are particularly relevant to normative social influence upon individual judgment. We shall not elaborate the theoretical rationales for the hypotheses, since they are for the most part obvious and they follow from other theoretical writings (e.g., 4, 5).

Hypothesis I.

Normative social influence upon individual judgments will be greater among individuals forming a group than among an aggregation of individuals who do not compose a group.[3]

---

[1] By positive expectations we mean to refer to those expectations whose fulfillment by another leads to or reinforces positive rather than negative feelings, and whose nonfulfillment leads to the opposite, to alienation rather than solidarity; conformity to negative expectations, on the other hand, leads to or reinforces negative rather than positive feelings.

[2] The term *another* is being used inclusively to refer to "another person," to a "group," or to one's "self." Thus, a normative social influence can result from the expectations of oneself, or of a group, or of another person.

[3] Generally one would also expect that group members would be more likely to take the judgments of other group members as trustworthy evidence for forming judgments about reality and, hence, they would be more susceptible to informational social influence than would nongroup members. The greater trustworthiness usually reflects more experience of the reliability of the judgments of other members and more confidence in the benevolence of their motivations. However, when group members have had no prior experience together and when it is apparent in both the group and nongroup situations that the others are motivated and in a position to report correct judgments, there is no reason to expect differential susceptibility to informational social influence among group and nongroup members.

That is, even when susceptibility to informational social influence is equated, we would predict that the greater susceptibility to normative social influence among group members would be reflected in the greater group influence upon individual judgment. This is not to say that individuals, even when they are not group members, may not have some motivation to conform to the expectations of others—e.g., so as to ingratiate themselves or so as to avoid ridicule.

Hypothesis II.

Normative social influence upon individual judgment will be reduced when the individual perceives that his judgment cannot be identified or, more generally, when the individual perceives no pressure to conform directed at him from others.

Hypothesis III.

Normative social influence to conform to one's own judgment will reduce the impact of the normative social influence to conform to the judgment of others.

Hypothesis IV.

Normative social influence to conform to one's own judgment from another as well as from oneself will be stronger than normative social influence from oneself.

Normative social influence from oneself to conform to one's own judgment may be thought of as an internalized social process in which the individual holds expectations with regard to his own behavior; conforming to positive self-expectations leads to feelings of self-esteem or self-approval while nonconformity leads to feelings of anxiety or guilt. In general, one would expect that the strength of these internalized self-expectations would reflect the individual's prior experiences with them as sources of need satisfaction—e.g., by conforming to his own judgments or by self-reliance he has won approval from such significant others as his parents. As Hypothesis IV indicates, we believe that contemporaneous social pressure to conform to one's own judgment may supplement, and perhaps be even stronger than, the individual's internalized pressure to conform to his own judgment.

Two additional hypotheses, dealing with the effect of difficulty of judgment, are relevant to one of the experimental variations. They follow:

Hypothesis V.

The more uncertain the individual is about the correctness of his judgment, the more likely he is to be susceptible to both normative and informational social influences in making his judgment.

Hypothesis VI.

The more uncertain the individual is about the correctness of the judgment of others, the less likely he is to be susceptible to informational social influence in making his judgment.[4]

METHOD

Subjects.

One hundred and one college students from psychology courses at New York University were employed as *S*s. The study was defined for the *S*s as an experimental study of perception.

Procedure.

We employed the experimental situation developed by Asch (1) with certain modifications and variations which are specified below. For detailed description of the procedures utilized by Asch and replicated in this experiment, Asch's publication should be consulted. The basic features of the Asch situation are: (*a*) the *S*s are instructed that they are participating in a perceptual experiment, wherein they have to match accurately the length of a given line with one of three lines; (*b*) correct judgments are easy to make; (*c*) in each experimental session there is only one *naive S*, the other participants, while ostensibly *S*s, are in fact "stooges" who carry out the experimenter's instructions; (*d*) each participant (i.e., the naive *S* and the stooges) has to indicate his judgments publicly; (*e*) on 12 of the 18 perceptual judgments the stooges announce wrong and unanimous judgments, the errors of the stooges are large and clearly in error; (*f*) the naive *S* and the stooges are in a face-to-face relationship and have been previously acquainted with one another.[5]

---

[4] Although we have no data relevant to this hypothesis, we present it to qualify Hypothesis V and to counteract an assumption in some of the current social psychological literature. Thus, Festinger (5) has written that where no physical reality basis exists for the establishment of the validity of one's belief, one is dependent upon social reality (i.e., upon the beliefs of others). Similarly, Asch (2) has indicated that group influence grows stronger as the judgmental situation diminishes in clarity. The implication of Hypothesis VI is that if an individual perceives that a situation is objectively difficult to judge—that others as well as he experience the situation in the same way (i.e., as being difficult and as having uncertainty about their judgments)—he will not trust their judgments any more than he trusts his own. It is only as his confidence in their judgments increases (e.g., because he deems that agreement among three uncertain judges provides more reliable evidence than one uncertain judge) that the judgments of others will have informational social influence. However (at any particular level of confidence in the judgment of others), one can predict that as his confidence in his own judgment decreases he will be more susceptible to normative social influence. With decreasing self-confidence there is likely to be less of a commitment to one's own judgment and, hence, less influence not to conform to the judgments of others.

[5] Inspection of the Asch situation would suggest that informational social influence would be strongly operative. As Asch has put it (2, p. 461):

To test the hypotheses set forth in the foregoing section, the following experimental variations upon Asch's situation were employed:

1. The face-to-face situation.   This was an exact replication of Asch's situation except for the following minor modifications: (*a*) Only three stooges, rather than eight, were employed;[6] (*b*) the *S* and the stooges were unacquainted prior to the experiment; and (*c*) two series of 18 judgments were employed. In one series (the visual series), the lines were physically present when the *S* and the stooges announced their judgments; in the other series (the memory series), the lines were removed before any one announced his judgment. In the memory series, approximately three seconds after the lines were removed the first stooge was asked to announce his judgment. The sequences of visual and memory series were alternated so that approximately half the *S*s had the memory series first and half had the visual series first.

2. The anonymous situation.   This situation was identical with the face-to-face situation except for the following differences: (*a*) Instead of sitting in the visual presence of each other, the *S*s were separated by partitions which prevented them from talking to each other or seeing one another; (*b*) Instead of announcing their judgments by voice, the *S*s indicated their judgments by pressing a button; (*c*) No stooges were employed. Each *S* was led to believe he was Subject No. 3, and the others were No. 1, No. 2, and No. 4. He was told that when the experimenter called out "Subject No. 3" he was to indicate his

The subject knows (a) that the issue is one of fact; (b) that a correct result is possible; (c) that only one result is correct; (d) that the others and he are oriented to and reporting about the same objectively given relations; (e) that the group is in unanimous opposition at certain points with him.

He further perceives that the others are motivated to report a correct judgment. In such a situation, the subject's accumulated past experience would lead him to expect that he could rely on the judgments of others, especially if they all agreed. That is, even if his eyes were closed he might feel that he could safely risk his life on the assumption that the unanimous judgments of the others were correct. This is a strong informational social influence and one would expect it to be overriding except for the fact that the subject has his eyes open and receives information from a source which he also feels to be completely trustworthy—i.e., from his own perceptual apparatus. The subject is placed in strong conflict because the evidences from two sources of trustworthy information are in opposition.

In the Asch situation, it is apparent that, in addition to informational social influence, normative social influence is likely to be operating. The naive *S* is in a face-to-face situation with acquaintances and he may be motivated to conform to their judgments in order to avoid being ridiculed, or being negatively evaluated, or even possibly out of a sense of obligation. While it may be impossible to remove completely the impact of normative social influence upon any socialized being, it is evident that the Asch situation allows much opportunity for this type of influence to operate.

[6] Asch found that three stooges were about as effective in influencing the *S*s as eight.

judgment by pressing one of three buttons (A, B, or C) which corresponded to what he thought the correct line was. When an S pressed a given button, a corresponding bulb lit on his own panel and on a hidden master panel. Presumably the appropriate bulb also lit on the panels of each of the other Ss, but, in fact, the bulbs on any S's panel were not connected to the buttons of the other Ss. When the experimenter called for the judgments of Subject No. 1, of Subject No. 2, and of Subject No. 4, a concealed accomplice manipulated master switches which lit bulbs on each of the S's panels that corresponded to judgments presumably being made by these respective Ss. Subjects No. 1, No. 2, and No. 4 were, in effect, "electrical stooges" whose judgments were indicated on the panels of the four naive Ss (all of whom were Subject No. 3) by an accomplice of the experimenter who manipulated master switches controlling the lights on the panels of the naive Ss. The pattern of judgments followed by the "electrical stooges" was the same as that followed by the "live stooges" in the face-to-face situation. (d) In providing a rationale for being labeled Subject No. 3 for each of the naive Ss, we explained that due to the complicated wiring setup, the S's number had no relation to his seating position. Implicitly, we assumed that each S would realize that it would be impossible for the others to identify that a judgment was being made by him rather than by any of two others. However, it is apparent from postexperiment questionnaires that many of the Ss did not realize this. It seems likely that if we had made the anonymous character of the judgments clear and explicit to the Ss, the effects of this experimental variation would have been even more marked.

3. The group situation. This situation was identical to the anonymous situation except that the subjects were instructed as follows:

This group is one of twenty similar groups who are participating in this experiment. We want to see how accurately you can make judgments. We are going to give a reward to the five best groups—the five groups that make the fewest errors on the series of judgments that you are given. The reward will be a pair of tickets to a Broadway play of your own choosing for each member of the winning group. An error will be counted any time one of you makes an incorrect judgment. That is, on any given card the group can make as many as four errors if you each judge incorrectly or you can make no errors if you each judge correctly. The five groups that make the best scores will be rewarded.

4. The self-commitment variation. This variation was employed in both the face-to-face and anonymous situations. In it, each S was given a sheet of paper on which to write down his judgment before he was exposed to the judgments of the others. He was told not to sign the sheet of paper and that it would not be collected at the end of the experiment. After the first series of 18 judgments, the Ss threw away their sheets. The Ss did not erase their recorded judgments after each trial as they did in the Magic Pad self-commitment variation.

4A. The Magic Pad self-commitment variation. This variation was employed in the anonymous situation. In it, each S was given a Magic Writing Pad on which to write down his judgment before he was exposed to the judgments of the others. After each S had been exposed to the judgment of the others and had indicated his own judgment, he erased his judgment on the Magic Writing Pad by lifting up the plastic covering. It was made convincingly clear to the *S* that only he would ever know what he had written down on the pad.

5. The public commitment variation. This variation was employed in both the face-to-face situation and in the anonymous situation. In it, the *S*s followed the same procedure as in the self-commitment variation except that they wrote down their initial judgments on sheets of paper which they signed and which they knew were to be handed to the experimenter after each series of 18 judgments.

RESULTS

The primary data used in the analysis of the results are the errors made by the *S*s which were in the direction of the errors made by the stooges. We shall present first the data which are relevant to our hypotheses; later we shall present other information.

Hypothesis I.

The data relevant to the first hypothesis are presented in Table 1. The table presents a comparison of the anonymous situation in which the individuals were motivated to act as a group with the anonymous situation in which there was no direct attempt to induce membership motivation; in both situations, no self or public commitment was made. The data provide strong support for the prediction that the normative social influence upon individual judgments will be greater among individuals forming a group than among individuals who do not compose a group. The average member of the group made more than twice as many errors as the comparable individual who did not participate in the task as a member of a group.

Qualitative data from a postexperimental questionnaire, in which we asked the *S* to describe any feelings he had about himself or about the others during

Table 1 MEAN NUMBER OF SOCIALLY INFLUENCED ERRORS IN INDIVIDUAL JUDGMENT AMONG GROUP MEMBERS AND AMONG NONMEMBERS

EXPERIMENTAL TREATMENT	N	MEMORY SERIES	VISUAL SERIES	TOTAL
Group, anonymous, no commitment	15	6.87	5.60	12.47
Nongroup, anonymous, no commitment	13	3.15	2.77	5.92
		*p VALUES**		
		.01	.05	.001

* *Based on a t test, using one tail of the distribution.*

the experiment, also support Hypothesis I. Seven out of the fifteen Ss in the "group" condition spontaneously mentioned a felt obligation to the other group members; none of the individuals in the nongroup condition mentioned any feeling of obligation to go along with the others.

Hypothesis II.

To test the second hypothesis, it is necessary to compare the data from the face-to-face and anonymous situations among the individuals who were otherwise exposed to similar experimental treatments. Tables 2 and 3 present the relevant data. It is apparent that there was less social influence upon individual judgment in the anonymous as compared with the face-to-face situation. This

Table 2 MEAN NUMBER OF SOCIALLY INFLUENCED ERRORS IN INDIVIDUAL JUDGMENT IN THE ANONYMOUS AND IN THE FACE-TO-FACE SITUATIONS

		NO COMMITMENT		
SITUATION	*VISUAL*	*MEMORY*	*TOTAL*	*N*
Face-to-face	3.00	4.08	7.08	13
Anonymous	2.77	3.15	5.92	13
		SELF-COMMITMENT		
SITUATION	*VISUAL*	*MEMORY*	*TOTAL*	*N*
Face-to-face	.92	.75	1.67	12
Anonymous	.64	.73	1.37	11
		PUBLIC COMMITMENT		
SITUATION	*VISUAL*	*MEMORY*	*TOTAL*	*N*
Face-to-face	1.13	1.39	2.52	13
Anonymous	.92	.46	1.38	13

Table 3 *p* VALUES* FOR VARIOUS COMPARISONS OF SOCIALLY INFLUENCED ERRORS IN THE ANONYMOUS AND FACE-TO-FACE SITUATIONS

COMPARISON	*TOTAL ERRORS*
A vs. F	.001
A vs. F, no commitment	.001
A vs. F, self-commitment	.10
A vs. F, public commitment	.001
Interaction of commitment with A-F	.01

* *p values are based on t tests, using one tail of distribution, derived from analyses of variation.*

lessening of social influence is at the .001 level of statistical confidence even when the comparisons include the "commitment variations" as well as both the visual and the memory series of judgments. The interaction between the commitment variations and the anonymous, face-to-face variations, which is statistically significant, is such as to reduce the over-all differences between the anonymous and face-to-face situation; the differences between the face-to-face and the anonymous situations are most strongly brought out when there is no commitment. Similarly, if we compare the anonymous and face-to-face situations, employing the memory rather than the visual series, the effect of the normative influence upon judgments in the face-to-face situation is increased somewhat, but not significantly. That is, as we eliminate counter-normative influences (i.e., the "commitment") and as we weaken reality restraints (i.e., employ the "memory" rather than "visual" series), the normative influences in the face-to-face situation operate more freely.

The support for Hypothesis II is particularly striking in light of the fact that, due to faulty experimental procedure, the "anonymous" character of the anonymous situation was not sufficiently impressed on some of the Ss. For these Ss, the anonymous situation merely protected them from the immediate, visually accessible pressure to conform arising from the lifted eyebrows and expressions of amazement by the stooges in the face-to-face situation. Complete feeling of anonymity would probably have strengthened the results.

Hypotheses III and IV.

Tables 4, 5, and 6 present results showing the influence of the different commitment variations. The public and the self-commitment variations markedly reduce the socially influenced errors in both the face-to-face and anonymous situations. In other words, the data provide strong support for

Table 4 p VALUES* FOR VARIOUS COMPARISONS OF SOCIALLY INFLUENCED ERRORS IN THE DIFFERENT COMMITMENT TREATMENTS

COMPARISON	TOTAL ERRORS	ERRORS ON VISUAL SERIES	ERRORS ON MEMORY SERIES
No commitment vs. public commitment, F	.001	.01	.001
No commitment vs. self-commitment, F	.001	.01	.001
Self-commitment vs. public commitment, F	.01	NS	NS
No commitment vs. self-commitment, A	.001	.01	.01
No commitment vs. public commitment, A	.001	.01	.002
Self-commitment vs. public commitment, A	NS	NS	NS

* *p values are based on t tests, using one tail of the distribution, and derived from the analyses of variation.*

Table 5 MEAN NUMBER OF SOCIALLY INFLUENCED ERRORS IN JUDGMENTS
IN THE ANONYMOUS SITUATION AS AFFECTED BY THE COMMITMENT
VARIATIONS

| *NO COMMITMENT* | | | | | *MAGIC PAD SELF-COMMITMENT* | | | |
VISUAL	MEMORY	TOTAL	N		VISUAL	MEMORY	TOTAL	N
2.77	3.15	5.92	13		1.63	2.27	3.90	11

| *SELF-COMMITMENT* | | | | | *PUBLIC COMMITMENT* | | | |
VISUAL	MEMORY	TOTAL	N		VISUAL	MEMORY	TOTAL	N
.64	.73	1.37	11		.92	.46	1.38	13

Table 6 p VALUES* FOR VARIOUS COMPARISONS OF SOCIALLY INFLUENCED
ERRORS IN THE DIFFERENT COMMITMENT VARIATIONS

COMPARISON	TOTAL ERRORS	ERRORS ON VISUAL SERIES	ERRORS ON MEMORY SERIES
No commitment vs. Magic Pad self-commitment	.05	NS	NS
Magic Pad self-commitment vs. self-commitment	.005	NS	.05
Magic Pad self-commitment vs. public commitment	.001	NS	.01

* *p values are based on t tests using one tail of the distribution.*

Hypothesis III which asserts that normative social influence to conform to one's
own judgment will reduce the impact of the normative influence to conform to
the judgment of others.

The data with regard to the influence of self-commitment are ambiguous in
implication since the results of the two self-commitment variations—i.e., the
"Magic Pad self-commitment" and the "self-commitment"—are not the same.
The first self-commitment variation produced results which are essentially the
same as the public commitment variation, markedly reducing socially influenced
errors. The Magic Pad self-commitment variation produced results which were
different from the no commitment variation, reducing the errors to an extent
which is statistically significant; however, unlike the first self-commitment
variation, the Magic Pad self-commitment was significantly less effective than the
public commitment in reducing socially influenced errors.

Our hunch is that the Ss in the first self-commitment variation perceived the
commitment situation as though it were a public commitment and that this is
the explanation of the lack of differences between these two variations. That is,
writing their judgments indelibly supported the belief that "others can see what

I have written." The Ss in the Magic Pad self-commitment variation, on the other hand, were literally wiping their initial judgments away in such a manner that they would be inaccessible to anyone. Hence, in the Magic Pad variation, the normative influences to conform to one's own judgment had to be sustained by the S himself. Normative influences from the S's self (to be, in a sense, true to himself) were undoubtedly also operating in the noncommitment variation. What the Magic Pad did was to prevent the S from distorting his recollection of his independent judgment after being exposed to the judgments of the others. Further, there is a theoretical basis for assuming that the commitment to a judgment or decision is increased following the occurrence of behavior based upon it. Hence, the behavior of writing one's judgment down on the Magic Pad makes the original decision less tentative and less subject to change. However, it is apparent that this internally sustained influence to conform with one's own judgment was not as strong as the combination of external and self-motivated influences. These results support our fourth hypothesis.

Hypothesis V.

Table 7 presents a comparison of the errors made on the visual and on the memory series of judgments. It is apparent that the Ss were less influenced by the judgments of others when the judgments were made on a visual rather than on a memory basis. It is also evident from the data of Table 2 that the differences between the visual and memory series were reduced or disappeared when the Ss wrote down their initial, independent judgments. These results support our fifth hypothesis which asserts that the more uncertain the individual is about the correctness of his judgment, the more likely he is to be susceptible to social influences in making his judgment. Further support comes from the questionnaire data. Out of the 90 Ss who filled out questionnaires, 51 indicated that they were more certain of their judgment when the lines were visually present, 2 were more certain when they were absent, and 39 were equally certain in both instances.

Being exposed first to the memory series rather than the visual series had the effect of making the Ss more susceptible to social influence upon their judgments throughout both series of judgments. In other words, an S was more likely

Table 7 SOCIALLY INFLUENCED ERRORS IN INDIVIDUAL JUDGMENTS AS
AFFECTED BY THE STIMULUS TO BE JUDGED (VISUAL OR MEMORY)

	N	MEAN NUMBER OF ERRORS	"p" VALUE
Errors on visual series	99	2.20 ⎱	.005*
Errors on memory series	99	2.60 ⎰	
Total errors when visual series was first	51	4.12 ⎱	
Total errors when memory series was first	48	5.71 ⎰	.005

* Based on a t test of differences between visual and memory series for each subject.

to make socially influenced errors on the memory series and, having allowed himself to be influenced by the others on this first series of judgments, he was more likely to be influenced on the visual series than if he had not previously participated in the memory series. It is as though once having given in to the social influence (and it is easier to give in when one is less certain about one's judgment), the *S* is more susceptible to further social influences.

DISCUSSION

A central thesis of this experiment has been that prior experiments which have been concerned with "group" influence upon individual judgment have, in fact, only incidentally been concerned with the type of social influence most specifically associated with groups, namely "normative social influence." Our results indicate that, even when normative social influence in the direction of an incorrect judgment is largely removed (as in the anonymous situation), more errors are made by our *S*s than by a control group of *S*s making their judgments when alone.[7] It seems reasonable to conclude that the *S*, even if not normatively influenced, may be influenced by the others in the sense that the judgments of others are taken to be a more or less trustworthy source of information about the objective reality with which he and the others are confronted.

It is not surprising that the judgments of others (particularly when they are perceived to be motivated and competent to judge accurately) should be taken as evidence to be weighed in coming to one's own judgment. From birth on, we learn that the perceptions and judgments of others are frequently reliable sources of evidence about reality. Hence, it is to be expected that if the perceptions by two or more people of the same objective situation are discrepant, each will tend to re-examine his own view and that of the others to see if they can be reconciled. This process of mutual influence does not necessarily indicate the operation of normative social influence as distinct from informational social influence. Essentially the same process (except that the influence is likely to be unilateral) can go on in interaction with a measuring or computing machine. For example, suppose one were to judge which of two lines is longer (as in the Müller-Lyer illusion) and then were given information that a measuring instrument (which past experience had let one to believe was infallible) came up with a different answer; certainly one might be influenced by this information. This influence could hardly be called a normative influence except in the most indirect sense.

While the results of prior experiments of "group" influence upon perception can be largely explained in terms of non-normative social influence, there is little doubt that normative influences were incidentally operative. However, these were the casual normative influences which can not be completely eliminated from any human situation, rather than normative influences deriving from specific group membership. Our experimental results indicate that when a group situation is created, even when the group situation is as trivial and artificial as it was in our groups, the normative social influences are grossly increased, producing considerably more errors in individual judgment.

[7] Asch (2) reports that his control group of *S*s made an average of considerably less than one error per *S*.

The implications of the foregoing result are not particularly optimistic for those who place a high value on the ability of an individual to resist group pressures which run counter to his individual judgment. In the experimental situation we employed, the *S*, by allowing himself to be influenced by the others, in effect acquiesced in the distortion of his judgment and denied the authenticity of his own immediate experience. The strength of the normative social influences that were generated in the course of our experiment was small; had it been stronger, one would have expected even more distortion and submission.

Our findings, with regard to the commitment variations, do, however, suggest that normative social influences can be utilized to buttress as well as to undermine individual integrity. In other words, normative social influence can be exerted to help make an individual be an individual and not merely a mirror or puppet of the group. Groups can demand of their members that they have self-respect, that they value their own experience, that they be capable of acting without slavish regard for popularity. Unless groups encourage their members to express their own, independent judgments, group consensus is likely to be an empty achievement. Group process which rests on the distortion of individual experience undermines its own potential for creativity and productiveness.

SUMMARY AND CONCLUSIONS

Employing modifications of the Asch situation, an experiment was carried out to test hypotheses concerning the effects of normative and informational social influences upon individual judgment. The hypotheses received strong support from the experimental data.

In discussion of our results, the thesis was advanced that prior studies of "group" influence upon individual judgment were only incidentally studies of the type of social influence most specifically associated with groups—i.e., of normative social influence. The role of normative social influence in buttressing as well as undermining individual experience was considered.

REFERENCES

1. Asch, S. E. Effects of group pressure upon the modification and distortion of judgments. In H. Guetzkow (Ed.), *Groups, leadership and men.* Pittsburgh: Carnegie Press, 1951. Pp. 177–90.

2. Asch, S. E. *Social psychology.* New York: Prentice Hall, 1952.

3. Bovard, E. W. Group structure and perception. *J. abnorm. soc. Psychol.,* 1951, *46,* 398–405.

4. Deutsch, M. A theory of cooperation and competition. *Hum. Relat.,* 1949, *2,* 129–52.

5. Festinger, L. Informal social communication. *Psychol. Rev.,* 1950, *57,* 271–82.

6. Sherif, M. A study of some social factors in perception. *Arch. Psychol.,* 1935, *27,* No. 187.

Effects of Different Conditions of Acceptance upon Conformity to Group Norms

JAMES E. DITTES AND HAROLD H. KELLEY

Among the variables influencing a person's conformity to a group's norms, two interrelated factors are likely to be important: (*a*) the extent to which he is attracted to or values his membership in the group; and (*b*) the extent to which he feels that other members are attracted to or value him. With respect to the first, it has been demonstrated that the more highly a person is attracted to a group, the more he conforms to the face-to-face pressures operating within it (1, 3) and the more he resists counternorm communications from outside it (6). The experiment reported here attempts to hold constant this first variable and to determine the effects on conformity of the second.

A relationship of *mutual dependence* is presupposed between the individual and group. Just as the individual is dependent on other members (a relationship emphasized in research on attraction to or valuation of the group), they also, to some degree, depend upon him—his skills, knowledge, and general ability to contribute to group life. Through their behavior they can be expected to communicate the value they place on him (to be referred to as their *acceptance* of him) and their desire to have him continue as a member. The present research varies this information concerning a person's acceptance in a group and investigates the effects on his conformity to its norms.

The effect of either variable on conformity is probably mediated by various intervening acquired motives. We would assume that in our culture, conformity to group standards is generally learned as a means of satisfying many acquired motives, activation of which results, given appropriate conditions, in conformity behavior. The range of motives involved seems to include at least two fairly distinct clusters, one consisting of "approach" motives such as tendencies to help the group and to pattern one's self after admired persons, the other of anxiety-based motives such as desire to avoid social criticism and loss of membership.

It is probable that valuation of membership affects conformity through both kinds of motives, but that feelings of acceptance affect the person's sense of security about remaining in the group, which in turn affects primarily those motives based on anxiety. Assuming valuation constant, information communicated from fellow members that a person is little accepted by them increases his sense of insecurity, activating various acquired motives (to avoid social criticism, etc.), to which conformity behavior has been learned. Persons informed that they are well accepted in a group feel secure in their membership and have little anxiety-based motivation to conform.

Reprinted from Journal of Abnormal and Social Psychology, 53, *1956, 100–107. Copyright 1956 by the American Psychological Association and reproduced by permission.*

In the present investigation, we are interested in two kinds of such information: (*a*) information about *how much* the person is accepted and (*b*) information about *how stable* the acceptance evaluations are. Either item would be expected to influence insecurity. Because of practical limitations, it was not possible to carry out a factorial design permitting evaluation of the separate effects and interaction of these two variables. It was decided that an investigation of their joint effects would provide a better initial test of the fruitfulness of our analysis than a study of either variable alone. Throughout the report, the label "acceptance" applies to both these components.

The hypothesis we propose to test is: Among persons who attach equal importance to their membership in a group, those who receive information that they are only minimally accepted by their colleagues and that this evaluation is subject to change, possibly becoming worse, conform more than persons who receive information that they are highly accepted and that this situation is stable.

A similar hypothesis was tested by Kelley and Shapiro (5) who found it supported by correlational evidence that nonconformity was associated with high actual popularity or acceptance. But the hypothesis was not supported by the experimental manipulations of fictitious information about acceptance. It was suggested that this relationship was obscured because valuation of membership was not held constant. They found that information that one is poorly accepted affects not only his feelings of acceptance but also his subsequent valuation of the group. As our analysis suggests, a decline in valuation should decrease the "approach" motives which prompt conformity (e.g., desire to aid the group) thus offsetting any increase in other conformity-prompting motives resulting from the insecurity derived from feeling poorly accepted.

The present experiment was designed to avoid this obscuring effect in two ways: (*a*) It was attempted, with partial success, to keep valuation uniform by motivating all *S*s so highly to participate in the group that their valuation of membership would remain constantly high throughout the experiment. (*b*) Several degrees of acceptance were introduced, instead of two, with the expectation that even if valuation varied significantly between the extreme conditions of acceptance, it might remain uniform between more similar conditions, particularly with the conditions of relatively high acceptance. In this case the hypothesis could still be tested by comparing the conformity among persons in those degrees of acceptance for which valuation remained relatively uniform.

METHOD

Subjects. One hundred and three volunteers from the Yale freshman class met in 18 five- and six-man groups. Members of each group had no prior acquaintance with one another.

Incentives to motivate S*s to value and participate in their group, and instructions about possible rejection.* At the outset, each *S* agreed to work with his group in a contest against the other experimental groups. A cash prize and prestigeful recognition were offered as awards for the group best in efficiency, smoothness of working together, and soundness of decisions. These instructions carried the strong implication that unanimity in group decisions was highly desirable.

It was then announced that to guarantee an effectively working group, members would have the option of eliminating from their group any person who appeared detrimental to its success. For this purpose, subsequent tasks were to be interrupted periodically while each member anonymously rated each other one on this question:

How desirable is it that this person be kept in the group?

_____extremely desirable

_____very desirable

_____somewhat desirable

_____not very desirable, but he should be kept in

_____he should be rejected from the group

It was made to appear likely that some Ss would receive low ratings and that this would be unpleasant and penalizing for them: they would have to undergo the embarrassment of defending themselves in an open discussion of whether they should be rejected; rejection would carry the implication that the person was inadequate in his "social adaptability." (While the ratings were actually collected during the subsequent period, no S was ever discussed for rejection.)

Introduction of "delinquent gangs" problem and achievement of unanimous decision; interruptions to obtain ratings of others. In each group, an initial discussion concerned the relative worthiness of two gangs of juvenile delinquents, described in detailed simulated court records. A difference in the records insured that the same gang would be judged better in all groups, but this difference was slight enough that the decision could emerge only after considerable discussion. To heighten the tendency to conformity, the problem was described as being much like a jury's in that solution required the agreement of all. During the discussion, an observer kept a tally of each man's participation and whether his comments were for or against the gang ultimately favored by the group.

After general agreement was reached in free discussion, the norm was crystallized and registered by having the group rate the two gangs on several scales such that one gang was assigned labels such as "very deserving" and "fundamentally good"; and the other gang was characterized as "vicious," "malicious," etc. During this process E refused to record any rating until it was concurred in by every member. After this public agreement, Ss privately rated the gangs on different scales, to provide a measure of their initial acceptance of the group's characterization of the two gangs.

The discussion of the gangs was interrupted three times to permit the members to rate one another as to the desirability of their remaining in the group. Each time, E quickly thumbed through the ratings, pretended that no S had received low enough ratings to warrant discussing his possible rejection, and "discarded" the ratings into a wastebasket.

Introduction of different conditions of acceptance. At the end of the "gangs" discussion, E suggested a rest period. While Ss were relaxing, he casually inquired whether they'd be interested in seeing how they had been rated. Before anyone could object, *E* retrieved the slips from the wastebasket and distributed them. In this manner, each *S* was allowed to see privately what he thought to be the ratings made of him by the other members. These were in fact fictitious ratings prepared in advance and substituted for the originals in the wastebasket. So that *S*s would similarly interpret these ratings, *E* announced that he had noticed the average to be around "very desirable." In each group, one person found his ratings to be mostly higher than this average (*high* condition); two received ratings mostly at this average (*average* condition); two had ratings slightly below average (*low* condition); and one received ratings well below (*very low* condition). (In 5-man groups, only one of the intermediate conditions was represented by two persons.) Information about the probable stability of the ratings was provided by *E*'s statement, as though from experience with ratings in other groups, that the higher the rating the less likely it was to change; that low ratings were quite likely to change, possibly becoming higher or *even lower*. It was intended that as a result of this information, a person in the *high* condition would feel highly accepted, *and* that this was a stable situation. At the other extreme, a person in the *very low* condition was supposed to feel very little acceptance, *and* that his colleagues' evaluations might change, even becoming worse.

Before each session, the four conditions of acceptance were randomly assigned to positions around the discussion table. The 103 *S*s were distributed among the conditions as follows: 18 in *high*, 33 in *average*, 34 in *low*, and 18 in *very low*. The intermediate conditions were assigned more *S*s because greater variability of behavior was anticipated in them.

Additional information about the gangs, private judgments, and public discussion. After the fictitious ratings had been introduced and interpreted, the group proceeded to the second phase of the "gangs" problem. The purpose of this phase was to introduce pressure to deviate from the group consensus about the gangs and to determine each person's subsequent adherence to the norm, as indicated in his further private ratings of the gangs and in his opinions expressed in open discussion.

The pressure to deviate consisted of information suggesting that the unpreferred gang was superior to the previous evaluation, hinting at mitigating circumstances and desirable traits not clearly brought out in the original records. The *S*s privately evaluated the additional information by checking agreement or disagreement with evaluative statements that accompanied it. The tendency to discredit or "explain away" the new information was assumed to represent conformity with the group's original norm (these scores are reported as Gang Index 1). The *S*s also made additional ratings of the gangs after reading this information, one set anonymously and one set supposedly for public comparison (Gang Indices 2 and 3 respectively). To obtain an indication of each *S*'s speed of responding to the contradictory information, the observer noted the order in which *S*s finished making their evaluations and ratings.

Following the ratings, the group openly discussed the gangs for a short period during which were made observations comparable to those made during the initial discussion of the gangs.

Administration of number-judgment problem. A second situation for assessing conformity was next introduced, using a task requiring simple comparative judgments of numerosity—judging which of two squares contained more dots, the same problem used by Kelley and Shapiro (5). The problem was presented to *S*s working privately, in a series of eleven pairs of squares of decreasing difficulty, in which the correct answer was the same for the entire series. The *S*s were to share ideas and try to improve their group score by exchanging written messages between successive judgments. In fact, their messages were not delivered, but were intercepted and replaced by a standard set of messages which led each *S* to believe that all the other members of his group had decided that a given square, *A*, was the correct answer for the series. To heighten the pressure to conform to this consensus, the rule was imposed that the group would score points on any one of the eleven successive judgments only when the group was unanimously correct.

Pressure to deviate from the consensus was introduced by having the later pairs in the series provide increasingly clear evidence that the consensus was in error, that square *B* was the correct answer.

On each pair, *S* reported his "private opinion" (and degree of confidence in it) and also a "public vote" to be tallied toward the group score. These were summed over the last ten judgments (the ones made following receipt of messages indicating the group consensus), yielding Dot Index 1 for the private opinions (weighted by confidence) and Dot Index 2 for the public votes. It will be noted that these conformity indices may reflect two aspects of conformity: (*a*) initial acceptance of the apparent consensus and (*b*) continued adherence to it in the face of the contradictory evidence. Actually, there is little variability in conformity on the early judgments (the general level being high), so these indices reflect primarily the second aspect.

Subsequent measures. (*a*) The *S*s' perceptions of experimental conditions of acceptance were measured by a direct question immediately after they saw the ratings and at the end of the experiment, by recall of the ratings they had received. (*b*) Valuation of membership in the group: Immediately after receiving the ratings and also at the end of the experiment, *S*s answered short questionnaires containing items measuring their positive motivation to remain in their particular group, e.g., desire to be invited to further meetings, liking to work with the other members. (*c*) The *S*s' interpretations of conditions of acceptance: On a questionnaire given several months after the experiment, *S*s indicated how likely they considered it to be that they might be rejected, and the freedom they felt about expressing opinions contrary to the group's judgment.

Termination of experimental session. At the end of each session, the purpose and procedures of the experiment were disclosed and the *S*s were told that the ratings they had seen were fictitious. These disclosures were greeted with laughter, expressions of relief, and even a certain amount of disbelief. At no time did any *S* indicate that he had clearly doubted the genuineness of the ratings he had seen. Special care was taken to reinvolve as active and obviously accepted group members those *S*s who had been in the conditions of *low* and *very low* acceptance. The *S*s were requested to maintain secrecy during the remainder of the weeks scheduled for the experiment. Their excellent cooperation in this provides one of several indications of the favorable attitudes with which they left the experiment.

RESULTS

Direct Effects of Experimental Conditions

Perceived acceptance in group. The fictitious ratings clearly produced the intended differences among the experimental conditions in amount of perceived acceptance. The question, "From the point of view of the group, how desirable is it that you, yourself, be kept in?" ("extremely desirable" scored as 5 and "I should be rejected from the group" scored as 1), yielded average scores of 4.7, 3.8, 3.3, and 2.9, respectively for the *high, average, low,* and *very low* conditions. Analysis of variance reveals that the between-condition variance is significant at beyond the .001 level of confidence. Furthermore, at the end of the experiment, Ss were able to recall their ratings accurately. The recalled ratings did not differ significantly from those actually received.

Perceived likelihood of being rejected. Several questions dealing with perceived likelihood of being asked to leave the group and with preoccupation about this possibility serve largely to differentiate the *very low* condition from the other three, the *very low* Ss viewing rejection as more likely. The *very low's* differ significantly ($p < .01$) from each of the other conditions which do not differ significantly among themselves. These questions were asked only in the questionnaire given some months after the experiment so the results must be viewed with some reservations.

Valuation of membership. The efforts to keep all Ss highly attracted to the group were only partially successful. The *high* and *average* conditions showed the highest and approximately equal levels of attraction while the levels for the *low* and *very low* conditions were markedly lower, especially the latter. This effect was the same whether measured immediately after the ratings were distributed or at the end of the experiment. The total valuation scores yielded a between-condition variance which is significant at beyond the .001 level of confidence. Table 1 indicates the different valuation scores and the statistical significance of the differences between adjacent conditions.

Table 1 VALUATION OF GROUP MEMBERSHIP BY FOUR EXPERIMENTAL
CONDITIONS OF ACCEPTANCE

CONDITION OF ACCEPTANCE	HIGH	AVERAGE	LOW	VERY LOW
Average valuation of membership in group	40	39.5	37	35.5
Significance of difference between adjacent conditions	$p > .50$	$p < .0001$		$p < .0001$

Because valuation of membership was kept uniform only for *high* and *average* conditions, major interest in the subsequent results will be in comparisons of these two conditions. In these, we may expect there to be little interaction of valuation with our two main variables, acceptance and conformity.

Effects on Participation

The *S*s in the *very low* condition reduced their participation in the discussion of the delinquent gangs by about 50 per cent after seeing the ratings ($p < .01$ for the change from the prior amount of participation). In contrast, *average* acceptance tended to result in increased participation, the difference between before and after being significant at the .09 level of confidence. The amount of participation after the ratings were received, expressed as a percentage of the amount of prior participation, is as follows: 93 per cent, 131 per cent, 118 per cent, and 56 per cent, respectively for *high, average, low,* and *very low.*

Effects on Conformity

Conformity in responding to questionnaires. Average values of the conformity indices derived from the questionnaires used with the two tasks are presented in Table 2, high positive scores indicating high conformity, negative scores low conformity. The gang-judgment indices were adjusted to take account of individual differences in initial conformity to the group decisions and intergroup differences in conformity behavior.[1] The three separate gang indices were summed to give an over-all gang-judgment score. Also the five different measures were combined into an over-all conformity score by counting for each *S* the number of his scores on the five measures which were above the average of his experimental group. The average of these numbers for each experimental condition is presented in the last line of Table 2. Because the theoretical interest centers on the *high* and *average* conditions by virtue of their having the highest and approximately equal levels of valuation of membership, *p* values are given in Table 2 for differences between them. Since the two low conditions show the same tendency to be lower than the *average, p* values are also presented for the differences between their combined mean and that of the *average.*

[1] The scores on initial acceptance of the group decisions on the gangs were obtained before the experimental manipulations of acceptance and, as might be expected, an analysis of them reveals no differences approaching significance among the *S*s who later found themselves in the different conditions. In order to eliminate these initial individual differences from the measures of subsequent conformity, each *S*'s score on initial acceptance was subtracted from each of the three later measures of opinion. Analysis of variance of each of these difference scores showed that the 18 experimental groups differed significantly in mean level of conformity and also in variability. These effects presumably reflect slightly different definitions of the norm and differing pressures to conform which developed during different experimental sessions. To eliminate these differences, on each measure of the gang judgment each *S* was given a standard score representing the amount of his conformity with reference to the mean and standard deviation of his particular experimental group. As noted in the text, the dot-judgment scores, based only on behavior occurring after the experimental manipulations, reflect both initial acceptance of the norms and resistance to contrary evidence, though largely the latter. It was not necessary to transform them to standard scores because they did not vary significantly among experimental sessions with regard either to means or variances.

Table 2 AVERAGE CONFORMITY SCORES FOR THE FOUR EXPERIMENTAL
CONDITIONS OF ACCEPTANCE*

CONFORMITY INDEX	EXPERIMENTAL CONDITIONS OF ACCEPTANCE				p VALUES FOR	
	HIGH	AVER-AGE	LOW	VERY LOW	HIGH VS. AVER-AGE	AVERAGE VS. LOW AND VERY LOW
Gang judgments:						
1	−.22	.07	.10	−.09		
2	−.41	.32	−.10	.09	<.02	.10
3	−.31	.20	−.07	.04	<.10	
Over-all gang	−.92	.57	−.05	.02	<.05	
Dot judgments:						
1	39.0	43.4	33.2	36.4		.02
2	7.7	8.2	7.2	6.7		<.05
Over-all Conformity	2.5	3.2	2.5	2.6	.06	<.05

* *Positive values indicate high conformity; negative values, low conformity. The significance of the difference between conditions on the over-all conformity index was tested with chi square, dividing those who were above their group mean on a majority of the five indices from the remainder. A t test was used to test the significance of the other differences noted.*

In general, Ss receiving ratings of *average* acceptability tended to show more conformity behavior than did Ss receiving ratings of *high* acceptability. The results with *low* and *very low* conditions are less uniform, possibly for reasons connected with their rather low valuation of membership. They showed less conformity than the *average* and more than the *high* condition on gang judgments, and less than either of the other two on dot judgments.

The three indices of conformity on gang judgments were found to be significantly intercorrelated, as were the two indices on dot judgments. Significant correlations between gang and dot measures were found only for the *high* and *average* conditions and these had values of around .50. Despite this low degree of consistency between the two types of conformity behavior, Table 2 shows that the difference in conformity between *high* and *average* conditions of acceptance is consistent over the two somewhat different tasks.

A less direct indication of conformity gives results supporting those of Table 2. An observer noted the order in which the Ss at each session completed the task of evaluating the additional information that suggested that the group's decision on the gangs was inaccurate. It might be assumed that persons oriented most strongly toward conforming would give less attention to the new information and make quick judgments simply on the basis of the previously established norm; and that persons less motivated to conform would give more conscientious attention to the information and hence complete the task more slowly. The average rank order of finishing the task is as follows: 4.2, 2.7, 3.8, and 3.1, for *high, average, low,* and *very low,* respectively. The condition of *average* acceptance was fastest, indicating, on the basis of the above assumptions, most conformity; the *high* condition was slowest indicating least conformity. The difference between these two is significant at the .05 level of confidence, using a chi-square analysis that divided Ss into slowest and fastest halves.

Conformity in open discussion. In Table 2, the measures intended to tap private opinions (Gang Index 1 and 2; Dot Index 1) and those supposed to reflect public expression (Gang Index 3 and Dot Index 2) reveal essentially similar trends over the four conditions of acceptance. However, as compared with the quasi-public nature of the latter measures, analysis of actual public expressions of opinion shows a somewhat different pattern of conformity from that noted in Table 2. (This finding suggests that the questionnaire results mainly reflect private conformity.) In the discussion of the gangs after the additional information had been read, there was a general decrease in the proportion of comments that expressed conformity to the group's earlier preference for one gang over the other. (Before the information, 88 per cent of the comments involving opinion were favorable to the group norm; afterward, only 49 per cent were so.) This decrease was less for the *very low* condition than for the others; i.e., in their actual public remarks, the *very lows* conformed more closely to the original norm than any of the other conditions. The scores[2] for the *high, average, low,* and *very low* conditions, respectively, were: −.55, −.47, −.52, and −.23, with the greater negative number indicating the greater deviation from the norm. Chi-square analysis, dividing *S*s at the over-all median into high and low changers, shows that the difference between *very low* and the other conditions taken together is significant at the .08 level. The difference between any other condition and the rest does not approach significance.

This result receives partial confirmation from responses to a question about how free the *S* would have felt to express an opinion contrary to the group opinion. *Very low S*s report more hesitancy in this respect than do *High S*s ($p = .07$) and the other conditions report intermediate degrees.

DISCUSSION

To simplify the reader's task of assimilating the results and trends reported above, they are summarized verbally in Table 3. We now consider the interpretation of these findings. In several respects, they are consistent with the hypothesized relationship between acceptance and conformity. However, the total pattern of results suggests that the relationship depends on more complex intervening variables than had been anticipated.

One set of data consistent with the hypothesis is provided by the comparison of the *high* and *average* conditions. Since the relation between acceptance and conformity is likely to be obscured if valuation varies, as previously discussed, the hypothesis can be clearly tested only by comparing conditions having fairly similar levels of valuation—in this experiment, the *high* and *average* conditions. Between these two, higher conformity behavior was exhibited by the condition of lower and less stable acceptance. The available evidence does not indicate, however, any difference between *high* and *average S*s in feelings of insecurity about their membership. If these groups actually do not differ in this respect, the higher conformity of the *average S*s must be explained on some other basis

[2] The score for each *S* represents the proportion of his total remarks in the later discussion which were pronorm, minus the proportion of his total remarks in the earlier discussion which were pronorm, plus the proportion of antinorm remarks in the earlier discussion, minus the proportion of antinorm remarks in the later discussion.

Table 3 DIGEST OF THE RESULTS OF THE FOUR EXPERIMENTAL
CONDITIONS OF ACCEPTANCE

VARIABLE	EXPERIMENTAL CONDITION OF ACCEPTANCE			
	HIGH	AVERAGE	LOW	VERY LOW
Perceived acceptance	High	Average	Low	Very Low
Perceived likelihood of being rejected				Higher than any other condition
Valuation of membership	Moderate	Moderate	Low	Very Low
Participation in group discussion		Highest		Lowest
Speed of reacting to counternorm information		Faster than any other condition		
Conformity in questionnaire responses (private?)	Low	High	Low	Low
Conformity in public statements				Higher than any other condition
Felt freedom to express deviant opinion	Highest			Lowest

than the one underlying our hypothesis: that they would be more motivated to avoid rejection. Their total pattern of behavior—high conformity on the questionnaires, rapid reactions to counternorm information, and heightened participation in the discussion after learning of their acceptance—is perhaps more suggestive of a desire to improve their social standing. The *S* in the *average* condition places considerable value upon the group, but at the same time, is not completely accepted in it. Since *E*'s comments indicate there is some possibility that his acceptance status may change, we might expect him to try to attain complete acceptance. Eager participation and uncritical conformity to the norms would presumably facilitate this improvement in status. That this conformity extends even to the expression of private opinions on the questionnaire is understandable if we consider that there may be a general tendency for upward-mobility-oriented persons to identify with and take over the values of higher status individuals (7).

The behavior exhibited by the *very lows* is much more consistent with our initial notion of anxiety-motivated conformity. In general, and in accord with prior findings (4, 5), group membership loses its attractiveness for persons little valued by their colleagues.[3] Along with this loss goes a decline in tendency to

---

[3] This raises interesting theoretical questions which cannot be discussed here: Is acceptance by others one of the prerequisites for desiring membership in a group? Why does valuation not decline with the change from *high* to *average* conditions, but drops sharply for the lower degrees of acceptance? Is this a level-of-aspiration effect, in which the motivation to stay in the group declines only as the possibility of success in this effort drops below some critical value?

accept the group's norm, at least in quasi-private settings. In the extreme case, however, where acceptance is so low that actual rejection is presumably an imminent possibility, anxiety about rejection is especially high and the result seems to be a pattern of guarded public behavior, i.e., the *very lows* withdrew from open participation in the discussion and showed the highest amount of conformity in the opinions they did publicly voice. Avoidance of rejection, which is presumably motivated by penalties particularly attached to rejection (embarrassment, suffering failure in front of the *E*), is of course a variable different from the positive motivation to participate in the group; so anxiety over rejection may have been high for the *very lows*, even though they had little positive motivation to stay in the group. (The questionnaire some months after the experiment indicated that the desire to be kept in the group and not be rejected had been as high for the *very lows* as for the other conditions, while at the same time, their estimate of the likelihood of this event had been higher.) Their public conformity, then, may reflect a relatively high motivation to avoid rejection. That they exhibit a high public conformity but little private acceptance is consistent with Festinger's hypothesis that this particular pattern of conformity results when the attractiveness of group membership is low, but people are constrained to stay in the group by external threats or barriers against leaving (2).

In brief, our results suggest two processes linking conditions of acceptance to conformity. For persons who value a group, are less than completely accepted in it, but have some possibility of achieving complete acceptance, conformity facilitates such a gain in acceptance. Their conformity is unquestioning and extends to private opinions as well as to public behavior. On the other hand, persons who are on the brink of unwelcome rejection manifest conformity only at the public level, presumably as a means of forestalling such rejection.

The major variable in this experiment—security and degree of acceptance—is, from several points of view, an aspect of what is commonly called "status." We might therefore expect our results to shed some light on the problem of the relationship between status and conformity. In general, we doubt that this relationship is ever a simple one. Our results and interpretations suggest that to predict conformity from status, clarity is first needed as to the conditions under which conformity is to be observed, whether they involve surveillance by other members or relative privacy. Then, it must be asked whether the observed differences in status are associated with differences in (*a*) valuation of membership, (*b*) security in membership, and (*c*) motivation to improve one's acceptance. Under some conditions, as when low status is associated with relatively high insecurity about membership, it seems likely that status is inversely related to public conformity. But if there is a marked difference between high and low status persons in their valuation of membership, as a result of greater privileges and satisfactions being associated with higher status, status and conformity may be correlated positively.

Undoubtedly, a number of other factors also affect this relationship. For example, it is easy to imagine instances where special motives directed toward conformity would be operative for high status persons, but not for low status members. One such case would be that where the opinions of a high status member have carried inordinate weight in the setting of group standards so that they happen to coincide with his private preferences. What appears as conformity in his behavior may actually be motivated by private considerations that preceded the acceptance of his behavior as the norm. Another instance may be when special conformity demands are made of high status persons, for example, because of the special symbolic value their conformity may possess.

These considerations indicate that many factors affect the relation between status and conformity. In some instances, the relationship may be direct; in other, inverse; and in still others, perhaps, nonexistent. We believe the specific situations and results will be most intelligible when analyzed in terms of factors such as those suggested above.

SUMMARY

In experimental groups of Ss, two different norms were developed: one concerning a social value judgment; the other, a simple perceptual judgment. The Ss were experimentally made to feel different degrees of being accepted by the other members and were then given opportunities and incentives to deviate from the norms. Subsequent conformity, participation, and attitudes toward the group were studied in relation to the different conditions of acceptance.

The results point to two contrasting patterns of conformity evoked by different conditions of acceptance. The first appears to consist of a high degree of genuine adherence to the norms, as indicated by unquestioning conformity extending even to conditions of privacy, and a higher-than-average motivation to participate in group discussion. This pattern appeared for the experimental condition in which subjects enjoyed somewhat less than complete acceptance but probably saw the possibility of gaining this status. It is interpreted as based on strong positive attachment to the group and motivation to improve one's status therein.

The second pattern is marked by high conformity only under public conditions. It occurred for the experimental condition of lowest acceptance, in which Ss saw total rejection as being a likely possibility. The interpretation is made that although Ss in this condition have lost much of their positive motivation to conform to group standards (indicated by their very low valuation of membership and reflected in their low private conformity), they may nevertheless be concerned about the negative consequences accompanying rejection (at least, under the conditions represented in this experiment). Public conformity is seen as a way of forestalling this unpleasant eventuality.

REFERENCES

1. Back, K. W. Influence through social communication. *J. abnorm. soc. Psychol.*, 1951, *46*, 9–23.

2. Festinger, L. An analysis of compliant behavior. In M. Sherif and M. O. Wilson (Eds.), *Group relations at the crossroads*. New York: Harper, 1953. Pp. 232–55.

3. Festinger, L., Schachter, S., & Back, K. *Social pressures in informal groups*. New York: Harper, 1950.

4. Jackson, J. Analysis of interpersonal relations in a formal organization. Unpublished doctor's dissertation, Univer. of Michigan, 1952. Reported in D. P. Cartwright and A. F. Zander (Eds.), *Group dynamics.* Evanston: Row, Peterson, 1953. P. 424.

5. Kelley, H. H., & Shapiro, M. M. An experiment on conformity to group norms where conformity is detrimental to group achievement. *Amer. sociol. Rev.,* 1954, *19,* 667–77.

6. Kelley, H. H., & Volkart, E. H. The resistance to change of group-anchored attitudes. *Amer. sociol. Rev.,* 1952, *17,* 453–65.

7. Lewin, K. Self-hatred among Jews. In *Resolving social conflicts.* New York: Harper, 1948. Pp. 186–200.

Ethnocentrism and the Acceptance of Negro Support in a Group Pressure Situation

MILTON MALOF AND ALBERT J. LOTT

This study was designed to determine whether or not a highly prejudiced person would accept the support of a Negro in a group pressure situation that produces conflict and self-doubt. Persons high and low in prejudice, as measured by the California E Scale, were placed in group situations in which the effects of prejudice on conformity, and on the acceptance of social support from Negro and white partners could be studied. Use was made of the Asch (1951) line judging procedure, which is interpreted as setting up contradictory pressures between an individual's perceptual experience and social consensus. Each experimental group was composed of one critical subject who was white and five confederates, of whom four were white and one was Negro. After being confronted for some time with a contrary majority of five, the critical subject was given support either by the Negro or a white confederate.

The original conception of ethnocentric ideology (Adorno, Frenkel-Brunswik, Levinson, & Sanford, 1950) leads to the prediction that highly prejudiced individuals will manifest more conformity behavior than low prejudiced individuals. The highly ethnocentric person is characterized as one who idealizes and is submissive to ingroup standards. In addition, the E Scale contains some acquiescence variance as well as content variance (Chapman & Campbell, 1959), and it is therefore further expected that a person scoring high on the E Scale will be more susceptible to influence attempts than one scoring low. Since Asch (1951) has found that the amount of yielding to an objectively incorrect majority decreases when the minority subject is supported in his judgments by one group

Reprinted from Journal of Abnormal and Social Psychology, 65, *1962, 254–58. Copyright 1962 by the American Psychological Association and reproduced by permission.*

member, lessened conformity may also, then, be expected of a highly ethnocentric subject, but only when he is joined by a white partner and not by a
Negro. The ethnocentric individual, with his strong negative, stereotyped views
of Negroes, should reject the support of a Negro group member and show no
significant decrease in conformity responses.

The hypotheses tested in the present investigation are derived from the
general position of Adorno et al. (1950) but also provide a test of another set of
propositions. The work of Rokeach (1960) suggests that racial prejudice is a
special case of a more general belief prejudice. In other words, people do not
reject other people primarily on the basis of race or ethnic categories, but rather
"in terms of how congruent or incongruent others' belief systems are" to their
own. By systematically pitting belief characteristics of people against their
ethnic characteristics, Rokeach has shown that preference or rejection of others,
by southerners as well as northerners, is influenced more by belief similarity and
dissimilarity than by race. Applying these findings to the present problem,
highly prejudiced persons would not be expected to differ from low prejudiced
persons in accepting social support from a Negro as readily as from a white
partner. If the Asch (1951) situation may be considered as one which violates a
critical subject's belief in the veridicality of his own perception of simple stimuli,
he should, according to Rokeach, accept the support of anyone who sees things
his way and the racial characteristics of the supporting person should be of
secondary importance.

A third approach which attempts to predict the behavior of prejudiced
individuals is that of Pettigrew (1961) who has emphasized the importance of
the situation in understanding interracial behavior and has suggested that, for
predictions in this area, the concept of social adjustment may be more useful
than personality variables. He maintains that most individuals will shift their
responses in an interracial situation to conform to the demands of that situation,
which include the norms of the community. The situation resistant, or defiant,
individual is the one who holds extreme racial attitudes and the one for whom
these attitudes are highly salient. Most persons, however, will be situation bound
and behave in accord with prevailing custom. It is difficult to derive explicit
predictions from the Pettigrew formulation with respect to the present experimental situation primarily because it is not clear whether the situation resistant
individual can be detected by high scores on the E Scale, or by means of depth
interviews, or whether he can only be identified when his behavior is consistent
over a number of different interracial situations.

The specific hypotheses tested in the present study, based on the personality
oriented (Adorno et al., 1950) approach to ethnocentrism, are as follows:

Hypothesis 1. When placed in a social pressure situation, highly prejudiced
persons will conform more than persons low in prejudice.

Hypothesis 2. If an individual low in prejudice is offered social support in such
a situation by one other member of the group, such support will be accepted as
readily from a white as from a Negro partner.

Hypothesis 3. An individual high in prejudice will accept support from a white
group member but will reject it from a Negro. Acceptance of support is defined

by a decrease in conformity to the inaccurate judgments of the majority, while rejection of support is defined by no change in such conformity behavior.

METHOD

Subjects

Sixty white males from classes in introductory psychology at the University of Kentucky served as critical subjects. In the experiment proper, each was a member of a six-person group formed for the purpose of the study. Forty-one white males from the same classes and six Negro males from other classes voluntarily aided the investigators by participating in the groups as confederates.

Procedure and Materials

A week or more prior to the experimental situation, the E Scale was adminis-tered to all introductory psychology students by laboratory assistants. The experimenter was not linked with this procedure in any way. A mean total ethnocentrism score and a mean Negro ethnocentrism score (based on the six Negro items only) were computed for each subject. Thirty subjects who were highly prejudiced, i.e., who had high general E scores and high Negro E scores were then selected. The mean item score[1] for these subjects, on both scales, ranged from 5.1 to 7.0, the maximum score possible. For this group as a whole, the mean E score was 5.04, the mean Negro E score was 5.54. Thirty other subjects, low in both general and Negro prejudice, were also selected. These subjects scored from 3.0 to 1.0, the lowest possible score, on both scales. Group means were 2.37 and 1.67 on the general E and Negro E scales, respectively.

Four experimental conditions, with 15 critical subjects in each, were: High E-Negro partner, High E-white partner, Low E-Negro partner, and Low E-white partner. In one condition, a Negro partner (confederate) broke away from the majority in the middle of the experiment and began announcing correct estimates of the line stimuli; in the second condition, the partner playing this role was one of the white confederates.

The experimental task, materials, and instructions were taken from Asch (1956). When a subject arrived at the place of the experiment, he found some or all of the confederates ostensibly waiting for the experiment to begin. When everyone was present, the experimenter asked the group to take seats at a table in the order that their names had been called. The experimenter explained that the seating order was randomized to insure that each person had an equal opportunity to sit in any seat. The critical subject always occupied the sixth seat. The "partner's" position was randomized among the second, third, fourth, and fifth seats. After the experimenter read the instructions, some confederates

---

[1] Six response categories were utilized which were scored 7, 6, 5, 3, 2, 1 according to whether a subject strongly agreed, moderately agreed, slightly agreed, slightly disagreed, moderately disagreed, or strongly disagreed, respectively. If an item was not answered it received a score of 4.

asked clarifying questions to enhance the impression that they were new to the situation. The partner was Negro or white depending upon the experimental condition.

When the session was over, the critical subject was interviewed. Five questions were asked, designed to determine whether or not the subject knew the situation was rigged and if he was aware of the presence of a "partner." All subjects said they were aware that one group member shared their judgments during the last part of the experiment. A replacement was obtained for one subject who detected the nature of the deception.

The measure of conformity utilized was simply the number of responses which a critical subject made, with or without a partner, which were incorrect, and either in agreement with the incorrect judgment made by the majority or a "compromise" judgment (choice of the intermediate line). All subjects made 18 line judgments without a partner and 18 with a partner. Twelve in each instance were critical trials where the unanimous majority gave an incorrect judgment. On the other 6 trials, which were interspersed among the critical trials, the majority gave correct judgments.

RESULTS

The range of conformity responses (raw scores) for the High E subjects, combining those in the Negro, and white, partner conditions, was from 0 to 12, while that for the Low E subjects, similarly combined, was 0 to 4. The maximum score possible was 12 since 12 trials were given without a partner and with incorrect majority judgments. These scores were analyzed by means of the median test (Siegel, 1956). The relevant data are given in Table 1. The resultant chi square was found to be 16.3 ($p < .001$), indicating that the High E subjects made significantly more conformity responses in the face of a unanimous majority than did Low E subjects, which confirms the first hypothesis.

Table 1 CONFORMITY RESPONSES OF CRITICAL SUBJECTS BEFORE OBTAINING A PARTNER'S SUPPORT

EXPERIMENTAL CONDITION	NUMBER OF SUBJECTS AT OR BELOW MEDIAN[a]	NUMBER OF SUBJECTS ABOVE MEDIAN	N
Low E	25	5	30
High E	9	21	30
	$x^2 = 16.3, p < .001$		
Low E-white partner	11	4	15
Low E-Negro partner	14	1	15
	Fisher's exact test, $p = .10$		
High E-white partner	5	10	15
High E-Negro partner	4	11	15
	Fisher's exact test, $p = .38$		

[a] *Median number of conformity responses for Low E and High E subjects combined = 1.0, for Low E subjects = 0, and for High E subjects = 3.0.*

Prior to testing the second and third hypotheses, relative to the acceptance of Negro and white partners by Low and High E subjects, a check was made to see whether the two Low E groups, and the two High E groups, had the same initial levels of conformity. Table 1 presents the conformity scores for the two groups within each of the ethnocentrism levels. Using Fisher's exact probability test (Siegel, 1956), with each distribution divided at the median (3.0 for the High E and 0 for the Low E groups), the probability that the two Low groups are different was found to be .10 (two-tailed) and that the two High groups are different, .38 (two-tailed). It is concluded, therefore, that between the two Low E groups and between the two High E groups there were no significant differences in conformity behavior prior to the entry of a partner into the situation.

The second hypothesis predicted that an individual low in prejudice would accept support from a Negro as readily as from a white partner. Fisher's exact probability test was utilized to compare the yielding scores of the Lows with white partners with the yielding scores of the Lows with Negro partners for the 12 critical trials on which correct judgments were made by a partner. The number of scores above and below the median made by subjects in each of the two groups is given in Table 2. The difference was found not to be significant ($p = .46$), thus supporting the hypothesis.

Table 2 CONFORMITY RESPONSES OF CRITICAL SUBJECTS AFTER OBTAINING A PARTNER'S SUPPORT

EXPERIMENTAL CONDITION	NUMBER OF SUBJECTS AT OR BELOW MEDIAN[a]	NUMBER OF SUBJECTS ABOVE MEDIAN	N
Low E-white partner	10	5	15
Low E-Negro partner	12	3	15
	Fisher's exact test, $p = .46$		
High E-white partner	12	3	15
High E-Negro partner	7	8	15
	Fisher's exact test, $p = .10$		

[a] *Median number of conformity responses for Low E subjects = 0; that for High E subjects = 0.*

The third hypothesis, that a highly prejudiced subject will accept support from a white partner, but reject it from a Negro was also tested by use of the exact probability test. Dividing the conformity score distribution at the median, the High E subjects who were offered support by a white partner were compared with the High E subjects who were offered support by a Negro partner. These data are shown in Table 2. Since the probability that the scores of these two groups were different was found to be .10, the null hypothesis cannot be rejected. This finding is contrary to our prediction. It can be seen from Table 2, however, that, although the difference was not a significant one, there were more High E subjects who made zero conformity responses with a white partner than with a Negro partner. Two additional analyses were therefore performed. For both of the High E groups conformity behavior in the condition of no partner was compared with that in the condition of partner present, by means of the Wilcoxon matched-pairs signed-ranks test (Siegel, 1956). In both cases the obtained T was equal to 0 ($p < .01$, two-tailed) indicating that there was a significant drop in number of conformity responses for the High E subjects as they went from a situation where they were opposed by a unanimous majority to one where they were supported by one other member of the group, regardless of his race. The number of white partner and Negro partner subjects who decreased, increased, or made the same number of conformity responses with a partner as they had without one are shown in Table 3.

Table 3 CHANGE IN CONFORMITY BEHAVIOR OF HIGH E SUBJECTS FROM THE CONDITION OF NO PARTNER TO THE CONDITION OF PARTNER PRESENT

EXPERIMENTAL CONDITION	NUMBER OF SUBJECTS WHO CONFORMED LESS WITH PARTNER PRESENT	NUMBER OF SUBJECTS WHO CONFORMED MORE WITH PARTNER PRESENT	NUMBER OF SUBJECTS WHO DID NOT CHANGE WITH PARTNER PRESENT	N
High E-white partner	13	0	2	15
High E-Negro partner	10	0	5	15

DISCUSSION

The greater amount of conformity in a group pressure situation which was found true of high ethnocentric as compared with low ethnocentric subjects supports our first hypothesis and the basic notion that the ethnocentric person will obey ingroup "requirements" and submit to ingroup standards. That he appears to perceive even a contrived ingroup as superior in judgment ability and worthy of following is an indication of the extent to which he will idealize and be influenced by ingroup pressures generally. The greater amount of conformity of the high ethnocentric person may also be interpreted as a behavioral indication of an acquiescence factor that appears to be associated with the measurement of ethnocentrism.

The low prejudiced subjects behaved as was expected, both in conforming less than high prejudiced subjects initially when faced with an incorrect unanimous majority, and then in reducing this conformity when joined by either a white or Negro partner. The latter finding supports Hypothesis 2.

The highly prejudiced subjects also accepted the support of both Negro and white partners. This finding contradicts the third hypothesis and thus tends to question the adequacy of the Adorno et al. (1950) framework from which the prediction stemmed. The results obtained on the High E subjects fit more neatly into the Rokeach (1960) approach to interracial behavior in which belief congruence is regarded as a more important determiner of the acceptance of others than racial or ethnic characteristics. Thus highly prejudiced subjects would have been expected to accept the support of a Negro partner, as they did, when the Negro provided agreement for perceptual judgments.

The clear, but nonsignificant, trend in the direction of greater acceptance of the white partner than the Negro partner by the highly prejudiced subjects, is consistent with the Adorno et al. (1950) approach but can also be explained by Rokeach (1960). He found that, when belief is held constant, white subjects tend to prefer their own racial group to the Negro group. Although belief similarity is the most important criterion of acceptance, when both a Negro and a white person agree with a white individual there is a clear tendency for the white person to be accepted more than the Negro.

What implications do the results of the present study have for Pettigrew's (1961) position? They suggest that a high score on the E Scale will not identify a prejudiced person who is situation resistant. What is needed is a set of operations by means of which such an individual may be detected other than by observing his behavior in interracial situations. It is possible that there are few persons who will overtly exhibit prejudice in the face of contrary situational pressures and that these are persons whose prejudice is part of a more general pathology.

The present investigation supports the frequently noted phenomenon that prediction of behavior from elicited verbal attitudes will not be successful without some consideration of the situation in which the behavior will take place. Verbal attitudes may be good predictors of other elicited verbal attitudes as has been shown, for example, by Greenberg (1961), who found a significant positive correlation between the E Scale and an integration attitude scale. However, when a behavioral expression of an attitude is called for, the situational characteristics seem to assume great importance in determining how the attitude will, in fact, be expressed. The present study indicates that known prejudicial attitudes do not provide adequate grounds for making accurate behavioral predictions in certain interracial situations.

SUMMARY

Highly prejudiced individuals and other individuals low in prejudice, as measured by the California E Scale, served as critical subjects in an experiment utilizing the Asch (1951) line judging task. After being opposed by a unanimous majority for some time, subjects received support of either a Negro or white confederate. Predictions, based on the Adorno et al. (1950) conception of ethnocentric ideology, were that: (a) when faced with an opposed unanimous majority, high ethnocentric subjects would manifest more conformity behavior than low E subjects; (b) low E subjects would accept support equally from a white or Negro confederate; (c) high E subjects would accept support from a white but not a Negro confederate.

The first two predictions were confirmed but high ethnocentric subjects were also found to accept significant amounts of support from Negro, as well as white, confederates. Acceptance of support is defined as a decrease in conformity responses with the partner present.

REFERENCES

Adorno, T. W., Frenkel-Brunswik, Else, Levinson, D. J., & Sanford, R. N. *The authoritarian personality*. New York: Harper, 1950.

Asch, S.   Effects of group pressure upon the modification and distortion of judgment. In H. Guetzkow (Ed.), *Groups, leadership and men.* Pittsburgh: Carnegie Press, 1951. Pp. 177–90. (Also in D. Cartwright & A. Zander (Eds.), *Group dynamics: Research and theory.* Evanston, Ill.: Row, Peterson, 1953, Pp. 151–62.

Asch, S.   Studies of independence and conformity. *Psychol. Monogr.,* 1956, *70* (9, Whole No. 416).

Chapman, L., & Campbell, D.   The effect of acquiescence response-set upon relationships among the F Scale, ethnocentrism, and intelligence. *Sociometry,* 1959, *22,* 153–61.

Greenberg, H.   The development of an integration attitude scale. *J. soc. Psychol.,* 1961, *54,* 103–9.

Pettigrew, T.   Social psychology and desegregation research. *Amer. Psychologist,* 1961, *16,* 105–12.

Rokeach, M.   *The open and closed mind.* New York: Basic Books, 1960.

Siegel, S.   *Nonparametric statistics for the behavioral sciences.* New York: McGraw-Hill, 1956.

8

ATTITUDE FORMATION
AND CHANGE—
THEORETICAL BACKGROUND

Reconciling Conflicting Results Derived from Experimental and Survey Studies of Attitude Change

CARL I. HOVLAND

Two quite different types of research design are characteristically used to study the modification of attitudes through communication. In the first type, the *experiment*, individuals are given a controlled exposure to a communication and the effects evaluated in terms of the amount of change in attitude or opinion produced. A base line is provided by means of a control group not exposed to the communication. The study of Gosnell (1927) on the influence of leaflets designed to get voters to the polls is a classic example of the controlled experiment.

In the alternative research design, the *sample survey*, information is secured through interviews or questionnaires both concerning the

Reprinted from The American Psychologist, 14, *1959, 8–17. Copyright 1959 by the American Psychological Association and reproduced by permission.*

336

respondent's exposure to various communications and his attitudes and opinions on various issues. Generalizations are then derived from the correlations obtained between reports of exposure and measurements of attitude. In a variant of this method, measurements of attitude and of exposure to communication are obtained during repeated interviews with the same individual over a period of weeks or months. This is the "panel method" extensively utilized in studying the impact of various mass media on political attitudes and on voting behavior (cf., e.g., Kendall & Lazarsfeld, 1950).

Generalizations derived from experimental and from correlational studies of communication effects are usually both reported in chapters on the effects of mass media and in other summaries of research on attitude, typically without much stress on the type of study from which the conclusion was derived. Close scrutiny of the results obtained from the two methods, however, suggests a marked difference in the picture of communication effects obtained from each. The object of my paper is to consider the conclusions derived from these two types of design, to suggest some of the factors responsible for the frequent divergence in results, and then to formulate principles aimed at reconciling some of the apparent conflicts.

DIVERGENCE

The picture of mass communication effects which emerges from correlational studies is one in which few individuals are seen as being affected by communications. One of the most thorough correlational studies of the effects of mass media on attitudes is that of Lazarsfeld, Berelson, and Gaudet published in *The People's Choice* (1944). In this report there is an extensive chapter devoted to the effects of various media, particularly radio, newspapers, and magazines. The authors conclude that few changes in attitudes were produced. They estimate that the political positions of only about 5% of their respondents were changed by the election campaign, and they are inclined to attribute even this small amount of change more to personal influence than to the mass media. A similar evaluation of mass media is made in the recent chapter in the *Handbook of Social Psychology* by Lipset and his collaborators (1954).

Research using experimental procedures, on the other hand, indicates the possibility of considerable modifiability of attitudes through exposure to communication. In both Klapper's survey (1949) and in my chapter in the *Handbook of Social Psychology* (Hovland, 1954) a number of experimental studies are discussed in which the opinions of a third to a half or more of the audience are changed.

The discrepancy between the results derived from these two methodologies raises some fascinating problems for analysis. This divergence in outcome appears to me to be largely attributable to two kinds of factors: one, the difference in research design itself; and, two the historical and traditional differences in general approach to evaluation characteristic of researchers using the experimental as contrasted with the correlational or survey method. I would like to discuss, first, the influence these factors have on the estimation of overall effects of communications and, then turn to other divergences in outcome characteristically found by the use of the experimental and survey methodology.

Undoubtedly the most critical and interesting variation in the research *design* involved in the two procedures is that resulting from differences in definition of exposure. In an experiment the audience on whom the effects are being evaluated is one which is fully exposed to the communication. On the other hand, in naturalistic situations with which surveys are typically concerned, the outstanding phenomenon is the limitation of the audience to those who *expose themselves* to the communication. Some of the individuals in a captive audience experiment would, of course, expose themselves in the course of natural events to a communication of the type studied; but many others would not. The group which does expose itself is usually a highly biased one, since most individuals "expose themselves most of the time to the kind of material with which they agree to begin with" (Lipset et al., 1954, p. 1158). Thus one reason for the difference in results between experiments and correlational studies is that experiments describe the effects of exposure on the whole range of individuals studied, some of whom are initially in favor of the position being advocated and some who are opposed, whereas surveys primarily describe the effects produced on those already in favor of the point of view advocated in the communication. The amount of change is thus, of course, much smaller in surveys. Lipset and his collaborators make this same evaluation, stating that:

As long as we test a program in the laboratory we always· find that it has great effect on the attitudes and interests of the experimental subjects. But when we put the program on as a regular broadcast, we then note that the people who are most influenced in the laboratory tests are those who, in a realistic situation, do not listen to the program. The controlled experiment always greatly overrates effects, as compared with those that really occur, because of the self-selection of audiences *(Lipset et al., 1954, p. 1158).*

Differences in the second category are not inherent in the design of the two alternatives, but are characteristic of the way researchers using the two methods typically proceed.

The first difference within this class is in the size of the communication unit typically studied. In the majority of survey studies the unit evaluated is an entire program of communication. For example, in studies of political behavior an attempt is made to assess the effects of all newspaper reading and television viewing on attitudes toward the major parties. In the typical experiment, on the other hand, the interest is usually in some particular variation in the content of the communications, and experimental evaluations much more frequently involve single communications. On this point results are thus not directly comparable.

Another characteristic difference between the two methods is in the time interval used in evaluation. In the typical experiment the time at which the effect is observed is usually rather soon after exposure to the communication. In the survey study, on the other hand, the time perspective is such that much more remote effects are usually evaluated. When effects decline with the passage of time, the net outcome will, of course, be that of accentuating the effect obtained in experimental studies as compared with those obtained in survey researches. Again it must be stressed that the difference is not inherent in the designs as such. Several experiments, including our own on the effects of motion pictures (Hovland, Lumsdaine, & Sheffield, 1949) and later studies on the "sleeper effect" (Hovland & Weiss, 1951; Kelman & Hovland, 1953), have studied retention over considerable periods of time.

Some of the difference in outcome may be attributable to the types of communicators characteristically used and to the motive-incentive conditions operative in the two situations. In experimental studies communications are frequently presented in a classroom situation. This may involve quite different types of factors from those operative in the more naturalistic communication situation with which the survey researchers are concerned. In the classroom there may be some implicit sponsorship of the communication by the teacher and the school administration. In the survey studies the communicators may often be remote individuals either unfamiliar to the recipients, or outgroupers clearly known to espouse a point of view opposed to that held by many members of the audience. Thus there may be real differences in communicator credibility in laboratory and survey researches. The net effect of the differences will typically be in the direction of increasing the likelihood of change in the experimental as compared with the survey study.

There is sometimes an additional situational difference. Communications of the type studied by survey researchers usually involve reaching the individual in his natural habitat, with consequent supplementary effects produced by discussion with friends and family. In the laboratory studies a classroom situation with low postcommunication interaction is more typically involved. Several studies, including one by Harold Kelley reported in our volume on *Communication and Persuasion* (Hovland, Janis, & Kelley, 1953), indicate that, when a communication is presented in a situation which makes group membership salient, the individual is typically more resistant to counternorm influence than when the communication is presented under conditions of low salience of group membership (cf. also, Katz & Lazarsfeld, 1955, pp. 48–133).

A difference which is almost wholly adventitious is in the types of populations utilized. In the survey design there is, typically, considerable emphasis on a random sample of the entire population. In the typical experiment, on the other hand, there is a consistent overrepresentation of high school students and college sophomores, primarily on the basis of their greater accessibility. But as Tolman has said: "college sophomores may not be people." Whether differences in the type of audience studied contribute to the differences in effect obtained with the two methods is not known.

Finally, there is an extremely important difference in the studies of the experimental and correlational variety with respect to the type of issue discussed in the communications. In the typical experiment we are interested in studying a set of factors or conditions which are expected on the basis of theory to influence the extent of effect of the communication. We usually deliberately try to find types of issues involving attitudes which are susceptible to modification through communication. Otherwise, we run the risk of no measurable effects, particularly with small-scale experiments. In the survey procedures, on the other hand, socially significant attitudes which are deeply rooted in prior experience and involve much personal commitment are typically involved. This is especially true in voting studies which have provided us with so many of our present results on social influence. I shall have considerably more to say about this problem a little later.

The differences so far discussed have primarily concerned the extent of overall effectiveness indicated by the two methods: why survey results typically show little modification of attitudes by communication while experiments indicate marked changes. Let me now turn to some of the other differences in generalizations derived from the two alternative designs. Let me take as the second main area of disparate results the research on the effect of varying distances between the position taken by the communicator and that held by the recipient of the communication. Here it is a matter of comparing changes for persons who at the outset closely agree with the communicator with those for others who are mildly or strongly in disagreement with him. In the naturalistic situation studied in surveys the typical procedure is to determine changes in opinion following reported exposure to communication for individuals differing from the communicator by varying amounts. This gives rise to two possible artifacts. When the communication is at one end of a continuum, there is little room for improvement for those who differ from the communication by small amounts, but a great deal of room for movement among those with large discrepancies. This gives rise to a spurious degree of positive relationship between the degree of discrepancy and the amount of change. Regression effects will also operate in the direction of increasing the correlation. What is needed is a situation in which the distance factor can be manipulated independently of the subject's initial position. An attempt to set up these conditions experimentally was made in a study by Pritzker and the writer (1957). The method involved preparing individual communications presented in booklet form so that the position of the communicator could be set at any desired distance from the subject's initial position. Communicators highly acceptable to the subjects were used. A number of different topics were employed, including the likelihood of a cure for cancer within five years, the desirability of compulsory voting, and the adequacy of five hours of sleep per night.

The amount of change for each degree of advocated change is shown in Fig. 1. It will be seen that there is a fairly clear progression, such that the greater the amount of change advocated the greater the average amount of opinion change produced. Similar results have been reported by Goldberg (1954) and by French (1956).

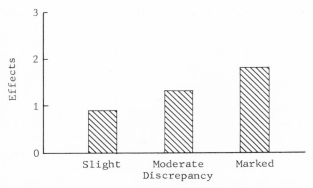

Fig. 1. Mean opinion change score with three degrees of discrepancy (deviation between subject's position and position advocated in communication). [*From Hovland & Pritzker, 1957*]

But these results are not in line with our hunches as to what would happen in a naturalistic situation with important social issues. We felt that here other types of response than change in attitude would occur. So Muzafer Sherif, O. J. Harvey, and the writer (1957) set up a situation to simulate as closely as possible the conditions typically involved when individuals are exposed to major social issue communications at differing distances from their own position. The issue used was the desirability of prohibition. The study was done in two states (Oklahoma and Texas) where there is prohibition or local option, so that the wet-dry issue is hotly debated. We concentrated on three aspects of the problem: How favorably will the communicator be received when his position is at varying distances from that of the recipient? How will what the communicator says be perceived and interpreted by individuals at varying distances from his position? What will be the amount of opinion change produced when small and large deviations in position of communication and recipient are involved?

Three communications, one strongly wet, one strongly dry, and one moderately wet, were employed. The results bearing on the first problem, of *reception*, are presented in Fig. 2. The positions of the subjects are indicated on the abscissa in letters from A (extreme dry) to H (strongly wet). The positions of the communication are also indicated in the same letters, *B* indicating a strongly dry communication, *H* a strongly wet, and *F* a moderately wet. Along the ordinate there is plotted the percentage of subjects with each position on the issue who described the communication as "fair" and "unbiased." It will be seen that the degree of distance between the recipient and the communicator greatly influences the evaluation of the fairness of the communication. When a communication is directed at the pro-dry position, nearly all of the dry subjects consider it fair and impartial, but only a few per cent of the wet subjects consider the identical communication fair. The reverse is true at the other end of the scale. When an intermediate position is adopted, the percentages fall off sharply on each side. Thus under the present conditions with a relatively ambiguous

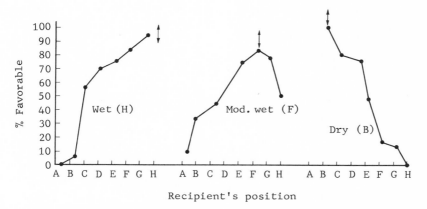

Fig. 2. Percentage of favorable evaluations ("fair," "unbiased," etc.) of wet (*H*), moderately wet (*F*), and dry (*B*) communications for subjects holding various positions on prohibition. Recipients position range from *A* (very dry) to *H*(very wet). Position of communications indicated by arrow. [*From Hovland, Harvey, & Sherif, 1957*]

communicator one of the ways of dealing with strongly discrepant positions is to *discredit* the communicator, considering him unfair and biased.

A second way in which an individual can deal with discrepancy is by distortion of what is said by the communicator. This is a phenomenon extensively studied by Cooper and Jahoda (1947). In the present study, subjects were asked to state what position they thought was taken by the communicator on the prohibition question. Their evaluation of his position could then be analyzed in relation to their own position. These results are shown in Fig. 3 for the moderately wet communication. It will be observed that there is a tendency for individuals whose position is close to that of the communicator to report on the communicator's position quite accurately, for individuals a little bit removed to report his position to be substantially more like their own (which we call an "assimilation effect"), and for those with more discrepant positions to report the communicator's position as more extreme than it really was. This we refer to as a "contrast effect."

Now to our primary results on opinion change. It was found that individuals whose position was only slightly discrepant from the communicator's were influenced to a greater extent than those whose positions deviated to a larger extent. When a wet position was espoused, 28% of the middle-of-the-road subjects were changed in the direction of the communicator, as compared with only 4% of the drys. With the dry communication 14% of the middle-of-the-roaders were changed, while only 4% of the wets were changed. Thus, more of the subjects with small discrepancies were changed than were those with large discrepancies.

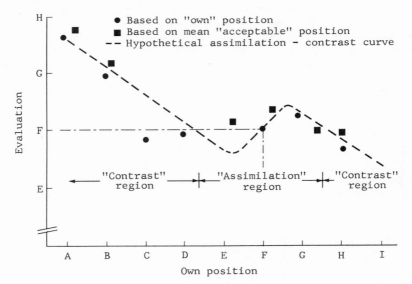

Fig. 3. Average placement of position of moderately wet communication (*F*) by subjects holding various positions on the issue, plotted against hypothetical assimilation-contrast curve. [*From Hovland, Harvey, & Sherif, 1957*]

These results appear to indicate that, under conditions when there is some ambiguity about the credibility of the communicator and when the subject is deeply involved with the issue, the greater the attempt at change the higher the resistance. On the other hand, with highly respected communicators, as in the previous study with Pritzker using issues of lower involvement, the greater the discrepancy the greater the effect. A study related to ours has just been completed by Zimbardo (1959) which indicates that, when an influence attempt is made by a strongly positive communicator (i.e., a close personal friend), the greater the discrepancy the greater the opinion change, even when the experimenter made a point of stressing the great importance of the subject's opinion.

The implication of these results for our primary problem of conflicting results is clear. The types of issues with which most experiments deal are relatively uninvolving and are often of the variety where expert opinion is highly relevant, as for example, on topics of health, science, and the like. Here we should expect that opinion would be considerably affected by communications and furthermore that advocacy of positions quite discrepant from the individual's own position would have a marked effect. On the other hand, the types of issues most often utilized in survey studies are ones which are very basic and involve deep commitment. As a consequence small changes in opinion due to communication would be expected. Here communication may have little effect on those who disagree at the outset and function merely to strengthen the position already held, in line with survey findings.

A third area of research in which somewhat discrepant results are obtained by the experimental and survey methods is in the role of order of presentation. From naturalistic studies the generalization has been widely adopted that primacy is an extremely important factor in persuasion. Numerous writers have reported that what we experience first has a critical role in what we believe. This is particularly stressed in studies of propaganda effects in various countries when the nation getting across its message first is alleged to have a great advantage and in commercial advertising where "getting a beat on the field" is stressed. The importance of primacy in political propaganda is indicated in the following quotation from Doob:

The propagandist scores an initial advantage whenever his propaganda reaches people before that of his rivals. Readers or listeners are then biased to comprehend, forever after, the event as it has been initially protrayed to them. If they are told in a headline or a flash that the battle has been won, the criminal has been caught, or the bill is certain to pass the legislature, they will usually expect subsequent information to substantiate this first impression. When later facts prove otherwise, they may be loath to abandon what they believe to be true until perhaps the evidence becomes overwhelming *(Doob, 1948, pp. 421–422).*

A recent study by Katz and Lazarsfeld (1955) utilizing the survey method compares the extent to which respondents attribute major impact on their decisions about fashions and movie attendance to the presentations to which they were first exposed. Strong primacy effects are shown in their analyses of the data.

We have ourselves recently completed a series of experiments oriented toward this problem. These are reported in our new monograph on *Order of Presentation in Persuasion* (Hovland, Mandell, Campbell, Brock, Luchins, Cohen, McGuire, Janis, Feierabend, & Anderson, 1957). We find that primacy is often *not* a very significant factor when the relative effectiveness of the first side of an issue is compared experimentally with that of the second. The research suggests that differences in design may account for much of the discrepancy. A key variable is whether there is exposure to both sides or whether only one side is actually received. In naturalistic studies the advantage of the first side is often not only that it is first but that it is often then the only side of the issue to which the individual is exposed. Having once been influenced, many individuals make up their mind and are no longer interested in other communications on the issue. In most experiments on order of presentation, on the other hand, the audience is systematically exposed to both sides. Thus under survey conditions, self-exposure tends to increase the impact of primacy.

Two other factors to which I have already alluded appear significant in determining the amount of primacy effect. One is the nature of the communicator, the other the setting in which the communication is received. In our volume Luchins presents results indicating that, when the same communicator presents contradictory material, the point of view read first has more influence. On the other hand, Mandell and I show that, when two different communicators present opposing views successively, little primacy effect is obtained. The communications setting factor operates similarly. When the issue and the conditions of presentation make clear that the points of view are controversial, little primacy is obtained.

Thus in many of the situations with which there had been great concern as to undesirable effects of primacy, such as in legal trials, election campaigns, and political debate, the role of primacy appears to have been exaggerated, since the conditions there are those least conducive to primacy effects: the issue is clearly defined as controversial, the partisanship of the communicator is usually established, and different communicators present the opposing sides.

Time does not permit me to discuss other divergences in results obtained in survey and experimental studies, such as those concerned with the effects of repetition of presentation, the relationship between level of intelligence and susceptibility to attitude change, or the relative impact of mass media and personal influence. Again, however, I am sure that detailed analysis will reveal differential factors at work which can account for the apparent disparity in the generalizations derived.

INTEGRATION

On the basis of the foregoing survey of results I reach the conclusion that no contradiction has been established between the data provided by experimental and correlational studies. Instead it appears that the seeming divergence can be satisfactorily accounted for on the basis of a different definition of the communication situation (including the phenomenon of self-selection) and differences in the type of communicator, audience, and kind of issue utilized.

But there remains the task of better integrating the findings associated with the two methodologies. This is a problem closely akin to that considered by the members of the recent Social Science Research Council summer seminar on *Narrowing the Gap Between Field Studies and Laboratory Studies in Social Psychology* (Riecken, 1954). Many of their recommendations are pertinent to our present problem.

What seems to me quite apparent is that a genuine understanding of the effects of communications on attitudes requires both the survey and the experimental methodologies. At the same time there appear to be certain inherent limitations of each method which must be understood by the researcher if he is not to be blinded by his preoccupation with one or the other type of design. Integration of the two methodologies will require on the part of the experimentalist an awareness of the narrowness of the laboratory in interpreting the larger and more comprehensive effects of communication. It will require on the part of the survey researcher a greater awareness of the limitations of the correlational method as a basis for establishing causal relationships.

The framework within which survey research operates is most adequately and explicitly dealt with by Berelson, Lazarsfeld, and McPhee in their book on *Voting* (1954). The model which they use, taken over by them from the economist Tinbergen, is reproduced in the top half of Fig. 4. For comparison, the model used by experimentalists is presented in the lower half of the figure. It will be seen that the model used by the survey researcher, particularly when he employs the "panel" method, stresses the large number of simultaneous and

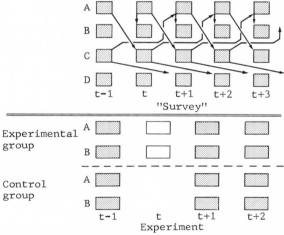

Fig. 4. TOP HALF: "Process analysis" schema used in panel research. (Successive time intervals are indicated along abscissa. Letters indicate the variables under observation. Arrows represent relations between the variables.) [*From Berelson, Lazarsfeld, & McPhee, 1954*]

BOTTOM HALF: Design of experimental research. (Letters on vertical axis again indicate variables being measured. Unshaded box indicates experimentally manipulated treatment and blank absence of such treatment. Time periods indicated as in top half of chart.)

interacting influences affecting attitudes and opinions. Even more significant is its provision for a variety of "feedback" phenomena in which consequences wrought by previous influences affect processes normally considered as occurring earlier in the sequence. The various types of interaction are indicated by the placement of arrows showing direction of effect. In contrast the experimentalist frequently tends to view the communication process as one in which some single manipulative variable is the primary determinant of the subsequent attitude change. He is, of course, aware in a general way of the importance of context, and he frequently studies interaction effects as well as main effects; but he still is less attentive than he might be to the complexity of the influence situation and the numerous possibilities for feedback loops. Undoubtedly the real life communication situation is better described in terms of the survey type of model. We are all familiar, for example, with the interactions in which attitudes predispose one to acquire certain types of information, that this often leads to changes in attitude which may result in further acquisition of knowledge, which in turn produces more attitude change, and so on. Certainly the narrow question sometimes posed by experiments as to the effect of knowledge on attitudes greatly underestimates these interactive effects.

But while the conceptualization of the survey researcher is often very valuable, his correlational research design leaves much to be desired. Advocates of correlational analysis often cite the example of a science built on observation exclusively without experiment: astronomy. But here a very limited number of space-time concepts are involved and the number of competing theoretical formulations is relatively small so that it is possible to limit alternative theories rather drastically through correlational evidence. But in the area of communication effects and social psychology generally the variables are so numerous and so intertwined that the correlational methodology is primarily useful to suggest hypotheses and not to establish causal relationships (Hovland et al., 1949, pp. 329–340; Maccoby, 1956). Even with the much simpler relationships involved in biological systems there are grave difficulties of which we are all aware these days when we realize how difficult it is to establish through correlation whether eating of fats is or is not a cause of heart disease or whether or not smoking is a cause of lung cancer. In communications research the complexity of the problem makes it inherently difficult to derive causal relationships from correlational analysis where experimental control of exposure is not possible. And I do not agree with my friends the Lazarsfelds (Kendall & Lazarsfeld, 1950) concerning the effectiveness of the panel method in circumventing this problem since parallel difficulties are raised when the relationships occur over a time span.

These difficulties constitute a challenge to the experimentalist in this area of research to utilize the broad framework for studying communication effects suggested by the survey researcher, but to employ well controlled experimental design to work on those aspects of the field which are amenable to experimental manipulation and control. It is, of course, apparent that there are important communication problems which cannot be attacked directly by experimental methods. It is not, for example, feasible to modify voting behavior by manipulation of the issues discussed by the opposed parties during a particular campaign. It is not feasible to assess the effects of communications over a very long span of time. For example, one cannot visualize experimental procedures for answering the question of what has been the impact of the reading of *Das Kapital* or *Uncle Tom's Cabin*. These are questions which can be illuminated by historical and sociological study but cannot be evaluated in any rigorous experimental fashion.

But the scope of problems which do lend themselves to experimental attack is very broad. Even complex interactions can be fruitfully attacked by experiment. The possibilities are clearly shown in studies like that of Sherif and Sherif (1953) on factors influencing cooperative and competitive behavior in a camp for adolescent boys. They were able to bring under manipulative control many of the types of interpersonal relationships ordinarily considered impossible to modify experimentally, and to develop motivations of an intensity characteristic of real-life situations. It should be possible to do similar studies in the communication area with a number of the variables heretofore only investigated in uncontrolled naturalistic settings by survey procedures.

In any case it appears eminently practical to minimize many of the differences which were discussed above as being not inherent in design but more or less adventitiously linked with one or the other method. Thus there is no reason why more complex and deeply-involving social issues cannot be employed in experiments rather than the more superficial ones more commonly used. The resistance to change of socially important issues may be a handicap in studying certain types of attitude change; but, on the other hand, it is important to understand the lack of modifiability of opinion with highly-involving issues. Greater representation of the diverse types of communicators found in naturalistic situations can also be achieved. In addition, it should be possible to do experiments with a wider range of populations to reduce the possibility that many of our present generalizations from experiments are unduly affected by their heavy weighting of college student characteristics, including high literacy, alertness, and rationality.

A more difficult task is that of experimentally evaluating communications under conditions of self-selection of exposure. But this is not at all impossible in theory. It should be possible to assess what demographic and personality factors predispose one to expose oneself to particular communications and then to utilize experimental and control groups having these characteristics. Under some circumstances the evaluation could be made on only those who select themselves, with both experimental and control groups coming from the self-selected audience.

Undoubtedly many of the types of experiments which could be set up involving or simulating naturalistic conditions will be too ambitious and costly to be feasible even if possible in principle. This suggests the continued use of small-scale experiments which seek to isolate some of the key variables operative in complex situations. From synthesis of component factors, prediction of complex outcomes may be practicable. It is to this analytic procedure for narrowing the gap between laboratory and field research that we have devoted major attention in our research program. I will merely indicate briefly here some of the ties between our past work and the present problem.

We have attempted to assess the influence of the communicator by varying his expertness and attractiveness, as in the studies by Kelman, Weiss, and the writer (Hovland & Weiss, 1951; Kelman & Hovland, 1953). Further data on this topic were presented earlier in this paper.

We have also been concerned with evaluating social interaction effects. Some of the experiments on group affiliation as a factor affecting resistance to counternorm communication and the role of salience of group membership by Hal Kelley and others are reported in *Communication and Persuasion* (Hovland et al., 1953).

Starting with the studies carried out during the war on orientation films by Art Lumsdaine, Fred Sheffield, and the writer (1949), we have had a strong interest in the duration of communication effects. Investigation of effects at various time intervals has helped to bridge the gap between assessment of immediate changes with those of longer duration like those involved in survey studies. More recent extensions of this work have indicated the close relationship between the credibility of the communicator and the extent of postcommunication increments, or "sleeper effects" (Hovland & Weiss, 1951; Kelman & Hovland, 1953).

The nature of individual differences in susceptibility to persuasion via communication has been the subject of a number of our recent studies. The generality of persuasibility has been investigated by Janis and collaborators and the development of persuasibility in children has been studied by Abelson and Lesser. A volume concerned with these audience factors to which Janis, Abelson, Lesser, Field, Rife, King, Cohen, Linton, Graham, and the writer have contributed will appear under the title *Personality and Persuasibility* (1959).

Lastly, there remains the question on how the nature of the issues used in the communication affects the extent of change in attitude. We have only made a small beginning on these problems. In the research reported in *Experiments on Mass Communication*, we showed that the magnitude of effects was directly related to the type of attitude involved: film communications had a significant effect on opinions related to straightforward interpretations of policies and events, but had little or no effect on more deeply intrenched attitudes and motivations. Further work on the nature of issues is represented in the study by Sherif, Harvey, and the writer (1957) which was discussed above. There we found a marked contrast between susceptibility to influence and the amount of ego-involvement in the issue. But the whole concept of ego-involvement is a fuzzy one, and here is an excellent area for further work seeking to determine the theoretical factors involved in different types of issues.

With this brief survey of possible ways to bridge the gap between experiment and survey I must close. I should like to stress in summary the mutual importance of the two approaches to the problem of communication effectiveness. Neither is a royal road to wisdom, but each represents an important emphasis. The challenge of future work is one of fruitfully combining their virtues so that we may develop a social psychology of communication with the conceptual breadth provided by correlational study of process and with the rigorous but more delimited methodology of the experiment.

REFERENCES

Berelson, B. R., Lazarsfeld, P. F., & McPhee, W. N. *Voting: A study of opinion formation in a presidential campaign.* Chicago: Univer. Chicago Press, 1954.

Cooper, Eunice, & Jahoda, Marie. The evasion of propaganda: How prejudiced people respond to anti-prejudice propaganda. *J. Psychol.,* 1947, *23,* 15–25.

Doob, L. W. *Public opinion and propaganda.* New York: Holt, 1948.

French, J. R. P., Jr. A formal theory of social power. *Psychol. Rev.,* 1956, *63,* 181–94.

Goldberg, S. C. Three situational determinants of conformity to social norms. *J. abnorm. soc. Psychol.,* 1954, *49,* 325–29.

Gosnell, H. F. *Getting out the vote: An experiment in the stimulation of voting.* Chicago: Univer. Chicago Press, 1927.

Hovland, C. I. Effects of the mass media of communication. In G. Lindzey (Ed.), *Handbook of social psychology.* Vol. II. *Special fields and applications.* Cambridge, Mass.: Addison-Wesley, 1954. Pp. 1062–1103.

Hovland, C. I., Harvey, O. J., & Sherif, M. Assimilation and contrast effects in reactions to communication and attitude change. *J. abnorm. soc. Psychol.,* 1957, *55,* 244–52.

Hovland, C. I., Janis, I. L., & Kelley, H. H. *Communication and persuasion.* New Haven: Yale Univer. Press, 1953.

Hovland, C. I., Lumsdaine, A. A., & Sheffield, F. D. *Experiments on mass communication.* Princeton: Princeton Univer. Press, 1949.

Hovland, C. I., Mandell, W., Campbell, Enid H., Brock, T., Luchins, A. S., Cohen, A. R., McGuire, W. J., Janis, I. L., Feierabend, Rosalind L., & Anderson, N. H. *The order of presentation in persuasion.* New Haven: Yale Univer. Press, 1957.

Hovland, C. I., & Pritzker, H. A. Extent of opinion change as a function of amount of change advocated. *J. abnorm. soc. Psychol.,* 1957, *54,* 257–61.

Hovland, C. I., & Weiss, W. The influence of source credibility on communication effectiveness. *Publ. opin. Quart.,* 1951, *15,* 635–50.

Janis, I. L., Hovland, C. I., Field, P. B., Linton, Harriett, Graham, Elaine, Cohen, A. R., Rife, D., Abelson, R. P., Lesser, G. S., & King, B. T. *Personality and persuasibility.* New Haven: Yale Univer. Press, 1959.

Katz, E., & Lazarsfeld, P. F. *Personal influence.* Glencoe, Ill.: Free Press, 1955.

Kelman, H. C., & Hovland, C. I. "Reinstatement" of the communicator in delayed measurement of opinion change. *J. abnorm. soc. Psychol.,* 1953, *48,* 327–35.

Kendall, Patricia L., & Lazarsfeld, P. F. Problems of survey analysis. In R. K. Merton & P. F. Lazarsfeld (Eds.), *Continuities in social research: Studies in the scope and method of "The American Sodier."* Glencoe, Ill.: Free Press, 1950. Pp. 133–96.

Klapper, J. T. *The effects of mass media.* New York: Columbia Univer. Bureau of Applied Social Research, 1949. (Mimeo.)

Lazarsfeld, P. F., Berelson, B., & Gaudet, Hazel. *The people's choice.* New York: Duell, Sloan, & Pearce, 1944.

Lipset, S. M., Lazarsfeld, P. F., Barton, A. H., & Linz, J. The psychology of voting: An analysis of political behavior. In G. Lindzey (Ed.), *Handbook of social psychology.* Vol. II. *Special fields and applications.* Cambridge, Mass.: Addison-Wesley, 1954. Pp. 1124–75.

Maccoby, Eleanor E. Pitfalls in the analysis of panel data: A research note on some technical aspects of voting. *Amer. J. Sociol.,* 1956, *59,* 359–62.

Riecken, H. W. (Chairman) Narrowing the gap between field studies and laboratory experiments in social psychology: A statement by the summer seminar. *Items Soc. Sci. Res. Council,* 1954, *8,* 37–42.

Sherif, M., & Sherif, Carolyn W. *Groups in harmony and tension: An integration of studies on intergroup relations.* New York: Harper, 1953.

Zimbardo, P. G. Involvement and communication discrepancy as determinants of opinion change. Unpublished doctoral dissertation, Yale University, 1959.

Modes of Resolution of Belief Dilemmas

ROBERT P. ABELSON

INTRODUCTION

This is a paper about intrapersonal conflict resolution. We first identify the kind of conflict to be considered.

There are two levels of analysis of intrapersonal conflict: the action level and the belief level, the former dealing with external motor responses and the latter with internal affective and cognitive processes. Particular instances of conflict may, for theoretical convenience, be localized at one or another of these levels. For example, one may ask how a person acts when simultaneously motivated to approach and to avoid an external object (3, 9, 10). Or one may ask instead what happens to the cognitive representation of an external object when the object simultaneously incurs favorable and unfavorable cognitions (12). The present paper is addressed to the latter type of question. We shall not consider the problem of whether and how the action level is to be reduced to the belief level or vice versa. We only consider conflicts between one belief and another or, more generally, conflicts within a belief structure. The term "belief dilemma" is intended to enforce the distinction between the variety of conflict here considered and conflict in general.

BELIEF DILEMMAS

The model of cognitive structure to be described is similar at various points to other recent models (6, 8, 13).

First, we imagine a cognitive representation, a "cognitive element," corresponding to any attitude object. Associated with such a cognitive element is a numerical value, positive if the object is liked, negative if the object is disliked. Next, we suppose that between each pair of cognitive elements there may exist some kind of perceived relation. Assigned to each relation is another numerical value, positive if the relation is "associative," negative if the relation is "dissociative" (11). Examples of associative relations are: is, has, includes, likes, helps, produces, implies. Examples of dissociative relations are: avoids, hates, hinders, defeats, destroys, is incompatible with. A zero value indicates a null, or irrelevant, relation.

Given an attitude issue or "conceptual arena" (1), a certain set of cognitive elements would be relevant for a given individual. The set of relevant elements and the particular relations among them define the *content* of the individual's belief system on the issue. The form, or *structure*, of belief may be expressed independently of the content according to the array of numerical affect values and relation values defined above.

A belief structure may or may not contain inconsistencies. By inconsistency is meant not logical inconsistency but psychological inconsistency, or, as it has been variously referred to, imbalance (7), incongruity (12, 13), or dissonance (5). We shall use the term "imbalance."

Heider (7), Festinger (5), and Osgood and Tannenbaum (12) have all postulated a motivation for the reduction of imbalance. There is said to be a tendency, a pressure, toward the attainment of cognitive balance. An essential qualification to this postulate has been pointed out by Abelson and Rosenberg (1). There are innumerable inconsistencies in anyone's belief system which may lie dormant and unthought about. Pressure toward cognitive balance, if always operative on all cognitive elements, would produce much more balance in belief systems than one finds empirically. It is much more plausible to assume that this pressure operates only when the issue is salient; that is, when the issue is being "thought about," or, if this is too rational a terminology, when "cognitive work" is applied on the issue. General methods for identifying the presence of imbalance in a structure of any size have been given elsewhere (1, 4). Here we confine our analysis to a simple case of imbalance: two elements and the relation between them.

There are six possible cases to be considered: two positively valued objects, related associatively or related dissociatively; one positively valued object and one negatively valued object, related dissociatively or related associatively; and two negatively valued objects, related associatively or related dissociatively. In each of these three pairs of cases, the first possibility is balanced, the second one is imbalanced. This may be clarified by reference to Figure 1.

An imbalanced dyad will be said to constitute a belief dilemma when the intensity of affect toward the objects is strong and when the dyad is often salient (i.e., often present in thought).

MODES OF RESOLUTION

Four possible modes of resolution are specified below. Each can manifest itself in several ways. The modes are labeled: (*a*) denial, (*b*) bolstering, (*c*) differentiation, and (*d*) transcendence.

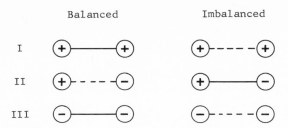

Fig. 1. Cognitive structures with two elements and one relation. An unbroken line symbolizes an associative (positive) relation; a broken line a dissociative (negative) relation.

The mechanism of denial aims toward the conversion of a structure on the right into one on the left, either through change of affect toward the element ("denial of the element") or change in the sign of the relation ("denial of the relation").

Denial refers to a direct attack upon one or both of the cognitive elements or the relation between them. The value felt toward the object, whether positive or negative, is denied, or the opposite is asserted; or the sign of the relation between the elements is explained away, or the opposite is asserted. Examples are: the man on a diet professing that he never liked rich foods anyway, the groom convincing himself of his avid belief in his bride's religion, John Calvin interpreting the scriptures to show that Christ never really condemned usury. If an attempt at denial is successful, it will convert an imbalanced structure into a balanced one. However, denial attempts may run into various difficulties, as, for example, when the denial is too great a distortion of reality or conflicts with other elements in the larger belief system. For example, the Boston colonists faced in 1773 with the odious taxation on tea went so far as to vote that "it is the sense of this Body that the use of tea is improper and pernicious." It is unlikely that this denial of the desirability of tea, albeit effective in encouraging group action, was effective in suppressing the taste for tea of the individuals concerned.

The mechanism called "bolstering" consists of relating one or the other of the two cognitive objects in a balanced way to other valued objects (Fig. 2), thereby minimizing the relative imbalance in the structure. This mechanism plays an important part in Festinger's theory of cognitive dissonance (5). He points out many situations in which the introduction of new cognitive elements is useful in reducing dissonance. This is a mechanism not for eliminating imbalance entirely but only for drowning it out, so to speak. Examples are: the smoker who is worried about lung cancer telling himself that smoking is extremely enjoyable, good for his nerves, and socially necessary; and the proponent of a large standing army, unwelcome in peacetime, claiming that it is good character training for the nation's youth. The mechanism of bolstering may be used in conjunction with the mechanism of denial. For example, in the example of the large standing army the advocate might also say that the large standing army was not contrary to peaceful purposes; in fact, it aided the cause of peace to have a large standing army.

Original structure   Bolstered structure

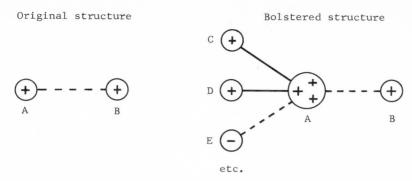

etc.

Fig. 2.   The mechanism of bolstering in reducing cognitive imbalance. In the bolstered structure (right) the units *AC, AD, . . .* are all balanced. The relative effect of the imbalanced unit *AB* is thus reduced.

The two mechanisms listed thus far have the property that they preserve the identity of the cognitive elements. The meaning of the attitude objects remains the same even though attitude toward the objects may be weakened by denial or strengthened by bolstering. Another mode of resolution arises if we consider the possibility of differentiation of the cognitive elements. An element may be split into two parts with a strong dissociative relation between the parts. To see how this mechanism might restore cognitive balance, consider the issue of hydrogen-bomb testing. For many people, continued hydrogen-bomb testing is positively valued, but poisoning of the atmosphere is negatively valued. These two cognitive objects are associatively related—there is a causal connection of some degree. This dyad is therefore imbalanced. But there is bomb testing and there is bomb testing: one might differentiate this attitude object into two—testing "dirty bombs" and testing "clean bombs." It is only the testing of dirty bombs that contributes to poisoning of the atmosphere; the testing of clean bombs presumably does not. Thus the imbalance is resolved. To take another example, the facts of evolution, positively valued, are contradictory to the Bible which is also positively valued. But there are two Bibles: the Bible as literally interpreted and the Bible as figuratively interpreted. The Bible as figuratively interpreted is not contradictory to the facts of evolution but may be seen as concordant with them. In a third example, from an experiment by Asch (2), subjects who feel unfavorable toward "politicians" are confronted with a highly prestigeful source who glorifies the political profession. Many subjects get off the hook by differentiating statesmen (good politicians) from ward-heelers (bad politicians). In these examples one element is differentiated into two parts, a new part and an old part. The old part retains the relation with the other element in the structure, but the affect toward it is changed. The new part, on the other hand, retains the old affect toward the differentiated element, but the sign of the relation with the other element is changed. These changes are reviewed in Figure 3.

It is interesting to note the large number of dimensions along which objects can be differentiated. They may be differentiated according to the internal

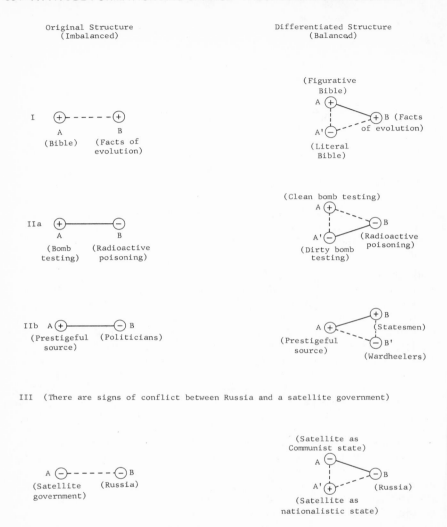

Fig. 3. The mechanism of differentiation in restoring cognitive balance

content of the object, the object as viewed in a social context versus a personal context, the object as it is versus as it should be, the object as it is versus the object as it will be, etc.

The mechanism of transcendence is in a sense obverse to the mechanism of differentiation. Elements, instead of being split down, are built up and combined into larger units organized on a superordinate level, as indicated in Figure 4. For example, the dilemma pitting science against religion is transcended by the consideration that both the rational man and the spiritual man must be jointly cultivated to reach a fuller life or a better society or a deeper understanding of the universe. Thus the dilemma is transcended by imbedding the conflicting

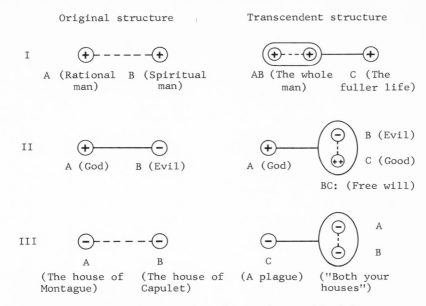

Fig. 4. The mechanism of transcendence in restoring cognitive balance

parts in a new concept instrumental to some higher purpose. The theosophical dilemma of God's presumed permissiveness toward evil is sometimes resolved by appeal to transcendent concepts. In the intriguing case study (6) of a group of individuals who prepared for a cataclysm that never occurred, it is reported that the group leader offered a transcendent resolution for the belief crisis: the cataclysm was said to have been stayed by God because of the group's devotion.

CHOICE AMONG THE MODES OF RESOLUTION

Presumably, the individual with an imbalanced cognition will strive to choose among the various modes of resolution. Imbalanced structure would then be under a variety of pressures to change. The theoretical specification of which particular changes are likely to take place is a complex problem. Several working propositions are sketched here. A more rigorous theory is in the process of development.

Proposition 1.—There will be a hierarchy of resolution attempts in general proceeding in the following order: denial, bolstering, denial, differentiation, and transcendence.

The hierarchy of resolution attempts is based upon the relative ease of achieving success with each of the methods. The reason denial appears twice in the listing is that there are usually two points in the process at which denial may enter. If we consider the situation in which imbalance is introduced by forced or accidental exposure to propaganda or opinions seeking to establish new cognitive relations or to contradict previously held affect values, a first opportunity for denial may arise by a rejection of the relevance of the new material. If the initial denial fails, bolstering will be attempted and then another attempt at denial, this time buttressed by further thought about the issue. The presumption here is that denial and bolstering are simpler cognitive mechanisms than differentiation and transcendence, although they are not necessarily more effective in reducing cognitive imbalance. Differentiation is difficult because it requires intellectual ability, flexibility, and because, when there is strong affect toward a cognitive object, it is not easily split apart. Transcendence is presumably still more difficult, for it requires the existence of a compelling superordinate structure in which a given imbalance may be imbedded.

Proposition 2.—When two cognitive elements stand in imbalanced relation to each other and the affect toward one is more intense than toward the other, the tendency will be to apply bolstering toward the more intensely affected element and/or denial toward (*a*) the less intensely affected element and/or (*b*) the relation between the elements.

Proposition 2a.—The probability that an attempt will be made to bolster an element is high if other elements relevant to it are strong and stand in balanced relation to it (Fig. 2) and is low if other relevant elements are weak or stand in imbalanced relation to it.

Corollary.—Elements for which the individual's affect is intensely socially supported are readily subject to bolstering attempts when caught in a strong dilemma.

Proposition 2b.—The probability that an attempt will be made to deny an element is high if other relevant elements are strong and stand in imbalanced relation to it and is low if other relevant elements are weak or stand in balanced relation to it.

Corollary.—Elements with which considerable shame or guilt is associated (e.g., elements connoting the overindulgence of appetites) are readily subject to denial attempts when caught in a strong dilemma (i.e., when firmly related in imbalanced fashion to a strongly affected element). See Example 1.

Example 1

Note.—The element *C* must be compelling for the resolution to be stable. If original positive affect toward *B* is strong, the stability of the attempted resolution is jeopardized.

Proposition 2c.—Relations between cognitive elements are readily denied when the external evidence for the relation is remote, ambiguous, under suspicion of bias, or dependent upon specific circumstances which can readily be perceived as inapplicable in general.

Proposition 2d.—A relation between cognitive elements A and B is readily subject to denial attempts when there is available an element A', formally similar to A and standing in associative relation with it, such that *the relation between* A' *and* B *is of opposite sign as between* A *and* B, *and is stronger*.

Proposition 2e.—A relation between cognitive elements A and B is readily subject to denial attempts when there is available an element A', formally similar to A, yet standing psychologically in dissociative relation to A, such that *the relation between* A' *and* B *is of the same sign as between* A *and* B, *but stronger* (the "mote-beam" technique).

See Example 2 (from the point of view of a liberal but very proud southerner).

Proposition 3.—If the affects toward two cognitive elements which stand in imbalanced relation to each other are nearly equal and the resolutions suggested in Proposition 2 fail, the converse resolutions will be attempted; that is, there will be attempts to bolster the less intense element and/or to deny the more intense element.

Proposition 4.—The classical relationship between the intensity and extremity of attitude may be explained in terms of a succession of dilemma resolutions in individual histories with the attitude object.

Explanation: The mechanism of bolstering used in the service of dilemma resolution increases the intensity of affect toward the object. An object which has been repeatedly bolstered is therefore the object of an intense attitude. But repeated bolstering also increases the extremity of attitude. In bolstering, the attitude object is connected with other objects. New reasons and supports are given for it; it is seen to be instrumental to other values; it is seen to be supported by various people and groups. In short, it is imbedded in a cognitive system of ever widening circumference. If scope of cognitive support is equated with extremity of attitude, then the relationship between extremity and intensity follows.

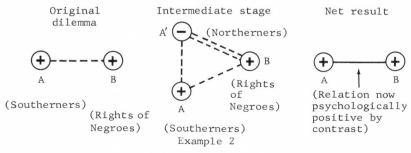

Example 2

Those individuals who do not invoke bolstering will in general be the ones with moderate attitudes of low intensity.

Proposition 5.—If, in the search for new elements to bolster an original element in imbalance, further imbalance is created (usually because the new elements are imbalanced with each other), differentiation of the original element is encouraged.

See Example 3 (it is pointed out to an individual that universal public school education, by being compulsory, violates the democratic ideal of individual free choice—some parents might want to keep children out of school).

Proposition 6.—When an element is differentiated it is crucial to the maintenance of the resolution that the old part and the new part of the element be strongly dissociated.

Proposition 7.—Transcendent resolutions are likely to be invoked only in the case of chronically insoluble dilemmas. However, once a transcendent resolution is achieved, it may be found applicable to a variety of dilemmas.

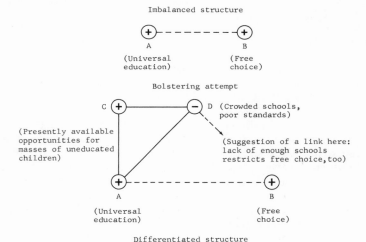

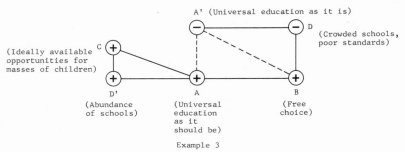

Example 3

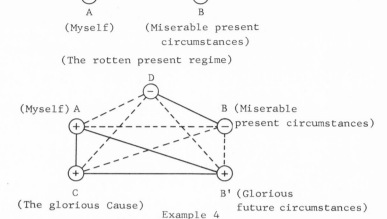

Example 4

Proposition 8.—Mass propaganda efforts seek dilemma resolutions effective for a large number of people simultaneously.

See Example 4 (a nation in a period of hard times).

Revolutionary propaganda aims to bolster *A* and differentiate *B* along a time dimension. The dissociated parts of *B* are each doubly bolstered, as follows:

(English translation: "You are now part of the glorious Cause. Reject with us your miserable present circumstances. Look forward to the glorious future when all will be different. The rotten present regime despises you and is responsible for your misery. The Cause will attack the regime and lead you to the glorious future. The regime will try to prevent this but we shall triumph.")

Explicit in this analysis is the reason revolutionists should be so concerned over public apathy. Those "Indifferents" who are not dissatisfied with their present circumstances have no dilemma to resolve, and consequently the propaganda does not "take" (unless the Indifferents can be convinced that their situation is indeed grim).

REFERENCES

1. Abelson, R. P., and Rosenberg, M. J. "Symbolic Psychologic: A Model of Attitudinal Cognition." *Behavioral Science,* III (1958), 1–13.

2. Asch, S. E. "Studies in the Principles of Judgments and Attitudes: II. Determination of Judgments by Group and Ego Standards." *Journal of Social Psychology*, XII (1940), 433–65.

3. Brown, J. S. "Principles of Intrapersonal Conflict. *Conflict Resolution*, I (1957), 135–54.

4. Cartwright, D., and Harary, F. "Structural Balance: A Generalization of Heider's Theory." *Psychological Review*, LXIII (1956), 277–93.

5. Festinger, L. *Theory of Cognitive Dissonance.* Evanston, Ill.: Row, Peterson & Co., 1957.

6. Festinger, L., Riecken, H., and Schachter, S. *When Prophecy Fails.* Minneapolis: University of Minnesota Press, 1956.

7. Heider, F. "Attitudes and Cognitive Organization." *Journal of Psychology,* XXI (1946), 107–12.

8. ———. *The Psychology of Interpersonal Relations.* New York: John Wiley & Sons, 1958.

9. Lewin, K. "Environmental Forces in Child Behavior and Development." In C. Murchison (ed.), *A Handbook of Child Psychology.* Worcester, Mass.: Clark University Press, 1931.

10. Miller, N. "Experimental Studies of Conflict." In J. McV. Hunt, (ed.), *Personality and the Behavior Disorders.* New York: Ronald Press Co., 1944.

11. Osgood, C. E., Saporta, S., and Nunnally, J. C. "Evaluative Assertion Analysis." *Litera,* III (1956), 47–102.

12. Osgood, C. E., and Tannenbaum, P. H. "The Principle of Congruity in the Prediction of Attitude Change." *Psychological Review,* LXII (1955), 42–55.

13. Osgood, C. E., Suci, G. T., and Tannenbaum, P. H. *The Measurement of Meaning.* Urbana: University of Illinois Press, 1957.

Persistence and Regression of Changed Attitudes: Long-Range Studies

THEODORE M. NEWCOMB

I.

One-half score and seven years ago, here in Philadelphia, I read a paper before this society. It was properly, which is to say polysyllabically, titled—something about autistic hostility—and its manuscript pages numbered just 28. Doubtless I would long since have forgotten about it had I not discovered, several years later, that another man had stolen my central idea, some five-score years before I was born. The name of the thief was William Blake, and a striking feature of *his* paper was that its total number of *words* was just 28. Let me quote them:

> I was angry with my friend:
> I told my wrath, my wrath did end.
> I was angry with my foe:
> I told it not, my wrath did grow.

Reprinted from The Journal of Social Issues, 19, *1963, 3–14. Copyright 1963 by the Society for the Psychological Study of Social Issues and reproduced by permission.*

Though I'm not sure that Blake would accept the phrasing, our common theme had to do with the change and persistence of attitudes. What I, at least, was trying to say was that one's attitudes toward another person are not likely to change if one so manipulates one's environment that one cannot add to or correct one's information about that person. Today I shall pursue a similar theme, though in a somewhat different direction.

One's attitude toward something is not only a resultant of one's previous traffic with one's environment but also a determinant of selective response to present and future environments. Viewed in the latter way, existing attitudes may determine one's selection among alternative environmental settings, and these in turn may serve to preserve or undermine the very attitudes that had been initially responsible for one's selection among the alternatives. Insofar as attitudes are self-preserving, such tendencies to select a supportive environment would, if empirically supported, provide an important explanation of their persistence. In its most general form, the hypothesis would run somewhat as follows: Existing attitudes are most likely to persist, other things equal, when one's environment provides most rewards for their behavioral expression. But this platitudinous proposition ("things persist when conditions are favorable to their persistence") is not very interesting, and is probably not even testable. A more interesting and more testable form of the proposition would take account of both change and persistence, both of attitudes and of environmental supportiveness. In particular, it would say something about a changed selection of environments following attitude change, about the ways in which the recently formed attitude is or is not reinforced by the new environment, and about the persistence of the attitude in both supportive and hostile environments. Such a proposition, in its simplest form, would run somewhat as follows: A recently changed attitude is likely to persist insofar as it leads to the selection of subsequent environments that provide reinforcements for the behavioral expression of the changed attitude.

Among the many possible forms of environmental reinforcements of behavioral expressions of attitudes, I shall consider a single class: behavior on the part of other people that one perceives as supportive of one's own attitudes. With few exceptions, such support comes from persons or groups toward whom one is positively attracted, according to the principles of what is perhaps most frequently known as balance theory (Cf. Heider, 1958; Brown, 1962; Newcomb, 1963). I am, in short, about to defend the limited proposition that a recently changed attitude is most likely to persist if one of its behavioral expressions is the selection of a social environment which one finds supportive of the changed attitude. This proposition differs from the one about autistic hostility primarily in that persistence of a recently acquired attitude depends upon continuing rather than cutting off sources of information about the attitude-object.

II.

There are various ways in which such a proposition might be tested in the laboratory. But insofar as one is interested, as I have been, in long-range effects, one will make use of "natural" settings. I shall therefore cite a few findings from two of my own studies, mentioning only briefly the less immediately relevant one (1961), which involved the daily observation of two populations of 17 male students, all initial strangers to one another, who lived intimately together for four-month periods. The only attitudes of these subjects that showed much change, from first to last, were their attractions toward each other—attitudes which had not even existed, of course, before their initial encounters in this research setting. Expressions of interpersonal attraction during the first week or two were highly unstable, but after about the fifth week they showed only slow and slight changes (Cf. Newcomb, 1963).

Under the conditions of this research, imposed environments (in the form of arbitrarily assigned rooms, roommates, and floors) had no consistent effects beyond the first week or two in interpersonal preferences. That is, one could predict little or nothing about interpersonal attraction from the fact of being roommates or floormates. Self-selected interpersonal environment, however, was closely associated with interpersonal attraction. At all times later than the first week or two, pairs of subjects who were reported by others to belong to the same voluntary subgroups were almost invariably pairs whose members chose each other at very high levels of attraction. If this seems to be a commonplace observation (as indeed it is), let me remind you of my reason for reporting it; interpersonal environments are not only consequences of existing attraction but also sources of future attraction. It is an everyday phenomenon that, having developed differential attitudes toward one's several acquaintances, one manipulates one's interpersonal environment, insofar as one can, to correspond with one's interpersonal preferences. And insofar as one is successful, chances are that the preferences will be further reinforced. My data, showing stability both of preferences and of voluntarily associating subgroups following the first month or so, indicate that exactly this was occurring. The fact that it is an everyday occurrence enhances rather than negates the importance of the principle involved, namely, that a recently acquired attitude will persist insofar as it results in the selection of an environment that is supportive of that attitude.

III.

I now turn to a totally different set of data, or rather to two sets of data from the same subjects, obtained over an interval of more than 20 years. The earlier responses were obtained between 1935 and 1939 at Bennington College (Newcomb, 1943); the later ones, obtained in 1960 and 1961, were from almost all of the subjects who had been studied for three or more consecutive years during the 1930's. To be specific, out of 141 former students in this category who in 1960 were alive, resident in continental United States, and not hopelessly invalided, 130 (scattered in 28 states) were interviewed, and 9 of the remaining 11 completed more or less parallel questionnaires. The interview dealt primarily with their present attitudes toward a wide range of public-affairs issues, with attitudes of their husbands and other contemporary associates, and with their histories and careers since leaving the College.

Before telling you some of the follow-up findings, I ought to report a few of the original ones. During each of four consecutive years (1935-36 through 1938-39), juniors and seniors were on the average markedly less conservative than freshmen in attitude toward many public issues of the day. Studies of the same individuals over three- and four-year intervals showed the same trend, which was not attributable to selective withdrawal from the College. Comparisons with other colleges showed almost no intercollege differences in freshmen attitudes, but much less conservatism at Bennington than at the other institutions on the part of seniors. Individual studies showed that at Bennington nonconservatism was rather closely associated with being respected by other students, with participation in college activities, and with personal involvement in the College as an institution. The relatively few malcontents were, with surprisingly few exceptions, those who held conservative attitudes toward public issues.

Given these initial findings, one of my concerns in planning the follow-up study was the following: Under what conditions would individuals who had become less conservative during their college years remain relatively nonconservative 20-odd years later, and under what conditions would they "regress" to relatively conservative positions? (As to the problem of comparing attitudes toward one set of issues in the 1930's with those toward quite different issues in the 1960's, I shall for present purposes note only that at both times we used indices of relative, not absolute standing: each subject is compared with the same set of peers.)

By way of noting the general pattern of persistence vs. regression on the part of the total population, I shall first compare one early with one later datum. In the 1940 presidential election, 51% of our interview sample who reported a preference for either major candidate chose the Democrat, F. D. Roosevelt, and 49% the Republican, W. Willkie. Twenty years later, the comparable figures were 60% for J. F. Kennedy and 40% for R. M. Nixon. No single election, of course, provides a very good test of what might be termed "general conservatism concerning public affairs," but at any rate this particular comparison does not suggest any conspicuous regression toward freshman conservatism. This conclusion is also supported by the following finding: In six consecutive presidential elections (1940 through 1960), an outright majority of our interviewees (51%) reported that they had preferred the Republican candidate either once or never, whereas only 27% of them had preferred that candidate as many as five times out of the six times.

The problem of regressive effects can also be approached by comparing relative conservatism on the part of the same individuals over the interval of 20-odd years. In terms of party or candidate preference in 1960, the degree of individual stability is startling. As shown in Table 1, individuals who were in the

Table 1 PRESIDENTIAL PREFERENCES IN 1960, ACCORDING TO QUARTILES OF PEP SCORES ON LEAVING COLLEGE IN THE LATE 1930S

PEP QUARTILE	NIXON PREFERRED	KENNEDY PREFERRED	TOTAL
1 (least conservative)	3	30	33
2	8	25	33
3	18	13	31
4 (most conservative)	22	11	33
TOTAL	51	79	130

least conservative quartile of the total population, on graduating, preferred Kennedy by frequencies of 30 to 3, and those in the next quartile by 25 to 8; 83% of this half of the population preferred Kennedy 20 years later, while 37% of the initially more conservative half preferred Kennedy after 20 years. Political party preferences, and also an index of general political conservatism, showed about the same relationship to political conservatism more than two decades earlier. These data provide no support for a prediction of general regression— either toward previous conservatism or in the statistical sense of regression toward the mean.

Other evidence concerning the general nonconservatism in this population in the early 1960's includes the following:

77% of them considered themselves "liberal" or "somewhat liberal," as compared with 17% who were "conservative" or "somewhat conservative";
76% "approved" or "strongly approved" of "Medicare" for the aged under Social Security;
61% "approved" or "strongly approved" of admitting Red China into the United Nations.

These and other data suggest that the population as a whole is now far less conservative than is to be expected in view of its demographic characteristics. Its socio-economic level may be judged from these facts: (1) 77% of the 117 respondents who were or had been married were judged by the interviewer to be at least "fairly well-to-do," with annual incomes of not less than $20,000; and (2) of 113 mothers in the population, 65% had sent at least one of their children to a private school. In religious background, about three-quarters of them were Protestants (more than half of whom were Episcopalian), and less than 10% were either Catholic or Jewish. According to information assembled for me by the Survey Research Center of the University of Michigan,* the proportion of Protestant women college graduates at the income level of this population who in 1960 expressed a preference for Kennedy over Nixon was less than 25—as compared with 60% of this alumnae population.

I shall now revert to my earlier theme: If this population is now less conservative than one might expect, to what extent is this explainable in terms of its members' selection of post-college environments that were supportive of nonconservative attitudes? It proves to be very difficult to categorize total environments from this point of view, and so for the present I shall limit myself to a single aspect of post-college environments: husbands. I am making no assumptions here except that (1) husbands were indeed a part of their wives' environments; (2) wives had had something to do with selecting this part of their environments; and (3) husbands, as environmental objects, were capable of being either supportive or nonsupportive of their wives' attitudes.

Nearly 80% of our respondents both had a husband and were able to report on his attitudes toward most of the issues with which we were concerned, during all or most of the past 20 years; one reason for placing a good deal of confidence in their reports is that they seem highly discriminating, as indicated by such responses as these: "I don't think I know how he'd feel on that particular issue,"

*By my colleague Philip Converse, to whom I am most grateful.

or "Now on *that* one he doesn't agree with me at all." Here are some summaries concerning all husbands whose wives were willing to attribute attitudes toward them (nearly all wives on most issues):

54% of the husbands in 1960 favored Kennedy over Nixon;
64% of them either "approved" or "strongly approved" of "Medicare" for the aged under Social Security;
57% of them either "approved" or "strongly approved" of admitting Red China into the United Nations.

And so it is almost as true of husbands as of wives that they are less conservative than is to be expected in view of their demographic characteristics: husbands' and wives' demographic characteristics are taken to be identical except for a very few couples differing in religious background, and their present attitudes are highly similar (90% of 1960 presidential preferences by pairs of spouses, for example, being reported as the same in 1960). It would hardly seem to be a matter of sheer chance that a set of men who are less conservative than is to be expected are married to a set of women of whom just the same thing is true. It seems necessary, therefore, to assume that attitudes toward public affairs had something to do with husbands' and wives' reciprocal selection of one another, or with post-marital influence upon one another, or with both. Here is one statistical support for this assumption: the correlation between wives' scores on an instrument labeled Political and Economic Progressivism, as of their graduating from college in the late 1930's, with the number of Republican candidates that their subsequent husbands voted for between 1940 and 1960 was .32; this does not account for much of the variance, but its p value is $< .0005$.

Another interesting finding has to do with the number of women in our interview sample whose husbands had attended Ivy League colleges; one would expect this proportion to be high, since so many of the women's fathers and brothers had attended these colleges. The actual frequency turned out to be just 50%. These Ivy League husbands' voting preferences in 1960, however, turned out to be much more like their wives' preferences than like their classmates' preferences: 52% of husbands whose wives were able to state a preference were for Kennedy—which is to say that they did not differ at all in voting preferences from all non-Ivy League husbands. This total set of facts can best be interpreted as follows: Our Bennington graduates of the late 1930's found their husbands in the kinds of places where their families expected them to be found, but they selected somewhat atypical members of these "proper" populations of eligibles; they tended not to have conservative attitudes that were then typical of these populations.

One evidence of this atypical selection is to be seen in the occupational distribution of these womens' husbands. Only 38% of all husbands are classifiable as "in management or business," the remaining 62% representing for the most part a wide range of professions (especially college teaching, entertainment, and the arts) and public employment (especially in government). Husbands in these two general categories (management and business vs. all others) differed sharply in their voting preferences in 1960; of the 113 husbands whose wives attributed preferences to them, 26% of those in management and business preferred Kennedy, and 68% of all other husbands preferred Kennedy. In sum, these women's husbands had typically come from "the right" places but a majority of them did not have "the right" attitudes or occupational interests.

If, therefore, I were to select a single factor that contributed most to these women's maintenance of nonconservative attitudes between the late 1930's and early 1960's, I think it would be the fact of selecting husbands of generally nonconservative stripe who helped to maintain for them an environment that was supportive of their existing attributes.

IV.

Now I shall turn from the total population of interviewees to some comparisons of subpopulations. The most crucial of these, from the point of view of my proposition about supportive environments, are to be found within the population of nonconservatives on leaving college in the late 1930's: What seems to be the differences between those who do and those who do not remain nonconservative in the early 1960's? Such comparisons will have to be impressionistic, since numbers of cases are small.

Among 22 individuals previously labeled as clearly nonconservative in their third or fourth year of attendance at the College, just half belong in the same category now. Only three of them are clearly conservative today, the remaining eight being classified as intermediate. Here are these wives' descriptions of their husbands' political positions over the years:

3 presently conservative wives: 3 Republican husbands (100%)
7 presently intermediate wives: 3 Republican husbands (42%)
8 presently nonconservative wives: 2 Republican husbands (25%)

Of the three presently conservative women, none mentions having engaged in activities related to political or other public issues; of the eight who are intermediate, six mention some activity of this kind, but they identify their activity only in such general terms as "liberal" or "Democratic Party"; of the 11 still nonconservative women, eight mention such activities, more than half of them specifying such "causes" or organizations as labor unions, civil liberties, the ADA, or the NAACP.

Each interviewee was also asked about the general orientation of "most of your friends" toward political and other public affairs. More than half (12) of the 22 women originally labeled as clearly nonconservative described their environment of friends as "liberal," in spite of the fact that most of them lived in suburbs or other geographical areas not generally renowned for liberalism. Interestingly enough, those who are now relatively conservative answered this question in just about the same way as did those who are still relatively nonconservative. The 16 women originally labeled as clearly conservative, on leaving college, answered this question somewhat differently; more than half of them (9) described their environment of friends as predominantly "conservative," but answers differed with the present attitudes of the respondents. That is, those who are now, in fact, relatively conservative with near-unanimity describe their friends as conservative, whereas those who are now relatively nonconservative consider a substantial proportion or even most of their friends to be "liberal." Thus only those who were quite conservative in the late 1930's and who still remain so see themselves surrounded by friends who are primarily conservative.

In sum, nearly all of the still nonconservative women mention either husbands or public activities (most commonly both) that have served to support and maintain previously nonconservative attitudes, while none of the three formerly nonconservative but presently conservative women mentions either husband or public activities which have served to maintain earlier attitudes.

What about attitude persistence on the part of those who, after three or four years in college, were still relatively conservative? Sixteen of those who were then labeled conservative were interviewed in the early 1960's, ten of them being categorized as still conservative and three as now nonconservative. Only one of the nonchangers reported having a husband who was a Democrat, and in this lone case he turned out to have voted for Nixon in 1960. Two of the three changers, on the other hand, report husbands who were Democrats and Kennedy voters in 1960. Only two of the persistent conservatives mentioned public activities presumably supportive of their attitudes (in behalf of the Republican Party, in both cases); eight of the ten described most of their friends either as conservative or as Republicans. The conditions that favor the persistence of conservatism over the 20-odd years are thus about the same as those that favor the persistence of nonconservatism: supportive environments in the form of husbands, local friends, and (for the nonconservatives but not the conservatives) in the form of associates in activities related to public issues.

There is a special sub-population of students who, as of graduating in the late 1930's, were candidates for regression; that is, they became much less conservative during their college years. Of these, about one-third (9 of 28) were among the most conservative half of the same population in the early 1960's, and may be regarded as regressors, in some degree at least. Eight of these potential regressors were, for various reasons, unable to report on husbands' preferences. Among the remaining 19 respondents, five were actual regressors, four of whom reported their husbands to be Republicans or "conservative Republicans." Among 14 actual non-regressors reporting, ten described their husbands as Democrats or "liberal Democrats," two referred to them as "Republicans who have been voting Democratic," and only two call their husbands Republicans. These are highly significant differences: the actual regressors can pretty well be differentiated from the nonregressors merely by knowing their husbands' present attitudes. By this procedure only 3 of 19, or 16% of all predictions would not have been correct.

This total set of data suggests that either regression and persistence of attitudes as of leaving college are, over the years, influenced by husbands' attitudes, or early post-college attitudes had something to do with the selection of husbands, or both. In either case, both regression and persistence are facilitated by the supportiveness of husbands.

V.

If there is any very general principle that helps to account for this whole range of phenomena (both my 1946 and my 1963 versions), I believe that it is to be found in an extended version of "balance theory," as originally outlined by

Heider (1946, 1958). Heider's formulations are formulated in individual and phenomenological terms; a balanced state is a strictly intrapersonal, psychological state. But it is also possible to conceptualize an objective, multi-person state of balance, referring to the actual relationships among different persons' attitudes, regardless of the person's awareness of each other. Such a concept is psychologically useful not only because it describes an actual, existing situation—an environment of which each person is himself a part, as suggested by Asch (1952)—but also because it describes a relationship which, given reasonably full and accurate communication, comes to be accurately perceived. My own recent work on the acquaintance process has been interesting to me primarily because it inquires into the processes by which and the conditions under which *intra*personal states of balance come to correspond with *inter*personal ones. As outlined by Heider, and subsequently by many others (Cf. Brown *et al.*, 1962), the processes by which imbalanced states serve as goals toward the attainment of balanced ones include both internal, psychological changes and external modifications of the environment. Thus, one may achieve a balanced state with the important figures in one's social environment—whether by selecting those figures, by modifying one's own attitudes, or by influencing others' attitudes—and at the same time continue to perceive that environment accurately.

According to such an extended, *inter*personal concept of balance, an imbalanced state under conditions of continued interaction is likely to be an unstable one, simply because when it is discovered it arouses *intra*personal imbalance on the part of one or more of the interactors, and this state arouses forces toward change. Given marked attitude change on the part of one but not the other member of a dyad actually in balance with respect to that attitude, imbalance results. This was what typically happened to students at Bennington College vis-à-vis their parents, in the 1930's. A common way in which they attempted to reduce imbalance was by avoidance—not necessarily of parents but of the divisive issues as related to parents. As Heider might say, unit formation between issue and parents was broken up, and psychological imbalance thus reduced. Such a "solution" resembles autistic hostility in that it involves a marked restriction of communication.

But this solution, as many of my subjects testified, was not a particularly comfortable one. Hence, it would hardly be surprising if many of them, during early post-college years, were in search of environments that would provide less uncomfortable solutions—or, better yet, more positively rewarding ones. An ideal one, of course, would be a husband who was rewarding as a supporter of one's own attitudes as well as in other ways.

And so, vis-à-vis parents and fellow-students at first, and later vis-à-vis husbands (or perhaps working associates), forces toward balance were at work. Specifically, support from important people concerning important issues came to be the rule, and its absence the exception. Support sometimes came about by changing one's own attitudes toward those of needed supporters, or, more commonly, by selecting supporters for existing attitudes. The latter stratagem represented not merely an automatic tendency for attitudes to perpetuate themselves. More significantly, I believe, it represents an adaptation to a world that includes *both* persons and issues. Such a dual adaptation can be made, of course, by sacrificing one's stand on the issues (regression). But if the dual adaptation is to be made without this sacrifice, then an interpersonal world must be selected (or created) that is supportive—in which case we can say that the attitude has been expressed by finding a supportive environment.

According to my two themes (of *1946* and *1963*) an existing attitude may be maintained by creating environments in which *either* new information can be avoided *or* in which other persons support one's own information. In either case, the fate of an attitude is mediated by the social environment in which the individual attempts to maintain or to restore balance regarding that same attitude. Insofar as that environment excludes disturbing information or provides reinforcing information, the attitude persists. And insofar as the selection or the acceptance of that environment is a consequence of holding the attitude, we have a steady-state, self-maintaining system.

VI.

If you will pardon an autobiographical reference I should like to tell you, finally, one of my reasons for choosing my present topic. When, just 17 years ago tomorrow, I read my paper on autistic hostility at the annual meeting of this Society, one of the persons in the audience—as I observed with both delight and consternation—was the man in whose memory we meet today, Kurt Lewin. A few hours later, as we were both waiting for another session to begin, he asked me if he might publish my paper. Though I cannot remember for certain, I suspect that in my eagerness to accept his offer I did not stop to ask in what journal he planned to publish it, but to have appeared in the first issue of Volume I of *Human Relations* is to this day a matter of no small pride to me.

Kurt Lewin did not, alas, live to see even the first issue of the journal that he did so much to launch. But even today he is constantly looking over my shoulder, just as he did when I was revising that now-ancient paper for publication—for him. I like to think that, were he alive, he would be curious as to what I had done, over the years, with the notion of autistic hostility. And so, though I cannot tell him, I can report to you, at a meeting in his honor, one of the things that I have done with it.

REFERENCES

Asch, S. E. *Social Psychology*. New York: Prentice-Hall, 1952.

Brown, R. Models of attitude change. In Brown, R., Galanter, E., Hess, E. H., & Mandler, G. *New Directions in Psychology*. New York: Holt, Rinehart & Winston, 1962.

Heider, F. Attitudes and cognitive organization. *J. Psychol,* 1946, *21,* 107–12.

———. *The Psychology of Interpersonal Relations*. New York: Wiley, 1958.

Newcomb, T. M. *Personality and Social Change.* New York: Holt, Rinehart & Winston, 1943.

———. Autistic hostility and social reality. *Human Relations,* 1947, *1,* 69–86.

———. *The Acquaintance Process.* New York: Holt, Rinehart & Winston, 1961.

Primacy Versus Recency in Persuasion as a Function of the Timing of Arguments and Measures

CHESTER A. INSKO

Is the greater persuasive effect more likely to be produced by the first or the second opposing communications successively presented to a recipient? According to convention the case in which the initial communication has the greater effect is called one of primacy, and the case in which the final communication has the greater effect is called one of recency. Common sense lends support to both primacy and recency effects. It is better "to get your side of the argument in first," but also it is better "to have the last word."

In a recent study Miller and Campbell (1959) formulated and tested a theory of primacy versus recency that seems to be a definite advance on previous work (Hovland, Mandell, Campbell, Brock, Luchins, Cohen, McGuire, Janis, Feierabend, & Anderson, 1957). Miller and Campbell assumed that the persuasive impact of a communication is a function of its retention and thus derived predictions from the Ebbinghaus forgetting curve about the circumstances under which primacy and recency effects may be expected. Underwood (1948) had previously shown that for verbal learning the relative superiority of the second of two lists with respect to retention decreases as the time between learning and testing becomes greater, a direct consequence of the nature of the Ebbinghaus curve. With a long enough time interval the forgetting curves for both lists reach asymptote, and recency is not found.

Miller and Campbell's view of the implications of the Ebbinghaus curve as it applies to two competing communications is presented in Figure 1, drawn on the assumption of no interaction between communications, and an initial primacy advantage for the first communication. In Condition 1 the two communications are presented in immediate succession with a measure of opinion directly following the second communication; in Condition 2 the communications are presented in succession with a measure of opinion a week after the second communication; in Condition 3 the communications are presented a week apart with a measure of opinion directly following the second communication; in Condition 4 they are presented a week apart with a measure of opinion a week after the second communication. On the basis of these curves Miller and Campbell predicted that the relative recency effect in the four conditions would fall in the following order: $3 > 4$, $3 > 1$, $3 > 2$, $1 > 2$, and $4 > 2$.

In their data based on prosecution and defense arguments in a summarized law case, this prediction was exactly upheld with respect to relative recency effects on the measure of opinion, but less precisely with respect to retention. Condition 1 did not show more recency than Condition 2, and furthermore,

Reprinted from Journal of Abnormal and Social Psychology, 69, 1964, 381–391. Copyright 1964 by the American Psychological Association and reproduced by permission.

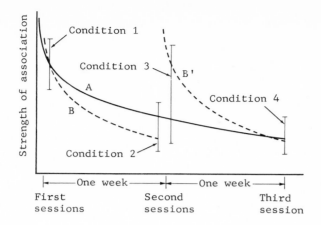

Fig. 1. Hypothetical forgetting curves for two competing communications with an added primacy effect (Miller & Campbell, 1959, p. 2); the primacy effect is represented by the higher initial starting point and final asymptote of Curve A in comparison with Curve B or B'. (The initial communication is represented by Curve A, and the second by either Curve B or B'.)

Condition 2 showed neither primacy nor recency (not primacy as expected); and Condition 4 showed recency (while neither primacy nor recency was expected). And finally the average within-groups correlation between the opinion and recall scores was −.10, insignificantly different from zero.

These results are rather curious. One would not have been surprised if predictions based on the Ebbinghaus curve had been upheld for retention but not for opinion. But just the opposite happened. Some of the difficulty could conceivably lie in the measure of retention used. Rather than a multiple-choice or recognition test, perhaps a straight recall test would have been better. Recall rather than recognition is, after all, the process that is assumed to mediate effects on opinion as measured at times subsequent to exposure to the persuasive communications.

Thomas, Webb, and Tweedie (1961) attempted to test the hypothesis that primacy may be obtained under conditions of delayed measurement. Using two communications concerned with the issue of whether or not it was advisable to use a new anticancer serum routinely in medical practice they failed to obtain significant results under conditions of either familiarity or nonfamiliarity.

But Miller and Campbell's expectation that the curve for the first of two communications should level off at a higher asymptote than the curve for the second communication is not an integral or necessary part of their theory. It merely incorporates what they regarded as an empirical generalization, one that would seem to have a dubious support. The rest of the theory may still be substantially correct. If so, one major aspect of the determinants of primacy and recency effects would be accounted for in terms of more general phenomena of human learning and recall. The present study seeks to test Miller and Campbell's theory employing recall as a measure of retention and a wider range of temporal intervals between communications and measures, respectively.

METHOD

Subjects

The subjects, primarily sophomores, were obtained from an introductory psychology course at the University of California. The assignment of groups to conditions was randomly determined. To fill the requirements of the design, 48 groups each of 7 subjects ($N = 336$) were used. Sixty-seven subjects were randomly eliminated from 35 of the groups in order to obtain equal Ns.

Communications

To assure lack of any prior familiarity with the issues, a summarized law case was used for the experimental communications. In the tape recordings, the same speaker was used to present the summaries of both prosecution and defense arguments pertaining to a supposedly real bigamy trial. The communications were the same as those used in previous research (Insko, 1962). Both of the communications were one-sided and approximately 850 words in length. Each communication, respectively, summarized the testimony of a series of six prosecution or six defense witnesses. The testimony of these witnesses pointed simply to the guilt or to the innocence of the defendant; it did not attempt to discredit or contradict the testimony of the opposing side.

Response Measures

Opinion was measured on a 9-point graphic scale on which low values indicated belief in the innocence and high values belief in the guilt of the defendant.

Retention was measured by having subjects recall the content of the two communications one at a time. For each communication subjects were given a separate sheet of paper with space provided for them to identify and recall the testimony of each of the six prosecution or defense witnesses. The recall material was rated by two independent judges. Subject's recall for each witness received two possible points for identification of the witness and two possible points for presentation of the witness' testimony. Incomplete or distorted identification of the witness and incomplete or distorted presentation of the testimony were each given one point. With six witnesses on each side, perfect recall received a score of 24 in each case. The scoring of relative primacy or recency of recall involved subtracting the defense score from the prosecution score for each subject, to yield a possible range of difference scores from −24 to +24.

After listening twice to the taped communications, 30 judges (undergraduates) rated each of the prosecution and defense witnesses in terms of importance in supporting the respective case on a 5-point graphic scale from "not important" to "extremely important." For certain analyses, the mean importance rating for each witness thus obtained was multiplied by the subject's recall score for that witness. Summing the weighted recall scores for the defense witnesses and subtracting them from the sum of weighted recall scores for the prosecution witnesses produced a total weighted recall score for each subject.

Procedure

Upon entering the room subjects were given an instructional sheet to read which informed them that the experiment was concerned with jury deliberation, and that after hearing a tape-recorded presentation of the summary arguments of the prosecution and defense, they were to deliberate the case. Microphones were set up in the room supposedly for the purpose of recording the deliberation. After the subjects finished reading the instructions, the experimenter read them aloud and commented upon them extensively. The prosecution and defense communications were played either one immediately after the other, 2 days apart, 1 week apart, or 2 weeks apart. Recall and opinion were measured either immediately after the second communication, or 2 days, or 1 week after the second communication.

If the subjects were in a group that was to return a second time they were told that the first session was intended primarily as an orientation to familiarize them with the general purposes and procedures of the experiment. During the second session, if the subjects were in a group that was to return a third time, they were told, after hearing the second communication, that the experimenter had decided that deliberation or discussion could best be studied if it were carried on entirely within one uninterrupted hour. The subjects were specifically asked not to discuss the trial either among themselves or with other people until the time of deliberation.

Five independent variables were manipulated in the experiment: order of communications—prosecution-defense or defense-prosecution; time between communications—none, 2 days, 1 week, or 2 weeks; time between second communication and recall and opinion measures—none, 2 days, or 1 week; order of measures—opinion-recall or recall-opinion; and order of recall measures—prosecution-defense or defense-prosecution. The latter two variables were tied so that opinion-recall always went with defense-prosecution recall, and recall-opinion always went with prosecution-defense recall. The design thus called for 48 different conditions: 2 x 4 x 3 x 2.

RESULTS

The mean opinion and recall scores for each of the 48 groups are presented in Table 1. An opinion score greater than 5 indicates agreement with the prosecution and a score less than 5 indicates agreement with the defense. The recall scores were obtained by subtracting the defense recall score from the prosecution recall score, and adding 10 to eliminate minus signs. Thus, a score greater than 10 indicates superior recall of the prosecution and a score less than 10 indicates superior recall of the defense. The recall scores are the mean of the scores obtained by two independent raters. The Spearman-Brown corrected reliability of the rating is +.98. No incompletely filled out forms were obtained. However, approximately 5% of the subjects failed to return for either the second or the third session. The subjects not returning were fairly randomly distributed over the 44 groups in which there was either a second or a third session.

Table 1 SUMMARY OF THE EXPERIMENTAL DESIGN AND RESULTS

	TIME BETWEEN COMMUNICATIONS											
	NONE			2 DAYS			1 WEEK			2 WEEKS		
	TIME BETWEEN SECOND COMMUNICATION AND MEASURES											
	NONE	2 DAYS	1 WEEK	NONE	2 DAYS	1 WEEK	NONE	2 DAYS	1 WEEK	NONE	2 DAYS	1 WEEK
Recall opinion												
Prosecution-defense												
Group number	1	2	3	4	5	6	7	8	9	10	11	12
M opinion	6.66	4.33	4.09	4.31	4.23	3.91	4.20	5.34	4.53	2.89	3.59	5.14
M recall	17.14	11.29	11.50	6.86	9.43	12.71	8.50	9.50	11.50	8.50	10.14	13.07
Defense-prosecution												
Group number	13	14	15	16	17	18	19	20	21	22	23	24
M opinion	4.61	4.30	4.03	5.36	5.70	4.53	5.57	5.31	5.19	5.66	5.14	4.33
M recall	12.93	14.00	10.64	17.14	10.21	14.86	13.71	14.93	10.50	19.71	13.50	10.29
Opinion-recall												
Prosecution-defense												
Group number	25	26	27	28	29	30	31	32	33	34	35	36
M opinion	4.01	4.04	4.37	4.94	4.44	4.84	4.01	4.16	4.99	3.33	5.10	4.14
M recall	7.00	14.71	11.50	9.86	9.50	11.57	6.43	6.86	11.93	4.43	9.43	12.71
Defense-prosecution												
Group number	37	38	39	40	41	42	43	44	45	46	47	48
M opinion	4.86	4.30	5.21	5.24	4.86	3.59	5.53	5.19	5.19	5.54	4.93	4.01
M recall	12.64	9.14	13.86	13.07	14.14	11.43	17.07	14.21	10.64	13.71	11.14	11.79

Note. –N = 7 for all groups.

Analysis of Temporal Effects: t Tests and Trend Analyses

By ignoring the order of opinion and recall measures (collapsing the data across this variable), and by taking the differences between corresponding scores for the two orders of communications we are able to examine the pattern of primacy and recency over time. Since a high score indicates agreement with or superior recall of the prosecution, recency is indicated when communications presented in a defense-prosecution order result in a higher score than communications presented in a prosecution-defense order. The opposite effect, of course, is evidence for primacy.

For both the opinion and the recall data the mean differences between the prosecution-defense and defense-prosecution orders, together with the *t* values relating to these differences, are presented in Table 2. The average within-group variance for all 48 groups was used in the denominator of the *t*'s. In those groups in which the measures follow immediately after the second communication, the recency effect for both recall and opinion increases as the time between communications increases. For the opinion data the recency effect is significant in the 1- and 2-week groups, and for the recall data there is a significant recency effect in the 2-day, 1-week, and 2-week groups. In the groups with a time lapse both between the two communications and between the second communication and the measures, the recency effect becomes progressively less as the interval between the second communication and the measures increases, with one exception. The exception is a nonsignificant reversal of the opinion scores in the groups with a 2-day interval both between communications and between the second communication and measures.

With respect to the groups in which the second communication immediately follows the first, no striking trends appear as the time interval between the second communications and the measures increases. As it was originally stated, though without evident justification, Miller and Campbell's (1959) theory predicted that the immediate measure groups should show more recency than the 1-week measure groups. The data show the opposite effect, although not significantly so.

These temporal effects upon primacy-recency are graphically presented for the opinion data in Figure 2 and for the recall data in Figure 3. The ordinates of these graphs represent net recency, as the differences between the sums of defense-prosecution and prosecution-defense orders of presentation. The abscissas represent time elapsed between the first communication and measurement. The dotted lines running between 0 and 14 days connect data points for the groups in which measures were administered immediately after the second communication, and graphically portray the effect of varying the interval between the communications. The solid lines connecting with the dotted lines at 0, 2, 7, and 14 days on the abscissa represent the effect of varying the interval between the second communication and the measures. An analysis of each of the five trends was carried out by a technique proposed by Grandage (1958) for computing the orthogonal coefficients of unequal intervals, with results presented in the figures adjacent to the appropriate curves.

According to Miller and Campbell's theory the memory for the persuasive impact of a communication should follow the negatively accelerated function of

Table 2 *t* Tests Results

	TIME BETWEEN COMMUNICATIONS											
	NONE			2 DAYS			1 WEEK			2 WEEKS		
	TIME BETWEEN SECOND COMMUNICATION AND MEASURES											
	NONE	*2 DAYS*	*1 WEEK*	*NONE*	*2 DAYS*	*1 WEEK*	*NONE*	*2 DAYS*	*1 WEEK*	*NONE*	*2 DAYS*	*1 WEEK*
Opinion												
M difference	0.60a	0.12b	0.39b	0.68b	0.94b	0.32a	1.44b	0.50b	0.43b	2.49b	0.69b	0.47a
t	1.02			1.16	1.60		2.46*			4.26**	1.18	
Recall												
M difference	0.72b	1.43a	0.74b	6.74b	2.71b	1.00b	7.92b	6.39b	1.14a	10.24b	2.54b	1.85a
t		1.02		4.81**	1.94		5.66**	4.56**		7.31**	1.81	1.32

Note. – In each case, df = 288.
a Primacy.
b Recency.
* p < .05.
** p < .01.

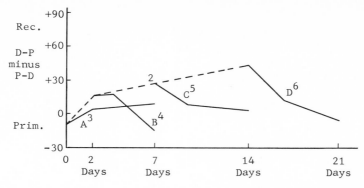

Fig. 2. Recency and primacy in persuasion as a function of the time between communications (dotted line) and the time between the second communication and the measures (solid line). (Point A refers to the delayed measurement conditions with no time between communications; Point B, to the delayed measurement conditions with 2 days between communications; Point C, to the delayed measurement conditions with 7 days between communications; and Point D, to the delayed measurement conditions with 14 days between communications. Each data point is based on the difference between a prosecution-defense order of presentation group of 14 subjects and a defense-prosecution order of presentation group of 14 subjects. Point 2: linear $F = 13.68$ ($p < .01$), deviation from linearity $F = .62$ (*ns*); Point 3: variable $F = .77$ (*ns*); Point 4: linear $F = 6.15$ ($p < .01$), deviation from linearity $F = 5.30$ ($p < .01$), quadratic $F = 4.58$ ($p < .05$), deviation from curvature $F = 6.68$ ($p < .01$); Point 5: variable $F = .95$ (*ns*); Point 6: linear $F = 11.41$ ($p < .01$), deviation from linearity $F = 1.58$ (*ns*), quadratic $F = 12.84$ ($p < 0.1$), deviation from curvature $F = .10$ (*ns*).)

the Ebbinghaus curve. In the theoretical situation in which two communications are exactly equated in terms of persuasiveness, the recency effect of a time interval between the communications is equal to the difference in the heights of the two curves. With immediate measurement and increasing time between first and second communications the recency effect should increase as the curve for the first communication drops, but then should level off as the curve for the first communication reaches asymptote. Our index of the theoretical difference between the two curves is, of course, the difference between measures for the two orders of presentation. Thus, in the immediate measurement groups, the curve representing time between communications should rise with negative acceleration and eventually reach asymptote as the theoretical curve for the first communication reaches asymptote; i.e., should be quadratic in form. In the delayed measurement groups in which there is some time between communications, the curves should drop with negative acceleration and eventually reach asymptote as the theoretical curves for both communications reach asymptote; i.e., should also be quadratic in form. We thus expect a rising quadratic curve with increasing time between the second communication and the measures.

Considering first the trend lines in the two graphs representing time between communications (dotted lines), it is apparent that the trends for recall and

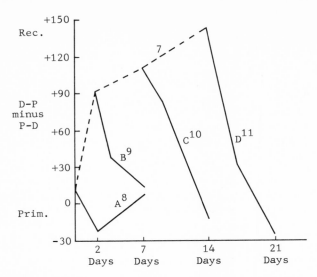

Fig 3. Recency and primacy in recall as a function of the time between communications (dotted line) and of the time between the second communication and the measures (solid lines). (Point A refers to the delayed measurement conditions with no time between communications; Point B, to the delayed measurement conditions with 2 days between communications; Point C, to the delayed measurement conditions with 7 days between communications; and Point D, to the delayed measurement conditions with 14 days between communications. Each data point is based on the difference between a prosecution-defense order of presentation group of 14 subjects and a defense-prosecution order of presentation group of 14 subjects. Point 7: linear $F = 18.51$ ($p < .01$), deviation from linearity $F = 3.55$ ($p < .05$), quadratic $F = 3.03$ (ns); Point 8: variable $F = .77$ (ns); Point 9: linear $F = 7.06$ ($p < .01$), deviation from linearity $F = 1.84$ (ns), quadratic $F = 8.47$ ($p < .01$), deviation from curvature $F = .44$ (ns); Point 10: linear $F = 23.67$ ($p < .01$), deviation $F = .33$ (ns); Point 11: linear $F = .33$ (ns), quadratic $F = 37.50$ ($p < .01$), deviation from curvature $F = .86$ (ns).)

opinion are only roughly the same shape. Both trends have significant linear Fs, but the F for deviation from linearity in the case of the recall trend is also significant, even though the quadratic F is not. Both curves do show a break in direction at the 2-day interval, and negative acceleration thereafter. It is probable that if even greater time between communications had been provided, both curves would have arrived at a stable or quasi-stable asymptote.

The trend lines for delayed measurement (solid lines) dropping from the 14-day interval to the 21-day interval in the two graphs (representing the effect of delayed measures after communications separated by 14 days) appear to be fairly similar in form. Both trends have highly significant quadratic Fs, and insignificant quadratic deviation Fs. The opinion trend is one of the unusual kinds in which both the linear and quadratic Fs are significant, and the deviations from both are not significant. The quadratic F, however, is larger than the linear F.

Although the delayed measurement lines for the group with 7-day intervals between communications get progressively lower (toward primacy) on both graphs, they do not appear to have at all the same shape. The opinion trend, in fact, does not show significant variance of any sort, and the recall trend is significantly linear.

For the groups with 2-day intervals between communications, the delayed measurement lines on the two graphs do not even get progressively lower with the passage of time. Both lines show greatest relative primacy 7 days after the second communication. The opinion and recall trends both show significant linear and quadratic Fs. The linear deviation and quadratic deviation Fs are both significant for opinion, but not for recall.

For the groups without a time interval between communications, neither of the delayed measurement lines for recall or opinion has significant variance. As was mentioned earlier, in this case Miller and Campbell predict a significant trend in the direction of primacy or of decreasing recency.

Analyses of Variance

A summary of analyses of variance for the measures of both opinion and recall is presented in Table 3. The total between-groups Fs in both analyses are significant warranting the evaluation of the t's and Fs as previously reported. The

Table 3 SUMMARY OF ANALYSES OF VARIANCE FOR MEASURES OF OPINION AND RECALL

SOURCE	df	OPINION		RECALL	
		MS	F	MS	F
Time between communications (A)	3	2.87	1.20	11.82	
Time between second communication and measures (B)	2	2.37		8.47	
Order of measures (C)	1	0.83		82.51	6.02*
Order of communications (D)	1	24.05	10.07**	698.63	50.95**
A × B	6	2.62	1.10	7.86	
A × C	3	0.39		15.98	1.17
A × D	3	3.91	1.64	80.26	5.85**
B × C	2	0.68		52.05	3.80*
B × D	2	7.00	2.93	318.70	23.24**
C × D	1	0.00		3.14	
A × B × C	6	3.81	1.60	43.92	3.20**
A × B × D	6	5.19	2.17*	60.39	4.40**
A × C × D	3	6.26	2.62	19.58	1.43
B × C × D	2	1.07		12.19	
A × B × C × D	6	2.25		70.02	5.11**
Total between	47	3.65	1.53*	64.75	4.72**
Within	288				
Total	335				

* $p \leqslant .05.$
** $p \leqslant .01.$

single most important F from the standpoint of Miller and Campbell's theory is the triple interaction between order of communications, time between communications, and time between the second communication and measures. These Fs, which are significant for both the opinion and recall data, correspond to the finding that recency increases with the time between communications, and decreases with the time between the second communication and measures. The significance of the main effect for order of communications in both sets of data corresponds to the fact that most of the order effects were in the direction of recency.

Six additional Fs are significant only for recall. Two of these, the interactions between order of communications, on the one hand, and both the time between communications and the time between the second communication and measures, on the other, are reasonable in the context of Miller and Campbell's theory. According to the first, the longer the time between communications the greater the recency effect; and according to the second, the longer the time between the second communication and the measures, the less the recency effect. Miller and Campbell's theory states that the longer the time between communications the greater the recency effect, if there is immediate measurement, and that the longer the time between the second communication and the measures the less the recency effect, if there has been enough time between communications to produce a recency effect. The fact that each of the temporal variables when taken alone should have a significant effect upon the primacy-recency differences indicates the power of these variables.

Several or perhaps all of the remaining four Fs involve the phenomenon of response interference, although interpretation is made difficult because the variables concerning order of measurement are tied. Two of the Fs that involve order of measurement nevertheless make some sense if we interpret the effects as a resultant of the order of recall, prosecution-defense or defense-prosecution, ignoring the tied variable of whether opinion or recall is measured first.

The first of these Fs is a main effect for order of measures. The direction of the effect is such that there is more recall of the prosecution in the prosecution-defense order of recall than in the defense-prosecution order. If we assume that the act of recalling one communication interferes with the subsequent recall of a second communication, then whichever communication is recalled first should be recalled better. This is exactly what happened. The second F, the interaction between the order of measures and the time between the second communication and the measures, indicates that the superior recall of the first recalled communication effect is most evident immediately following the second communication, less evident 2 days after the second communication, and slightly reversed 1 week after the second communication. The effect of response interference might reasonably be expected to be most apparent during the period in which fairly rapid forgetting is occurring, and least apparent or nonexistent during the period in which forgetting is beginning to reach a stable asymptote. After longer time intervals when response interference is not a factor, the communication recalled second may benefit from associations aroused during the prior recall of the first communication.

The two remaining significant Fs defy theoretical interpretation: the triple interaction between order of measures, time between communications, and the time between the second communication and the measures, and the quadruple interaction between order of measures, order of communications, time between communications, and time between the second communication and the measures.

An analysis of variance of the weighted recall scores yielded results, except for two Fs, that were very similar to those of the analysis of variance of the unweighted recall scores. The F for order of measures is significant only for the unweighted scores, and the F for time between communications is significant only for the weighted scores ($p < .05$). The latter corresponds to a finding that there is relatively more recall of the prosecution witnesses in the short than the long time intervals between communications.

Correlational Analyses

The simple direct correlation between the two dependent variables, opinion and retention, is $+.24$ ($p < .01$), and the correlation between opinion and weighted recall is $+.26$ ($p < .01$), insignificantly larger. It had originally been expected that the weighting of the recall scores in terms of judged importance would increase the correlation with opinion. Inasmuch as the corrected reliability for the 30 obtained judgments of the importance of the prosecution and defense witnesses is $+.99$ and $+.96$, respectively, this failure cannot be attributed to unreliability. On the other hand, the manner in which the weights were applied was entirely arbitrary, and the range of importance for the witnesses on either side was not very great; every witness seemed to be fairly damning to the opposition's case.

The within-cell correlations between opinion and recall vary between $-.59$ and $+.72$, and average a nonsignificant $+.10$ by Fisher's z transformation. When weighted recall scores are used, the corresponding values vary between $-.67$ and $+.83$, and average a significant $+.15$ ($p < .05$). The two average within-cell correlations, however, do not differ significantly from each other. Whether the average within-cell correlations differ significantly from the zero-order correlations is not known since no test of significance has been developed for such a comparison. One possible reason for the difference in magnitude between the zero-order correlations and the average within-cell correlations is the restriction in the range of the variables within each cell. But according to McNemar (1954), there is no satisfactory way to "correct" for the restriction in range of *both* the involved variables. Inasmuch as 20 out of 48 of the unweighted and 19 out of 48 of the weighted within-cell correlations are negative, such a correction could have only a small effect on the average within-cell correlation.

The basic assumption of Miller and Campbell's theory is that opinion is a function of retention. Although in the present study retention is operationally indexed through recall, and opinion through the marking of a rating scale, it is not to be supposed that retention is nothing but recall, or that opinion is nothing but the marking of a rating scale. In addition to measuring retention, recall also facilitates and emphasizes it, and in addition to measuring opinion, the marking of a rating scale also crystallizes and emphasizes it. This being the case, the assumption that opinion is a function of retention leads to the prediction that there should be a greater correlation between measures of opinion and retention in the recall-opinion order of measurement than in the

opinion-recall order of measurement. The contrary assumption, equally compatible with the relationships thus far reported, that retention is a function of
opinion leads to the opposite prediction.

The test is made still more relevant by the fact that there is a degree of
commitment to an opinion once the subjects have marked the rating scale due to
the fact that they are under the impression that they are subsequently going to
debate or discuss the issue. In any event, the average within-cell correlation is
+.17 in the recall-opinion order and +.03 in the opinion-recall order. These
correlations do not differ significantly from zero or from each other. For the
weighted recall scores the correlation with opinion is +.17 in the recall-opinion
order and +.13 in the opinion-recall order.

CONCLUSION AND DISCUSSION

Miller and Campbell's (1959) theory conceptualizes retention as an intervening
variable accounting for temporal effects in persuasive communications. According to the theory, changes in opinion over time should parallel those in retention, and measures of opinion should correlate positively with those of
retention. We shall examine in turn the results with regard to each of these
expectations.

With regard to opinion as a function of the timing of communications and
measurement, the results generally support the Miller and Campbell theory. We
can safely generalize that the longer the time interval between two opposing
persuasive communications to which a person has been exposed, the greater the
recency effect on opinion measured immediately after the second communication, and the longer the time elapsed from this second communication to the
time that opinion is measured, the less the recency effect.

But the data fail to support Miller and Campbell's prediction that delayed
measurement in the groups with no time between communications should
produce a primacy effect or less recency than occurs without the delay. In this
respect our results are in agreement with those of Thomas et al. (1961), who also
failed to obtain a primacy effect with delayed measurement. Miller and
Campbell predicted a primacy effect under these circumstances because they
believed that the forgetting curve for the first communication starts at a
somewhat higher level than the forgetting curve for the second communication,
a difference that becomes observable only with delayed measurement when the
curve for the first communication has leveled off at a higher asymptote. Since
this postulated effect is not an integral or necessary part of their theory its
disconfirmation does not disturb the remainder of their analyses relating opinion
to retention effects.

The results with regard to retention as a function of the timing of communications and measurement were similar to those for opinion. The longer the time
interval between two opposing communications to which a person has been
exposed, the greater the recency effect on retention measured immediately after
the second communication; and the longer the time elapsed from this second
communication to the time that retention is measured, the less the recency
effect. The data again failed to support the prediction that delayed measurement
in the groups with no time between communications produces a primacy effect

or less recency than occurs without the delay. These results agree in all respects with those of Miller and Campbell.

The predictions concerning the shapes of the opinion and recall functions over time are only roughly supported. Many of the curves either are linear or have significant linear components when they should be quadratic. It should be noted, however, that the number of cases at any one data point is fairly small (each point plots the difference between two groups of 14 subjects each), and that the time intervals may not have covered a sufficient range to show the true shape of the curves. The forgetting of the single first communication had clearly not reached asymptote after 2 weeks, a condition essential to producing curvature in the function of the differences between recall of the first and second communications.

The correlational results involve the notorious ambiguity inherent in the interpretation of any correlation. That retention causes opinion is, of course, the basic assumption of Miller and Campbell's theory. That opinion causes retention is, however, a derivation of Festinger's (1957) theory of cognitive dissonance. For a person to remember the content of a persuasive argument with which he does not agree should arouse dissonance, which could be reduced through appropriate forgetting. Some such process may conceivably occur after the subject has heard both communications and agreed with one or the other. We attempted to test for the validity of these two opposing assumptions by examining the differences between the average within-cell correlation in the recall-opinion and opinion-recall groups. The results were indecisive.

The fact that in the analyses of variance, sources of variance proved significant for recall that were not significant for opinion is also troublesome for any simple assumption that retention causes opinion. Both opinion and retention may covary as a function of the timing of communications and measures, without one being causally prior to the other. The smaller size of the average within-cell correlations between opinion and recall, relative to the zero-order correlations, suggests such an interpretation.

It is only through further research that the causal sequence can be disentangled. For instance, the assumption that retention causes opinion leads to the prediction that if forgetting of the first of two opposing communications is produced through experimentally manipulated interference, a recency effect should follow. And the assumption that opinion causes recall leads to the prediction that the greater the degree of experimentally produced commitment to an opinion, the lower the degree to which the content of the opposing communication will be recalled.

REFERENCES

Festinger, L. *A theory of cognitive dissonance*. Evanston, Ill.: Row, Peterson, 1957.

Grandage, A. Orthogonal coefficients for unequal intervals. *Biometrics* 1958, *14*, 287–89.

Hovland, C. I., Mandell, W., Campbell, Enid H., Brock, T., Luchins, A. S., Cohen, A. R., McGuire, W. J., Janis, I. L., Feierabend, Rosalind L., & Anderson, N. H. *The order of presentation in persuasion*. New Haven: Yale Univer. Press, 1957.

Insko, C. A. One-sided versus two-sided communications and countercommunications. *J. abnorm. soc. Psychol.*, 1962, *65*, 203–6.

McNemar, Q. *Psychological statistics.* New York: Wiley, 1954.

Miller, N., & Campbell, D. T. Recency and primacy in persuasion as a function of the timing of speeches and measurements. *J. abnorm. soc. Psychol.*, 1959, *59*, 1–9.

Thomas, E. J., Webb, Susan, & Tweedie, Jean. Effects of familiarity with a controversial issue on acceptance of successive persuasive communications *J. abnorm. soc. Psychol.*, 1961, *63*, 656–59.

Underwood, B. J. Retroactive and proactive inhibition after five and forty-eight hours, *J. exp. Psychol.*, 1948, *38*, 29–38.

9

ATTITUDE CHANGE

The Paradox of De Facto Selective Exposure Without Preferences for Supportive Information

DAVID O. SEARS

In this paper the plan is to (A) present the basic hypotheses about selective exposure and review briefly the most recent research evidence on them, (B) consider whether or not this evidence may be trusted, (C) suggest some implications of these outcomes for attitude change and consistency theory, and (D) attempt to reconcile the results of laboratory and field findings on selective exposure.

A. BASIC HYPOTHESES AND RECENT RESEARCH

Four basic propositions have been tested in experimental work on selective exposure. They are these: (1) people seek supportive information; (2) people avoid nonsupportive information; (3) both tendencies occur more frequently with greater cognitive dissonance; and (4) both tendencies occur more frequently when the individual has little confidence in his initial opinion. Freedman and Sears (1965a) reviewed relevant research published through mid-1965, and concluded that available evidence did not favor any of these four propositions. First let us briefly consider whether or not subsequent research forms a more conclusive picture.

Four studies have tested whether or not people seek supportive information. One by Brock (1965) on smoking and lung cancer indicated they do, as did one of three conducted by Mills (1965a, b) in a market survey situation. The same studies provide evidence on whether or not people avoid nonsupportive information. Mills reports significant avoidance in two experiments (Mills, 1965a) but not in a third (1965b), and Brock (1965) found no evidence for avoidance. So in each case only two of the four relevant studies yielded positive evidence. It might be noted parenthetically that most experiments theoretically designed to test separately 'seeking' and 'avoiding' tendencies have not successfully done so, due to the absence of an adequate neutral baseline (Rhine, 1967a).

Relative preferences for supportive and nonsupportive information were also tested in three studies by Lowin (1967a, b) and in studies by Lowe and Steiner (1968) and Thayer (1968). In each case no significant preference emerged. In two other studies (Clarke and James, 1967b), the data are potentially relevant to this question (and supportive information appears to have been preferred somewhat) but the necessary significance tests are not given. All in all, the picture seems to remain a mixed one.

Several attempts have been made at manipulating cognitive dissonance. In three studies, Mills attempted to vary the revocability, importance, and difficulty of making a decision (1965a, b). Selectivity increased with greater decision difficulty in one case (1965b), but his other four variations had no effect. Lowe and Steiner (1968) varied the revocability and importance of a decision and found increased importance actually *decreased* selectivity, while revocability had no effect. Rhine (1967b) varied the similarity of candidates' positions in the 1964 campaign to the subjects' perceptions of their positions (though this variation would appear not to be as directly relevant to dissonance arousal, since the subjects' own positions and candidate preferences were not considered). Avoidance of dissonant information increased with greater dissonance, but the seeking of consonant information did not. A surprising finding in this study was that selectivity was actually lower in the Dissonance-Arousal experimental groups than in the No-Dissonance control group. Also, some evidence is produced for a curvilinear relationship between dissonance arousal and selectivity, which Rhine elsewhere (1967a) argues is the more appropriate derivation from dissonance theory. Nevertheless, the data on the effects of dissonance arousal remain essentially ambiguous.

The fourth proposition has received the most attention. It predicts an interaction between confidence in one's initial opinion and selectivity. Highly confident people are supposed to seek nonsupportive information, confident that they can refute it. People with little confidence should avoid nonsupportive information and seek the reassurance conveyed by supportive information. The corollary is that among difficult-to-refute arguments, supportive information should be preferred to nonsupportive information. Among easily refuted arguments, nonsupportive information should be preferred (Lowin, 1967a, b).

The evidence on this fourth notion again is mixed, unfortunately. Canon (1964) and Freedman (1965a) conducted virtually identical studies manipulating confidence; Canon obtained the predicted interaction, but Freedman found no trace of it, though obtaining similar results to Canon's in other respects. Mills (1965a, b) varied the ease of making a choice, and hence presumably the confidence with which it was made. In one case there were no differences, while in the second confidence affected preference for supportive information but not avoidance of nonsupportive information. Lowin (1967a) and Thayer (1968) varied the subject's confidence in his own judgment, but both found that this variation did not affect subsequent selectivity.

The corollary hypothesis, dealing with message refutability or message strength, has met with more success. In one experiment, greater preference for supportive information was obtained under conditions of high communicator credibility than under low credibility (Lowin, 1967a). And in a mail survey during the 1964 election campaign, Lowin (1967b) found strong supportive and weak nonsupportive messages preferred to strong nonsupportive and weak supportive messages. In a second mail survey, though, the hypothesis was supported in only one of four comparisons (Lowin, 1967b).

Of the eight relevant studies, therefore, two support the confidence hypothesis, two are mixed, and the remaining four fail to support it. It should be noted, however, that no study has yet obtained the converse; i.e., a *positive* relationship between manipulated confidence and selectivity.

In sum, recent research offers no grounds for modifying the conclusions reached in the earlier review. The evidence does not systematically favor any of the four propositions listed.

B. THE INSENSITIVITY POSSIBILITY

It has been repeatedly noted that people are primarily exposed to supportive information in nature, and that most audiences do in fact overrepresent those who initially agree with the communicator. This state of affairs may be termed 'de facto selectivity.' The problem is to reconcile these observations with the apparent burden of the experimental research reviewed above.

There are two obvious possibilities. First, the experimental work may have been badly done, and simply be insensitive to the true differences that are there. Second, there may in fact be no general preference for supportive information, whether under neutral, high-dissonance, or low-confidence conditions. That is, the experimental work may accurately reflect a true state of no differences. Let us consider these two possibilities in turn. First, what grounds might there be for thinking that the experimental work has overlooked true differences?

1. Stimulus Situation

It would be hard to fault the theoretical relevance of stimulus materials that have been used. However, one general problem is insuring that the subject really believes he will be exposed to his choice. Brock (1965) has found greater selectivity with actual exposure choices than with abstract 'interest' ratings. Lowin (1965), on the other hand, obtained approximately the same results from ratings-in-the-abstract and actual requests for information. In previous studies, one or the other procedure has been used, but it is not obvious that one systematically induced more selectivity than the other. Thus the point does not seem to account for the general lack of selectivity in experimental studies. However, it is a useful criticism; exposure choices have often been quite artificial.

2. Confoundings

The supportiveness of a particular exposure alternative has often been confounded with other very obvious factors. Perhaps the most common confounding is with practical utility. A given piece of information often is of practical utility when it is supportive, and of little utility when nonsupportive. Experiments done in market research settings (cf. Mills, 1965a, b) are particularly prone to this confounding, and may artifactually produce selectivity. However, it is not clear that selectivity has generally been *blocked* by confoundings.

3. Self-consciousness

Most people do not like to think they are unwilling to hear 'the other side of the argument.' Thus to maximize the chance of obtaining selectivity, one should not ask the subject's opinion and then his exposure preference immediately thereafter. The subject is likely to resist claiming too strong a preference for anything bolstering his beliefs. Ideally the two should be measured in separate sessions. This precaution has almost never been taken, however. Lowin (1967b) did, but at the expense of obtaining exposure preferences in mail surveys, thus getting a rather small return. Sears and Freedman (1963) measured opinions privately. The norm has been, however, to take both measures publicly and more or less contiguously—thus probably suppressing some selectivity.

4. Sampling Distortions

In the grand tradition of American psychology, the subjects in laboratory exposure experiments have almost invariably been lower division college students drawn from introductory psychology classes. The obvious danger of this selection is that something special may be working against selectivity in this population. And there is good reason to fear such a bias. A major explicit goal of undergraduate education is to train students to view supportive and nonsupportive information alike with a critical but informed eye. It is regarded as cowardice to avoid discrepant information, and as a sign of intellectual maturity the ability to take it in and argue it down. This obviously ought to work against getting selective exposure effects.

However, few researchers have attempted to draw upon other populations, and even these have generally wound up with college-educated and other staunchly middle class groups (Ehrlich *et al.*, 1957; Adams, 1961; Freedman & Sears, 1963). Still, there is some evidence in favor of this interpretation. These latter field studies have been more inclined to report selectivity than have laboratory studies with college student subjects.

As a final note, that old bugaboo of research on dissonance theory, the mystery of the disappearing sample, plagues even research on selective exposure. Brock (1965) found that he had to reject 37 per cent of his subjects, while Lowin (1965), using a mail return technique, lost 76 per cent of his respondents. Normally sample shrinkage is lamented mainly for form; we are so accustomed to using bizarre samples (college sophomores) that the bizarreness of our subsamples hardly seems important, particularly when the selection seems unsystematic across conditions. It may be more important in exposure research, however. Lowin (1965) found strong partisans more selective *and* more likely to return their questionnaires; hence the drop-out rate may determine one's final results.

5. Conclusion

In the absence of compelling reasons to the contrary, one would normally conclude that available data provide the best key to some underlying truth. However there might seem to be special reasons in this case for mistrusting available data. Too many of the methodological shortcomings of this research would seem to operate in a single direction: to minimize selective exposure. This might give grounds for feeling that additional research, conducted in a more thorough and careful manner, would present quite a different picture.

This argument, a common one in psychology when intuitively pleasing hypotheses are not supported, raises a more basic question of statistical inference, however. Normally we assume that probability values are based on what would probably happen if a given experiment were replicated many times; i.e., what would happen in the long run. Yet what in fact do we assume if a series of studies obtain no differences, and finally one does support the hypothesis? The norm seems to be to reject the prior series as having been poorly conducted, with inadequate manipulations, impotent designs, poor sampling, etc. This occurs whether the prior series were 'pilots' of our own or others' finished products. The final study is accepted as finally having proven the point, and the others are rejected as not having been fair tests.

Obviously, though, there must come a point when one starts to take negative results seriously. The question comes down to how many well-conducted studies obtaining positive results will be required to balance the numerous less well-conducted studies already completed and obtaining negative results (and journal editors' not unreasonable biases against negative results must be considered in the balancing).

C. IMPLICATIONS: THE TRUE NULL HYPOTHESIS POSSIBILITY

The second general possibility is that in fact little or no preference for supportive information exists, whether under neutral, high-dissonance, or low-confidence conditions. If this were true, what implications would it have for the three most relevant research areas: attitude change, motivation, and mass communications?

1. Defending Commitments

In the context of consistency theory, selective exposure is thought of as one of the many ways in which people protect themselves from disagreeable information. It has an especially prominent place in this list of mechanisms because it is clearly the most primitive and least adaptive. Rebellious children place their hands over their ears and flout their angry parents, claiming they can hear not a word of scolding. News photographs of the aftermath of a disaster often portray the relatives of dead persons holding their hands over their eyes as if the tragedy would not be real if unseen. In hysteria the sense organ responsible for offensive stimulation is symptomatically closed off, as in hysterical blindness or anesthesia. These are cases in which persons used extraordinarily primitive defenses.

There are other defenses that block veridical reception of information. The most commonly noted are selective perception, selective learning, and selective retention. It is interesting that the same empirical problems arise with these mechanisms as with selective exposure. For example, there is currently some doubt that the early selective learning findings are replicable. In six recent experiments, Waly and Cook (1966) and Greenwald and Sakumura (1967) failed to find any tendency for subjects to learn supportive arguments more easily than nonsupportive arguments. And it has not been difficult at all to find conditions under which nonsupportive material is learned more readily than supportive material. Jones and Aneshansel (1956) found this to occur when subjects expected to be required to produce counterarguments or debate an opponent. Later, Canon (1964) and Freedman (1965c) found exposure to dissonant arguments preferred when the subject expected to be required to counter an unknown set of dissonant arguments. Similarly, Jones and Kohler (1958) anticipated Lowin's (1967a, b) exposure findings by showing that implausible discrepant arguments were learned more readily than implausible supportive arguments (though Waly and Cook, 1966, have failed to replicate this finding).

Efforts to demonstrate that perceptual distortions operate in the service of affective preferences have also met with relatively little success throughout psychology. Methodological artifacts have been difficult to surmount (cf. Solomon & Howes, 1951). In communications research, distortion effects have been obtained, and often in the predicted direction. However, they usually have been of discouragingly minor magnitude (Hovland, Harvey, & Sherif, 1957; Manis, 1961a), and have not been responsive to such straightforward variations as the discrepancy (Harvey, Kelley, & Shapiro, 1957) or ambiguity (Manis, 1961b) of the informational input.

So the empirical data on all these 'avoidance' defenses appear to share a common set of problems: counterexamples are easily found, methodological problems abound, and the magnitude of effect often seems minor. This might lead to a tentative conclusion that the 'avoidance' defenses are relatively unpopular mechanisms for defending beliefs and behavioral commitments. Presumably they are commonly used to defend the organism against severe forms of psychological stress, such as the threat of death, bodily violation, or the loss of a love object (Janis, 1958; Greenstein, 1965). The indicated empirical question has not been posed: When will threat produce the avoidance of veridical information processing, and when will it induce mechanisms involving cognitive or affective change? That is, what distinguishes between the conditions for selective learning, perception, and exposure, and the conditions for opinion change, source derogation, etc.?

If the tentative conclusion is accepted, that in everyday life people do not generally utilize information-avoidance techniques as a way of softening the impact of unpleasant information, then two additional directions for further research are indicated. One is added attention to the dynamics of influence resistance. If people resist influence by confronting information and rejecting it, the important questions have to do with the process by which that happens. Brock and Balloun's (1967) ingenious experiments on attention to persuasive communications seem to represent a productive approach in this respect. Another is increased attention to nondefensive information seeking. Research on exposure has been excessively sterile because of a preoccupation with selectivity in the service of partisan preferences. Thus little is known about what actually contributes to information seeking. The major exposure problem faced by public affairs communicators is not in reaching their enemies, but in reaching anyone at all. Low absolute rates of exposure, rather than widespread selectivity, are the primary obstacles to influence. And little is known about the determinants of variations in absolute rates of exposure.

2. Homeostatic Hedonism

In common with numerous other psychological theories, the consistency theories seem to rest on an assumption that tension-reduction or minimization of stimulation is a major aim of the human organism. Thus the organism is supposed to avoid stimulating or tension-inducing kinds of information, and seek information that reduces tension. In studies on exposure this simple-minded view clearly does not hold; there seem to be just as many instances in which the stimulation-increasing information is preferred.

It may well be that the wrong question is being asked. Implicitly the question of a general preference for supportive information pits man's defensiveness against his curiosity. Which one has won out in his nature is of little interest, because both are obviously strong (see Chapter 16). This conclusion seems likely not to be altered no matter how many subsequent studies are done. The more important question is what determines which tendency will be dominant under any given set of conditions. Similarly, to ask whether or not the organism will respond defensively when threatened, as has been done in varying dissonance arousal, simply misses the point. It would be astonishing if the organism did not respond to threat. The challenge is to try to predict what *kind* of defense will be stimulated.

One qualification should be imposed on this general criticism, however. There may be some cultural value in knowing what specific kinds of choices people generally make, just as it is of some interest to know whether Americans prefer Bonanza to Shakespeare. It tells us something about our culture. This may be especially relevant for our thinking about a democratic political system, since we are accustomed to assuming that the voter prepares to exercise his franchise by informing himself about each alternative.

3. De Facto Selectivity

In nature, the pattern appears to be, in general, one of people being exposed primarily to positions with which they already agree. The usual explanation is that people actively seek supportive information and avoid nonsupportive information. If this hypothesis is rejected as inconsistent with experimental data, what explanations for de facto selectivity remain?

a. De facto selectivity doesn't exist either. One possibility is that de facto selectivity has also been oversold as a general characteristic of communication situations. Sears and Freedman (1967) have critically examined some of the most widely cited data on this point, and indeed it turns out not to be as overwhelming an effect as often suggested. The effect often occurs for one set of partisans but not the other, to be based upon rather small differences, or to be explicable by invoking other variables known to be strongly correlated with exposure (e.g., education). Nevertheless, it appears that de facto selectivity occurs often enough that it deserves additional attention (see Chapter 79).

b. Public economic control. A more sophisticated version of the original selective exposure hypothesis might hold that people use their economic power, whether consciously or unconsciously, to reward their friends and punish their enemies. For example, a community may impose its political beliefs on its newspapers by failing to subscribe to or patronize the advertisers of deviationist newspapers. The trouble with this idea is that it takes too simple-minded a view of the economics of mass communication. The 'loser' in economic competition usually merges with a paper of virtually identical editorial policy. What is eliminated most easily is redundancy rather than diversity. In any event this hypothesis depends upon the psychological hypothesis we have rejected, so no more need be said about it here.

c. Sycophantic communicators. A related idea, ingeniously tested by Zimmerman and Bauer (1956), is that communicators choose only to tell their audiences what the audience wishes to hear. No doubt this principle accounts for the variations in communications addressed by a given communicator to several audiences. The trouble is that such variations are too small to account for de facto selectivity. The President may emphasize one aspect of a policy before one audience and another before a second, but he supports the same policy alternative in both cases. Billy Graham does not suddenly turn agnostic when he addresses a sophisticated college student audience. Fluctuations from audience to audience are simply not gross enough to account for de facto selectivity. So this explanation is inadequate.

d. Asymmetric availabilities. Perhaps people are always selecting information from a skewed set of alternatives. That is, the typical information choice may be from a set of many supportive and a few nonsupportive communications. Even random sampling from such a skewed set of alternatives would produce de facto selectivity. Why might supportive generally be much more readily available than nonsupportive information? Two reasons seem especially salient.

The first reason involves the *ubiquity of consensus.* As Henessey has pointed out, ". . . most people agree with most other people about most things" (1965, p. 154). This in itself makes it more difficult to find nonsupportive than supportive communications. This general consensus holds in a broad sense for mankind in general on a great many issues; e.g., regarding the assertion that the world is round. On more controversial issues, consensus is no less impressive, though it tends to be limited to our immediate social and informational environment. It would be much harder for most of us to find pro-Soviet information, or information on the opposite side of the race issue from our own, than supportive views on these issues. Each of us lives in what is largely a supportive environment, even on the most divisive and controversial of issues. Hence we are rarely given a 'fair chance' to select nonsupportive information.

The main reason for this is that we get most of our opinions from our immediate environments. Hence they are bound to reflect the biases of our environments (Greenwald & Sakumura, 1967; Zajonc, 1965). A person growing up in Alabama is likely to form a favorable opinion of Governor Wallace, while the same person, if raised in Massachusetts, would be likely not to. Since the environment was biased in favor of one position prior to opinion formation, the best guess is that it will be biased in the same way afterwards. And the information alternatives from which the individual samples should be skewed in the same way, producing almost by necessity greater availability of supportive than nonsupportive alternatives.

Diabolical manipulators also maximize de facto selectivity. Some especially powerful communicators can deliberately structure the individual's information alternatives such that his opportunity to choose nonsupportive information is slight indeed. Examples of this kind come to mind easily. The most extreme are totalitarian regimes: the Mainland Chinese regime has severely restricted deviationist literature throughout its period in office; the Roman Catholic Church has made various sporadic efforts over the years to prevent its parishoners from coming into contact with non-Catholic or anti-Catholic ideas (cf. The *Index Librorum Prohibitorum*); even the not altogether totalitarian United States government often restricts public exposure to embarrassing information.

People with considerably less power over communication channels also may effect some restrictions. Conservative merchants attempt to place their newspaper advertising in the place that will both do the most for sales and strengthen the hand of conservative communicators; liberally oriented intellectuals tend to restrict the exposure of college students to nonliberal ideas, and so forth. Apparently much more benign censors are the timid parents who prevent sadistic, cynical, or erotic literature from falling into the hands of small children. Small children in America therefore are rather naive (Easton & Dennis, 1965) about the realities of social existence, given this continuing diet of supportive information. Each of these examples, then, represents a group of communicators who are able to control the exposure alternatives of particular individuals, specifically restricting them to a choice among numerous supportive alternatives mixed with only occasional nonsupportive possibilities.

e. Confounding supportiveness with other attractions. Many information alternatives are overchosen because of attractive features which are irrelevant to, but systematically associated with, their supportiveness. These other attractions are of course many; the following are a few examples of the more important ones.

First, the *perceived truth value* of supportive communications is greater than that of nonsupportive material. Presumably one of the major reasons why people seek information is to find out what is true. The more likely a communication is to indicate the truth, the more attractive it should be. On controversial issues there are two ideal guides. One is a source who is invariably on the side of the good, and the other is a source who invariably chooses the more iniquitous alternative. For example, John F. Kennedy and Robert Welch served these two functions for Democratic subjects in 1963 (Sears, 1965a). If both kinds of sources were equally common, then supportive and nonsupportive communicators would be equally valuable as guides to truth.

As it happens, however, there seem to be more positive guides than negative guides. Numerous Democratic politicians were regarded by Democratic subjects in 1963 as reliable indicators of the correct side of issues, whereas only an occasional Republican politician was regarded as an equally infallible guide to the *incorrect* side. The bulk of Republican leaders (and the Republican Party as a whole) were regarded as sometimes right and sometimes wrong, and therefore as uninformative about the correct side of an issue in most specific instances (Sears, 1965b). Many supportive communicators (Democrats) were useful guides, but only a few nonsupportive communicators (Republicans) were useful. And as a general rule, therefore, the individual who is seeking truth or a correct position is better off sampling sources of information who are generally supportive than sampling sources who are generally nonsupportive.

Another obvious feature is *practical utility*. A mother offered a choice between a speech on how environment affects children's personalities (a position with which she agrees) and one arguing the importance of heredity (with which she disagrees) will certainly choose the former (Adams, 1961). Why? Because information about the environment's impact may be of some practical help to her. Similarly, a choice between information about a product one owns and a product one does not own surely will result in preference for the former (Mills, 1965a, b). The more one knows about a new possession the better, from a practical standpoint. This apparently holds even before the choice: one wants to read about a product one soon will choose, and thus possess, more than about a product one soon will reject, and thus not possess (Mills, 1965c). And when expecting to debate, discuss one's views with others, or transmit one's views to others, supportive information is likely to be sought more than when expecting to read privately about the issue or receive someone else's views (Clarke & James, 1967; Brock & Fromkin, in press). The reason is that one wants to gather information that will help in the task of the moment, not that one needs to shore up a shaky position. These are likely not to be isolated exceptions; rather, examples of a general correlation in nature between utility and supportiveness.

The ways in which propagandistic appeals are distributed in society cause people with certain general kinds of *taste* to be exposed to certain kinds of political views, willy-nilly. An ex-Texan who listens to hillbilly music in Los Angeles is likely to be exposed to right-wing propaganda; the college professor who listens to classical music on FM is going to hear more liberal appeals. Upper middle-class business and professional people subscribe to the New York *Times* rather than the *Daily News*, or the Los Angeles *Times* rather than the *Herald-Examiner*, for obvious social and informational reasons. However, it is doubtful that these decisions rest much on editorial policy. Rather, they rest on long-term habits of taste and preference, normally irrelevant to (but empirically correlated with) political and social opinions.

Finally, the *practical details of self-exposure* are usually less complicated for supportive information. One is more likely to be informed of supportive mass meetings, transportation and companionship are usually easier to arrange, and so on. Just in the normal course of the day's events, without departing from the normal routine, it is easier to be advised of when supportive meetings or TV programs are available, where meetings are, and so on.

Numerous other variables could be mentioned. These seem to be among the most important reasons, however, why supportive information is particularly attractive, quite aside from its ability to reassure or bolster beliefs.

D. CONCLUSIONS

1. There is considerable evidence indicating that in nature, exposure is generally somewhat greater to supportive than to nonsupportive information.

2. There is no empirical evidence indicating a general preference for supportive information over nonsupportive information, regardless of whether the test is conducted under neutral, high-dissonance, or low-confidence conditions.

3. Attempts to explain the ineffectiveness of mass communications in field settings should concentrate upon low absolute rates of exposure and upon resistance to communications the individual processes more or less accurately, and deemphasizes barriers to accurate reception based upon active avoidance of disagreeable information.

4. The most probable explanations for de facto selectivity have to do with the unusual availability of supportive information, and with the likelihood that supportiveness is, in nature, correlated with other attractive features of information; e.g., truthfulness, usefulness, and so on.

Communicator Credibility and Communication Discrepancy as Determinants of Opinion Change

ELLIOT ARONSON, JUDITH A. TURNER, AND J. MERRILL CARLSMITH

Recent experiments in the area of communication and persuasion have shown that a number of variables affect the success of an influence attempt. One such variable is the credibility of the communicator. Experimental results have shown unequivocally that there is a positive relationship between the credibility of the communicator and the extent of opinion change (Arnet, Davidson, & Lewis, 1931; Haiman, 1949; Hovland & Weiss, 1952; Kelman & Hovland, 1953; Kulp, 1934). Another variable of obvious importance is the extent of the discrepancy between the opinion advocated by the communicator and the precommunication opinion of the recipient. However, experiments dealing with this variable have yielded contradictory results. Several investigators have found that the degree of induced opinion change varies as a positive function of the degree of discrepancy (Cohen, 1959; Goldberg, 1954; Hovland & Pritzker, 1957; Zimbardo, 1960). However, other investigators have found evidence for resistance to change when the discrepancy is extreme (Cohen, 1959; Fisher & Lubin, 1958; Hovland, Harvey, & Sherif, 1957).

Some attempts have been made to explain these inconsistent findings. Hovland et al. (1957), for example, have suggested that there is a linear relationship between discrepancy and opinion change only when the audience is not highly involved with the topic of the communication. They assert that when involvement is high, the function is curvilinear—that with great discrepancies there is little opinion change.

A different explanation, based upon the theory of cognitive dissonance (Festinger, 1957), was proposed by Festinger and Aronson (1960). They suggested that the apparently inconsistent findings could be explained by an interaction between discrepancy and credibility. According to Festinger and Aronson, when an individual finds that an opinion advocated by a credible communicator is discrepant from his own opinion he experiences dissonance. His cognition that he holds a particular opinion is dissonant with his cognition that a credible communicator holds a somewhat different opinion. The greater the discrepancy between his own opinion and the opinion advocated by the communicator, the greater the dissonance. Generally, a person might reduce this dissonance in at least four ways: He could change his own opinion to bring it closer to that of the communicator; change the communicator's opinion to bring it closer to his own opinion; seek support for his opinion by finding other people who hold similar opinions; derogate the communicator—that is, make the opinion of the communicator nonapplicable to his own by discounting the ability of the communicator to have a valuable opinion on the topic. However, in most experimental influence situations, a communication is delivered either by a noninteracting speaker or in the form of a written message. Hence, it is impossible for the recipient to influence the communicator's opinion. In addition, the recipient is usually a member of a noninteracting audience. Hence, he is unable to seek immediate social support. Therefore, in this type of situation, the recipient may reduce dissonance by changing his own opinion or by derogating the communicator.

The magnitude of dissonance increases as a function of the discrepancy. Thus, if dissonance were reduced by opinion change alone, then the degree of opinion change would increase as a direct function of the extent of discrepancy. But dissonance can also be reduced by derogating the communicator; as with opinion change, the tendency to derogate the communicator should likewise increase as a direct function of the extent of the discrepancy. Moreover, it seems reasonable to assume that at the extremes, opinion changes and derogation of the communicator are clear alternatives. A person is not likely to change his opinion in the direction of a communicator whom he has sharply derogated; similarly, he is not likely to derogate a communicator who had induced a major change in his opinion.[1]

What conditions will maximize dissonance reduction through opinion change rather than derogation? Credibility seems to be crucial. If a communicator has perfect credibility, he cannot be derogated (by definition). Here, dissonance can be reduced only by opinion change. In this situation, dissonance theory would predict that degree of opinion change would vary as a direct function of the extent of discrepancy. This prediction received support from an experiment by Zimbardo (1960). In this experiment, if the communicator was the best friend of the recipient, she was able to induce the greatest opinion change when the discrepancy was the greatest; this was true even when the advocated position was described previously by the recipient as unreasonable and indefensible.

At the other extreme, if a communicator has no credibility, he can be derogated completely (by definition). In this case, there would be no opinion change regardless of the degree of discrepancy, since a discrepant statement would not arouse dissonance.

Consider a communicator of mild credibility. Here, both opinion change and derogation can be used to reduce dissonance. If a communication is relatively close to the opinion of the recipient, the existing dissonance can be reduced easily by a slight shift in opinion. On the other hand, if the discrepancy is great, a person can reduce dissonance much more easily by derogating the communicator. That is, if the position advocated by a mildly credible communicator is extreme, it may appear quite unrealistic to the recipient. If this were the case, it is unlikely that he would change his attitude very much. Instead, he might reduce dissonance by deciding that the communicator is unrealistic—or stupid, naive, untruthful, etc.

This experiment was designed to investigate the conditions under which changing one's opinion and derogating the communicator are chosen as alternative methods of reducing the dissonance which is created when an individual is

---

[1] This is true *only* at the extremes. Theoretically if neither opinion change nor derogation is extreme, dissonance may be reduced by a combination of both processes.

exposed to an opinion which is discrepant from his own. Suppose subjects are exposed to persuasive communications at various distances from their original positions, and for some subjects the communicator is presented as highly credible (virtually indisparageable), while for other subjects the communicator is presented as mildly credible (easily disparageable). For each level of communicator credibility, we may predict a different function relating discrepancy to opinion change. Thus, it should be possible to construct a family of curves reflecting opinion change as a function of communicator credibility and degree of discrepancy. In the ideal case—the case of a communicator who is perfectly indisparageable—opinion change should be a linear function of discrepancy. The larger the degree of opinion change advocated, the greater the dissonance, and hence, the greater the opinion change. As the communicator becomes less credible, and derogation becomes a possible avenue of dissonance reduction, we predict that the curve will decline near the extreme end. As the discrepancy becomes large, derogation will be an easier method of dissonance reduction than opinion change, and consequently, there would be little or no opinion change and great derogation of the communicator. As the communicator becomes even less credible, the curve representing opinion change will begin to decline at a point closer to the origin (zero discrepancy). Finally, in the ideal case of zero credibility, the curve should be completely flat. Moreover, the curve for a highly credible communicator should be higher at all points of discrepancy. This follows because a highly credible communicator can arouse greater dissonance and hence induce greater opinion change; dissonance introduced by a communicator of low credibility can be more easily reduced by disparaging the communicator than by changing opinions. (See Figure 1 for theoretical and actual curves.)

PROCEDURE

In order to test these hypotheses, an experiment was designed which had the following characteristics:

1. The subjects were exposed to a persuasive communication which was identical for all groups except for the extent of the discrepancy and the credibility of the communicator.
2. The task was such that the original opinions of the subjects fell at the same position on some continuum so that the amount of change advocated could be determined independently of the initial position of the subject.
3. The subsequent opinions of the subjects as well as the amount of derogation of the communicator were measured.

The subjects were 112 female college students[2] who were paid volunteers for "an experiment in esthetics." They met in small groups, ranging in size from two to seven. The subjects were told that the experimenter was interested in studying

---

[2] Actually, 115 subjects participated in the experiment. The data from 3 were discarded because the experimental sanction against intercommunication was not observed; one of the subjects announced loudly (within earshot of the others) that she disagreed with the author of the essay.

how people evaluate poetry. They were first asked to rank order nine stanzas from obscure modern poems, all of which contained alliteration. The criterion for ranking was stated ambiguously: "the way the poet uses form to aid in expressing his meaning." Next, each subject was asked to read a two-page essay entitled "The Use of Alliteration in Poetry." This communication consisted mostly of general statements about the uses and abuses of alliteration in poetic writing. The final half page consisted of an illustration of the points made in the essay; that is, the ideas stated in the essay were applied in the evaluation of a particular stanza. For each subject, the stanza that was used as an illustration was the one that she had originally ranked as the eighth-best stanza.

For approximately one-third of the subjects there was a small discrepancy between her opinion of the stanza and the communicator's opinion; for approximately one-third of the subjects there was a moderate discrepancy; and for approximately one-third of the subjects there was an extreme discrepancy. The discrepancy was created by having the communication state that the poem was better than the subject had indicated in her first ranking. The slight discrepancy was established by introducing the stanza as average; the communication asserted that half of the stanzas were better, half worse. The medium discrepancy was established by introducing the stanza as one of the better examples; it was stated that two of the others were superior. The large discrepancy was established by introducing the stanza as the best example of the use of alliteration in the sample. In summary, the subjects were faced with a discrepancy of either three, five, or seven rank-order positions between their ranking of the crucial stanza and that of the communicator.

In each of these three conditions, some of the subjects read communications supposedly written by a highly credible source—an expert on poetry; the others read virtually identical essays, supposedly written by a student. T. S. Eliot was chosen as the expert or highly credible source. It was assumed that his importance as both a poet and a critic would be well known to the subjects and, therefore, that it would be relatively difficult for them to discount his judgment of the poems. In the mildly credible condition, the communication was attributed to a Miss Agnes Stearns, who was described as a student at Mississippi State Teachers College. The subjects were told that Miss Stearns planned to become a high school English teacher—that she had composed the essay and had asked the experimenter (her cousin) to show it to the subjects. In all conditions, subjects were told that the experimenter was interested in seeing whether the communication would help them to evaluate poetry.

After the subjects had read the essay, they were told that their initial ranking was used merely to acquaint them with the poetry and with the ranking procedure. The experimenter explained that now that they were familiar with the ranking technique, they should carefully rank the poems a second time according to the same criterion. Finally, they were asked to evaluate the essay by indicating on a seven-point scale the strength of their agreement or disagreement with 14 evaluative statements about the essay and the author (e.g., the coherence of the essay, the reasonableness of the author, etc.). These evaluative statements constituted our measure of disparagement.

At the end of the session, the purpose of the experiment and the need for deception were discussed.

RESULTS

According to the theory, the highly credible communicator should produce greater opinion change when he advocates a more extreme position. The greater the discrepancy between his opinion and the opinion of the recipient, the greater the opinion change. On the other hand, the mildly credible communicator should produce greater opinion change with increasing discrepancy only up to a point; as his position becomes more extreme, recipients will resort to disparagement rather than opinion change as a means of reducing dissonance.

Table 1 shows the mean opinion change in each of the six conditions. It is apparent that the highly credible communicator was more successful in inducing opinion change than the mildly credible communicator at every point of discrepancy. Moreover, in the High Credibility condition, opinion change increases with degree of discrepancy. The mildly credible communicator is not only less able to induce opinion change, but actually induces less change with a large discrepancy than with a moderate discrepancy.

Table 1 MEAN OPINION CHANGE

COMMUNICATOR	DISCREPANCY		
	SMALL	*MEDIUM*	*LARGE*
Highly credible	2.50	4.06	4.14
	(16)[a]	(16)	(14)
Mildly credible	1.19	2.56	1.41
	(21)	(23)	(22)

	DIFFERENCES BETWEEN CONDITIONS OF DISCREPANCY FOR EACH COMMUNICATOR[b]		
	SMALL–MEDIUM	*MEDIUM–LARGE*	*SMALL–LARGE*
Highly credible	2.25*	0.11	2.45*
Mildly credible	2.42**	2.06*	0.39

CONDITION	DIFFERENCES BETWEEN COMMUNICATORS FOR EACH CONDITION OF DISCREPANCY[b]		
	SMALL	*MEDIUM*	*LARGE*
High Credibility – Mild Credibility	2.49**	2.22*	4.37***

[a] *n's appear in parentheses.*
[b] *t values.*
* *p <.05, two-tailed*
** *p <.02.*
*** *p <.001.*

Figure 1 shows a family of theoretical and actual curves for this situation. The degree of discrepancy is plotted on the abscissa, and the degree of opinion change is plotted on the ordinate. We have predicted a different curve for each degree of communicator credibility. The 45-degree line is a theoretical curve representing the "perfectly credible" communicator, perhaps unattainable experimentally. In response to such a communicator, disparagement is impossible, so that opinion change is the only means of reducing dissonance. The horizontal line is a theoretical curve representing the "perfectly incredible" communicator. In this case, the recipient would experience no dissonance regardless of the extent of the discrepancy between his opinion and that advocated by the communicator. The other two curves show intermediate degrees of credibility. These curves are empirical, representing the opinion change of the subjects in this experiment. As the communicator is made less credible, the curve is lowered at all points (since more disparagement takes place at all points, reducing some of the dissonance). Similarly, as the communicator is made less credible, the curve reaches its maximum sooner (as disparagement replaces opinion change as the major method of reducing dissonance).

To some extent, the results involving the derogation of the communicator lend support to this analysis. The results pertinent to derogation are presented in Table 2. It is clear that subjects derogated the mildly credible communicator to a greater extent than the highly credible communicator. This was the case irrespective of the degree of the discrepancy; for each condition of discrepancy, the difference between the derogation of the highly credible and mildly credible communicators is highly significant. These results are not unequivocal, however. As can be seen from inspection of Table 2, there was no difference in derogation among the various conditions of discrepancy in the Mildly Credible condition. These data do not support our theoretical analysis. That is, although we have demonstrated that credibility and discrepancy do interact to produce opinion change as predicted, our analysis suggests systematic differences in the derogation of the communicator within the Mildly Credible condition. Specifically, it was predicted that in the Mildly Credible condition, with high discrepancy,

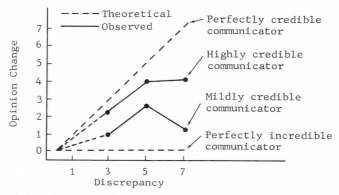

Fig. 1. Opinion change as a function of credibility and extent of discrepancy—theoretical and observed curves.

Table 2 DEROGATION OF THE COMMUNICATOR

COMMUNICATOR	DISCREPANCY		
	SMALL	MEDIUM	LARGE
Highly credible	31.75	29.31	32.43
Mildly credible	60.10	58.04	56.00

derogation would be used in lieu of opinion change as a means of reducing dissonance. Thus, if our analysis is correct, subjects in this condition appear to have ended the experiment carrying a barrel full of dissonance. This is an unenviable circumstance—for the theorists as well as the subjects. There appears to be no easy theoretical explanation for this datum. Methodologically, it is possible that our measure of derogation was not a very good one. It may have been sensitive enough to induce the subjects to playback the instructions, leaving those in the Mildly Credible condition more derogatory than those in the Highly Credible condition. But our measure may not have been sensitive enough to reflect fine distinctions within the Mildly Credible condition. Similarly, it is well known that college students are often reluctant to make extremely negative statements about a fellow student. That is, in the Mildly Credible condition, there may have been a ceiling effect in the disparagement scale; the degree of derogation may have been maximal even when the communicator's position was not discrepant. Thus, subjects in this condition may have privately derogated the communicator without expressing it in writing. Although these methodological explanations are convenient from our point of view, they are hardly conclusive. Further research may suggest alternative explanations for these particular results.

Reconciliation of Results with Previous Findings

The main body of results supports the theoretical analysis and suggests a reconciliation of previous contradictory findings. It is a reasonable assumption that each of the previous experiments examined only one of the family of theoretical functions outlined above. We may at least tentatively support such an assumption by a brief analysis of the disparageability of the communicators used in these studies.

Let us first examine some studies which found a linear relationship between opinion change and degree of discrepancy. As previously mentioned, Zimbardo (1960) used as a communicator a person who was not only a close friend of the subject, but one who was also a proven expert in the area of the communication. Clearly, this communicator was highly credible. Hovland and Pritzker (1957) described their communicator as "respected by the recipient, and hence an authoritative source of opinion." Goldberg (1954) used, as an expert, the combined previous judgments of the subject himself and one or more peers. It seems reasonable that such a combined judgment (of from two to four people, *including* the subject himself) would be difficult to disparage.

In contrast, Hovland et al. (1957), who found decreasing opinion change with an extreme discrepancy, used a communicator without describing him to the subject. To quote the authors, there was "ambiguity about the credibility of the communicator." Fisher and Lubin (1958), who found a similar effect, used a single unexpert peer as a communicator. It seems apparent that such a communicator was relatively easy to disparage.

In Cohen's (1959) experiment the communicator was defined only by a description of the communication. When the communication was described as "difficult and subtle," "arguments . . . related in a complex fashion," Cohen found increasing opinion change with increasing discrepancy. However, when the communication was described as "easy to grasp," he found less opinion change with high discrepancy. It may be assumed that a communicator who has been able to compose a complex, difficult, and subtle argument is perceived as more intelligent and, hence, more credible than a communicator whose argument is simple and easy to grasp. Moreover, it is difficult to disparage a communicator after one has been told that one might not be able to understand the communication, since disliking the communication may be tantamount to failing to understand it.

REFERENCES

Arnet, C. C., Davidson, Helen H., & Lewis, H. N. Prestige as a factor in attitude change. *Sociol. soc. Res.*, 1931, *16*, 49–55.

Cohen, A. R. Communication discrepancy and attitude change. *J. Pers.*, 1959, *27*, 386–96.

Festinger, L. *A theory of cognitive dissonance*. Evanston, Ill.: Row, Peterson, 1957.

Festinger, L., & Aronson, E. The arousal and reduction of dissonance in social contexts. In D. Cartwright & A. Zander (Eds.), *Group dynamics: Research and theory*. (2nd ed.) Evanston, Ill.: Row, Peterson, 1960. Pp. 214–31.

Fisher, S., & Lubin, A. Distance as a determinant of influence in a two-person serial interaction situation. *J. abnorm. soc. Psychol.*, 1958, *56*, 230–38.

Goldberg, S. C. Three situational determinants of conformity to social norms. *J. abnorm. soc. Psychol.*, 1954, *49*, 325–29.

Haiman, F. S. An experimental study of the effects of ethos in public speaking. *Speech Monogr.*, 1949, *16*, 190–202.

Hovland, C. I., Harvey, O. J., & Sherif, M. Assimilation and contrast effects in reactions to communication and attitude change. *J. abnorm. soc. Psychol.*, 1957, *55*, 244–52.

Hovland, C. I., & Pritzker, H. A. Extent of opinion change as a function of change advocated. *J. abnorm. soc. Psychol.*, 1957, *54*, 257–61.

Hovland, C. I., & Weiss, W. The influence of source credibility on communication effectiveness. *Publ. Opin. Quart.*, 1952, *15*, 635–50.

Kelman, H. C., & Hovland, C. I. "Reinstatement" of the communicator in delayed measurement of opinion change. *J. abnorm. soc. Psychol.*, 1953, *48*, 327–35.

Kulp, D. H. Prestige as measured by single-experience changes and their permanency. *J. educ. Res.*, 1934, *27*, 663–72.

Zimbardo, P. G. Involvement and communication discrepancy as determinants of opinion conformity. *J. abnorm. soc. Psychol.*, 1960, *60*, 86–94.

Facilitating Effects of "Eating-While-Reading" on Responsiveness to Persuasive Communications

IRVING L. JANIS, DONALD KAYE, AND PAUL KIRSCHNER

It is commonly assumed that people are more likely to yield to persuasion at a time when they are eating or drinking than at a time when they are not engaged in any such gratifying activity. Salesmen, business promoters, and lobbyists often try to "soften up" their clients by inviting them to talk things over at a restaurant or cafe. Representatives of opposing economic or political groups, when unable to settle their disputes while seated formally around a conference table, may find themselves much more amenable to mutual influence, and hence more conciliatory, while seated comfortably around a dinner table.

Little systematic research has been done, as yet, to determine the conditions under which pleasant stimulation will augment the acceptance of persuasive communications. One might expect that when the communicator is the perceived source of the gratifying stimulation, a more favorable attitude toward him will ensue, which would tend to lower the recipient's resistance to his persuasive efforts (see Hovland, Janis, & Kelley, 1953, pp. 19–55). But a more complicated situation often arises at educational symposia, political conventions, cocktail parties, and informal dinners where: (a) the donor (that is, the person who is perceived as being responsible for the gratification) is *not* the communicator and (b) the donor does *not* endorse the persuasive communications that happen to be presented at the particular time when the recipients are being indulged. If a positive gain in effectiveness is found to occur under these condtiions, where the gratifying activity is entirely extraneous to the content, source, or endorsement of the communications, a number of important theoretical questions will arise— questions concerning some of the basic processes of attitude change which will require systematic experimental analysis. For example, when eating has a facilitating effect on acceptance of persuasive messages, does it always depend entirely upon the heightened motivation of the recipients to conform with the donor's wishes? If so, a positive outcome under nonendorsement conditions will be paradoxical unless it turns out that there is a general tendency for people to assume, consciously or unconsciously, that the donor would like them to be influenced by whatever communications are presented (even though he explicitly says that he does not endorse the point of view being expressed). Or does the extraneous gratification operate as a source of reinforcement independently of the recipient's attitude toward the donor? If this is the case, we might be led to assume that the food corresponds to an "unconditioned stimulus," and its facilitating effects might be accounted for in terms of the laws of conditioning.

The latter theoretical possibility is suggested by Razran's (1940) brief research note, published 25 years ago, in which he gave a summary statement of the following two experimental observations: (a) an increase in ratings of "personal approval" occurred when a series of sociopolitical slogans were presented to experimental subjects while they were enjoying a free lunch and (b) a decrease in such ratings occurred when the slogans were presented while the subjects were being required to inhale a number of unpleasant, putrid odors. In his report, however, Razran does not mention certain important details, such as whether the experimenter was the donor of the free lunch and whether he said anything to the subjects about his personal attitude toward the slogans.

So far as the authors have been able to ascertain, no subsequent experiments have been published pertinent to checking Razran's observations. Nor has any published research been found bearing on the related questions of whether or not (and under what limiting conditions) extraneous pleasant or unpleasant stimulation can affect the degree to which a recipient will accept a series of persuasive arguments that attempt to induce him to change a personal belief or preference.

As a preliminary step toward reopening experimental research on the above-mentioned set of theoretical problems, the present study was designed to investigate the alleged phenomenon of enhanced communication effectiveness arising from "eating-while-reading." The research was designed primarily to answer the following question: If an experimenter gives the subjects desirable food and drink but states explicitly that the persuasive messages to be presented are ones with which he does not necessarily agree, will there be a significant increase in acceptance from the gratifying activity of eating that accompanies exposure to the communications?

METHOD AND PROCEDURE

Experimental Design

The basic design involved randomly assigning the subjects to two different experimental conditions. One was a condition in which a substantial quantity of food was offered to the subjects during the time they were engaged in reading a series of four persuasive communications. Upon entering the experimental room, the subjects found the experimenter imbibing some refreshments (peanuts and Pepsi-Cola) and they were offered the same refreshments with the simple explanation that there was plenty on hand because "I brought some along for you too." The contrasting "no-food" condition was identical in every respect except that no refreshments were in the room at any time during the session.

The same measures of opinion change were used in the two experimental groups and also in a third group of *unexposed controls*, who were included in the study in order to obtain a base line for ascertaining the effectiveness of each communication per se. The subjects randomly assigned to the control condition were given the same pre- and postcommunication questionnaires, separated by the same time interval as in the other two experimental conditions, but without being exposed to any relevant communications.

The Communications and the Opinion Measures

On the basis of extensive pretesting, we prepared four communications, each of which advocated an unpopular point of view and had been found to be capable of inducing a significant degree of opinion change. These communications were attributed to fictitious authors who were described as journalists or news commentators. The main conclusions, all of which involved quantitative predictions or preferences about future events, were as follows:

1.   It will be more than 25 years before satisfactory progress can be expected in the search for a cure for cancer.
2.   The United States Armed Forces do not need additional men and can be reduced to less than 85% of their present strength.
3.   A round-trip expedition to the moon will be achieved within the next decade.[1]
4.   Within the next 3 years, three-dimensional films will replace two-dimensional films in practically all movie theaters.

In order to assess opinion changes, four key questions were included in both the pre- and the postcommunication questionnaires, each of which asked the subject to express his opinion in the form of a quantitative estimate (for example, "How many years do you think it will be before an extremely effective cure is found for cancer so that cancer will no longer be a major cause of death? About _____ years.")

Experiments I and II: Similarities and Differences

The same experimental design, described above, was used in two separate experiments, during successive semesters at the same college. In all essential features the first (Experiment I) was identical with the second (Experiment II) in that exactly the same experimental variations were used along with the same instructions, the same communications, and the same pre- and post-communication questionnaires. But the two experiments differed in several minor ways. The main difference was that in Experiment I the time interval between the precommunication questionnaire and exposure to the communications was about 2 months; whereas in Experiment II the precommunication questionnaire was given at the beginning of the experimental session, immediately preceding the communications.

In Experiment I, the initial questionnaire was administered in regular undergraduate class sessions. It was introduced as a "survey of student opinions" and the key questions were embedded among numerous filler questions on a variety of other controversial issues. After a period of 2 months, the subjects were contacted by telephone and asked to be unpaid volunteers for a study on reading preferences. The vast majority volunteered and each subject was seen in a private interview session, at the beginning of which he was randomly assigned to the

---

[1] This study was carried out before the major developments in space flights had occurred, at a time when few people were optimistic about the rate of technical progress in this field. In response to the moon-flight question on the initial questionnaire, almost all the students gave estimates of 10 years or more before a successful round-trip flight could be expected.

"food with communication" condition or the "no food with communication" condition or the unexposed control condition. After answering the final set of postcommunication questions, each subject was briefly interviewed concerning his reactions to the experimental situation.

In Experiment II, the same essential procedures were used except for the fact that the precommunication questionnaire was given at the beginning of the experimental session. Another minor difference was that the unexposed controls were given some extracts from a popular magazine on irrelevant topics, which took approximately the same reading time as the four persuasive communications. Moreover, unlike the unexposed controls in Experiment I, those in Experiment II were given the same food in the same way as in the main experimental condition, so that they too were eating while reading the (irrelevant) articles.

In addition to the three conditions that were set up to replicate the essential features of Experiment I, a fourth experimental condition was introduced in Experiment II in order to investigate a subsidiary problem, namely, the effects of extraneous *unpleasant* stimuli. The fourth experimental group, while reading the four persuasive communications, was exposed to an unpleasant odor (produced by a hidden bottle of butyric acid), for which the experimenter disclaimed any responsibility.

In both experiments, the experimenter explained that the purpose was to assess the students' reading preferences. He asserted that he did *not* endorse the communications and casually mentioned that he happened to agree with certain of the ideas expressed and not with others (without specifying which). He asked the subjects to read the articles as though they were at home reading a popular magazine. In line with the alleged purpose, the postcommunication questionnaire in both Experiments I and II included 20 filler questions asking for interest ratings of the articles (for example, ratings of how much interest they would expect the average college student to have in each topic).

Subjects

A total of 216 Yale undergraduate students were used in the two experiments. In Experiment I, 35 men were in the unexposed control group, 32 in the "no food with communication" condition, and 33 in the "food with communication" condition. In Experiment II, the corresponding numbers were 23, 31, and 31, respectively. There were also 31 subjects in the fourth experimental group exposed to the "unpleasant" condition.

RESULTS

In both experiments, observations of the subjects' eating behavior in the "food" condition showed that every one of them ate at least one handful of peanuts and drank at least one-half glass of the soft drink. The main findings concerning the effects of eating desirable food on the acceptance of the four persuasive communications are shown in Table 1. In general, the results indicate that "eating-while-reading" has a facilitating effect on the amount of opinion change. In Experiment I, the differences between the food and no-food conditions are

Table 1 Opinion Changes Induced by Exposure to Four Persuasive Communications under Two Different Conditions: "Food" versus "NoFood" Given by the Experimenters

% OPINION CHANGE

COMMUNICATION TOPIC	EXPERIMENT I		EXPERIMENT II		COMBINED DATA FROM EXPERIMENTS I AND II	
	NO FOOD (N = 32)	FOOD (N = 33)	NO FOOD (N = 31)	FOOD (N = 31)	NO FOOD (N = 63)	FOOD (N = 64)
1. Cure for cancer						
Positive change	68.7	81.8	80.7	93.5	74.6	87.4
Negative change	21.8	12.1	3.2	0.0	12.7	6.3
No change	9.5	6.1	16.1	6.5	12.7	6.3
Total	100.0	100.0	100.0	100.0	100.0	100.0
Net change	46.9	69.7	77.5	93.5	61.9	81.1
p	=.11		<.10		<.05	
2. Preferred size of United States Armed Forces						
Positive change	65.6	81.8	29.0	51.6	47.6	67.2
Negative change	9.4	0.0	0.0	0.0	4.8	0.0
No change	25.0	18.2	71.0	48.4	47.6	32.8
Total	100.0	100.0	100.0	100.0	100.0	100.0
Net change	56.2	81.8	29.0	51.6	42.8	67.2
p	<.05		<.05		<.01	

Table 1 Continued

COMMUNICATION TOPIC	EXPERIMENT I		EXPERIMENT II		COMBINED DATA FROM EXPERIMENTS I AND II	
	NO FOOD (N = 32)	FOOD (N = 33)	NO FOOD (N = 31)	FOOD (N = 31)	NO FOOD (N = 63)	FOOD (N = 64)
3. Round trip to moon						
Positive change	53.2	75.9	48.4	58.0	50.8	67.2
Negative change	21.9	12.1	19.4	12.9	20.6	12.5
No change	24.9	12.0	32.2	29.1	28.6	20.3
Total	100.0	100.0	100.0	100.0	100.0	100.0
Net change	31.3	63.8	29.0	45.1	30.2	54.7
p	=.05		=.20		<.05	
4. Three dimensional movies						
Positive change	68.7	75.9	74.2	77.4	71.5	76.6
Negative change	21.8	12.1	0.0	6.5	11.1	9.4
No change	9.5	12.0	25.8	16.1	17.4	14.0
Total	100.0	100.0	100.0	100.0	100.0	100.0
Net change	46.9	63.8	74.2	70.9	60.4	67.2
p	=.20		=.40		<.20	

% OPINION CHANGE

consistently in the predicted direction for all four communications, two of which are significant at the .05 level. (All p values are one-tailed and were obtained on the basis of the formula for assessing the difference between two net percentage changes, given by Hovland, Lumsdaine, & Sheffield, 1949.) The results for Experiment II show differences in the same direction for three of the four communications, two of which are significant at the .10 level. There is a very small, nonsignificant difference in the reverse direction on the fourth communication.

The p values based on the combined data from both experiments, shown in the last column of Table 1, can be regarded as a satisfactory summary of the overall outcome inasmuch as: (a) the numbers of cases in each experiment are almost equal; and (b) the two experiments differed only in minor features that are irrelevant to the main comparison under investigation. The combined data show that all four communications produced differences in the predicted direction and for three of them the differences are large enough to be statistically significant. Thus, the results support the conclusion that, in general, the extraneous gratification of eating while reading a series of persuasive communications tends to increase their effectiveness.

That each communication was effective in inducing a significant degree of opinion change, whether presented under food or no-food conditions, is indicated by the comparative data from the unexposed controls. In both experiments, the control group showed very slight positive changes, if any, on each of the four key questions and the amount of change was always significantly less than the corresponding net change shown by the food and no-food experimental groups.[2] There were no consistent differences between the control group in Experiment I and the one in Experiment II, which indicates that the different time intervals between the before and after measures and the other minor procedural differences between the two experiments had no direct effect on the opinion measures.

The condition of unpleasant stimulation introduced into Experiment II had no observable effect on the amount of opinion change. The net changes obtained from the group exposed to the foul odor ($N = 31$) were as follows: cancer cure, 67.7%; size of armed forces, 25.8%; round trip to moon, 38.7%; three-dimensional movies, 64.5%. These values differ only very slightly from those obtained from the group exposed to the no-food condition in Experiment II (see Table 1); none of the differences are large enough to approach statistical signifi-

[2] In all but one instance, the net change shown by the unexposed controls was not significantly different from zero. The one exception occurred in the control group in Experiment I with respect to the first issue (cancer cure), on which a significant net change of −34% was found. This change, however, was in the reverse direction from that advocated by the communication (probably as a consequence of optimistic publicity concerning new advances in cancer research that appeared in the newspapers during the months between the before and after questionnaires). Thus, on this item, as well as on the other three, the control group showed significantly less change in the expected direction than the two experimental groups.

An analysis of responses to the precommunication questionnaire from both experiments showed that initially, on each of the four key opinion questions, there were only very slight, nonsignificant differences among the experimental and control groups. None of the results in Table 1 and none of the other observed differences in amount of opinion change are attributable to initial differences.

cance. As expected, however, all the net changes for the unpleasant odor condition are smaller than those for the food condition and in two of the four instances the differences are statistically significant at beyond the .05 level.

DISCUSSION

Our finding that the extraneous gratifying activity of eating tended to increase the degree to which the accompanying persuasive messages were accepted may prove to have important implications for the psychology of attitude change, especially if subsequent research shows that the gains tend to be persistent, giving rise to sustained modifications of personal beliefs or preferences. Since the control group in Experiment II (which received food along with irrelevant communications) showed net opinion changes that were practically zero and were significantly less than those shown by the main experimental group, the food alone appears to have had no direct effect on any of the opinion measures. Hence the observed outcome seems to implicate psychological processes involved in the *acceptance* of persuasive influences.

Our results on the positive effects of food are similar to Razran's (1940) findings on the increase in favorable ratings of sociopolitical slogans induced by a free lunch. Razran has indicated that he regards his observations as evidence of Pavlovian conditioning, resulting from the contiguity of the conditioned stimuli (the slogans) and the unconditioned pleasant stimuli (food). Before accepting any such interpretation, however, further investigations are needed to check systematically on the possibility that the change in acceptability is brought about by creating a more favorable attitude toward the donor. We attempted to minimize this possibility in both Experiments I and II by having the experimenter give the subjects an introductory explanation in which he clearly stated that he was not sponsoring the persuasive communications. Despite this attempt, however, the subjects may have ignored or forgotten his remarks and assumed that he was sponsoring them. We have no evidence bearing directly on this matter, but we did note that in the informal interviews conducted at the end of each experimental session, many more favorable comments about the experimenter were made by the subjects who had been in the food condition than by those who had been in the no-food condition.

Our failure to confirm Razran's findings on the negative effects of *unpleasant* stimulation might be accounted for in terms of attitude toward the experimenter. In Razran's experiment, the experimenter "required" the subjects to sniff the putrid odors, and hence he might have been directly blamed for the unpleasant stimulation; whereas in our Experiment II, the unpleasant odor was presented as an accidental occurrence for which the experimenter was not responsible. Further experimental analysis is obviously needed to determine if the effects of pleasant and unpleasant stimulation observed in our experiment are dependent upon whether or not the experimenter is perceived as the causal agent.

The fact that the experimenter himself participated in eating the food might have influenced the subjects' perceptions of the general atmosphere of the reading session and hence needs to be investigated as a possible variable, independently of the subjects' food consumption. The limiting conditions for positive effects from "eating-while-reading" also require systematic investigation, particularly in relation to unpleasant interpersonal stimuli, such as those provoking embarrassment, outbreaks of hostility, or other forms of emotional tension that could counteract the positive atmosphere created by the availability of desirable food.

It is also important to find out whether variations in the experimenter's endorsement of the communications play a crucial role in determining the facilitating effects of the proferred food. For example, if subsequent research shows that the experimenter's positive versus negative endorsements make a difference, then an explanation in terms of increased motivation to please the donor will be favored, rather than a simple conditioning mechanism, and a more complicated explanation will be required to account for the positive effects obtained under conditions where the experimenter explicitly detaches himself from sponsorship of the communications.[3] These implications are mentioned to illustrate the new lines of research suggested by comparing the results from the present experiment with those from Razran's earlier study.

REFERENCES

Hovland, C. I., Janis, I. L., & Kelley, H. H. *Communication and persuasion.* New Haven: Yale Univer. Press, 1953.

Hovland, C. I., Lumsdaine, A. A., & Sheffield, F. D. *Experiments on mass communication.* Princeton: Princeton Univer. Press, 1949.

Razran, G. H. S. Conditioned response changes in rating and appraising sociopolitical slogans. *Psychological Bulletin,* 1940, *37,* 481.

[3] The potential importance of positive versus negative endorsement by the experimenter as an interacting variable was suggested by some unexpected results obtained in a pilot study by Dabbs and Janis, which was carried out as a preliminary step toward replicating the present experiment under conditions where the experimenter indicates that he personally *disagrees* with the persuasive communications. The pilot study results led us to carry out a new experiment in which we compared the effects of eating-while-reading under two different endorsement conditions (the experimenter agreeing or disagreeing with the communications). A report on the effects of the interacting variables, as revealed by the data from the Dabbs and Janis experiment, is currently being prepared for publication.

Effects of Varying the Recommendations in a Fear-Arousing Communication

JAMES M. DABBS, JR., AND HOWARD LEVENTHAL

A number of studies have investigated the effects of fear arousal on persuasion. Although the majority report that fear increases persuasion, the picture is not completely clear. Facilitating effects of fear on persuasion have been reported in studies of dental hygiene practices (Haefner, 1965; Leventhal & Singer, 1966; Singer, 1965), tetanus inoculations (Leventhal, Jones, & Trembly, in press; Leventhal, Singer, & Jones, 1965), safe driving practices (Berkowitz & Cottingham, 1960; Leventhal & Niles, 1965), and cigarette smoking (Insko, Arkoff, & Insko, 1965; Leventhal & Watts, 1966; Niles, 1964). However, under increasing levels of fear Janis and Feshbach (1953) observed no increase in acceptance of beliefs about the proper type of toothbrush to use, and Leventhal and Niles (1964) observed some decrease in acceptance of a recommendation to stop smoking. All these results are based on verbal measures of *attitude* change.

The picture is even less clear when one considers actual *behavior* change. The study on tetanus by Leventhal et al. (1965) reports that some minimal amount of fear is necessary for behavior change, but that further increases in fear do not affect change. The later study by Leventhal et al. (in press) reports a slight tendency for increases in fear to increase behavior change. In the studies of dental hygiene practices, Janis and Feshbach (1953) reported decreased behavior change under high fear, while Singer (1965) found no main effect of fear. In the study on smoking by Leventhal and Watts (1966) high fear simultaneously increased compliance with a recommendation to cut down on smoking and decreased compliance with a recommendation to take an X-ray.

The present study attempted to account for some of these divergent findings. It is reasonable to expect that the behavior being recommended by a persuasive communication is of critical importance (Leventhal, 1965). Recommendations that are seen as effective in controlling danger may be accepted more readily as fear is increased, while ineffective recommendations may be rejected rationally or may produce reactions of denial (Janis & Feshbach, 1953) or aggression (Janis & Terwilliger, 1962). Additionally, rejection of a recommended behavior may occur if subjects have become afraid of the behavior itself (Leventhal & Watts, 1966).

Recommendations presented as part of fear-arousing communications vary in their effectiveness in controlling danger and in the unpleasantness associated with them. For example, brushing the teeth offers no guarantee of preventing decay, while taking a chest X-ray can lead to the unpleasant discovery of lung cancer. An audience might well reject recommendations which are ineffective in warding off danger or which are difficult, painful, or apt to bring unpleasant consequences. Recommendation factors have been invoked post hoc to explain research findings, but have not been manipulated and studied directly.

In the present study fear was manipulated by presenting differing discussions of the danger of tetanus. Inoculations and booster shots were recommended for protection against tetanus. Under high and low levels of fear, inoculation was portrayed so that it would be seen as more or less *effective* in preventing tetanus and more or less *painful* to take (these manipulations were orthogonal). Subjects' intentions to take shots and their actual shot-taking behavior were used to measure compliance with the recommendations.

It was expected that compliance would be greater when shots were highly effective or not painful. These factors might produce simple main effects or they might interact with level of fear. It seemed more likely that the latter would be the case—that increased fear would make subjects either more or less sensitive to differences in the recommendations.

METHOD

Subjects and Design

Letters were sent to all Yale College seniors asking them to participate in a study to be conducted jointly by the John Slade Ely Center, a local research organization, and the Department of University Health. The study was presented as a survey of student health practices at Yale and an evaluation of some health-education materials. An attempt was then made to contact all seniors by telephone for scheduling.

Of approximately 1,000 students who received letters, 274 were scheduled and run in the experiment. Seventy-seven of these were excluded because they had been inoculated since the preceding academic year, and 15 were excluded because of suspicion, involvement in compulsory inoculation programs, allergic reactions to inoculation, or religious convictions against inoculation. The final usable N was 182.

Each subject received a communication which was intended to manipulate perceived effectiveness and painfulness of inoculation. Three levels of fear (including a no-fear control level), two levels of effectiveness, and two levels of pain were combined in a $3 \times 2 \times 2$ factorial design. The n's for the resulting 12 conditions ranged from 11 to 20, with smaller n's in the no-fear control conditions.

Procedure

Experimental sessions were conducted in a classroom with groups ranging in size from 1 to 12. Subjects within each session were randomly assigned to conditions. Control (no-fear) conditions were run separately because of the brevity of the control communications.

Questionnaires containing medical items and personality premeasures were administered at the beginning of the session. Subjects then read a communication on tetanus and gave their reactions to it in a second questionnaire. They were assured that all their responses would be kept confidential.

Communications

Communications were 10-page pamphlets which discussed the danger of tetanus and the effectiveness and painfulness of inoculation.[1] All pamphlets gave specific instructions on how to become inoculated and were similar in style and content to those used by Leventhal et al. (1965) and Leventhal et al. (in press).

Fear. Low-fear material described the very low incidence of tetanus and indicated that bleeding from a wound usually flushes the poison-producing bacilli out of the body. A case history was included which reported recovery from tetanus following mild medication and throat-suction procedures. High-fear material indicated that tetanus can be contracted through seemingly trivial means and that if contracted the chances of death are high. A high-fear case history was included which reported death from tetanus despite heavy medication and surgery to relieve throat congestion. Black-and-white photographs were included in the low-fear material and color photographs in the high-fear material. The discussion of tetanus and case history were omitted entirely from control (no-fear) communications.

Effectiveness. The effectiveness manipulation stressed either the imperfections or the unusual effectiveness of inoculation. Low-effectiveness material stated that inoculation is generally effective and about as adequate as the measures available to deal with other kinds of danger. It pointed out, however, that no protection is perfect and that there is a possibility that even an inoculated person will contract tetanus. High-effectiveness material described inoculation as almost perfect and as far superior to methods available to deal with other kinds of danger. It emphasized that inoculation reduces the chances of contracting tetanus, for all practical purposes, to zero. All communications reported that a new type of inoculation was available at the Department of University Health which would provide protection against tetanus for a period of 10 years.

Pain. To produce fear of the recommended behavior, it was pointed out that inoculation against tetanus has always been painful. Subjects were told that the new inoculation requires a deep intramuscular injection of tetanus toxoid and alum precipitate, making the injection even more painful than before and the local reaction longer lasting. The discussion of pain was presented to subjects as a forewarning so that the discomfort would not take them by surprise. This discussion was omitted from pamphlets in the no-pain conditions.

Specific instructions on how to get a shot and a map showing the location of the Department of University Health were included in all pamphlets. Subjects were encouraged to get a shot or at least to check on whether or not they needed one.

---

[1] Communications have been deposited with the American Documentation Institute. Order Document No. 9011 from ADI Auxiliary Publications Project, Photoduplication Service, Library of Congress, Washington, D. C. 20540. Remit in advance $2.00 for microfilm or $3.75 for photocopies and make checks payable to Chief, Photoduplication Service, Library of Congress.

Measures

Most questions on the pre- and postcommunication questionnaires were answered on 7-point rating scales. The precommunication questionnaire contained medical questions and four personality measures (susceptibility, coping, anxiety, and self-esteem). The susceptibility measure was made up of three items which asked subjects how susceptible they felt toward common illnesses, toward unusual diseases, and toward illness and disease in general. Three items used to measure coping asked subjects whether they tended to tackle problems actively or to postpone dealing with them. The problems concerned subjects' health habits, their everyday lives as students, and their decisions regarding summer activities. The anxiety scale was made up of 10 true-false items from the Taylor (1953) Manifest Anxiety scale.

The self-esteem measure was similar to that used by Dabbs (1964). Subjects rated themselves on 20 adjectives and descriptive phrases and then rated each of the 20 items as to its desirability. Eight items were classified as desirable and 12 as undesirable on the basis of mean ratings from the entire sample of subjects. Using this group criterion of desirability, each subject's self-esteem score was defined as the sum of his ratings of himself on the undesirable items subtracted from the sum of his ratings on the desirable items. (It was subsequently discovered that 12 subjects in the present study had participated in the earlier study by Dabbs, and the correlation between their self-esteem scores in the two studies was .62, $p < .01$. This correlation, despite a lapse of 3 years and changes in the measuring instrument, suggests this type of measure is reasonably stable.)

The postcommunication questionnaire included checks on each of the experimental manipulations, a 10-item mood adjective check list, and questions on intentions to take shots, the importance of shots, and the likelihood of contracting tetanus. The subject's evaluation of the pamphlet and the date and place of his last tetanus shot were obtained on this questionnaire.

A measure of behavioral compliance with the recommendations was obtained from shot records of the Department of University Health. Subjects were counted as complying if they took tetanus shots between the experimental sessions and the end of the semester, about 1 month later. When contacted by letter and phone, no subjects reported receiving shots at places other than the Department of University Health. A few reported that they had tried to take shots and had been told they did not need any. These subjects were counted as having taken shots, but their data are presented separately in Footnote 2 below.

RESULTS

Main Effects of the Manipulations

Compliance with the recommendations was unaffected by the manipulations of effectiveness and pain. The manipulation of fear, however, influenced both intentions to take shots ($F_{2,179} = 4.85$, $p < .01$) and actual shot-taking behavior[2] $(F = 3.39, p < .05)$. The effects were linear (Table 1), with compliance being greatest under high fear. The consistency of subjects' responses is indicated by high biserial correlations between intention and behavior measures within high-fear $(r_b = .62, p < .01)$ and low-fear $(r_b = .68, p < .01)$ conditions; no correlation was computed for the control conditions since only three control subjects took shots.

Table 1 COMPLIANCE WITH RECOMMENDATIONS

	CONTROL (NO FEAR)	LOW FEAR	HIGH FEAR
Mean intentions to take shots	4.12	4.73	5.17
Proportion of Ss taking shots	.06	.13	.22
N	48	62	72

Table 2 shows that the fear manipulation increased feelings of fear, as it was intended to do. It also increased feelings of interest and nausea, belief in the severity of tetanus and the importance of taking shots, and desire to have additional information. None of these measures were affected by the manipulations of effectiveness or pain.

Both effectiveness and pain were successfully manipulated. Check questions showed that subjects in the high-effectiveness conditions felt inoculation was more effective than did those in the low-effectiveness conditions $(\overline{X}_{high} = 6.7,$ $\overline{X}_{low} = 5.8, F_{1,170} = 105.85, p < .01)$. Subjects in the pain conditions felt shots would be more painful $(\overline{X}_{pain} = 4.1, \overline{X}_{no\ pain} = 2.3, F_{1,170} = 74.56, p < .01)$ and reported more "mixed feelings" about taking shots $(F_{1,170} = 7.20, p < .01)$ than did subjects in the no-pain conditions. But the clear perception of differences in effectiveness did not affect subjects' intentions to take shots, nor did increasing the anticipated painfulness of shots decrease intentions to take them. In fact, there was a slight tendency for painfulness to strengthen intentions to be inoculated $(F_{1,170} = 2.72, p = .10)$.

Correlations among Responses

Only within the high-fear condition did reported fear correlate with intentions to take shots $(r = .23, p < .01)$. A scatterplot of scores revealed that the

[2] "Shot-taking behavior" combines 20 subjects who took shots and 7 who reported trying to take shots. These two categories are distributed similarly across the fear treatment conditions: 2, 6, and 12 subjects took shots; and 1, 2, and 4 subjects tried to do so.

An arc sine transformation of the proportions in Table 1 was used (Winer, 1962). This made it possible to test the significance of the differences between groups against the *base-line variance* of the transformation (see Gilson & Abelson, 1965). Base-line variance has a theoretical value which does not depend on computations from observed data. In the present case this value is given by the reciprocal of the harmonic mean number of cases on which each proportion is based, or $1/59 = .0169$.

Table 2 OTHER REACTIONS TO FEAR MANIPULATION

	CONTROL	LOW FEAR	HIGH FEAR	F[a]
Fear[b]	7.74	9.25	12.19	21.50**
Feelings of nausea	1.27	1.24	1.90	7.95**
Feelings of interest	4.48	4.70	5.39	6.12**
Evaluation of the severity of tetanus	4.64	4.83	5.34	3.86*
Feelings of susceptibility to tetanus	3.46	3.99	4.25	3.31*
Evaluation of the importance of shots	5.85	6.16	6.52	6.44**
Desire for more information about tetanus	3.08	2.68	3.57	3.90*

[a] *F ratios are computed from three-way analyses of variance. In each analysis df = 2/170 (approximately).*
[b] *"Fear" represents the sum of three items: feelings of fear, fear of contracting tetanus and fear produced by the pamphlet.*
* *$p < .05$.*
** *$p < .01$.*

high-fear condition increased the range of reported fear and that the positive correlation could be attributed to subjects in the extended portion of the range (those scoring higher than 13 on a 19-point composite scale). These extreme subjects all showed strong intentions to take shots, while other subjects in the high-fear condition sometimes did and sometimes did not intend to take shots. This pattern suggests that fear and acceptance of a recommendation are more closely associated when fear is relatively high, though acceptance may occur at any level of reported fear.

Unlike fear, anger was negatively associated with intent to take shots. The over-all within-class correlation between anger and intentions was $-.18$ ($p < .05$). This correlation remained essentially the same within different levels of the fear treatment, but became increasingly negative as the recommendation was portrayed as less effective and more painful (Table 3). Both the row and column differences in Table 3 are significant[3] (for rows, $CR = 2.02$, $p < .05$); for columns, $CR = 2.81$, $p < .01$). It should be emphasized that these are correlational differences only. Low effectiveness and high pain did not increase the mean level of anger or decrease intentions (or decrease actual shot taking). The ranges of anger and intention scores also did not differ among the four conditions.

Personality Differences

None of the premeasures on personality (susceptibility, coping, anxiety, self-esteem) were significantly correlated with intentions to take shots, nor did the

---

[3] Significance of these differences was tested after applying Fisher's z' transformation to the correlation coefficients.

Table 3 CORRELATIONS BETWEEN ANGER AND INTENTIONS TO TAKE SHOTS
UNDER VARYING PORTRAYAL OF RECOMMENDATIONS

| | EFFECTIVENESS | |
	LOW	*HIGH*
Pain		
Low	−.29	.15
High	−.52	−.18

correlations vary systematically across the 12 experimental conditions. However, differences were observed when subjects were split at the median into groups high and low on self-esteem. Figure 1 shows intentions to take shots among high- and low-self-esteem subjects. The only significant effect within this data (other than the main effect of fear) is the interaction between self-esteem and fear level ($F_{2,166} = 4.74$, $p < .01$). Subjects low in self-esteem increased their intentions to take shots from control to low-fear conditions, then showed no further increase under high fear. Subjects high in self-esteem, on the other hand, showed increased intentions only from low- to high-fear conditions.

DISCUSSION

A positive relationship between fear arousal and persuasion was observed. Increases in the intensity of the fear manipulation were associated with increases in attitude and behavior change, with high correlations between intentions to take shots and actual shot taking. These findings are similar to those of Leventhal et al. (in press), who reported a slight tendency for shot taking to increase as fear was raised from low to high levels.

Subjects' beliefs about the effectiveness of inoculation did not affect their compliance; they responded equally well to recommendations portrayed as low and high in effectiveness. This may be because even the low-effective recommendation was rated relatively high in effectiveness (5.8 on a 7-point scale). However, the manipulation was sufficient for subjects to perceive significant differences between low and high effectiveness, and the failure of this variable to influence compliance suggests caution in using it to reconcile divergent results of studies on fear arousal and persuasion (Janis & Leventhal, in press; Leventhal, 1965; Leventhal & Singer, 1966).

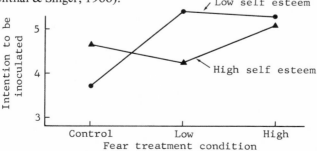

Fig. 1. Self-esteem differences in reactions to the communications on tetanus.

The description of pain produced mixed feelings about shots, but did not prevent subjects from taking them. Perhaps this is because the discomfort of inoculation is negligible in comparison with the pain of tetanus itself. A stronger manipulation of anticipated "painfulness" was unintentionally introduced in the study by Leventhal and Watts (1966), who created fear of smoking by showing a film in which a chest X-ray led to the discovery of cancer and to surgical removal of a lung. The authors suggested that decreased X-ray taking in this condition was more likely caused by fear of the consequences of an X-ray than by defensive reactions to the fear-arousing material on cancer. The present findings do not invalidate their conclusion, but they limit the range of situations to which such an explanation might apply. Subjects apparently do not respond to small variations in the effectiveness or unpleasantness of a recommended course of action. Unless a compelling deterrent exists, people who anticipate danger prefer to do something rather than nothing.

This last statement is qualified by differences in the behavior of high- and low-self-esteem subjects. Low-self-esteem subjects showed high compliance with the recommendations in both high- and low-fear conditions, while high-self-esteem subjects showed high compliance only in the high-fear condition. In addition, personality measures of self-esteem and coping were significantly correlated ($r = .49$, $p < .01$) in the present study, as they were in the study reported by Dabbs (1964). One might conclude that high-self-esteem subjects are more active and aggressive in dealing with their environment and have developed more skill in meeting dangers with appropriate protective actions. Thus, they may recognize inoculation to be more appropriate when the danger of tetanus is greater, while low-self-esteem subjects may accept the position of the communication that inoculation is appropriate regardless of the magnitude of danger. An alternative possibility is that some differences characteristically associated with self-esteem simply disappear when there is an urgent need to combat danger (as there was with the high-fear communication).

In the conditions where inoculation was depicted as ineffective or painful, anger was negatively associated with intentions to be inoculated. It is possible that increased anger in these conditions would have lowered compliance. But since anger and compliance did not covary as the fear treatment was increased, there appears to be no causal relationship between them. It seems more likely that anger does not decrease compliance, but that under certain conditions it provides the justification for noncompliance. Under other conditions—as when recommended behaviors are highly effective, not painful, and not a reasonable target for anger—noncompliance may have to be justified in some other manner.

All the present findings could have been influenced by several factors which were not varied. For example, all subjects received the manipulations of perceived danger, effectiveness, and pain in the same order. Learning about the dangers of tetanus first may have caused some subjects to ignore differences in the effectiveness and painfulness of inoculation. In addition, all subjects were asked after reading the communications whether or not they intended to be inoculated. One might expect that stating an intention to be inoculated would commit the subject to following this course of behavior later on. However, the findings of Leventhal et al. (1965) and Leventhal et al. (in press) indicate that specific instructions must be present before intentions will be translated into behavior. Since all subjects in the present study did receive specific instructions, the high correlations between intentions and behavior may be due to this factor.

Finally, while fear and persuasion were associated, the evidence of any causal relationship between them is tenuous. As in most studies of fear arousal and attitude change, the communications used were complex ones. They discussed the damage tetanus can cause and the likelihood of contracting it. They differed in fearfulness, interest, and feelings of nausea evoked. They also differed in length, type of language used, and amount of information about tetanus. With such confounding it is impossible to attribute increases in attitude change solely to increases in fear. This is an inherent difficulty when fear is manipulated by the use of differing descriptions of danger. Another approach should be developed by anyone wishing to manipulate fear independently of other aspects of a persuasive communication.

REFERENCES

Berkowitz, L., & Cottingham, D. R. The interest value and relevance of fear-arousing communications. *Journal of Abnormal and Social Psychology*, 1960, *60*, 37-43.

Dabbs, J. M., Jr. Self-esteem, communicator characteristics, and attitude change. *Journal of Abnormal and Social Psychology*, 1964, *69*, 173-81.

Gilson, C., & Abelson, R. P. The subjective use of inductive evidence. *Journal of Personality and Social Psychology*, 1965, *2*, 301-10.

Haffner, D. P. Arousing fear in dental health education. *Journal of Public Health Dentistry*, 1965, *25*, 140-46.

Insko, C. A., Arkoff, A., & Insko, V. M. Effects of high and low fear-arousing communications upon opinions toward smoking. *Journal of Experimental Social Psychology*, 1965, *1*, 256-66.

Janis, I. L., & Feshbach, S. Effects of fear-arousing communications. *Journal of Abnormal and Social Psychology*, 1953, *48*, 78-92.

Janis, I. L., & Leventhal, H. Human reactions to stress. In E. Borgatta & W. Lambert (Eds.), *Handbook of personality theory and research*. New York: Rand McNally, in press.

Janis, I. L., & Terwilliger, R. An experimental study of psychological resistances to fear-arousing communications. *Journal of Abnormal and Social Psychology*, 1962, *65*, 403-10.

Leventhal, H. Fear communications in the acceptance of preventive health practices. *Bulletin of the New York Academy of Medicine*, 1965, *41*, 1144-68.

Leventhal, H., Jones, S., & Trembly, G. Sex differences in attitude and behavior change under conditions of fear and specific instructions. *Journal of Experimental Social Psychology*, in press.

Leventhal, H., & Niles, P. A field experiment on fear arousal with data on the validity of questionnaire measures. *Journal of Personality*, 1964, *32*, 459-79.

Leventhal, H., & Niles, P. Persistence of influence for varying durations of threat stimuli. *Psychological Reports*, 1965, *16*, 223-33.

Leventhal, H., & Singer, R. P. Affect arousal and positioning of recommendations in persuasive communications. *Journal of Personality and Social Psychology*, 1966, *4*, 137-46.

Leventhal, H., Singer, R. P., & Jones, S. Effects of fear and specificity of recommendations upon attitudes and behavior. *Journal of Personality and Social Psychology,* 1965, *2,* 20–29.

Leventhal, H., & Watts, J. C. Sources of resistance to fear-arousing communications on smoking and lung cancer. *Journal of Personality,* 1966, *34,* 155–75.

Niles, P. The relationships of susceptibility and anxiety to acceptance of fear-arousing communications. Unpublished doctoral dissertation, Yale University, 1964.

Singer, R. P. The effects of fear-arousing communications on attitude change and behavior. Unpublished doctoral dissertation, University of Connecticut, 1965.

Taylor, J. A. A personality scale of manifest anxiety. *Journal of Abnormal and Social Psychology,* 1953, *48,* 285–90.

Winer, B. J. *Statistical principles in experimental design.* New York: McGraw-Hill, 1962.

Effectiveness of Emotional Role-Playing in Modifying Smoking Habits and Attitudes

IRVING L. JANIS AND LEON MANN

The persistence of undesirable habits such as heavy smoking and overeating, despite the desire of many people to modify their overindulgences, poses a major challenge for research on attitude change. The problem of smoking has attained prominence because of the incongruity between the average smoker's continuance of the habit and his knowledge that it might cause lung cancer. In general it appears that rational appeals, making use of cogent scientific evidence, have little sustained effect, if any, on the cigarette smoker. Even when influenced by persuasive messages that vividly convey the threatening consequences of the smoking habit, most smokers are affected only temporarily and usually return to the habit within a few days, bolstering their original attitude by minimizing, distorting, or denying the content of the message. It is a well-known fact that the cancer scare promoted by repeated publicity campaigns in the mass media during the past decade has had little residual effect on the American population and the consumption of cigarettes has continued to increase (Toch, Allen, and Lazer, 1961; Cannell and MacDonald, 1956; Greenberg, 1964).

A number of individual cases have been observed, nevertheless, in which dramatic conversions took place as a result of direct personal encounters with the threat, as in the case of physicians, cancer scientists, and the relatives of

Reprinted from Journal of Experimental Research in Personality, *1,* 1965, *84–90. Copyright 1965 by the American Psychological Association and reproduced by permission.*

cancer victims (Snegireff and Lombard, 1959; Lawton and Goldman, 1961). It seems probable that when people stop smoking after direct encounters with cancer victims, it is partly because of an empathic reaction involving the realization that, if it can happen to others, it can happen to themselves. A marked change in attitude and behavior is likely to occur if a smoker can no longer relegate the feared consequences to the category of remote or irrelevant dangers.

The present study was devised to investigate the possibility that the technique of role-playing, which has been found to be effective in facilitating attitude change, might be used in a way that would provide an empathic "contact" experience similar to the type of direct contact that occasionally leads to a spectacular conversion. Several experiments (e.g., Culbertson, 1957; Janis and King, 1954, 1956; Kelman, 1953) have shown that when a person verbalizes a belief or judgment to others he becomes more inclined to accept it himself. The role-playing procedure in these experiments requires the person to take the part of a rational advocate of a position contrary to his personal opinions, so that he is induced to scan the opposing viewpoint and to improvise new arguments. Thus the person finds himself examining belief systems that were formerly sealed off, as he conscientiously executes the task of examining the other side of the issue. It is quite possible, however, for a person to carry out a cognitive role-playing assignment in a defensive way with a minimum of emotional involvement and with covert denial of the relevance of what he is saying to his personal outlook. This type of defensiveness might explain why modest success was attained in Horn's (1960) study, which was a unique attempt to use a role-playing technique for the purpose of trying to influence smoking habits. In Horn's experiment, high school students took the role of providing information to their parents on the dangers of smoking and this led to only a small decrease in the number of students who would have otherwise commenced smoking.

When rational appeals fail, some degree of success in modifying deep-seated habits may nevertheless be achieved by vivid emotional appeals that personalize the threat, as in the case of audiences exposed to dramatic "scare" films depicting the suffering and mutilation of cancer victims (Janis, in press). It seems plausible, therefore, to expect that some comparable degree of success in breaking through the defensive facade might be attained by using an "emotional" type of role-playing, which induces the person to become empathically involved in a life-like situation. "Emotional" role-playing in this case consists of a standardized psychodramatic procedure in which the E induces the S to give an improvised emotional performance by asking him to act out a fictitious calamity as though it were really happening, using props and other staging devices to enhance the illusion of reality. One of the unique features of this type of role-playing procedure is that the E enters directly into dramatic dialogues with the S, following a standardized script that he has memorized, and thus is able to focus the S's attention on the emotionally arousing features of the distressing episode that is being enacted.

In the present study, the form of emotional role-playing we devised requires the S to play the role of a medical patient who has just completed a series of intensive medical examinations and has asked the physician to tell the truth about the diagnosis. Enacting the role of the physician, the *E* informs the "patient" that the diagnosis is cancer of the lung, that a lung operation will have to be undergone as soon as possible, and that cigarette smoking must be given up immediately. The role-playing setting and the *E*'s script were designed to facilitate the arousal of fantasies and personalized images of being victimized by lung cancer, with the expectation that when the threat cannot be readily denied or ignored the person may begin for the first time to experience some genuinely fearful anticipations that "it *could* happen to me."

In the literature on psychodrama, there are a few anecdotal accounts of the clinical use of similar role-playing procedures which appear to have been helpful in the treatment of delinquents and other types of "problem" cases (e.g., Moreno, 1957; Corsini, 1958); but so far as we know, the present study represents the first systematic attempt to investigate the effectiveness of emotional role-playing in modifying attitudes and habits.

METHOD

Subjects

The *S*s were 26 women, 18-23 years of age, all of whom volunteered to participate in a research study under the auspices of their local State College. None of them knew that the purpose had anything to do with changing their smoking habits. They were screened by telephone to make sure they were moderate or heavy smokers (i.e., were consuming at least 15 cigarettes per day). The rationale given for asking about their smoking habits was simply that the study involved playing a role that required the person to be a smoker.

Subjects were randomly assigned to one of two conditions: 14 were placed in the experimental group (role-players) and 12 in the control group (non-role-playing "judges," exposed to the same instructions and information).

Experimental Procedures

The young women in both the experimental and control groups were told at the beginning of the session that role-playing is sometimes used as a research technique to create life-like situations when it is difficult to make direct observations of real-life behavior, such as the emotional reactions of patients in a doctor's office. The *E* then explained that the purpose of the research was to study two important problems concerning the human side of medical practice, namely how patients react to bad news and how they feel about a doctor's advice to quit an enjoyable habit like smoking.

On the pretext that *E* would best understand *S*'s performance of the role of a patient if he knew her personal opinions on relevant topics, a premeasure of attitudes toward smoking was administered. The questionnaire contained 15 items which assessed *S*'s beliefs about smoking and cancer, her feelings of concern about being a smoker, and her intention to modify or continue the habit.

The procedures up to this point were identical for both experimental and control *S*s, but after the initial questionnaire only those assigned to the experimental condition were given the emotional role-playing instructions. Each *S* in the latter group was asked to imagine that *E* was a doctor who was treating her for a "bad cough that was not getting any better." She was to make believe that this was her third visit to his office, and that she had come this time to be informed of the results of X-rays and other medical tests. The *E* gave a brief sketch of five different scenes and *S* was asked to act out each one as realistically as possible:

Scene 1. Soliloquy in waiting room: The *S* is asked to give her thoughts out loud, expressing worry while awaiting the doctor's diagnosis and feeling conflicted about whether or not to smoke a cigarette.

Scene 2. Conversation with the physician as he gives the diagnosis: In acting out the standard (memorized) script of the physician's role, *E* begins by informing the patient that he will tell her the whole truth, since this is what she had requested last time. He goes on to say that a definite diagnosis can now be made on the basis of the X-ray and sputum tests and that, unfortunately, it is bad news. Pointing to an actual chest X-ray obtained from the Pathology laboratory, he explains that there is a small malignant mass in the patient's right lung; an operation therefore is needed as soon as possible. He encourages the *S* to ask questions. In the course of this conversation, *E* again refers to *S*'s former request for all the facts and then informs her of the fact that there is only a moderate chance for a successful outcome from surgery for this condition.

Scene 3. Soliloquy while physician phones for a hospital bed: The *S* is again asked to express aloud her thoughts and feelings about the bad news while *E* is telephoning in a distant part of the room.

Scene 4. Conversation with the physician concerning arrangements for hospitalization: Continuing to act on the basis of the standard script, *E* gives detailed information about reporting to the hospital the following morning and asks several questions about the patient's family and personal circumstances. He informs her that she should expect to be in the hospital at least six weeks because surgery of the chest takes a long time to heal.

Scene 5. Conversation with the physician about the causes of lung cancer: The *E* raises some questions about the patient's smoking history and asks her if she is aware of the connection between smoking and cancer. Then *E* discusses with the patient the urgent need to stop smoking immediately and encourages her to speak freely about the difficulties she expects to encounter in trying to give up the habit at this time, now that she knows it is essential.

Control Group

In this group *S*s were given no opportunity to role play, but were exposed to the very same information as the experimental group. This was done by asking each *S* to listen to an authentic tape recording of a role-playing session.

When the initial questionnaire about smoking was administered, these *S*s were told that, since people's judgments are sometimes influenced by their personal habits and opinions, *E* wanted to find out how they felt about the various issues raised in the five scenes that were about to be heard. The control *S*s were told that the recording was to be judged in terms of the quality of the role-player's performance and the intensity of her emotional involvement in the role. The particular tape that was played for this purpose was of 25 minutes' duration (the average amount of time for the role-playing activity) and was selected because of its exceptionally dramatic and emotional quality.

After hearing the tape, the control *S*s were given a questionnaire containing some items requesting them to evaluate the role-player's performance and other items asking them to report their own reactions to the recording.

Follow-Up Interview

At the end of the session, *S*s in both groups were again given the questionnaire containing items about attitudes toward smoking. Each *S* was told that the main purpose was to ask some additional questions about her reactions to the procedure she had just gone through, but that some of the questions would be the same as those asked earlier, all of which should be answered, "according to how you think and feel right now."

As each *S* was leaving, *E* mentioned that he would phone her when the results of the experiment became available in order to provide a summary report. Nothing whatsoever was said about a follow-up interview. Then, two weeks after the session, *E* telephoned *S* and reported briefly about various types of comments the *S*s had made about different types of role-playing procedures that had been tried out, without suggesting that any changes in personal smoking habits had occurred or were to be expected. As an after-thought, *E* inquired whether *S* had thought about the experiment and—if modification in amount of smoking was not spontaneously mentioned—he asked whether her own smoking behavior had changed in any way during the past two weeks.

RESULTS AND DISCUSSION

Immediate Attitude Changes

Both groups were initially similar in attitudes toward smoking, the differences on all items in the initial questionnaire being very slight and nonsignificant. After playing the role of a cancer victim, however, the *S*s in the experimental group showed marked changes in attitude as compared with the control group. The findings for the first four items in Table 1 indicate that the role players showed a significantly greater increase in anti-smoking attitudes than the controls on all four of the indicators used to assess the immediate effects of the experimental treatment: (a) personal belief that smoking leads to lung cancer ($p < .01$), (b) expectation that "much harm can come to me from my smoking" ($p < .01$), (c) willingness to try to give up smoking ($p < .01$), and (d) expressed intention to stop smoking immediately ($p < .05$).[1]

[1] All probability values are for a one-tailed test of significance, since the direction of the differences was predicted by the hypothesis that emotional role-playing is more effective in modifying attitudes and habits than passive exposure to the same information.

Table 1 COMPARISONS BETWEEN EXPERIMENTAL (ROLE-PLAYING) GROUP AND CONTROL GROUP ON ATTITUDE CHANGE AND HABIT CHANGE

ITEMS	GROUP[a]	MEAN SCORE BEFORE ROLE PLAY	MEAN SCORE AFTER ROLE PLAY	NET CHANGE	t TEST
1. Belief that smoking causes lung cancer	Experimental	4.50	5.86	1.36	2.78**
	Control	4.17	4.17	0	
2. Fear of personal harm from smoking	Experimental	4.36	6.00	1.64	2.93**
	Control	4.25	4.33	0.08	
3. Willingness to attempt modification of smoking	Experimental	2.57	4.50	1.93	2.73**
	Control	2.42	3.00	0.58	
4. Intention to quit smoking	Experimental	2.79	5.08	2.29	2.05*
	Control	2.50	3.58	1.08	
5. Number of cigarettes smoked daily	Experimental	24.1	13.6[b]	−10.5	1.84*
	Control	21.7	16.9[b]	− 4.8	

[a] $N = 14$ in experimental group, $N = 12$ in control group.
[b] This measure was obtained two weeks after the session, whereas the other four measures were obtained immediately after the role playing performance (or control condition).
 * $p < .05$.
** $p < .01$.

Changes in Smoking Habits Reported Two Weeks Later

One of the major aims of the study was to investigate whether emotional role-playing can produce a conversion-like experience that would lead to a marked and persistent change in actual smoking habits. The results for the fifth item in Table 1 show that initially, before being exposed to the experimental treatments, there was a negligible difference in the amount of daily cigarette consumption reported by the two groups ($p < .40$). In the follow-up interview conducted two weeks after each experimental session, the role-players reported an average decrease of 10.5 in their daily cigarette consumption, whereas the controls reported an average decrease of only 4.8; this difference is statistically significant at beyond the 5% confidence level. The comparatively large drop found for the role-playing group is not attributable to a few extreme cases: The majority of the role-players (10 of the 14 women) reported a sizeable decrease, whereas the majority of the controls (7 of the 12 women) reported no change at all.

Although one must be somewhat skeptical about *S*s' verbal reports about their current cigarette consumption, the findings supplement the attitude data in indicating that emotional role-playing was *differentially* more effective in producing manifestations of change than the control condition, which passively exposed the *S*s to the same informational inputs and "demand" characteristics. That the *S*s' verbal reports about the drop in their cigarette consumption were probably quite genuine is strongly suggested by additional comments they made about the difficulties they were having in avoiding the temptation to resume smoking, and the special efforts they were making to implement their decision to cut down on smoking. (E.g., "I made a pact with friends to put 30¢ in the bank for every day I don't smoke.")

Fear as the Mediating Source of Motivational Changes

The arousal of fear appears to have been a mediating factor in producing the observed changes in attitudes and reported behavior. This interpretation is strongly suggested by some additional evidence obtained during the role-playing and control sessions. In response to two additional items on the immediate post-treatment questionnaire, the role-players reported much more fear about their health than the controls ($t = 2.37, p < .05$) and also expressed much more worry about lung cancer ($t = 2.81, p < .01$).

The *E*'s observational notes also indicate that the role players displayed considerable affect arousal during their performance, including tremors, trembling, and flushing. These manifestations of fear impressed us as being far beyond the call of duty, even for whole-hearted adherents of the Stanislavski method of acting. The *E*'s observational notes on the control group, on the other hand, indicated that these *S*s showed considerable interest while listening to the dramatic tape recording, but with signs of only a very mild degree of emotional arousal as compared with the role-players, several of whom continued to show signs of being severely shaken long after the performance was over. Spontaneous comments made by almost every role-player at the end of the session indicated awareness of fear arousal: e.g., "You scared me to death"; "I was really getting scared"; "That just shook me up—it does scare me—it does!"

Further evidence of the plausibility of attributing the major motivational impact of the role-playing procedure to fear arousal is provided by correlational data indicating a positive association between reported level of fear about health (regardless of experimental condition) and subsequent reported modification of smoking habits ($X^2 = 4.53, df = 1, p < .05$).

For many Ss, the intense emotional experience that occurred while playing the role of the cancer victim appears to have functioned as a "last straw" which impelled them to transform their "good intentions" into action. One role-player put it this way: "This is the oomph I needed for giving up"; while another asserted, "I heard so much about the dangers of smoking, and then one more thing and that was it."

The passively exposed control group, in contrast, expressed more disbelief and affective detachment. On the post-treatment questionnaire, for example, the controls were much more likely than the role-players to agree with the following assertions: (a) that a causal relation between smoking and cancer has *not* been proven ($t = 2.19, p < .05$); (b) that the seriousness of lung cancer has been exaggerated ($t = 2.05, p < .05$); (c) that smoking is "just another one of those risks" ($t = 2.26, p < .05$); (d) that individual susceptibility rather than smoking is the important factor in lung cancer ($t = 3.66, p < .01$); and (e) that continuing to smoke does *not* imply any "lack of control and will power" ($t = 1.71, p < .10$). Along with their efforts to minimize the relevance of the well-publicized scientific evidence concerning the link between smoking and cancer, the control Ss were more likely to react negatively toward those who convey the unpleasant information, as indicated by their relatively strong endorsement of the statement "I feel very annoyed when people warn me about the dangers of smoking" ($t = 2.68, p < .01$).

In the follow-up interviews, there were also some indications that the emotional role-playing procedure had activated, over the two-week interval, an increase in vigilance as well as a heightened need for reassurance, in line with theoretical expectations concerning the nature of reflective fear (Janis, 1962). Specifically, three types of fear-related changes were spontaneously mentioned by the role-players while talking with E on the telephone:

1. Increased awareness of the literature on smoking and lung cancer: e.g., "After I saw you so many articles popped out at me"; "I'm more aware of the symptoms and I think about it. . .; and [I would like to get a] book on the warning signs of cancer."

2. Active attempts to obtain reassurance: e.g., "I got scared—I'm glad I did—I went to a doctor for a check-up"; and "I'm planning to go and get an X-ray."

3. Continued realization of personal vulnerability: e.g., "If I'd kept smoking I'm sure something would have happened to me, with my luck"; "Driving home afterwards I got scared—[I thought] what if it would be me—how would I actually react to getting lung cancer?"; "I've really thought about it—especially because Grandmother had cancer—there is a weak spot in the family."

The comments indicating awareness of personal vulnerability, made spontaneously by a few role-players during their follow-up interview, were very similar in content to those that had been made by many role-players immediately after their performance. For example, one girl reported, "I felt after a while I wasn't acting, it was really true"; another commented, "It makes it sound so near"; a third said, "I started to think, this could be me—really!"

Although the role-playing activity as a whole had an impressive emotional quality, certain parts of the psychodramatic sequence seemed to be particularly salient to the Ss as concrete representations of the threat. In response to the question, "Which part made the greatest impression on you?" several role-players mentioned the immediate threat of hospitalization, and a few spontaneously mentioned that the coughing symptoms described in the script were applicable to themselves. (E.g., "I really do have that cough and it's bad in the morning"; and "I felt I was in the part because I do cough.")

This phenomenon of becoming deeply impressed by specific disturbing details from enacting the fictional role of a cancer victim suggests that the procedure may entail more than merely a novel or dramatic way of eliciting attention to the relevant information. During the performance unpleasant outcomes such as pain, physical incapacity, hospitalization and death seem to acquire in fantasy a personal reality that is usually resisted when people are told about these same threatening outcomes in the usual types of warning communications.[2]

Thus, the qualitative observations supplement the quantitative data on attitude change in suggesting that the techniques of emotional role-playing may prove to be an exceptionally successful means for arousing potentially adaptive fear reactions, breaking through the defensive facade that normally prevents many people from taking account of their personal vulnerability to objective sources of danger. As yet we do not know how persistent the effects of emotional role-playing will prove to be, but this question is now being investigated by a follow-up study on the Ss in this experiment, which will provide information about their smoking habits over a two-year period.

REFERENCES

Cannell, C., and MacDonald, J. The impact of health news on attitudes and behavior. *Journalism Quarterly,* 1956, *33,* 315–23.

2The finding that the controls modified their attitudes and smoking habits to some extent indicates that listening to the information and dramatic presentation in the tape recording of a role-playing session may also have been quite effective with Ss of the type used in this experiment, even though it produced less change than the role-playing procedure. Pilot studies carried out with other types of Ss suggest that young college women may be especially receptive to anti-smoking communications. It is quite possible, therefore, that the results obtained from the role-playing may be partly dependent on the predispositions of the sample used in the investigation. For example, in an older sample, with more deeply ingrained habits and greater inhibitions about acting in a make-believe situation, less involvement and accordingly less change would be expected. Replications of the present study with different types of persons are obviously essential before any firm conclusions can be drawn as to how successful the emotional role-playing technique would be in smoking clinics or in any large-scale program to modify the smoking habits of various sectors of the population.

Corsini, R. Psychodrama with a psychopath. *Group Psychotherapy*, 1958, *11*, 33–39.

Culbertson, F. Modification of an emotionally held attitude through role-playing. *Journal of Abnormal and Social Psychology*, 1957, *54*, 230–33.

Greenberg, D. S. Tobacco: After publicity surge, Surgeon General's Report seems to have little enduring effect. (News and Comment). *Science*, 1964, *145*, 1021–22.

Horn, D. Modifying smoking habits in high school students. *Children.* 1960, *7*, 63–65.

Janis, I. Psychological effects of warnings. In D. Chapman and G. Baker (Eds.), *Man and society in disaster.* New York: Basic Books, 1962.

Janis, I. *The contours of fear: Psychological studies of war, disaster, illness, and experimental stress.* New York: Wiley (in press).

Janis, I., and King, B. The influence of role-playing on opinion-change. *Journal of Abnormal and Social Psychology,* 1954, *49*, 211–18.

Kelman, H. Attitude change as a function of response restriction. *Human Relations,* 1953, *6*, 185–214.

King, B., and Janis, I. Comparison of the effectiveness of improvised vs. non-improvised role-playing in producing opinion changes. *Human Relations,* 1956, *9*, 177–86.

Lawton, M., and Goldman, A. Cigarette smoking and attitude toward the etiology of lung cancer. *Journal of Social Psychology,* 1961, *54*, 235–48.

Moreno, J. The psychodrama. In J. E. Fairchild (Ed.), *Personal problems and psychological frontiers.* New York: Sheridan House, 1957.

Snegireff, K., and Lombard, O. Smoking habits of Massachusetts physicians. *New England Journal of Medicine,* 1959, *261*, 603.

Toch, H., Allen, T., and Lazer, W. Effects of cancer scares: the residue of the news impact. *Journalism Quarterly,* 1961, *38*, 25–34.

The Chinese Indoctrination Program for Prisoners of War: A Study of Attempted "Brainwashing"

EDGAR H. SCHEIN

In this paper I shall try to present an account of the 'typical' experiences of United Nations prisoners of war in Chinese Communist hands, and to interpret these experiences in a social-psychological framework. Before the return of United Nations prisoners, the "confessions" of such prominent men as Cardinal Mindszenty and William Oatis had already aroused considerable interest in so-called brainwashing. This interest was heightened by the widespread rumors

Reprinted from Psychiatry: Journal for the Study of Interpersonal Processes *(1956) 19: 149–72. Copyright 1956 by the William Alanson White Psychiatric Foundation and reproduced by permission.*

of collaboration among United Nations prisoners of war in Korea. Following their repatriation in August 1953, a rash of testimonial articles appeared in the weekly magazines, some attempting to show that the Chinese Communist techniques were so terrifying that no one could withstand them, others roundly condemning the collaborative activities of the so-called "progressives"[1] as having been selfishly motivated under conditions in which resistance was possible. These various accounts fall short because they are too emotionally charged to be objective, and because they fail to have any generality, since they are usually based on the personal experiences of only one man.

The data upon which this paper is based were gathered in an attempt to form a generalized picture of what happened to the average man from the time he was captured until the time he was repatriated. The data were collected during August 1953 at Inchon, Korea, where the repatriates were being processed, and on board the U.S.N.S. General Black in transit to the United States from September 1 to September 16.

The method of collecting the data was, in the main, by intensive interviews conducted in Inchon, where the author was a member of one of the processing teams.[2] In the course of the processing, relatively objective tests and projective tests were also given the men;[3] but intensive interviewing was felt to be preferable for gathering the data presented here, because the material to be obtained was highly novel, and because the men had been through a highly traumatic situation which might make the eliciting of *any* information very difficult. It was also recognized that the men might find it difficult to remember, might be reluctant to relate certain of their experiences, and might retrospectively falsify many events.

Of approximately 20 repatriates selected at random at different stages of the repatriation, each was asked to tell in chronological order and in as great detail as possible what had happened to him during his captivity. Emphasis was placed on what the Chinese or North Koreans *did* in their handling of the prisoners and how the men reacted. The men were particularly encouraged to relate the reactions of *others*, in order to avoid arousing anxiety or guilt over their own behavior and thereby blocking the flow of memories. The interviews varied in length from two to four hours.

From these interviews a picture emerged which was recorded in the form of a composite or typical account of the capture and imprisonment experience. This account was then given to three psychiatrists[4] who together had interviewed 300 men assigned to them at random. It was their job to delete material which, on the basis of their information, was false and to add details which had not been revealed in my 20 interviews.

[1] Commonly called *pro's* by their fellow prisoners.

[2] As part of the processing, psychiatric interviews were initiated at Inchon during the two or three days that the men were there. The procedure of processing has been described in detail by Henry A. Segal in "Initial Psychiatric Findings of Recently Repatriated Prisoners of War," *Amer. J. Psychiatry* (1954) 111:358–363.

[3] The results of this testing will be reported on in part by H. D. Strassman, Margaret Thaler, and E. H. Schein in "A Prisoner of War Syndrome: Apathy as a Reaction to Severe Stress," *Amer. J. Psychiatry* (1956) 112:998–1003.

[4] These were Dr. Harvey Strassman, Dr. Patrick Israel, and Dr. Clinton Tempereau; their assistance in reading and commenting on the manuscript was extremely valuable.

On board ship I was present at a large number of psychiatric interviews and group therapy sessions, and engaged in many informal discussions with repatriates. Extended late evening "bull sessions" with repatriates were particularly informative.[5]

Many of the traumatic prison-camp experiences could probably not be fully communicated through verbal interviews. However, I believe that the data are sufficiently inclusive and reliable to provide a reasonably accurate account of prisoner-of-war experiences. The picture presented is not to be viewed as the experience of any single person nor as the experience of all the men. Rather, it represents a composite or typical account which, in all its details, may or may not have been true for any one prisoner.

THE PRISONER-OF-WAR EXPERIENCE

Capture, the March, and Temporary Camps

United Nations soldiers were captured by the Chinese and North Koreans at all stages of the Korean conflict, although particularly large groups were captured during November and December, 1950. The conditions under which men were captured varied widely. Some men were captured by having their positions overrun or surrounded; others ran into road blocks and were cut off; still others fought for many days on a shifting front before they succumbed. The situation in the front lines was highly fluid, and there was a good deal of confusion on both sides. When a position was overrun, the men often scattered and became disorganized.

While the initial treatment of prisoners by the North Koreans was typically harsh and brutal—they often took the prisoner's clothing, gave him little if any food, and met any resistance with immediate severe punishment or death—the Chinese, in line with their over-all indoctrination policy, often tried to create an atmosphere of friendliness and leniency. Some men reported that their Chinese captors approached them with outstretched hands, saying, "Congratulations! You've been liberated." It was made clear to the man that he could now join forces with other "fighters for peace." Often the Chinese soldiers pointed out to their captives how lucky they were not to have been captured by the North Koreans. Some men reported incidents of Chinese beating off North Koreans who were "trying to hurt" American prisoners, or of punishing their own guards for being too rough or inconsiderate. The men were usually allowed to keep their clothing, and some consideration was given to the sick and wounded. However, the food and medical attention were only slightly better than that provided by the North Koreans.

For the first six to twenty-four hours after capture, a man was usually in a state of dazed shock, unable to take any kind of integrated action and, later, unable to report any kind of feeling he had had during this period. Following this, he expected death or torture at the hands of his captors, for rumors that this would happen had been widely circulated in the front lines, often based on

---

[5] The reliability of the material was further checked against the complete Army files on the total group of repatriates.

stories of men who had fallen into North Korean hands. These fears were, however, quickly dispelled by the friendly attitude of the Chinese soldiers; and this friendly attitude and the emphasis on "peace" was the first and perhaps most significant step in making the prisoner receptive to the more formal indoctrination which was to come later.

In the next weeks or months the prisoner was exposed to great physical hardship and to a series of psychological pressures which amounted to a cyclical reactivation of fears and their relief by actual events or by extravagant promises. Implicit in most of what the Chinese said and did was the suggestion that these stresses could be brought to an end by the adoption of a "cooperative" attitude by the prisoner, although at first it was not clear just what this meant.

The men were collected behind the lines and were marched north in groups of varying sizes. The men marched only at night, averaging about 20 miles, and were kept under strict cover in the daytime. Conditions on the march were very hard. Most men reported having great difficulty eating strange and badly prepared foods; however, they were often reminded, whether true or not, that they were getting essentially the same rations as the average Chinese foot soldier. Medical care was almost nonexistent, but this too was depicted as being equally true for Chinese soldiers because of supply shortages. Almost all the men had diarrhea, many had dysentery, and most of them suffered from exposure. Every day would find a few more dead.

Although the columns were not well guarded, few escapes were attempted because the men were too weak, did not know the terrain, were on the whole poorly organized, and were afraid of the North Koreans. The few who did escape were almost always returned to the group within a short time.

During these one- to two-week marches the men became increasingly disorganized and apathetic. They developed a slow plodding gait, called by one man a "prisoner's shuffle." Lines of authority tended to break down, and the prevailing attitude was "every man for himself." Open competition for food, clothing, and shelter made the maintenance of group ties almost impossible. Everything that happened tended to be frustrating and depriving, yet there was no ready outlet for hostility, and no opportunity for constructive resistance. The only *realistic* goal was to get to prison camp where, it was hoped, conditions would be better.[6]

Uppermost in the men's minds were fantasies of food—memories of all the good meals they had had in the past, or plans for elaborate menus in the future. The only competing fantasies concerned loved ones at home, or cars, which seemed symbolically to represent the return to their homes and to freedom.

Arrival at one of the temporary camps was usually a severe disappointment. Many men reported that the only thing that had kept them going on the march was the hope of improved conditions in the camp; but they found the food as

[6] Not all of the men participated in such severe marches. Those captured in 1951 and 1952 were sometimes taken north by truck or under less severe conditions. The sick and wounded were given somewhat more consideration, although never much in the way of medical aid. Numerous incidents were reported of Chinese guards helping men, occasionally even carrying them.

It should also be mentioned that the North Korean civilians seemed ambivalent toward the prisoners. Many of them were sadistic, but many others helped the Americans by hiding them or giving them food and clothing.

bad as ever, living conditions more crowded than before, and a continued lack of consideration for the sick and wounded. Moreover, there was now nothing to do but sit and wait. The news given the men was mostly false, playing up Communist military victories, and was, of course, particularly demoralizing. Many of the men became extremely apathetic and withdrawn, and according to some reports these apathy states sometimes became so severe as to result in death.[7]

The Chinese continually promised improvements in conditions or early repatriation, and failures of these promises to materialize were blamed on obstructions created by United Nations air activity or lack of "cooperation" among the prisoners. It was always made clear that only certain prisoners could hope to get a break: those who "did well," "cooperated," "learned the truth," and so on. The Chinese distributed propaganda leaflets and required the men to sing Communist songs. Apparently even guards were sensitized to finding potential collaborators among the prisoners by observing their reactions to such activities. Outright indoctrination was not attempted on the marches and in the temporary camps, but those men who finally reached one of the permanent camps were ill-prepared physically and psychologically for the indoctrination pressures they were about to face.

Life in the Permanent Prisoner-of-War Camp

Most of the permanent camps were parts of small Korean villages, often split into several compounds in different parts of the village. The camps were sometimes surrounded by a fence, by barbed wire, or by natural barriers, although sometimes not enclosed at all. While guards were posted at key places, they were not sufficiently plentiful to prevent escapes or excursions to other parts of the village. The camp usually consisted of a series of mud huts in which the men slept on the floor or on straw matting, and a schoolhouse or other permanent building which was used as administrative headquarters, for lectures, and for recreation. The various Chinese officer and enlisted billets were usually scattered through the village. Mess and latrine facilities were very inadequate, and conditions were crowded, but far better than in the temporary camps.

In camp the men were segregated by race, nationality, and rank, and were organized into companies, platoons, and squads. The squads varied in size from 10 to 15 men, who usually shared the same living area. No formal organization was permitted among the prisoners; thus, the Chinese put their own personnel in charge of the platoons and companies, and appointed certain prisoners as squad leaders without consideration of rank.

Although the daily routine in camp varied, the average prisoner arose at dawn, was required to do calisthenics for an hour or more, was assigned to various details—such as gathering wood, carrying water, cooking, repairing roads, burying other prisoners, and general maintenance of the camp—and then was given a breakfast of potato soup or some form of cereal at around eight o'clock. The rest of the morning and afternoon was usually spent on indoctrination or details. Whether there was a midday meal depended on the attitude of the prisoner, the supply of food, and the general state of the political situation. The

[7] For a more complete description of these apathy reactions, see reference footnote 3.

main meal was served around five o'clock and usually consisted of vegetables, grains, rice, and occasional bits of pork fat or fish. For men on such a meager diet, details involving many miles of walking or very hard work were especially exhausting.

Recreation varied with the camp and with the political situation. During the first year or so, a heavy emphasis was placed on indoctrination, and recreation was restricted to reading Communist literature, seeing propaganda films, and playing such games as checkers and chess. As the truce talks progressed and repatriation became a possibility, conditions in the camps improved generally. Less emphasis was placed on indoctrination and more leeway was given to the prisoners to engage in recreation of their own choice. The improvement in living conditions made physical recreation more feasible, and the men were permitted to devise athletic fields and equipment. Intercamp "Olympics" conducted by the Chinese—and used by them for their own propaganda purposes—drew wide participation among the more athletically inclined, regardless of their political sentiments.

There are few data available concerning the sexual activities of the prisoners. There were Korean women available in the villages, but men seldom visited them. Reports of homosexuality were very infrequent.

THE INDOCTRINATION PROGRAM

All of these conditions in the permanent camp were, in actual practice, interlocked with the indoctrination program. This program cannot be viewed as a collection of specific techniques routinely applied, but rather as the creation of a whole set of social conditions within which certain techniques operated. Whether the Chinese manipulation of the social setting to create certain effects was intentional can only be conjectured; intentional or not, it was an important factor in such success as the indoctrination program achieved.

The Removal of Supports to Beliefs, Attitudes, and Values

On matters of opinion, people tend to rely primarily on the opinions of others for determination of whether they themselves are "right" or "wrong"—whether these opinions of others are obtained through mass media of communication or through personal interaction. All of the prisoners' accustomed sources of information concerning daily events on a local, national, or international level were cut off by the Chinese, who substituted their own, usually heavily biased, newspapers, radio broadcasts, and magazines. *The Daily Worker* from various cities was available in the camp libraries, as were numerous magazines and journals from China, Poland, Russia, and Czechoslovakia. The radio news broadcasts heard usually originated in China. And the camp headquarters had no scruples concerning accuracy in the news announcements made over the camp public-address system.

The delivery of mail from home was systematically manipulated; the evidence indicates that all mail which contained information about the war or the truce talks, or which contained favorable personal news, was withheld, while letters containing no general information, or bad personal news, were usually delivered.

Personal contact with visitors from outside the camps was very limited, mainly restricted to Communist news correspondents. For most prisoners, there was simply no way to find out accurately what was going on in the world.

The Chinese also attempted to weaken the means of consensual validation by undermining personal contacts among the men. First of all, the men were segregated by race, apparently in order to put special indoctrination pressure on members of certain minorities, especially Negroes. The men were also segregated by rank, in what appeared to be a systematic attempt to undermine the internal structure of the group by removing its leaders. Thus the noncommissioned officers, who were at first in the enlisted camps, were put into a special camp when the Chinese found out that they were quite effective in keeping the other men from various kinds of collaboration. It was reported that this segregation was often followed by a considerable increase in collaboration, particularly among the younger enlisted men.

The Chinese emphasized that rank was no longer of any significance; the entire group was now part of a wider "brotherhood"—the earlier mentioned "fighters for peace"—in which, under communism, everyone was to be equal. The Chinese sometimes put particularly young or inept prisoners in command of the squads to remind the men that former bases of organization no longer counted. While such a procedure aroused only resistance and hostility in most of the prisoners, undoubtedly a few malcontents welcomed the opportunity to gain occupancy of the favored positions that had never been available to them before.

There was also persistent emphasis on undermining all friendships, emotional bonds, and group activities. For instance, the Chinese prohibited all forms of religious expression and ruthlessly persecuted the few chaplains or others who tried to organize or conduct religious services. Bonds to loved ones at home were weakened by the withholding of mail, as the Chinese frequently pointed out to the men that the lack of mail meant that their friends and relatives no longer cared for them.

The systematic use of Chinese spies and also informers from prisoner ranks made it possible for the Chinese to obtain detailed information about almost all activities going on in camp. The men reported that the Chinese were forever sneaking around their quarters and listening to conversations or observing activities from hidden posts, and they also knew that some of their number were acting as informers. These circumstances helped to create a feeling of general distrust, and the only fully safe course was to withdraw from all intimate interaction with other prisoners.

When any semblance of effective organization appeared spontaneously among the men, the Chinese would usually immediately remove and segregate the leaders or key figures; and informal groups which might have supported resistance activities were also usually systematically broken up. The few that were not broken up either were not effective or died because of lack of internal support, thus indicating that this system of social control was highly effective. Usually groups were formed for one of three purposes—to plan for and aid in escapes, to prevent men from collaborating, or for social reasons. According to most reports, the groups organized around escape were highly ineffective. Usually such groups were quickly liquidated by being physically broken up. A few poorly planned escapes were attempted, but the marginal diet, the strangeness of the surrounding terrain, and the carefully built-up fear of the North

Koreans all served to minimize escapes. When an escape did occur, the Chinese usually recovered the man easily by offering a bag of rice to anyone turning him in. The groups organized to keep men from collaborating, or to retaliate against them if they did, were usually composed of some of the more outspoken and violent resisters. One such group, labelled the "Ku Klux Klan" by the Chinese because of its militant policy, appeared to be composed mainly of men who had served some time in prison for various infractions of camp rules. They threatened potential collaborators through anonymous notes, but the number of incidents in which they followed through was relatively small. Usually the Chinese discovered their plans and, whenever they became dangerous, disrupted their activities. The third type of group consisted of prisoners who were solely interested in each other's company; one such group, made up primarily of older prisoners, was called "The Old Soldiers' Home."

A few groups remained intact even though the Chinese knew about them, perhaps because the Chinese did not consider them very dangerous, or because their leaders, as spokesmen for the prisoners, provided a valuable sounding board whenever the Chinese wanted to know how the group would react to certain changes in policy. The latter, in fact, gave such groups some power, but if this power was ever misused—that is, if the group supported an escape attempt or a theft of food, for instance—the group was quickly liquidated and its leaders were imprisoned or moved to another camp.

Various other groupings of men existed, some, such as the squad, for administrative reasons, others to support various Chinese enterprises. Soon after capture, the Chinese made a concerted effort to recruit men for a number of "peace committees" whose purpose it was to aid in the indoctrination by conducting personal interviews with resistant prisoners and to deter any resistance activity. They also were charged with such propaganda missions as the preparation of leaflets, peace petitions, and scripts for radio broadcasts—all under the guise of running such innocuous camp activities as recreation. An intercamp peace organization was also formed to draw up peace appeals and petitions to be submitted to the United Nations, carrying, of course, the endorsement of a large number of prisoners.

The members of the camp peace committees and the delegates to intercamp peace rallies were usually selected by a pseudo-democratic method. However, the men who ended up in the key positions were usually those the Chinese wanted, or, in any case, approved of—that is, men who were willing to cooperate with the Chinese, and who had sincerely or falsely convinced their captors that they were sympathetic to the Communist cause. Sometimes the election was held over and over again until the right man was chosen. At other times the men resigned themselves to the fact that all would go more smoothly if they selected at the beginning the man the Chinese wanted, for the group could be dissolved at will anyway.

Each camp also had a number of other committees operating under the peace committee. They were responsible for the daily routine affairs of the camp, such as sanitation, food, recreation, study, and entertainment. The number of noncollaborators who were allowed to be members appeared to depend on the mood of the Chinese and the degree to which they wanted to keep in touch with prisoner opinions. It is likely that with the general improvement in camp conditions in 1952 and 1953, the membership of the various committees became more representative. The peace committees were, by then, largely defunct; they had been exploited as much as possible by the Chinese and no longer served any function in their propaganda campaigns.

Various social groups formed by pro's were left intact—perhaps as a reminder to other prisoners that one way to enter into meaningful relationships with others was through common political activities for the Communists.

One of the most significant facts about the few types of groups that did exist in camp is that they were highly unstable from an internal point of view because of the possible presence of informers and spies. Mutual distrust existed especially in the peace committees and in groups sanctioned by the Chinese, because no member was ever sure whether any other member was really a pro or was just pretending to "go along." If a man was pretending, he had to hide this carefully lest a real pro turn him in to the Chinese. Yet a man who sincerely believed in the Chinese peace effort had to hide this fact from others who might be pretenders, for fear they might harm him directly or blacklist him for the future, at the same time convincing other pro's that he really was sincere.

The members of resistance groups and social groups also had to be wary of each other, because they never knew whether the group had been infiltrated by spies and informers. Furthermore, the fact that the group might be broken up at any time tended to keep any member from becoming too dependent on, or close to, another.[8]

From the point of view of this analysis the most important effect of the social isolation which existed was the consequent emotional isolation which prevented a man from validating any of his beliefs, attitudes, and values through meaningful interaction with other men at a time when these were under heavy attack from many sources, and when no accurate information was available.

Direct Attacks on Beliefs, Attitudes, and Values

The chief method of direct indoctrination was a series of lectures that all prisoners had to attend at some time during their imprisonment. These lectures were given daily and lasted from two to three hours. Each camp had one or more political instructors who read the lectures from a prepared text. Often one instructor read while another seemed to follow a second copy of the text, as if to make sure that the right material was being presented. The lectures were direct, simple, black-and-white propaganda. They attacked the United Nations and particularly the United States on various political, social, and economic issues, at the same time glorifying the achievements of the Communist countries, and making strong appeals for "peace."

Most men reported that the anti-American material was naïve and seldom based on adequate or correct information about the United States. Even the pro-Communist arguments were sometimes weak and susceptible to attack. Occasionally a well-educated prisoner debated points on communism successfully with instructors who had little knowledge of the classical works of communism.

---

[8] Segal (reference footnote 2) has aptly described such prisoner groups as "groups of isolates."

Usually the instructors presented the neo-Communist views of writers such as Mao Tse-tung and were unable to counter the arguments of prisoners who knew Marx and Lenin. The number of prisoners with sufficient education to engage in such arguments was, however, extremely small.

The constant hammering at certain points, combined with all the other techniques used—and in a situation where the prisoners had no access to other information—made it likely that many of the Chinese arguments did filter through enough to make many of the men question some of their former points of view. It is also likely that any appeal for "peace," no matter how false, found a receptive audience among combat-weary troops, especially when it was pointed out that they were fighting on foreign soil and were intervening in a civil war which was "none of their business." Both lectures and didactic "interrogations" emphasized detailed predictions of what would happen to the prisoners upon repatriation, some of which turned out to be accurate.[9] The Chinese implied that certain problems which would arise would be the result of the "weakness" or "unfairness" of the democratic ideology.

Another direct technique was the distribution of propaganda leaflets and the showing of Communist films glorifying the accomplishments of the Communist regime in Russia and China, and pointing out how much more had been done by communism for the peasant and laborer than by the capitalist system. While such films might have been highly ineffectual under ordinary circumstances, they assumed considerable importance because of the sheer lack of any other audio-visual material.

Perhaps the most effective attack on existing values, beliefs, and attitudes was the use of testimonials from prisoners who were ostensibly supporting Communist enterprises. These included peace petitions, radio appeals, speeches, and confessions. The use of such testimonials had a double effect in that it further weakened group ties while presenting pro-Communist arguments. As long as the men unanimously rejected the propaganda, each of them could firmly hold to the position that his beliefs must be right, even if he could not defend them logically. However, *if even one other man became convinced, it was no longer possible to hold this position.* Each man was then required to begin examining his beliefs and was vulnerable to the highly one-sided arguments that were repeatedly presented.

Of particular importance were the germ-warfare confessions which were extracted from a number of Air Force officers and enlisted men. The Chinese made a movie of one or two of the officers giving their testimony to the "international" commission which they had set up to investigate the problem, and showed this movie in all the camps. Furthermore, one or two of the officers personally went from camp to camp and explained how United Nations forces had used these bombs; this made a powerful impression on many men who had, until then, dismissed the whole matter as a Chinese propaganda project. The great detail of the accounts, the sincerity of the officers, the fact that they were freely going from camp to camp and did not look as if they were then or had

---

[9] The various problems that faced repatriates have been discussed by Segal, reference footnote 2, and by Robert J. Lifton in "Home by Ship: Reaction Patterns of American Prisoners of War Repatriated from North Korea," *Amer. J. Psychiatry* (1954) *110:* 732–39.

previously been under any duress made it difficult for some men to believe that the accounts could be anything but true.

While it is difficult to determine how many men were convinced that the United Nations forces had used germ bombs, it is evident that serious doubts arose in the minds of many, and some admitted being still in doubt even some weeks after their repatriation. Unquestionably, personal testimonials were on the whole a far more effective propaganda weapon than any amount of direct lecturing, although they both played a part in the over-all indoctrination. In general, the older and more experienced prisoners were less susceptible to this kind of propaganda. One sergeant stated that the following kinds of reasons prevented him and others from falling for germ-warfare charges: first, germ bombs are tactically impractical and ineffective; second, the United States would probably not abandon its ethics, and germ bombs would not be consistent with those ethics; and third, even if the United States were to use weapons previously not considered ethical, it would use atom bombs in preference to germ bombs.

The Chinese also used Koreans to give testimonials concerning the barbarity of the United Nations; in one instance women and children told one of the peace committees how United Nations planes had dropped toys which exploded when children tried to pick them up. It is difficult to evaluate the effects of such propaganda, but it is not likely that many prisoners believed stories of such extremity.

Indirect Attacks on Beliefs, Attitudes, and Values

In the direct attacks which I have been discussing, the source of propaganda was external. In the indirect attacks, a set of conditions was created in which each prisoner of war was encouraged to participate in a way that would make it more possible for him to accept some of the new points of view. One attempt to accomplish this was by means of group discussions following lectures.

Most lectures ended with a series of conclusions—for example, "The South Koreans started the war by invading North Korea," or "The aim of the capitalist nations is world domination." The men were then required to break up into squads, go to their quarters, and discuss the material for periods of two hours or more. At the end of the discussion each squad had to provide written answers to questions handed out during the lecture—the answers, obviously, which had already been provided in the lecture. To "discuss" the lecture thus meant, in effect, to rationalize the predetermined conclusions.[10]

A monitor was assigned to each squad to "aid" the men in the discussion, to make sure that they stayed on the proper topic, and to collect the answers and make sure that they were the "right" ones. Initially, the monitor for most squads was an English-speaking Chinese, but whenever possible the Chinese turned the job over to one of the squad members, usually the one who was most

---

[10] During the last year or so of imprisonment, many of the features of indoctrination which earlier had been compulsory were put on a voluntary basis. Any prisoners who were interested in learning more about communism could attend special lectures and group discussions. The men who participated in such voluntary programs were known as "self-study pro's" and were given many privileges not accorded to other prisoners.

cooperative or sympathetic to the Communist point of view. If one or more members of the squad turned in "wrong" answers—for example, saying that the North Koreans had invaded South Korea—the entire squad had to listen to the lecture again and repeat the group discussion. This procedure might go on for days. The Chinese never tired of repeating the procedure over and over again, apparently believing that group discussion had a better chance of success in converting men to their point of view than individual indoctrination.

The success of such discussions often depended on the degree of supervision. If the monitor was lax, the groups would talk about anything but the required material. But a prisoner-of-war monitor who was actively pro-Communist or a Chinese who had a good understanding of English idiom might obtain considerable discussion. Even when an issue was actively discussed, in many cases it probably reinforced the United Nations position by providing an opportunity for the men to obtain some consensual validation. But in other cases, the deliberation on points of view other than the one they had always held caused them to question certain beliefs and values which in the past had not led to satisfactory conditions for them.

A second means of indirect attack was interrogation. Interrogations were carried on during all stages of internment, but their apparent function and the techniques utilized varied from time to time. Almost all men went through lengthy and repetitive military interrogations, but failure to answer questions seldom led to severe physical punishment. Instead, various psychological pressures were applied. For instance, all information supplied was cross-checked against earlier interrogations and against the information from other men. If an answer did not tally with other information, the respondent had to explain the discrepancy. Continuous pressure to resolve contrary answers often forced a man to tell the truth.

The Chinese tried to create the impression that they could obtain *any* information from *anyone* by the following interrogation technique: If a man continued to refuse to answer a question, despite great fatigue and continued repetition of the question, the interrogator would suddenly pull out a notebook and point out to the man the complete answer to the question, sometimes in astonishingly accurate detail. The interrogation would then move on to a new topic and the same procedure would be repeated, until the man could not assess whether there was indeed *anything* that the Chinese did *not* know. In most cases the man was told that others had already given information or "confessed," so why should he hold back and suffer?[11]

A further technique was to have the man write out the question and then the answer. If he refused to write it voluntarily, he was asked to copy it from the notebooks, which must have seemed like a harmless enough concession. But the information which he had copied could then be shown to another man as evidence that he had given information of his own volition. Furthermore, it could be used to blackmail him, because he would have a hard time proving that he had merely copied the material.

---

[11] Many men reported that they felt the Chinese were boasting when they told what they knew—that they were very proud of their ability as interrogators and felt a need to show off to their captives.

Another type of interrogation to which almost all men were subjected involved primarily nonmilitary information. The Chinese were very curious about all aspects of life in the Western world and asked many questions about it, often in great detail. They also endeavored, by means of printed forms, to obtain a complete personal history from each prisoner, with particular emphasis on his social-cultural background, his class status, his and his parents' occupational histories, and so on. The purpose was apparently to determine which prisoners' histories might predispose them toward the Communist philosophy and thus make them apt subjects for special indoctrination.

Most men did not give accurate information. Usually the prisoner filled out the form in terms of fictitious characters. But later he would be required to repeat the entire procedure and would usually be unable to remember his earlier answers. He would then be confronted with the discrepancies and would be forced into the fatiguing activity of having to invent justification after justification to resolve them.

If and when the Chinese felt that they had obtained a relatively true account, it was used in discussion between the interrogator and the prisoner to undermine the prisoner's beliefs and values. Various points in the life history were used to show a man the "errors" of his past life—for example, that he or his parents had been ruthless capitalists exploiting workers, yet had really received only meager benefits from such exploitation. The Chinese were particularly interested in any inconsistencies in the life histories and would focus discussion on them in order to bring to light the motivations involved. Whenever possible, any setbacks that a man had experienced economically or socially were searchingly analyzed, and the blame was laid on the capitalistic system.

The fact that many men were unclear about why they were fighting in Korea was a good lever for such discussions. The interrogator or instructor could point out the basic injustices of foreign intervention in a civil war, and simultaneously could arouse longings for home and the wish that the United Nations had never taken up the fight in the first place. It was not difficult to convince some men that being in Korea was unfair to the Koreans, to themselves, and to their familes who wanted them home.

Interrogations might last for hours, days, or even weeks. In some cases the interrogator lived with his subject and tried to create an atmosphere of warmth and friendliness. The main point seemed to be to get the prisoner talking, no matter what he was talking about. The discussions sometimes became effective didactic sessions because of the friendly relationship which the interrogator built up. If there were any weaknesses or inconsistencies in a man's belief systems, once he lowered his guard and began to examine them critically, he was in danger of being overwhelmed by the arguments of the instructor. This did not, of course, occur typically. For many men such critical self-evaluation served as a reinforcement to their own beliefs and actually enabled them to expose weaknesses in the Communist arguments.

Another effective technique for getting the men to question their own beliefs and values was to make them confess publicly to wrongdoings and to "criticize" themselves. Throughout the time that the men were in camp they were required to go through these rituals over and over again, no matter how trivial the offense. These offenses usually were infractions of camp rules. Soon after the men had arrived in permanent camp they were given copies of the camp rules and were required to sign a statement that they would abide by them. Most of the men were far too hungry and cold to read several pages of script covering every aspect of camp life in such minute detail that it was practically impossible not to break one of the rules from time to time. For example, an elaborate set of rules governed where in camp a man was allowed to expectorate.

Sooner or later a minor or major infraction of the rules would occur. The man would be immediately brought up before the camp commander, where his offense would be condemned as a serious crime—one for which he, the commander would point out, could be severely punished, if it were not for the lenient Chinese policy. In line with the great show which the Chinese made of treating the prisoner as a responsible person, the fact that he had agreed in writing to abide by the rules would be emphasized. The prisoner could not now say that he had not read the rules, for this would expose him to further embarrassment. The camp commander would then ask whether the man would admit that he had broken the rule, whether he was sorry that he had done so, and whether he would promise not to behave in such a "criminal" manner in the future. If the offender agreed, which seemed at the time to be harmless enough and an easy way to get off, he would be asked to write out a confession.

Sometimes this ended the matter. But frequently the man was required to read his confession to a group of prisoners and to follow it by "self-criticism," which meant that the description of the wrong deed had to be analyzed in terms of the wrong *idea* that lay behind it, that the self had to be "deeply and sincerely" criticized in terms of a number of reasons why the idea and deed were "wrong," and that an elaborate set of promises about future conduct had to be made, along with apologies for the past. Such public self-effacement was a humiliating and degrading experience, and it set a bad precedent for other men who had been attempting to resist getting caught in this net.

Writing out confessions, reading them, and criticizing oneself for minor misconduct in camp did not seem too great a concession at first when viewed against the possibility of physical punishment, torture, or imprisonment. However, these techniques could become a psychological torture once the initial concession had been made. A man who had broken a rule and had gone through the whole ritual of criticism would shortly afterward break another rule, which would arouse increased hostility on the part of the Chinese and lead to correspondingly greater demands for confession and self-criticism. Men who had confessed at first to trivial offenses soon found themselves having to answer for relatively major ones.[12]

It should be pointed out, however, that the prisoners found numerous ways to obey the letter but not the spirit of the Chinese demands. For example, during public self-criticism sessions they would often emphasize the wrong words in the sentence, thus making the whole ritual ridiculous: "I am sorry I

---

[12] It can be seen that such a technique of "training" a man to confess can ultimately lead to the demand that he confess not only to misdeeds and the "wrong" ideas which lay behind them, but also to "wrong" thoughts and feelings which had not even resulted in action. In conjunction with public self-appraisal, prisoners were also often encouraged to keep diaries of their activities and thoughts. Usually only those prisoners who seriously studied communism kept diaries.

called Comrade Wong *a no-good son-of-a-bitch*." Another favorite device was to promise never to "get caught" committing a certain crime in the future. Such devices were effective because even those Chinese who knew English were not sufficiently acquainted with idiom and slang to detect subtle ridicule.

There is also some evidence that the Chinese used enforced idleness or solitary confinement to encourage prisoners to consider the Communist point of view. One of the few activities available, in such circumstances, was to read Communist literature and books by Western authors who directly or indirectly attacked capitalism. The camp libraries were wholly made up of such literature. Those who did not have the strength or inclination to go on physically taxing details found themselves with no alternative but to spend their time reading pro-Communist material. In addition, some read because they felt so emotionally isolated from other prisoners that they could enjoy only solitary activities.

The Eliciting of Collaboration by Rewards and Punishments

For a number of propaganda purposes the Chinese seemed to want certain men to cooperate in specific ways, without caring whether they accepted communism or not. These men did not seem to enjoy as much status as other pro's and were cast off by the Chinese as soon as they had ceased to be useful. Such collaboration was elicited directly by a system of rewards and incentives on the one hand, and threats and punishments on the other.

While it is dangerous to relate complex human behavior to a simple pattern of rewards and punishments, the repatriates' accounts of life in the prisoner-of-war camps make possible a considerable number of inferences concerning the 'positive' and 'negative' aspects of the social environment, which were important in eliciting the kind of behavior the Chinese wanted. It was made clear to all prisoners, from the time of their capture on, that cooperation with the Chinese would produce a more comfortable state of affairs, while noncooperation or open resistance would produce a continuing marginal existence. Which rewards were of primary importance to the men varied with their current condition. On the marches and in the temporary camps physical conditions were so bad that more food, any medication, any clothing or fuel, better and less crowded living conditions, and the like constituted a powerful reward. Promises of early repatriation, or at least of marked improvement of conditions in the permanent camps, were powerful incentives which were chronically exploited.

In the permanent camps there was some improvement in the physical conditions, so that basic necessities became less effective incentives. The promise of early repatriation continued to be a great incentive, however, despite the fact that it had been promised many times before without result. Communicating with the outside world now became a major concern. To let those at home know they were alive, some prisoners began to collaborate by making slanted radio broadcasts or filling their letters with propaganda or peace appeals in order to make sure that they were sent.

As conditions continued to improve, some of the luxury items and smaller accessories to living assumed greater significance. Cigarettes, combs, soap, candy, small items of clothing, a cup of hot tea, a drink of liquor, fresh fruit, and other items of this kind were sought avidly by some men.[13] Obtaining such items from the Chinese was inextricably linked with the degree to which the prisoner was willing to "cooperate." Any tendency toward "cooperation" was quickly followed by an increase in material rewards and promises for the future.

In some cases rewards were cleverly linked with participation in the indoctrination. For example, highly valued prizes such as cigarettes or fresh fruit were offered for essays dealing with certain aspects of world politics. The winning entries were published in the camp newspaper or magazine. Usually the winning entry was selected on the basis of its agreement with a Communist point of view, and the winner was usually someone well on the road to collaboration anyway, but the whole competition succeeded in getting the men to participate—to consider the various sides of an issue and to examine their previous views critically.

The Chinese also used rewards and punishments to undermine group organization. For example, shortly after capture, a number of men were led to believe that if they made radio broadcasts to the United Nations lines they would be repatriated early. The content of the broadcasts was not specified, but the men agreed to make them in the hope of letting their relatives know that they were alive. These men were then conspicuously assembled in front of other prisoners and were taken to a special location some distance away, where the broadcasts were to be made. In the meantime, other prisoners were encouraged to believe that these men were obtaining special privileges because they were "cooperating" in bringing "peace" to Korea.

The actual content of the radio messages turned out to be a peace appeal which tacitly condemned the United Nations, and a statement that the prisoners were being well treated by the Chinese. When the men saw the messages that they were to read, some of them refused to make the broadcast, despite threats of severe punishment. Other men agreed to make the broadcast but tried to code a message into the prescribed text, and still others hoped that the recipients of the broadcasts would somehow know that they were under duress. At least their families would know that they were alive if they broadcasted something.

When these men rejoined the other prisoners, they found that they had aroused the suspicion and hostility of many, especially since the Chinese showed their "appreciation" by ostentatiously bestowing favors on them. In order to retain these special privileges—and having in any case incurred the hostility or even ostracism of their own group—some of these men continued to collaborate, rationalizing that they were not really harming the United Nations cause. They became self-appointed secret agents and attempted to infiltrate the Chinese hierarchy to gather "intelligence information," in which capacity they felt that they could actually aid the United Nations cause.

Among the most effective rewards used by the Chinese were special privileges and certain symbolic rewards, such as rank and status in the prison hierarchy. Perhaps the most important of the privileges was freedom of movement; the pro's had free access to the Chinese headquarters and could go into town or

---

[13] A number of men reported that black-market activities flourished among the prisoners. Those items of value which men did not wish to use themselves were bartered or sold to other men. Even valuable medicines could sometimes be obtained only by bartering with pro's who had obtained them from the Chinese.

wherever they wished at any time of the day or night. They were given certain preferred jobs, such as writing for the camp newspaper, and were excused from the more unpleasant chores around the camp. They were often consulted by the Chinese in various policy matters. They received as a status symbol a little peace dove to be worn in the lapel or a Mao Tse-tung button which served as an identification badge. And many rewards were promised them for the future; they were told that they were playing a vital role in the world-wide movement for "peace," and that they could enjoy positions of high rank in this movement if they stayed and continued to work for it.

If one asks why men "fell" for this kind of line—why they were able to believe this kind of promise—one must look to the circumstances described earlier. These men had no sources of contrary information to rely on, and once they had collaborated even a little they were ostracized by their buddies, thus losing the support of the group which might have kept them from collaborating further.

Just as the probability of collaborative behavior could be increased through the use of rewards, the probability of resistance could be decreased through negative or painful stimulation. Usually threats of punishment were used when prisoners refused to "cooperate," and actual punishment was meted out for more aggressive resistance. Threats of death, nonrepatriation, torture, reprisals against families, reduction in food and medication, and imprisonment were all used. While the only one of these threats which was carried out with any degree of consistency was imprisonment, which sometimes involved long periods of solitary confinement, the other threats were nevertheless very effective and the possibility that they might be carried out seemed very real. Especially frightening was the prospect of nonrepatriation, which seemed a likely possibility before the prisoner lists were exchanged at Panmunjom. The threat of death was also effective, for the men knew that they could be killed and listed officially as having died of heart failure or the like.[14] With regard to food and medication, the men could not determine whether they were actually being punished by having these withheld, or whether the meager supply was merely being reserved for "deserving" prisoners.

An effective threat with officers was that of punishing the whole group for which the officer was responsible if he personally did not "cooperate." The incidence of such group punishment was not revealed in the accounts, but it is clear that if an officer did "cooperate" with the Chinese, he was able both to relieve his own fears and to rationalize his cooperation as being the only means of saving the men for whom he was responsible.

Reinforcing all these threats was the vague but powerful fear of the unknown; the men did not know what they were up against in dealing with the Chinese and could not predict the reactions of their captors with any degree of reliability. The only course that led to a consistent reduction in such tension was participation in Chinese enterprises.

---

[14]There is evidence that the Chinese sometimes staged "executions" in order to elicit cooperation. A prisoner might be marched out into a field, an empty gun placed to his head, and the trigger actually pulled. This procedure first created a state of high anxiety and then a state of grateful relief when it was discovered by the prisoner that he would not be executed after all.

Overt punishment varied with the offense, with the political situation, and with the person administering it. Shortly after capture there were numerous incidents of brutality, most of them committed by North Koreans. During early interrogations the Chinese frequently resorted to minor physical punishment such as face-slapping or kicking when answers were not forthcoming, but a prisoner who continued to be silent was usually dismissed without further physical punishment.

Physical punishments in permanent camps had the effect of weakening rather than injuring the men. They varied from severe work details to such ordeals as standing at attention for long periods; being exposed to bright lights or excessive cold; standing on tiptoe with a noose around the neck; being confined in the "cage," a room too small to allow standing, sitting, or lying down; being thrown in the "hole," a particularly uncomfortable form of solitary confinement; or being kept in filthy surroundings and denied certain essentials for keeping clean. Those who were *chronically* uncooperative were permanently segregated from the rest of the group and put into special camps where more severe forms of discipline backed by harsher punishments were in effect. Basically, the "lenient policy" applied only to those men whom the Chinese hoped they could use.

More common forms of punishment for minor infractions were social in character, intended to degrade or embarrass the prisoner in front of his fellows. Public confessions and self-criticisms were the outstanding forms of such punishment, with blackmail being frequently used if a prisoner had once collaborated to any extent. There is *no* evidence that the Chinese used any drugs or hypnotic methods, or offered sexual objects to elicit information, confessions, or collaborative behavior. Some cases of severe physical torture were reported, but their incidence is difficult to estimate.

General Principles in All Techniques

Several general principles underlay the various phases of the Chinese indoctrination, which may be worth summing up at this point. The first of these was *repetition.* One of the chief characteristics of the Chinese was their immense patience in whatever they were doing; whether they were conducting an interrogation, giving a lecture, chiding a prisoner, or trying to obtain a confession, they were always willing to make their demand or assertion over and over again. Many men pointed out that most of the techniques used gained their effectiveness by being used in this repetitive way until the prisoner could no longer sustain his resistance. A second characteristic was the *pacing of demands.* In the various kinds of responses that were demanded of the prisoners, the Chinese always started with trivial, innocuous ones and, as the habit of responding became established, gradually worked up to more important ones. Thus after a prisoner had once been "trained" to speak or write out trivia, statements on more important issues were demanded of him. This was particularly effective in eliciting confessions, self-criticism, and information during interrogation.

Closely connected with the principle of pacing was the principle of constant *participation* from the prisoner. It was never enough for the prisoner to listen and absorb; some kind of verbal or written response was always demanded. Thus if a man would not give original material in question-and-answer sessions, he was asked to copy something. Likewise, group discussions, autobiographical statements, self-criticisms, and public confessions all demanded an active participation by the prisoner.[15]

In their propaganda campaign the Chinese made a considerable effort *to insert their new ideas into old and meaningful contexts.* In general this was not very successful, but it did work for certain prisoners who were in some way not content with their lot in the United States. The obtaining of autobiographies enabled each interrogator to determine what would be a significant context for the particular person he was dealing with, and any misfortune or setback that the person had suffered served as an ideal starting place for undermining democratic attitudes and instilling communistic ones.

No matter which technique the Chinese were using, they always structured the situation in such a way that the correct response was followed by some form of *reward*, while an incorrect response was immediately followed by *threats* or *punishment.* The fact that the Chinese had complete control over material resources and had a monopoly of power made it possible for them to manipulate hunger and some other motives at will, thereby giving rewards and punishments their meaning.

Among the various propaganda techniques employed by the Chinese, their use of *prestige suggestion* was outstanding. The average prisoner had no way of disputing the germ-warfare confessions and testimonials of Air Force officers, or the conclusions of an investigation of the germ-warfare charges by ostensibly impartial scientists from many nations.

Among the positive propaganda appeals made, the most effective was probably the *plea for peace.* The Chinese presented an antiwar and laissez-faire ideology which strongly appealed to the war-weary combat soldier.

In addition, the Chinese used a number of *manipulative tricks,* which were usually successful only if the prisoner was not alert because of fatigue or hunger. One such trick was to require signatures, photographs, or personal information for a purpose which sounded legitimate, then using them for another purpose. Some prisoners reported that they were asked to sign "camp rosters" when they first arrived in camp and later found that they had actually signed a peace petition.

In essence, the prisoner-of-war experience in camp can be viewed as a series of problems which each man had to solve in order to remain alive and well integrated. Foremost was the problem of physical privation, which powerfully motivated each man to improve his living conditions. A second problem was to overcome the fears of nonrepatriation, death, torture, or reprisals. A third

---

[15] The Chinese apparently believed that if they could once get a man to participate he was likely to continue, and that eventually he would accept the attitudes which the participation expressed. However, it may have also been true that the interrogators, for instance, were in danger of losing face with their own group if they could not produce concrete evidence that they had obtained some information; at times they seemed to want any kind of answers, so long as they had something to show in headquarters as proof that they had done their job. Similarly, the material obtained at the end of the group discussions was perhaps used as evidence that the instructors were doing their jobs properly. Thus it is possible that part of the aim was a check by the Chinese on each other.

problem was to maintain some kind of cognitive integration, a consistent outlook on life, under a set of conditions where basic values and beliefs were strongly undermined and where systematic confusion about each man's role in life was created. A fourth problem was to maintain a valid position in a group, to maintain friendship ties and concern for others under conditions of mutual distrust, lack of leadership, and systematically created social disorganization. The Chinese had created a set of conditions in which collaboration and the acceptance of communism led to a resolution of conflicts in all these areas.

REACTIONS TO THE INDOCTRINATION

It is very difficult to determine after the fact what happend in this highly complex and novel situation—what it was really like for the men who had to spend several years in the Chinese prisoner-of-war camps. Each set of experiences had a highly personal and unique flavor to it, making generalized conclusions difficult.

I may illustrate the problem by discussing *ideological change* and *collaboration*. Both of these were responses to the indoctrination, broadly conceived, *but neither necessarily implies the other*. It was possible for a man to collaborate with the enemy without altering his beliefs, and it was equally possible for a man to be converted to communism to some degree without collaborating.

Obviously, it is necessary to define these responses, even though any precise definition will to some degree distort the actual events. *Collaboration* may be defined as any kind of behavior which helped the enemy: signing peace petitions, soliciting signatures for peace petitions, making radio appeals, writing radio scripts, writing false information home concerning conditions in the camps (or recording statements to this effect), writing essays on communism or working for the Communist-controlled newspaper, allowing oneself to be photographed in "rigged" situations, participating in peace rallies or on peace committees, being friendly with the enemy, asking others to cooperate with the enemy, running errands for the enemy, accepting special privileges or favors, making false confessions or pro-enemy speeches, informing on fellow prisoners, divulging military information, and so on.

Nothing about ideological conversion is implied in this definition. A man who engaged in any of these collaborative behaviors because he wanted an extra cigarette was just as much a collaborator as one who did so because he wanted to further the Communist cause. Moreover, the definition does not take into account the temporal pattern of such behavior. Many men collaborated at one time during their imprisonment when one set of conditions existed, but did not collaborate at other times under other conditions. The man who moved from collaboration to resistance was obviously different from the man who moved from resistance to collaboration. Perhaps most important of all, this definition says nothing about the particular pattern of motivations or circumstances that drove a man to the first collaborative act and subsequently into a situation in which it was difficult to stop collaborating.

Yet such a concept of collaboration has an advantage in its reference to *overt* behavior. It was such behavior which the other men in camp reacted to and which often formed the basis for later judgments of a man by his government, family, and friends, although different motives were often imputed by different sources for such behavior. The motives that lay behind the behavior are of obvious importance and must be understood, but it should also be recognized that conjectures of motives are more precarious than analyses of behavior.

Ideological change may be defined as a reorganization of political beliefs, which could vary from acquiring mild doubts concerning some aspects of the democratic ideology to the complete abandonment of this ideology and a total embracing of communism. The latter I shall label *conversion*. The problem of measuring the *degree* of ideological change is complicated by the lack of good behavioral criteria for measuring such a process of reorganization of beliefs. One might be tempted to say that anyone could be termed a convert who actively attempted to convince others of the worth of communism, who took all the advanced courses in camp, and who was able to demonstrate in his overt behavior a disregard for democratic values. But such behavior might also characterize a relatively intelligent man who had begun to read Communist literature out of boredom, only to find that both his friends and the Chinese took this as evidence of his genuine interest in communism. He might then be ostracized by his friends and pressed into collaboration by the Chinese, who, it was rumored, severely punished anyone who deceived them.

Of all the prisoners, 21 refused repatriation; one might assume that these represent the total number of converts, but such a criterion is inadequate on at least two grounds. On the one hand, some converts would undoubtedly have been sent back to the United States to spread communism and form a potential fifth column. On the other hand, some collaborators who had not changed ideologically might have been afraid to return, knowing that court-martial proceedings and personal degradation probably awaited them.

One might think that the identification of such men could be made successfully by others who were collaborators and possibly converts. However, anyone who had been and remained a convert would *not* identify other converts. On the other hand, a collaborator who had repudiated communism and his own collaborative activities would be likely to implicate as many others as possible in order to make his own behavior look better. Allegations from known collaborators are therefore very unreliable.

Thus it is more difficult to determine how the prisoners responded to indoctrination techniques ideologically than it is to determine what overt collaboration occurred. What the prisoners *did* is, relatively speaking, a matter of fact; why they did it is a matter of conjecture. In presenting a classification of types of reactions and the motivation patterns or situations that elicited them, one must rely primarily on the *consensus* of the accounts of the repatriates and must recognize the possible biases that can arise in such an analysis after the fact. I am not implying that each prisoner could be placed into one of the categories to be presented below; it is more likely that each man fell into several categories at any given time, and, moreover, that his motivation-situation complex shifted as different sets of circumstances presented themselves.

The "Get-Alongers"

The predominant reaction of prisoners was to establish a complex compromise between the demands of the Chinese and the demands of their own ideology. This kind of behavior was labeled "playing it cool" by the men, and consisted primarily in a physical and emotional withdrawal from all situations which might arouse basic conflict. Men who reacted in this way were unwilling to do anything that did not have to be done, and learned after some months to 'suspend' their feelings about most events, no matter how provoking they might be. This was not an easy adjustment to maintain, since the prisoner had to make some concessions to the Chinese to avoid the more severe physical or psychological pressures, at the same time avoiding cooperating to such an extent as to arouse the suspicion and hostility of his fellow prisoners. The safest course was to withdraw emotionally both from the Chinese and from the rest of the prisoner group; this withdrawal was made easier by the apathy and physical weakness induced by life under marginal conditions.[16]

Most of the men who achieved this kind of compromise successfully without too great a toll on their personality were well integrated and retained secure and stable group identifications from before their prisoner-of-war experience. Their judgment concerning the extent to which they could collaborate safely had to be relatively unimpaired, and they had to be able to evaluate objectively and dispassionately threats made by the Chinese.

At the beginning, while the noncommissioned officers were still in the enlisted camps, many of them were able—partly because of their strong identification with the Army, and partly because of their wider experience—to help the other men carry out such a compromise solution. In many situations they were able to give advice that appears to have been sound from all points of view; thus they would help the other men compose answers to questions that would be sufficiently pro-Communist to satisfy the Chinese but not extreme enough to arouse the suspicion of other prisoners or to be called treasonable. They would also advise the other men on the wisdom of cooperating in the lectures, of trying to escape, and so on.

The Resisters

A number of men developed chronic resistance as their main mode of behavior in camp, refusing to go along with even the most trivial of Chinese requests. This lack of cooperation varied from passive resistance to active, organized obstructionism. Such men were a great trial to the Chinese, who labeled them "reactionaries" and either imprisoned them, if they felt they had some justification, or segregated them in special camps. According to the dynamics involved, these men seem to have fallen into four somewhat separate classes.

---

[16] For Puerto Ricans and other foreign nationals whose knowledge of English was very shaky, the problem was easily solved. These men conveniently forgot what little English they knew, and, because the Chinese did not have instructors who could speak their languages, they were permitted to withdraw to a relatively comfortable existence of doing details or routine chores. A few others successfully convinced the Chinese that they were illiterate or in some other way incapacitated for study. Some men resolved the conflict by volunteering for all the heavy or unpleasant details, but obviously such a solution was available only to the physically strong and healthy.

The obstructionist.—These men were characterized by a life-long pattern of indiscriminate resistance to all forms of authority,[17] and had histories of inability to get along in the United Nations Army just as they were unable to get along with the Chinese. They openly defied any attempt to get them to conform, and performed deeds which other prisoners considered heroic, such as withstanding severe torture. Usually these men spent a major part of their internment in the camp prison, in solitary confinement, or in the "hole."

The idealist or martyr.—These men had unusually powerful identifications with groups whose ideology demanded that they actively resist all forms of pressure from the Chinese. The best example would be the man who was deeply religious and whose faith demanded absolute noncooperation with a "Godless enterprise" of the type the Chinese represented.

The anxious guilt-ridden person.—This was the man who was afraid of his own inclination to be tempted by the positive rewards that the Chinese offered for collaboration, and who could handle these impulses only by denying them and overreacting in the other direction. He was chronically guilt-ridden over his unpatriotic and antisocial impulses and absolved himself by indulging in exaggerated forms of resistance.

The well-integrated resistance leader.—Probably the majority of resistors fell into this class, although there is no way to estimate their number. Because of extensive experience in difficult situations and a thorough understanding of the military, they were able systematically to organize other men and to set important precedents for resistance. Most of the commissioned and noncommissioned officers fell into this group.[18] The chief characteristic of these men seemed to be their ability to make valid judgments concerning possible courses of action in a situation in which there was little information on which to base such judgments. They had to be able to guess what Chinese reactions would be, what United Nations reactions would be, and most important, how to handle the other prisoners.

The Cooperators

This group is the most difficult to delineate, since I am attempting to include not only those whom the Chinese considered progressives but all those who collaborated to any significant extent. The accounts of prisoners concerning men who collaborated make possible the discrimination of six somewhat separate patterns of motivation for such behaviors.

The weakling.—This was the man who was chronically unable to resist any form of authority, and who was unable to withstand any degree of physical or

[17] This pattern has been well described by Lifton, reference footnote 9.

[18] I have already mentioned the role of noncommissioned officers in helping the "get-alongers" to maintain a compromise role; my mention of them here is an illustration of the fact that this is not a classification of the men, as such, but a classification of behavior. Thus, just as the noncommissioned officers displayed leadership in many instances in compromise, so they also functioned as resistance leaders whenever possible.

psychological discomfort. Such men probably became collaborators very soon after their internment, with a minimum of ideological involvement, because it was the easiest way. They often found that the more they collaborated, the more collaboration was demanded of them. They were highly susceptible to threats of blackmail by the Chinese, who could exhibit the evidence of their collaboration to the other prisoners or the United Nations authorities. From the point of view of these men, collaboration was an acceptable adjustment under the physical strains of internment, and they developed elaborate rationalizations to justify their behavior and to convince themselves that they would not suffer for it in the future.

The opportunist.—These men exploited the role of pro for all its material benefits, again without any ideological involvement, and with little consideration for the future welfare of themselves or others. They were characterized chiefly by their lack of stable group identifications either inside or outside the Army. They met all situations as they arose and tried to make the most out of them for themselves.

The misguided leader.—A minority of commissioned and noncommissioned officers engaged in various types of collaborative activities under the firm impression that they were furthering the United Nations cause and resisting the enemy. Their primary error was one of judgment. They reasoned that the best way to resist indoctrination was to go along with it, to find out what the Chinese were up to, to get into the inner circle so as to better plan resistance. In most cases, they managed merely to set a bad precedent for other prisoners, who felt that if their superiors were getting special privileges they should be getting them as well. These officers, like others, found that once they had begun to collaborate it was difficult to stop. Some of these men were probably weakling types who personally preferred the path of least resistance, but who, because of their responsible positions, had to develop adequate rationalizations. They could not see that their course of action was highly inappropriate; they saw only a justification which met their own needs.

The bored or curious intellectual.—Of the very small number of men who had superior education, some turned to Communist literature out of boredom or curiosity, and then found that they had aroused both the hostility of their own group and the expectations of the Chinese that they would collaborate. Only a few managed to interest themselves in the Communist literature without falling into this dilemma. More often, material rewards for the intellectual's interest resulted in his ostracism from his own group, and drove him in the direction of collaboration. Some of these men were fooled by the promise of early repatriation in return for collaboration, and they felt that their collaboration would be sufficiently minor not to damage their own futures. These men, like those previously described, seldom became ideologically confused or converted. Essentially they used bad judgment in an ambiguous situation.

The 'low-status' person.—The man who was most vulnerable *ideologically* was one who had never enjoyed any kind of secure or rewarding status position either in his home community or in the Army. This type included the younger and less intelligent, the malcontent, and the man whose social reference groups made the attainment of status difficult—that is, the member of various racial, religious, national, or economic minority groups. These men had little realization of the benefits of democracy because they had never experienced them in a meaningful way. They felt that the society was more to blame for their failures than they were. Such men were ready to give serious consideration to an ideology that offered remedies for their misfortunes. As pro's within the Communist hierarchy they could, for the first time, enjoy some measure of status and privilege, and the Chinese wisely promised them important roles in the future of the "peace movement." Some of these men were probably among those who declined repatriation—perhaps out of fear, when they realized how seriously they had jeopardized their position in the Army and at home, perhaps in order to stay with the cause which had for the first time allowed them to be important. It is difficult to determine whether such men underwent a complete ideological conversion, but there is no doubt that they gave serious consideration to the Communist cause, at least to the limit of their intellectual capacity.[19]

The accounts of the repatriates were unclear regarding the reactions of members of the various minority groups, especially the Negroes. The Communist technique of segregating the Negroes and giving them special indoctrination was probably a tactical error. Many Negroes felt that if they were going to be segregated they might as well be segregated in the United States—that there was nothing new or better about communism in this respect. Moreover, the propaganda given them was too extreme; even the very low-status Negro knew that his circumstances in the United States were not as bad as the Communists painted them.

However, because of the low-status category of most of the Negroes, the positive appeals made to them must have struck responsive chords in some. They had an opportunity to be leaders and to enjoy fully equal status if they became pro's, and they could rationalize that they would be able to improve the position of their race by participating in Communist peace movements which advocated equality. It is not possible to determine to what extent these positive appeals outweighed the deterrents, and thus to estimate the degree to which ideological change occurred among the Negroes. In any case, the Chinese probably could have persuaded more Negroes to collaborate and to embrace communism had they not made the fundamental errors of segregation and poor propaganda.

The Communist sympathizer.—This was the man who, even before he had joined the Army, was sympathetic to the Communist cause and who, therefore, felt no conflict about his course of action in the prisoner-of-war camp. However, if there were loyal Communists in the camps, it is unlikely that the Chinese

---

[19] The men who were most vulnerable to ideological appeals were not necessarily the ones the Chinese encouraged to become pro's. There is considerable evidence that the Chinese were quite selective in giving important jobs to prisoners and that they favored more mature and stable ones. Thus the younger, less intelligent, and less stable person was exploited by the Chinese in the same manner as he had probably been exploited before. The Chinese made what use they could of such men and then rejected them when they ceased to be useful.

divulged their identity by calling them pro's, since they would be of far more use as undercover agents.

Attitudes toward Progressives

The reaction of most men toward the pro's was one of perplexity, fear, and hostility. They could not understand how anyone could "swallow the junk" the Chinese were presenting, yet they were afraid that they too might be swayed, for among the pro's were many men like themselves. If the pro was a "weak-minded guy" or a man who did not have the stamina to resist the physical pressures, other men felt some sympathy for him, but at the same time they resented the extra privileges that his weakness gained for him. If the pro was perceived to be an opportunist, he was hated and threatened with retaliation during internment or following repatriation. If the pro was a person who had status or rank, the men felt perplexed and afraid; they could not decide what they themselves should do especially if such a pro tried to convince them that it was acceptable to collaborate.

The pro's were very conspicuous in camp by their identification symbols, by their special privileges—which they did not hesitate to flaunt—and by the fact that they usually congregated around camp headquarters. This made them ideal scapegoats and targets for hostility.

They were ostracized by the other prisoners who often refused even to carry on conversations with each other when a pro was present, forcing the pro's into interaction with each other. Thus they tended to form tightly knit groups, which continued even after the end of their internment. The men accused the pro's of informing, imputed to them many motives about which they themselves felt guilty, and attributed any punishment they suffered to some report by a pro. They threatened the pro's with physical violence, but were usually prevented by the Chinese from carrying out such threats. Later, on board ship, the men frequently said that they would now "get even," but the low rate of incidents suggests that no realistic plans underlay the threats. Perhaps most men felt too guilty about their own actual or fantasied collaboration to be comfortable about retaliating against those who had succumbed to the temptations.

The attitudes of the pro's varied with their motivations. Those who had been tricked or "seduced" into collaborating before they could fully realize the consequences remained aloof from other prisoners because they felt guilty and afraid. The opportunists or low-status prisoners felt their collaboration to be entirely justified by the prisoner-camp situation and viewed noncollaborators as "fools who don't know a good thing when they see it." They tried to persuade others to collaborate—in some cases because they sincerely believed part of the Chinese propaganda, and in other cases because they knew that the Chinese would reward them still further if they succeeded. Many pro's tried hard to remain liked both by the Chinese and by the other prisoners, but few succeeded. Since the Chinese presented themselves as benevolent captors, the pro's were the only group in camp who could consistently be used as an outlet for all the hostility engendered by the prison-camp situation.

THE EFFECTIVENESS OF THE INDOCTRINATION TECHNIQUES

By disrupting social organization and by the systematic use of reward and punishment, the Chinese were able to elicit a considerable amount of collaboration. This is not surprising when one considers the tremendous effort the Chinese made to discover the weak points in individual prisoners, and the unscrupulousness with which they manipulated the environment. Only a few men were able to avoid collaboration altogether—those who adopted a completely negativistic position from the moment of capture without considering the consequences for themselves or their fellow prisoners. At the same time the number of men who collaborated to a sufficient extent to be detrimental to the United Nations cause was also very small. The majority collaborated at one time or another by doing things which seemed to them trivial, but which the Chinese were able to turn to their own advantage. Such behavior did not necessarily reflect any defection from democratic values or ideology, nor did it necessarily imply that these men were opportunists or neurotics. Often it merely represented poor judgment in evaluating a situation about which they had little information, and poor foresight regarding the reactions of the Chinese, other prisoners, and people back home.

The extent to which the Chinese succeeded in converting prisoners of war to the Communist ideology is difficult to evaluate because of the previously mentioned hazards in measuring ideological change, and because of the impossibility of determining the *latent* effects of the indoctrination. In terms of *overt* criteria of conversion or ideological change, one can only conclude that, considering the effort devoted to it, the Chinese program was a failure. Only a small number of men decided to refuse repatriation—possibly for reasons other than ideological change[20]—and it was the almost unanimous opinion of the prisoners that most of the pro's were opportunists or weaklings. One can only conjecture, of course, the extent to which prisoners who began to believe in communism managed to conceal their sympathies from their fellows and the degree to which repatriates are now, as a result of their experience, predisposed to find fault with a democratic society if they cannot make a go of it.

It is difficult to determine whether to attribute this relative failure of the Chinese program to the inadequacy of their principles of indoctrination, to their technical inefficiency in running the program, or to both these factors. In actual practice the direct techniques used were usually ineffective because many of the Chinese instructors were deficient in their knowledge of Western culture and the English language. Many of their facts about America were false, making it impossible for them to obtain a sympathetic audience, and many of their attempts to teach by means of group discussion failed because they were not sensitive to the subtle ways in which prisoners managed to ridicule them by sarcasm or other language devices. The various intensive pressures brought to

[20] A discussion of some background factors in the lives of these men is presented by Virginia Pasley in *21 Stayed*; New York, Farrar, Strauss & Cudahy, 1955. Unfortunately her study is inconclusive because she did not investigate the background factors in a control group of men who decided to be repatriated.

bear on single prisoners and the fostering of close personal relationships between prisoner and instructor were far more effective in producing ideological change, but the Chinese did not have nearly enough trained personnel to indoctrinate more than a handful of men in this intensive manner.

The technique of breaking up both formal and spontaneous organization was effective in creating feelings of social and emotional isolation, but it was never sufficiently extended to make the prisoners completely dependent on the Chinese. As long as the men lived and "studied" together, there remained opportunities for consensual validation and thus for resisting indoctrination. However, as a means of social control this technique was highly effective, in that it was virtually impossible for the prisoners to develop any program of organized resistance or to engineer successful communication with the outside by means of escapes or clandestine sending out of information.

The most powerful argument against the intellectual appeal of communism was the low standard of living which the men observed in the Korean villages in which they lived. The repatriates reported that they were unable to believe in a system of values which sounded attractive on paper but which was not practiced, and they were not impressed by the excuse that such conditions were only temporary.

Most men returned from prison camp expressing a strong anti-Communist feeling and a conviction that their eyes had, for the first time, been opened to the real dangers of communism. Many men who had taken little interest in politics before returned with the feeling that they now knew what the United States was fighting for in Korea, and expressed a willingness to continue the fight wherever necessary. Hostility toward the Communists was expressed in such violent proposals as blowing up the *Daily Worker* building or deporting all registered Communists to Korea so that they could see the system in operation firsthand. The repatriates' attitude implied that anything labeled "Communist" had to be destroyed, and anything or anyone against communism had to be supported to the greatest possible extent; types of communism or types of approaches in dealing with communism were not evaluated separately.

It was, of course, difficult to determine the strength and stability of sentiments expressed a few days or weeks after repatriation. In some men these feelings undoubtedly represented an attempt to overcome the guilt that they felt for having collaborated or wavered in their beliefs. In other men they represented simply the accumulated hostility of two to three years of unrelieved frustration and deprivation. But, curiously, this hostility was seldom verbalized against the Chinese as such; it was always the Communists or the pro's who were the targets. The men were confused about the Chinese because they were so inconsistent; they never felt that they could understand or predict the Chinese reaction to anything.

In summary, it can be said that the Chinese were successful in eliciting and controlling certain kinds of behavior in the prisoner population. They were less successful in changing the beliefs of the prisoners. Yet this lack of success might have been due to the inefficiency of a program of indoctrination which could have been highly effective had it been better supported by adequate information and adequately trained personnel.

Collaboration with the enemy occurs to a greater or lesser extent in any captive population. It occurred in the Japanese and German prisoner-of-war camps during World War II. But never before have captured American soldiers faced a *systematic effort* to make them collaborate and to convert them to an alien political ideology. The only precedent in recent history was the handling of political prisoners by the Nazis, described by Bettelheim.[21] By means of extreme and degrading physical and psychological torture the Nazis attempted to reduce the prison population to an "infantile" state in which the jailer would be viewed with the same awe as the child views his father. Under these conditions, the prisoners tended, in time, to identify with the punitive authority figures and to incorporate many of the values they held, especially with respect to proper behavior in camp. They would curry the favor of the guards, would imitate their style of dress and speech, and would attempt to make other prisoners follow camp rules strictly.

It is possible that such a mechanism also operated in the Chinese prison camps. However, the Nazis attempted, by brutal measures, to reduce their prisoners to docile slave laborers, while the Chinese attempted, by using a "lenient policy" and by treating the prisoners as men in need of "education," to obtain converts who would actively support the Communist point of view. Only those prisoners who showed themselves to be "backward" or "reactionary" by their inability to see the fundamental "truths" of communism were treated punitively.

The essence of this novel approach is to gain complete control over those parts of the physical and social environment which sustain attitudes, beliefs, and values, breaking down interactions and emotional bonds which support the old beliefs and values, and building up new interactions which will increase the probability of the adoption of new beliefs and values. If the only contacts a person is permitted are with persons who *unanimously* have beliefs different from his own, it is very likely that he will find at least some among them with whom, because of growing emotional bonds, he will identify and whose beliefs he will subsequently adopt.

Is the eliciting of collaborative behavior in itself sufficient to initiate the process of ideological change? One might assume that a person who had committed acts consonant with a new ideology might be forced to adopt this ideology in order to rationalize his behavior. This might happen especially if the number of possible rationalizations were limited. The situation in the prison camps, however, allowed the men to develop rationalizations which did not necessarily involve Communist premises. Furthermore, it is likely that whatever rationalizations are adopted, they will not acquire the permanence of beliefs unless supported by social reinforcements. When the prisoners reentered the democratic setting, most of them gave up whatever Communist premises they might have been using to rationalize their collaboration and found new rationalizations that attempted to explain, from the standpoint of democratic premises, why they had collaborated. Apart from the technical difficulties the

[21] Bruno Bettelheim, "Individual and Mass Behavior in Extreme Situations," *J. Abnormal and Social Psychol.* (1943) *38*: 417–52.

Chinese experienced in running their indoctrination program, they were never able to control social interactions to a sufficient extent to reinforce in meaningful social relationships the Communist rationalizations for collaboration.

Taken singly, there is nothing new or terrifying about the specific techniques used by the Chinese; they invented no mysterious devices for dealing with people. Their method of controlling information by controlling the mass media of communication has been a well-known technique of totalitarian governments throughout history. Their system of propagandizing by means of lectures, movies, reading materials, and testimonials has its counterparts in education and in advertising. Group discussions and other methods requiring participation have their counterparts in education and in psychiatry. The possibility that group discussion may be fundamentally superior to lectures in obtaining stable decisions by participants has been the subject of extensive research in American social psychology. The Chinese methods of interrogation have been widely used in other armies, by the police, by newspaper reporters, and by others interested in aggressively eliciting information. Forced confessions and self-criticism have been widely used techniques in religious movements as a basis for conversion or as a device to perpetuate a given faith. The control of behavior by the manipulation of reward and punishment is obviously the least novel of all the techniques, for men have controlled each other in this way since the beginning of history.

Thus the only novelty in the Chinese methods was the attempt *to use a combination of all these techniques and to apply them simultaneously* in order to gain complete control over significant portions of the physical and social environment of a group of people. Such an ambitious effort applied on such a large scale is probably unique in the Communist movement, and perhaps in the *Chinese* Communist movement. In order to understand and evaluate this attempt to create ideological uniformity, it is necessary to view the techniques cited in terms of a social-psychological model which does justice to the complexity of this combination. Attempts such as Meerloo's[22] or Winokur's[23] to conceptualize the process of brainwashing in terms of a simple conditioning or learning model seem not only to be premature, but to ignore the most important factor—the simultaneous application of many techniques of social and behavioral control.

Before brainwashing can be properly understood, far more information must be gathered on its operation within China and within the Communist party as a whole; factors which the Chinese have succeeded in manipulating must be built into social-psychological researches on social conformity and attitude change; theoretical models must be constructed which will give a properly weighted emphasis to the variety of factors which probably operate in brainwashing; and personality concepts must be developed which can be used convincingly to categorize the behavior of people subjected to an attack on their most fundamental beliefs and values.

And most important, those who are attempting to understand brainwashing must look at the facts objectively, and not be carried away by hysteria when

[22] Joost A. M. Meerloo, "Pavlovian Strategy as a Weapon of Menticide," *Amer. J. Psychiatry* (1954) 110: 809–813.

[23] George Winokur, "'Brainwashing'—A Social Phenomenon of Our Time," *Human Organization* (1955) 13: 16–18.

another country with a different ideology and with different ultimate ends succeeds in eliciting from a small group of Americans behavior that is not consonant with the democratic ideology.

The Relative Efficacy of Various Types of Prior Belief-Defense in Producing Immunity Against Persuasion

WILLIAM J. McGUIRE AND DEMETRIOS PAPAGEORGIS

The disconcerting vulnerability of people's convictions in forced exposure situations provides a provocative contrast to the relative ineffectiveness of the voluntary exposure persuasion campaigns conducted over the mass media (Hovland, 1959). The high effectiveness of forced exposure situations is seen in laboratory experiments, face-to-face discussion, and political indoctrination of captive audiences (United Kingdom Ministry of Defense, 1955; United States Senate, 1956). The various election studies (Berelson, Lazarsfeld, & McPhee, 1954), on the other hand, indicate the relatively small effects of indoctrination campaigns depending on the voluntary exposure of the audience. The student of persuasive communication is inclined to attribute this contrast, at least in part, to the fact that people characteristically defend their convictions by avoiding exposure to counterarguments. This postulate of self-selected exposure to arguments so as to avoid receipt of information at variance with one's already formed opinions has been too widely discussed in the recent literature to need development here (Festinger, 1957; Janis, 1957; Klapper, 1957).

While defense-by-avoidance is likely to be highly effective for belief maintenance so long as the person can adequately regulate his own exposure to arguments, it has the disadvantage of leaving him poorly prepared to resist counterarguments should he be involuntarily exposed to them. Living in an ideologically monolithic environment, the person tends to underestimate the vulnerability of his beliefs and the likelihood of their being attacked. Hence, he will have had little motivation or practice in developing supporting arguments to bolster his belief or in preparing refutations for the unsuspected counterarguments. This postulate of defense-by-avoidance, and its implication of a deficiency in both practice and motivation for developing belief resistance, suggested several hypotheses regarding the immunizing effectiveness of alternative types of prior belief-defense, before forced exposure to massive doses of counterarguments.

Reprinted from Journal of Abnormal and Social Psychology, 62, *1961, 327–37.* *Copyright 1961 by the American Psychological Association and reproduced by permission.*

The first of these hypotheses is suggested by the closely analogous health problem of the person who has been brought up in so aseptic an environment that he has failed to develop resistance to infection and, hence, although appearing in very good health, proves quite vulnerable when suddenly exposed to a massive dose of an infectious virus. The disease resistance of such a person might be raised by either of two procedures: he might be given supportive therapy—good diet, exercise, rest, etc.—designed to better his physical condition; or alternatively, he might be given an inoculation of the infectious virus itself (in a weakened form) such as would stimulate, without overcoming, his defenses. With respect to developing immunity to specific diseases, the inoculation procedure is generally more effective.

Pursuing this medical analogy into the area of resistance to persuasion, it is hypothesized that the "supportive therapy" approach of pre-exposing a person to arguments in support of his belief has less immunizing effectiveness than the "inoculation" procedure of pre-exposing him to weakened, defense stimulating forms of the counterarguments. This prediction is made primarily for the case of widely accepted cultural beliefs, since the person's inclination to avoid exposure to counterarguments is likely to have been successful with such uncontroverted beliefs. However, even with regard to a culturally controversial issue, it would be predicted on the basis of the postulate of defense-by-avoidance that a person would tend to choose his associates so as to remain within an ideologically homogeneous subpopulation. Studies of political behavior (Berelson et al., 1954) demonstrate this social homogeneity even with respect to so controversial an issue as presidential preference during the quadrennial United States campaigns.

The hypothesized superiority of pre-exposure to weakened counterarguments runs counter to recommendations frequently repeated in investigations of prisoner-of-war behavior during the Korean conflict (Kinkead, 1959; United States Senate, 1956). The readiness of American personnel under prison camp conditions to surrender their prior convictions regarding proper behavior has been attributed to the failure of our formal and informal instructional institutions—home, school, army, etc.—to provide these soldiers with sufficient knowledge of "American" ideals and the reasons for maintaining them. Consequently, it was concluded, such vulnerability can be reduced in the future if our schools and other institutions teach more explicitly the reasons for maintaining these beliefs. The present hypothesis predicts that, on the contrary, pre-exposure to the counterarguments themselves (in weakened form) is more effective as an immunizing agent than is the presentation of arguments supporting the cultural truism.

A second hypothesis follows from the postulate of defense-by-avoidance and its implication that the person, due to a lack of practice, is inept at defending his beliefs when the necessity arises. In the case of such beliefs, the requirement that the person actively participate, without guidance, in the defense should have a deleterious effect on the amount of immunity to later persuasion that the defense confers. Very likely the person cannot employ such an opportunity for participation effectively and the time could be more efficiently used in presenting him with already developed defensive material. Furthermore, such required participation should tend to be so difficult a task as to interfere with the reception of any defensive material presented, and to bring home to him forcibly how unable he is to defend his belief, thus tending to weaken rather than strengthen his confidence in it. Other theoretical formulations leading to this second hypothesis are considered in later discussion. Also to be considered later are some theoretical implications of the forced compliance studies and of studies involving active recitation during learning that might seem to lead to the opposite prediction.

A third hypothesis involves an interaction effect between the two main variables, type of defense and amount of participation. The requirement of active participation should be less detrimental with the supportive type of defense than with the type involving pre-exposure to counterarguments. This prediction was based on two considerations, one having to do with motivation, the other with the danger of overexposure to counterarguments, during the defense.

Although the second hypothesis points to a net negative effect from a requirement of active participation under the present situation, one component of the participation effect is likely to be beneficial, namely, its effect on motivation. By postulation, the person is not only unprepared, but also unmotivated to defend the supposedly unassailable cultural truisms prior to any attack. Hence, having to make an observable contribution during the defensive session should tend to supply some useful extrinsic motivation for working seriously at the defensive task. The lack of intrinsic motivation (and the consequent beneficial contribution of the requirement for active participation) is likely to be more pronounced in the supportive defense condition, which is likely to appear to involve belaboring the obvious. The pre-exposure to (weakened) counterarguments involved in the other defense suggests that the "truism" might indeed be assailable, and, hence, provides more intrinsic motivation for working seriously at the defensive task than does the supportive defense.

A second consideration leading to the predicted interaction effect involves the possibility that the active participation condition, being less under the experimenter's control, might overexpose the person to the dangerous material involved in the weakened counterarguments. This possible basis of the predicted interaction effect (as well as theoretical considerations leading to the prediction of an opposite interaction effect) are discussed more fully in connection with the results obtained.

METHOD

General Procedure

The experiment was represented to the subjects as a study of the relationship between reading and writing skills. Each subject took part in two one-hour experimental sessions. The first was designed to give the subject various types of belief-immunizing treatments; the second, 2 days later, exposed him to strong counterarguing messages attacking the beliefs.

First session. In the first, or "immunizing," session, each subject was given defensive treatments on two beliefs. The first defensive treatment involved assigning him a belief that is almost universally held by his peers and instructing him (under experimentally varied conditions) to write a 20-minute essay defending that belief.

After the 20 minutes were up the subjects were given the second immunizing treatment, which involved reading for 5 minutes a 1,000-word essay (of an experimentally varied type) on another cultural truism and then answering a series of comprehension questions about the material read.

The subject's final task in the first session was to complete an attitude questionnaire designed to measure strength of belief in the cultural truisms. The subject was told to indicate his own belief, regardless of the positions taken in the essays that had been assigned to him, purportedly to allow us to check on whether the person's beliefs about the particular subject matter used in the test had any effect on his performance level. The belief scores obtained on the immunized issues in this first session questionnaire furnished a measure of the direct effect of the defensive treatments themselves, prior to the second session presentation of the strong counterargument messages.

Second session.   The subject took part 48 hours later in a second session which involved presentation of three 1,000-word essays containing strong counter-arguments against each of the two previously defended, and one additional belief. After being allowed 5 minutes for reading each of these three messages, the subject was required to answer a series of multiple-choice questions on their contents. Finally the subject was once again given the opinion questionnaire just described, and told to indicate his present personal belief, whatever might have been argued in any of the previous essays. The beliefs which the subjects indicated on these questionnaires on the immunized and unimmunized beliefs provided the measure of the effectiveness of the various immunizing conditions.

At the end of the experiment considerable effort was expended to inform the subject of the nature of the study and of the deceits used. Particular stress was put on the fact that the immunization and counterargument messages were both constructed for propaganda purposes and that no weight should be given to any argument simply because it had been included in one of these propaganda messages.

Independent Variables

Amount of active participation in the defense.   The main manipulation of the degree of active, unguided participation was the already described reading vs. writing variation, the writing condition, of course, being defined as requiring more active participation than the reading. Within each of these conditions there was a further manipulation of the variable. There were passive and active subtypes of the reading condition: half of the subjects were told simply to read the material silently for 5 minutes, so as to be able later to answer questions testing their comprehension of it, the other half were instructed in addition to select and underline the one sentence in each paragraph most fully and succinctly summarizing that paragraph. The passages read were identical in active and passive subtypes, each consisting of a 1,000-word, five-paragraph essay defending one of the cultural truisms. The first paragraph summarized four arguments and each of the following paragraphs developed one of these in detail.[1] Within the writing condition also, there were two variations—guided and unguided writing. Half the subjects were given an outline summarizing four defensive arguments that could be used, and the other half received no such guiding outline.

Type of defense. Two types of defensive material were employed. In half the treatments, the prior defense involved presenting the subject with arguments supporting the cultural truism to which he initially adhered; in the other half, it involved exposure to possible counterarguments against the truism together with refutations of these counterarguments. In the reading conditions both of these types of defenses took the form of 1,000-word, five-paragraph essays, each essay presenting four supporting arguments, or mentioning and then refuting four counterarguments. In the writing-from-outline participation condition, the two types of defense involved presenting the subject either with one-sentence synopses of each of four supporting arguments or with four two-sentence synopses, each mentioning a counterargument and an argument refuting it. In the writing-without-outline participation condition, the subjects in the supportive conditions were instructed to write an essay giving arguments in support of the truism, and those in the refutational, an essay mentioning and refuting possible counterarguments against the truism.

Design

Each subject served in an experimental condition on each of four cultural truisms. On one, he received neither the defensive treatment in the first session nor the strong counterargument treatment in the second (to provide an index of the base-levels of the beliefs). On another, he received no defensive treatment in the first session, only the strong counterarguments in the second (to provide a measure of the effect of the attack in the absence of prior defense). On the other two beliefs, he received both the prior defensive and subsequent strong counterargument treatment. The pair of defensive treatments given any one subject was not assigned completely at random: each subject received one reading and one writing defense. (Since 20 minutes were allowed for writing and only 5 for reading, this restriction was imposed to assure that all subjects served the same amount of time in the immunization session.) Hence, effects involving reading vs. writing conditions constitute intrasubject comparisons, while the other effects involve cross-subject comparisons. For this reason, in the results presented below, different parts of the variance are used as the "error" terms for the two classes of effects. The fact that this design required each subject to serve in four conditions is the reason that materials were developed on four different issues. These issues were rotated systematically around conditions from subject to subject.

[1] The complete text of all the communications, defensive and counterargumentative, used in this study has been deposited with the American Documentation Institute. Order Document No. 6745 from ADI Auxiliary Publications Project, Photoduplication Service, Library of Congress; Washington 25, D.C., remitting in advance $1.75 for microfilm or $2.50 for photocopies. Make checks payable to: Chief, Photoduplication Service, Library of Congress.

Issues

On the basis of an earlier survey of student opinions (involving different subjects from those serving in the experiment) four issues were selected from an initial pool of 20, all of which dealt with health topics. Since the hypotheses dealt particularly with cultural truisms, the criteria for selection were extremeness and homogeneity of precommunication beliefs. The health area was found to be particularly fertile of such beliefs among college students. The beliefs selected were the following: "Everyone should get a chest X-ray each year in order to detect any possible tuberculosis symptoms at an early stage"; "The effects of penicillin have been, almost without exception, of great benefit to mankind"; "Most forms of mental illness are not contagious"; "Everyone should brush his teeth after every meal if at all possible." For brevity's sake, these four issues are henceforth referred to by the following letters, respectively: T (tuberculosis), P (penicillin), M (mental illness), and D (dental).

The subjects indicated their beliefs in these statements by marking an "X" in the appropriate space on a 15-interval graphic scale that looked as follows:

| Definitely | Probably | Uncertain | Probably | Definitely |
| FALSE | FALSE | | TRUE | TRUE |

The subjects were told to make an "X" in the space that best indicated their belief about the truth of the statement. The preliminary survey data showed that if we scale these intervals from 1-15 going towards the right, the mean belief on each of the four issues was over 13, with the mode at 15.

Subjects

A total of 130 subjects participated in both sessions of the experiment. These were all unpaid students in freshman rhetoric courses at the University of Illinois. Data for 16 additional subjects who took part in the first (immunization) session, but did not appear for the second (counterargument) session are omitted from the analysis. Since the rhetoric course is required of almost all freshman students who enter any college of the university, the subjects probably constitute a representative sample (as regards age, sex, intelligence, etc.) of first-semester freshman students in all colleges of this large state university.

RESULTS

General Effects

The control data from the first session indicate that the initial beliefs were extreme and homogeneous, amounting, as intended, to cultural truisms. Even though the beliefs were already at the high initial level of 13.26 points on the 15-point scale (see Table 1), the eight defensive conditions did further strengthen them, moving them up to about 50% of the remaining scale distance ($p < .001$).

Despite their unqualified initial acceptance the beliefs proved highly vulnerable to the massive counterarguments in the second session, which reduced them from the 13.26 point level of the first session to 6.64 points ($p < .001$) when not preceded by any immunization treatment. Even with prior immunization, the strong counterarguments lowered the beliefs considerably (see Table 2) though the mean effect of the eight immunization treatments was to attenuate their effect by about one-third ($p < .001$). These eight treatments differed considerably among themselves in regard to both direct strengthening effects (see Table 1) and immunizing effects (see Table 2). We turn now to this question of comparative effects.

Comparative Efficacy of Supportive and Refutational Defense

Both types of defense had significant direct strengthening effects on the beliefs, prior to the presentation of the strong counterargument messages but, as can be seen in Table 1, the supportive defense was slightly more effective ($p < .10$) in this regard than the refutational.

Regarding immunizing effectiveness, on the other hand, the refutational defense was superior ($p < .001$) to the supportive, as can be seen in Table 2. In fact, the supportive defense had hardly any immunizing effect. The 7.39 point level to which the strong counterarguments reduce the beliefs after the four supportive defenses is only slightly ($p = .16$) higher than the 6.64 point level to which they were reduced after no defense at all. Even the most effective supportive defense (writing-with-outline) was superior to no-defense only on the .13 level of significance; and the poorest supportive defense (writing-without-outline) was actually (though trivially) worse than no defense at all, as can be seen in Table 2.

Comparative Efficacy of the Different Participation Conditions

The defensive treatments clearly lost effectiveness to the extent that they required the subject's unguided active participation in the defense. This detrimental effect is seen most clearly if we consider the major manipulation of participation, reading vs. writing. The reading conditions had a greater ($p = .05$) direct strengthening effect (see Table 1), and even more pronounced, a greater ($p < .001$) immunization effect (see Table 2).

All four of the comparisons between minor manipulations of participation were in the same direction. Passive reading proved superior to reading-and-underlining in regard to both direct strengthening and immunization. Likewise, writing-from-outline proved more effective than writing-without-outline in both these respects. While all four effects were in the same direction and agreed with the significant effect of the main (reading vs. writing) manipulations of participation their magnitudes (which can be seen in Tables 1 and 2) fall short of conventional significance levels.

Table 1 BELIEFS AFTER IMMUNIZATION BUT BEFORE EXPOSURE TO STRONG COUNTERARGUMENTS
(15 = ABSOLUTE AGREEMENT; 1 = ABSOLUTE DISAGREEMENT)

ISSUES	IMMUNIZATION CONDITION								
	READING				WRITING				CONTROL (NO IMMUNIZATION)
	SUPPORTIVE		REFUTATIONAL		SUPPORTIVE		REFUTATIONAL		
	PASSIVE	UNDERLINE	PASSIVE	UNDERLINE	OUTLINE	NO OUTLINE	OUTLINE	NO OUTLINE	
D	14.75	15.00	15.00	14.50	14.11	13.83	13.57	14.57	13.39
M	15.00	14.22	13.14	12.71	14.62	14.33	13.00	12.22	13.22
P	14.67	12.62	14.67	15.00	14.11	14.11	13.71	12.67	13.41
T	14.22	14.89	14.22	14.14	14.83	14.38	14.30	14.50	13.02
Weighted mean	14.62	14.16	14.34	14.13	14.38	14.19	13.71	13.46	13.26
Total N	32	32	35	31	32	32	31	35	260

Table 2 BELIEFS AFTER BOTH IMMUNIZATION AND EXPOSURE TO THE STRONG COUNTERARGUMENTS
(15 = ABSOLUTE AGREEMENT; 1 = ABSOLUTE DISAGREEMENT)

		IMMUNIZATION CONDITION								
	STRONG COUNTERARGUMENTS ONLY (NO IMMUNIZATION)	READING				WRITING				CONTROL (NO IMMUNIZATION OR COUNTERARGUMENTS)
		SUPPORTIVE		REFUTATIONAL		SUPPORTIVE		REFUTATIONAL		
ISSUES		PASSIVE	UNDERLINE	PASSIVE	UNDERLINE	OUTLINE	NO OUTLINE	OUTLINE	NO OUTLINE	
D	4.74	8.25	9.50	12.70	10.00	9.00	9.17	7.57	7.57	12.88
M	7.06	6.17	5.33	11.14	10.86	8.75	4.89	8.71	7.33	11.50
P	8.62	8.78	11.62	11.10	13.86	7.67	7.56	9.71	10.89	13.44
T	6.42	6.33	5.11	11.00	10.29	5.67	5.25	10.30	11.40	12.69
Weighted mean	6.64	7.47	7.63	11.51	11.13	7.94	6.53	9.19	9.46	12.62
Total N	130	32	32	35	31	32	32	31	35	130

Interaction between Type of Defense and Participation

The interaction between type of defense (supportive vs. refutational) and participation (reading vs. writing) is in the predicted direction but of a magnitude that attains only borderline significance. The superiority of reading over writing is greater with the refutational than with the supportive defense, in regard to both direct strengthening effect ($p = .10$) and immunizing effect ($p = .08$), as can be seen in Tables 1 and 2.

The interaction effect emerges more clearly when we contrast writing-from-outline—with regard to which there is a double reason for expecting the predicted interaction—with the other three participation conditions. This condition has the greatest immunizing effectiveness of the four with the supportive type of defense and the least of the four with the refutational defense, the interaction being significant at the .03 level.

DISCUSSION

In the case of each of the three predicted effects there were alternative theoretical bases for predicting the same effect or, in some cases, the opposite effect. These alternative formulations, together with subsidiary findings are considered in the following sections which take up each of the predicted effects in turn. The probable limits of valid generalization of each of the obtained effects are also discussed.

Type-of-Defense Effects

The finding that the direct strengthening effect was greater with presentation of supporting arguments than with pre-exposure to refuted counterarguments calls attention to the danger that the refutational defense (or any defensive procedure involving pre-exposure to the counterarguments, however weakened) might have the direct effect of slightly weakening the belief by acquainting the subject with unsuspected counterarguments. Should this be the case, a practical question would arise regarding the advisability of exposing a large population to such an immunization procedure when only a small, unpredictable sample is likely ever to be exposed to the subsequent massive dose of counterarguments. The data indicate, however, that no such direct "boomerang" effect occurred. On the contrary, the scores presented in Table 1 show that the refutational treatments had the immediate effect of strengthening the belief by 0.65 points ($p = .02$).

The finding of a reversed relationship between the immediate direct strengthening effect and the immunizing effectiveness of the refutational as compared with the supportive defense, raises the question of how well the immunizing effectiveness of a treatment can be predicted from its immediate apparent strengthening effect. The results over the eight defensive conditions indicate that immunization is very poorly predicted by the direct strengthening effect: over all eight defensive conditions, the rank order coefficient of correlation between immediate strengthening and subsequent resistance is actually negative ($p = -0.38$). Hence, the initial strength of belief or the amount of induced strengthening is a very poor indicator of conferred resistance to subsequent strong counterarguments. Some treatments (e.g., the refutational defenses) that appear to leave the beliefs relatively weak actually confer on them hidden reserves of resistance, while other treatments (e.g., the supportive defenses) that seem to have much strengthened the beliefs have actually left them "paper tigers."

The supportive vs. refutational manipulation in this study is quite similar to the one- vs. two-sided argument manipulation in previous studies (Hovland, Lumsdaine, & Sheffield, 1949; Lumsdaine & Janis, 1953). Their one-sided condition is much the same as our supportive; their two-sided condition is, however, a less close analog to our refutational. While their two-sided defense involved the supportive arguments plus some lesser mention of counterarguments either unsupported or refuted, our refutational defense involved no supportive arguments, only some mention of counterarguments with detailed refutations thereof. The obtained superiority of the refutational defense in this study suggests that the previously found superiority of the two-sided messages may have been due solely to their having pre-exposed the subjects to the weakened counterarguments, without the concomitant exposure to the supporting arguments having been necessary. Whether the concomitant presentation of the supporting arguments does confer any additional effect, and under what circumstances—for example, before or after or intermingled with the weakened counterarguments—remains a question for subsequent research.

There are theoretical reasons for not generalizing the obtained immunizing superiority of the refutational over the supportive defense beyond certain of the conditions that obtained in the present experiment. One such restriction derives from the type of belief used, namely, those culturally regarded as being truisms almost beyond debate. Beliefs of this type are the most likely to have been overprotected against counterarguments in the past and, hence, particularly in need of resistance-stimulating pre-exposure to weakened forms of the counterarguments before massive exposure to strong forms. The moderation of less extreme beliefs may result from the obscurity or unimportance of the issue or, in the case of an important issue, to the person's having perceived reasons both for and against the belief. In the latter case, the person should be more prepared for strong counterarguments and, hence, the refutational defense may prove relatively less effective than we found with initially extreme beliefs.

A further restriction on the generality of the immunizing superiority of the refutational defense derives from the time parameters of the present study. Immunizing effectiveness was measured over the very brief interval of 48 hours. Presumably conferred immunity dissipates with time so that the effectiveness of all conditions would diminish as the interval between the defensive treatments and the presentation of the strong counterarguments lengthened. The question remains whether there might be different decay rates depending on how the immunity was conferred.

Another reservation about the obtained immunizing effectiveness of the refutational defense derives from the fact that in the present study the strong counterarguments subsequently presented to the subject were the very counterarguments previously refuted in the defensive session. The question arises whether the refutational defense has any general immunizing effect—lessening the subsequent belief-weakening impact not only of strong forms of the same counterarguments but of alternate counterarguments as well. Once again the medical field supplies an analogy in the question of whether inoculation with a weakened form of one strain of a virus produces immunity to other strains as well. At least two possible bases for expecting a generalized immunity effect from exposure to refutational arguments can be suggested. First, pre-exposure to the weakened counterargument may, by making the subject more aware of the vulnerability of his belief, stimulate him to develop supporting arguments and to think up and refute other counterarguments. Second, the earlier experience of seeing some counterarguments refuted may lessen the impressiveness of all subsequently-received counterarguments against the belief.

The refutational defense used in the present experiment constitutes just one example of a larger class, namely, immunization by pre-exposure to the counterarguments in weakened forms, thus stimulating, without overwhelming, the subject's defenses before he is exposed to strong forms of the counterarguments. The counterarguments might be weakened during the inoculation treatment by less drastic procedures than the explicit refutations used here. They might, for example, be presented as emanating from a negatively valenced source or as endorsed by a negative reference group. Or opposition to them might be registered as coming from the subject's peer groups, or prestige figures, or the general consensus. Alternatively, these counterarguments might simply be stated without supporting evidence or with patently specious supporting evidence. Use of these alternative treatments involving pre-exposure to arguments that are weakened less completely than the explicit refutation carries the risk that the counterarguments might be so strongly presented in the immunizing session that they actually weaken the belief. On the other hand, the exposure to somewhat stronger forms than used in this experiment might be more stimulating to the person's defenses, and thus develop greater resistance to a subsequent massive dose of counterarguments.

This question, concerning the optimal strength of exposure to counterarguments during the immunizing session, raises a theoretical issue regarding the underlying mechanism of the immunity conferred. (The same issue also arose in the discussion of the specificity of the conferred immunity—whether just against the same counterarguments to which pre-exposed, or others as well.) One possible mechanism is that pre-exposure strengthens the belief by stimulating the subject to develop supporting arguments for maintaining his belief. Alternatively, the prior experience of seeing the weakness of counterarguments may lessen the perceived credibility of the later strong forms of counterarguments. If the former mechanism is paramount, pre-exposure to relatively strong counterarguments (up to the point of strength where they begin to overwhelm, rather than stimulate the subject's defenses) would be optimal. If the latter mechanism is the more important, then the more weakened the counterarguments during the pre-exposure, the greater the conferred immunity.

Effects of Requiring Participation

The superiority of the low over high participation conditions with respect to both direct strengthening and conferred immunity was found in all six of the possible independent comparisons. Since the direction of this effect is so clear-cut and yet might seem unexpected in the light of some previous studies on the effects of active participation, discussion seems in order regarding the postulated mechanisms and regarding relevant distinctive features of the present study.

The hypothesis that the defense of a cultural truism would be less effective to the extent that the believer is required to participate in it actively was based on the assumption that the believers are poorly prepared for such a task. The assumption receives support not only from the confirmation of the hypothesis, but also from the incidental evidence that the obtained participation was very poor in both quantity and quality. In the no outline condition, the essays were typically very meager. About half of the subjects (34 out of the 67) in this condition produced only one or no defensive argument. In the outline condition, the arguments tended to be unelaborated reiterations of the points presented in the outline. The poor quality of these essays leaves a strong impression that the defensive session tended to be largely wasted on the writing condition. Indeed, some suggestion is offered that the poorness of the subject's performance may have raised doubts in his own mind regarding the validity of his belief, in the finding (see Table 2) that after the subject was called upon without the benefit of any guiding outline to write a defensive essay giving arguments in support of his belief, the strong counterarguments reduced the beliefs more than after no defense at all.

A related basis for the obtained detrimental effect of requiring active participation derives from the limited time allowed for the defense in this study. Given that the person was poorly prepared to exercise initiative in defending his overprotected beliefs, the mechanics of the participation task may have usurped time needed for elicitation and absorption of the defensive material itself. Such stimulus-reception interference due to the requirement of participation could account for the superiority of passive reading over active (which required the subject to analyze and select the crucial clause in each paragraph, besides reading the material within an only moderately long, 5-minute interval). This factor could also be involved in the obtained superiority of both reading conditions over the writing conditions. Despite the quadruple time allowance of 20 minutes in the writing condition, it was apparently felt by the subjects to be less adequate for the task than was the 5-minute period allowed for the reading task. On a post-experimental questionnaire, 46 of the 130 subjects complained about insufficient time for writing the essay, and only 18 for the reading task ($p < .01$, by a chi square test). However, while this situation raises the theoretical question of whether the writing condition might prove relatively more effective should the time restriction be removed, it leaves a clear answer of practical importance: even though the time allowance was four times as great in the writing as in the reading conditions, the writing conditions still produced less immunity than the reading.

Another, alternative interpretation of the obtained superiority of the reading over writing conditions has been suggested by Carl Hovland (in a personal communication). Hovland suggests that this manipulation may have affected perceived source credibility and, hence, (Hovland & Weiss, 1951), the persuasive impact of the defensive messages. Even though no explicit indication of message source was given in any of the immunization communications, there was probably a strong tendency for the subject to assume that the essays presented for reading came from a high prestige source since their subject matter was rather technical and involved specialized information, and, stylistically, they were well organized and literate. Since in the writing conditions, the arguments came from the subject himself (who was likely to be well aware of his lack of competence in the area) they were unlikely to gain as much from source credibility as in the reading condition. Even in the writing-from-outline condition in which the arguments were presented to the subject, they were presented in a telegraphic style that quite likely detracted from their prestigefulness. The factor of source prestige may at least partially explain the obtained superiority of the reading over writing conditions. However, this explanation accounts less adequately than does the earlier one for the findings in forced compliance experiments (discussed below) of the opposite effect. In those studies active participation was found to augment persuasive effectiveness even though the experiments do not differ greatly from the present one in regard to source-credibility.

In generalizing the obtained negative relation between immunizing effectiveness and amount of active participation in the defense, it is important to note that the present study involved beliefs with which the subject was in complete agreement at the outset and which were practically unquestioned in his culture so that the subject was unpracticed in their defense. There are two lines of research that lead us to expect that the relative value of active participation would be greater in the case of controversial, frequently argued beliefs of lower initial strength.

A number of studies have shown that in situations of forced compliance, active participation is more efficacious than passive reading in converting the person to a new belief that had initially been rejected. Kelman's work (1953) on response restriction, Janis and King's (1954) and King and Janis' (1956) work on active role playing and improvisation, Festinger's (1957) work on behavioral commitment and Lewin's (1958), and Hovland, Campbell, and Brock's (1957) work on public decision all furnish instances of the indoctrination value of overt participation. Likewise, practitioners of consent engineering, including essay contest sponsors, evangelists, indoctrinators of prisoners-of-war, etc. have long been acting on the postulate that overt participation increases opinion change. In these previous instances, however, the defended belief is rather disparate from the subject's own initial belief whereas in the case of the cultural truisms used in this experiment the subject tends to be in such complete initial agreement with the proposition that little potential remains for further internalization from the active participation. Also, in the studies cited the active participation requirement usually came just after the subject received a persuasive message that served as a guide for his participation.

A second line of research, from the learning area, also suggests that it would be unwise to generalize the present finding of a detrimental effect from active participation beyond the case of infrequently argued beliefs. The classic study by Gates (1917) and several subsequent studies have demonstrated that a greater amount of learning occurs under conditions of active recitation than of passive reading. Since opinion change is positively related to message comprehension

(McGuire, 1957), the Gates study suggests that active participation in the defense would produce greater strengthening of the belief. That the opposite result was found is not surprising in view of the type of material involved in the present participation task. Since the subjects were unpracticed in defending the beliefs, the task was difficult and they were on an early segment of the learning curve, conditions under which the learning contribution of active participation has been found to be small or even negative (Kimble & Wulff, 1951; Krueger, 1930). Furthermore, the material was meaningful, which again has been found to diminish the benefits from active participation (Peterson, 1944).

Interaction Effect

The interaction hypothesis received the least impressive confirmation of the three predictions. However it received its most substantial support when the writing-from-outline participation condition, in which both the postulated mechanisms (lack of need for extrinsic motivation and danger of overexposure to the counterarguments) are operative, is contrasted with the other three participation conditions. This finding suggests that both mechanisms contribute to the effect, since the condition in which only one mechanism (lack of extrinsic motivation) is operative, writing-without-outline, falls between this condition and the conditions (reading) in which neither mechanism is operative, in regard to the superiority of refutational over supportive defense.

The interaction effect predicted and obtained in this study cannot be generalized to situations that fail to present the refutational material in such wise that the subject perceives it as a defense of his belief, and not an attack on it. (There is always some danger, which must be minimized for the present interaction effect to occur, that the refutational defense, since it mentions the counterarguments at the outset, may be misperceived by the subject as an attack on his belief.) The basic postulate of defense-by-avoidance underlying the present study would indicate that where the refutational defense is likely to be initially misinterpreted by the subject as an attack on his belief, the subject should tend to avoid exposing himself to it (Janis, 1957). Hence, in such ambiguous situations the opposite direction of interaction would be predicted, namely, that the extrinsic pressure to expose oneself to the defensive material, in the requirement of overt participation, would be more important with the refutational than the supportive defense. Such interaction should be increasingly pronounced as the subject's confidence in his belief declines (Brodbeck, 1956; Festinger, 1957).

SUMMARY

It was postulated that people characteristically defend their beliefs (particularly cultural truisms) by avoiding exposure to contradictory information, with the result that in forced exposure situations these untried beliefs prove highly vulnerable to persuasion. Since the person is unmotivated to develop a defense of his belief to the extent that he considers it invulnerable, it was hypothesized that such beliefs are more effectively immunized against persuasion by pre-exposure to counterarguments (in a weakened form that stimulates, without overcoming, the receiver's defenses) than by pre-exposure to arguments supporting the belief. Second, since the person is unpracticed in the defense of such beliefs, it was predicted that the immunizing pretreatments would lose effectiveness to the extent that they required the person to participate actively, without guidance, in the defense. Finally an interaction effect was predicted such that the detrimental effect of requiring active participation is greater with the defense involving pre-exposure to the counterarguments than with the supportive defense.

The subjects were 130 college freshmen who took part in two experimental sessions. In the first, they received immunizing treatments on various strongly held health beliefs. Type of defense (pre-exposure vs. supportive) and amount of participation in the defense were varied orthogonally. The subjects' beliefs were then measured to ascertain the direct effects of the defensive treatments. In the second session, the subjects were exposed to strong counterarguments on both immunized and nonimmunized beliefs and then the final beliefs were measured to ascertain the comparative immunizing effectiveness of the defensive treatments.

Both of the predicted main order effects were confirmed at the .001 level. Some support ($p = .08$) was also found for the predicted interaction effect. The defensive treatments, besides conferring immunity against subsequent counterarguments, also had an immediate direct strengthening effect on the beliefs ($p = .01$), but the amount of direct strengthening was not predictive of the latent resistance to counterarguments conferred by these treatments.

REFERENCES

Berelson, B., Lazarsfeld, P. F. & McPhee, W. N. *Voting.* Univer. Chicago Press, 1954.

Brodbeck, May. The role of small groups in mediating the effects of propaganda. *J. abnorm. soc. Psychol.,* 1956, *52,* 166–70.

Festinger, L. *A theory of cognitive dissonance.* Evanston: Row, Peterson, 1957.

Gates, I. A. Recitation as a factor in memorizing. *Arch. Psychol., NY,* 1917, *6,* No. 40.

Hovland, C. I. Reconciling conflicting results derived from experimental and survey studies of attitude change. *Amer. Psychologist,* 1959, *14,* 8–17.

Hovland, C. I., Campbell, Enid H., & Brock, T. Effect of "commitment" on opinion change following communication. In C. I. Hovland (Ed.), *The order of presentation in persuasion.* Vol. 1. New Haven: Yale Univer. Press, 1957. Pp. 23–32.

Hovland, C. I., Lumsdaine, A. A., & Sheffield, F. D. *Experiments on mass communication.* Princeton: Princeton Univer. Press, 1949.

Hovland, C. I., & Weiss, W. The influence of source credibility on communication effectiveness. *Publ. opin. Quart.,* 1951, *15,* 635–50.

Janis, I. L. Motivational effects of different sequential arrangements of conflicting arguments: A theoretical analysis. In C. I. Hovland (Ed.), *The order of presentation in persuasion.* Vol. 1. New Haven: Yale Univer. Press, 1957. Pp. 170–86.

Janis, I. L., & King, B. The influence of role-playing on opinion change. *J. abnorm. soc. Psychol.,* 1954, *49,* 211–18.

Kelman, H. C.   Attitude change as a function of response restriction. *Hum. Relat.*, 1953, *6*, 185–214.

Kimble, G. A., & Wulff, J. J.   *Participation and guidance during the learning session.* (Audio-vis. Div., HRRL, AFRDC) Washington, D. C.: Bolling Air Force Base, 1951.

King, B., & Janis, I. L.   Comparison of the effectiveness of improvised versus non-improvised role-playing in producing opinion change. *Hum. Relat.*, 1956, *9*, 177–86.

Kinkead, E.   *In every war but one.* New York: Norton 1959.

Klapper, J.   What do we know about the effects of mass communication: The brink of hope. *Publ. opin. Quart.*, 1957, *21*, 453–74.

Krueger, L. C.   The relative effect of interspersing a recall at different stages of learning. *Arch. Psychol., NY*, 1930, *18*, 15–25.

Lewin, K.   Group decision and social change. In Eleanor Maccoby, T. M. Newcomb, & E. L. Hartley (Eds.), *Readings in social psychology.* New York: Holt, 1958. Pp. 197–211.

Lumsdaine, A. A., & Janis, I. L.   Resistance to "counter-propaganda" produced by one-sided and two-sided "propaganda" presentation. *Publ. opin. Quart.*, 1953, *17*, 311–18.

McGuire, W. J.   Order of presentation as a factor in "conditioning" persuasiveness. In C. I. Hovland (Ed.), *The order of presentation in persuasion.* Vol. 1. New Haven: Yale Univer. Press, 1957. Pp. 98–114.

Peterson, H. A.   Recitation or recall as a factor in the learning of long prose selections. *J. educ. Psychol.*, 1944, *35*, 220–28.

United Kingdom Ministry of Defense.   *Treatment of British prisoners of war in Korea.* London: HM Stationery Office, 1955.

United States Senate (84th Congress, 2nd Session), Committee on Government Operations, Permanent Subcommittee on Investigations. *Communist interrogation, indoctrination and exploitation of American military and political prisoners.* Washington, D. C.: United States Government Printing Office, 1956.

10

DISSONANCE

AND ATTITUDE-DISCREPANT

BEHAVIOR

The Effects of Severity of Initiation on Liking for a Group: A Replication

HAROLD B. GERARD AND GROVER C. MATHEWSON

The experiment by Aronson and Mills (1959), in which a positive relationship was found between the severity of initiation into a group and subsequent liking for that group, is open to a variety of interpretations other than the one the authors give. The purpose of the experiment to be reported here was an attempt to rule out some of the more cogent of these alternative interpretations.

The observation that people often tend to value highly things for which they have suffered or expended a great deal of effort can be interpreted as having been due to dissonance reduction. The hypothesized process involved assumes that knowledge held by the person that he had suffered

Reprinted from Journal of Experimental Social Psychology, 2, *1966, 278–87. Copyright 1966 by Academic Press, Inc., and reproduced by permission.*

or expended a great deal of effort for a desired goal is inconsistent with knowledge that the goal or certain aspects of it are worthless. Such inconsistencies produce psychological dissonance which is unpleasant and the individual will attempt to reduce this unpleasantness by cognitive work. In this case he can either distort his beliefs about the amount of suffering or effort he expended by coming to believe that it was less than he had previously thought or he can distort his belief about the worthlessness of aspects of the goal by coming to believe that these aspects were really not worthless. In their study, Aronson and Mills attempted to create a laboratory situation in which the latter hypothesized process could be examined. Let us review that experiment in some detail so that we may then point up the basis for the other interpretations of the data.

The subjects were college coeds who were willing to volunteer for a series of group discussions on the psychology of sex. The ostensible purpose of the study was presented to the subject as having to do with the investigation of group dynamics. Before any prospective member could join one of the discussion groups she was given a "screening test" to determine her suitability for the group. The severity of this screening test (or initiation) was varied; in the "severe" treatment the subject read obscene literature and a list of dirty words out loud to the experimenter (who was a male), whereas in the "mild" condition the subject read sexual material of an innocuous sort. The subject was told that the screening test had been necessary in order to weed out people who were too shy to discuss topics related to sex. After the initiation, each experimental subject was informed that she had passed the test and was therefore eligible for membership in the group. She was led to believe that the group she was to join had been formed several weeks ago and that she was to take the place of a girl who had to drop out. Her "participation" in her first meeting with the group was limited to "overhearing" via headphones what was presented to her as an ongoing discussion by the group on aspects of sexual behavior in animals. The reason she was given for not being able to participate actively in the discussion was that the other three girls had prepared for the discussion by reading a book on the sexual behavior of animals. It was also suggested to her that overhearing the discussion without participating in it would give her an opportunity to get acquainted with how the group operates. What she heard was not an ongoing discussion but was instead a standardized recorded discussion on the sexual behavior of animals that was extremely boring and banal. The discussion was contrived to be worthless in order to maximize the dissonance of the subject in the "severe" initiation group, since the knowledge that she had suffered to get into the group would be dissonant with finding out that the discussion was worthless.

After hearing the taped recording, the subject was asked to evaluate the discussion and the participants on a number of semantic differential-type scales. A control group was also run in which the subjects evaluated the discussion without having received any initiation whatsoever. The findings of the experiment supported the derivation from dissonance theory, namely that the subjects in the "severe" treatment evaluated the discussion more favorably than did the "mild" or control subjects. A dissonance theory interpretation conceives of the "severe" initiation as confronting the subject with the "problem" of having suffered for something that was later found to be worthless and the prediction is based upon how that problem is "solved." One of the reasons why the results are important and provocative is that they are exactly opposite to what a strict application of secondary reinforcement theory would predict in which it would be expected that the unpleasantness of the initiation would "rub off" and generalize to the discussion.

While the results are consistent with dissonance theory, they lend themselves to a variety of other, quite plausible interpretations. For example, there is an entire *family* of interpretations that derives from the fact that the content of the initiation and the content of the discussion are so closely related, both having to do with sex. One could argue that the initiation aroused the girls sexually to a greater extent in the "severe" as compared with the "mild" treatment and they were therefore more anxious to get into the group in order to pursue the discussion of sex. Along similar lines, one could also argue that the girls in the "severe" treatment did not know the meaning of some of the dirty four-letter words and believed that they could find out their meaning by joining the discussion group. This is a variation of the uncertainty-affiliation hypothesis. Still another possibility is that the subjects in the "severe" treatment were intrigued by the obscene material and the dirty words and may have believed that, if not now, sometime in the future these things would be discussed by the group. One could continue to list related interpretations based upon the assumed arousal of one or another motive in the "severe" treatment that might be satisfied by joining the discussion group (thus making the group more attractive).

Another possible interpretion, a "relief" hypothesis, is that the reading of the obscene material built up anxiety which was subsequently reduced by the banal, innocuous material of the group discussion. Since the discussion was responsible for reducing the anxiety, it took on positive value for the subject in the "severe" treatment.

Schopler and Bateson (1962) find partial support for a "dependency" interpretation of the Aronson and Mills findings. Following Thibaut and Kelley (1959), Schopler and Bateson suggest that, as contrasted with the "mild" initiation, the "severe" initiation induced in the subject dependence upon the experimenter. This, according to them, occurred because the experimenter had "moved" the subject in the "severe" treatment through a "wide range of outcomes," consisting of the unpleasant shock and the pleasantness associated with the pride experienced by the "severe" subject upon learning that she had passed the test. Subjects in the "mild" condition had not experienced this range of pleasantness of outcome and hence were less dependent. Also, their argument continues, somehow the subject assumed that the experimenter expected her to like the discussion. Due to the assumed differential dependency induced by the initiation treatments, the subject in the "severe" treatment was more concerned with pleasing the experimenter than was the subject in the "mild" treatment and hence attempted to a greater extent to meet his expectations by indicating to him that she liked the discussion.

Chapanis and Chapanis (1964) suggest an "afterglow" hypothesis to explain the data. All subjects in the experiment were told that they had passed the embarrassment test. Presumably, subjects in the "severe" treatment perceived the test as being more difficult than did subjects in the "mild" treatment and, according to Chapanis and Chapanis, they therefore may have had a greater sense of accomplishment. This self-satisfaction somehow "rubbed off" onto other aspects of the task situation, including, presumably, the group discussion. This might then account for the "severe" subjects' more positive disposition toward the discussion.

Still another, even more plausible interpretation of quite a different sort, is that any experience following the "severe" initiation, which we assume was unpleasant, would by contrast seem more pleasant than it would following the "mild" initiation. It is important that this rather simple "contrast" hypothesis, which is a compelling explanation of the Aronson and Mills data, be ruled out, if possible.

A problem in the experiment related to the first set of interpretations concerns the nature of the initiation itself. Was the "severe" initiation really more unpleasant than the "mild" one? The authors do not report any check of the success of the experimental manipulation in producing differences in unpleasantness. Without the assurance that this all-important requirement was met, certain other interpretations of the data are quite plausible. It is not unlikely that many of the subjects in the "severe" treatment found the experience pleasant and exciting.

The experiment we shall report here is an attempt to replicate, not so much in fact but in spirit, the Aronson and Mills study, in order to counterpose the dissonance interpretation of the results against the other interpretations discussed above.

METHOD

An Overview of the Design

Two basic treatments were compared, one in which the subject received electrical shocks as part of an initiation procedure and one in which she received shocks as part of a psychological experiment, the "noninitiate" treatment. Within each of these treatments, half of the subjects received strong shocks and half received weak shocks. Half of the "severe" and half of the "mild" initiates were told that they had passed the screening test whereas the other half of each were not told whether they had passed. After the shocks, all subjects heard and then evaluated a boring and worthless group discussion about cheating in college. The "initiates" believed that this was a recording of a previous meeting of the group that they were slated to join, whereas the "noninitiates" evaluated the discussion as just one of a series of stimuli to which they were being exposed.

Procedure

The subjects were 48 female undergraduate volunteers contacted at random from the student body of the University of California at Riverside. All subjects were first contacted by telephone. During the telephone contact a subject selected to be an "initiate" was asked whether or not she would like to volunteer for a discussion club that was to discuss the problem of morals on university campuses. The "noninitiates" were asked, during the telephone contact, whether they would like to volunteer to be a subject in a psychological experiment. Thus, half of the subjects reported to the laboratory believing that they were going to be members of a discussion club whereas the other half believed that they were participating in a psychological experiment. The procedure followed during the experimental session was essentially the same for both "initiates" and "non-initiates." The "noninitiate" condition was introduced in an attempt to rule out the "contrast" and "relief" hypotheses. If the unpleasant experience represented by the initiation was not seen as instrumental to joining the discussion club and the same effect was found as in the Aronson and Mills experiment, both alternative explanations would receive support. If, however, the "initiates" showed the effect and the "noninitiates" did not, both the "contrast" and "relief" hypotheses would have been effectively ruled out. We might expect a secondary reinforcement effect in the "noninitiate" condition which would manifest as a negative relationship between the unpleasantness of the shocks and the evaluation of the discussion, the assumption being that the effect produced by the shocks would generalize to the discussion.

When the "initiate" arrived in the laboratory she was seated in an isolation booth and was told:

"In the past we have had considerable difficulty with some of the girls who have joined these discussion clubs. The problem is that some people cannot maintain an attitude of objectivity during the discussion. When this happens, naturally the discussion tends to deteriorate and emotions run very high. In order to avoid this difficulty in the future we have just instituted a screening test to weed out those girls who would tend to let their emotions run away with them during a discussion. You are the first person to whom we will be administering the test which is a very good one that has been used by psychologists for many years. It consists of determining your physiological reaction to a series of stimuli. We do this by hooking you up to these electrodes [the experimenter shows the subject a pair of dummy GSR electrodes] that detect changes in your skin resistance during the test which is done with the aid of this recorder [the experimenter shows the subject a small strip-chart recorder]. By your response on this chart we can tell how objective you are likely to be under conditions represented by the morals discussion."

The subject was told that she was the first one to take the test in order to eliminate the possibility that she would want to be in the group in order to compare her reactions to the test with those of the girls already in the discussion group.

The "noninitiate" was told when she arrived at the laboratory, "You are going to be a subject in a psychological experiment which involves your being exposed to a variety of different kinds of stimuli. We are going to determine your reaction to these stimuli with the aid of these electrodes [the experimenter shows the subject the GSR electrodes] which are hooked up to this instrument [the experimenter shows the subject the strip chart recorder]."

All subjects were hooked up to the electrodes and received exactly the same sequence of stimuli which was designed to be a credible screening test for the "initiate." The sequence consisted of a spray of perfume from an atomizer placed in the ceiling of the subject's booth, a series of slides of paintings projected on the wall in front of the subject's booth [the paintings were: Roualt, *The Apprentice*; Picasso, *Madame Picasso, Portrait of A. Vollard, Figure by the Sea*; La Tour, *Self Portrait*; Matisse, *Landscape*; and Klee, *Girl Possessed*]. Each painting was presented for 15 seconds with a 15-second pause between presentations. After all of the paintings were shown, the subject was fitted with headphones and heard the shooting sequence in Copland's ballet, *Billy the Kid*. Finally, the subject received the critical stimuli which were a series of three shocks delivered 15 seconds apart by a Lafayette inductorium. In the "severe" treatment the shocks were quite strong whereas in the "mild" treatment they were barely supraliminal. This method of varying suffering would be more likely, on the face of it at least, to produce greater uniformity of psychological state within each of the two suffering levels than the method used by Aronson and Mills. Using electric shock to produce suffering effectively separates the content of the initiation from the content of the discussion. If the Aronson and Mills effect were to be found by using shock this would rule out the family of interpretations that are all based upon the similarity of content of the two phases of the experiment.

Aronson and Mills informed all of their subjects that they had passed the screening test. The subject, thus, had acquired that for which she had suffered. It was inappropriate in the present experiment to inform the "noninitiates" as to how they had done in responding to the sequence of stimuli since they had not been told that they were taking a test. In order to control for this difficulty, half of the "initiates" were told, after receiving the shocks, that they had passed the screening test, whereas the other half were treated like the "noninitiates" by not receiving any feed-back concerning their performance on the screening test. This "told" vs. "not-told" factor was counterbalanced across the "severe" and "mild" initiates. More importantly, this treatment also enables us to test the Chapanis and Chapanis "afterglow" hypothesis, the plausibility of which is based on the assumption that the pleasure experienced in passing the severe initiation generalized to the group discussion. If those subjects who were told that they had passed showed the Aronson and Mills effect and those who were not given this information did not show the effect, the "afterglow" explanation would be supported. The Schopler and Bateson "dependence" hypothesis would also be supported if the Aronson and Mills effect replicated in the "told" but not in the "not-told" treatment, since the assumed broader range of outcomes experienced by the "severe" subject depends on the pleasure experienced by the subject upon learning that she had passed the test.

All subjects then listened to a five-minute tape recording of three girls having a discussion of cheating in college. This discussion was absolutely worthless, consisting mostly of hemming, hawing, clearing of throats, and pauses. The "initiate" was told that this was a recording of a previous discussion of the group that she was slated to join. The "noninitiate" was merely asked to listen to the discussion as one of the sequence of stimuli. Aronson and Mills presented the recording as an ongoing discussion. This difference in procedure in our "initiate" treatment did not seem to us to be critical.

In the final phase of the experiment, all subjects evaluated the discussion using semantic differential-type scales similar to those used by Aronson and Mills. Eight scales dealt with the qualities of the participants and eight with qualities of the discussion itself. Each scale was numbered from 0 to 15, the polarity of the scales being alternated in order to counteract any response bias. After this evaluation sheet was filled out, the subject was administered a post-experimental questionnaire which asked her to rate the pleasantness or unpleasantness of the various stimuli. The subject's evaluation of the shocks on this questionnaire was, of course, the check on the manipulation of suffering.

RESULTS

The two shock levels clearly induced different degrees of pleasantness. The post-questionnaire contained a 7-point scale on which the subject rated the pleasantness of the shocks. The difference between the two shock conditions was extremely large ($p < .001$ by chi-square)[1] with the majority of subjects in the "severe" condition indicating that the shocks were "extremely unpleasant." No subjects in the "mild" treatment found the shocks more than only "mildly unpleasant."

The discussion evaluation data are shown in Table 1. The figures in the table represent the means of the pleasantness ratings for both the participant and the discussion evaluation, summed over the eight scales used for each. Tables 2 and 3 present the analysis of variance for each of the two evaluations. We see a clear main effect of the initiation factor. When the subject anticipated joining the group whose discussion she had heard, she tended to evaluate both the discussion and the participants more highly than she did when there was no such expectation. This shows a general "effort effect" in line with dissonance theory. There was also a main effect of severity that is accounted for by the "initiates." The crucial degree of freedom that concerns us here is the interaction between initiation and severity which also yields a significant F-ratio. A t test applied within the "initiates" and within the "noninitiates" shows that both trends, which are opposite, are significant, the trend in the "initiate" treatment being stronger ($p < .01$) than the trend in the "noninitiate" treatment ($p < .05$). Whether or not the "initiate" received feedback about her performance on the screening test (the "told" vs. "not-told" variations) appears not to have interacted with severity of the shock. We do see, however, that for the participant evaluation there does seem to be a main effect of feedback. Informing the subject that she had passed the test appears to have reduced the evaluation of the participants.

Since there was some variation in both the "severe" and "mild" shock conditions in the perception of unpleasantness by the subject, we were in a position to do an internal analysis of the data by examining the correlation between *perceived* severity of the shock and liking for the group discussion. On the basis of dissonance theory we would expect a positive relationship only within the "initiate" condition. The overall correlation with the "initiate" treatment is .52 for the participant rating and .45 for the discussion rating ($p < .01$ for both correlation coefficients). The corresponding correlations in the "noninitiate" treatment are .03 and .07.

---

[1] Chi-square was used as a test of significance because the distribution in the "severe" treatment was skewed.

Table 1 THE EFFECTS OF SEVERITY OF SHOCK, INITIATION, AND FEEDBACK ON EVALUATION OF THE GROUP DISCUSSION

| | INITIATE | | | | NONINITIATE | |
| | MILD SHOCK | | SEVERE SHOCK | | MILD SHOCK | SEVERE SHOCK |
	TOLD	NOT TOLD	TOLD	NOT TOLD		
Participant rating	11.5	26.1	31.1	41.0	19.8	13.2
Discussion rating	11.0	15.6	27.0	28.2	9.1	5.8

a *The larger the number, the more favorable the evaluation.*

Table 2 ANALYSIS OF VARIANCE OF THE PARTICIPANT EVALUATION

SOURCE	SS	df	MS	F**
Initiation (I)	1276	1	1276	8.28
Severity (S)	1045	1	1045	6.78
I × S	1504	1	1504	9.77
Told (T)	1201	1	1201	7.80
S (I) × T^a	45	1	45	
Error	6471	42	159	

a *Interaction of feedback (Told vs. Not-told within the initiate condition).*
b $F.05 = 4.07, F.01 = 7.27.$

Table 3 ANALYSIS OF VARIANCE OF THE DISCUSSION EVALUATION

SOURCE	SS	df	MS	F
Initiation (I)	1811	1	1811	13.22
Severity (S)	850	1	850	6.20
I × S	835	1	835	6.09
Told (T)	69	1	69	
S (I) × T	23	1	23	
Error	5774	42	137	

DISCUSSION

The data from the experiment strongly support the "suffering-leading-to-liking" hypothesis and effectively rule out a number of other interpretations of the original experiment by Aronson and Mills. Our data for the "initiate" treatment are much stronger than those in the first experiment. This is probably attributable to the shock manipulation which undoubtedly produced more uniform within-treatment levels of suffering. The fact that the content of our suffering manipulation was divorced from the content of the group discussion eliminates the family of interpretations of the Aronson and Mills data that invoke some motive for wanting to affiliate that would be assumed to be greater in the "severe" than in the "mild" initiation treatment. The fact that there was an interaction between the initiate and severity factors eliminates the "contrast" and "relief" hypotheses. Both hypotheses predict the same difference under the "initiate" and the "noninitiate" treatments. We see instead an effect within the "noninitiate" treatment that supports a secondary reinforcement interpretation; the more severe the shock the *less* did the subject like the discussion. The internal correlational analysis adds further support for the "suffering-leading-to-liking" hypothesis and further weakens the "contrast" and "relief" hypotheses, since within the "initiate" treatment the greater was the perceived suffering the greater did the subject like the group discussion, whereas no such relationship was found within the "noninitiate" treatment.

Both the Chapanis and Chapanis "afterglow" and the Schopler and Bateson "dependence" hypotheses depend upon the subject having had a success experience after learning that she had passed the screening test. This success experience is presumed to have been greater in the "severe" than in the "mild" initiation treatment. Greater liking for the discussion under the "severe" initiation should therefore, according to both hypotheses, occur under the "told" but not under the "not-told" treatment. The lack of such an interaction effectively rules out both hypotheses.

Feedback did have a main effect on the evaluation of the participants. The high evaluation of the participants in the "not-told" as compared with the "told" condition may reflect a desire to be in the group. When informed that she had passed the screening test and would be in the group, the subject reduced her evaluation. Objects that a person is not sure he can have may appear more attractive to him under certain circumstances than similar objects that he already possesses. Having suffered or expended effort in order to acquire the object may be just such a circumstance. This effect was not predicted and our interpretation, therefore, must be considered as highly speculative.

REFERENCES

Aronson, E., and Mills, J. The effect of severity of initiation on liking for a group. *Journal of Abnormal and Social Psychology*, 1959, *59*, 177–81.

Chapanis, N. P., and Chapanis, A. Cognitive dissonance: five years later. *Psychological Bulletin*, 1964, *61*, 1–22.

Schopler, J., and Bateson, N. A dependence interpretation of the effects of a severe initiation. *Journal of Personality*, 1962, *30*, 633–49.

Thibaut, J., and Kelley, H. H. *The social psychology of groups.* New York: Wiley, 1959.

Long-Term Behavioral Effects of
Cognitive Dissonance

JONATHAN L. FREEDMAN

Since the publication of *A Theory of Cognitive Dissonance* (Festinger, 1957), a large number of studies have been conducted to test a variety of deductions from the theory. Although not all of the results have been positive, in general the published research has supported the basic theory (see Brehm and Cohen, 1962, for a review).

There is, however, one quite serious limitation in this research. Virtually all of the results supporting dissonance theory have involved attitudes of one sort or another as measured by paper and pencil questionnaires, and all of the significant effects were found a very short time after the experimental manipulation. The authors of these studies have made the explicit or implicit assumption that the same results would also hold for appropriate behavioral measures and that with sufficiently powerful manipulations the effects would endure for some time. Unfortunately, there is little or no evidence supporting such an assumption.

Only two published studies have aroused dissonance in an attempt to produce behavioral changes. Although both of these (Cohen, Greenbaum, and Mansson, 1963; and Wieck, 1964) report positive results, the experimental situations were quite unusual; and the effects were obtained very soon after the manipulation. The data on long-term effects are less consistent. Aronson and Carlsmith (1963) report that 45 days after an initial manipulation there was still some tendency for a dissonance effect to remain. Opposed to this is the result of a study by Walster (1964). Postdecisional changes in attitudes were taken at various intervals after a choice, and it was found that after ninety minutes attitudes were the same as before the decision was made.

The issue of whether or not dissonance theory applies to important, enduring, behavior is particularly important because of the nature of the theory. It is clearly a cognitive theory, and is stated in terms of thoughts, opinions, beliefs, etc. A person's awareness of his own behavior is a cognitive element and fits into the theoretical framework, but the theory does not deal directly with the behavior itself. It is assumed, of course, that changes in cognitions will tend to produce corresponding changes in relevant behavior and vice versa; but as Festinger has recently pointed out (1964), this remains to be shown. The present study, therefore, was designed primarily to demonstrate that the arousal and subsequent reduction of cognitive dissonance can affect relatively important behavior and that this effect can endure over a reasonably long period of time.

One of the most ubiquitous and important problems in behavior modification is the attempt to shape a child's behavior so that it is in accordance with the moral, legal, and social values of society. It is relatively easy to make the child

Reprinted from Journal of Experimental Social Psychology, 1, *1965, 145–55.*
Copyright 1965 by the Academic Press, Inc., and reproduced by permission.

behave correctly when he is offered a reward or threatened with punishment, but this is far from enough. For the socialization process to be successful, the child must also behave correctly in the absence of any such direct pressure, and this is considerably more difficult to accomplish. It has been suggested (Aronson and Carlsmith, 1963; Festinger and Freedman, 1964; Mills, 1958) that the theory of cognitive dissonance provides one possible framework within which to consider this problem.

Attempts to shape a child's behavior often occur in a type of forced compliance situation. The child is told not to do something[1] and is under varying amounts of pressure to obey. The parent or authority giving this restriction may strengthen it with a promise of a reward if the child obeys, a threat of punishment if he does not obey, or some other justification for obeying such as that the toy is fragile and may break if not used correctly. Any of these justifications may vary in magnitude. The rewards may be large or small, the threats mild or severe, the reasons good or bad, etc. If the child obeys the restriction, he is in a potentially dissonant situation because he wanted to perform the forbidden act but did not. As in other forced compliance situations, the greater the justification for obeying, the less dissonance should be aroused (cf. Festinger and Carlsmith, 1959; Freedman, 1963; Rabbie, Brehm, and Cohen, 1959; etc.).

Consider a situation in which a child is told not to play with a very attractive, desirable toy, and is threatened with either mild or severe punishment for disobeying. If he obeys, all those factors which made him want to play with the toy are dissonant with the knowledge that he did not play with it. However, these factors are to some extent balanced by those factors which justified not playing with it. With a severe threat, the child has a very good justification for not playing since if he played, he would have been punished severely. Since there is little or nothing dissonant about refraining from playing even with a desirable toy in order to avoid severe punishment, little or no dissonance should be aroused under a severe threat condition. With a mild threat, on the other hand, the child does not have as good a reason for refraining. If the threat is mild enough relative to the desirability of the toy, a considerable amount of dissonance should be aroused. Regardless of the absolute level of threat, more dissonance should be aroused by obeying under mild than under severe threat.

Any dissonance that is aroused may be reduced either by decreasing the desire to play with the toy or by increasing the justification for not playing with it. The most direct and obvious way of accomplishing the former is to devalue the forbidden toy or increase the value of other, nonforbidden toys or activities. Aronson and Carlsmith (1963) and Turner and Wright (1964) have recently demonstrated in a situation similar to the one described above that a forbidden toy is devalued more under mild than under severe threat. The justification for not transgressing may be increased by magnifying the perceived dangerousness of the act, by enhancing the value of the prohibiting agent, by accepting the adult's evaluation of the act as wrong, or by a variety of similar changes in the perception of the situation.

---

[1] The same arguments would hold for situations in which the child is told to do something, but for purposes of this paper the discussion will refer only to the case in which the authority attempts to prevent certain behavior.

The important point for our purpose is that any of these modes of dissonance reduction would tend to make the child less likely to play with the toy in the future. A lessening in the value of the toy, an increase in the value of the authority, an acceptance of the moral value that playing with that toy was wrong will all decrease the child's tendency to play with the toy. All these modes of dissonance reduction should be reflected in one specific type of behavior—to the extent that these modes of reduction occur the child should have less inclination to play with the toy, and he should be less likely to play with it even if the original threat were no longer salient or had been removed entirely.

It should be recalled that less dissonance should be aroused by obeying under severe than under mild threat, and correspondingly, less dissonance reduction should occur in the severe threat condition. Thus, if children refrain from playing with the toy under either severe or mild threat and are then given another opportunity to play with the toy with the threats removed, more of the children in the mild threat than in the severe condition should refrain from playing in this second session.

One final point should be made. The arousal of dissonance in this situation depends upon the lack of justification for obeying the restriction. If the child never considers transgressing because he perceives the pressure against this to be too great, no dissonance should be aroused. In other words, the child must face and resist temptation in order for dissonance to be produced. If, for example, the parent made the threat, even a mild threat, but never gave the child a chance to transgress, little or no dissonance would be aroused.

The analysis in terms of cognitive dissonance may now be summarized. A child is told not to play with a toy and is threatened with severe or mild punishment if he transgresses. If he is put into a situation in which he is tempted to play with it and he does not, greater dissonance will be aroused under mild than under severe threat. If there is then another opportunity to play with the toy and the threats are removed, those children who resisted temptation under mild threat will be less likely to play with the toy than those who resisted under severe threat. This difference between mild and severe threat will not occur if the child was not exposed to temptation in the first place. The present experiment was done to test this prediction with the additional specification that the effect could be demonstrated 3 or more weeks after the initial dissonance manipulation.

METHOD

Design

Children were told not to play with a very desirable toy under either high or low threat for disobeying, and were given a five minute free period during which the toy was present and available. During this period half of Ss in each threat condition were left alone with the toy (experimental groups); half were not left alone (control groups). Ratings of the attractiveness of the forbidden toy and four other toys were taken before the threat instructions were given and after the free period. Several weeks later the threats were nullified by a second E and

Ss were again given the opportunity to play with the forbidden toy. There were thus four groups: experimental mild and severe threat (EM and ES), and control mild and severe threat (CM and CS). The mild and severe threats served as high or low justification for obeying in the first session, and the major prediction was that fewer Ss in the EM than in the ES condition would play with the toy during the second session. The control groups were included to assess the direct effect of the threat instructions. There was presumably little or no temptation during the first session of the control condition because E was present. Since only those Ss who resisted temptation should feel any dissonance, the predicted superiority of the mild threat instructions should appear in the experimental conditions but not in the control conditions.

Procedure

The Ss were 89 boys in the second to fourth grades in the Carmel and Springer schools in Los Altos, California. They were run individually and randomly assigned to conditions. Four Ss (two in each of the experimental conditions) violated the prohibition by playing with the toy in the first session and were not included in the analysis, and two more were absent and could not be seen in the second session. The remaining 83 Ss were divided equally among the four conditions except that the CS had 20 Ss and the other groups had 21 Ss.

The procedure in the first session was quite similar to that employed by Aronson and Carlsmith (1963). The S was told that the study concerned children's preferences among various toys. He was asked to indicate his liking of each of five toys on a scale ranging from 0 ("very, very bad toy") to 100 ("very, very good toy") by pointing to a place on the scale. The five toys were a cheap plastic submarine, an extremely expensive, battery controlled robot, a child's baseball glove, an unloaded Dick Tracy toy rifle, and a Tonka tractor. The robot was the toy which was forbidden in order to maximize the temptation to transgress. It was placed on the floor with its control handle on a table, and the other toys were laid out neatly on the table. The toys were demonstrated briefly by E in the order listed above, and were then rated by S in the same order. The E recorded the ratings on a separate sheet.

At this point the procedure diverged for the various conditions. For the experimental Ss, E pretended to remember that he had an errand to do and said that he had to leave for about 10 minutes. For the control Ss, E said that he had something to do and would be busy for about 10 minutes working in the room.

In the low threat conditions E continued, "While I'm gone (or busy) you can play with the toys if you want. You can play with any of them except the robot (pointing to it). Do not play with the robot. It is wrong to play with the robot." The high threat conditions had these same instructions with the addition of the following: "If you play with the robot I'll be very angry and will have to do something about it." Note that Ss are told that it is "wrong" to play with the robot, and also that the severe threat condition depends primarily on an ambiguous, vague threat to "do something about it." It was felt that this would probably be more threatening and would be less susceptible to disbelief than any specific threat.

The E then left the room in the experimental conditions, or worked at some papers in the room in the control conditions. A concealed electric timer was attached to the control switch on the robot so that it would indicate whether or not the robot was turned on, and if so, for how long. At the end of only five minutes, E returned to the room (or finished his work), told S that we wanted a second rating of the toys, and said that sometimes ratings change and sometimes they did not change, and that S should rate them as he felt about them now. After the second rating, S was thanked, told not to talk about the study with anyone else, and sent back to his class. This first session was run by a male E.

The second session was arranged to make it appear unrelated to the first. The interval between the two sessions ranged from 23 to 64 days (Christmas vacation interrupted the course of the study) with a mean interval of 39.8 days. There were no appreciable differences among the groups in either the range of time intervals or the mean interval. This session was run by a female E who was not described as coming from Stanford, whereas the male E who ran the first session was explicitly from Stanford. The same experimental room was used to make the presence of the toys plausible, but the furniture was rearranged somewhat. The toys were in the far corner of the room placed in a disorderly manner. The control switch for the robot was draped carelessly over a music stand, and the other toys were scattered around.

The E, who did not know what group S was in, asked him to sit at the table and told him that she wanted him to copy some drawings. She then administered five cards of the Bender Gestalt (Bender, 1938) which S copied while E timed his responses. After the Bender was finished, E said that she had to score it and might want to ask S some questions about it. She said that while she was doing that, if S wanted he could play with any of the toys that someone had left in the room (pointing to the toys). This was delivered rather casually, and she then pretended to begin scoring the test. If, as happened occasionally, S continued to sit at the table, E repeated that S could play with the toys, and finally she said that she would prefer it if S did not watch her. Most Ss played with some of the toys, but as will be discussed later, a few did not play with any. If S asked specifically if he could play with the robot, E responded that as far as she was concerned he could play with any of the toys. As before, the timing apparatus timed if and how long S played with the robot, and E also recorded from the stopwatch how many seconds the toy was running. Unfortunately, part-way through the experiment, the robot broke down and would no longer operate. This, of course, made time scores meaningless since S would immediately discontinue playing with the robot as soon as it was obvious that it was not working. Therefore, the major data are simply whether or not S pressed the control switch.

Table 1 NUMBER IN EACH CONDITION WHO PLAYED WITH ROBOT IN SECOND SESSION

GROUP	LOW THREAT		HIGH THREAT	
	PLAYED	DID NOT PLAY	PLAYED	DID NOT PLAY
Experimental	6	15	14	7
Control	14	7	13	7

At the end of four minutes, E said she was finished scoring the drawings and that S had done quite well. She thanked him and urged him not to talk about the study. This concluded the experiment.

RESULTS

Our original basic assumption was that less dissonance would be aroused by resisting temptation under high justification than under low justification, and that this difference would be reflected in subsequent behavior. In particular, it was predicted that the mild threat experimental condition (EM) would produce more dissonance than the severe threat experimental (ES) and that fewer Ss in the EM than in the ES would play with the forbidden toy in the second session. The relevant data are presented in Table 1, which shows the number of Ss in each group who played with the robot in the second session. It may be seen that more than twice as many Ss in the ES condition as in the EM condition played with the previously forbidden toy. This difference is in the predicted direction and is significant ($X^2 = 6.11$, $p < .02$). In other words, the use of a mild threat in the first session more effectively prevented subsequent transgression than the use of a severe threat.

Since the presence of E during the first session should have been sufficient justification by itself to prevent the arousal of dissonance, no difference was expected between the mild and severe threat control conditions. Regardless of the severity of the threat, Ss should have felt little dissonance; and the two groups should therefore not have differed in amount of transgression during the second session. The results are consistent with this analysis—the amount of transgression in the two control conditions was virtually identical.

No prediction was made regarding differences between the experimental severe threat condition and the control groups, because the exact strength of the threat was undetermined. If the severe threat had by itself been sufficient to preclude the arousal of any dissonance, the additional justification provided by E's presence would not have made any difference. If, however, the severe threat were not this effective, additional justification could have further reduced the amount of dissonance; and the control groups would show greater transgression than the experimental severe threat group. Since the actual results show no differences between the control groups and the experimental severe threat group, it appears that the severe threat provided enough justification for not playing with the toy so that little or no dissonance was aroused.

Included in the data presented in Table 1 are some Ss who did not play with any toys in the second session. It might be argued that these Ss are not resisting the temptation to play with the robot, but rather are not interested in playing with the toys. In a sense these Ss should not be included among those who do not play with the forbidden toy since they do not play with any toy. As may be seen in Table 2, removing these Ss from the analysis does not change the main effect appreciably. The difference between EM and ES conditions is still in the predicted direction and significant ($X^2 = 5.51$, $p < .02$). There is a slight tendency for the CM Ss to transgress more than the CS Ss. Although this difference is not significant, it suggests that the effect in the experimental

Table 2 Number in Each Condition Who Played with Robot in Second Session, with *S*s Who Played with No Toys Omitted from Data

| | MILD THREAT | | SEVERE THREAT | |
GROUP	PLAYED	DID NOT PLAY	PLAYED	DID NOT PLAY
Experimental	6	12	14	4
Control	14	1	13	7

conditions may have occurred despite some direct effect of the threat which operated in the direction opposite to the effect of the dissonance manipulation.

The other major data are presented in Table 3 which shows the changes in evaluations of the toys from the beginning to the end of the first experimental session. The toys were rated on a scale ranging from 0 ("very, very bad toy") to 100 ("very, very good toy"). If dissonance were aroused by not playing with the forbidden toy, one possible way of reducing it would have been to devalue the forbidden toy or increase the value of the other toys. This would make the forbidden toy relatively less attractive and would decrease the temptation to play with it. As may be seen, all of the groups change their ratings significantly in the direction of dissonance reduction. This change need not, however, have been due to dissonance reduction. In the first place, the initial ratings of the robot were so high (all above 90) that an increase in its rating was highly unlikely. In addition, almost all *S*s played with some of the toys but not the robot. The relative increase in the other toys might therefore have been due to greater familiarity with them, or some other factor associated with having used them.

Table 3 Mean Changes in Ratings of Toys

GROUP		ROBOT	OTHERS	TOTAL CHANGE IN DIRECTION OF DISSONANCE REDUCTION[a]
Experimental	Mild threat	−5.48[b]	+7.72	13.20
	Severe threat	−4.28	+5.90	10.18
Control	Mild threat	−4.00	+5.31	9.31
	Severe threat	−4.84	+5.93	10.77

[a] *The sum of the decrease in rating of the robot and the mean increase in rating of the other toys.*
[b] *All changes are significantly different from no change at p <.05. None of the differences between experimental groups approaches significance.*

A more meaningful way of considering these data is to compare the various groups in amount of change. Presumably the greater the dissonance that was aroused, the more change in the direction of dissonance reduction that should have occurred. Therefore, the mild threat experimental group should show more dissonance reduction than the other groups. On both individual measures and the overall change measure, the EM group does show the most change in the direction of dissonance reduction; but none of these differences are significant. Thus, although the results are consistent with the dissonance analysis, they do not provide significant support for it.

This lack of significance is in contrast with the results of the study by Aronson and Carlsmith (1963) in which a forbidden toy was devalued significantly more under mild threat than under severe threat conditions. The experimental situations are not, however, exactly comparable. In the present study the forbidden toy, the robot, was intentionally made much more attractive than any of the other toys in order to maximize the temptation to play with it. It was so much more desirable than the other toys (it was rated an average of more than ten points higher than the closest toy) that devaluing it below the other toys must have been extremely difficult and unrealistic. It seems likely that re-evaluating the toys was not an efficient or practical mode of dissonance reduction in the present experiment and was not employed to any great extent.

DISCUSSION

Although the difference in amount of transgression between the high and low threat experimental groups is clearly consistent with the prediction from dissonance theory, other explanations of this difference are possible. A more severe threat might have called more attention to the forbidden toy or made it seem more attractive, and this would tend to make the severe threat Ss play with the toy more than did the mild threat Ss. Or, E may have been liked more or believed more when he made a mild threat than when he made a severe threat, and his original commands would have been obeyed more in the former condition. Any of these explanations sounds plausible, and there are probably a number of other reasonable possibilities that could explain the difference between the high and low threat experimental conditions.

It should be noted, however, that the control Ss received exactly the same threat instructions as the corresponding experimental Ss, and that all Ss went through exactly the same procedure with one crucial difference. In the experimental conditions, E left the room and gave S a chance to play with the forbidden toy without being observed; in the control conditions, E did not leave the room. Any explanation of the results must therefore account for the fact that only when E leaves the room during the first session do the threats have differential effects on subsequent behavior. The explanations offered above clearly would require differences in both experimental and control conditions and may thus be ruled out; and most other explanations based on surmises about the differential meaning, plausibility or direct effect of the threat instructions would probably also be eliminated.

The results do fit the analysis in terms of cognitive dissonance. When Ss are given a mild threat and they resist temptation, more dissonance is produced than when they resist temptation because of a severe threat. This dissonance may be reduced in a number of ways, all of which would tend to make S refrain from playing with the toy in the future even in the absence of any threat. Since more dissonance is aroused in the low threat condition, more dissonance reduction occurs in that condition; and the low threat *S*s should refrain from playing to a greater extent than should the high threat *S*s.

When *E* remains in the room, there is no temptation to play with the forbidden toy since *S* would surely get caught. Therefore, no dissonance is aroused in either high or low threat control conditions; and the two should not differ. The lack of difference between control groups is clearly consistent with the dissonance analysis and would seem to make alternative explanations somewhat difficult.

The results thus strongly support the predictions based on the theory of cognitive dissonance. They provide a clear demonstration that the theory does apply to behavioral as well as attitudinal changes and that the arousal and reduction of differential amounts of dissonance can have a significant effect even after an interval of just under 6 weeks.

Since the data on changes in ratings of the toy indicated that this was not a major mode of dissonance reduction in the present situation, it might be interesting to speculate on what the primary mode of reduction was. One provocative possibility is that at least in part dissonance was reduced by an acceptance of the idea that it was wrong to play with the forbidden toy. In other words, the subject may have provided himself with moral justification for obeying the restriction. This would tend to make him less likely to play with the toy in the second session, even though another *E* said it was all right to play with it.

As Festinger and Freedman have pointed out (1964), one implication of this is that inculcating moral values will be most successful if a minimal amount of justification of any kind is offered for the relevant behavior. If the goal is to make a child accept the values of society, he should not be given a great many logical reasons supporting the valued behavior, nor threatened with severe punishment or eternal damnation if he transgresses, nor promised great rewards, eternal or otherwise, for obeying. Rather, he should be given just enough justification to cause him to obey in the presence of the justification; and then his acceptance of the value itself will be maximal. This analysis of the development of moral values is, of course, highly speculative, and the present study offers no evidence directly supporting it. The present result and that reported by Mills (1958) are, however, consistent with the analysis, and it is hoped that it will be tested more directly by additional research.

SUMMARY

The study was conducted to investigate whether or not the arousal of cognitive dissonance can produce long-term behavioral effects. Children were told not to play with a very desirable toy under high or low threat, and were left alone with the toy. Those who did not play with it were given a second opportunity to play with the toy several weeks later, with the original threat removed. The prediction was that those subjects who had resisted temptation under mild threat would be less likely to play with the toy in this second session than would those who had resisted under severe threat. The results supported this prediction.

REFERENCES

Aronson, E., and Carlsmith, J. M. The effect of the severity of threat on the devaluation of forbidden behavior. *J. abnorm. soc. Psychol.*, 1963, *66*, 584–88.

Bender, Lauretta. A visual motor gestalt test and its clinical use. Research Monogr. No. 3, *Amer. Orthopsychiat. Assoc.*, 1938.

Brehm, J. W., and Cohen, A. R. *Explorations in Cognitive Dissonance*. Wiley: New York, 1962.

Cohen, A. R., Greenbaum, C. W., and Mansson, H. H. Commitment to social deprivation and verbal conditioning. *J. abnorm. soc. Psychol.*, 1963, *67*, 410–21.

Festinger, L. *A theory of cognitive dissonance*. Stanford, Calif.: Univer. Press, 1957.

Festinger, L. Behavioral support for opinion change. *Pub. Opin. Quart.*, 1964, *28*, 404–17.

Festinger, L., and Carlsmith, J. Cognitive consequences of forced compliance. *J. abnorm. soc. Psychol.*, 1959, *58*, 203–10.

Festinger, L., and Freedman, J. L. Dissonance reduction and moral values. In *Personality Change* (Worchel and Byrne, ed.). New York: Wiley, 1964.

Freedman, J. L. Attitudinal effects of inadequate justification. *J. Pers.*, 1963, *31*, 371–85.

Mills, J. Changes in moral attitudes following temptation. *J. Pers.*, 1958, *26*, 517–31.

Rabbie, J. M., Brehm, J. W., and Cohen, A. R. Verbalization and reactions to cognitive dissonance. *J. Pers.*, 1959, *27*, 407–17.

Turner, Elizabeth A., and Wright, J. C. The effects of severity of threat and perceived availability on the attractiveness of objects. Unpublished manuscript, 1964.

Walster, Elaine. The temporal sequence of post-decision processes. In *Conflict, decision and dissonance* (L. Festinger, ed.). Stanford, Calif,: Univer. Press, 1964. Pp. 112–28.

Wieck, K. E. Reduction of cognitive dissonance through task enhancement and effort expenditure. *J. abnorm. soc. Psychol.*, 1964, *68*, 533–39.

Studies in Forced Compliance:
I. The Effect of Pressure for Compliance on Attitude Change Produced by Face-to-Face Role Playing and Anonymous Essay Writing

J. MERRILL CARLSMITH, BARRY E. COLLINS,
AND ROBERT L. HELMREICH

An encouragingly large body of literature has appeared in recent years which suggests that inducing a person to adopt a counterattitudinal position causes him to change his attitude in the direction of the position adopted. Unfortunately, there is a growing disagreement concerning the relationship between the size of the incentive which is used to induce the person to adopt a counterattitudinal position and the amount of attitude change. The empirical question is straightforward: Does increasing the amount of incentive offered to a person to engage in counterattitudinal role playing *increase* or *decrease* the amount of attitude change which results from that role playing? Theoretically, there are two opposing predictions which correspond to each of the opposite empirical results.

Dissonance-Theory Prediction

Dissonance theory (Festinger, 1957) predicts that the greater the inducement offered to the subject to adopt a position with which he does not agree, the less the resultant attitude change. The reasoning behind this prediction is spelled out in some detail by Festinger (Ch. 4) and by Festinger and Carlsmith (1959, pp. 203–204). Briefly, the argument goes as follows: The two cognitions "I believe X" and "I am publicly stating that I believe not X" are dissonant. However, all pressures, threats, and rewards which induce one to state that he believes "not X" are consonant with the cognition "I am publicly stating that I believe not X." Consequently, the greater the pressures, threats, or rewards, the more consonant cognitions the individual holds, and the lower the magnitude of the dissonance. Since one primary means of dissonance reduction in this situation is to change one's attitude in the direction "not X," it follows that the larger the reward for stating "not X," the *less* the resultant attitude change in that direction should be.

Incentive or Reinforcement Theory Prediction

On the other hand, various forms of "incentive theory" (Janis & Gilmore, 1965), "consistency theory" (Rosenberg, 1965), or "reinforcement theory" argue that the greater the incentives for the counterattitudinal role playing, the greater should be the resultant attitude change. Thus, advocates of this position state:

... the significance of a reward received for writing a counterattitudinal essay ...

Reprinted from Journal of Personality and Social Psychology, 4, *1966, 1–13.* *Copyright 1966 by the American Psychological Association and reproduced by permission.*

would be different from that claimed in dissonance theory: such a reward would, in proportion to its magnitude, be likely to have a positive effect both upon the development and the stabilization of the new cognitions. From this it would be predicted that with the removal of the biasing factors the degree of attitude change obtained after the subjects have written counterattitudinal essays will vary directly, rather than inversely, with the amount of reward [Rosenberg, 1965, p 331].

... two separate kinds of mediation are ... conceivable: the *expectation* of payment for counterattitudinal advocacy may operate as an incentive and thus affect the quality of the arguments advanced in support of new cognitions; the *receipt* of payment may operate as a reinforcement that further fosters the internalization of the counterattitudinal cognitions ... [Rosenberg, 1965, p. 39].

[Janis and Gilmore, 1965, make a similar argument:] According to this "incentive" theory, when a person accepts the task of improvising arguments in favor of a point of view at variance with his own personal convictions, he becomes temporarily motivated to think up all the good positive arguments he can, and at the same time suppresses thoughts about the negative arguments which are supposedly irrelevant to the assigned task. This "biased scanning" increases the salience of the positive arguments and therefore increases the chances of acceptance of the new attitude position [pp. 17–18].

Empirical Controversy

Let us briefly review some of the experiments which have dealt with this question. The first such experiment was conducted by Kelman (1953), who asked seventh-grade students to write essays favoring one or another kind of comic book. Different subjects were offered different amounts of incentive to adopt the opposite position of the one they actually held. He found that, among subjects who complied with the request, there was more attitude change among those who were offered a low incentive than among those who were offered a high incentive. Although such a finding is in line with the prediction made by dissonance theory, the fact that many fewer subjects complied with the request in the low-incentive group than in the high-incentive group leaves open the possibility that self-selection may have affected the results. Also, since incentives were offered for compliance and for noncompliance, it is not always easy to identify the "high-incentive" conditions.

In order to check on this possibility, Festinger and Carlsmith (1959) carried out an experiment where the subject was offered varying amounts of money to publicly adopt a counterattitudinal position. Specifically, the subjects were requested to tell a waiting girl (actually a confederate) that an experiment that they had just participated in was interesting and exciting. (In fact, the experiment had been dull and boring.) Subjects were told that the experimenter's assistant, who usually performed this role, had, unexpectedly, failed to show up, and subjects were offered either $1 or $20 to perform this task, and to be on call for a possible similar task in the future. Festinger and Carlsmith found that subjects who had been paid only $1 changed their attitudes more in the direction of the position they had publicly advocated than did $20 subjects.

Although this finding provides good support for the dissonance-theory prediction, several criticisms have been directed toward the experiment. Most of these criticisms argue that the $20 inducement was inordinately large, and would produce guilt, suspicion, or some other reaction which would interfere with the attitude change. To counter this criticism, Cohen (Brehm & Cohen, 1962) carried out a similar experiment using smaller amounts of money. In this experiment, subjects were approached in their rooms by a fellow student who asked them to write an essay in favor of the actions of the New Haven police. (Most students privately disagreed with this position.) Subjects were offered either $.50, $1, $5, or $10 for writing such an essay. After writing the essays the subjects' attitudes toward the police actions were assessed. Cohen's results fit closely with the dissonance-theory predictions; there was decreasing attitude change with increasing amounts of incentive for performing the counter-attitudinal behavior. Taken together, the Festinger and Carlsmith and Cohen experiments support the empirical generality of the negative relationship between incentive and attitude change predicted by dissonance theory.

Several more recent experiments, however, have cast some doubt on the generality of the dissonance-theory interpretation of these results. In the first of these experiments (Janis & Gilmore, 1965) subjects were asked to write an essay which argued that all college students should be required to take an extra year of mathematics and of physics. In an attempt to show that the results obtained by Festinger and Carlsmith were due to the use of an "extraordinarily large reward of $20 [which] might have unintentionally generated some degree of suspicion or wariness," they repeated the use of $1 and $20 as rewards. They also added a variation in the sponsor of the project. In one case, the sponsor was described as a new publishing company, in the other as a research organization on the behalf of a number of universities. Unfortunately, they made two major changes in the offering of money, which prevents a direct comparison with the Festinger and Carlsmith experiment. Rather than offering subjects the money as payment *and* as a retainer for possible future work, they made no mention of any possible future work. In addition, whereas in the Festinger and Carlsmith study the money was offered for performing a task for which a sudden, unexpected, and pressing need had arisen, Janis and Gilmore offered this money for a task which was being done by several people, and which many other people might have done just as well. These two factors may have contributed to the fact that Janis and Gilmore report that their subjects perceived the money as a surprising and inappropriate payment.

Janis and Gilmore found that—with their technique of presentation—variations in monetary reward produced no differences in attitude change. Whether this failure to replicate is due to these changed techniques of presentation or due to suspicion and negative feelings is an empirical question.

The one finding that Janis and Gilmore do report is an interaction between role playing and sponsorship conditions. In the role-playing conditions, the public welfare sponsorship produced significantly more attitude change than did the commercial sponsorship; in the control conditions, there was no significant difference. Unfortunately, the role-playing subjects differed from the control subjects not only by virtue of the fact that they wrote an essay against their position, but also because they were given a few "general questions," for example, "Considering the type of career you are likely to be in, how might a background in physics and math enable you to function more adequately?" Such questions might well serve as a persuasive communication, and the difference between the sponsorship conditions would then be attributable to prestige or "demand" effects of the more positive sponsor.

The finding from Janis and Gilmore which is of major interest for our purposes here is the failure to find an effect of incentive on attitude change where the large incentive was designed especially to arouse suspicion. In a more recent experiment, Elms and Janis (1965) were able to detect some effects of incentive under similar circumstances—effects which tended to go in the opposite direction from that predicted by dissonance theory. Varying amount of incentive, nature of sponsorship, and presence or absence of role playing in a 3 x 2 x 2 factorial, Elms and Janis asked subjects to write an anonymous essay advocating that qualified United States students should be sent to study in Russia for 4 years. The alleged sponsor of the research program was a private firm hired by the Soviet Embassy in one condition (negative sponsorship), while in the other condition the firm had been hired by the United States State Department (positive sponsorship). Subjects were paid either $.50, $1.50, or $5 to write an essay counter to their position. Only 1 of the 10 experimental groups showed significant attitude change. This was the group paid $10 under favorable sponsorship conditions. This group showed more attitude change than those subjects paid $.50. (However, the relationship is not linear. These $.50 subjects showed more—although not significantly—change than those subjects paid $1.50.) Under unfavorable sponsorship conditions, there were no significant effects. The $.50-$10 comparison for favorable sponsorship is the opposite of that predicted by dissonance theory, and is interpreted by Elms and Janis as being in support of "incentive theory."

Stronger evidence for increasing attitude change with increasing incentive is reported by Rosenberg (1965). His study, which is similar to Cohen's (Brehm & Cohen, 1962) study, asked subjects to write essays advocating that the Ohio State football team be banned from playing in the Rose Bowl (a strongly counterattitudinal position). Rosenberg changed Cohen's procedure by separating the "compliance inducer" from the posttester. The person who asked the subject to write the essay was not the same person as the experimenter who gathered the information on the subject's attitudes following the manipulation. In addition to a control condition, in which subjects wrote no counterattitudinal essay, there were three levels of reward for writing the essay—$.50, $1, and $5. The results of the experiment were exactly the opposite of Cohen's—the group paid $5 changed their attitudes much more than did the groups paid $.50 or $1, who in turn changed more than the control condition.

Unfortunately, the interpretation of these results must remain equivocal. As Nuttin (1964) points out:

Rosenberg's study is, like most replications, not a "duplicate" of Cohen's study, but a very complex chain of interactions which are functionally more or less equivalent or similar to the ones Cohen investigated. Not only the attitude object itself but also the social status of the E and the experimental situation as a whole were quite different in both studies .... Notwithstanding this, Rosenberg interprets his discrepant findings as due to *his* definition of the difference between the two experiments [pp. 4ff. for other critical discussion of Rosenberg's study].

The most recent study of this problem is a large experiment by Nuttin (1964), for which only preliminary results are available. Nuttin ran 20 experimental conditions in which he essentially attempted to replicate both studies, adding what he felt had been missing control groups in Rosenberg's study. The most clearcut results he reports are on his replication of the Rosenberg study, where he finds exactly the opposite of what Rosenberg found. Thus, even when some degree of "perceptual separation" is maintained, Nuttin finds identical results to those of Cohen—the larger the incentive, the less the attitude change. However, Nuttin was unable to replicate the Festinger and Carlsmith results.

Since most of the criticisms which are applied to one individual study do not apply to the others, the meaning of all studies, in concert, is not clear. At the very least, these data suggest that the original formulation of the attitude-change process by Festinger and Carlsmith was incomplete. At the most, they suggest that the dissonance results were due to trivial artifacts. Because of the many differences in procedure among these various studies, it would be worthwhile to study differences in procedure which might have produced different results.

There are, of course, many differences, but let us turn our attention to just one. Contrast the Festinger and Carlsmith experiment with, say, that of Elms and Janis. In the study by Festinger and Carlsmith, the subject is asked to make a public statement (at least in front of one other person) which conflicts with his private belief. Furthermore, the person to whom he is making this statement is *unaware* that this is in fact in conflict with the private belief. Such a situation is certainly one in which dissonance would be aroused.

Consider on the other hand the position of the subject in the Elms and Janis experiment. He is being asked to write an essay in favor of a position which he does not agree with. He is assured that his essay will be kept anonymous—no one will ever know that he wrote it except the experimenter. And the experimenter— the only person to read the essay—knows full well that the essay does *not* express the subject's private opinion. The experimenter, in essence, is asking him whether he has the intellectual ability to see some arguments on the opposite side of the issue from that which he holds. It can be argued that writing such an essay will create no dissonance. Stated in an extreme form, the question is whether the cognition "I am, for good *reasons*, listing some arguments in favor of the position 'not-X' is dissonant with the cognition 'I believe X.' " It is plausible that, especially among college students, the cognition that one is listing such arguments is not at all dissonant with the cognition that one believes the opposite. Rather, the ability intellectually to adopt such a position is the hallmark of the open-minded and intellectual.

The argument in the paragraph above is not altogether different from the emphasis which Brehm and Cohen (1962) have placed on the role of commitment in the arousal of dissonance. A person who is merely writing arguments in favor of a position, but who has not committed himself to that position, would not experience dissonance *about the fact that he was writing arguments*. This is not to say that there may not be dissonance of some other kind, or that there may not be other nondissonance processes operating to produce attitude change as a result of writing these arguments. For example, insofar as the arguments he produces are good ones, there is dissonance aroused between the cognition—

"This good argument in favor of not X exists" and the cognition "I believe X." This dissonance-theory process sounds quite similar to the incentive-theory process which Janis and Gilmore posit to explain attitude change produced by role playing. The point to be made here is that writing an anonymous essay may not produce dissonance *of the particular kind* studied by Festinger and Carlsmith, and that the predictions from dissonance theory about incentive effects may not be relevant in such situations.

In order to test this post hoc explanation, we attempted to design an experiment which would demonstrate that the results reported by Festinger and Carlsmith could be repeated under appropriate conditions, whereas the opposite kind of results might be expected under different conditions.

One further difference between experiments which have obtained results consistent with the dissonance-theory predictions and those experiments which have not has been the theoretical predilection of the experimenters. With the exception of the work of Nuttin, the results in line with dissonance-theory predictions have been obtained by experimenters who were to some extent identified with dissonance theory and who might be expected to "hope for" results consistent with dissonance theory. The converse has been true of experimenters who have obtained results inconsistent with dissonance theory. In light of the increasing interest in subtle effects of so-called "experimenter bias" (Rosenthal, 1965) we carried out the present experiment using two experimenters of different theoretical backgrounds. One of the experimenters (JMC) was presumably identified with a dissonance-theory approach; the other (BEC) was somewhat identified with a more behavioristic or reinforcement theory approach.

The basic design of the experiment to be reported here is a 2 x 2 x 4 factorial. Subjects were asked to adopt a counterattitudinal position in two very different ways. Half of the subjects were asked to lie to a confederate in a face-to-face confrontation. They were asked to tell a confederate that a decidedly dull task was, in fact, interesting—a manipulation essentially identical to that of Festinger and Carlsmith. The other half of the subjects were asked to write an anonymous essay in favor of the same position—an essay which would ostensibly be used to help the experimenter prepare another description which would then be presented to future subjects. Half of the subjects were run by each experimenter. Finally, experimental subjects were paid one of three different amounts of money for performing the task, while a control group was paid no additional money and performed no counterattitudinal responses.

METHOD

Subjects

An advertisement was placed in the local paper offering to pay high school age students (14–18) $2.50 for 2 hours of participation in a psychological experiment. When males called the listed number, they were given appointments for the experiment. Females were put on a "waiting list."

Two hundred and two male subjects participated in the experiment. A total of 11 subjects were eliminated from the reported results. Four subjects (2 pairs of brothers) were discarded because, in the judgment of the experimenter administering the posttest, they did not comprehend the meaning of the 11-point rating scale. Typically they expressed strong approval or disapproval and then chose a number on the opposite end of the scale. The posttester did not know which condition the subject was in, and, therefore, could not bias the results by selective elimination. Four more subjects (2 $.50 role play, 1 $1.50 role play, and 1 $.50 essay) were discarded because they did not follow through on the assigned role play or essay. Typically they admitted the task was dull and stated that they had been asked to say it was interesting. Only 1 subject showed any detectable sign of suspicion, and he was eliminated before he took the posttest. One subject accidentally saw the confederate in conversation with one of the experimenters. Finally, 1 subject, when he heard from the confederate that her friend "told her it was kind of dull," called in the experimenter and suggested that the accomplice be assigned to a control group since she knew the task was dull.

The subjects were extremely heterogeneous. They ranged from those who could barely master the complexities of an 11-point scale or could produce only 20 or 25 words of essay in 10 minutes to numerous prep-school students and children from professional families. The sample included a substantial number of Negroes.

Setting and Personnel

The study was conducted in six rooms of the Yale Psycho-Educational Clinic over a 3-week period. The five personnel conducting the experiment were the two principal investigators (BEC and JMC, who alternated as "project director" and "posttester"), a graduate assistant who served as experimenter (RLH), a receptionist, and a female high school age accomplice.

Overview of Design

The basic procedure was similar to that used by Festinger and Carlsmith (1959). Experimental subjects were asked either to write an essay or to tell a second, presumably naïve, subject that the experimental task was fun, interesting, exciting, and enjoyable. The subjects knew from their own experience with the task that it was dull and uninteresting. Subjects were paid an *additional* $5, $1.50, or $.50 to role play or write the essay. Control subjects were paid no additional money and were not asked to role play or write an essay. One-half of the subjects were run with BEC as project director and JMC as posttester, and the other half were run with the roles reversed. Attitudes toward the experimental task were then measured in a posttest-only design. The accomplice rated the several dimensions of the role-play performance, and the transcripts of the role plays and the essays were rated on a number of variables by three judges.

Procedure

All subjects. On arriving at the building, each subject was greeted by the receptionist who verified his age and high school status and conducted him to an experimental room furnished with desk, chairs, and writing materials. After the subject had waited alone for several minutes, the experimenter entered the room, introduced himself as Mr. Helmreich, and announced that he was ready to start the experiment. The experimenter then explained that the experiment itself would only take a little over an hour and that since subjects were being paid for 2 hours' participation, arrangements had been made for every subject to take part in a record survey being conducted in the building by a "man from some consumer research outfit in New York." At this point, the subject was presented with the experimental task—20 5-page booklets of random numbers. Each booklet had a cover sheet which instructed the subject to strike out each occurrence of two of the digits (e.g., 2s and 6s) contained in the booklet. The subject was told that he should work at a comfortable rate, correct mistakes, and continue working until stopped by the experimenter. The experimenter then explained that he would describe the purpose of the study when he stopped the subject on completion of the task. The subject was then left alone to work for an hour. The supply of booklets left with the subject was many times the number which could be completed in an hour. The task itself was designed to be so dull and repetitious that the subject would leave with a generally negative feeling.

At the end of an hour, the experimenter reentered the room and told the subject that he could stop as the experiment was completed. The experimenter then seated himself next to the subject and said he would explain the purpose of the study. The experimenter described the project as a largescale study designed to investigate how a person's prior expectation of the nature of a task might affect the amount and accuracy of work performed. The subject was told that the project was investigating the best ways to describe routine tasks so that people would be motivated to work hard and accurately. Each subject was told that he was in a control condition and, therefore, had been given no expectation about how pleasant the task would be. He was told that his group would serve as the standard comparison for other groups which were given positive expectations.

At this point the explanations began to differ according to the experimental condition to which the subject was assigned. Four different procedures were used: role-play control, role-play experimental, essay control, and essay experimental.

Role-play control subjects. Subjects in this condition were told that subjects in the other condition were introduced by the experimenter to a high school boy named Anderson who, presumably, had just finished the experimental task. In fact, continued the experimenter, the boy was paid by the experimenter to say the task was fun, interesting, exciting, and enjoyable. The experimenter remarked that after the paid assistant had been with a subject in the other condition 2 minutes, telling the subject how the experiment was fun, interesting, etc., the experimenter would return to the room, excuse the assistant, and start the subject on the same random-number task. The experimenter pointed out that a high school age assistant was necessary in order to make the description of the task plausible.

At this point, the experimenter asked if the subject had any questions concerning the purpose of the study. After dealing with any questions, the experimenter stated that the project director (BEC or JMC) would like to thank him. The experimenter then left the room and returned with the project director, who then gave the termination speech.

Role-play experimental subjects. In this condition, as the experimenter was finishing the same description given to role-play control subjects and asking for questions, the project director knocked on the door, entered the room, excused himself, and asked the experimenter if he knew where Anderson was. After the experimenter replied that he had not seen him, the director remarked that a subject was waiting in a condition where he was supposed to be told that the task was fun and interesting. He then asked the experimenter if he knew how to get in touch with Anderson and received a negative reply. After a pause, the director asked the experimenter if the subject with him was finished. The experimenter replied that the subject had completed the task and that he was explaining the purpose of the study. The director then remarked that perhaps the subject could help them; that, as the experimenter had no doubt explained, Anderson had been hired to tell some of the waiting subjects that the task was fun, interesting, exciting, and enjoyable. The subject was told that he could help the director out of a jam by describing the task in those terms to a girl who was waiting to start the experiment. The director said that since he was in a bind, he could pay $.50 ($1.50, $5) for doing this job. After the subject agreed (every subject agreed to undertake the task), the experimenter was sent to obtain the proper amount of money and a receipt form. While the experimenter was gone, the director rehearsed the points (fun, interesting, exciting, enjoyable) that the subject was to make to the waiting confederate. After the experimenter returned, the subject took his money, signed a receipt, and was conducted by the director to another room where the female confederate was waiting, ostensibly to start the experiment.

The director told the confederate that the subject had just finished the experiment and that he would tell her something about it. He then left, saying he would be back in a couple of minutes. The girl said little until the subject made some positive remarks about the task, then remarked that a friend of hers had taken the test and had not said much about it except that it was rather dull. Most subjects attempted to counter this evaluation, and the accomplice listened quietly accepting everything the subject said about the task. The interaction between the subject and the accomplice was recorded on a concealed tape recorder.

After 2 minutes, the director returned to the room, told the accomplice that the experimenter would be in to get her started on the experiment and led the subject from the room. The director then gave the termination speech common to all subjects.

Essay control subjects. Procedures in this condition were the same as in the role-play control condition except that subjects were told that subjects in the other condition read a short essay describing the task positively. The experimenter stated that after reading the essay, subjects in this other group were given the same random-number task. After answering any questions concerning the purpose of the study, the experimenter brought in and introduced the project director who gave the termination speech.

Essay experimental subjects. In this condition, subjects were treated in the same manner as essay controls until the project director was introduced. At this point the director seated himself beside the subject, stated that he had a problem and that the subject might be able to help. He remarked that, as the experimenter described, some subjects in other conditions read an essay describing the task as fun, interesting, exciting, and enjoyable. But he further commented that the experimenters were unhappy with this essay. The director felt that the essays were unsatisfactory because they did not sound like they had been written by high school students and that they did not have the perspective of someone who had taken the experiment. The experimenters had decided to write a new description of the task and felt that the best way to proceed would be to ask a few of the subjects to write positive descriptions of the task. He emphasized that no other subjects would read these essays because he would merely use them as sources of phrases and ideas for an essay which he, the director, would write. He then added that since they were "in a bind" he could pay the subject $.50 ($1.50, $5) to write a 5- or 10-minute description of the task. After the subject agreed to do so (all subjects agreed to write the essay), the experimenter was sent to obtain the proper amount of money and a receipt form. While the experimenter was gone, the director rehearsed with the subject the points that he should make in the essay—that the task was fun, interesting, exciting, and enjoyable. After the experimenter returned, the subject took his money, signed a receipt, and followed the director to another office where he was given paper and pen and told to write for 5 or 10 minutes. He was to press a buzzer which would notify the director when he was finished. The subject was then left alone, and an electric timer was started in the adjoining office. The subject stopped the timer when he pressed the buzzer to signify that he had finished the essay. If the subject had not completed the essay by the end of 15 minutes, the director appeared in the room and told him that he had been working about 15 minutes and should finish up in the next couple of minutes. If still working, subjects were told to stop at the end of 17 minutes (1,000 seconds). After collecting the essay, the director gave the termination speech.

Termination speech. (Identical for all subjects.) While walking away from the experimental room, the director remarked that, as the experimenter had mentioned, a man from Consumer Research Associates had asked if he could have the subjects rate some records since the experiment did not last the full 2 hours. He stated that he did not know much about what the survey was about, but he would show the subjects where to go. As in the Festinger and Carlsmith (1959) study, the experimenter then states, "I certainly hope you enjoyed the experiment. Most of our subjects tell us they did." He then directed the subject to the posttest room, thanked him, and made a strong request for secrecy about the experiment. It was clear to the subject that the experiment was over at this point.

Posttest. The subject then arrived at a comfortably appointed office labeled Consumer Research Associates on the door. As the subject entered the office, he was greeted by the posttester (BEC or JMC) who introduced himself as Ted

Johnson of Consumer Research Associates. Johnson then ushered the subject into the office and seated him before a desk. Next to the desk was a portable record player equipped with stereo earphones. The desk itself was littered with papers bearing Consumer Research Associates' letterhead and titled "Teen Age Market Survey—Connecticut." Johnson introduced the posttest by saying that his company was interested in the type of music teen-agers listened to and the types of music they liked for specific activities. He added that this was important because teen-agers bought 68% of the records sold in this country.

The subject was then asked to listen to a "practice" record for 30 seconds. Johnson then asked the subject to rate the practice record on several questions. He explained the use of an 11-point scale running from −5 to +5 using a graphic illustration of the scale. The subject rated the record as to how much he liked it generally, how much he would like to listen to it on a date, how much he would like to dance to it, and how much he would like to study by it—each rating on the 11-point scale. After the practice record, Johnson announced that they were ready to start the survey. As he started to hand the earphones to the subject he stated:

Oh. There is one thing I forgot. As you might imagine, the kind of mood you are in and the kind of experiences you have just had might influence the ratings you give in a situation like this. [The preceding spoken slowly to give the subject opportunity to agree.] If you had a splitting headache, you would not like much of anything we played through those earphones. [Subjects usually laughed—the volume was moderately high.] So I do want to ask you a question or two about that sort of thing. I don't know much about what they are doing up there, but would you say the test they had you working on was sort of pleasant or unpleasant? [slight pause] As a matter of fact, why don't we put it in terms of the same scale we used for the records? A minus 5 would be very unpleasant and a plus 5 would be very pleasant.

Since the subject had already used the rating scale for the practice record, the other five questions were covered quickly, and the subject immediately began to listen to the first "survey record." The word "test" was used in each question to make sure that the subjects were reacting to the experimental task only, and not the total experiment.

The six questions asked in the posttest were:

1. How pleasant did you find the test?
2. Was it an interesting test?
3. Did you learn anything from the test?
4. Would you recommend the test to a friend?
5. Would you describe the test as fun?
6. What is your general overall mood at the present time?

In each case a +5 represented a highly positive reaction and a −5 a strongly negative reaction. All subjects seemed convinced about the genuineness of the posttest; several hesitated to discuss the test because the project director had cautioned them to secrecy.

RESULTS

There are 15 subjects in each of the four control groups, and 11 subjects in all but one of the 12 experimental groups. There are only 10 subjects in the $.50, BEC, essay cell. The results can be discussed in three broad categories: the six questions in the posttest, measures evaluating the quality of the role-play performance and of the essays, and experimenter effects.

Posttest Variables

The mean response for each of the six questions in the posttest is shown in Table 1. Consider first the questions dealing with words the subject actually used while role playing or essay writing—"How interesting would you say the test was?" and "How much fun would you say the test was?" Table 1 shows that both essay and role-play control subjects found that the test, or random-number task, was uninteresting ($M = -1.2$) and not much fun ($M = -1.4$).

Table 1 MEANS FOR POSTTEST VARIABLES COLLAPSED OVER EXPERIMENTERS

	CONTROL	$.50	$1.50	$5.00
Interesting				
RP	−1.43	1.23	−0.86	−1.18
E	−1.00	−0.86	1.32	2.41
Fun				
RP	−1.43	0.76	−0.81	−1.10
E	−1.28	−0.80	1.62	1.55
Fun plus interesting				
RP	−2.71	1.81	−1.62	−2.19
E	−2.14	−1.80	3.24	3.95
Pleasant				
RP	0.77	1.18	0.82	1.55
E	0.93	0.86	2.14	2.55
Learn anything				
RP	−0.37	−0.50	−2.00	−0.32
E	−2.27	−0.10	−0.41	−0.64
Recommend				
RP	2.53	2.50	1.59	2.27
E	2.33	2.38	2.50	3.56
Mood				
RP	1.83	2.18	2.27	3.41
E	2.83	2.19	3.32	3.36

Note. − Scores from single questions range from −5 (extremely negative toward the task) to +5 (extremely positive). Fun plus interesting can range from −10 to +10. RP = role play; E = essay.

Our major hypotheses concerned the differential effects of pressure for compliance in the role-playing and essay-writing situations. Specifically, it was anticipated that subjects who engaged in a face-to-face confrontation (role play) would show a *negative* relationship between money offered for the role playing and attitude change. Thus subjects offered $.50 to role play should show maximal change, followed by subjects offered $1.50, and then those offered $5; the control subjects should, of course, be lowest.

Subjects who had written counterattitudinal essays, on the other hand, should show exactly the opposite trend. In this case, those subjects paid $5 should be most positive toward the task, followed in order by subjects paid $1.50, subjects paid $.50, and control subjects. In other words, the hypothesis anticipates a *positive* relationship between attitude change and money for subjects who wrote essays.

Figures 1 and 2 reveal two facts. First, it can be seen that subjects who adopted a counterattitudinal position, whether this was done by publicly announcing the position or by privately writing an essay adopting the position, changed their attitudes to bring them into line with the counterattitudinal position. That is, they felt that the experiment had been relatively more fun and interesting than did control subjects.

Moreover, both hypotheses are strongly confirmed. The amount of money offered to adopt this counterattitudinal position had sharply different effects for role players and essay writers. When a subject is asked to publicly adopt a position which he does not privately believe in a face-to-face confrontation, he changes his attitude less if he is paid large amounts of money to adopt this position. Thus subjects paid $5 thought that the experiment was much less interesting and fun than did subjects paid $.50. An analysis of variance showed that the test for linear trend in the role-playing conditions was significant at the .05 level or better (see Table 2).

When a subject is asked to write a private essay which disagrees with his beliefs, however, the effect is exactly the opposite. The more the subject is paid to write this essay, the more his attitude changes in the direction of the position he is adopting. Thus, subjects paid $5 thought the experiment was more fun and interesting than did subjects paid $.50. Again an analysis of variance shows a significant linear trend in the hypothesized direction (see Table 2).

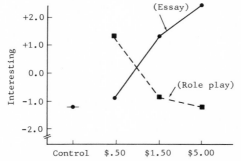

Fig. 1. Responses to posttest question on interesting. (The value drawn for the control group represents the average on all control groups.)

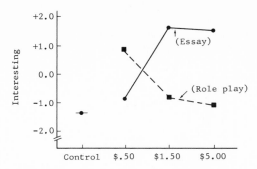

Fig. 2. Responses to posttest question on fun. (The value drawn for the control group represents the average of all control groups.)

In general, essay subjects evidenced more attitude change. This finding should be interpreted with some caution, however. A glance at Figures 1 and 2 suggests that, if the study had used only $.50 incentives, it would have been the role-play subjects who evidenced the most attitude change.

As can be seen from the last line in Table 2, the two a priori hypotheses and the role play-essay main effect account for most of the between-cell variance for fun and interesting. The fact that these 3 degrees of freedom (out of a total of 15) account for so much of the variance indicates the unimportance of experimenter main effects and higher order interactions.

As Festinger and Carlsmith found, this effect seems to be quite specific to the particular words used in adopting the counterattitudinal position. When subjects were asked how pleasant the experiment had been, or how much they had learned from it, or whether they would recommend it to a friend, there were no effects in the role-playing conditions, and only one significant effect in the essay-writing condition (see Tables 1 and 2). Only the questions asking the subjects how interesting and how much fun the experiment had been seem to show the effects of role playing which are predicted.

Subjects were also asked to rate their general mood, and on this question an interesting trend appears. Although the effect of incentive is not significant for either essay-writing or role-playing subjects taken individually, the trend is identical in both cases, so that there is a significant main effect of money. As inspection of Table 1 shows, the more subjects were paid, the better the mood they were in at the end of the experiment, irrespective of whether they were paid to write essays or to engage in face-to-face role playing. Such an effect may seem hardly surprising for the subjects who wrote essays. Essay subjects said that they were in a better mood after they had been paid $5; they also said that the experiment had been more fun and more interesting.

However, subjects who had engaged in face-to-face role playing and were paid $5 said that they were in a better mood, but thought that the experiment had been *less* fun and *less* interesting than subjects paid $.50. Thus, the results for essay-writing subjects might be interpreted as a simple generalization: they had been paid more money, were consequently in a better mood, and consequently rated the experiment as more fun and more interesting. Such a possible effect is,

Table 2 A PRIORI HYPOTHESES FOR POSTTEST VARIABLES PLUS MAIN EFFECT FOR ROLE PLAY-ESSAY

	INTERESTING	FUN	FUN PLUS INTERESTING	PLEASANT	LEARN ANYTHING	RECOMMEND	GENERAL MOOD
Role play, rank-order linear trend	8.1**	5.4*	7.1*	<1	<1	<1	<1
Essay, rank-order linear trend	18.1***	13.6***	19.3***	8.5***	1.6	1.6	2.0
Role play versus essay (from Table 3)	5.0*	4.0*	5.7*	2.7	<1	1.0	2.9
Percentage of between-cell variance contributed by 3 hypotheses	73	73	74	63	23	23	20

Note. – Unweighted mean solution. Error term from Experimenter × Role Play-Essay × Money analysis (Table 3).
* $p < .05$.
** $p < .01$.
*** $p < .005$.

Table 3 EXPERIMENTER, ROLE PLAY-ESSAY, AND MONEY STANDARD ANALYSES ($2 \times 2 \times 4$ ANALYSIS OF VARIANCE)

SOURCE	df	INTERESTING	FUN	FUN PLUS INTERESTING	PLEASANT	LEARN ANYTHING	RECOMMEND	MOOD
Role play versus essay	1	5.05*	3.98*	5.73*	2.69	<1	1.02	2.90
Money	3	3.05*	2.90*	3.42*	2.60	<1	<1	3.17*
Interaction	3	7.04**	4.74**	7.15**	1.28	1.60	<1	<1
MS_e		9.91	9.75	31.64	5.14	15.67	10.05	4.22
df error		175	167[a]	167[a]	175	175	175	175

Note. – Since none of the experimenter main effects and none of the experimenter interactions reached the .05 level (only 1 of 28 reached the .10 level), they have been omitted from the table. The unweighted mean solution was used.
[a] The fun measure was not included in the posttest until 8 subjects (all in different cells) had been run. Consequently the N for fun and for fun plus interesting is only 183.
* $p < .05$.
** $p < .01$.

of course, impossible for the role-playing subjects. The more they were paid, the better the mood they were in, but the less they thought the experiment was fun and interesting. Such a finding is especially interesting in view of the interpretation of the results of Festinger and Carlsmith offered by several writers (e.g., Elms & Janis, 1965) which focuses on the hypothesis that subjects paid $20 failed to show attitude change because they felt anxious or guilty. Insofar as this question about mood can tap some of these presumed feelings, we find that contrary to this hypothesis, the more subjects are paid for performing a task like this, the better they feel.

Role-Play and Essay Performance

Evidence on the subjects' actual performances was gathered when all three authors independently rated the essays and transcripts of the role plays. Transcriptions of role-play performance were rated on the following six scales:

1. Persuasiveness and emphasis before the accomplice remarks that she has heard the task is dull.
2. Persuasiveness and emphasis after remark.
3. Overall positiveness.
4. Overall persuasiveness and conviction.
5. Percent of time spent on assigned topic.
6. Dissociation of self from content of message.

Ratings by the accomplice are also available on role-play subjects for the first four scales and for:

5. Apparent conflict.
6. Signs of discomfort.

Essays were rated on the following four scales:

1. Emphasis used in making points.
2. The extent to which the subject went beyond the statements given and created reasons in support of his general theme.
3. Overall quality and persuasiveness.
4. Apparent effort (with an attempt to control for ability).

It was anticipated that, if any differences were found at all, high incentives should improve the quality of both role-play and essay performance. (Control groups were, of course, omitted from all analyses, and separate analyses were performed for essay and role-play measures.) The interjudge reliabilities were typically in the 70s and 80s, and the various performance measures were highly correlated among themselves. None of these ratings of role-play transcripts showed even a .10 trend in any analysis of variance. Similarly, evaluations of the content of the essays show no glimmer of a difference among treatment groups. Also, there is no evidence that any of the measures of role-play or essay performance were correlated with posttest attitudes. According to the ratings made by the accomplice, role-play subjects showed highest conflict when they were paid only $.50 (the $F = 5.58$, $p < .01$, for the 2×3 Experimenter $\times$

Money analysis of variance). But this is the only "quality of performance" accomplice rating which shows any sign of a money effect.

Experimenter Effects

The results from the two experimenters are remarkably similar. The Fs for experimenter main effects and experimenter interactions are, in general, smaller than might be expected by chance. There are two variables, however, which produced significant experimenter effects: the accomplice's ratings of conflict (necessarily for role-play subjects only since it is an accomplice rating) and the "number of words used once" measure. According to the accomplice's ratings of conflict, subjects run by BEC indicated more conflict than those run by JMC ($p < .05$). Since the role play occurred before the subject met the posttester, we can safely assume the effect was created in the experimental manipulations and not in the posttest. Posttest attitudes show no parallel trend.

Subjects were told to use four words: interesting, exciting, enjoyable, and fun. Each role play and essay was scored for the number of these words which were used at least once. Both role-play ($p < .05$) and essay ($p < .01$) subjects run by BEC used more words than subjects run by JMC in both conditions. This effect is easily understood in terms of the heavier emphasis placed on the four words by BEC. In contrast to JMC, he asked the subjects to repeat the words back to him after he had stated them to the subjects. For the *role-play subjects only*, subjects run by JMC tended to use more words in high-incentive conditions, while BEC's subjects show no such trend (interaction $p < .05$). The attitude data show no patterns similar to any of those revealed by the number of words measure.

DISCUSSION

As can be seen in Figures 1 and 2, the major hypotheses from the study have been dramatically confirmed. There is one set of circumstances where increasing pressure for compliance leads to smaller amounts of attitude change. A subject who was enticed to make a patently false statement before a peer who believed the subject was sincere showed less attitude change with increased pressure for compliance. Figures 1 and 2 clearly indicate that the comparison between the $.50 group and the $1.50 group is the more crucial for role-play subjects. The highly significant difference between these two relatively small rewards represents a very strong replication of the original Festinger and Carlsmith study. These results, taken in conjunction with those of Cohen (Brehm & Cohen, 1962), make it highly unlikely that the original Festinger and Carlsmith result is an artifact of the unusual magnitude of the $20 reward.

It is equally clear, however, that there is another set of circumstances in which increasing pressure for compliance produces more attitude change. A subject who wrote an anonymous essay (to be read only by the experimenter) showed more attitude change with increasing pressure for compliance. This dramatic interaction is quite consistent with the theory outlined in the introduction.

The results for the experimenter manipulation are also encouraging. The two experimenters produced remarkably similar effects. It is clearly the case that the differing theoretical orientations of the experimenters—and their somewhat different expectations about the outcomes—had no effect whatsoever on attitude change.

What remains unspecified, however, is the crucial difference between the role-play and essay-writing conditions. The following list describes just a few of the many components in the complex manipulation used in this study: The essays were written while the role plays were oral; the role-play sessions lasted for a maximum of 2 minutes while the essay sessions lasted for a maximum of 17 minutes; as a result of the differing justifications used to entice compliance, role-play subjects performed under somewhat more "hectic" or "crisis" circumstances than essay subjects; finally, if looked at from the subjects' perspective, the social consequences or implications of the compliant act differed greatly between the two conditions. In the essay condition, the only reader of the essays would be the experimenter, who understood why the essay had been written. In the role-play condition, however, the audience—the experimental accomplice—presumably believed that the subject was sincere when he said that the task was fun, interesting, exciting, and enjoyable. It seems quite clear that the latter condition is more dissonance producing.

What is unclear from dissonance theory, however, is why the essay condition should show an *increasing* amount of attitude change with increased incentive. If there is no dissonance at all produced in the essay condition, then the different incentives should have no effect on attitude change—there should, in fact, be no attitude change. If the amount of effort is greater for high-incentive subjects, then dissonance theory can predict a positive relationship between the amount of incentive and attitude change. *If* subjects in the high incentive conditions exerted more effort, then this greater effort should lead to greater dissonance in the high-incentive conditions, and, consequently, greater attitude change. A long and careful examination of both essays and role-play performance, however, unearthed no evidence whatsoever that the high-incentive essays were in any way superior. The fact that the finished product in the high-incentive condition is not better, of course, does not imply that the students did not try harder. Subjects were given four words to repeat, and there was little else that they could do other than repeat the four words and include them in complete sentences. It is possible that an increased effort in the high-incentive condition would not be reflected in higher quality essays.

It is probably necessary to turn somewhere other than dissonance theory for an explanation of the positive relationship between pressure for compliance and attitude change. One very plausible explanation of our results for the essay-writing subjects is a simple generalization phenomenon. We know that the more subjects were paid the better the mood they were in. It would not be surprising if this good mood generalized to the task they had been doing, so that they would report that the task had been more fun and interesting. This explanation would assume that in the role-playing conditions, this tendency to generalize was overcome by the dissonance produced.

Alternatively, it is possible that the theoretical orientation proposed by Hovland (Hovland, Lumsdaine, & Sheffield, 1949) and Janis (Janis & Gilmore,

1965) is needed in order to explain the attitude change in the essay condition. But, as we understand them, these theories also must predict that the performance in the high-incentive condition will be superior in some way to the performance in low-pressure conditions. Nor do they make clear why the opposite effect should be found in the role-play conditions.

One final point should be made about the sensitivity of the incentive manipulation. A quick glance at Figures 1 and 2 indicates that the results would have appeared quite different had the $.50 group been omitted. There would have been no incentive effects for either essay or role-play subjects, and there would have remained only the main effect indicating that essay subjects showed more attitude change than role-play subjects.

Finally, it should be noted that our results for the role-playing subjects are consistent with several other experiments using different techniques for varying pressure for compliance. Studies on the use of strong or weak threats to induce counterattitudinal behavior (Aronson & Carlsmith, 1963; Freedman, 1965; Turner & Wright, 1965) have consistently shown more attitude change when weaker pressures are applied for compliance. Another kind of evidence comes from experiments by Freedman (1963) in which he shows more attitude change when little justification is provided for the counterattitudinal behavior than when high justification is provided.

REFERENCES

Aronson, E., & Carlsmith, J. M. Effect of the severity of threat on the devaluation of forbidden behavior. *Journal of Abnormal and Social Psychology,* 1963, *66*, 584–88.

Brehm, J. W., & Cohen, A. R. *Explorations in cognitive dissonance.* New York: Wiley, 1962.

Elms, A., & Janis, I. Counter-norm attitudes induced by consonant versus dissonant conditions of role-playing. *Journal of Experimental Research in Personality*, 1965, *1*, 50–60.

Festinger, L. *A theory of cognitive dissonance.* Stanford: Stanford University Press, 1957.

Festinger, L., & Carlsmith, J. M. Cognitive consequences of forced compliance. *Journal of Abnormal and Social Psychology*, 1959, *58*, 203–10.

Freedman, J. L. Attitudinal effects of inadequate justification. *Journal of Personality,* 1963, *31*, 371–85.

Freedman, J. L. Long-term behavior effects of cognitive dissonance. *Journal of Experimental Social Psychology*, 1965, *1* 145–55.

Hovland, C. I., Lumsdaine, A. A., & Sheffield, F. D. *Experiments on mass communication.* Princeton: Princeton University Press, 1949.

Janis, I. L., & Gilmore, J. B. The influence of incentive conditions on the success of role playing in modifying attitudes. *Journal of Personality and Social Psychology*, 1965, *1*, 17–27.

Kelman, H. C. Attitude change as a function of response restriction. *Human Relations*, 1953, *6*, 185–214.

Nuttin, J. M., Jr. Dissonant evidence about dissonance theory. Paper read at Second Conference of Experimental Social Psychologists in Europe, Frascati, Italy, 1964.

Rosenberg, M. J. When dissonance fails: On eliminating evaluation apprehension from attitude measurement. *Journal of Personality and Social Psychology*, 1965, *1*, 28–42.

Rosenthal, R. On the social psychology of the psychological experiment: The experimenter's hypothesis as unintended determinant of experimental results. *American Scientist*, 1963, *51*, 268–83.

Turner, E. A., & Wright, J. C. Effects of severity of threat and perceived availability on the attractiveness of objects *Journal of Personality and Social Psychology*, 1965, *2*, 128–32.

The Temporal Sequence of Post-Decision Processes

ELAINE WALSTER

This experiment was performed in order to obtain evidence bearing directly on the hypothesis that immediately following a decision there is a temporary period in which the person experiences regret. The clearest and most direct way in which this hypothesis can be examined is to have subjects make a decision and then to remeasure the attractiveness of the alternatives at varying intervals of time following the decision. If the regret phenomenon occurs, one should find that in a period soon after the decision the chosen alternative becomes *less* attractive and the rejected alternative *more* attractive than they had been before the decision. After this, of course, if the theory is correct, one would obtain the usual evidence of dissonance reduction.

The consideration of such a design, however, brings us face to face with a difficult problem. There have been many studies concerned with post-decision dissonance reduction, all of which have remeasured the attractiveness of the alternatives very soon after the decision. They have all yielded evidence that dissonance reduction occurs. Clearly, if we are to maintain the hypothesis about the regret period in the face of the evidence from these experiments, we are forced to contend that, at least in those experiments, the regret period was very fleeting indeed. The question of design then becomes: How can we construct a decision situation in which the regret phase in the post-decision process is relatively long-lasting?

If one examines the characteristic situation used in previous experiments, some clues concerning the answer to this question may be obtained. Typically, these experiments have presented subjects with a choice between two alternatives, both of which were positive in nature and possessed no negative attributes at all. If a person is offered a choice between two phonograph records as a gift, for example, even if one of them is not very well liked, there is nothing negative about having it. At a minimum, if the person does not like the gift he gets, he can throw it away and he is no worse off than before. In addition, of course, the decision is not a very important one for the person. It has few consequences of any lasting nature for him. It seems reasonable to conjecture that in this kind of situation dissonance reduction proceeds very rapidly and regret is very momentary.

The attempt was made, consequently, to find a situation in which subjects could be offered a decision between alternatives that had both positive and negative aspects, that would be reasonably important to the subject, and in which the decision would have lasting consequences. Furthermore, one would want to be able to employ this decision situation in a well-controlled context. It would be necessary to measure the attractiveness of the alternatives before the decision and, assigning subjects to conditions at random, remeasure the attractiveness at different lengths of time after the decision. One would also want to control the activity of the subject and his interactions with others during the entire period between initial measurement and final measurement.

Fortunately, we were able to obtain the cooperation of the Sixth Army District Reception Center at Fort Ord, California. Arrangements were made to use as subjects in the experiment men who were drafted into the Army. They were each to be given a choice of which of two occupational specialties they wanted to be assigned to for their two years in the service. Certainly, such a decision, affecting two years of their lives, is reasonably important; the descriptions of the occupational specialties could be written so as to emphasize both positive and negative aspects of each alternative; and dissonance reduction in this situation should not be a particularly easy affair. In short, this seemed a reasonable situation for testing the validity of the hypothesis about post-decision regret. The details of, and the reasons for, the experimental procedure are given below.

PROCEDURE

Two hundred and seventy-seven draftees who reported for processing at the Fort Ord Reception Center were used as subjects. Each subject was run in the experiment within a day or two of his arrival at the Reception Center—before he had gone far enough in his initial processing to have any information about his probable job assignment in the Army. Men who had enlisted, or who for any other reason had something to say about their job assignment, were excluded from the sample. Men were made available for the experiment on weekends and on days when there were so many arrivals at the Reception Center that not all of them could be processed. In this way, the study did not interfere with the normal processing activity at the Reception Center, nor did it prolong the time any man spent there.

The Army personnel were asked to select men to assign to the study who had had at least some high school education but who had not completed college. It was felt that the job selections to be offered would be most appropriate for men with intermediate education. Frequently, however, information on educational level was not available to the Army personnel at the time they assigned men to the study and so this selection on educational criteria was not rigorous. In our total sample, six subjects had had no high school education at all and fifteen had completed college.

Early in the course of running the experiment it was realized that most of the alien draftees and many of the Spanish-speaking men had difficulty understanding the instructions and had trouble in making the ratings required of them. Consequently, we requested the Army personnel to exclude such subjects in the future. Nineteen Spanish-speaking and four alien draftees who had already been run in the experiment were discarded from the sample.

Five subjects at a time were run through the experiment. A uniformed driver met the five men at the Reception Center and drove them to the experimental building, about ten minutes away. During the drive he told them that they had been randomly selected for a special job placement program that the Army was conducting and that they would receive a definite job assignment some time during the day. The driver also commented that although the jobs the special placement program had to offer were, perhaps, not as good as those they might have in civilian life, they were better than those the men could hope to get under the regular job placement program. These comments were intended to make the men believe that, whatever job they were assigned that day, it was definite and as good as or better than anything else they could get.

As soon as the driver arrived at the experimental building, he assembled the men and introduced them to the two experimenters standing in the doorway. Experimenter 1 then explained to the men:

As he has probably told you, we're working for the Army on a special experimental program of job placement. You were more or less randomly selected from men in your educational category. Today, I'm going to interview each one of you. I can only see one of you at a time, so while you're waiting for your interview, Miss Turner (Experimenter 2) will be getting some other necessary information from you. She'll ask you to fill out some questionnaires concerning the kind of jobs you've held, the things you like and dislike in a job, and so forth.

O.K. [*Pointing to the closest man*] I'll be seeing you first. Miss Turner will tell the rest of you what to do.

The first subject was then led into the large room where Experimenter 1 conducted all the interviewing. Experimenter 2 took each of the other four men to separate small cubicles in the experimental building. When all four men had been seated, Experimenter 2 distributed Questionnaire 1 which asked the men about their previous job and educational experience.

At the same time, in the main experimental room, Experimenter 1 asked the first subject to be seated. On the table in front of the subject's chair was a large chart titled "How Much Would You Like to Work at This Job in the Army for the Next Two Years?" Underneath the title was a 31-point scale. The highest point on the scale (Point 1) was labeled "Would like extremely much." Point 31 was labeled "Would dislike extremely much."

Experimenter 1 then explained to the subject:

Today we're interested in getting a fairly precise idea of how attractive a number of jobs that the Army is especially interested in seem to you. So, I'll tell you a little bit more about 10 different jobs. I'd like you to think about these jobs and decide how much you'd like to work at each one during your next two years in the Army. Do take into account all those personal things and preferences that make you want one job more than another. You will be assigned to one of these jobs, and I'll be able to tell you which one you got before you leave today.

To help you to give us a pretty clear idea of how you feel about each of these jobs, we've made up this scale.

The scale on the chart was then explained to the subject; some civilian job titles, printed on arrow-shaped cards, were placed at various points on the scale by the experimenter to demonstrate further how the scale was to be used. At this point, the subject was encouraged to ask questions.

Experimenter 1 then picked up a packet of 10 arrow-shaped cards, each having an Army job title and job description printed on it. She told the subject:

Now whichever of these jobs you're assigned to, you will have to go to school for from six to eight weeks to learn how to do that job in the Army manner.

Now I'll read the job description that's printed on each arrow along with you. Then take your time and decide how much you like each job, and then put the arrow at the right spot. If you should change your mind as we go along, and feel that some job should be rated higher or lower, naturally, it's all right to change that job's position. However, it's probably a good idea to reread the description of the job you're thinking of changing, because sometimes the reason you think you've made a mistake is that you've forgotten some of the things that are involved in the job.

Take as much time as you want. We're anxious to get a really accurate idea both of how much you like each job relative to the others, and how much you like each job absolutely; that is, exactly at which of the points on the scale you think it belongs.

Experimenter 1 then read the 10 job titles and descriptions to the subject, pausing after each description so the subject could place a titled arrow at the appropriate point on the scale.

These job descriptions were written so that each job appeared to have a few really desirable and a few really undesirable features. It was hoped that this obvious mixture of good and bad elements in each job would increase the amount of dissonance subjects experienced and make dissonance reduction more difficult.

When the subject had finished placing all 10 job arrows, the experimenter suggested:

Now that you've seen all the jobs, it's probably a good idea to reread the job descriptions and make sure you get everything just where you want it. Sometimes we just can't give you the jobs you like most, and so we'd like to know how you feel about every one of the jobs.

When this subject had finished his final ratings of the jobs, Experimenter 1 took him to a separate cubicle and then returned to the large experimental room to record where on the 31-point scale he had rated each of the 10 jobs. This initial interview usually took 12 to 15 minutes.

Experimenter 1 then called in the second subject from his cubicle to the large experimental room and followed a procedure identical to that followed for the first subject. At the same time, Experimenter 2 asked Subject 1 to fill out Questionnaire 1, which the other subjects had completed earlier, and asked Subjects 3 through 5 to fill out Questionnnaire 2.

Approximately every 15 minutes another subject was interviewed by Experimenter 1 and the remaining subjects were given the next in a series of four questionnaires to fill out. The purpose of these questionnaires was primarily to keep the subject occupied while Experimenter 1 was interviewing the other men. Also, the questionnaires, taken from material contained in the subtests of the Strong Vocational Interest Inventory, helped make the later job selection seem more plausible.

Subjects filled out questionnaires and were interviewed according to the following sequence:

TIME SCHEDULE	SUBJECT 1	SUBJECT 2	SUBJECT 3	SUBJECT 4	SUBJECT 5
1st 15 min.	Interview	Ques. 1	Ques. 1	Ques. 1	Ques. 1
2nd 15 min.	Ques. 1	Interview	Ques. 2	Ques. 2	Ques. 2
3rd 15 min.	Ques. 2	Ques. 2	Interview	Ques. 3	Ques. 3
4th 15 min.	Ques. 3	Ques. 3	Ques. 3	Interview	Ques. 4
5th 15 min.	Ques. 4	Ques. 4	Ques. 4	Ques. 4	Interview

The purpose of the initial interview was to obtain a measure of how each subject evaluated each job before he was faced with a decision. The next step was to select two jobs and to offer the subject a choice between them. Ideally, it would have been desirable to offer each subject a choice between jobs that he had rated near the middle of the scale, with the initial ratings separated by a constant amount and identical for all subjects. To approach this as closely as possible without discarding too many subjects, Experimenter 2 examined the initial ratings of each subject and selected the two jobs he should be offered according to the following criteria:

1. The job the subject liked best was never used as one of the alternatives for choice. Similarly, none of the three least attractive jobs was used. When possible, the next to the most attractive job was also avoided.

2. No job rated above 6 on the attractiveness scale ("Would like very much") or below 18 (between "Would like and dislike equally" and "Would dislike fairly much") was ever offered as one of the two choice alternatives.

3. Within the above restrictions, two jobs were selected to offer the subject that were rated approximately five units apart on the 31-point scale. If there were no two jobs rated five units apart that satisfied the other criteria, jobs rated six units apart were used. If this too were not possible, jobs rated four units apart, seven units apart, or three units apart were used.

If none of these conditions could be met, the subject was not used in the experiment. Altogether, ten subjects were discarded because no pair of jobs could be offered them under the above set of restrictions.

After Experimenter 2 had made the selection of which jobs should be offered to each subject, Experimenter 1 called the first subject back into the experimental room.

She stated:

Well, by now we can give you some definite information about your Army assignment for the next two years. We've examined all the preferences you expressed to me, the scores on the tests you took for Miss Turner, and considered your background information and job experience.

You understand that in the Army, job assignment is in large part determined by what jobs the Army has to fill at any given time. In this experimental job placement program, we are trying to work out a really good compromise between what you can do, what you want to do, and what jobs we have to fill. The very best we can do for you, considering your test scores and the Army's needs, is to offer you a choice between these two jobs.

Experimenter 1 then handed the subject the arrows (containing job titles and job descriptions) for the two jobs between which he was to decide and reread the descriptions to him.

Experimenter 1 then concluded: "As soon as you decide which of the two jobs you want, tell me. I can definitely assign you to whichever one you choose for your time in the Army."

If the subject asked why he had not been offered the job he ranked first in the initial interview, Experimenter 1 told him that the main determinant could have been his test scores, the Army's current needs, or the qualifications of the other draftees. For specific information he was told that he would have to see Miss Turner. It was stressed, however, that these were the only jobs available to him.

Subjects were randomly assigned to one of four experimental conditions, the only difference between the conditions being the interval of time allowed to elapse between the decision and the remeasurement of the attractiveness of the jobs. One-fourth of the subjects rerated the jobs immediately after the decision. The others rerated the jobs after an interval of four minutes, 15 minutes, or 90 minutes.

If the subject was assigned to the "Immediate Condition," the experimenter continued:

O.K. There are a couple of other things I'd like you to do. The next thing I'd like you to do will in no way affect your Army assignment, but it will help us in developing and improving our job placement program.

By now you've had quite a bit of time to think about these jobs [*pointing to the 10 jobs*], and jobs in general, and you've probably thought of a lot of things that make a job good or bad that just didn't occur to you before. What we'd like you to do is to rerate all these jobs now that you've had a reasonable length of time to think about them.

The subject was then handed a 10-page questionnaire, each page exactly like the chart on which he had rated the jobs during his first interview.

Experimenter 1 continued:

The scale they've provided is just like the one you used earlier, only there's a separate rating page for each job. If you'd write the job number up at the top of each page, we'd know which one you are talking about. Then just draw an arrow at that place which most accurately represents how you feel about each job, *right at this moment*.

If the subject had been assigned to the four-minute, 15-minute, or 90-minute condition, then, after saying "O.K. There are a couple of other things I'd like you to do," Experimenter 1 added, "but there's some work I have to do first. If you'd just wait 'right here' (four-minute condition), or 'across the hall in your room' (15-minute and 90-minute conditions), I'll get back to you just as soon as I can. Sometimes it takes quite a while. Don't worry, I haven't forgotten you." The experimenter then left the subject alone with nothing to do for the appropriate number of minutes.

When Experimenter 1 returned (after four minutes, 15 minutes, or 90 minutes), she followed the same procedure described for the immediate condition.

RESULTS

If the phenomenon of post-decision regret is a real one, and if evidence of it exists in this experiment, it should be reflected in a drawing together of the two alternatives soon after the decision is made. That is, sometime in the immediate post-decision period the chosen alternative should *decrease* in attractiveness and the rejected alternative *increase* in attractiveness. This, of course, should be followed by the usual spreading apart of the alternatives that is the normal evidence of dissonance reduction.

The experiment was designed in ignorance, of course, of the time interval at which post-decision regret would be at its maximum. That is, it was theoretically conceivable that regret would be seen as soon as the decision was made. It was also theoretically conceivable that it could take a little time before the regret would develop to measurable quantities. For this reason we included an immediate condition, a four-minute-delay condition, and a 15-minute-delay condition. Conceivably, it could take as long as 15 minutes, or even longer, for regret to develop. We simply did not know ahead of time. The 90-minute condition was included to make sure that we had at least one interval long enough for recovery from regret to occur and for the effects of dissonance reduction to be evident. The interval of 90 minutes was chosen as the longest time that it seemed at all feasible to keep a person sitting alone in a small room with nothing to do but wait.

Before we look at the data, there is one decision that must be made about the analysis. Of the 244 subjects from whom usable data were obtained, 51 (21 per cent), when asked to make a choice, chose the job that they had originally rated as the *less* attractive of the two they were offered. This is, of course, a rather high percentage of such inversions. In any experiment of this type a certain number of inversions will occur because new considerations of a major character occur to the subject between the time of making the rating and the time of making the decision. There are also, usually, some subjects who make the ratings on a rather abstract basis, but who, when faced with the decision, suddenly consider the alternatives in a new light of reality. In addition to this, in the current experiment there were undoubtedly many subjects who simply did not understand the rating scale fully, some who did not listen to or did not adequately comprehend the job descriptions, and some who were simply not interested. It must be remembered that the subjects comprised a very hetero-geneous population, many of them being run through the experiment on the very first day that they reported to the Army Reception Center.

Whatever the reasons for the inversions, they represent a difficulty for analysis. It represents something of a distortion to disregard them or simply to throw them together for analysis with data from other subjects. Since there are so many subjects who show inversions, their data will be presented separately. Since these subjects come about equally from all conditions, this does not interfere with any comparison among the four conditions and, by presenting their data separately, we can determine whether they show the same trends as the other subjects. The data for the 193 subjects who chose the alternative they had rated as *more* attractive will be presented first, and then the other data will be examined for comparison.

Table 5.2 presents the data on ratings of the chosen and rejected alternatives for the major portion of the sample, namely, those who chose the job they had originally rated as more desirable. The first two columns of figures show the pre-decision ratings of the two alternatives. It is, of course, no surprise that these

Table 5.2 MEAN RATINGS OF CHOSEN AND REJECTED ALTERNATIVES FOR SUBJECTS WHO CHOSE THE MORE ATTRACTIVE JOB

EXPERIMENTAL CONDITION	PRE-DECISION RATINGS		CHANGE FROM PRE-DECISION TO POST-DECISION RATINGS		CHANGE IN DISCREPANCY
	CHOSEN	REJECTED	CHOSEN	REJECTED	
Immediate (N = 48)	9.80	15.09	.70	.00	.71
Four Minutes (N = 48)	9.79	15.02	−.37	−.97	−1.34
Fifteen Minutes (N = 48)	10.04	14.98	1.56	.58	2.14
Ninety Minutes (N = 49)	9.91	14.84	.67	−.36	.31

Note: Change scores are indicated as positive if they are in the direction of dissonance reduction and as negative if they are in the opposite direction. Thus, changes toward greater attractiveness of the chosen alternative and toward less attractiveness of the rejected alternative are scored as positive changes.

figures are so similar from condition to condition, since there were rather narrow limits within which the two jobs offered could have been rated and, in addition, subjects were assigned to conditions at random. The third and fourth columns of figures show the changes from the pre-decision to the post-decision ratings of each alternative. The last column shows the total amount of dissonance reduction that occurred.

A glance at the figures in this last column of Table 5.2 shows that there is, indeed, a period of post-decision regret followed by appreciable dissonance reduction. In the condition in which the alternatives were rerated immediately after the decision, there is a relatively small change of .71 in the direction of dissonance reduction, a change that is not significantly different from zero ($t = 1.38$). Those subjects who rerated the jobs after a four-minute delay period show the opposite of dissonance reduction, namely, regret. In this condition the chosen alternative decreases somewhat in attractiveness while the rejected alternative increases in attractiveness. The total change of −1.34 is significantly different from zero at the 7 per cent level ($t = 1.80$) and significantly different from the change obtained in the immediate condition at the 2 per cent level ($t = 2.26$).

It does, then, seem that in this experiment evidence of post-decision regret exists and that it takes a little time for this regret phenomenon to show itself. If one examines the data for those subjects who rerated the jobs after a delay of 15 minutes, one observes, furthermore, that the period of post-decision regret is, indeed, a temporary one. After 15 post-decision minutes have elapsed there is no more evidence of regret but rather clear evidence of the usual dissonance reduction. By this time the chosen alternative is rated as more attractive and the rejected alternative as less attractive than they were initially. The total change of 2.14 is significantly different from zero ($t = 2.90$) and from the four-minute condition ($t = 3.32$). It is clear that we did, indeed, obtain post-decision regret followed by dissonance reduction. The various experimental conditions are significantly different from one another in a clear and unequivocal manner. For example, an analysis of variance on all four experimental conditions yields an F of 3.99, which, for three and 189 degrees of freedom, is significant beyond the 1 per cent level.

The data for the 90-minute-delay condition, however, provide a rather surprising result. Instead of continuing to obtain dissonance reduction equal to or greater than that obtained in the 15-minute-delay condition, one finds that after 90 minutes have elapsed there is no evidence of any dissonance reduction at all. The change of .31 is not significantly different from zero and, because of increased variability in this condition, is not clearly different from either the 15-minute condition ($t = 1.69$) or the four-minute condition ($t = 1.52$). It is difficult to understand this result, although there are some good hunches that can be offered. We will, however, postpone our discussion of the perplexing 90-minute condition temporarily.

Let us first turn our attention to the data obtained from those subjects who chose the job they had initially rated as the less attractive of the two they were offered. These data are presented in Table 5.3. It is clear from a glance at the last column in the table, which presents the total change in discrepancy between the two alternatives, that the absolute magnitude of these changes is very large.

Table 5.3   MEAN RATINGS OF CHOSEN AND REJECTED ALTERNATIVES FOR
SUBJECTS WHO CHOSE THE LESS ATTRACTIVE JOB

EXPERIMENTAL CONDITION	PRE-DECISION RATINGS		CHANGE FROM PRE-DECISION TO POST-DECISION RATINGS		CHANGE IN DISCREPANCY
	CHOSEN	REJECTED	CHOSEN	REJECTED	
Immediate (N = 12)	14.78	10.18	4.70	2.03	6.73
Four minutes (N = 13)	14.93	10.62	1.58	3.53	5.11
Fifteen Minutes (N = 13)	14.46	10.03	3.50	3.62	7.12
Ninety Minutes (N = 13)	15.04	10.56	2.99	2.44	5.43

Undoubtedly, this is simply a reflection of the fact that for these subjects the initial rating is relatively meaningless. For these data one must simply ignore the absolute magnitude of the results and look just at the comparison among conditions. It may be seen that the results go in exactly the same direction as the previous results we discussed. From the immediate condition to the four-minute condition the change in discrepancy decreases, from four minutes to 15 minutes it increases, and by 90 minutes it has decreased again. The numbers of cases are rather small, and the variability for these subjects is quite large. None of these differences is statistically significant. The only point to be made is that these subjects show largely the same pattern of results as the others, even duplicating the perplexing problem of the 90-minute condition.

What are some of the possible reasons for the results from the 90-minute condition? The first inclination, on obtaining a result that is so surprising from a theoretical point of view, is to suspect some purely technical methodological inadequacy. In this particular experiment there is a natural inclination to suspect that in the 90-minute condition, the very long period of sitting alone in a small room with nothing to do may have introduced boredom, anger, resentment, or any of a number of other factors that might have contributed to the obtained result. This may or may not be true, but the best judgment we can make is that it is not true. Let us look closely at some aspects of the "boredom" explanation to see why this judgment seems reasonable.

It is conceivable that after 90 minutes of sitting alone in a small room, these subjects felt angry with the Army. This experience may have confirmed all their worst expectations, with the result that they may have felt that everything in the Army is terrible, including the possible jobs. If this explanation had any validity at all, we would expect that the average post-decision rating of the jobs not involved in the choice would be considerably lower for subjects in the 90-minute-delay condition than for subjects in the other conditions. This, however, is not the case. The average post-decision ratings of the jobs not involved in the choice were 15.89, 15.35, 15.51, and 15.51 for the four conditions—differences which are certainly indistinguishable from one another.

Another possible aspect of the "boredom" explanation is that being bored and having lost interest in the whole proceedings, the subjects in the 90-minute-delay condition stop discriminating among jobs on the post-decision ratings. That is, out of boredom or, perhaps, anger, they make their second ratings in a perfunctory manner, essentially saying that everything is the same. To check on this possibility we computed the standard deviation of each subject's post-decision ratings of the jobs. If they stopped cooperating and stopped discriminating among jobs, we would expect this to be reflected in a smaller dispersion of the individual's ratings. This again is not true. The four conditions are almost identical.

Nowhere could any evidence be found to support a contention of methodological inadequacy in the 90-minute condition. Consequently, we have come to the conclusion that it is probably a real effect. But if it is a real effect, what does it mean? Is dissonance reduction just a temporary matter? This seems unlikely. Although there has been little done concerning long-range effects of dissonance reduction, what we do know would certainly argue against the disappearance of all effects within 90 minutes. Ninety minutes may be a long time to sit doing nothing in a room but, after all, it is a short amount of time in which to expect a rather pervasive process to be completely nullified.

This still, however, leaves us with no answer to the perplexing result of the 90-minute condition. And we can give no good answer—not in the sense of an answer that can be supported with data. We can however, offer what seems to us to be a good hunch. We think the answer lies in the great difficulty of reducing dissonance in this experimental situation. Let us look at this more carefully. In choosing this particular context for doing this experiment, we were motivated primarily by our intuitive notions concerning the conditions under which regret would be rather pronounced and would last for a sufficiently long time so that we could measure it. Intuitively, it seemed to us that this would happen if the decision were important, the alternatives possessed a mixture of good and bad characteristics, and dissonance reduction was very difficult. The idea was that under such circumstances the post-decision dissonance would be large and, if dissonance reduction were difficult and took time, that focusing on the dissonance in order to reduce it would produce the regret phase. If dissonance reduction were too easy, the regret phase might be very fleeting.

We were probably very successful in creating a situation in which dissonance reduction was, indeed, difficult. At least we know that we did obtain a period in which post-decision regret appeared. We probably created a situation in which only a limited amount of dissonance could be reduced by most subjects. Under most ordinary "real-life" circumstances, the person would go talk to others about it, seek new information, and generally try to get informational and social support for the process of further reducing dissonance. In our experiment this was impossible. The person was left entirely on his own resources. There was no new information obtainable and there was no one else he could even talk to about it. It is possible that after some dissonance had been reduced, the continued focusing on the remaining dissonance without further successful dissonance reduction could produce the effect obtained in the 90-minute condition.

If this is the correct explanation, there are certain implications. If one were to set up a situation in which dissonance reduction was even more difficult, almost impossible, the effect of focusing on and unsuccessfully trying to reduce the dissonance might result in a steady increase in the importance of the dissonance and a steady narrowing of the discrepancy between the alternatives. If in our experimental situation the subjects had been provided with more leeway, people to talk to, things to read about the Army and its jobs—anything that would have aided dissonance reduction—the results of the 90-minute condition might have been different.

SUMMARY

An experiment was conducted to test the hypothesis that:

1. Shortly after having made a decision, the subject, because of the salience of dissonance, will experience a period in which the chosen alternative seems less attractive and the rejected alternative more attractive than they were prior to the decision.
2. This "regret" period will be followed by the customary dissonance-reduction process and the spreading apart of the alternatives in terms of attractiveness.

The subjects in the experiment had to make a decision that was rather important and would affect two years of their lives. Reratings of alternatives were obtained immediately after the decision for some subjects, four minutes afterward for some, 15 minutes afterward for others, and 90 minutes afterward for still others.

The data showed clear evidence of "regret" four minutes after the decision. Fifteen minutes after the decision, recovery had occurred and there was clear evidence of dissonance reduction. Surprising results were obtained from those subjects measured 90 minutes after the decision. There was no evidence here of any dissonance reduction.

11

COMPLIANCE,

OBEDIENCE,

AND ALTRUISM

Behavioral Study of Obedience

STANLEY MILGRAM

Obedience is as basic an element in the structure of social life as one can point to. Some system of authority is a requirement of all communal living, and it is only the man dwelling in isolation who is not forced to respond, through defiance or submission, to the commands of others. Obedience, as a determinant of behavior, is of particular relevance to our time. It has been reliably established that from 1933–45 millions of innocent persons were systematically slaughtered on command. Gas chambers were built, death camps were guarded, daily quotas of corpses were produced with the same efficiency as the manufacture of appliances. These inhumane policies may have originated in the mind of a single person, but they could only be carried out on a massive scale if a very large number of persons obeyed orders.

Reprinted from Journal of Abnormal and Social Psychology, 67, *1963, 371–78. Copyright 1963 by the American Psychological Association and reproduced by permission.*

Obedience is the psychological mechanism that links individual action to political purpose. It is the dispositional cement that binds men to systems of authority. Facts of recent history and observation in daily life suggest that for many persons obedience may be a deeply ingrained behavior tendency, indeed, a prepotent impulse overriding training in ethics, sympathy, and moral conduct. C. P. Snow (1961) points to its importance when he writes:

When you think of the long and gloomy history of man, you will find more hideous crimes have been committed in the name of obedience than have ever been committed in the name of rebellion. If you doubt that, read William Shirer's "Rise and Fall of the Third Reich." The German Officer Corps were brought up in the most rigorous code of obedience . . . in the name of obedience they were party to, and assisted in, the most wicked large scale actions in the history of the world [p. 24].

While the particular form of obedience dealt with in the present study has its antecedents in these episodes, it must not be thought all obedience entails acts of aggression against others. Obedience serves numerous productive functions. Indeed, the very life of society is predicated on its existence. Obedience may be ennobling and educative and refer to acts of charity and kindness, as well as to destruction.

General Procedure

A procedure was devised which seems useful as a tool for studying obedience (Milgram, 1961). It consists of ordering a naive subject to administer electric shock to a victim. A simulated shock generator is used, with 30 clearly marked voltage levels that range from 15 to 450 volts. The instrument bears verbal designations that range from Slight Shock to Danger: Severe Shock. The responses of the victim, who is a trained confederate of the experimenter, are standardized. The orders to administer shocks are given to the naive subject in the context of a "learning experiment" ostensibly set up to study the effects of punishment on memory. As the experiment proceeds the naive subject is commanded to administer increasingly more intense shocks to the victim, even to the point of reaching the level marked Danger: Servere Shock. Internal resistances become stronger, and at a certain point the subject refuses to go on with the experiment. Behavior prior to this rupture is considered "obedience," in that the subject complies with the commands of the experimenter. The point of rupture is the act of disobedience. A quantitative value is assigned to the subject's performance based on the maximum intensity shock he is willing to administer before he refuses to participate further. Thus for any particular subject and for any particular experimental condition the degree of obedience may be specified with a numerical value. The crux of the study is to systematically vary the factors believed to alter the degree of obedience to the experimental commands.

The technique allows important variables to be manipulated at several points in the experiment. One may vary aspects of the source of command, content and form of command, instrumentalities for its execution, target object, general social setting, etc. The problem, therefore, is not one of designing increasingly more numerous experimental conditions, but of selecting those that best illuminate the *process* of obedience from the sociopsychological standpoint.

Related Studies

The inquiry bears an important relation to philosophic analyses of obedience and authority (Arendt, 1958; Friedrich, 1958; Weber, 1947), an early experimental study of obedience by Frank (1944), studies in "authoritarianism" (Adorno, Frenkel-Brunswik, Levinson, & Sanford, 1950; Rokeach, 1961), and a recent series of analytic and empirical studies in social power (Cartwright, 1959). It owes much to the long concern with *suggestion* in social psychology, both in its normal forms (e.g., Binet, 1900) and in its clinical manifestations (Charcot, 1881). But it derives, in the first instance, from direct observation of a social fact; the individual who is commanded by a legitimate authority ordinarily obeys. Obedience comes easily and often. It is a ubiquitous and indispensable feature of social life.

METHOD

Subjects

The subjects were 40 males between the ages of 20 and 50, drawn from New Haven and the surrounding communities. Subjects were obtained by a newspaper advertisement and direct mail solicitation. Those who responded to the appeal believed they were to participate in a study of memory and learning at Yale University. A wide range of occupations is represented in the sample. Typical subjects were postal clerks, high school teachers, salesmen, engineers, and laborers. Subjects ranged in educational level from one who had not finished elementary school, to those who had doctorate and other professional degrees. They were paid $4.50 for their participation in the experiment. However, subjects were told that payment was simply for coming to the laboratory, and that the money was theirs no matter what happened after they arrived. Table 1 shows the proportion of age and occupational types assigned to the experimental condition.

Personnel and Locale

The experiment was conducted on the grounds of Yale University in the elegant interaction laboratory. (This detail is relevant to the perceived legitimacy of the experiment. In further variations, the experiment was dissociated from the university, with consequences for performance.) The role of experimenter was played by a 31-year-old high school teacher of biology. His manner was impassive, and his appearance somewhat stern throughout the experiment. He was dressed in a gray technician's coat. The victim was played by a 47-year-old accountant, trained for the role; he was of Irish-American stock, whom most observers found mild-mannered and likable.

Table 1 DISTRIBUTION OF AGE AND OCCUPATIONAL TYPES IN THE EXPERIMENT

OCCUPATIONS	20–29 YEARS n	30–39 YEARS n	40–50 YEARS n	PERCENTAGE OF TOTAL (OCCUPA-TIONS)
Workers, skilled and unskilled	4	5	6	37.5
Sales, business, and white-collar	3	6	7	40.0
Professional	1	5	3	22.5
Percentage of total (Age)	20	40	40	

Note. – Total N = 40

Procedure

One naive subject and one victim (an accomplice) performed in each experiment. A pretext had to be devised that would justify the administration of electric shock by the naive subject. This was effectively accomplished by the cover story. After a general introduction on the presumed relation between punishment and learning, subjects were told:

But actually, we know *very little* about the effect of punishment on learning, because almost no truly scientific studies have been made of it in human beings.

For instance, we don't know how *much* punishment is best for learning–and we don't know how much difference it makes as to who is giving the punishment, whether an adult learns best from a younger or an older person than himself–or many things of that sort.

So in this study we are bringing together a number of adults of different occupations and ages. And we're asking some of them to be teachers and some of them to be learners.

We want to find out just what effect different people have on each other as teachers and learners, and also what effect *punishment* will have on learning in this situation.

Therefore, I'm going to ask one of you to be the teacher here tonight and the other one to be the learner.

Does either of you have a preference?

Subjects then drew slips of paper from a hat to determine who would be the teacher and who would be the learner in the experiment. The drawing was rigged so that the naive subject was always the teacher and the accomplice always the learner. (Both slips contained the word "Teacher,") Immediately after the drawing, the teacher and learner were taken to an adjacent room and the learner was strapped into an "electric chair" apparatus.

The experimenter explained that the straps were to prevent excessive movement while the learner was being shocked. The effect was to make it impossible for him to escape from the situation. An electrode was attached to the learner's wrist, and electrode paste was applied "to avoid blisters and burns." Subjects were told that the electrode was attached to the shock generator in the adjoining room.

In order to improve credibility the experimenter declared, in response to a question by the learner: "Although the shocks can be extremely painful, they cause no permanent tissue damage."

Learning task. The lesson administered by the subject was a paired-associate learning task. The subject read a series of word pairs to the learner, and then read the first word of the pair along with four terms. The learner was to indicate which of the four terms had originally been paired with the first word. He communicated his answer by pressing one of four switches in front of him, which in turn lit up one of four numbered quadrants in an answer-box located atop the shock generator.

Shock generator. The instrument panel consists of 30 lever switches set in a horizontal line. Each switch is clearly labeled with a voltage designation that ranges from 15 to 450 volts. There is a 15-volt increment from one switch to the next going from left to right. In addition, the following verbal designations are clearly indicated for groups of four switches going from left to right: Slight Shock, Moderate Shock, Strong Shock, Very Strong Shock, Intense Shock, Extreme Intensity Shock, Danger: Severe Shock. (Two switches after this last designation are simply marked XXX.)

Upon depressing a switch: a pilot light corresponding to each switch is illuminated in bright red; an electric buzzing is heard; an electric blue light, labeled "voltage energizer," flashes; the dial on the voltage meter swings to the right; various relay clicks are sounded.

The upper left-hand corner of the generator is labeled Shock Generator, Type ZLB, Dyson Instrument Company, Waltham, Mass. Output 15 Volts–450 Volts.

Details of the instrument were carefully handled to insure an appearance of authenticity. The panel was engraved by precision industrial engravers, and all components were of high quality. No subject in the experiment suspected that the instrument was merely a simulated shock generator.[1]

---

[1] A related technique, making use of a shock generator, was reported by Buss (1961) for the study of aggression in the laboratory. Despite the considerable similarity of technical detail in the experimental procedures, both investigators proceeded in ignorance of the other's work. Milgram provided plans and photographs of his shock generator, experimental procedure, and first results in a report to the National Science Foundation in January 1961. This report received only limited circulation. Buss reported his procedure 6 months later, but to a wider audience. Subsequently, technical information and reports were exchanged. The present article was first received in the Editor's office on December 27, 1961; it was resubmitted with deletions on July 27, 1962.

Sample shock. Each naive subject is given a sample shock on the shock generator, prior to beginning his run as teacher. This shock is always 45 volts, and is applied by pressing the third switch of the generator. The shock is applied to the wrist of the naive subject, and has its source in a 45-volt battery wired into the generator. This further convinces the subject of the authenticity of the generator.

Shock instructions. The subject is told to administer a shock to the learner each time he gives a wrong response. Moreover—and this is the key command—the subject is instructed to "move one level higher on the shock generator each time the learner flashes a wrong answer." He is also instructed to announce the voltage level before administering a shock. This serves to continually remind subjects of the increasing intensity of shocks administered to the learner.

Preliminary and regular run. Pretests revealed that the procedure of reading words and administering shocks requires some practice before it can be handled smoothly. Therefore, immediately preceding the regular run, the teacher is given a preliminary series of 10 words to read to the learner. There are 3 neutral words in the practice series (i.e., words that the learner answers correctly), so that shocks are administered for 7 of the words, with the maximum shock at 105 volts (moderate shock). Almost all subjects master the procedure by the time the preliminary run is over.

Subjects are then presented with a second list, and are told that the procedure is the same as for the first list; the experimenter adds, however:

When you get to the bottom of the list, repeat it over again, and continue giving shocks, until the learner has learned all the pairs correctly.

The experimenter instructs the subject to,

start from 15 volts and increase the shock level one step each time the learner gives a wrong answer.

Feedback from the victim. In all conditions the learner gives a predetermined set of responses to the word pair test, based on a schedule of approximately three wrong answers to one correct answer. In the present experimental condition no vocal response or other sign of protest is heard from the learner until Shock Level 300 is reached. When the 300-volt shock is administered, the learner pounds on the wall of the room in which he is bound to the electric chair. The pounding can be heard by the subject. From this point on, the learner's answers no longer appear on the four-way panel.

At this juncture, subjects ordinarily turn to the experimenter for guidance. The experimenter instructs the subject to treat the absence of a response as a wrong answer, and to shock the subject according to the usual schedule. He advises the subjects to allow 5–10 seconds before considering no response as a wrong answer, and to increase the shock level one step each time the learner fails to respond correctly. The learner's pounding is repeated after the 315-volt shock is administered; afterwards he is not heard from, nor do his answers reappear on the four-way signal box.

Experimenter feedback. At various points in the experiment the subject may turn to the experimenter for advice on whether he should continue to administer shocks. Or he may indicate that he does not wish to go on. It was important to standardize the experimenter's responses to these inquires and reactions.

If the subject indicated his unwillingness to go on, the experimenter responded with a sequence of "prods," using as many as necessary to bring the subject into line.

Prod 1: Please continue, *or* Please go on.
Prod 2: The experiment requires that you continue.
Prod 3: It is absolutely essential that you continue.
Prod 4: You have no other choice, you *must* go on.

The prods were always made in sequence: Only if Prod 1 had been unsuccessful, could Prod 2 be used. If the subject refused to obey the experimenter after Prod 4, the experiment was terminated. The experimenter's tone of voice was at all times firm, but not impolite. The sequence was begun anew on each occasion that the subject balked or showed reluctance to follow orders.

Special prods. If the subject asked if the learner was liable to suffer permanent physical injury, the experimenter said:

Although the shocks may be painful, there is no permanent tissue damage, so please go on. [Followed by Prods 2, 3, and 4 if necessary.]

If the subject said that the learner did not want to go on, the experimenter replied:

Whether the learner likes it or not, you must go on until he has learned all the word pairs correctly. So please go on. [Followed by Prods 2, 3, and 4 if necessary.]

Dependent Measures

The primary dependent measure for any subject is the maximum shock he administers before he refuses to go any further. In principle this may vary from 0 (for a subject who refuses to administer even the first shock) to 30 (for a subject who administers the highest shock on the generator). A subject who breaks off the experiment at any point prior to administering the thirtieth shock level is termed a *defiant* subject. One who complies with experimental commands fully, and proceeds to administer all shock levels commanded, is termed an *obedient* subject.

Further records. With few exceptions, experimental sessions were recorded on magnetic tape. Occasional photographs were taken through one-way mirrors. Notes were kept on any unusual behavior occurring during the course of the experiments. On occasion, additional observers were directed to write objective descriptions of the subjects' behavior. The latency and duration of shocks were measured by accurate timing devices.

Interview and dehoax. Following the experiment, subjects were interviewed; open-ended questions, projective measures, and attitude scales were employed. After the interview, procedures were undertaken to assure that the subject would leave the laboratory in a state of well being. A friendly reconciliation was arranged between the subject and the victim, and an effort was made to reduce any tensions that arose as a result of the experiment.

RESULTS

Preliminary Notions

Before giving an account of the experimental results, it is instructive to consider how persons predict others will perform when commanded to administer powerful shocks to another person. Fourteen Yale seniors, all psychology majors, were provided with a detailed description of the experimental situation. They were asked to reflect carefully on it, and to predict the behavior of 100 hypothetical subjects. More specifically, they were instructed to plot the distribution of obedience of "100 Americans of diverse occupations, and ranging in age from 20 to 50 years," who were placed in the experimental situation.

There was considerable agreement among the respondents on the expected behavior of hypothetical subjects. All respondents predicted that only an insignificant minority would go through to the end of the shock series. (The estimates ranged from 0 to 3%; i.e., the most "pessimistic" member of the class predicted that of 100 persons, 3 would continue through to the most potent shock available on the shock generator—450 volts.) The class mean was 1.2%. The question was also posed informally to colleagues of the author, and the most general feeling was that few if any subjects would go beyond the designation Very Stong Shock.

Result of Experiment I

Subjects accept situation. With few exceptions subjects were convinced of the reality of the experimental situation, that they were administering shocks to another person, and the most potent shocks were extremely painful. In the post-experimental interview subjects were asked: "How painful to the learner were the last few shocks that you administered to him?" Subjects were instructed to indicate their answers on a printed 14-point scale ranging from "Not at all painful" to "Extremely painful." The modal response was 14 (Extremely painful) with the mean at 13.42.

Signs of extreme tension. Many subjects showed signs of nervousness in the experimental situation, and especially upon administering the more powerful shocks. In a large number of cases the degree of tension reached extremes that are rarely seen in sociopsychological laboratory studies. Subjects were observed to sweat, tremble, stutter, bite their lips, groan, and dig their finger-nails into their flesh. These were characteristic rather than exceptional responses to the experiment.

One sign of tension was the regular occurrence of nervous laughing fits. Fourteen of the 40 subjects showed definite signs of nervous laughter and smiling. The laughter seemed entirely out of place, even bizarre. Full-blown, uncontrollable seizures were observed for 3 subjects. On one occasion we observed a seizure so violently convulsive that it was necessary to call a halt to the experiment. The subject, a 46-year-old encyclopedia salesman, was seriously embarrassed by his untoward and uncontrollable behavior. In the post-experimental interviews subjects took pains to point out that they were not sadistic types, and that the laughter did not mean they enjoyed shocking the victim.

Distribution of scores. It had been conjectured that persons would not, in general, agree to administer shocks beyond the level designated as Very Strong Shock. The distribution of maximum shocks for this experiment is shown in Table 2. The obtained distribution of scores deviates radically from the prediction.

Upon command of the experimenter, each of the 40 subjects went beyond the expected breakoff point. No subject stopped prior to administering Shock Level 20. (At this level–300 volts–the victim kicks on the wall and no longer provides answers to the teacher's multiple-choice questions.)

Of the 40 subjects, 5 refused to obey the experimental commands beyond the 300-volt level. Four more subjects administered one further shock, and then refused to go on. Two broke off at the 330-volt level, and 1 each at 345, 360, and 375 volts. Thus a total of 14 subjects defied the experimenter. It is instructive to reprint their remarks at the point of defiance, as transcribed from the tape recordings:

[0124] I think he's trying to communicate, he's knocking . . . . Well it's not fair to shock the guy . . . these are terrific volts. I don't think this is very humane . . . . Oh, I can't go on with this; no, this isn't right. It's a hell of an experiment. The guy is suffering in there. No, I don't want to go on. This is crazy. [Subject refused to administer more shocks.]

[0123] He's banging in there. I'm gonna chicken out. I'd like to continue, but I can't do that to a man . . . . I'm sorry I can't do that to a man. I'll hurt his heart. You take your check . . . . No really, I couldn't do it.

These subjects were frequently in a highly agitated and even angered state. Sometimes, verbal protest was at a minimum, and the subject simply got up from his chair in front of the shock generator, and indicated that he wished to leave the laboratory.

Of the 40 subjects, 26 obeyed the orders of the experimenter to the end, proceeding to punish the victim until they reached the most potent shock available on the shock generator. At that point, the experimenter called a halt to the session. (The maximum shock is labeled 450 volts, and is two steps beyond the designation: Danger: Severe Shock.) Although obedient subjects continued to administer shocks, they often did so under extreme stress. Some expressed reluctance to administer shocks beyond the 300-volt level, and displayed fears similar to those who defied the experimenter; yet they obeyed.

Table 2 DISTRIBUTION OF BREAKOFF POINTS

VERBAL DESIGNATION AND VOLTAGE INDICATION	NUMBER OF SUBJECTS FOR WHOM THIS WAS MAXIMUM SHOCK
Slight Shock	
15	0
30	0
45	0
60	0
Moderate Shock	
75	0
90	0
105	0
120	0
Strong Shock	
135	0
150	0
165	0
180	0
Very Strong Shock	
195	0
210	0
225	0
240	0
Intense Shock	
255	0
270	0
285	0
300	5
Extreme Intensity Shock	
315	4
330	2
345	1
360	1
Danger: Severe Shock	
375	1
390	0
405	0
420	0
XXX	
435	0
450	26

After the maximum shocks had been delivered, and the experimenter called a halt to the proceedings, many obedient subjects heaved sighs of relief, mopped their brows, rubbed their fingers over their eyes, or nervously fumbled cigarettes. Some shook their heads, apparently in regret. Some subjects had remained calm throughout the experiment, and displayed only minimal signs of tension from beginning to end.

DISCUSSION

The experiment yielded two findings that were surprising. The first finding concerns the sheer strength of obedient tendencies manifested in this situation. Subjects have learned from childhood that it is a fundamental breach of moral conduct to hurt another person against his will. Yet, 26 subjects abandon this tenet in following the instructions of an authority who has no special powers to enforce his commands. To disobey would bring no material loss to the subject; no punishment would ensue. It is clear from the remarks and outward behavior of many participants that in punishing the victim they are often acting against their own values. Subjects often expressed deep disapproval of shocking a man in the face of his objections, and others denounced it as stupid and senseless. Yet the majority complied with the experimental commands. This outcome was surprising from two perspectives: first, from the standpoint of predictions made in the questionnaire described earlier. (Here, however, it is possible that the remoteness of the respondents from the actual situation, and the difficulty of conveying to them the concrete details of the experiment, could account for the serious underestimation of obedience.)

But the results were also unexpected to persons who observed the experiment in progress, through one-way mirrors. Observers often uttered expressions of disbelief upon seeing a subject administer more powerful shocks to the victim. These persons had a full acquaintance with the details of the situation, and yet systematically underestimated the amount of obedience that subjects would display.

The second unanticipated effect was the extraordinary tension generated by the procedures. One might suppose that a subject would simply break off or continue as his conscience dictated. Yet, this is very far from what happened. There were striking reactions of tension and emotional strain. One observer related:

I observed a mature and initially poised businessman enter the laboratory smiling and confident. Within 20 minutes he was reduced to a twitching, stuttering wreck, who was rapidly approaching a point of nervous collapse. He constantly pulled on his earlobe, and twisted his hands. At one point he pushed his fist into his forehead and muttered: "Oh God, let's stop it." And yet he continued to respond to every word of the experimenter, and obeyed to the end.

Any understanding of the phenomenon of obedience must rest on an analysis of the particular conditions in which it occurs. The following features of the experiment go some distance in explaining the high amount of obedience observed in the situation.

1. The experiment is sponsored by and takes place on the grounds of an institution of unimpeachable reputation, Yale University. It may be reasonably presumed that the personnel are competent and reputable. The importance of this background authority is now being studied by conducting a series of experiments outside of New Haven, and without any visible ties to the university.

2. The experiment is, on the face of it, designed to attain a worthy purpose—advancement of knowledge about learning and memory. Obedience occurs not as an end in itself, but as an instrumental element in a situation that the subject construes as significant, and meaningful. He may not be able to see its full significance, but he may properly assume that the experimenter does.

3. The subject perceives that the victim has voluntarily submitted to the authority system of the experimenter. He is not (at first) an unwilling captive impressed for involuntary service. He has taken the trouble to come to the laboratory presumably to aid the experimental research. That he later becomes

an involuntary subject does not alter the fact that, initially, he consented to participate without qualification. Thus he has in some degree incurred an obligation toward the experimenter.

4. The subject, too, has entered the experiment voluntarily, and perceives himself under obligation to aid the experimenter. He has made a commitment, and to disrupt the experiment is a repudiation of this initial promise of aid.

5. Certain features of the procedure strengthen the subject's sense of obligation to the experimenter. For one, he has been paid for coming to the laboratory. In part this is canceled out by the experimenter's statement that:

Of course, as in all experiments, the money is yours simply for coming to the laboratory. From this point on no matter what happens, the money is yours.[2]

6. From the subject's standpoint, the fact that he is the teacher and the other man the learner is purely a chance consequence (it is determined by drawing lots) and he, the subject, ran the same risk as the other man in being assigned the role of learner. Since the assignment of positions in the experiment was achieved by fair means, the learner is deprived of any basis of complaint on this count. (A similar situation obtains in Army units, in which—in the absence of volunteers—a practicularly dangerous mission may be assigned by drawing lots, and the unlucky soldier is expected to bear his misfortune with sportsmanship.)

7. There is, at best, ambiguity with regard to the prerogatives of a psychologist and the corresponding rights of his subject. There is a vagueness of expectation concerning what a psychologist may require of his subject, and when he is overstepping acceptable limits. Moreover, the experiment occurs in a closed setting, and thus provides no opportunity for the subject to remove these ambiguities by discussion with others. There are few standards that seem directly applicable to the situation, which is a novel one for most subjects.

8. The subjects are assured that the shocks administered to the subject are "painful but not dangerous." Thus they assume that the discomfort caused the victim is momentary, while the scientific gains resulting from the experiment are enduring.

9. Through Shock Level 20 the victim continues to provide answers on the signal box. The subject may construe this as a sign that the victim is still willing to "play the game." It is only after Shock Level 20 that the victim repudiates the rules completely, refusing to answer further.

These features help to explain the high amount of obedience obtained in this experiment. Many of the arguments raised need not remain matters of speculation, but can be reduced to testable propositions to be confirmed or disproved by further experiments.[3]

The following features of the experiment concern the nature of the conflict which the subject faces.

10. The subject is placed in a position in which he must respond to the competing demands of two persons: the experimenter and the victim. The conflict must be resolved by meeting the demands of one or the other; satisfac-

---

[2] Forty-three subjects, undergraduates at Yale University, were run in the experiment without payment. The results are very similar to those obtained with paid subjects.

[3] A series of recently completed experiments employing the obedience paradigm is reported in Milgram (1964).

tion of the victim and the experimenter are mutually exclusive. Moreover, the resolution must take the form of a highly visible action, that of continuing to shock the victim or breaking off the experiment. Thus the subject is forced into a public conflict that does not permit any completely satisfactory solution.

11.   While the demands of the experimenter carry the weight of scientific authority, the demands of the victim spring from his personal experience of pain and suffering. The two claims need not be regarded as equally pressing and legitimate. The experimenter seeks an abstract scientific datum; the victim cries out for relief from physical suffering caused by the subject's actions.

12.   The experiment gives the subject little time for reflection. The conflict comes on rapidly. It is only minutes after the subject has been seated before the shock generator that the victim begins his protests. Moreover, the subject perceives that he has gone through but two-thirds of the shock levels at the time the subject's first protests are heard. Thus he understands that the conflict will have a persistent aspect to it, and may well become more intense as increasingly more powerful shocks are required. The rapidity with which the conflict descends on the subject, and his realization that it is predictably recurrent may well be sources of tension to him.

13.   At a more general level, the conflict stems from the opposition of two deeply ingrained behavior dispositions: first, the disposition not to harm other people, and second, the tendency to obey those whom we perceive to be legitimate authorities.

REFERENCES

Adorno, T., Frenkel-Brunswik, Else, Levinson, D. J., & Sanford, R. N.   *The authoritarian personality*. New York: Harper, 1950.

Arendt, H.   What was authority? In C. J. Friedrich (Ed.), *Authority*. Cambridge: Harvard Univer. Press, 1958. Pp. 81–112.

Binet, A.   *La suggestibilité*. Paris: Schleicher, 1900.

Buss, A. H.   *The psychology of aggression*. New York: Wiley, 1961.

Cartwright, S. (Ed.)   *Studies in social power*. Ann Arbor: University of Michigan Institute for Social Research, 1959.

Charcot, J. M.   *Oeuvres complétes*. Paris: Bureaux du Progrès Medical, 1881.

Frank, J. D.   Experimental studies of personal pressure and resistance. *J. gen. Psychol.*, 1944, *30*, 23–64.

Friedrich, C. J. (Ed.)   *Authority*. Cambridge: Harvard Univer. Press, 1958.

Milgram, S.   Dynamics of obedience. Washington: National Science Foundation, 25 January 1961. (Mimeo)

Milgram, S.   Some conditions of obedience and disobedience to authority. *Hum. Relat.*, 1965.

Rokeach, M.   Authority, authoritarianism, and conformity. In I. A. Berg & B. M. Bass (Eds.), *Conformity and deviation*. New York: Harper, 1961. Pp. 230–57.

Snow, C. P.   Either-or. *Progressive*, 1961(Feb.), 24.

Weber, M.   *The theory of social and economic organization*. Oxford: Oxford Univer. Press, 1947.

Compliance Without Pressure:
The Foot-in-the-Door Technique

JONATHAN L. FREEDMAN AND SCOTT C. FRASER

How can a person be induced to do something he would rather not do? This question is relevant to practically every phase of social life, from stopping at a traffic light to stopping smoking, from buying Brand X to buying savings bonds, from supporting the March of Dimes to supporting the Civil Rights Act.

One common way of attacking the problem is to exert as much pressure as possible on the reluctant individual in an effort to force him to comply. This technique has been the focus of a considerable amount of experimental research. Work on attitude change, conformity, imitation, and obedience has all tended to stress the importance of the degree of external pressure. The prestige of the communicator (Kelman & Hovland, 1953), degree of discrepancy of the communication (Hovland & Pritzker, 1957), size of the group disagreeing with the subject (Asch, 1951), perceived power of the model (Bandura, Ross, and Ross, 1963), etc., are the kinds of variables that have been studied. This impressive body of work, added to the research on rewards and punishments in learning, has produced convincing evidence that greater external pressure generally leads to greater compliance with the wishes of the experimenter. The one exception appears to be situations involving the arousal of cognitive dissonance in which, once discrepant behavior has been elicited from the subject, the greater the pressure that was used to elicit the behavior, the less subsequent change occurs (Festinger & Carlsmith, 1959). But even in this situation one critical element is the amount of external pressure exerted.

Clearly, then, under most circumstances the more pressure that can be applied, the more likely it is that the individual will comply. There are, however, many times when for ethical, moral, or practical reasons it is difficult to apply much pressure when the goal is to produce compliance with a minimum of apparent pressure, as in the forced-compliance studies involving dissonance arousal. And even when a great deal of pressure is possible, it is still important to maximize the compliance it produces. Thus, factors other than external pressure are often quite critical in determining degree of compliance. What are these factors?

Although rigorous research on the problem is rather sparse, the fields of advertising, propaganda, politics, etc., are by no means devoid of techniques designed to produce compliance in the absence of external pressure (or to maximize the effectiveness of the pressure that is used, which is really the same problem). One assumption about compliance that has often been made either explicitly or implicitly is that once a person has been induced to comply with a small request he is more likely to comply with a larger demand. This is the

Reprinted from Journal of Personality and Social Psychology, 4, *1966, 195–202. Copyright 1966 by the American Psychological Association and reproduced by permission.*

principle that is commonly referred to as the foot-in-the-door or gradation technique and is reflected in the saying that if you "give them an inch, they'll take a mile." It was, for example, supposed to be one of the basic techniques upon which the Korean brainwashing tactics were based (Schein, Schneier, & Barker, 1961), and, in a somewhat different sense, one basis for Nazi propaganda during 1940 (Bruner, 1941). It also appears to be implicit in many advertising compaigns which attempt to induce the consumer to do anything relating to the product involved, even sending back a card saying he does not want the product.

The most relevant piece of experimental evidence comes from a study of conformity done by Deutsch and Gerard (1955). Some subjects were faced with incorrect group judgments first in a series in which the stimuli were not present during the actual judging and then in a series in which they were present, while the order of the memory and visual series was reversed for other subjects. For both groups the memory series produced more conformity, and when the memory series came first there was more total conformity to the group judgments. It seems likely that this order effect occurred because, as the authors suggest, once conformity is elicited at all it is more likely to occur in the future. Although this kind of conformity is probably somewhat different from compliance as described above, this finding certainly lends some support to the foot-in-the-door idea. The present research attempted to provide a rigorous, more direct test of this notion as it applies to compliance and to provide data relevant to several alternative ways of explaining the effect.

EXPERIMENT I

The basic paradigm was to ask some subjects (Performance condition) to comply first with a small request and then 3 days later with a larger, related request. Other subjects (One-Contact condition) were asked to comply only with the large request. The hypothesis was that more subjects in the Performance condition than in the One-Contact condition would comply with the larger request.

Two additional conditions were included in an attempt to specify the essential difference between these two major conditions. The Performance subjects were asked to perform a small favor, and, if they agreed, they did it. The question arises whether the act of agreeing itself is critical or whether actually carrying it out was necessary. To assess this a third group of subjects (Agree-Only) was asked the first request, but, even if they agreed, they did not carry it out. Thus, they were identical to the Performance group except that they were not given the opportunity of performing the request.

Another difference between the two main conditions was that at the time of the larger request the subjects in the Performance condition were more familiar with the experimenter than were the other subjects. The Performance subjects had been contacted twice, heard his voice more, discovered that the questions were not dangerous, and so on. It is possible that this increased familiarity would serve to decrease the fear and suspicion of a strange voice on the phone and might accordingly increase the likelihood of the subjects agreeing to the larger request. To control for this a fourth condition was run (Familiarization) which attempted to give the subjects as much familiarity with the experimenter as in the Performance and Agree-Only conditions with the only difference being that no request was made.

The major prediction was that more subjects in the Performance condition would agree to the large request than in any of the other conditions, and that the One-Contact condition would produce the least compliance. Since the importance of agreement and familiarity was essentially unknown, the expectation was that the Agree-Only and Familiarization conditions would produce intermediate amounts of compliance.

METHOD

The prediction stated above was tested in a field experiment in which housewives were asked to allow a survey team of five or six men to come into their homes for 2 hours to classify the household products they used. This large request was made under four different conditions: after an initial contact in which the subject had been asked to answer a few questions about the kinds of soaps she used, and the questions were actually asked (Performance condition); after an identical contact in which the questions were not actually asked (Agree-Only condition); after an initial contact in which no request was made (Familiarization condition); or after no initial contact (One-Contact condition). The dependent measure was simply whether or not the subject agreed to the large request.

Procedure

The subjects were 156 Palo Alto, California, housewives, 36 in each condition, who were selected at random from the telephone directory. An additional 12 subjects distributed about equally among the three two-contact conditions could not be reached for the second contact and are not included in the data analysis. Subjects were assigned randomly to the various conditions, except that the Familiarization condition was added to the design after the other three conditions had been completed. All contacts were by telephone by the same experimenter who identified himself as the same person each time. Calls were made only in the morning. For the three groups that were contacted twice, the first call was made on either Monday or Tuesday and the second always 3 days later. All large requests were made on either Thursday or Friday.

At the first contact, the experimenter introduced himself by name and said that he was from the California Consumers' Group. In the Performance condition he then proceeded:

We are calling you this morning to ask if you would answer a number of questions about what household products you use so that we could have this information for our public service publication, "The Guide." Would you be willing to give us this information for our survey?

If the subject agreed, she was asked a series of eight innocuous questions dealing with household soaps (e.g., "What brand of soap do you use in your kitchen sink?") She was then thanked for her cooperation, and the contact terminated.

Another condition (Agree-Only) was run to assess the importance of actually carrying out the request as opposed to merely agreeing to it. The only difference between this and the Performance condition was that, if the subject agreed to answer the questions, the experimenter thanked her, but said that he was just lining up respondents for the survey and would contact her if needed.

A third condition was included to check on the importance of the subject's greater familiarity with the experimenter in the two-contact conditions. In this condition the experimenter introduced himself, described the organization he worked for and the survey it was conducting, listed the questions he was asking, and then said that he was calling merely to acquaint the subject with the existence of his organization. In other words, these subjects were contacted, spent as much time on the phone with the experimenter as the Performance subjects did, heard all the questions, but neither agreed to answer them nor answered them.

In all of these two-contact conditions some subjects did not agree to the requests or even hung up before the requests were made. Every subject who answered the phone was included in the analysis of the results and was contacted for the second request regardless of her extent of cooperativeness during the first contact. In other words, no subject who could be contacted the appropriate number of times was discarded from any of the four conditions.

The large request was essentially identical for all subjects. The experimenter called, identified himself, and said either that his group was expanding its survey (in the case of the two-contact conditions) or that it was conducting a survey (in the One-Contact condition). In all four conditions he then continued:

The survey will involve five or six men from our staff coming into your home some morning for about 2 hours to enumerate and classify all the household products that you have. They will have to have full freedom in your house to go through the cupboards and storage places. Then all this information will be used in the writing of the reports for our public service publication, "The Guide."

If the subject agreed to the request, she was thanked and told that at the present time the experimenter was merely collecting names of people who were willing to take part and that she would be contacted if it were decided to use her in the survey. If she did not agree, she was thanked for her time. This terminated the experiment.

RESULTS

Apparently even the small request was not considered trivial by some of the subjects. Only about two thirds of the subjects in the Performance and Agree-Only conditions agreed to answer the questions about household soaps. It might be noted that none of those who refused the first request later agreed to the large request, although as stated previously all subjects who were contacted for the small request are included in the data for those groups.

Our major prediction was that subjects who had agreed to and carried out a small request (Performance condition) would subsequently be more likely to comply with a larger request than would subjects who were asked only the larger request (One-Contact condition). As may be seen in Table 1, the results support the prediction. Over 50% of the subjects in the Performance condition agreed to

Table 1 PERCENTAGE OF SUBJECTS COMPLYING WITH
LARGE REQUEST IN EXPERIMENT I

CONDITION	%
Performance	52.8
Agree-Only	33.3
Familiarization	27.8*
One-Contact	22.2**

Note. – N = 36 for each group. Significance levels represent differences from the Performance condition.
* p < .07.
** p < .02.

the larger request, while less than 25% of the One-Contact condition agreed to it. Thus it appears that obtaining compliance with a small request does tend to increase subsequent compliance. The question is what aspect of the initial contact produces this effect.

One possibility is that the effect was produced merely by increased familiarity with the experimenter. The Familiarization control was included to assess the effect on compliance of two contacts with the same person. The group had as much contact with the experimenter as the Performance group, but no request was made during the first contact. As the table indicates, the Familiarization group did not differ appreciably in amount of compliance from the One-Contact group, but was different from the Performance group (χ^2 = 3.70 p < .07). Thus, although increased familiarity may well lead to increased compliance, in the present situation the differences in amount of familiarity apparently were not great enough to produce any such increase; the effect that was obtained seems not to be due to this factor.

Another possibility is that the critical factor producing increased compliance is simply agreeing to the small request (i.e., carrying it out may not be necessary). The Agree-Only condition was identical to the Performance condition except that in the former the subjects were not asked the questions. The amount of compliance in this Agree-Only condition fell between the Performance and One-Contact conditions and was not significantly different from either of them. This leaves the effect of merely agreeing somewhat ambiguous, but it suggests that the agreement alone may produce part of the effect.

Unfortunately, it must be admitted that neither of these control conditions is an entirely adequate test of the possibility it was designed to assess. Both conditions are in some way quite peculiar and may have made a very different and extraneous impression on the subject than did the Performance condition. In one case, a housewife is asked to answer some questions and then is not asked them; in the other, some man calls to tell her about some organization she has never heard of. Now, by themselves neither of these events might produce very much suspicion. But, several days later, the same man calls and asks a very large favor. At this point it is not at all unlikely that many subjects think they are being manipulated, or in any case that something strange is going on. Any such reaction on the part of the subjects would naturally tend to reduce the amount of compliance in these conditions.

Thus, although this first study demonstrates that an initial contact in which a request is made and carried out increases compliance with a second request, the question of why and how the initial request produces this effect remains unanswered. In an attempt to begin answering this question and to extend the results of the first study, a second experiment was conducted.

There seemed to be several quite plausible ways in which the increase in compliance might have been produced. The first was simply some kind of commitment to or involvement with the particular person making the request. This might work, for example, as follows: The subject has agreed to the first request and perceives that the experimenter therefore expects him also to agree to the second request. The subject thus feels obligated and does not want to disappoint the experimenter; he also feels that he needs a good reason for saying "no"—a better reason than he would need if he had never said "yes." This is just one line of causality—the particular process by which involvement with the experimenter operates might be quite different, but the basic idea would be similar. The commitment is to the particular person. This implies that the increase in compliance due to the first contact should occur primarily when both requests are made by the same person.

Another explanation in terms of involvement centers around the particular issue with which the requests are concerned. Once the subject has taken some action in connection with an area of concern, be it surveys, political activity, or highway safety, there is probably a tendency to become somewhat more concerned with the area. The subject begins thinking about it, considering its importance and relevance to him, and so on. This tends to make him more likely to agree to take further action in the same area when he is later asked to. To the extent that this is the critical factor, the initial contact should increase compliance only when both requests are related to the same issue or area of concern.

Another way of looking at the situation is that the subject needs a reason to say "no." In our society it is somewhat difficult to refuse a reasonable request, particularly when it is made by an organization that is not trying to make money. In order to refuse, many people feel that they need a reason—simply not wanting to do it is often not in itself sufficient. The person can say to the requester or simply to himself that he does not believe in giving to charities or tipping or working for political parties or answering questions or posting signs, or whatever he is asked to do. Once he has performed a particular task, however, this excuse is no longer valid for not agreeing to perform a similar task. Even if the first thing he did was trivial compared to the present request, he cannot say he never does this sort of thing, and thus one good reason for refusing is removed. This line of reasoning suggests that the similarity of the first and second requests in terms of the type of action required is an important factor. The more similar they are, the more the "matter of principle" argument is eliminated by agreeing to the first request, and the greater should be the increase in compliance.

There are probably many other mechanisms by which the initial request might produce an increase in compliance. The second experiment was designed in part to test the notions described above, but its major purpose was to demonstrate the effect unequivocally. To this latter end it eliminated one of the important problems with the first study which was that when the experimenter made the second request he was not blind as to which condition the subjects were in. In this study the second request was always made by someone other than the person who made the first request, and the second experimenter was blind as to what condition the subject was in. This eliminates the possibility that the experimenter exerted systematically different amounts of pressure in different experimental conditions. If the effect of the first study were replicated, it would also rule out the relatively uninteresting possibility that the effect is due primarily to greater familiarity or involvement with the particular person making the first request.

EXPERIMENT II

The basic paradigm was quite similar to that of the first study. Experimental subjects were asked to comply with a small request and were later asked a considerably larger request, while controls were asked only the larger request. The first request varied along two dimensions. Subjects were asked either to put up a small sign or to sign a petition, and the issue was either safe driving or keeping California beautiful. Thus, there were four first requests: a small sign for safe driving or for beauty, and a petition for the two issues. The second request for all subjects was to install in their front lawn a very large sign which said "Drive Carefully." The four experimental conditions may be defined in terms of the similarity of the small and large requests along the dimensions of issue and task. The two requests were similar in both issue and task for the small-sign, safe-driving group, similar only in issue for the safe-driving-petition group, similar only in task for the small "Keep California Beautiful" sign group, and similar in neither issue nor task for the "Keep California Beautiful" petition group.

The major expectation was that the three groups for which either the task or the issue were similar would show more compliance than the controls, and it was also felt that when both were similar there would probably be the most compliance. The fourth condition (Different Issue-Different Task) was included primarily to assess the effect simply of the initial contact which, although it was not identical to the second one on either issue or task, was in many ways quite similar (e.g., a young student asking for cooperation on a noncontroversial issue). There were no clear expectations as to how this condition would compare to the controls.

METHOD

The subjects were 114 women and 13 men living in Palo Alto, California. Of these, 9 women and 6 men could not be contacted for the second request and are not included in the data analysis. The remaining 112 subjects were divided about equally among the five conditions (see Table 2). All subjects were contacted between 1:30 and 4:30 on weekday afternoons.

Two experimenters, one male and one female, were employed, and a different one always made the second contact. Unlike the first study, the experimenters actually went to the homes of the subjects and interviewed them on a face-to-face basis. An effort was made to select subjects from blocks and neighborhoods that were as homogeneous as possible. On each block every third or fourth house was approached, and all subjects on that block were in one experimental condition. This was necessary because of the likelihood that neighbors would talk to each other about the contact. In addition, for every four subjects contacted, a fifth house was chosen as a control but was, of course, not contacted. Throughout this phase of the experiment, and in fact throughout the whole experiment, the two experimenters did not communicate to each other what conditions had been run on a given block nor what condition a particular house was in.

The small-sign, safe-driving group was told that the experimenter was from the Community Committee for Traffic Safety, that he was visiting a number of homes in an attempt to make the citizens more aware of the need to drive carefully all the time, and that he would like the subject to take a small sign and put it in a window or in the car so that it would serve as a reminder of the need to drive carefully. The sign was 3 inches square, said "Be a safe driver," was on thin paper without a gummed backing, and in general looked rather amateurish and unattractive. If the subject agreed, he was given the sign and thanked; if he disagreed, he was simply thanked for his time.

The three other experimental conditions were quite similar with appropriate changes. The other organization was identified as the Keep California Beautiful Committee and its sign said, appropriately enough, "Keep California Beautiful." Both signs were simply black block letters on a white background. The two petition groups were asked to sign a petition which was being sent to California's United States Senators. The petition advocated support for any legislation which would promote either safer driving or keeping California beautiful. The subject was shown a petition, typed on heavy bond paper, with at least 20 signatures already affixed. If she agreed, she signed and was thanked. If she did not agree, she was merely thanked.

The second contact was made about 2 weeks after the initial one. Each experimenter was armed with a list of houses which had been compiled by the other experimenter. This list contained all four experimental conditions and the controls, and, of course, there was no way for the second experimenter to know which condition the subject had been in. At this second contact, all subjects were asked the same thing: Would they put a large sign concerning safe driving in their front yard? The experimenter identified himself as being from the Citizens for Safe Driving, a different group from the original safe-driving group (although it is likely that most subjects who had been in the safe-driving conditions did not notice the difference). The subject was shown a picture of a very large sign reading "Drive Carefully" placed in front of an attractive house. The picture was taken so that the sign obscured much of the front of the house and completely concealed the doorway. It was rather poorly lettered. The subject was told that: "Our men will come out and install it and later come and remove it. It makes just a small hole in your lawn, but if this is unacceptable to you we have a special mount which will make no hole." She was asked to put the sign up for a week or a week and a half. If the subject agreed, she was told that more names than necessary were being gathered and if her home were to be used she would be contacted in a few weeks. The experimenter recorded the subject's response and this ended the experiment.

RESULTS

First, it should be noted that there were no large differences among the experimental conditions in the percentages of subjects agreeing to the first request. Although somewhat more subjects agreed to post the "Keep California Beautiful" sign and somewhat fewer to sign the beauty petition, none of these differences approach significance.

The important figures are the number of subjects in each group who agreed to the large request. These are presented in Table 2. The figures for the four experimental groups include all subjects who were approached the first time, regardless of whether or not they agreed to the small request. As noted above, a few subjects were lost because they could not be reached for the second request, and, of course, these are not included in the table.

Table 2 PERCENTAGE OF SUBJECTS COMPLYING WITH LARGE REQUEST IN EXPERIMENT II

| ISSUE[a] | TASK[a] | | | |
	SIMILAR	N	DIFFERENT	N
Similar	76.0**	25	47.8*	23
Different	47.6*	21	47.4*	19
	One-Contact 16.7 ($N = 24$)			

Note. — Significance levels represent differences from the One-Contact condition.
[a] Denotes relationship between first and second requests.
* $p < .08$.
** $p < .01$.

It is immediately apparent that the first request tended to increase the degree of compliance with the second request. Whereas fewer than 20% of the controls agreed to put the large sign on their lawn, over 55% of the experimental subjects agreed, with over 45% being the lowest degree of compliance for any experimental condition. As expected, those conditions in which the two requests were similar in terms of either issue or task produced significantly more compliance than did the controls (χ^2's range from 3.67, $p < .07$ to 15.01, $p < .001$). A somewhat unexpected result is that the fourth condition, in which the first request had relatively little in common with the second request, also produced more compliance than the controls ($\chi^2 = 3.40, p < .08$). In other words, regardless of whether or not the two requests are similar in either issue or task, simply having the first request tends to increase the likelihood that the subject will comply with a subsequent, larger request. And this holds even when the two requests are made by different people several weeks apart.

A second point of interest is a comparison among the four experimental conditions. As expected, the Same Issue-Same Task condition produced more compliance than any of the other two-contact conditions, but the difference is not significant (χ^2's range from 2.7 to 2.9). If only those subjects who agreed to the first request are considered, the same pattern holds.

DISCUSSION

To summarize the results, the first study indicated that carrying out a small request increased the likelihood that the subject would agree to a similar larger request made by the same person. The second study showed that this effect was quite strong even when a different person made the larger request, and the two requests were quite dissimilar. How may these results be explained?

Two possibilities were outlined previously. The matter-of-principle idea which centered on the particular type of action was not supported by the data, since the similarity of the tasks did not make an appreciable difference in degree of compliance. The notion of involvement, as described previously, also has difficulty accounting for some of the findings. The basic idea was that once someone has agreed to any action, no matter how small, he tends to feel more involved than he did before. This involvement may center around the particular person making the first request or the particular issue. This is quite consistent with the results of the first study (with the exception of the two control groups which as discussed previously were rather ambiguous) and with the Similar-Issue groups in the second experiment. This idea of involvement does not, however, explain the increase in compliance found in the two groups in which the first and second request did not deal with the same issue.

It is possible that in addition to or instead of this process a more general and diffuse mechanism underlies the increase in compliance. What may occur is a change in the person's feelings about getting involved or about taking action. Once he has agreed to a request, his attitude may change. He may become, in his own eyes, the kind of person who does this sort of thing, who agrees to requests made by strangers, who takes action on things he believes in, who cooperates with good causes. The change in attitude could be toward any aspect of the situation or toward the whole business of saying "yes." The basic idea is that the change in attitude need not be toward any particular issue or person or activity, but may be toward activity or compliance in general. This would imply that an increase in compliance would not depend upon the two contacts being made by the same person, or concerning the same issue or involving the same kind of action. The similarity could be much more general, such as both concerning good causes, or requiring a similar kind of action, or being made by pleasant, attractive individuals.

It is not being suggested that this is the only mechanism operating here. The idea of involvement continues to be extremely plausible, and there are probably a number of other possibilities. Unfortunately, the present studies offer no additional data with which to support or refute any of the possible explanations of the effect. These explanations thus remain simply descriptions of mechanisms which might produce an increase in compliance after agreement with a first request. Hopefully, additional research will test these ideas more fully and perhaps also specify other manipulations which produce an increase in compliance without an increase in external pressure.

It should be pointed out that the present studies employed what is perhaps a very special type of situation. In all cases the requests were made by presumably nonprofit service organizations. The issues in the second study were deliberately noncontroversial, and it may be assumed that virtually all subjects initially sympathized with the objectives of safe driving and a beautiful California. This is in strong contrast to campaigns which are designed to sell a particular product, political candidate, or dogma. Whether the technique employed in this study would be successful in these other situations remains to be shown.

REFERENCES

Asch, S. E.Effects of group pressure upon the modification and distortion of judgments. In H. Guetzkow (Ed.), *Groups, leadership and men; research in human relations*. Pittsburgh: Carnegie Press, 1951, Pp. 177–90.

Bandura, A., Ross, D., & Ross, S. A. A comparative test of the status envy, social power, and secondary reinforcement theories of identificatory learning. *Journal of Abnormal and Social Psychology*, 1963, *67*, 527–34.

Bruner, J. The dimensions of propaganda: German short-wave broadcasts to America. *Journal of Abnormal and Social Psychology*,1941, *36*, 311–37.

Deutsch, M., & Gerard, H. B. A study of normative and informational social influences upon individual judgment. *Journal of Abnormal and Social Psychology, 1955, 51,* 629–36.

Festinger, L., & Carlsmith, J. Cognitive consequences of forced compliance. *Journal of Abnormal and Social Psychology*, 1959, *58*, 203–10.

Hovland, C. I., & Pritzker, H. A. Extent of opinion change as a function of amount of change advocated. *Journal of Abnormal and Social Psychology*, 1957, *54*, 257– 61.

Kelman, H. C., & Hovland, C. I. "Reinstatement" of the communicator in delayed measurement of opinion change. *Journal of Abnormal and Social Psychology*, 1953, *48*, 327–35.

Schein, E. H., Schneier, I., & Barker, C. H. *Coercive pressure*. New York: Norton, 1961.

Some Effects of Guilt on Compliance

J. MERRILL CARLSMITH AND ALAN E. GROSS

Most research concerned with how to get a person to comply has been carried out in situations where there is a great deal of external pressure for compliance. In many studies, the extent of the pressures is obvious (e.g., Asch, 1951; Deutsch & Gerard, 1955). Other studies have used the immense pressure of the experimenter-subject relationship. For example, Milgram's (1964) remarkable demonstrations of obedience are all carried out in the context of an experimenter ordering a subject to comply. In these, and in most other studies of compliance, the focus has been on variables affecting compliance within this framework of strong external pressure.

Reprinted from Journal of Personality and Social Psychology, 11, *1969, 232–39.* *Copyright 1969 by the American Psychological Association and reproduced by permission.*

The research described here studies how one can get compliance without these external pressures. This is of interest for several reasons. First of all, it is often necessary, for financial, ethical, practical, or other reasons, to apply only minimal external pressure when attempting to obtain compliance. Second, it has become clear from much of the research stemming from dissonance theory (e.g., Brehm & Cohen, 1962; Carlsmith, Collins, & Helmreich, 1966; Festinger & Carlsmith, 1959) that in order to get maximal attitude change following compliance, it is important to have as little pressure for compliance as is consistent with obtaining that compliance. All of this work has ignored the question of how to get compliance with minimal pressure. In all cases the compliance was obtained within the experimenter-subject relationship, with an experimenter requesting that the subject comply. As Orne (1962) pointed out, compliance is virtually guaranteed under these circumstances. In the dissonance studies, variations in pressure for compliance are obtained by adding a number of additional external pressures (e.g., money) for some of the subjects.

More recently, there has been some interest in the question of obtaining compliance with minimal pressure. Wallace and Sadalla (1966) attempted to persuade subjects to volunteer for an experiment involving painful shocks. Some of their subjects were induced to break an expensive machine before the request was made; for other subjects the machine was broken but the subject was not responsible. Subjects who had broken the machine were significantly more likely to volunteer for the unpleasant experiment than subjects who had not. Unfortunately, 30% of the subjects never broke the machine, so that such a comparison is confounded by self-selection.

A similar finding is reported incidentally by Brock and Becker (1966). Again, student subjects were induced to press a button which either destroyed the experimenter's apparatus or emitted a slight puff of smoke. Following this, the experimenter asked them to sign a petition advocating doubling tuition at the University. No subjects in the low-damage condition were willing to sign the petition. About 50% of the subjects in the high-damage condition were willing to sign it.

Both of these experiments suggest that guilt may cause a sharp increase in compliance. Unfortunately, in both experiments the request was made by the experimenter who was fully aware of the subject's condition. We may expect compliance to be strongly affected by the persuasiveness or perseverance of an experimenter's request, as well as by more subtle variations in his behavior. Accordingly, the possibility of some experimenter bias creeping in is disquieting. Nevertheless, the experiments do strongly suggest that guilt may play an important role in inducing compliance.

In the first experiment reported here, the authors tried to assess the effects of three different variables which might be thought to produce compliance. In all cases, the request for compliance was made by someone who was not an experimenter, and the request was not made as part of an experiment.

One variable of some interest in the compliance paradigm is the status of the person making the request for compliance. Accordingly, some of the subjects in the present study were asked to comply by someone of higher status than themselves; others were asked to comply by someone of lower status. A second variable, which might be expected to interact with status, is the presence or absence of a witness to the request. Finally, the authors wished to study the effects of guilt, and thus induced some of the subjects to deliver painful electric shocks to the person making the request.

To summarize, the first experiment employed a $2 \times 2 \times 2$ factorial design to test the effects of three variables on the likelihood that a subject will comply to a request. The requester had either been shocked or not shocked (by the subject) prior to the request; he was introduced as either a high-or low-status person; and the request was made either privately or witnessed by an experimenter.

EXPERIMENT I: METHOD

Overview of Design

The dependent measure was the extent to which the subject was willing to comply to a request by a confederate who had just served as learner in a bogus experiment. Subjects were assigned the role of "teacher" in a learning situation, and were instructed to throw a large knife switch whenever the learner made a mistake. The switch merely sounded a buzzer, but half of the subjects had been told that closing the switch also caused the learner to receive painful electric shocks. After the experiment was completed, the learner, who had been described as being drawn from either a high- or low-status pool of subjects, presented a request to the subject either privately or in the presence of the experimenter.

Subjects

Male students of Foothill College were offered $2 to participate in a 45-minute learning experiment to be conducted at the Stanford University Psychology Department. Forty-eight students were recruited, and data from 40 subjects, 5 randomly assigned to each of eight conditions of the $2 \times 2 \times 2$ design, were used. Data from 8 subjects were eliminated from the analysis, 7 because they suspected that the confederate or his request were part of the experimental design, and 1 because he did not believe that the confederate was actually being shocked. None of the results reported below is altered if these subjects are included in the analysis.

Apparatus

The experimental room contained three tables and an impressive array of wiring and electrical equipment. Two booths, one for the learner-confederate, and one for the teacher-subject, faced each other on the center table. The learner's booth was equipped with response switches which turned on corresponding lights in the teacher's booth, a panel of feedback lights which were activated by switches on the teacher's side, and a book containing 15 patterns, described as a standard concept-formation task.

In addition, a respirometer tube which was connected to a pen recorder, and palm electrodes with leads running to a Fels dermohmmeter, were present at the learner's side. In shock conditions the palm contacts were described to the subject as electrodes hooked up to a shock generator; in nonshock conditions they were called palm recorders connected to a skin-resistance measuring device. The purpose of this equipment was simply to make it credible to the subject that the confederate's responses were the main focus of the experiment.

Aside from the complementary switches and panels necessary for viewing the learner's responses and feeding him back "correct answers," the subject's booth contained controls labeled "correct" and "error." The subject was instructed to use these switches to reinforce the learner positively when he was correct, and to give him negative feedback after trials which included at least one error. Pushing the positive button turned on a large green light in both booths, and closing the negative knife switch sounded a loud buzzer which operated for 1 second at 1-second intervals. The third table, which was empty except for pencils and a letter basket, was used for making the request after the learning trials.

Procedure

When subjects arrived they were informed that they would be working with another man who would arrive in a few minutes. Meanwhile the experimenter explained the rationale for assigning the subject to the role of teacher:

What we're trying to find out is what kinds of things affect the way people solve problems which require them to learn fairly difficult concepts. One thing we already know for sure is that certain kinds of feedback information can improve a subject's performances. But, we think *who* gives the feedback information also makes a big difference; that is, we think learners may respond in different ways to different teachers. As you probably know, the teacher or trainer who gives the feedback in these kinds of studies is almost always an experimental psychologist or at least an advanced graduate student, but in this series that we're running now we want to find out how our subjects react and learn when they *know* that a feshman or sophomore junior college student like yourself is acting as the instructor—the one who gives the feedback.

At this point the experimenter remarked that the experiment would be particularly interesting because a special group of men had been recruited to act as learners. The experimenter then manipulated the status of the requester by identifying the group as (*a*) "young executives from Lockheed who have been selected for a special management development program" or (*b*) "unemployed men who were high school dropouts and are now being processed for eligibility in the Federal Job Training Program." The experimenter then explained exactly what the subject was to do during the learning trials:

He [the learner] is going to work on this standard concept-formation task. Your job will be to feed back the correct answer on each of the 15 trials like this [experimenter demonstrates switches]. You record his answers here [subject is handed a form which includes a list of correct responses and columns for recording the learner's responses. The learner's source group—"federal unemployment" or "management development"—and the learning method— "shock" or "negative feedback"—were prominently written in at the top of the page], and then feed back the correct configuration by using these switches which activate his lights. If he is completely correct you give him about 2 seconds of positive feedback like this [experimenter demonstrates switch which operates green light], but if he is wrong—that is, if he made any mistakes on the trial—you throw this negative feedback switch which sounds a loud buzzer. . . .

In the shock conditions the experimenter continued:

and activates that shock apparatus [points at dermohmmeter] which will administer shocks to Mr. Rawlins' hands. I'll show you how it works when we look at his side of the apparatus. We regulate these shocks so that they are pretty painful and unpleasant—otherwise we can't really see how they affect the learning process—but there is absolutely no permanent tissue damage resulting from these shocks, so don't worry about that. [Experimenter and subject walk around table to learner's booth.] . . . We also attach one of these electrodes to each of the subject's palms. As you can see, these are hooked to the generator in order to apply the shock voltage at a level which is as painful as we can get commensurate with the subject's safety. He's already had a dose of the shock last week, so he knows what it feels like.

In nonshock conditions, the experimenter explained that a buzzer signal given after wrong responses sometimes has a facilitating effect on learning, and when the subject was shown the electrodes on the learner's side of the table, he was told "they will be attached to each of the subject's palms . . . it measures skin resistance much in the same way as they do with lie detectors."

After the subject was reseated at his booth, questions about the procedure were answered, after which the experimenter opened a door leading to a room where the confederate was waiting, greeted him, and introduced him to the subject.

The two booths were arranged so that no visual contact could be made between learner and teacher while they were seated. The experimenter then briefly recapitulated the procedure. In both shock and nonshock treatments the buzzer was ambiguously referred to as negative feedback in the presence of the confederate—for example,

Just like last time, when the answers don't match—when you're wrong—the teacher throws his negative feedback switch. Just a second, let me check this [the experimenter glances at some dials]. OK, let's see if the switch is working. [to teacher] Remember, just give three bursts of negative feedback.

After the buzzer sounded three times, the experimenter said humorously to the learner, "Well, I guess that's working all right."

The confederate's responses were programmed so that he appeared to be learning the concept toward the end of the series. Nevertheless, he was completely correct only six times during the 15 trials, so that all subjects were required to throw the negative feedback switch nine times. Four of the nine times that he made an error, the confederate kicked the table in response to the buzzer. This lent realism to the shock conditions; subjects in nonshock conditions could attribute the slight movement to a change of position, if they noticed it at all.

Request

After the fifteenth trial the experimenter removed the confederate's palm contacts, and asked him to sit at another table to fill out a "concept-formation questionnaire." As soon as the confederate began writing, the experimenter seated the subject at the same table, paid him, and asked him to complete a receipt which called for address, telephone number, and other personal information. The receipt form was designed to occupy the subject for 1 or 2 minutes. Both the confederate and the subject were told that the experiment was over, and that they were free to leave when they finished filling out the forms which they were to put in a letter basket on the table.

In witness conditions, the experimenter began adjusting the apparatus while hovering near the table and obviously attending to the request. Near the beginning of the request, the confederate turned to the experimenter and asked, "Am I bothering you?" to which the experimenter replied, "No, I was just interested in what you were saying." In no-witness conditions, the experimenter excused himself and left the room, closing the door after him. A concealed microphone allowed him to listen to the request from another nearby room.

A few seconds after the experimenter either left the room or began adjusting equipment, the confederate completed his questionnaire, put it in the letter basket, and haltingly began his rehearsed request. After engaging the subject's attention, the confederate identified himself as a member of a committee that was attempting to prevent a freeway from being built through the redwood trees in Northern California[1] He explained that people were needed to telephone potential signers of a petition to save the trees. After displaying several stacks, each made up of 50 index cards containing names and phone numbers, he requested that the subject help with this task:

What's involved is just to phone the people and say there is this petition and would they be interested in signing it. So, what I was wondering was if you'd be willing to call some of these people, but you wouldn't have to call up 50 of them if you didn't have time. As I say, it takes a minute or two for each one. Would you be willing to call some of these people for us?

If the subject refused to help, the confederate put the cards in his pocket and left the room. If the subject agreed to make some phone calls, he was asked, "How many of them do you think you could do? As I say, we've got 50 of them, but any number you could do would be a help."

Shortly after the subject refused, or complied and specified the number of calls, the experimenter (who then reentered the room in nonwitness conditions) interrupted, and asked the confederate to wait in another room because he had

---

[1] In view of recent publicity and concern about redwoods in California, it seems worthwhile to mention that the first experiment was carried out in March, 1965; the second experiment was carried out in August, 1965. At that time, there was relatively little concern about redwoods; none of the subjects had heard anything more than vague talk about conservation groups.

"forgotten to ask the subject some questions." After the experimenter determined whether or not it was suspected that the request had been part of the design, he explained the actual purpose of the experiment to the subject, and invited him to return at a later date to pick up a copy of the results.

This procedure effectively prevented the confederate from knowing whether the subject was in the shock or nonshock condition. He was also ignorant as to whether he (the confederate) was of high or low status. It was, of course, impossible for him to be ignorant as to whether or not there was a witness present. The fact that the person making the request was blind (on at least two of the three variables) seems to us a critically necessary feature for studying compliance. As pointed out by Aronson and Carlsmith (1968), bias cannot affect interactions if the experimenter is blind on one of the interacting variables.

RESULTS AND DISCUSSION

The results can be summarized simply. Neither the status of the person making the request nor the presence of a witness had any effect on compliance. Both of these variables also failed to interact with each other or with the presence or absence of shock. When the subject had shocked the confederate prior to the request for compliance, however, there was a striking increase in the amount of compliance elicited. Whereas 25% of the subjects agreed to make some phone calls in the control conditions, 75% of the subjects who had just administered a shock to the confederate agreed to make some calls. A Fisher exact test on this difference yields a probability of .004. Table 1 shows the mean number of phone calls accepted in each of the eight conditions. Table 2 shows an analysis of variance of the data. Again, we see that the effect of delivering a shock to the person who makes the request for compliance is highly significant; no other effects even approach significance.

Not only was the probability of compliance higher in the shock conditions, there was also a tendency for the *level* of compliance to be higher. Among those subjects who did comply, the mean number of phone calls agreed to was 32 in the shock conditions, and 16 in the nonshock conditions ($t = 1.93, p < .10$). Of the 20 compliant subjects, 7 agreed to take the whole stack of 50 cards; all of these were in the shock conditions.

Although this experiment provides convincing evidence that delivering a shock to another person will markedly increase the likelihood of subsequent

Table 1 MEAN NUMBER OF PHONE CALLS ACCEPTED

| | SHOCK | | NONSHOCK | |
| | REQUESTER'S STATUS | | REQUESTER'S STATUS | |
CONDITION	HIGH	LOW	HIGH	LOW
E present	26	16	6	2
E not present	25	29	5	3

Table 2 ANALYSIS OF VARIANCE

SOURCE	df	MS
Shock (A)	1	4,000
Status (B)	1	90
Witness (C)	1	90
A × B	1	0
A × C	1	90
B × C	1	160
A × B × C	1	90
Within cell error	32	279.38
Total	39	

compliance to that person, the interpretation is somewhat ambiguous. At least three alternative explanations come immediately to mind. First, it may be that people will in general comply with a request from a person whom they see as unfortunate. Since the confederate has just been subjected to a series of painful shocks, it may be that the subjects feel sorry for him, sympathetic towards him, and comply with his request in order to make his life a little more pleasant.

Alternatively, it may be that the subjects feel very guilty about having administered a series of painful shocks to another person, and will engage in compliant behavior for anyone who asks them to help in a good cause. This explanation suggests that the person feels guilty, or that his self-image has been tarnished, and that compliance with another may be a good way to alleviate the guilt or to gild the image. A third possible interpretation, related to the last, is that the subject wants to make restitution. Having injured the confederate by delivering painful shocks to him, he wishes to compensate for this by doing a favor for him. For convenience these three interpretations will be referred to as the sympathy, the generalized guilt, and the restitution explanations.

Since each of these is perfectly plausible in the original study, a second experiment was carried out designed to differentiate among them and to provide a sharper theoretical picture of the forces involved. The second experiment used a procedure quite similar to the first, but added a third person to the interaction—a witness. Several of the possible permutations of one person asking another to comply allow one to distinguish among the three possible interpretations offered.

EXPERIMENT II: METHOD

Overview

The setting for this experiment was essentially the same as for the first. There were, however, three people in the experimental room (two of whom were confederates). Just as before, one person was the teacher for a simple concept-learning experiment, and this teacher either did or did not deliver shocks to a learner. A third person, the witness, served as an observer and his ostensible task was to record all of the responses and feedback. After the learning phase of the experiment was completed, one person was excused, and the subject and one confederate were left alone for a moment to fill out some forms. After a moment, the confederate described the campaign to save the redwoods and asked the subject to make some phone calls to help him.

There were four experimental conditions. Two were an exact replication of the previous experiment. In the control condition, the learner made the compliance request of the teacher, and no mention was made of electric shock. In the restitution condition, the learner made the request of the teacher, and the teacher had just delivered nine electric shocks. In the generalized guilt condition, the witness made the request of the teacher, after the teacher had delivered shocks to the learner. Finally, in the sympathy condition, the learner, who had just received the shocks, made the request of the witness, who had observed, but not delivered, the shocks. Since the true subject was always the person of whom the request was made, he was sometimes in the role of teacher and sometimes of witness. The confederates took the other two roles.

Various comparisons among the conditions make it possible to distinguish among the three possible explanations listed above. Thus, if the generalized guilt condition is significantly higher than the control condition, we can rule out the restitution explanation. Comparing the sympathy condition with the restitution condition enables us to find out whether or not sympathy is a possible explanation.

Again, we felt that it was crucial that the person making the request be blind as to the condition the subject was in. This presents some difficulties, since it also implies that he did not even know what role he was playing. However, the confederate was effectively blinded so that in no case did he know what condition the subject was in.

Subjects

Forty-seven male Foothill College students were paid $2 to participate in the study which was disguised as a learning experiment. Data for 7 subjects were discarded; 3 did not believe that the learner was shocked, 2 could not correctly identify the role of the requester, 1 suspected that the request was part of the experiment, and 1 would not respond to the request without first consulting his parents. The remaining 40 subjects were divided equally among four experimental conditions.

The experimental setting was the same as in the first experiment, except that the table was partitioned into three parts, one for each of the participants. The participants could not see each other when seated. The subject and one confederate arrived for the experiment first. This confederate was always the one who made the request and will be referred to as the "requesting confederate." He and the subject were introduced and spent a minute or two together so that this confederate would be salient for the subject. Then the subject was taken upstairs to the experimental room and the confederate was asked to wait outside "since you were in the experiment last week and know how it works." The experiment was explained to the subject, and his role was made clear, Special efforts were made to also make clear what the role of the first confederate would be. After the experiment had been explained to the subject, both confederates were brought in. The "requesting confederate" always sat at the same place and actually played the same role, although the subject was told that the confederate played whatever role the experimental condition called for. Before the "requesting confederate" was brought into the room, the apparatus was moved (without knowledge of the subject) so that it appeared the same to the "requesting confederate" in all conditions. Thus the "requesting confederate" was blind as to the experimental condition, but in the prior briefing of the subject a great deal of stress was placed on who played what role so that the subject would know who was making the request at the end of the experiment.

After all participants were seated the instructions were briefly reviewed. The experimenter pointed to each spot as he reviewed the instructions so that again the subject was reminded of which confederate was playing the role. The "requesting confederate" could not see the experimenter during this period. The learning phase of the experiment was identical to the previous experiment, except that the witness recorded everything which took place. After this was completed, the experimenter announced that the experiment was over, excused one confederate, and asked the subject and the "requesting confederate" to fill out some receipt forms. He then left the room. While the subject and the confederate were filling out the forms, the confederate made his request for compliance, just as in the first study.

Following this, the experimenter returned, asked the subject for any suspicions he might have had, and ascertained that the subject knew what role the "requesting confederate" had played. He then explained the true purpose of the experiment.

RESULTS AND DISCUSSION

The results of the experiment are shown in Table 3, which lists the average number of phone calls the subjects agreed to make in each of the four conditions. A one-way analysis of variance shows highly significant treatment effects ($F = 7.03$, $df = 3/36$, $p < .001$). It may be seen that the result of the first experiment replicates nicely. Restitution subjects accept an average of 23.5 phone calls; controls accept only 13 ($t = 1.39$, $df = 36$, ns). The smaller number of subjects in these two cells prevented the difference from being significant, although the difference is of roughly the same order of magnitude as in the first experiment. Much of the difference in the absolute values of the two control

Table 3

EXPERIMENTAL CONDITION	REQUEST-ING CON-FEDERATE'S ROLE	S's ROLE	FEEDBACK	M NO. PHONE CALLS ACCEPTED
Control	Learner	Teacher	Buzzer	13.0
Sympathy	Learner	Witness	Shock	6.5
Restitution	Learner	Teacher	Shock	23.5
Generalized guilt	Witness	Teacher	Shock	39.0

groups is accounted for by one aberrant subject in the control condition in the second experiment who agreed to make 50 calls.

The results are even clearer when we consider the other conditions, and ask whether guilt, restitution, or sympathy is playing the predominant role. Subjects in the generalized guilt condition, where a witness, who has observed the whole interaction, makes the request, agree to make an average of 39 calls. This group is significantly higher than any of the other three conditions ($t \geq 2.05, p \leq .05$).

The sympathy condition, on the other hand, produces less compliance than any other condition. In this case, the subject is present when a confederate ostensibly receives the painful electric shocks, but has nothing to do with delivering them. When this confederate later asks the subject to comply, the average number of phone calls accepted is only 6.5, a value which is significantly less than either of the conditions in which the subject actually delivers the shock. Thus a person who has just received a series of painful shocks can elicit compliance only from the person who has administered the shocks, not from a witness to the experience.

Experiment II was designed to distinguish between guilt, restitution, and sympathy interpretations of the large amount of compliance produced by shocking another person. The answer seems clear. Sympathy in itself elicits surprisingly little compliance. In fact, those nonguilty subjects who witnessed a victim receiving shocks were slightly less willing to accede to the victim's request than were control subjects. It appears that guilt arising from personal implication is a necessary precondition for obtaining compliance in this situation. Subjects who were personally responsible for the shocks (restitution and generalized guilt conditions) agreed on the average to phone 31.25 people, whereas subjects who did not administer shocks (sympathy and control conditions) agreed to only 9.75 phone calls ($t = 3.97, p < .001$).

Although Experiment I demonstrated that people will attempt to alleviate guilt by complying with the person they feel guilty about, the strong compliance obtained in the generalized guilt condition makes it clear that guilt can lead to compliance even when there is no opportunity to make amends to the injured party. Restitution does not appear to be a necessary component of the guilt-compliance relationship. At first it appears that the witness' knowledge that the subject had hurt the confederate might be critical in explaining these results— that the subject wants to show the witness that he really is a kind and helpful person in order to repair his social image. However, a recent series of experiments by Freedman, Wallington, and Bless (1967) demonstrates compliance effects in similar situations when the request was made by someone who had no knowledge of the subject's transgression.

It is surprising that the generalized guilt condition produces *more* compliance than the restitution condition. Although the comparison between these two conditions is slightly confounded (the witness had not received shock the week before whereas the learner had), the result strongly suggest that there is some other factor which is reducing the tendency to comply in the restitution condition. This unexpected increase in compliance to the witness may reflect a tendency to avoid the victim. Continued contact with the victim could result in uncomfortable feelings of obligation or serve as an unpleasant reminder to the subject that he had voluntarily pushed the shock button. Freedman et al. (1967)

provide some evidence to support the avoidance interpretation. The experimenters contrived to induce the subject to knock over a stack of supposedly carefully indexed note cards. Later, when subjects were asked to assist in a public opinion survey, subjects who did not have to associate with the graduate student who owned the cards complied more than nonguilty controls. There were no differences between experimental and control subjects when the request involved working closely with the graduate student victims. A related interpretation is that voiced by several of the present subjects—that the confederate was taking advantage of a situation which had given him some power. As one subject said, "I didn't like that guy. He knew he had me in a situation where I owed him something and he took advantage of it by asking me to make all those phone calls for him." This is also consistent with Lerner's (1965) finding that if a person has inflicted suffering on someone, he is likely to devalue the victim.

Taken together with other recent work (e.g., Freedman et al, 1967), these two experiments provide convincing evidence that a very powerful technique for obtaining compliance is to first induce a person to do something which harms another person. The second experiment reported here suggests that guilt about the action is the mediating factor in producing this compliance, and that the compliance need not be to the person who was hurt. The wide variety of methods of hurting another person which have been used in experiments reporting this relationship, including destroying a machine (Brock & Becker, 1966; Wallace & Sadalla, 1966), costing another person green stamps (Berscheid & Walster, 1967), upsetting the order of a graduate student's index cards (Freedman et al., 1967), and lying (Freedman et al., 1967), give the result substantial empirical generality.

It is not clear, however, why compliance to the types of requests that are typically made in these experiments is so effective in alleviating the guilt. The fact that the compliance need not be to the person who is responsible for the guilt suggests that an interpretation based on bolstering the subject's self-image may be the most productive. All of the subjects in these experiments had been asked to comply by engaging in some behavior which was of fairly high social desirability, that is, helping another person gather names for a petition. Because of this, compliance is likely to give a subject positive information about himself. It would be of interest in clarifying the processes involved in this guilt-compliance relationship to see if the same effect holds when the subject is asked to engage in some negative behavior. For example, are subjects who are made guilty likely to comply with another person who asks them to cheat?

REFERENCES

Aronson, E., & Carlsmith, J. M. Experimentation in social psychology. In G. Lindzey & E. Aronson (Eds.), *The handbook of social psychology*. (2nd. ed.) Reading, Mass.: Addison-Wesley, 1968.

Asch, S. E. Effects of group pressure on the modification and distortion of judgments. In H. Guetzkow (Ed.), *Groups, leadership, and men*. Pittsburgh: Carnegie, 1951.

Berscheid, E., & Walster, E. When does a harm-doer compensate a victim? *Journal of Personality and Social Psychology*, 1967, 6, 435–41.

Brehm, J., & Cohen, A. R. *Explorations in cognitive dissonance.* New York: Wiley, 1962.

Brock, T. C., & Becker, L. A. "Debriefing" and susceptibility to subsequent experimental manipulations. *Journal of Experimental Social Psychology*, 1966, *2*, 314–23.

Carlsmith, J. M., Collins, B. E., & Helmreich, R. K. Studies in forced compliance: I. The effect of pressure for compliance on attitude change produced by face-to-face role playing and anonymous essay writing. *Journal of Personality and Social Psychology*, 1966, *4*, 1–13.

Deutsch, M., & Gerard, H. G. A study of normative and informational social influence upon individual judgment. *Journal of Abnormal and Social Psychology*, 1955, *51*, 629–36.

Festinger, L., & Carlsmith, J. M. Cognitive consequences of forced compliance. *Journal of Abnormal and Social Psychology*, 1959, *58*, 203–11.

Freedman, J. L., Wallington, S. A., & Bless, E. Compliance without pressure: The effect of guilt. *Journal of Personality and Social Psychology*, 1967, *7*, 117–24.

Lerner, M. J. The effect of responsibility and choice on a partner's attractiveness following failure. *Journal of Personality*, 1965, *33*, 178–87.

Milgram, S. Group pressure and action against a person. *Journal of Abnormal and Social Psychology*, 1964, *69*, 137–43.

Orne, M. On the social psychology of the psychological experiment. *American Psychologist*, 1962, *17*, 776–83.

Wallace, J., & Sadalla, E. Behavioral consequences of transgression: I. The effects of social recognition. *Journal of Experimental Research in Personality*, 1966, *1*, 187–94.

Group Inhibition of Bystander Intervention in Emergencies

BIBB LATANÉ AND JOHN M. DARLEY

Emergencies, fortunately, are uncommon events. Although the average person may read about them in newspapers or watch fictionalized versions on television, he probably will encounter fewer than half a dozen in his lifetime. Unfortunately, when he does encounter one, he will have had little direct personal experience in dealing with it. And he must deal with it under conditions of urgency, uncertainty, stress, and fear. About all the individual has to guide him is the secondhand wisdom of the late movie, which is often as useful as "Be brave" or as applicable as "Quick, get lots of hot water and towels!"

Under the circumstances, it may seem surprising that anybody ever intervenes in an emergency in which he is not directly involved. Yet there is a strongly held

Reprinted from Journal of Personality and Social Psychology, 10, *1968, 215–21. Copyright 1968 by the American Psychological Association and reproduced by permission.*

cultural norm that individuals should act to relieve the distress of others. As the Old Parson puts it, "In this life of froth and bubble, two things stand like stone—kindness in another's trouble, courage in your own." Given the conflict between the norm to act and an individual's fears and uncertainties about getting involved, what factors will determine whether a bystander to an emergency will intervene?

We have found (Darley & Latané, 1968) that the mere perception that other people are also witnessing the event will markedly decrease the likelihood that an individual will intervene in an emergency. Individuals heard a person undergoing a severe epileptic-like fit in another room. In one experimental condition, the subject thought that he was the only person who heard the emergency; in another condition, he thought four other persons were also aware of the seizure. Subjects alone with the victim were much more likely to intervene on his behalf, and, on the average, reacted in less than one-third the time required by subjects who thought there were other bystanders present.

"Diffusion of responsibility" seems the most likely explanation for this result. If an individual is alone when he notices an emergency, he is solely responsible for coping with it. If he believes others are also present, he may feel that his own responsibility for taking action is lessened, making him less likely to help.

To demonstrate that responsibility diffusion rather than any of a variety of social influence processes caused this result, the experiment was designed so that the onlookers to the seizure were isolated one from another and could not discuss how to deal with the emergency effectively. They knew the others could not see what they did, nor could they see whether somebody else had already started to help. Although this state of affairs is characteristic of many actual emergencies (such as the Kitty Genovese murder in which 38 people witnessed a killing from their individual apartments without acting), in many other emergencies several bystanders are in contact with and can influence each other. In these situations, processes other than responsibility diffusion will also operate.

Given the opportunity to interact, a group can talk over the situation and divide up the helping action in an efficient way. Also, since responding to emergencies is a socially prescribed norm, individuals might be expected to adhere to it more when in the presence of other people. These reasons suggest that interacting groups should be better at coping with emergencies than single individuals. We suspect, however, that the opposite is true. Even when allowed to communicate, groups may still be worse than individuals.

Most emergencies are, or at least begin as, ambiguous events. A quarrel in the street may erupt into violence, but it may be simply a family argument. A man staggering about may be suffering a coronary or an onset of diabetes; he may be simply drunk. Smoke pouring from a building may signal a fire; on the other hand, it may be simply steam or air-conditioning vapor. Before a bystander is likely to take action in such ambiguous situations, he must first define the event as an emergency and decide that intervention is the proper course of action.

In the course of making these decisions, it is likely that an individual bystander will be considerably influenced by the decisions he perceives other bystanders to be taking. If everyone else in a group of onlookers seems to regard an event as nonserious and the proper course of action as nonintervention, this consensus may strongly affect the perceptions of any single individual and inhibit his potential intervention.

The definitions that other people hold may be discovered by discussing the situation with them, but they may also be inferred from their facial expressions or their behavior. A whistling man with his hands in his pockets obviously does not believe he is in the midst of a crisis. A bystander who does not respond to smoke obviously does not attribute it to fire. An individual, seeing the inaction of others, will judge the situation as less serious than he would if he were alone.

In the present experiment, this line of thought will be tested by presenting an emergency situation to individuals either alone or in the presence of two passive others, confederates of the experimenter who have been instructed to notice the emergency but remain indifferent to it. It is our expectation that this passive behavior will signal the individual that the other bystanders do not consider the situation to be dangerous. We predict that an individual faced with the passive reactions of other people will be influenced by them, and will thus be less likely to take action than if he were alone.

This, however, is a prediction about individuals; it says nothing about the original question of the behavior of freely interacting groups. Most groups do not have preinstructed confederates among their members, and the kind of social influence process described above would, by itself, only lead to a convergence of attitudes within a group. Even if each member of the group is entirely guided by the reactions of others, then the group should still respond with a likelihood equal to the average of the individuals.

An additional factor is involved, however. Each member of a group may watch the others, but he is also aware that the others are watching him. They are an audience to his own reactions. Among American males it is considered desirable to appear poised and collected in times of stress. Being exposed to public view may constrain an individual's actions as he attempts to avoid possible ridicule and embarrassment.

The constraints involved with being in public might in themselves tend to inhibit action by individuals in a group, but in conjunction with the social influence process described above, they may be expected to have even more powerful effects. If each member of a group is, at the same time, trying to appear calm and also looking around at the other members to gauge their reactions, all members may be led (or misled) by each other to define the situation as less critical than they would if alone. Until someone acts, each person only sees other nonresponding bystanders, and, as with the passive confederates, is likely to be influenced not to act himself.

This leads to a second prediction. Compared to the performance of individuals, if we expose groups of naive subjects to an emergency, the constraints on behavior in public coupled with the social influence process will lessen the likelihood that the members of the group will act to cope with the emergency.

It has often been recognized (Brown, 1954, 1965) that a crowd can cause contagion of panic, leading each person in the crowd to overreact to an emergency to the detriment of everyone's welfare. What is implied here is that a crowd can also force inaction on its members. It can suggest, implicitly but strongly, by its passive behavior, that an event is not to be reacted to as an emergency, and it can make any individual uncomfortably aware of what a fool he will look for behaving as if it is.

METHOD

The subject, seated in a small waiting room, faced an ambiguous but potentially dangerous situation as a stream of smoke began to puff into the room through a wall vent. His response to this situation was observed through a one-way glass. The length of time the subject remained in the room before leaving to report the smoke was the main dependent variable of the study.

Recruitment of subjects. Male Columbia students living in campus residences were invited to an interview to discuss "some of the problems involved in life at an urban university." The subject sample included graduate and professional students as well as undergraduates. Individuals were contacted by telephone and most willingly volunteered and actually showed up for the interview. At this point, they were directed either by signs or by the secretary to a "waiting room" where a sign asked them to fill out a preliminary questionnaire.

Experimental manipulation. Some subjects filled out the questionnaire and were exposed to the potentially critical situation while alone. Others were part of three-person groups consisting of one subject and two confederates acting the part of naive subjects. The confederates attempted to avoid conversation as much as possible. Once the smoke had been introduced, they stared at it briefly, made no comment, but simply shrugged their shoulders, returned to the questionnaires and continued to fill them out, occasionally waving away the smoke to do so. If addressed, they attempted to be as uncommunicative as possible and to show apparent indifference to the smoke. "I dunno," they said, and no subject persisted in talking.

In a final condition, three naive subjects were tested together. In general, these subjects did not know each other, although in two groups, subjects reported a nodding acquaintanceship with another subject. Since subjects arrived at slightly different times and since they each had individual questionnaires to work on, they did not introduce themselves to each other, or attempt anything but the most rudimentary conversation.

Critical situation. As soon as the subjects had completed two pages of their questionnaires, the experimenter began to introduce the smoke through a small vent in the wall. The "smoke" was finely divided titanium dioxide produced in a stoppered bottle and delivered under slight air pressure through the vent.[1] It formed a moderately fine-textured but clearly visible stream of whitish smoke. For the entire experimental period, the smoke continued to jet into the room in irregular puffs. By the end of the experimental period, vision was obscured by the amount of smoke present.

All behavior and conversation was observed and coded from behind a one-way window (largely disguised on the subject's side by a large sign giving preliminary instructions). If the subject left the experimental room and reported the smoke, he was told that the situation "would be taken care of." If the

---

[1] Smoke was produced by passing moisturized air, under pressure, through a container of titanium tetrachloride, which, in reaction with the water vapor, creates a suspension of tantium dioxide in air.

subject had not reported the presence of smoke by 6 minutes from the time he first noticed it, the experiment was terminated.

RESULTS

Alone condition. The typical subject, when tested alone, behaved very reasonably. Usually, shortly after the smoke appeared, he would glance up from his questionnaire, notice the smoke, show a slight but distinct startle reaction, and then undergo a brief period of indecision, perhaps returning briefly to his questionnaire before again staring at the smoke. Soon, most subjects would get up from their chairs, walk over to the vent, and investigate it closely, sniffing the smoke, waving their hands in it, feeling its temperature, etc. The usual alone subject would hesitate again, but finally walk out of the room, look around outside, and, finding somebody there, calmly report the presence of the smoke. No subject showed any sign of panic; most simply said, "There's something strange going on in there, there seems to be some sort of smoke coming through the wall . . . ."

The median subject in the alone condition had reported the smoke within 2 minutes of first noticing it. Three-quarters of the 24 people who were run in this condition reported the smoke before the experimental period was terminated.

Two passive confederates condition. The behavior of subjects run with two passive confederates was dramatically different; of 10 people run in this condition, only 1 reported the smoke. The other 9 stayed in the waiting room as it filled up with smoke, doggedly working on their questionnaire and waving the fumes away from their faces. They coughed, rubbed their eyes, and opened the window—but they did not report the smoke. The difference between the response rate of 75% in the alone condition and 10% in the two passive confederates condition is highly significant ($p < .002$ by Fisher's exact test, two-tailed).

Three naive bystanders. Because there are three subjects present and available to report the smoke in the three naive bystander condition as compared to only one subject at a time in the alone condition, a simple comparison between the two conditions is not appropriate. On the one hand, we cannot compare speeds in the alone condition with the average speed of the three subjects in a group, since, once one subject in a group had reported the smoke, the pressures on the other two disappeared. They legitimately could (and did) feel that the emergency had been handled, and any action on their part would be redundant and potentially confusing. Therefore the speed of the *first* subject in a group to report the smoke was used as the dependent variable. However, since there were three times as many people available to respond in this condition as in the alone condition, we would expect an increased likelihood that *at least* one person would report the smoke even if the subjects had no influence whatsoever on each other. Therefore we mathematically created "groups" of three scores from the alone condition to serve as a base line.[2]

[2] The formula for calculating the expected proportion of groups in which at least one person will have acted by a given time is $1 - (1 - p)^n$ where p is the proportion of single individuals who act by that time and n is the number of persons in the group.

In contrast to the complexity of this procedure, the results were quite simple. Subjects in the three naive bystander condition were markedly inhibited from reporting the smoke. Since 75% of the alone subjects reported the smoke, we would expect over 98% of the three-person groups to contain at least one reporter. In fact, in only 38% of the eight groups in this condition did even 1 subject report ($p < .01$). Of the 24 people run in these eight groups, only 1 person reported the smoke within the first 4 minutes before the room got noticeably unpleasant. Only 3 people reported the smoke within the entire experimental period.

Cumulative distribution of report times. Figure 1 presents the cumulative frequency distributions of report times for all three conditions. The figure shows the proportion of subjects in each condition who had reported the smoke by any point in the time following the introduction of the smoke. For example, 55% of the subjects in the alone condition had reported the smoke within 2 minutes, but the smoke had been reported in only 12% of the three-person groups by that time. After 4 minutes, 75% of the subjects in the alone condition had reported the smoke; no additional subjects in the group condition had done so. The curve in Figure 1 labeled "Hypothetical Three-Person Groups" is based upon the mathematical combination of scores obtained from subjects in the alone condition. It is the expected report times for groups in the three-person condition if the members of the groups had no influence upon each other.

It can be seen in Figure 1 that for every point in time following the introduction of the smoke, a considerably higher proportion of subjects in the alone condition had reported the smoke than had subjects in either the two passive confederates condition or in the three naive subjects condition. The curve for the latter condition, although considerably below the alone curve, is even more substantially inhibited with respect to its proper comparison, the curve of hypothetical three-person sets. Social inhibition of response was so great that the time elapsing before the smoke was reported was greater when

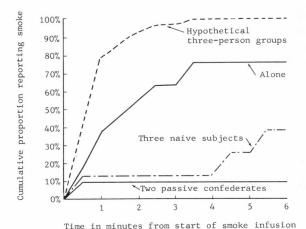

Fig. 1. Cumulative proportion of subjects reporting the smoke over time.

there were more people available to report it (alone versus group $p < .05$ by Mann-Whitney U test).

Superficially, it appears that there is a somewhat higher likelihood of response from groups of three naive subjects than from subjects in the passive confederates condition. Again this comparison is not justified; there are three people free to act in one condition instead of just one. If we mathematically combine scores for subjects in the two passive confederates condition in a similar manner to that described above for the alone condition, we would obtain an expected likelihood of response of .27 as the hypothetical base line. This is not significantly different from the .37 obtained in the actual three-subject groups.

Noticing the smoke. In observing the subject's reaction to the introduction of smoke, careful note was taken of the exact moment when he first saw the smoke (all report latencies were computed from this time). This was a relatively easy observation to make, for the subjects invariably showed a distinct, if slight, startle reaction. Unexpectedly, the presence of other persons delayed, slightly but very significantly, noticing the smoke. Sixty-three percent of subjects in the alone condition and only 26% of subjects in the combined together conditions noticed the smoke within the first 5 seconds after its introduction ($p < .01$ by chi-square). The median latency of noticing the smoke was under 5 seconds in the alone condition; the median time at which the first (or only) subject in each of the combined together conditions noticed the smoke was 20 seconds (this difference does not account for group-induced inhibition of reporting since the report latencies were computed from the time the smoke was first noticed).

This interesting finding can probably be explained in terms of the constraints which people feel in public places (Goffman, 1963). Unlike solitary subjects, who often glanced idly about the room while filling out their questionnaires, subjects in groups usually kept their eyes closely on their work, probably to avoid appearing rudely inquisitive.

Postexperimental interview. After 6 minutes, whether or not the subjects had reported the smoke, the interviewer stuck his head in the waiting room and asked the subject to come with him to the interview. After seating the subject in his office, the interviewer made some general apologies about keeping the subject waiting for so long, hoped the subject hadn't become too bored and asked if he "had experienced any difficulty while filling out the questionnaire." By this point most subjects mentioned the smoke. The interviewer expressed mild surprise and asked the subject to tell him what had happened. Thus each subject gave an account of what had gone through his mind during the smoke infusion.

Subjects who had reported the smoke were relatively consistent in later describing their reactions to it. They thought the smoke looked somewhat "strange," they were not sure exactly what it was or whether it was dangerous, but they felt it was unusual enough to justify some examination. "I wasn't sure whether it was a fire but it looked like something was wrong." "I thought it might be steam, but it seemed like a good idea to check it out."

Subjects who had not reported the smoke also were unsure about exactly what it was, but they uniformly said that they had rejected the idea that it was a fire. Instead, they hit upon an astonishing variety of alternative explanations, all sharing the common characteristic of interpreting the smoke as a nondangerous event. Many thought the smoke was either steam or air-conditioning vapors, several thought it was smog, purposely introduced to simulate an urban environment, and two (from different groups) actually suggested that the smoke was a "truth gas" filtered into the room to induce them to answer the questionnaire accurately. (Surprisingly, they were not disturbed by this conviction.) Predictably, some decided that "it must be some sort of experiment" and stoically endured the discomfort of the room rather than overreact.

Despite the obvious and powerful report-inhibiting effect of other bystanders, subjects almost invariably claimed that they had paid little or no attention to the reactions of the other people in the room. Although the presence of other people actually had a strong and pervasive effect on the subjects' reactions, they were either unaware of this or unwilling to admit it.

DISCUSSION

Before an individual can decide to intervene in an emergency, he must, implicitly or explicitly, take several preliminary steps. If he is to intervene, he must first *notice* the event, he must then *interpret* it as an emergency, and he must decide that it is his personal *responsibility* to act. At each of these preliminary steps, the bystander to an emergency can remove himself from the decision process and thus fail to help. He can fail to notice the event, he can fail to interpret it as an emergency, or he can fail to assume the responsibility to take action.

In the present experiment we are primarily interested in the second step of this decision process, interpreting an ambiguous event. When faced with such an event, we suggest, the individual bystander is likely to look at the reactions of people around him and be powerfully influenced by them. It was predicted that the sight of other, nonresponsive bystanders would lead the individual to interpret the emergency as not serious, and consequently lead him not to act. Further, it was predicted that the dynamics of the interaction process would lead each of a group of naive onlookers to be misled by the apparent inaction of the others into adopting a nonemergency interpretation of the event and a passive role.

The results of this study clearly support our predictions. Individuals exposed to a room filling with smoke in the presence of passive others themselves remained passive, and groups of three naive subjects were less likely to report the smoke than solitary bystanders. Our predictions were confirmed—but this does not necessarily mean that our explanation for these results is the correct one. As a matter of fact, several alternatives are available.

Two of these alternative explanations stem from the fact that the smoke represented a possible danger to the subject himself as well as to others in the building. Subjects' behavior might have reflected their fear of fire, with subjects in groups feeling less threatened by the fire than single subjects and thus being less concerned to act. It has been demonstrated in studies with humans (Schachter, 1959) and with rats (Latané, 1968; Latané & Glass, 1968) that togetherness reduces fear, even in situations where it does not reduce danger. In addition, subjects may have felt that the presence of others increased their ability to cope with fire. For both of these reasons, subjects in groups may have been less afraid of fire and thus less likely to report the smoke than solitary subjects.

A similar explanation might emphasize not fearfulness, but the desire to hide fear. To the extent that bravery or stoicism in the face of danger or discomfort is a socially desirable trait (as it appears to be for American male undergraduates), one might expect individuals to attempt to appear more brave or more stoic when others are watching than when they are alone. It is possible that subjects in the group condition saw themselves as engaged in a game of "Chicken," and thus did not react.

Although both of these explanations are plausible, we do not think that they provide an accurate account of subjects' thinking. In the postexperimental interviews, subjects claimed, *not* that they were unworried by the fire or that they were unwilling to endure the danger; but rather that they decided that there was no fire at all and the smoke was caused by something else. They failed to act because they thought there was no reason to act. Their "apathetic" behavior was reasonable—given their interpretation of the circumstances.

The fact that smoke signals potential danger to the subject himself weakens another alternative explanation, "diffusion of responsibility." Regardless of social influence processes, an individual may feel less personal responsibility for helping if he shares the responsibility with others (Darley & Latané, 1968). But this diffusion explanation does not fit the present situation. It is hard to see how an individual's responsibility for saving himself is diffused by the presence of other people. The diffusion explanation does not account for the pattern of interpretations reported by the subjects or for their variety of nonemergency explanations.

On the other hand, the social influence processes which we believe account for the results of our present study obviously do not explain our previous experiment in which subjects could not see or be seen by each other. Taken together, these two studies suggest that the presence of bystanders may affect an individual in several ways; including both "social influence" and "diffusion of responsibility."

Both studies, however, find, for two quite different kinds of emergencies and under two quite different conditions of social contact, that individuals are less likely to engage in socially responsible action if they think other bystanders are present. This presents us with the paradoxical conclusion that a victim may be more likely to get help, or an emergency may be more likely to be reported, the fewer people there are available to take action. It also may help us begin to understand a number of frightening incidents where crowds have listened to but not answered a call for help. Newspapers have tagged these incidents with the label "apathy." We have become indifferent, they say, callous to the fate of suffering others. The results of our studies lead to a different conclusion. The failure to intervene may be better understood by knowing the relationship among bystanders rather than that between a bystander and the victim.

REFERENCES

Brown, R. W. Mass phenomena. In G. Lindzey (Ed.), *Handbook of social psychology.* Vol. 2. Cambridge: Addison-Wesley, 1954.

Brown, R. *Social psychology.* New York: Free Press of Glencoe, 1965.

Darley, J. M., & Latané, B. Bystander intervention in emergencies: Diffusion of responsibility. *Journal of Personality and Social Psychology*, 1968, *8*, 377–83.

Goffman, E. *Behavior in public places.* New York: Free Press of Glencoe, 1963.

Latané, B. Gregariousness and fear in laboratory rats. *Journal of Experimental Social Psychology*, 1968, in press.

Latané, B., & Glass, D. C. Social and nonsocial attraction in rats. *Journal of Personality and Social Psychology*, 1968, *9*, 142–46.

Schachter, S. *The psychology of affiliation.* Stanford: Stanford University Press, 1959.